MEASUREMENT AND MEANING IN ECONOMICS

ECONOMISTS OF THE TWENTIETH CENTURY

General Editors: David Colander, *Christian A. Johnson Distinguished Professor of Economics, Middlebury College, Vermont, USA* and Mark Blaug, *Professor Emeritus, University of London, UK, Professor Emeritus, University of Buckingham, UK and Visiting Professor, University of Amsterdam, The Netherlands*

This innovative series comprises specially invited collections of articles and papers by economists whose work has made an important contribution to economics in the late twentieth century.

The proliferation of new journals and the ever-increasing number of new articles make it difficult for even the most assiduous economist to keep track of all the important recent advances. By focusing on those economists whose work is generally recognized to be at the forefront of the discipline, the series will be an essential reference point for the different specialisms included. Wherever possible, the articles in these volumes have been reproduced as originally published using facsimile reproduction, inclusive of footnotes and pagination to facilitate ease of reference.

A list of published and future titles in this series is printed at the end of this volume.

Measurement and Meaning in Economics

The Essential Deirdre McCloskey

Deirdre McCloskey

University Professor of the Human Sciences, University of Illinois at Chicago, USA

Edited and introduced by

Stephen Thomas Ziliak

Assistant Professor of Economics, Bowling Green State University, and Visiting Professor, Emory University, USA

ECONOMISTS OF THE TWENTIETH CENTURY

Edward Elgar
Cheltenham, UK • Northampton, MA, USA

Published by
Edward Elgar Publishing Limited
Glensanda House
Montpellier Parade
Cheltenham
Glos GL50 1UA
UK

Edward Elgar Publishing, Inc.
136 West Street
Suite 202
Northampton
Massachusetts 01060
USA

A catalogue record for this book
is available from the British Library

Library of Congress Cataloguing in Publication Data

McCloskey, Deirdre N.
     Measurement and meaning in economics : the essential Deirdre McCloskey / edited and introduced by Stephen Thomas Ziliak.
          p. cm. – (Economists of the twentieth century)
     Includes list of D.N. McCloskey's works.
     Includes index.
     1. Economics. 2. Rhetoric. I. Ziliak, Stephen Thomas, 1963– II. Title. III. Series.

HB71 .M3783 2001
330—dc21   00–067691

ISBN 1 85278 818 6 (cased)

Printed and bound by CPI Group (UK) Ltd, Croydon, CR0 4YY

Contents

Acknowledgements

The publishers wish to thank the following who have kindly given permission for the use of copyright material.

American Economic Association for 'Corn at Interest: The Extent and Cost of Grain Storage in Medieval England' with John Nash, *American Economic Review*, **74** (1), March 1984, 174–87; 'The Rhetoric of Economics', *Journal of Economic Literature*, **21** (2), June 1983, 481–517; 'The Standard Error of Regressions' with Stephen Thomas Ziliak, *Journal of Economic Literature*, **34**, March 1996, 97–114.

Association for Social Economics for 'Why I Am No Longer A Positivist', *Review of Social Economy*, **47** (3), Fall 1989, 225–38.

Blackwell Publishers for 'Did Victorian Britain Fail?', *The Economic History Review*, **23**, December 1970, 446–59; 'History, Differential Equations, and the Problem of Narration', *History and Theory*, **30** (1), 1991, 21–36.

Cambridge University Press for '1780–1860: A Survey' in *The Economic History of Britain, 1700–1860*, R. Floud and D.N. McCloskey (eds), 1994, 242–70; 'Bourgeois Virtue and the History of *P* and *S*', *The Journal of Economic History*, **58** (2), June 1998, 297–317.

Elsevier Science for 'English Open Fields as Behavior Towards Risk', *Research in Economic History*, **1**, Fall 1976, 124–70.

International Network for Economic Method for 'Economic Science: A Search Through the Hyperspace of Assumptions', *Methodus*, **3** (1), June 1991, 6–16.

Taylor and Francis for 'How the Gold Standard Worked, 1880–1913' with J. Richard Zecher, *The Monetary Approach to the Balance of Payments*, J.A. Frenkel and H.G. Johnson (eds), 1976, Allen and Unwin, 184–6, 192–208, abridged; 'Storytelling in Economics' in *Narrative in Culture*, C. Nash (ed.), 1990, Routledge, 5–22.

University of Chicago Press for 'Some Consequences of a Conjective Economics' in *Beyond Economic Man: Feminism and Economics*, M.A. Ferber and J.A. Nelson (eds), 1993, 69–93.

University of Wisconsin Press for 'How to Do a Rhetorical Analysis of Economics, and Why', 3–19, 'The Rhetoric of Scientism: How John Muth Persuades', 52–73 and 'The Lawyerly Rhetoric of Coase's *The Nature of the Firm*', 87–99 in *The Rhetoric of Economics*, 1998 (2nd ed.).

Editor's acknowledgement

I would like to thank the series editors, Mark Blaug and David Colander, and our managing editor at Edward Elgar Ltd, Dymphna Evans, for their enthusiastic and lightning-fast feedback. For the existence of a better introductory chapter I would like to acknowledge the discerning eyes of Neil Browne, Kevin Quinn, Yvonne Singh, and Jude Ziliak. With characteristic charity they improved measurements and clarified meanings in my prose. I was not smart enough to accept all their suggestions for improvement. Conversations with the cultural historian Rachel Buff were formative in both meanings of that word. For material assistance I thank: Bruce Caldwell, Leonard Carlson, John B. Davis, Barry Eichengreen, Ed Leamer, Paul Rubin, Warren Samuels, and Gretchen Voter (Blackwell Publishers). For so many things, scholarly and personal, I am indebted to my teacher, my collaborator, my friend – Deirdre McCloskey.

Introduction: D.N. McCloskey and the Rhetoric of a Scientific Economics

Stephen Thomas Ziliak

Economists have not experienced in their tribe anyone quite like Deirdre McCloskey. She is a conservative economist, a leading economic historian, a distinguished member of the profession, and a past-president and officer of professional organizations; she is the author or editor of 17 books and the author of more than 200 scientific articles; she is a founder of feminist economics, the New Economic Criticism, the New Economic History of Britain, the Project on Rhetoric of Inquiry (PoROI), and the International Cliometric Society – an association of quantitative economic historians; she is a popularizer of economics for *Scientific American*, *The Chronicle of Higher Education*, *The American Scholar*, *Lingua Franca*, *Common Knowledge*, the *Times Higher Education Supplement*, the *Eastern Economic Journal* and more; she is an activist for academic economics, an editor excelsior, a recipient of dozens of awards and named lectureships, and a holder of several named professorships in the United States and abroad. Recently, Deirdre McCloskey became Tinbergen Distinguished Professor of Erasmus University, Rotterdam, and most recently she has been named University Professor of the Human Sciences at the University of Illinois-Chicago.

Economists can tell a long story about their tribe. They'll tell how among them, one finds both the brilliant technician and the learned scholar. They'll tell how they play by the rules of the game. How they are content with the culture of the science. How they are predictable in their character, like Alfred Marshall could be, or like Marcus Welby, MD. But this conservative, Deirdre McCloskey, is a maverick, new to the ken, a discontent in her thinking about the methods and the philosophy of economics. She gave birth to a most unlikely field – 'the rhetoric of economics' – and she is raising it. She is radical in her persona. (The cliche will take hold.) Deirdre McCloskey loves economics. And among the lovers, she is the most fierce critic of economics as practiced.

McCloskey has said more than once that economics would improve if during sun-up economists would read more novels. She has invited novelistic thinking into our research on economic theory. Like the world-class physicist Richard Feynman, she's not joking: citing detailed textual examples, McCloskey finds a leading mathematical economist, Gerard Debreu, to be 'less precise and less self-critical than the better dress designers' ('How to Do' 1994 [1998], p. 6). An advocate of free markets and of methodological individualism, McCloskey can be found quoting Virginia Woolf, John Ruskin, Richard Rorty, Jurgen Habermas, Betty Friedan, John Dewey, and Stanley Fish – with affection. This quantitative economic historian gives keynote addresses at national conferences on rhetoric and composition. She has attended summer school for graduate students in literature. She teaches European students of management each summer in France. A former Director of Graduate Studies in Economics at the

University of Chicago, this same McCloskey changed her name in 1995 from 'Donald' to 'Deirdre,' and with it, her gender. She accepts invitations from colleges and universities all around the world to speak about how becoming a woman is changing the way she thinks about economics and history ('Some News' 1995; *New York Times* 1999). Her early thinking about the change of gender appears in *Crossing: A Memoir* (1999).

In most epochs the leading economists have been conservative in method and person. It's not so for the movers and shakers of other endeavors, a fact – McCloskey might say – italicizing the power of prudence in economic science. Painters have their Picasso and their Pollock. Einstein imagined moving trains and mountable light beams, and rewrote in physics the genesis of the possible. In the rare case the overlap of the person and the method is large, and largely transgressive. Think of the transgressions of Adrienne Rich, the eminent poet who continues to obliterate the boundaries of art and life, of the personal and the political (McCloskey knew her late husband, an economist at the Harvard Business School). Rich writes the poetry and the politics of her change in sexual preference after marriage and motherhood: 'I gave my tongue to love, and this makes it difficult to speak.' She wonders aloud about the Jewish identity which was in her family and yet hidden or scorned by her parents (Rich 1986).

A field can get by without a Rich-like transgression. Economics has. In contrast with other artists and scientists, the leading economists have done little transgressing in method or in self. One thinks of Parson Malthus who, Heilbroner assures us, was no prude. One thinks of Alfred Marshall, a Victorian bourgeois who was so embarrassed by his rhetoric that he hid the mathematics under cover of appendices. One thinks of the still-life editions of Samuelson's *Economics*, and of a style of economic theorizing that is stitched into *The Journal of Economic Theory*. One knows in advance of January's job market that Sears and Roebuck will suit the new PhD in Economics. The bohemian life of Leon Walras, a pioneer in general equilibrium theory, is mysterious (and mentionable) because rare (and French). But unlike the Parisians of the 1920s, and unlike the beat poets of the 1950s, the life of Walras as bohemian does not appear to have influenced his craft. He fetishized the logic of calculus.

In the theatre of scholarship Keynes is not seen to be an exception, either. Keynes was a personal friend of Virginia Woolf but he (mostly) kept separate from economic theory his voluminous classical learning and his thinking about gender and sexuality. Veblen is famously eccentric as scholar and figure but he barely kept a boot in the mainstream. Frank Knight comes close. The Moor never held an academic post. A census taker asks children in the Bronx to check Asian, white, Indian, black, Hispanic, or other. Those children whose 'homes' span the world and who see inside themselves a rainbow check 'other.' Economics has not met a McCloskey, distinguished in a conservative field and rhetorically 'other' on the same day.

By now it is obvious that McCloskey's critical work on economics – by which one usually means 'her work on rhetoric' – is more widely mentioned than is her work on economic history. And yet comparatively speaking her findings in rhetorical research are probably less known in the details. Ask an economic historian and she will tell you why land in medieval England was held in scattered plots. Ask an economist in another subfield and he has heard of 'the rhetoric of economics' but he will struggle to reap an economic simile. The economic historian may struggle, too, even when her training gives her a leg-up. Few economists will have read both the history and the criticism; such is the case with a phenomenon. It is my hope that this collection of essays will lessen the variance between what is said about McCloskey and what is read about McCloskey.

A census division of McCloskey's work into 'economics' and 'criticism' is crude. It corrupts the facts of what she was actually doing in the 1970s and 1980s in her work on the economics of Victorian entrepreneurship, open fields, the gold standard, interest rates, and the industrial revolution. The separation of economics and criticism corrupts the fact that her work on the rhetoric of economics is most relevant to one field: economics. The essays collected here present a test. Do New Keynesians and New Institutionalists not speak as critics in their scientific studies of gold? The distinguished economist Arnold Harberger says that in best practice economics the model will 'sing.' Harberger's form of praise gets repeated by other economists. Is it unreasonable, then, to imagine that Harberger's aesthetic of voice is relevant for understanding the discourse of economics? Imagine economics and criticism as one, living life in peace. And let their division have a life, too: we have to distinguish McCloskey's writings on the rhetoric of economics and calling that work 'criticism' shall serve. But who cares, really? Picasso's *Guernica* is no less important for the precedence of *Gertrude Stein*. And *The Structure of Scientific Revolutions* found its audience by virtue of Kuhn's ethos in normal science.

Making economists conscious of their language has been a central and abiding concern of McCloskey's. 'The Rhetoric of Economics' was published in the *Journal of Economic Literature*, the main barometer for the profession, in 1983. A prelude to the book of 1985, the intention of 'The Rhetoric of Economics' was to show how economists argue, and to suggest that economists think some about their speech. Interpreted as a work of philosophy, it was roundly attacked. The mismatch of expectations may have proved advantageous for the life of the work – it became, overnight, a cause célèbre.

The obstacles to fetching an audience were enormous. Rhetoric was not a concern. Rhetoric was in fact something to avoid: if you used it, you were no scientist, surely. You were an air head – and yes, your words were hot air. As McCloskey has noted, the average understanding of the word 'rhetoric' in 1983 was no different from that of journalists: a headline in Des Moines read 'Senate Campaign Mired in Rhetoric' (*Rhetoric of Economics* 1998, p. 5). Resistance was anticipated. Said McCloskey, 'The word "rhetoric" is doubtless an obstacle to understanding the point' – the point that figures of speech, all of them, have designs on their readers ('Rhetoric of Economics' 1983, p. 483; Chapter 8 this volume). Like that divorcee and front-porch-folk philosopher in Grace Paley's 'Distance,' D.N. McCloskey played the part of some 'crazy construction worker' trying to converse with 'fresh cement' (Paley 1974, p. 25). Even the philosophers of economics had no use for rhetoric, they believed. Married to a modernist philosophy of science, they were busy arguing about the claims of falsification. Or whether or not Econ had made the bedrock of science.

The talk, the arguing, is everything. Like poets and novelists, an economist is a writer with intent to persuade. Our words are not mere window dressing for interior clarities. Our shadow prices are not seen through a glassy mathematics of what comes naturally. Our words, our numbers, our algebras – they are what we know. Or better, they are what we are invited to know by the speaker with intent to persuade. In other words, in the scientific paper nothing – not window dressing or lambda for Lagrange – can be 'mere.' The language of the scientific paper does the scientific work, and therefore the language itself carries an ethical burden and an empirical character which should be examined by practitioners.

It's a good thing for *rhetoric* that the philosophers thought this *a philosophy*. It's a good thing because McCloskey was attempting Houdini-like an amazing feat. She chained herself to the philosophy of economics while trying to divert attention toward *the poetics* of economics. But her audience wasn't prepared to analyse the poetics, not in 1983. For to do so would be to put faith and ritual in a 'context of justification.' It would be to abandon the prescriptions of positivism, the practical philosophy of a scientific economics. Still, we stared at the chains, and inadvertently brought the rhetoric of economics to the surface.

At bottom, McCloskey asked economists to rethink the relationship between 'style' and 'substance.' Like other moderns, the economists of the twentieth century had imagined an epistemological divorce of style from substance. Modernist economists privileged, of course, the promise of the meat, the real stuff, the apparent substance that made the research worthy of its effort. Yet in works of economic history ('English Open Fields', pp. 125–6, 128; Chapter 2 this volume) and especially in criticism, McCloskey shows that substance and style are inseparable. (Showing what she means, beyond bald assertion, is a ritual raised to High Mass: an extended example is in 90 pages of *Economical Writing* (2000).) In 'How to do a Rhetorical Analysis of Economics, and Why,' to take one example, McCloskey shows 'the modern premise that content can be split from expression is mistaken' (p. 10; Chapter 10 this volume). Speaking in analogy with neoclassical economics, she says 'the two are yolk and white in a scrambled egg. Economically speaking, the production function for thinking cannot be written as the sum of two subfunctions, one producing "results" and the other "writing them up." The function [of thinking] is not separable' (p. 10). Good empiricist that she is, McCloskey proceeds to show in detail the inseparable bond of style and substance in modern master-works by Samuelson, Becker, Solow, Muth, Fogel, and Coase *(Rhetoric* 1998, chs. 3–6; see Chapters 12 and 13 this volume).

Among economists of the twentieth century it seems that only Keynes did not have to apologize for being a stylist. (He made it before the War.) Look around: economists have in 50 years dwindled their number of stylists to fewer than a dozen. Thus economists have had little to say about Keynes-the-stylist. It would require from substance-mongers some careful thinking about style. Keynes was a competent maker of metaphor, earnest as a dentist, and economists have found him to be quotable. But it is the allegorical phrase-making and story-telling that makes memorable the rhetoric of Keynes – his comic tale about 'the paradox of thrift,' for instance, and then most powerfully (or pathetically, in the classical sense of employing *pathos* in pursuit of a particular interest), the way he chiseled 'the failure of aggregate demand.' In *The Rhetoric of Economics* (1985 [1998]) McCloskey reveals just how much Keynes (and

Samuelson and Klein and Tinbergen and Smith and Marx and Walras and Hayek and Fisher and Newton) are speaking through us. Throughout the performance: exordium to peroration, beginning to end. No need to apologize. What McCloskey is saying, in effect, is that economists in authorial position, who hear voices when they write, are distilling their style from some academic scribbler of a few years back. We can't help it. The problem is that prior to the publication of 'The Rhetoric of Economics' (1983) most of us were sleepwalking during the process of distillation.

In truth, normal science is an exercise in studied ventriloquism. If the style is the man, and the man is a scientist, then Cowboy Bob Fogel will study his style. After all it is what one does with the undetermined figures of speech, all the little live things, that will make or break a novel piece of research. The introduction of Cartesian coordinates helped economists distinguish changes in demand from changes in quantity demanded and the like. The introduction of rhetoric helped economists distinguish changes in statistics and mathematics from changes in story and belief and the like. Indeed, McCloskey shows normal scientists that even in their most determined mathematical mood they'll use 'humanistic' figures of speech – persuading the science reader with appeals to ancient mysteries and common mythologies. Ironically, it may be that an author's appeals to mysteries and mythologies will elevate – and harden – some piece of the science. Take, for example, McCloskey's 'The Rhetoric of Scientism' (Chapter 12 this volume), in which she shows how a seminal but ill-written paper by John Muth slowed the spread of 'rational expectations.' Muth's teutonic and polysyllabic paper bestowed the bigger fame upon English translators Robert Lucas and Thomas Sargent. Yet Muth's idea that economic rationality could be applied toward beliefs about the future 'had magical powers over some' *(Rhetoric* 1998, p. 62). The magical reception raises no surprise when seen in the light of other magic, such as Euler's 'proof' of infinite addition (pp. 68–73). McCloskey finds that unproven parts of Muth's paper were received and repeated by Muth's translators and that the repetition itself has contributed largely to the 'truth' of the research that would follow. That readers needed to make a leap of faith – this time, by asking angels to do the math – helped John Muth persuade. In other words, even John Muth was part preacher, part folklorist, part poet of the infinite, and needed to be. McCloskey introduced the notion of *palimpsest* (though not the word) to a field that believed 'the data speak for themselves.' It's no small achievement for a single critic.

No one has measured how much McCloskey's talk about style and substance has altered the published scholarship in economics. It may be that a prerequisite for seeing the desired result is in practicing the desired result. But it can now be said that every economist has been told to consider the rhetoric of statistical significance – even if in the end both author and reader imitate slavishly the style of some academic scribbler, or some thoughtless editorial policy, of a few years back.

Sorry to say, that's what 70 per cent of us are doing: we're confusing statistical significance with economic significance, and sleepwalking through a thoughtless practice. Seventy per cent, that is, use *only* statistical significance. Ninety-six per cent misuse it. In 'The Standard Error of Regressions' (1996; Chapter 16 this volume), McCloskey and I report these and a dozen other depressing findings from our study of every paper using regression analysis in the 1980s in the *American Economic Review*. Things get worse: of the 70 per cent that confuse statistical significance with economic significance, *over 70 per cent fail to report or even measure the magnitudes of the purported relationships between economic variables* (p. 106). Tolstoy said that the greatest compliment one can pay an artist is imitation. Presumably he did not have in mind painting-by-numbers, or the science of Simon Sez. We hope to find improvement when we read all the papers of the 1990s. Our research on statistical practice has a policy implication. Journals caring about the health of the science shall profit by adding a question to their referee reports: 'Does the paper demonstrate economically significant findings?' At the time of this printing, half of us do not know. Simon Sez, ask about the meaning of your measurements.

You will hear economists of McCloskey's generation lament her rhetorical 'stuff,' wishing, with love and admiration, that she would 'come back to economics'. The lament is understandable: they cannot bear to give one of their best to full-time work in criticism. (Read 'Did Victorian Britain Fail?' (1970), a piece on entrepreneurship that is at bottom a plea for pacifism, and 'English Open Fields as Behavior Towards Risk' (1976), introduced as a piece of the new institutional economics at its beginning. You'll see what they mean (Chapters 1 and 2 this volume).) The lament is understandable and yet tragic. It tends to obstruct one's scholarship (economics has a rhetoric). It neglects the fact that McCloskey is exporting economics to other disciplines (recently, to Departments of English: Woodmansee and Osteen (eds) 1999). The lament stunts the intellectual growth of graduate students, who hang on Professor's every word (Klamer and Colander 1990). It censors conversations about economics – a discipline that in other regards will champion growth through freedom (Garnett (ed.) 1999). Worst of all the Rhetoric of Anti-Rhetoric tends to cut critical thinking out of the economics curriculum. Its professors and best-selling textbooks are stooping to lower and lower levels of Bloom's taxonomy:

Freedom, virtue. Tax vice.
Me Tarzan. You Jane.
Like banana smoothie? Come free with Mankiw book.
Do I get credit for this? Professor Tarzan, you're da' bomb!

He's da' bomb all right. But don't blame the student when she can't formulate a senior thesis. The professor of economics, in prideful ignorance of his rhetoric, is preaching freedom and self-reliance while clipping the wings of small birds.

McCloskey has more than one rhetorical perspective, more than one voice. If Italo Calvino and Grace Paley were to have stopped writing fiction and joined economics, they would have begun by imitating Deirdre McCloskey. In matters of purpose and style, it is better to imagine the philosophical self-reliance of Emerson and the perspectivalism of Nietzsche than it is fruitful to imagine Friedman or Fogel (West 1989, ch. 1; Lasch 1991, pp. 265–79; Kaufmann 1950 [1978], pp. 93–4). In the contemporary scene of social science fiction McCloskey's persona is better placed with pluralists Stanley Fish (in Law and English), Clifford Geertz (in Anthropology, Culture Studies, and Literature), George Marcus and James Clifford (in Ethnography and Fiction), and Stephen Jay Gould (in Paleontology and Just About Everything Else). In fact, Stanley Fish hired McCloskey in 1999 for the University of Illinois-Chicago, creating an academic Dream Team.

McCloskey's plurality of voices are unknown to economists who speculate from afar that rhetorical studies have nothing important to say about economics. But the fact that there is not one simple voice, a nameable McCliometrics, if you will, to scratch upon a philosopher's score card, is also missed by philosophers eager to stop the fast-break of rhetorical inquiry. While open to economic criticism, these philosophers favor analytical philosophy – a kind of 'blackboard economics' applied to questions of epistemology, ethics, and personal identity ('Economic Science' 1991, p. 10; Chapter 15 this volume). Often they have proven that the cat is on the mat (or some other existence theorem). McCloskey's response? Quote Virginia Woolf: 'Let a man get up and say, *Behold, this is the truth*, and instantly I perceive a sandy cat filching a piece of fish in the background. Look, you have forgotten the cat, I say' (Woolf 1931 in McCloskey's 'Some Consequences' 1993, p. 69; Chapter 14 this volume). In conjecture and in refutation McCloskey's voice is polyphonous: she is a Boothean anti-positivist and Neo-Aristotelian ('Rhetoric of Economics' 1983, pp. 482–4, 510; 'Not Positivist,' throughout; Chapter 7 this volume); a Feyerabend-type empiricist (McCloskey and Ziliak, 'Standard Error' (Chapter 16 this volume); Feyerabend 1981 [1988], pp. 142–7); a Habermasean theorist of speech communities (*Knowledge and Persuasion* 1994, pp. 99–101); a conservative Republican ('Bourgeois Virtue' 1994, pp. 182, 187; Chapter 6); a Rorty relativist (*Rhetoric* 1985 [1998], throughout); a Gothic economist, like John Ruskin or Beatrice Webb ('The Lawyerly' 1998, p. 98; *Knowledge and Persuasion* 1984, pp. 21–2); a (Max) Blackean student of metaphor ('Rhetoric' 1983, pp. 502–3; *Rhetoric* 1985, pp. 82–3; *If You're So Smart* 1991, p. 12); a Todorovian critic of narrative ('Storytelling in Economics' 1990, p. 20; *If You're So Smart* 1991, pp. 30–31); a (Kenneth) Burkean critic of neoclassical value theory ('The Dismal Science' 1989, pp. 100–101 and elsewhere); a proponent of dramatistic conceptions of human action, likened to the Austrian tradition ('Dismal Science,' pp. 100–101, 112); a model tester ('Gold Standard' 1976; Chapter 3); a Smithian virtue ethicist (*The Vices of Economists* 1996, pp. 128–30; 'Some Consequences' 1993, p. 85); a postmodern libertarian ('Rhetoric of Liberty' 1995); a nineteenth-century bourgeois, likened to Jane Austen ('Bourgeois Virtue' 1994, p. 184); an eighteenth-century bourgeois, likened to Benjamin Franklin (ibid, p. 179); a late positivist ('Does the Past?' 1976); an anarcho-feminist ('Some Consequences,' throughout; *Vices*, Ch. 5); a prototype of a small-town, white, Midwestern American, likened to Garrison Keilor and 'A Prairie Home Companion' ('Dismal Science,' p. 112; *If You're So Smart*, p. ix); a postmodern critic of power and knowledge, likened (with hesitations) to Michel Foucault ('Industrial Revolution' 1994, p. 269; *Knowledge and Persuasion*, Ch. 25). The list could be expanded, easily.

It's no wonder that critics have had a hard time keeping up with McCloskey. It was McCloskey who said that the division of labor is limited by the extent of speech in the market, turning Smith's insight on the specialization of labor and trade toward the faculty of speech (*Knowledge and Persuasion*, pp. 82, 372). Speaking is not cheap in the United States: McCloskey found that in 1988 persuasion alone was at least one-quarter of GDP (pp. 76–84). But the cost of persuasion does not explain why the talk between economics and the humanities cycles in a whisper and a sneer, a recession (p. 82). The recession is caused by artificial barriers to trade. It is difficult to find social scientists or philosophers who have read more than a few of the prerequisites for McCloskey's polyphony. One suspects that the literary meanings of broad generic moves, though fascinating, are slipping by. To take one example, McCloskey's 'Why I Am No Longer A Positivist' (Chapter 7) is a composite of Bertrand Russell's 'Why I am Not a Christian' and 'Why I am Not a Communist' (Russell [1957, 1956] 1961; cf. Booth 1974, Ch. 2). Complexities aside, McCloskey has circulated one open letter to the profession, easy to grasp:

Dear Junior Professors and Graduate Students,

Your potential is fantastic. Have courage. The Tenure Committee will respect you. Where to begin? Anywhere! Look at the 182 papers that Ziliak and I read in the *AER*: they need to be re-done. The textbooks – including my own *The Applied Theory of Price* – must be re-written. (You have to admit *that it is* a brilliant text. Relative to the new Tarzan and Jane model, you say. Okay fair enough.) But look, see: the historians, philosophers, journalists, citizens, dramatists, anthropologists, sociologists, and literary critics are dying for you to come off the blackboard and use economic theory in the real world – attend their seminars. Publish in their journals. Invite them to your seminars. Publish their papers in your journals.

There is so much to do dears, so much. I only hope that you won't blow it.

For the science, dears. For the science.

Love,

Deirdre

From the first book on British Iron and Steel (which won the David A. Wells Prize) to the memoir on gender crossing (which made the *New York Times*' Notable Books of the Year), McCloskey's voice has in parts remained constant (*Economic Maturity* 1973; *Crossing* 1999). As the essays here testify, McCloskey has been a constant advocate of some half-dozen ideas. She believes that economics is done best when it is historical; she favors retrodiction and stories with a moral. More Marcuse than Mises, McCloskey scorns the pretense and politics of prediction and control ('Victorian Britain' 1970; 'Gold Standard' [McCloskey and Zecher 1976]; 'Rhetoric' 1983, pp. 487–8; 'Storytelling' 1990). She believes that economics is done best when the historical perspective is long (as it is in 'Corn at Interest' [1984] (Chapter 4 this volume), where she and John Nash document the dramatic decline of interest rates, medieval to modern times; as it is in 'The Industrial Revolution' [1994] (Chapter 5 this volume), where she argues that free lunches are possible). She believes that economics is done best when the macroeconomics is open-economy ('Gold Standard;' 'Corn at Interest;' 'Industrial Revolution' 1994), when the paper asks and then measures How Big is a Big Effect? and What do You Mean, Significant? (all of Part I and Part II), when the middle classes are seen to be human and worthy ('Corn at Interest;' 'Bourgeois Virtue' 1994, 1998), when using fact and story and metaphor and logic (all of Part I; *Rhetoric* 1998, pp. 18–19), and when neoclassical, along the lines of Smith, Coase, Friedman, and Fogel.

McCloskey's 30 years of ethos-building in the mainstream suggests that one should locate her as a conventional scientist. To the heterodox economist McCloskey's ethos has been both the poison and the cure. Although heterodox economists are openly grateful for the freer dialogue that *The Rhetoric of Economics* has managed to create (now in five languages), they are severely critical of the conventional McCloskey, who dresses off-the-rack neoclassical. Saintly would not be too strong a description of both her cause and response. I am most familiar with the works of Marianne Ferber, Nancy Folbre, Ann Jennings, Julie Nelson, Diana Strassman, Albert Hirschman, Jack Amariglio, Neil Browne, Kevin Quinn, Philip Mirowski, Warren Samuels, Stephen Resnick, Richard Wolff, David Ruccio, Robert Heilbroner, William Milberg, and McCloskey's collaborator, Arjo Klamer. A brief introduction to their feminist, institutionalist, and Marxist voices can be found in Ferber and Nelson (eds), (1993); Samuels (ed.), (1990); de Marchi (ed.) (1992); Hirschman (1991); the new critical bibliography of *The Rhetoric of Economics* (1998, pp. 210–17); Part V, of *Knowledge and Persuasion* (1994; saints can get angry, too); Garnett (ed.) (1999), and Woodmansee and Osteen (eds), (1999). A similar mix of poison and cure is felt by outcast Austrians, who wish the conventional McCloskey would not go on defending data and utility functions (*Knowledge and Persuasion*, ch. 22).

Indeed when seen through the eyes of no small number of postmodernists, McCloskey's rhetoric is exposed to be old-fashioned, erroneous. After all, she believes we should reason about facts. She speaks neoclassically about a market-place of ideas. She professes the Chicago-school metaphors of value and exchange. All of this now in a postmodern rhetoric. Intolerance has at times prevailed. The English professor Wayne Booth, a hero of McCloskey's, gets booed by a gaggle of postmoderns at the meetings of the Modern Language Association. And as the postmodern economist Neil Browne has learned, invoking Booth's name can draw a hiss from a certain postmodern crowd. In other words the species of literary criticism that some economists fear is left-wing and radical in McCloskey is seen to be right-wing and 'scary' by folks in the humanities. An open field of inquiry can do well politically by avoiding some transgressions and McCloskey has done well in avoiding the larger land mines.

McCloskey is a self-conscious comedienne. She is the Calvino and Hobbes of economics, teaching moral lessons in a dialectical play of modern model-building and postmodern story-telling (Calvino 1957 [1959]; 1979 [1993]). 'Aunt Deirdre' reveals the foibles of 'the boys in the sandbox' (the boys being economists, mostly men, who pretend like *The Baron in the Trees* that scholarship can be done solely on the blackboard, that statistical significance is identical to economic significance, and that the economy can be engineered) while she delivers underneath it all a serious message (*Vices* 1996; Calvino 1957 [1959], p. 45). Economists had better get back to doing real science. Some of her readers are not laughing. In schoolyards of Massachusetts and Missouri things are so bad the AEA plays a laugh track every time a regression is run: 'HAH HAH! Whoa! heh heh heh.' But that's hardly reason for Aunt Deirdre to stop yelling from the kitchen: their *t*'s and sneers serve to strengthen the truth of her main point (*Vices*, ch. 1).

The comedienne is an optimist. She is not easy to grasp in this regard. McCloskey carries to conferences the cheer of a small-town mayor. If she were living in an age when intellectuals emphasized human nature instead of character, she would emphatically *not* keep the company of Hobbes or Calvin. Her prophets come in strange currency. She'd keep the company of Smith, Locke, Swift, Blake, Bloch, Rousseau,

Dickens, Macauley, and the Prince Kropotkin. She takes seriously and as a proposition the lives of Eric Hoffer and C.S. Lewis. It would be unfair to the facts to leave without mentioning Woody Guthrie and Jesus Christ. Indeed the 'Hobbes' part of the little joke is not apt: McCloskey does not assent to Hobbes' cynical view of human nature nor to its anti-social extensions that dominate game theory and parts of philosophy. She keeps nowadays the company of Adam Smith's *The Theory of Moral Sentiments* (1759 [19791]) and contemporary works on virtue ethics by Alasdair Macintyre and Phillipa Foot.

McCloskey-as-comic is an ironist and she has distinguished herself among critics of economics with a unique form. McCloskey's irony is not a 'smile of derision' as the historian Peter Gay (1974, p. 44) describes Edward Gibbon describing Roman subjects. A trace of derision can be found in McCloskey's irony. But more like Bernini's statues, her smile has baroque tongue-in-cheek, chiding the senators and chief patrons of economics while maintaining her own election to the senate. Unlike Veblen's, McCloskey's is not a stinker-in-a-coonskin cap irony. There is no slinging of insults from distant or disdainful locations. McCloskey's irony is ultimately embracing; it is the laughter of a best friend or a knowing wife, one who loves you despite your weaknesses. It's just that you can be better than you are. And because she happens to know a good deal about what you are up to, and because she is a vital part of your community, she is in a good position to say how you might do better.

McCloskey is asking us to stare hard at ourselves in the mirror but she wants us to do better than that. McCloskey wants us to interpret the rhetorics of our stare and of the mirror itself. (Anyone who believes a mirror to be neutral has not thought about the social and psychological implications of a hotel vanity, a periscope, Jeremy Bentham, a telescope, the zoo, John Berger, or a funnyhouse.) Our mirrors are not limited to models and regressions. Other people's money is a mirror. So is desire under constraint and *A Picture of Dorian Gray*. McCloskey is a far-reaching ironist, a provocateur. She creates mysteriously good feelings in the vanity of readers who will watch and listen. To her, the whole economy is rhetoric ('Industrial Revolution,' pp. 269–70; *Knowledge and Persuasion*, ch. 25).

At her best, McCloskey makes a passionate plea for preferred models and stories and findings while deconstructing the models and stories and findings. The achievement has implications for the practice of science. In 'History, Differential Equations, and the Problem of Narration' (1991, Chapter 11 this volume), McCloskey shows how historians share a style of argument with economists (and engineers) in linear and non-linear dynamics. The point of identifying the shared style of argument is to advance the learning of each. The basic difference between the two dynamics, linear and non-linear, is simple: if a 'path' of events (such as rocket trajectory or economic growth or women's liberation) is in fact non-linear, then small beginnings can have large effects. And if the true path is linear, then large effects can only stem from large beginnings.

Using a mix of differential equations and stories about Civil War battles, McCloskey makes the case: historians and economists argue alike. Therefore, historians and economists have a shared language for criticizing each other's stories. What dawns on the reader slowly and thrillingly about the rhetoric of the piece is that she uses small beginnings ('metaphors differ from stories') to make small points ('metaphor and story are linked by a theme') and she uses small beginnings ('metaphors differ from stories') to make big points ('humanists and economists need each other'). In other words, McCloskey uses the means of linear and non-linear dynamics to construct an argument about the narratival ends of linear and non-linear dynamics. The rhetoric of the rhetoric explains itself.

To put it differently, McCloskey offers her readers an *efferent* and an *aesthetic* way of reading any scholarly performance ('Storytelling,' p. 16; Rosenblatt 1978). The efferent way is to look for something tangible-seeming to take back to the office: a mathematical model of charitable giving, say, or some facts about the history of welfare dependence. The aesthetic reading emphasizes the poetry of the experience, the how-you-feel and what-you-feel from the dynamics of the piece. McCloskey's gift is in merging the two ways of reading, efferent and aesthetic. She makes the meaning of the model persuasive by using that very model to shape the narrative.

In the most general terms, McCloskey gives the reader an economics for thinking about the literature, and a literary criticism for thinking about the economy. One advantage of adopting this rhetorical posture is that everyday economists – not philosophers of science – become the important critics of economics (Nelson, Megill, and McCloskey (eds) 1987, ch. 1). The posture has moral implications. In McCloskey the theme is often moral, as it was in 1976 in 'English Open Fields as Behavior Towards Risk.' Once and again McCloskey's economic actors (here they are medieval peasants) ask: Is the economy I find in the paper the kind of economy I ought to live in? Is the author giving me a set of experiences that I would like to replicate in other parts of my life? The fiction here, working toward a persuasive history, is of men in the medieval peasantry. Holding land in scattered plots was good insurance in medieval England, McCloskey says, and contributed to your decency as a man (p. 165):

> [I]nsurance explains the gross facts of the persistence and decline of scattering; . . . it fits well with the view of medieval village life, long the orthodox view, that attributes fellow feeling and conservatism to medieval peasants. Peasants were conservative, to be sure, but not pointlessly so: a man is not a fool to insure himself against disaster by scattering his plots of land.

The questions that McCloskey's characters ask are the kinds of questions that many economists will ask at church or garden party but then routinely fail to ask while doing economics. Their rhetoric of motivation has become a robotic specification of Max U (a Vietnamese Jew, as McCloskey is fond of saying with a smile). McCloskey's questions begin to inquire about identity, the motivations of solidarity, and the plot of one's life, and are the kinds of questions that any economist can learn to ask by reading the works of Amartya Sen and Martha Nussbaum, Adam Smith's *The Theory of Moral Sentiments* (1759), Kenneth Burke's *A Rhetoric of Motives* (1950 [1969]), Wayne Booth's *The Company We Keep* (1988), James Agee and Walker Evans' *Let Us Now Praise Famous Men* (1939), Thorstein Veblen, any book by Albert Hirschman, nearly any piece of feminist economics, and this book. Max U is a dead metaphor. McCloskey believes that its resurrection could bring an understanding of love and other moral sentiments back into the core of market analysis. And economics back to science.

The Nietzsche scholar Walter Kaufmann makes a point about the benefits of reading

Nietzsche: 'We should not rashly take a well-phrased point for Nietzsche's ultimate position, but we often stand to gain if we ask ourselves *why* it should not be *ours*' (Kaufmann 1954 [1985], p. 1; emphasis in original). The point can be made about McCloskey, too, and should be. (For the world suffers no scarcity of scholars who would make their career off one or two phrases of a more brilliant mind.) One searches for parallels and in a coffee-house mood it is tempting to draw a parallel with Nietzsche. Each advocates a rhetorical approach; each celebrates a reasoned change of belief; each is an eccentric scholar of their time and generates more ideas than their detractors can keep up with; each employs an empiricist voice and fights against 'blackboard' science ('Economic Science' 1991). The McCloskey of *The Rhetoric of Economics* and of 'Some Consequences of a Conjective Economics' seems in places to share a vision with Nietzsche in what Nietzsche's translators have called 'the gay science' – anti-authoritarian, empirical, perspectival, playful, Dionysian (Kaufmann 1950 [1978], pp. 93–4). Still, Nietzsche was no town mayor. He died friendless. Unlike McCloskey in economics, Nietzsche strayed far from his home discipline, philology. By contrast, McCloskey's scholarship shall be seen as acts of propogation, the stuff of a pretty content soldier of the Scottish Enlightenment.

It may be useful to consider a parallel between McCloskey and a contemporary: the musician and actor, David Bowie. The comparison is unlikely. Economics is the science of scarcity; pop and rock music, the art of excess. Any likeness would not be conscious. The only rock song McCloskey can sing is 'I Walk the Line' by Johnny Cash. 'I keep a close watch on this heart of mine / I keep my eyes wide open all the time / I – mmmmm – mmmmm / how's it go?' (She knows lots of socialist hymns and songs of freedom from the Sixties.) It is unlikely, as much, that David Bowie has read 'Corn at Interest' or 'Did Victorian Britain Fail?' Of course one observer who out of politeness shall not be named whose name is Gertrude Himmelfarb might say that Bowie himself is proof: the existence of that demoralized renegade proves Victorian Britain failed. But like McCloskey in economics, David Bowie is solidly inside the mainstream of popular music while criticizing and expanding its borders from influences he finds outside of it. And like McCloskey in other human sciences, Bowie examines other cultural objects, attempting to enhance our understanding of them by showing what can be done with standard tropes in pop and rock.

A biography of McCloskey will probably pursue Bowie. But here it can be pointed out that by turns, 1960s–1990s, David Bowie was pushing the philosophical and the rhetorical boundaries of conservative, white male, pop and rock, through innovative uses of classical music, cross-dressing, computer technology, androgyny, Asian fashion, fairy tales, Grace Jones, minimalism, anti-essentialism, science fiction, film, feminism, punk rock, Pop Art, and Bing Crosby. Thus academic art historians find themselves speaking with punk rockers, and they both learn something. There is of course a multiplicity of selves in Bowie's attractions – an idea familiar to postmodern readers. That is Bowie's genius.

The parallel changes of David Bowie and Deirdre McCloskey, 1960s–1990s, would not be too difficult to draw. The drawing would follow McCloskey through Trotskyism, social history, Chicago school, cliometrics, institutionalism, international economics, international history, history of science, philosophy of science, sociology of science, Feyerabend, free markets, libertarianism, liberation, Rhetoric, rhetoric of science, classical languages, poetry, postmodernism, feminism, folk tales, free market feminism, bourgeoisie, Ben Franklin, virtues, bourgeois virtues, Jane Austen, transsexuality, Jesus, and human rights. Thus Marxist English professors find themselves at seminars with libertarian economists (Woodmansee and Osteen (eds), 1999), speaking of rhetoric, and they both learn something. That is McCloskey's genius.

The cultures of economics and rock have not been explored beyond the observation that Mick Jagger studied at the London School of Economics. (Here's a lesser-known connection, a rumor: the econometrician Richard Blundell is said to have played with the band that became Dublin's pop-punkers, The Boom Town Rats.) Strange as it may sound, understanding David Bowie may help one understand Deirdre McCloskey. It's the courageous use of self as metonymy for the message that is both shared and striking. Bowie makes the point famously in his song 'Changes' (1974):

> I turned to face myself . . . and these children / that you spit on / as they try to change their worlds / Are immune to your consultations / They're quite aware of what they're goin' through / Changes / Turn and face the strange . . . Changes / Pretty soon now you're gonna get older / Time may change me / But I can't trace time.

David Bowie, like Deirdre McCloskey, is rhetorically self-conscious, wide awake. Bowie's classic rock lyric sounds like McCloskey speaking to George Stigler and the positivist front. In 'Why I am No Longer a Positivist,' McCloskey complains that the introspective learning she (and Bowie) engage is literally ruled out by Stigler and the Old Guard, the positivists and other modern methodologists ('Not a Positivist' 1989, pp. 232, 236; 'Rhetoric' 1983, pp. 484, 488). And yet, as the chemist and philosopher Michael Polanyi, as Richard Rorty, as McCloskey, and as countless others have shown, in fact '[s]cientific knowledge is no different from other personal knowledge' ('Rhetoric' 1983, p. 488). It is through introspection on change of scene and of character that the narrators of the stories 'Changes' and 'Why I Am No Longer A Positivist' find – and justify – an important plot of history. A Stiglerian economist will not turn to face himself. His denial of an important tool of science – self-knowledge – will blind him to the bigger plots of economic history. He will confuse tastes with values (Hirschman 1984 [1995]), and he will believe that he lives in the best of all possible worlds.

An understanding of Deirdre McCloskey can be advanced by a reading of the poem 'Origins' by Adrienne Rich, the celebrated poet and sage of courageous transgressions. It is worth naming here at least three things for which Adrienne Rich is known publicly. Rich, a poet and divorced mother of three, came out as a lesbian and an anti-war activist (at a time well beyond her youth); the eminent poet reclaimed her family's Jewish identity, and wrote about the trauma (and necessity) of being 'split at the root' (in Lopate 1994, pp. 654–5); she also published poems about her sexuality, her gender identity, and her anti-war politics in a spoken-word poetry long before the spoken word was mainstream. 'Origins' can help one appreciate the role of transgression in what McCloskey achieves as economist and critic, taking attention properly away from the turning points.

> Turning points. We all like to hear about those. Points
> on a graph.

Sudden conversions. Historical swings. Some kind of
dramatic structure.
But a life doesn't unfold that way it moves
in loops by switchbacks loosely strung
around the swelling of one hillside toward another
one island toward another
A child's knowing a child's forgetting remain childish
till you meet them mirrored and echoing somewhere else
Don't ask me where I learned love
Don't ask me where I learned fear
Ask about the size of rooms how many lived in them
what else the rooms contained
what whispers of the histories of skin . . .
(Rich 1995, p. 63).

Apply 'Origins' to Deirdre McCloskey. One has more to gain by asking about the size of her rooms and how many live in them – a suggestion, it seems, as one listens to Rich, to ask about the spaces for conversation that McCloskey has opened up within and across the disciplines. Don't ask where she learned rhetoric. Don't ask where she learned she was a woman. Ask whose company she keeps, what good scholarship and what genuine friendships her life makes possible.

The economic historian Alexander Gerschenkron (who supervised McCloskey's dissertation at Harvard) cast serious doubt on the plausibility of W.W. Rostow's metaphor of economic development, 'take off' to 'sustained growth' (Gerschenkron 1952 [1962]; *If You're So Smart* 1991, ch. 5). More: Gerschenkron put the quietus to two centuries of philosophical thinking that economies have to develop in stages, Comte to Marx to Rostow (*If You're So Smart*, p. 76; Hirschman 1995, pp. 198–9). In like fashion, Gerschenkron would probably approve of the trivial role that Rich assigns to 'turning points,' to so-called stages, in personal development. Like Gerschenkron's, her story is a non-linear and feminist story to tell, and is therefore more difficult for economists to understand than are the linear stories of take-offs and spurts. The non-linear understanding is worth the investment. As Rich observed, '[it]'s a moving into accountability, enlarging the range of accountability' (in Lopate, p. 655). Perhaps McCloskey's most important contribution to the history of economics will come to be seen not in the rhetoric of economics or in economic history per se – these alone are worthy of highest distinction – but in the responsible modeling of a chameleon scholar, mirrored and echoing, in a mostly conifer field. (It's really beautiful, when one thinks of it, that we are speaking here not of a painter or a poet but a Chicago school economist.) A scholarly life, like a personal life, doesn't unfold in sudden conversions, quantitative history to literary criticism. Marxism to libertarianism. Male to female. A scholarly life moves in loops, in switchbacks loosely strung.

Improving Modernist Economics with the Gothic

What would an economics that took a full turn toward McCloskey look like? Some graduate schools still put a copy of Milton Friedman's positivist essay, 'The Methodology of Positive Economics' (1953), into the hands of first-year students. Friedman's essay is handed out in the same way that registration cards for the US

Army are handed out: round about age 18, or 22, you're told to sign up if you want to stay free (and maintain your citizenship). In the twenty-first century the essay will come to be seen as a minor remark on method during the Cold War of economic thought. But to have a consciousness about the essay one has to have read other essays in history and method, a discipline of mind which most graduate schools have let wither. Good graduate programs will not ban Friedman's essay: that would make the mistake of strategic deterrence that philosophical positivism has made. But every graduate student ought to develop a consciousness about the methods of economic science. If Adam Smith and Karl Marx were to become Co-Chairs of Economics, Berkeley or Chicago, you can be sure they'd agree. One could not begin graduate school with more vigor than by holding a couple of seminars on *Measurement and Meaning in Economics* and Friedman's 'The Methodology of Positive Economics.' The seminars could also serve as an excellent capstone for job-seeking PhDs.

We can summarize the practices of an economics which takes a full turn toward the 'Gothic' economics of Deirdre McCloskey. (In 'The Lawyerly Rhetoric of Coase's' one can see that McCloskey's architectural metaphor for best practice economics – Gothic – is not chosen randomly. Rather, McCloskey's Gothic stands figuratively atop the origins of modernism and postmodernism; namely, upon architecture [Lyotard 1984; 'The Lawyerly' 1998, p. 98].) Table 1 lists the main features: the first column, 'Economics now,' lists the central concerns of mainstream economics as it is currently practiced; the second column, 'Economics improved,' lists the concerns of an economics that gets back to science and to the wider conversations of humankind.

The details are in 17 books, 200 articles and, essentially, here. I don't agree with all the correlations of cure. McCloskey's style of economics will bring economists much closer to their subjects and yet we could get closer still: a gendered economics needs a racialized economics. (Quiz: Who was the first African American to study for the PhD in economics? For movements in this direction, and for the answer, permit me to mention the insightful papers assembled by Thomas Boston [1997a,b].) I will nevertheless tape this Table to my computer – call it my 'Things To Do' list. As science it will be more difficult than current practice. But then so is any practice that delivers unusually large rewards, intrinsic and extrinsic.

If the timing were different, this gathering together of scattered pieces could be called with novelty *Essays in Persuasion*, or simply, *Persuasion*. Unfortunately, *Essays in Persuasion* is already taken by Keynes' book of British economic history. (The precedence of Keynes did not stop one author from putting the name on a book of English literary criticism [Huntley 1981].) Unfortunately, again, *Persuasion* has on its side and against it Aristotelian rhetoric and the novel of McCloskey's beloved Jane Austen. Too bad the titles are famously taken. They cover a lot of McCloskey's range: British history, criticism, the gold standard, open fields, Austen, and Aristotle. Come to think of it, in a world that knows again the value of rhetoric, perhaps 'essays in persuasion' will become as common as 'principles of economics.' We could name McCloskey's works either way – essays in persuasion or principles of economics – and the parity would bring no real damage to the interests. In time. Meanwhile, *Measurement and Meaning in Economics* seems just about right.

Table 1 We're overdue for a new rhetoric of economic science

Economics Now emphasizes:	Economics Improved will emphasize:
Preference theory (*De gustibus non est disputandum*)	Metapreferences; character; dramatistic conceptions of self; preference formation
Constrained maximization	Stories about identity, including constrained choice (prudence), love, courage, justice, and temperance
Prediction	Retrodiction; historical inquiry
Steering the economy	Liberty
Efferent readings of scholarship	Efferent and aesthetic readings of scholarship
Closed economies	Open economies
Blackboard theory and logic	The whole 'rhetorical tetrad:' fact, story, logic, metaphor
Mathematical research	Mathematical research with real world evidence, with real world characters, with historical perspective, and with the discipline of ethical story-telling for making points about the real world
Mathematics as a 'solution' concept for real economies	Mathematics as legitimizing device for the self-image of the scientist; Mathematics as a helpful – sometimes most appropriate – logic
Sophisticated models	Styles which fit the idea and the occasion
Individualism	Individualism, with attention to solidarity and to identity politics
Statistical significance	Economic significance, though not abandoning statistical significance; simulation
Scholastic contributions	Interdisciplinary and courageous contributions
Autonomy	Social embeddedness
Monologue	Dialogue
Positivism and philosophical kin	Rhetorics of inquiry and other literary criticisms
Philosophical conservatism (consistency)	Philosophical self-reliance (even if that means changing one's beliefs; e.g., as in Hirschman's [1995] practice of 'self-subversion')

Table 1 (continued)

Economics Now emphasizes:	Economics Improved will emphasize:
Samuelson, Stigler, Arrow, Popper, Hayek, A.J. Ayer, Klein, Tinbergen, Descartes	Adam Smith, John Ruskin, Kenneth Burke, Fogel, Coase, Friedman, Ralph Waldo Emerson, Nietzsche, Paul Feyerabend, Nancy Folbre, Albert Hirschman, Barbara Bergman, Thomas Schelling, Alasdair MacIntyre, Mary Hesse, Martha Nussbaum, Richard Rorty, Wayne Booth, Barbara McClintock, Thomas Kuhn, Stephen Jay Gould, Michael Polanyi, Amartya Sen, Swift, Shaw, Balzac, Brecht, Hardy, Dickens, Ibsen, Austen, Frost
Patriarchy and essentialism	Feminism and anti-essentialism
Value neutrality (positive economics)	Ethics; moral economy (the classically rhetorical, accepting the fact that 'positive' and 'normative' are useless and harmful fictions)
'Objective' data from a CD-Rom	Multiple sources of data: tax records; employment records; administrative records; surveys; archives; questionnaires; ethnography; diaries; confessionals; self-constructed: think Beatrice Webb, Octavia Hill, J.R. Commons, Wassily Leontief
Faculty of reason	Faculty of speech and of reason

References

The cited works of D.N. McCloskey appear in the Appendix.

Agee, James and Walker Evans. *Let Us Now Praise Famous Men: Three Tenant Families* (Boston: Houghton Mifflin, 1939).
Booth, Wayne C. *Modern Dogma and the Rhetoric of Assent* (Chicago: University of Chicago Press, 1974).
Booth, Wayne C. *The Company We Keep: An Ethics of Fiction* (Berkeley: University of California Press, 1988).
Boston, Thomas. *A Different Vision: African American Economic Thought*, 2 vols (London: Routledge, 1997a), Vol. 1.
Boston, Thomas. *A Different Vision: Race and Public Policy*, 2 vols (London: Routledge, 1997b), Vol. 2.
Bowie, David. 'Changes' (1974), sound recording on David Bowie, *ChangesOneBowie* (New York: RCA Records, 1976).
Burke, Kenneth. *A Rhetoric of Motives* (Berkeley: University of California Press, 1950 [1969]).
Calvino, Italo. *The Baron in the Trees* (Orlando: Harcourt Brace, 1957 [1957]). Translated by William Collins Sons and Co.
Calvino, Italo. *If On A Winter's Night A Traveler* (New York: Alfred A. Knopf, 1981 [1993]). Translated by William Weaver.
de Marchi, Neil (ed.). *The Post-Popperian Methodology of Economics: Recovering Practice* (Boston and Dordrecht: Kluwer and Neijhoff, 1992).

Ferber, Marrianne, and Julie Nelson (eds). *Beyond Economic Man* (Chicago: University of Chicago Press, 1993).
Feyerabend, P.K. *Problems of Empiricism: Philosophical Papers, Volume 2* (Cambridge: Cambridge University Press, 1981 [1988]).
Friedman, Milton. 'The Methodology of Positive Economics', in *Essays in Positive Economics* (Chicago: University of Chicago Press, 1953).
Garnett, Robert Jr (ed.). *What Do Economists Know? New Economics of Knowledge* (London: Routledge, 1999).
Gay, Peter. *Style in History* (New York: Basic Books, 1974).
Gerschenkron, Alexander. *Economic Backwardness in Historical Perspective: A Book of Essays* (Cambridge, MA: Harvard University Press, 1952 [1962]).
Hirschman, Albert O. 'Against Parsimony: Three Easy Ways of Complicating Some Categories of Economic Discourse', in Stefano Zamagni (ed.), *The Economics of Altruism*, International Library of Critical Writings in Economics, vol. 48 (Aldershot, UK: Edward Elgar, 1992 [1995]), pp. 363–81. First published in *American Economic Review*, **74** (2, May 1984): 89–96.
Hirschman, Albert O. *The Rhetoric of Reaction: Perversity, Futility, Jeopardy* (Cambridge, MA: Harvard University Press, 1991).
Hirschman, Albert O. *A Propensity to Self-Subversion* (Cambridge, MA: Harvard University Press, 1995).
Huntley, Frank Livingstone. *Essays in Persuasion* (Chicago: University of Chicago Press, 1981).
Kaufmann, Walter. 'Introduction', in *The Portable Nietzsche* (Harmondsworth: Penguin, 1954 [1985]). Edited and translated by Walter Kaufmann.
Kaufmann, Walter. *Nietzsche: Philosopher, Psychologist, Antichrist* (Princeton: Princeton University Press, 1950 [1978]).
Klamer, Arjo, and David Colander. *The Making of an Economist* (Boulder: Westview Press, 1990).
Lasch, Christopher. *The True and Only Heaven: Progress and Its Critics* (New York: Norton, 1991).
Lopate, Phillip (ed.). *The Art of the Personal Essay: An Anthology from the Classical Era to the Present* (New York: Anchor Books, 1994).
Lyotard, Jean-Francois. *The Postmodern Condition: A Report on Knowledge* (Minneapolis: University of Minnesota, 1984). Translation from the French by Geoff Bennington and Brian Massumi.
Nelson, John S., Allen Megill, and D.N. McCloskey (eds). *The Rhetoric of the Human Sciences: Language and Argument in Scholarship and Public Affairs* (Madison: University of Wisconsin Press, 1987).
New York Times. 'Transsexual Economist Argues That Gender Determines Approach to Field', by Louise Uchitelle, 19 June 1999.
Paley, Grace. *Enormous Changes at the Last Minute* (New York: Farrar, Straus, Giroux, 1974).
Rich, Adrienne C. 'Split at the Root: An Essay on Jewish Identity' (1986), in Lopate (ed.), 1994, pp. 640–55.
Rich, Adrienne C. 'Origins', *Dark Fields of the Republic: Poems, 1991–1995* (New York: Norton, 1995).
Rosenblatt, Louise M. *The Reader, the Text, the Poem: The Transactional Theory of the Literary Work* (Carbondale: Southern Illinois University Press, 1978).
Russell, Bertrand. *The Basic Writings of Bertrand Russell* (New York: Simon and Schuster, 1961). Edited by Robert E. Egner and Lester F. Denonn.
Samuels, Warren J. (ed.). *Economics as Discourse: An Analysis of the Language of Economists* (Boston, Dordrect and London: Kluwer Academic, 1990).
Smith, Adam. *The Theory of Moral Sentiments* (Indianapolis: Liberty Classics, 1759 [1979]. Follows the 1853 'New Edition' by Henry G. Bohn. Introduction by E.G. West.
West, Cornel. *The American Evasion of Philosophy: A Genealogy of Pragmatism* (Madison: University of Wisconsin Press, 1989).
Woodmansee, Martha and Mark Osteen (eds). *The New Economic Criticism: Studies at the Intersection of Literature and Culture* (London: Routledge, 1999).

Preface: Personal Knowledge

Deirdre McCloskey

What's the unity? Steve Ziliak's 'Introduction' gives a characteristically insightful answer. He's asked me to give my own, cruder one here.

I've been most things in my life – a socialist, a positivist, a man. I don't regret my earlier versions. They've given me sympathy for the Other, I suppose, having been one. It has certainly been interesting to wander from high-school football player to college socialist to grad-school social engineer to husband and father and professor of this and that. I remember how impressed my own father was when a guidance counselor in my 8th grade told us that I had both verbal and mathematical ability and therefore could bring the Two Cultures together. My father was a professor, too, but hopeless at math (as a student of political science he got an A in Alvin Hansen's graduate course in economics at Harvard in 1946 by reading only the words between the diagrams and equations; even in 1946 that was difficult). My father was delighted, amazed, that his son could both write poetry and understand algebra. I've gradually come back, after putting away the literary side for a couple of decades while becoming competent in the quantitative side of the science, to the theme of exploring both sides together: there's the unity . . . in disunity.

But I wish I was better at whipping the dish into a smoother texture. It's simpler if you cook one thing, or can make it look like one thing at table. Your life will be easier to grasp. Some people – I think of Paul David of Stanford and All Souls – have such unified intellectual lives. Paul is still making the argument for indivisibilities he first noticed as a Harvard graduate student in the generation just before mine. His work coheres, and coheres, and coheres. Mine ramifies, and ramifies, and ramifies. His is an arrow; mine a branch. Isaiah Berlin long ago drew a distinction between hedgehogs and foxes: the hedgehogs know one big thing, the foxes many little things. I guess Paul is a hedgehog who wants to be a fox; I'm definitely a fox who wants to be a hedgehog.

All right, Deirdre. Answer the question. What's the unity? Make your case for hedgehogness, arrowness, the One Uniform Dish. This: I have always detested self-satisfied conventions, which makes me a radical of sorts. I'm an odd one, since I get just as annoyed at the self-satisfaction of the right as of the left or center. When I hear the phrase delivered with a smirk, 'It's obvious that,' I reach for my oomph. I have always believed in oomph. (I learned the other day that in the 1930s and 1940s oomph meant 'sex appeal;' that's nice, but I use it here in its more recent sense, something like 'force; strength of effect.') When I hear the words 'large' and 'significant' I reach for my yardsticks of oomphness. So from the earliest to the latest of the papers reprinted here you will see, I hope, that I'm a radical oomphist. There. I get very upset by the unsupported sneering that dominates academic life, the rhetoric of oomph-less ideology. I think a socialism needs to show that some new government intervention will do better than in the past. That's why I admire Baran and Sweezy's great (and mistaken) work: it tries to show that Marxism has oomph, rather than merely asserting it. A capitalism needs to show that competition actually works. That's why I admire Friedman's great (and mistaken) work: it tries to show that monetarism and free markets have oomph, though sometimes merely asserting it. A 'showing' in my little personal methodology involves actually thinking through the conventional arguments and then subjecting them to actual measurement. In short, it's science. As the Valley girls say: Duh. Or in Yiddish: So what else is new?

What's surprising is how few people want to do economic science. I get depressed by the rarity of people like Margaret Reid or Robert Fogel or Barbara Bergmann or Richard Caves. The great disappointments of my personal-intellectual life have been discovering that one hero or heroine after another turns out to be just another sneering ideologue, unwilling to take a chance with her conventional wisdom. Thus Bob Lucas; or George Stigler. I like to focus on Milton Friedman's most terrifying seminar question, 'How do you know?' (In my first week as an assistant professor at Chicago I was holding forth about the 'monopoly' of professional sports, a fact I had learned from Milton, when he himself looked up at me and inquired, 'How do you know? What makes you think that professional sports is a monopoly?' I had no idea. I could hardly reply, 'You told me so.') I've taken to telling graduate students that if they ask Milton's Question of every paragraph they write they will become good scientists; if of every sentence, great ones.

Of course if you accept without rethinking the convention that words and numbers are opposites the 'How do you know?' reduces to quantification. So for a long while I was a simpleminded positivist, until I noticed that the positivism didn't really get to the oomph. It's phony. The real reasons we come to scientific conclusions are not, say, proving existence theorems or finding statistically significant correlations. These matter a teensie bit. But mainly, I realized in the early 1980s (twenty years into the study of economics, so you can see I was a slow learner), the two bankrupt methods of modern economics are a small part of proper scientific persuasion.

I know it looks like my work splits into numbers and words, cliometrics and rhetoric. But don't you see, gentle reader, that both are radically oomphist? That both ask, 'How do you know?' Sometimes the answer is, 'Because total factor productivity was not hugely different between Britain and America,' or 'Because the correlation of yields in close fields is small enough to make scattering worthwhile.' And sometimes (more times than a simpleminded positivist would imagine, as I've come to realize) it is, 'Because of all the good reasons one might believe that markets are integrated internationally, they are integrated internationally, despite the insistence of one-instrument folk that they are not.' Or, 'Because the question is one of meaning, not of behavior.'

I'll keep trying to get the recipe for the dish right, a pound of quantification, a liter of poetics, a pinch of common sense. Is there unity? Will the dish ever make it to the table? I guess so, if I live long enough, even though I keep thinking at the last minute of new ingredients – feminism, Christianity, calibrated simulation. But please do stay. There's plenty to eat. Have a seat, now. May I get you something to drink?

PART I

WRITING HISTORICAL ECONOMICS AS IF MEASUREMENT MATTERED

[1]

Did Victorian Britain Fail?[1]

By DONALD N. McCLOSKEY

FEW beliefs are so well established in the credo of British economic history as the belief that the late Victorians failed. Statistical economists and literary historians, Englishmen and foreigners, late Victorians and moderns have accepted some version of it. The three senses in which Britain is said to have failed are that output grew too slowly because of sluggish demand, that too much was invested abroad because of imperfect capital markets, and that productivity stagnated because of inept entrepreneurship. The three are closely related. Slower growing demand, partly an inevitable consequence of new competition in world markets and partly an avoidable consequence of the shortcomings of British merchants and manufacturers, is said to have slowed British growth and, consequently, to have dulled the incentive to invest at home. The obstacles to investment were multiplied by imperfect capital markets, which channelled funds abroad to an even greater extent than warranted by the sluggish markets at home. In this milieu entrepreneurs had few opportunities to invest in new technologies. Again, however, the obstacles were multiplied by the inadequate response of the economy, for entrepreneurs were slow to take up even the limited opportunities open to them. Productivity, therefore, is said to have stagnated, worsening Britain's position in foreign markets, driving still more investment abroad, and closing the circle of failure. Few historians subscribe to the whole of this dismal tale, but many believe parts of it. The argument of this essay is that these beliefs are ill founded.

I

Since the early 'thirties when W. Hoffmann found that British industrial growth slowed noticeably after 1870, historians have suspected a failure in output growth. In a companion study to Hoffmann's, W. Schlote found that export growth also slowed after 1870. The correlation between industrial and export growth was suggestive and its discovery timely, for the new economics of the 'thirties seemed to provide it with a theoretical rationale. Aggregate demand, after all, determines output, and exports were a large part of Britain's aggregate demand. To many economists and historians it has seemed that this insight, though used by its discoverers to explain relatively brief periods of mass unemployment in the 'twenties and 'thirties, could also be used to explain the slow growth of the British economy in the forty years after 1870.[2]

[1] I should like to thank Professors P. David, S. L. Engerman, R. W. Fogel, P. Lindert, P. F. Mc-Gouldrick, J. R. Meyer, C. Pope, and R. Sylla for their comments on a version of this essay presented in January 1969 to the Purdue Conference on the Application of Economic Theory and Quantitative Techniques to Problems of Economic History.

[2] E.g. W. A. Lewis in *Economic Survey, 1919–1939* (1949), p. 74: "There can be little doubt that the main cause of the relative British stagnation was to be found in the export trade. In the first part of the nineteenth century the growth of British exports was astonishing..."; D. J. Coppock, 'The Climacteric of the 1890's: A Critical Note', *Manchester School*, XXIV (1956), 2: "The low rate of capital accumulation is explained partly by an exogenous decline in the rate of export growth, which reduced the incentive to invest."

One systematic use of the demand explanation of the late Victorian decline is a paper by J. R. Meyer, 'An Input–Output Approach to Evaluating British Industrial Production in the Late 19th Century'.[1] Because it makes the argument in a simple form and arrives at a concrete conclusion against which the significance of criticisms can be measured, it makes a particularly good text for an examination of the hypothesis. As Meyer puts the argument,

> Under almost any set of realistic assumptions, increments of industrial exports should increase the value of total production by more than their own value... This means that the indirect as well as direct effects of the late-nineteenth-century export decline must somehow be evaluated... About the best means now known for obtaining such measurements is the Leontief input-output table. The author has constructed such a table for the British economy of 1907... The level of industrial activity that would have been generated if exports had maintained the 1854–1872 rates of growth, everything else assumed unchanged, was found by replacing the actual exports with the theoretical exports [and using the input–output table] to arrive at the implied direct and indirect requirements of industrial output... the results tend to support the hypothesis that if the rate of growth in industrial exports had been maintained, the United Kingdom could have sustained its former high-level advance in industrial production... The input–output results ... [substantiate] the plausibility of retarded exports as an explanation of nineteenth-century stagnation in the United Kingdom.[2]

There are a number of criticisms of the argument that make it seem over-elaborate or incomplete but do not change its central conclusion. One such criticism is that the exercise in input–output analysis is unnecessary. If it is appropriate to speak of one rate of growth for all the many types of British exports, this rate will produce an identical rate of growth of gross output simply because the matrix of inter-industry requirements is assumed in input–output analysis to be a matrix of constants. And it is entirely appropriate to speak of one rate of growth of final demand in the present context. The hypothesis under consideration is that the falling average rate of growth of exports after 1870 retarded industrial production. The argument is not about the product composition of export growth but about its average rate, the one rate of growth that characterizes its behaviour. Little is gained by carrying out the input–output calculations, for the result that they will give has been assumed. Meyer's data imply, for example, that if exports had grown at 4·8 per cent per year from 1872 to 1907, as they did from 1854 to 1872, then industrial output would have grown at 4·7 per cent per year.[3] The near equality of the two rates is not surprising.

Although gross output and final demand must grow at the same rate if the assumptions of input–output analysis are met, they do not appear to have done so, and this is another difficulty with the argument. Hoffmann's index of industrial output, which is essentially a gross output index, grew at about 1·69 per

[1] *Explorations in Entrepreneurial History*, VIII (1955), 12–34, reprinted with revisions as ch. 5 in A. H. Conrad and J. R. Meyer, *The Economics of Slavery and Other Studies in Econometric History* (Chicago, 1964), to which subsequent references are made.
[2] Ibid. pp. 184–92, *passim*.
[3] Using Meyer's procedure, this is the rate of growth derived from increasing Hoffmann's index of industrial output including building in 1907 by the ratio of Meyer's hypothetical to actual industrial output in that year.

cent per year from 1872 to 1907 while real exports grew at 2·36 per cent and real national income at 2·40 per cent.[1] The difference of 0·7 per cent per year between the growth of final demand and gross output is inconsistent with the assumption in input–output analysis of fixed intermediate requirements. It took less and less intermediate output to produce the final output of the economy. Neglecting this development (which may with some justice be called "productivity change") will lead to an incorrect estimate of the hypothetical rate of growth of industrial output.

Neither of these criticisms, however, alters the broad conclusion. The hypothetical rate of growth of gross output as a whole (and industrial gross output as a part of it) can be recalculated using the more economical argument that its growth must equal the hypothetical growth of final demand minus the growth of the ratio of final demand to gross output. The rate of growth of exports from 1854 to 1872 is taken to be the hypothetical rate of growth of final demand from 1872 to 1907 in the relevant sense. It matters little whether exports alone or all of final demand (consumption, investment, exports, and government spending) are treated as the exogenous variable, for they grow at similar rates. The change in the ratio of final demand (Imlah's index) to gross output (Hoffmann's index) is calculated from the observed change in the period 1872–1907. Subtracting it from the hypothetical growth of final demand yields a gross output growth rate of 4·37 − 0·67 = 3·71 per cent per year from 1872 to 1907 had exports grown as they did from 1854 to 1872. This is indeed far above the growth-rate of 1·69 per cent per year in industrial output actually achieved from 1872 to 1907 and is higher even than the rate of 2·98 per cent per year achieved from 1854 to 1872. The emphasis on exports appears to be justified.[2]

The argument that Britain's output grew more slowly because of slower growing exports, however, assumes that aggregate demand alone determined output, when in fact there were constraints of supply.[3] Indeed, there is evidence that they were the only binding constraints. If faltering export demand after 1872 held back the growth of the British economy there would have been increasing unemployment as actual output, cut by the insufficiency of aggregate demand, fell more and more behind potential output. But unemployment after 1872 was low and did not increase with time: the trade-union figures suggest that unemployment late in the period 1872–1907 was lower than it was early in the period. The Victorian economy was at full employment and the growth of real output was determined by the growth of the factors of production, such as fixed capital and skilled labour, not by aggregate demand. This, then, is the decisive criticism of the demand theory: in the situation of the Victorian economy it is more plausible

[1] The Hoffmann index used here includes building (the results excluding building are virtually the same). Exports are Imlah's index, given in B. R. Mitchell, *Abstract of British Historical Statistics* (Cambridge, 1962), p. 328. National income is C. H. Feinstein's estimate (his net national income deflated by Bowley's retail price index), ibid. p. 367.

[2] An improvement in the terms of trade arising from faster-growing export demand is not a part of the demand hypothesis as it is usually stated. The argument that follows, therefore, abstracts from it.

[3] Since writing this I have discovered that D. H. Whitehead made essentially the same point about Meyer's argument in an interesting paper, 'The New Economic History: Counterfactuals and *Ceteris Paribus*', presented at the February 1968 Christchurch meeting of the Australian and New Zealand Association for the Advancement of Science.

to assume that supply created its own demand than that demand would have created its own supply.

The argument is that the hypothetical growth-rate of 3·71 per cent per year was impossible. Clearly, if all factors of production were inelastic in supply and if productivity change were exogenous, the achieved rate of growth would have been the limit of possibility. The question, then, is whether productivity change and the supplies of factors of production were responsive enough to the demands of the economy to permit a 3·71 per cent rate of growth.

The supply of labour was in all likelihood insufficiently responsive to the pressures of export demand in the late nineteenth century to permit so high a growth-rate. Unemployment was low and the rural pool of underemployed labour was by this time small.[1] Had all emigration from the United Kingdom ceased and had all these emigrants been of working age, the labour force might have grown at 1·6 per cent per year rather than at 1 per cent as it did from 1871 to 1911, but this is still low relative to the hypothetical growth of gross output.[2] If capital and labour were not substitutable, then, the slow growth of the labour force in the United Kingdom would have limited output growth. To put it the other way, had output grown at 3·71 per cent per year from 1872 to 1907 instead of 1·69 per cent the labour force at the end of the period would have had to have been twice as large as the actual labour force and two-fifths larger than the entire population aged 15 and over.[3]

If capital and labour *were* substitutable, an increase in capital per man could substitute in some degree for these improbable increases in the labour force. The magnitude of the necessary capital accumulation, assuming that the elasticity of substitution between capital and labour was unity, can be estimated from an equation of the sources of growth:

$$\bar{Q}_{go} = s_k \bar{K} + s_l \bar{L} + T'$$

in which $\bar{Q}_{go}$ is the proportional growth-rate of gross output in the economy, $\bar{K}$ and $\bar{L}$ the growth-rates of capital and labour, s_k and s_l their shares in national income, and T' the rate of productivity change defined to correspond with gross

[1] The only detailed employment statistics are for Great Britain, not the United Kingdom. Agricultural employment was only 8·5 per cent of the British work force in 1911 according to Mitchell, op. cit. p. 60. It is appropriate to take a year late in the period 1870–1914 because the proposition to be refuted asserts that there could have been substantially more re-employment of rural workers than was actually accomplished. Domestic service might have been another source of labour, although most of the workers were women with little alternative employment available (as their low wages suggest). In any case, in Great Britain the sum of employment in agriculture, domestic service, and personal service was 22·6 per cent of the labour force in 1911, contrasted with 41·5 per cent in the United States in 1910.—U.S. Bureau of the Census, *Historical Statistics of the United States, Colonial Times to 1957* (Washington, D.C., 1960), p. 74.

[2] The estimates of total employment in the United Kingdom are those of E. H. Phelps Brown and S. J. Handfield-Jones in 'The Climacteric of the 1890's: A Study in the Expanding Economy', *Oxford Economic Papers*, n.s. IV (1952), 298. The emigration estimates are those of Ferenczi and Willcox, given in Mitchell, op. cit. p. 50.

[3] Gross output in 1907 would have been twice what it actually was if it had grown at 3·71 per cent from 1872. If technology and the amount of capital per man were independent of the growth of the labour force, the actual ratio of gross output to employment in 1911 will serve as the ratio under the hypothetical conditions. Applying this ratio to the actual labour force raises it to 39·5 million.

output.[1] The growth equation can be solved for the rate of growth of capital,

$$\bar{K} = \frac{1}{s_k}[\bar{Q}_{go} - s_l \bar{L} - \bar{T}']$$

and placing the appropriate values in the right-hand side of the new equation yields the necessary rate:[2]

$$\bar{K} = \frac{1}{0 \cdot 442}[0 \cdot 0371 - 0 \cdot 52\,(0 \cdot 0102) - 0 \cdot 0050] = 0 \cdot 0609$$

This 6·09 per cent per year rate of capital growth is in the vicinity of four times the actual rate in the late nineteenth century.[3] The hypothetically higher capital growth would have had to have come from a great increase in the ratio of savings to income. Indeed, the disproportionate growth in capital would make the task more difficult because the capital–output ratio would rise, raising the savings ratio necessary for a given rate. Englishmen would have had to have saved about 42 per cent of their income—that is to say, an incredibly high proportion of it— for gross output to grow at its hypothetical rate of 3·71 per cent per year.[4]

The argument, of course, can be made the other way around: from a reasonable upper bound on the savings ratio one can deduce upper bounds on the growth of capital and output. An assumption about the outcome of such an exercise underlies much of the discussion of British opportunities at the end of the nineteenth century. As a matter of arithmetic higher savings are always possible, but the relevant historical question is whether the late Victorians were profligate in consumption compared with foreigners at the time or with Englishmen before.

[1] The constancy of the shares of labour, land, and capital over the period 1870–1914 suggests that a unitary elasticity of substitution is a reasonable approximation. A production function for gross output can be written

$$Q_{go} = F(K, L, Q_{go}^i, T')$$

in which Q_{go}^i is the quantity of intermediate material input corresponding to the particular degree of inter-industry detail chosen and T' is a parameter of technological change or time. The equation in the text can be derived from this production function. The shares attached to $\bar{K}$ and $\bar{L}$ are the shares in national income, not the shares in gross output. T' is about 0·005, using the data of the next two footnotes and the growth-rate of the Hoffmann index (1·69 per cent per year).

[2] The growth-rate of gross output is the hypothetical rate derived earlier. If the elasticity of substitution is one the shares of capital and labour will not change with different endowments. Consequently, the observed shares will be the shares under the hypothetical increase in the capital–labour ratio. The value 0·52 for labour is derived from the share of P. Deane and W. A. Cole's wages and salaries estimate in home-produced income (British Economic Growth, 1688–1959, Cambridge, 1964, p. 247) and the value 0·44 for capital is derived from the residual from 1·00 of land's share (based on Stamp's estimate of net property income) and labour's share. The rates of growth of labour (0·0102 each year) and productivity are also assumed to be the same under the new regime of rapid capital accumulation. The assumption that faster capital accumulation had little long-run effect on the rate of productivity change is justified by the pattern of productivity change reported below.

[3] The estimate of the growth of domestic fixed capital is 1·43 per cent per year, 1870–1910. Its derivation is explained below.

[4] The capital output ratio, v, must have averaged about 4·9 in 1870–1910 because domestic fixed capital formation was about 7 per cent of income (a low estimate) and the capital stock grew at about 1·43 per cent (7/1·43=4·9). This agrees roughly with Deane and Cole's estimates (op. cit. p. 274). In 1870, therefore, a 6·09 per cent growth of capital would require a savings ratio of (4·9) (6·09 per cent) =30 per cent. After 1870, with the capital stock growing at 6·09 per cent and national income at 4·34 per cent (the hypothetical growth rate of exports), v would rise from 4·9 at 6·09−4·34=1·75 per cent each year. By 1910 it would be 9·95 (!) and the required savings ratio would be (9·95) (6·09)=60·5 per cent. The geometric average of 30 and 60 is 42.

The evidence suggests that they were not. American savings ratios were higher than British ratios, but the difference was small. For example, from 1886 to 1900, by all accounts a period of low British savings, the British ratio of net investment to net national income averaged 10·4 per cent, while the American ratio averaged 13·7 per cent, a difference of 3·3 per cent of income.[1] Nor were savings a much higher share of national income before 1870: the savings ratio averaged 12·8 per cent from 1858 to 1873. Given the probable range of error in the estimates, the differences are insignificant. More important, if the order of magnitude of the deficiency in the savings ratio were 3 or 4 per cent of income, making up the deficiency would have had a small impact on the rate of growth of income. British emulation of the American standard of thrift, for example, would have raised the rate of growth of domestic capital by about a half of its former rate and the rate of growth of income by less than a tenth.[2] In other words, the route to significantly higher income growth by way of a rise in the savings ratio was not open to late Victorian England.

II

It is likely, then, that there were binding resource limitations on the growth of the British economy in the late nineteenth century. By reallocating resources, of course, any one sector of the economy could have grown faster: industry could have grown at the expense of services and exports at the expense of production for home consumption had labour and capital been allocated differently. The most popular target for hypothetical reallocation has been Britain's enormous holdings of capital abroad in the late nineteenth century. The common view is that if investors had been restrained from sending abroad a third of the savings available for capital formation, Britain would have been better off. It is clear that in this case Britain's domestic capital stock would have grown half as fast again. It is not clear, however, that exchanging domestic for foreign capital would have raised British national income. The question is how bringing capital home could be expected to increase income and how large the increase would have been.

If world capital markets were functioning efficiently, of course, a prohibition of investment abroad would have reduced British national income. Most of the supporters of the hypothesis of immiseration by capital exports have accepted the assumption that the enlightened self-interest of investors in perfect capital markets maximizes national income.[3] Their case has rested, therefore, on two themes:

[1] These years were chosen to include the years of very low saving in the 'nineties and to cover one and a half business cycles (in order to ensure that the average approximates the underlying trend). Net investment in the United Kingdom is estimated as the sum of Feinstein's net fixed investment series (Mitchell, op. cit. p. 373), Imlah's overall balance on current account (ibid. p. 334), and 40 per cent of the annual change in Feinstein's net national income (ibid. p. 367; this is the traditional way of estimating inventory investment). The ratio for the United States is S. Kuznets' estimate of net capital formation divided by his estimate of net national product for three quinquennia from 1887 to 1901 (U.S. Department of Commerce, op. cit. p. 143). It is more comprehensive than the estimate for the United Kingdom.

[2] Income growth rises less than in proportion to the rise in capital growth because there are other sources of growth, i.e. labour growth and technological change.

[3] Strictly speaking, the assumption is false. National income would have been maximized if Britain had acted as a monopolist in the export of capital, as M. Kemp points out in the chapter 'Foreign Lending and the National Advantage—The Lending Country' in his book *The Pure Theory of Inter-*

first, that investors were not enlightened; and, second, that capital markets were not perfect.

The main sort of unenlightened behaviour is said to have been investment in foreign projects with a high risk of default. Even J. M. Keynes, however, who led the attack in the 'twenties on investment abroad, did not base his argument on a supposition that Englishmen invested in risky projects abroad, any more than in risky projects at home, without demanding interest compensation for the risk. His primary point was, rather, that in default the physical capital abroad was lost to Englishmen: "If the Grand Trunk Railway of Canada fails its shareholders . . . we have nothing. If the Underground System of London fails its shareholders, Londoners still have their Underground System."[1] The significance of the point depends on the magnitude of the defaults and in the period 1870–1913, as A. K. Cairncross has observed,[2] they were small. Even in the 1870's, which was "probably the least remunerative decade in the sixty years before the war", defaults on investments abroad were "a comparatively small amount".[3] Defaults were not an important drain on British capital before the war.

The more common theme than the loss from default in the literature of immiseration by capital exports is the perversity of Britain's imperfect capital market. The City, the story goes, was expert at channelling British savings into foreign trade credit and railway bonds, but inexpert at serving the industrial hinterlands of Britain itself.[4] Keynes, for example, emphasized the Colonial Stock Act of 1900 and similar Acts before it which permitted British trust funds to be invested in colonial railway and governmental bonds, giving, he claimed, an artificial incentive to investment abroad. The effect was "to starve home developments by diverting savings abroad and, consequently, to burden home borrowers with a higher rate of interest than they would need to pay otherwise".[5]

The logic of this and similar arguments based on an artificial preference by some lenders for lending abroad is not compelling. If borrowers in the colonies

---

national Trade (Englewood Cliffs, N.J., 1964). The monopoly gain from restricting the export of capital, however, would have been trivial. A rough calculation using the assumptions described below suggests a gain of the order of one-tenth of 1 per cent of national income.

[1] J. M. Keynes, 'Foreign Investment and National Advantage', *Nation and Athenaeum*, xxxv (1924), 584–7.

[2] A. K. Cairncross, *Home and Foreign Investment, 1870–1913* (Cambridge, 1953), pp. 225–30.

[3] Ibid. p. 228. On p. 225 he remarks that "there were constant defaults ... but, for the most part, with the exception of those of the twenties and seventies, of a comparatively minor character." A complete case would require more definite information on defaults.

[4] C. P. Kindleberger put it: "Capital flows in channels, and these had been dug between London and the far reaches of the empire, but not between London and the industrial north."—*Economic Growth in France and Britain, 1851–1950* (Cambridge, Mass., 1964), p. 69. Cf. D. Landes, 'Technological Change and Industrial Development in Western Europe, 1750–1914', in M. Postan and H. J. Habakkuk, eds. *The Cambridge Economic History of Europe*, vi (Cambridge, 1965), 576. The belief in capital market imperfections is inconsistent with the conclusions of both Kindleberger and Landes that there was no shortage of capital to domestic industry. The imperfections, if effective, would have restricted the supply.

[5] Keynes, op. cit. p. 586. All of his arguments have more force in the 'twenties, when he formulated them, than in the decades before the war. On the other hand, he exaggerates the incentive given by the Trustee Acts to lending abroad. The Acts applied only to the minority of trust deeds that did not specify the form the lending was to take. Moreover, they permitted investment at home not only in consols but also in mortgages, railway bonds, and issues of local authorities. Cf. Cairncross, op. cit. pp. 89, 95, and C. K. Hobson, *The Export of Capital* (1914), p. 48.

were, in fact, offering lower interest rates than borrowers with similar credit standing at home, there would be an incentive for British lenders who, unlike the trustees, had no special motive for investing in colonial securities to move out of them into domestic securities, raising the low colonial interest rates. The evidence on the differential between home and foreign interest rates for securities of similar quality suggests that the common source of funds for home and foreign investment was, in fact, effective in equalizing the rates. Indeed, interest rates for securities abroad were normally slightly higher than securities at home with the same risk.[1]

The qualification "with the same risk" requires emphasis. In 1911–13 the average return on all capital at home was more than 10 per cent, while the return on capital abroad was less than 5 per cent.[2] The capital abroad, however, was held in safe bonds, while the capital at home had to be held on balance in equity. Englishmen owned their own capital stock and the risk of ownership required compensation in the form of a higher return than on the comparative safety of lending abroad. Englishmen who were willing to own capital received, through the leverage of loans from the faint-hearted, a return higher than the 10 per cent return on real capital, while bondholders received a lower return. Some, and perhaps all, of the difference between the return on real capital at home and bond capital abroad, then, was a reward for assuming risk.

Nonetheless, some of the difference may have been the result of imperfections in the capital market. In an imperfect capital market Britain would have gained by bringing some of her capital home. The net gain to national income from eliminating the gap caused by imperfections is represented by the shaded area in the diagram overleaf. The horizontal axis measures for 1911–13 capital at home, capital owned by citizens of the United Kingdom abroad, and foreign capital abroad[3] and the vertical axes the marginal products of capital at home and abroad. Income produced at home, since it is the total product of capital at home, is represented by the area under the solid curve of the marginal product of capital, while income from investments abroad, since it is the return on foreign bonds multiplied by the value of foreign bonds owned, is represented by the rectangle whose height is the return on foreign bonds.[4] The length G represents the

---

[1] Cf. Cairncross, op. cit. pp. 227–31.

[2] These estimates are based on the home-produced income accruing to capitalists and foreign investment earnings. The return at home agrees with the estimate by E. H. Phelps Brown and B. Weber for the entire period 1870–1912 ('Accumulation, Productivity, and Distribution in the British Economy, 1870–1938', *Economic Journal*, LXIII (1953), 263–88). The underlying capital stock estimates are discussed below.

[3] The domestic stock of capital in Great Britain was about £7,900 million in 1911–13, according to Deane and Cole, op. cit. p. 274 (based on H. Campion's income method estimate in *Public and Private Property in Great Britain* (1939). To their estimate I have added £500 million for Ireland (based on the relation between the United Kingdom and Great Britain in 1885 for capital in farming, industry, commerce, and finance (Deane and Cole, loc. cit.)). A capital stock of £8,400 million agrees roughly with the estimate of £8,100 million by Phelps Brown and Handfield-Jones, op. cit. p. 302. The stock of capital abroad on which Englishmen had a claim was about £4,000 million. This figure can be reached by capitalizing Imlah's yearly overseas investment earnings for 1911–13 (£188 million, Mitchell, op. cit. p. 334) at the prevailing interest rate on bonds (e.g. R. A. Lehfeldt's 'The Rate of Interest on British and Foreign Investment', *Statistical Journal* (1913) or American Railway bonds). Alternatively (and with the same result) Imlah's balance of payments on current account can be added year by year to the estimate of Cairncross for 1871 (op. cit. pp. 182–4). The relevant amount of foreign capital abroad can be taken at any reasonable magnitude, here £20,000 million, for it affects the results very little.

[4] The average for 1911–13 of Imlah's foreign investment earnings was £188 million (Mitchell, op. cit.

gap between the return on domestic and foreign bonds and is the chief point at issue. A gap of 6 per cent is an upper bound: it would be the true gap from imperfections only if none of the difference between the 10·7 per cent return on physical capital at home and the 4·7 per cent return on bond capital abroad was a premium for the risk of ownership. The gap, therefore, is taken to vary from 1 per cent to 6 per cent. Eliminating the gap would push the bond market to the

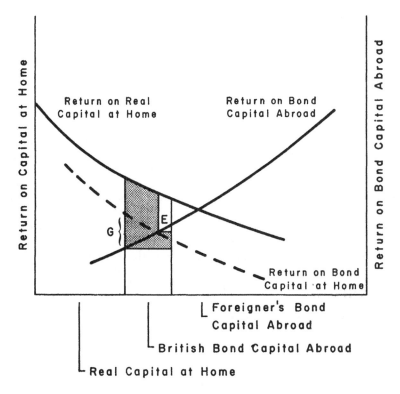

Fig. 1. *The Effect of Eliminating Imperfections in the Capital Market*

equilibrium E, reducing the return on physical capital at home and raising the return on bonds abroad.[1] Subtracting the old income at home and abroad from the new leaves the shaded area as the net gain.

The gain is small, even assuming great imperfections in the capital market, as shown in Table 1.[2]

---

p. 274). Subtracting this from Feinstein's net national income estimate leaves £1,980 million home-produced income.

[1] A reasonable estimate of the elasticity of the two curves involved, it can be shown, is the share of non-capital inputs in national income.

[2] The fall in the net gain for a gap larger than 3 per cent is not paradoxical. As more is borrowed abroad, the terms worsen.

Table 1. *The Effect of Eliminating Imperfections in the Capital Market*

Excess of home interest rate over 4·7% (%)	New capital at home (£ million)	New home income (£ million)	New income from abroad (£ million)	Additional income as % of old (%)
1	2,100	2,180	95	4·5
2	3,940	2,310	nil	6·5
3	5,560	2,420	86	7·3
4	7,040	2,500	178	7·0
5	8,380	2,560	266	5·5
6	9,530	2,600	350	3·5

Source: The procedure was to find the increment to capital at home, using the given data, that equilibrates the bond market. The details of the calculations are available from the author at the Department of Economics, University of Chicago, 1126 East 59th Street, Chicago, Illinois 60637.

The elimination of the largest possible imperfection during the period 1870–1913, even though it would have required enormous capital *imports*, would have raised income by the end of the period by only 7·3 per cent and would only have raised the rate of growth of income from 2·40 per cent per year to 2·58 per cent.

It has been argued that "the City of London and its financial institutions . . . were the greatest single threat to the prosperity of England."[1] The tiny increment to the growth of income from eliminating the threat suggests that this view is false. The United Kingdom exported a huge amount of capital in the period and it is tempting to believe that it could have drawn on this capital as a surplus for growth. In the light of the argument here, the temptation must be resisted.

The demand hypothesis of slower British growth, then, has a grave defect. Meyer's test, though flawed, appears at first to lend it support. But the demand hypothesis, in any form, assumes elastic supplies of labour and capital and these were not available. In late Victorian England there was no reserve army of unemployed, no pool of underemployed agricultural labour, no excessive consumption at home, and no profitless investment abroad. Had exports grown faster, output for domestic use would have grown slower: the total was fixed by the growth of resources and productivity.

III

The allegation of failure, therefore, must rest on slower-growing productivity. The measurement of how effectively an economy uses the resources available to it is a delicate matter with the best of information. With the poor quality of information available on the late Victorian economy, the task has seemed to some too difficult to attempt. They have passed on to reasons why Britain failed, taking as proven the fact of failure. It is not surprising that they have eschewed measurement, for the measures have given conflicting opinions on the course of pro-

[1] P. Rosenstein-Rodan at the International Economic Association conference on *Capital Movements and Economic Development* (1967), p. 68. The rapporteur says that Rosenstein-Rodan "drew attention to the major increase in the scale of British overseas investment during the few decades before World War I, and added that if this capital had been invested in England, England would have been much stronger." In the discussion, G. Leduc makes the same point about France. One of the papers they are discussing, B. Thomas' 'The Historical Record of International Capital Movements to 1913', concludes with a similar argument, but applies it, guardedly, only to the years 1900 to 1913.

ductivity change. One group, using Prest's deflated national income data, places the climacteric of productivity in the 'nineties while the other, using Hoffmann's index of industrial output, places it in the 'seventies. D. J. Coppock was the first to notice the divergence between the measures of national income and of industrial output. Remarking that "between 1875 and 1900 the two series are quite contradictory",[1] he chooses the industrial series and the earlier climacteric. C. Wilson leans the other way, but is disturbed by "the gap between the *apparent* slackening of economic growth and the better substantiated estimates of rising aggregate national income, a conundrum to which no really satisfactory answer has been given".[2]

The alleged conundrum is that industrial output grew slower than national income: Hoffmann's index grew at around 1·7 per cent per year from 1872 to 1907, while real national income was growing at 2 per cent or more per year. The coverage of the Hoffmann index, however, is surely smaller than the income estimates and the missing sectors may well have been growing faster.[3] Moreover, Hoffmann's index is essentially a gross output index. That is, although it uses value-added weights the basic data are gross, not net, outputs of the commodities. Hoffmann's index is not an index of national income originating in industry, as those who are puzzled by its lack of identity with national income appear to believe. By the argument developed earlier, therefore, Hoffmann's index *must* grow slower than national income: gross output and final output can grow at the same rate only if productivity change in the sense of a fall in the interindustry coefficient is nil.[4] There is, in short, no conundrum: there is no clear contradiction between Hoffmann's index and real income.

Coppock attempted to explain the divergence between Hoffmann's index and the measures of real income of Phelps Brown and Handfield-Jones[5] by arguing that the deflator of national income was too heavily weighted towards food and raw materials. Food and raw material prices were more volatile than more representative commodities, he said, falling faster before 1896 and rising faster after 1896, with the result that a change in trend of real national income appears in the 'nineties.[6] This criticism rests on an inappropriate set of weights for a price index of output. Noting that the weight on food in the Phelps Brown and Handfield-Jones price index is about 36 per cent, for example, he remarks that "it is obvious that the output of food bore no such relationship to national output."[7] The evi-

[1] Coppock, op. cit. p. 4.

[2] C. Wilson, 'Economy and Society in Late Victorian Britain', *Economic History Review*, 2nd ser. XVIII (1965), 193 (italics his).

[3] The coverage of the Hoffmann index is, of course, good. But a non-random sample, however large, yields biased estimates of the population characteristics. Wilson, op. cit., makes a convincing case that "miscellaneous industries and incorporeal functions" (as Giffen called them) were growing rapidly in this period. He mentions soap, retailing, and bicycles.

[4] Coppock's assertion that "a growth of some 0·5% or less per annum in industrial productivity [i.e. Hoffmann's index per man] cannot explain a growth of some 1·5% to 2·0% per annum in real income a head" (op. cit. p. 14) is, therefore, mistaken. There is no inconsistency between Hoffmann's index and the real national income estimates.

[5] Op. cit.

[6] A similar point was made by J. F. Wright in his review article on Deane and Cole, 'British Economic Growth, 1688–1959', *Econ. Hist. Rev.* 2nd ser. XVIII (1965), 397–412. Their use of Rousseaux's price index to deflate national income, he argues, produced a false rejuvenation of real national income after 1870.

[7] Op. cit. p. 16.

dence is the low share of income earned in agriculture. Income earned in an industry, however, is the sum of the rewards to labour, capital, and land inputs and is not in general equal to the sum of final expenditures on the product of the industry. It is not necessarily true that "what is relevant for a price index of final products is outputs not expenditures."[1] It appears from the context that Coppock means value added when he speaks of "outputs". With perfect data, prices weighted by expenditures shares would give exactly the same income deflator as prices weighted by value-added shares. There are no grounds for preferring one or the other, except when the data have been collected in one or the other fashion. In fact, because there are good indexes of final expenditure prices available (e.g. Bowley's cost of living index for consumption, Feinstein's gross investment deflator for investment, Imlah's export price index), it is convenient to construct a price index with final expenditure weights. It is the weight of each industry's product in final expenditure (gross national product) that the index of Phelps Brown and Handfield-Jones aims to reflect. Ironically, when after 1900 consumption data by product become available, they show that food, drink, and tobacco were almost exactly the 36 per cent of gross national product that Coppock believed was obviously too high.[2]

It is entirely appropriate, then, to use national product estimates, with their heavy weight on food, for measuring productivity. The table below gives some estimates of the home-produced gross national product of the United Kingdom for ten-year intervals from 1860 to 1910. The estimates of real gross national product were made by adding together the expenditures in the prices of 1900 by consumers, investors, government, and the rest of the world.

Table 2. *Real Gross National Product*

	Money G.N.P. £ million	Real G.N.P. £ million 1900 prices	Implicit price index	Growth-rate per year of real G.N.P. (% in previous decade)	Hoffmann's index of industrial output	Growth-rate per year of Hoffmann's index (%)
1860	841	720	116·7		34·2	
1870	1,156	999	115·7	3·27	43·4	2·38
1880	1,349	1,233	101·3	2·11	54·2	2·21
1890	1,500	1,634	91·7	2·82	65·5	1·91
1900	2,037	2,037	100·0	2·19	77·1	1·62
1910	2,265	2,211	102·5	0·806	86·5	1·14

Source: Details of the estimating procedures available from the author on request. Consumption for 1860–90 is based on the series of J. B. Jeffreys and D. Walters (in S. Kuznets, ed. International Association for Research in Income and Wealth, *Income and Wealth, Series V* (1955), p. 27), deflated by Bowley's ndex of the cost of living. Consumption for 1900–10 is based on D. A. Rowe's series given in Mitchell, op. cit. p. 371. Gross investment in 1900 prices is Feinstein's series (ibid. p. 373) and government expenditure is the estimate given by A. T. Peacock and J. Wiseman, *The Growth of Public Expenditure in the United Kingdom* (Princeton, N.J., 1961) at pp. 37 and 42. Real exports of commodities and invisibles minus real imports are based on Imlah's estimates (Mitchell, op. cit. pp. 331–3).

[1] Coppock, loc. cit.
[2] The consumption data are D. A. Rowe's, in Mitchell, op. cit. p. 370. The estimates of gross national product are Deane and Cole's in op. cit. p. 332. They are the sum of Rowe's consumption estimates and estimates of domestic fixed investment, net foreign investment, and public authorities expenditure. Food, drink, and tobacco expenditures were 36·3 per cent of gross national product from 1900 to 1909.

The striking feature of the growth of real product is its rapid growth before 1900 and its sharp deceleration afterwards. Unless the pattern of growth of inputs explains this break, the climacteric should be placed not in the 'seventies or 'nineties but in the 1900's. The growth of the relevant inputs, labour and capital, is exhibited in the next table.

Table 3. *Capital, Labour, and Productivity*

	Domestic capital value in 1900 prices (£ million)	Capital growth-rate per year (% in previous decade)	Labour (000's employed year after)	Labour growth-rate per year (%)	Productivity growth-rate per year (%)
1860	3,732		11,678		
1870	4,316	1·44	13,064	1·115	2·160
1880	5,057	1·60	14,450	1·025	0·872
1890	5,708	1·24	16,020	1·025	1·750
1900	6,657	1·54	17,740	1·025	0·982
1910	7,713	1·47	19,700	1·045	−0·383

Source: Details available from the author on request. The capital estimate is a decumulation of J. C. Stamp's estimate of the domestic capital stock (*British Incomes and Property* (1916), p. 404) by Feinstein's net fixed investment series (loc. cit.) and an estimate of inventory investment. Stamp's and Feinstein's estimates were adjusted for comparability. The labour series is an estimate given in Phelps Brown and Handfield-Jones, op. cit. p. 298. For the method of estimating the shares of labour and capital in home-produced income see above, p. 450, n. 2.

Both inputs are necessary for a meaningful measure of productivity: it is not appropriate, for example, to use the growth of output per man to draw inferences about the performance of the economy or a sector of it. Not surprisingly, the growth of the inputs is relatively steady, labour growing at about 1·05 per cent per year and capital at 1·45 per cent per year during the period. The last column shows the resulting measure of productivity change, that is, the growth of real product not attributable to the growth of capital or labour. Once again, there is a sharp deceleration after the turn of the century.

More important, however, is the sustained growth of productivity in the 'seventies, 'eighties, and 'nineties, for it was during these years that the conviction grew on Englishmen that they were falling behind the technology of Germany and, especially, the United States. As far as can be ascertained, however, productivity growth in the United States was of the same order of magnitude as in the United Kingdom: rates of 1 or 1·5 per cent per year are typical of the American as of the British economy at the time.[1] Given the uncertainties of the data for both countries, the most precise defensible statement is that there was little cause for alarm in the behaviour of British productivity.

The case for a late Victorian failure in productivity, then, appears weak. Indeed the failure, to be precise, was Edwardian. Nor is there any evidence that productivity responded to the growth of exports: real exports grew faster in the decade and a half before the First World War than they had since the 'sixties, yet productivity declined. Moreover, the correlation between capital accumulation

[1] J. W. Kendrick, for example, finds that productivity change averaged about 1·5 per cent per year from 1869 to 1909 in the United States. There are some difficulties with the data for 1869 and 1879. From 1889 to 1909 the measure averages about 1·3 per cent per year. See *Productivity Trends in the United States* (Princeton, N.J., 1961), p. 331.

and productivity change on which the demand theory of British failure rests is poor: capital accumulation was low in the 'eighties, for example, yet productivity growth was rapid.

A measure of productivity growth using national aggregates of output, labour, and capital, however, is a fragile foundation on which to erect theories of British success or failure. This is not because of the large size of the uncertainties in the data, although those compound the problem. The difficulty is that even with very good data the range of doubt in the result is large. This is a general problem and applies to the measure of productivity change used here as well as to the conceptually less complete measures used elsewhere. For example, the measure of productivity grew at $1 \cdot 2$ per cent per year from 1870 to 1900, a respectable pace. If the estimates in 1870 and 1900 of real gross national product, the stock of capital, the labour force, and the shares of capital and labour in national product are incorrect by as little as ± 3 per cent, however, the resulting estimate of productivity change will range from $0 \cdot 77$ per cent per year to $1 \cdot 62$ per cent, that is, by comparison with the United States, from failure to success.

The case for failure or success in the growth of productivity must rest ultimately on international comparisons of productivity in specific industries, not on the aggregate measures about which the controversy on British economic performance has hitherto revolved. The measure for each industry, of course, will be open to the same criticism, but if the errors for each industry are independent a set of many industry studies will constitute a sample of British behaviour from which more reliable inferences can be drawn. For the present, it is enough to show that the aggregate measures are consistent with success.

IV

It is implausible, then, to draw the lines of causation in late Victorian England from export demand to the output of the economy. The thesis expressed here is that the resources available to the economy were not elastic in supply and reallocation of them (capital abroad, for example) would have brought little or no additional growth. The growth of output depended on how productively the available resources were used. The measure of productivity suggests no great failure of Britain on this score. There was a dip of productivity in the 1900's, but it was too short, too late, and too uncertain to justify the dramatic description "climacteric". Nor does it support the notion that British businessmen were marking time from the 'seventies onward.[1] There is, indeed, little left of the dismal picture of British failure painted by historians. The alternative is a picture of an economy not stagnating but growing as rapidly as permitted by the growth of its resources and the effective exploitation of the available technology.

University of Chicago

---

[1] D. Landes, for example, asserts that "There is no doubt, that British industry was not so vigorous and adaptable from the 1870's on as it could have been."—Op. cit. p. 559.

[2]

ENGLISH OPEN
FIELDS AS BEHAVIOR
TOWARDS RISK

Donald N. McCloskey, UNIVERSITY OF CHICAGO

THE HISTORIOGRAPHY OF RISK

In much of England, from the earliest times to the nineteenth century, peasants held their land in many little scattered plots. Any description in the present state of knowledge is uncertain, but it is probably close to the mark to say that the typical villager in the Midlands of England, before the enclosures of the seventeenth and eighteenth centuries, held some 20 acres in the fields of his village in twenty or so separate locations. This is a most peculiar way to hold land, or at any rate so it has seemed to most observers of the system since the first enthusiasm for enclosure in the sixteenth century, because it appears to reduce output, a strange burden for a community near starvation to assume. The most obvious loss is the time spent wandering from plot to plot, but there are others of more consequence documented in some detail in the paper of which this is a continuation: the externalities of having close neighbors were high, the cost of fencing (and therefore of raising animals in private) high as well, and the system required the village to impose a clumsy common routine on all its members (McCloskey, 1975a). Although the output lost, by comparison with more consolidated holdings, was not as high as one might suppose from the intemperate language of improving pamphleteers, neither was it trivial. I have elsewhere used the typical increase in the rent of land after enclosure to estimate that the proportion of a village's output lost in the

124

17

seventeenth and eighteenth centuries was on the order of 13 percent (McCloskey, 1975b). In the centuries of full vigor of the open fields the output lost was no doubt lower, perhaps 10 percent. Yet why would a malnourished peasant throw away a tenth of his output?

Historians of medieval agriculture have for the most part answered this question in an off-hand way. It appears that the sharing of plow-teams, a spirit of egalitarianism, or the operation of inheritance laws, all of which have at one time or another held the field, fail to explain scattering. The one explanation that shows promise is that plots were scattered to insure against disaster.

The argument is that within a single English village there was enough variability in the yield of land in different locations and under different crops to make it desirable to hold a diversified portfolio of plots. The land and weather of England is notoriously variable, even over the two miles square or so of the typical village. A place with sandy soil on a rise would shed excessive rain while one with clay soil in a valley would hold insufficient rain; a place open to the wind would grow wheat likely to lodge if there were high winds and rain at harvest time but free of mold in a generally wet year, while a sheltered one would be relatively immune from windy disasters but less dry and more moldy on that account; and one place could be hit by flooding, insects, birds, rust, rabbits, moles, hail, hunting parties, thieves and wandering armies, to name a few more of the reasons an English peasant would want insurance, while another close by would go free.'A year of high prices for wheat might be a year of low prices for barley and oats, adding a price risk to the yield risk. When whole areas of a village were set aside for each crop, a natural result of scattering of holdings from other causes, the price risk would induce the peasant to hold land in all fields, for a man wanted bread, beer and feed for his animals regardless of the weather and would be averse to the risk of facing high prices he would assume were he to specialize in one crop and one crop area.

Further, before the seventeenth century risks were higher and the opportunities to avoid them more limited than they were to become later. The miserably low ratio of yield to seed before the agricultural revolution meant that a given percentage variation in the total crop was reflected in a larger percentage variation in the consumable crop, after allowing for seed. The techniques of drainage that have to some degree brought the effects of wet weather under control were unknown or expensive. High costs of transportation reduced the variety of weather represented in a given agricultural market and therefore raised the variability of prices above what it was to become in modern times. Futures markets for grain were rare. The market in loans to tide over a bad year was poorly developed. And if the peasant's wealth was not exclusively his seed and standing crop, the other assets he might have, from cattle to gold, were themselves subject to the high risks of natural disaster and random taxation. The inefficiencies of the open fields, in short, were payments on an insurance premium in a milieu in which agricultural yields were low and unpredictable and in which the costs of a shortfall—at best crushing debt or malnutrition and its associated diseases, at worst starvation—were high.

Risk aversion as a motive for scattering plots figures sometimes in studies of medieval, still more of modern, peasant agriculture. Although he did not, on this point, marshal the evidence, and leaned towards an explanation of scattering based on communal solidarity, Marc Bloch is exceptional among historians in emphasizing the force of risk aversion. The schemes for consolidation encouraged by French governments in the eighteenth century, he argued, were frustrated not only by the conservative and distrustful attitude of the peasants, but also by their concern "to reduce exposure to agrarian accidents . . . to a minimum by working plots scattered over the whole terrain." If the wheeled plow in the regions of heavy soils could explain the great length of plots, risk aversion could explain their narrowness and great number, even when light plows were used: "If the plots were dispersed . . . everyone had some hope of avoiding the full impact of natural or human disasters—hailstorms, plant diseases, devastation—which might descend upon a place without destroying it completely." (Bloch, 1966 [1931], pp. 233, 55.)

One must look outside the remote European past for much more testimony on the point. Scattering is a common feature of all manner of peasant agricultures, from Japanese paddies to Swiss meadows. Economists, government planners and the representatives of international agencies have generally viewed it as a valueless result of egalitarian inheritance systems, of irrational attachments to particular parcels, or of general hunger for land; as, in short, a pointless obstacle to agricultural progress on a par with sacred cows and excessive numbers of feast days, to be cleared away, if necessary by force, as soon as possible. Even so sympathetic and thorough a study as Kenneth Thompson's *Farm Fragmentation in Greece: The Problem and Its Setting* (1963) slips into this view.[1] He concedes that scattering reduces risk, but applies the argument only to fruit and vegetable crops, which are especially vulnerable to localized frosts and hailstorms. He treats the reason given by the inhabitants of one of his sample villages for their opposition to consolidation of plots—"Why should the plots be all together? We are more secure this way: fire, bad weather, etc."—as the prejudice of a benighted peasantry.[2]

In the Greek case and in other cases of scattered holdings past and present it has never been explained why peasants are so often opposed to consolidation if, as is commonly supposed, output was markedly higher when plots were consolidated. Since the English, French and Swedish examples of the eighteenth century, one government after another has passed laws designed to eliminate scattering by persuasion, subsidy, or compulsion, and it would be difficult to explain their painfully slow achievement of success if scattering had no advantage. The Dutch reallotment act of 1924, amended in 1938 and later, for example, made consolidation compulsory if a majority of either the landowners or the land voted by its owners favored it, and provided generous subsidies (all the costs incurred if the attempt to reallot the holdings failed). Nonetheless, in the early 1950's consolidation of plots in the Netherlands was far from complete (Vanderpol. In Parsons, *et al.*, pp. 548–54). The first of many consolidation acts in Germany was Hannover's in 1848, yet to this day farms in parts of Germany, especially the southwest, are scattered (Mayhew, 1973, pp. 178–99). Official concern with scattering, embodied at the state level in a series of consolidation acts, is half a century old in India, yet the problem (for so it is viewed) remains (Agarwal, 1971).

When they have looked beyond mere peasant conservatism or peasant jealousy for explanations of the opposition to consolidation a few historians and economists have come to emphasize risk aversion. Among the reasons Hungarian peasants rejected consolidation in the 1850's was their fear that natural disasters would destroy a family's whole crop (Molnar, 1971, II, p. 37). A century later, in a wholly different environment, as John W. Thomas, an economist with the Development Advisory Service, discovered, the logic was the same: in Bangladesh (then East Pakistan) in 1970 peasants "were strongly opposed to consolidation since fragmentation of land holdings was their prospective protection against loss of crops due to natural disasters," especially flooding that would leave high land (a mere six to ten feet above the rest) untouched.[3]

Anthropologists especially have been less liable than most historians and economists to dismiss opposition to consolidation as an irrational attachment to old forms. The Hopi Indians of the American Southwest in the 1930's scattered their plots of maize, the Katcina clan in one village holding six plots scattered over a 6 mile square area. As C. Daryll Forde explained:

> This dispersal is of very great practical importance since it reduces the risk of crop failure; where the crop on one group of fields may wither from drought or be washed away by floods there remains the chance that the others will be spared. In particular, disastrous floods rarely occur in all the flats in the same season. The lands close in to the mesa and those out in the middle are still more definitely reciprocal. In an abnormally wet year, when many of the latter are liable to be destroyed by the high floods, the scarp plots are well watered, while, on the other hand, in dry season when they in their turn are likely to be parched out, enough water is usually brought down by the streams to afford a harvest for the mid-valley fields (Forde, 1934, p. 234).

According to another anthropologist, Alan Hoben, scattering of plots by the Amhara farmer of Ethiopia "is highly desirable . . . for by providing him with fields of different qualities it enables him to diversify his crops and to reduce the risk of total crop failure." Attempts at imposing land reform on the Amhara have resulted in armed rebellion, most recently in 1967–68, when several hundred people were killed. Hoben remarks: "If a program of land reform is to be effective it must be based on a model . . . illuminating the rational process through which people make decisions about land instead of simply attributing these decisions to the dead hand of tradition." (Hoben, n.d., pp. 2, 11–12, and 34.) In view of such an attitude it is not surprising to find testimony of risk aversion causing scattering in a wide variety of anthropological studies, of Tanzania, for example, or of southwest Switzerland or of Brazil.[4] There is a good deal of testimony, in short, that the elementary wisdom of diversification in a dangerous world has appealed to peasant farmers and graziers as much as to urban ship owners and merchants. "Give a portion to seven, and also to eight," said Jesus, son of Sirach, "for thou knowest not what evil shall be upon the earth."

THE HISTORY OF RISK

Encouraging though it may be, testimony that aversion towards risk explains scattering elsewhere does not prove that it explains scattering in England. What is required is English evidence. English peasants never told why they scattered their holdings, perhaps because they or their rulers, speaking through the spare Latin of court rolls, could not be bothered to recite the obvious. Even if they had told why, of course, their testimony—"We are an egalitarian community of shareholders and wish to equalise class-by-class the quality as well as the quantity of land," or "We, like stockbrokers, wish to hold diversified portfolios"—would not be conclusive, for men are not always reliable reporters of their motives. Proofs of an explanation of scattering, then, must rely on its fit with facts other than direct testimony.

Chief among these facts is consolidation. Scattering was not always or everywhere present in England. By the eighteenth century open fields in their full-blown form were confined chiefly to a great triangle defined by Yorkshire in the north, Wiltshire in the south, and Norfolk in the east; yet open fields had once existed outside the triangle, in Cornwall, for example, or in Durham. And within the triangle some holdings or villages were consolidated before the eighteenth century or, indeed, before the fourteenth. An advantage that the hypothesis of risk aversion has over others is that risk can vary enough to explain these varying degrees of scattering, whereas the alternative hypotheses, of Germanic egali- tarianism or communal clearing or joint plowing, are reduced to making argu- ments for action at a distance. Partible inheritance, the leading contender since Joan Thirsk put the weight of her scholarship behind it, is a case in point (Thirsk, 1964 and 1973). The very place where partible inheritance among peasants survived the longest, the southeast of England, was among the first to consolidate; the very place where primogeniture began earliest, the Midlands, was among the last.

The hypothesis of risk aversion does not depend on action at a distance, for risk and the aversion to it moved during the widespread consolidations of the seven- teenth and eighteenth centuries in the right direction at the right time. The riskiness of yields due to disease and weather, for example, was being reduced by new varieties of corn in English agriculture from an early date. In the early seventeenth century there was developed in the south Midlands red-stalked wheat, more resistant to smut, a fungus which destroyed whole stands (Thirsk, 1967, p. 168). Early-ripening barley was another among many innovations of the seventeenth century that reduced risk, the risk in this case of wet, cold springs: barley could be sown in May rather than in March, yet still yield a crop (Thirsk, 1967, p. 170). The advances in the control of the water reaching the crop, that began with floating meadows in the seventeenth century and ended with the widespread use of underdrainage in the nineteenth, amounted to a reduction of the risk of unseasonable rain. Drainage is particularly difficult in regions with clay rather than sand or chalk soils, and it therefore comes as no surprise to find that clay characterized much of the soil of the Midlands, late enclosed. Clay is impermeable and holds a flood. Furthermore, it is dangerous to stir clay soils while they are still wet, because the soil acts then like clay in the hands of a potter, sticking to the plow and hardening on the ground into an unbreakable crust. About 1420 the anonymous English translator of a textbook on agriculture put the matter so: "The fenny feeld is not forto plowe./Lest all the yere it after be to tough/To plowe, eke, as men saith, noo thing wol growe/Thre yere on landes drier than ynough/And rain betwet," that is, nothing will grow for three years on [clay] lands that have become dry, then rained on, then plowed before becoming dry again (Lodge, 1873, p. 45).[5] A wet spring could make it impossible to prepare the land for barley, however rich the crop might be if the land could be plowed. It is significant, therefore, that in the two centuries from the middle of the seventeenth to the middle of the nineteenth, bracketing the most intense period of consolidation, corn production moved out of the wet clay valleys and onto the sands, chalks and high ground (Jones, 1964, pp. 110–28). This shift, in turn, was made possible by new and more reliable animal fodder (the turnip and, by the time of the Napoleonic Wars, the swedish turnip, which was drier and less subject to the risk of rot) and by improved transportation which brought bread to the specialized grazier and dairyman cheaply. And improved transportation itself reduced risk, by increasing the varieties of weather and soil represented in a single market area and therefore decreasing the variability of prices for the market as a whole.

There is some reason to believe that these events and others increased the uniformity of yields within a village, reducing the advantage of a diverse holding: controlling the flow of water in a field, eliminating partial theft and trampling of crops, and reducing the scattered attacks of mold and the like would make various parts of a scattered holding vary in yield more uniformly in the seventeenth century and after than they had before. There is some reason to believe, too, that agricultural innovations in the seventeenth century increased the cost of the insurance achieved by scattering. Flooding and draining a holding three or four times a year to yield a series of rich crops of hay is more difficult, though not impossible, if the holding is in scraps in the midst of other men's scraps than if the scraps are thrown together. Further, as an enthusiast for enclosure put it in 1769, "Land, which requires to be kept in Tillage, is less incommoded by the Open Field State, than that which is fit for Pasture or Dairy" (Homer, 1769, p. 8). The shift in many open-field regions from specializing in raising grain to specializing in raising livestock—and the greater importance of livestock in the life of mixed farms after the development of cheap winter fodder—would on this account be a reason for consolidation.

The central point, however, is that in the seventeenth and eighteenth centuries the new affluence of farmers and the new opportunities for employment outside of farming altogether reduced the value of insurance achieved by scattering. Gregory King believed that the family income of farmers and lesser freeholders was about £50 a year in 1688 (Thirsk and Cooper, [eds.], 1972, p. 780). Yet, to give an example from one locale which could be duplicated elsewhere, a thirty-acre farmer in mid-Essex by around 1700 held equipment, stock, furniture, jewelry, notes and cash at his death worth twice this figure.[6] Improvements in agricultural practice (among them, indeed, consolidation) made such accumulation of reserves against disaster possible. In Britain and the Low Countries, B. H. Slicher van Bath puts the resulting increase in yields of grain per bushel of seed from the sixteenth and seventeenth centuries to the turn of the nineteenth century at 50 percent, and Eric Kerridge puts it at a larger figure in England, concentrated before 1650 (Slicher van Bath, 1963, p. 16; Kerridge, 1968, pp. 330–331). The higher yields, moreover, reduced the probability of crop failures and reduced still further the probability of successive years of dearth, distressingly common when yield/seed ratios were low and the seed eaten in a hungry year. Little wonder, then, that the periodic crises of subsistence that have fascinated students of the *ancien régime* in France were by the seventeenth century unknown in England (Lastlett, 1965, pp. 113–114). And even when a man's harvest did fail, his income from the expanding industries of the countryside did not; at the end of the seventeenth century only 40 percent of the income of England and Wales was earned in agriculture (Deane and Cole, 1964, p. 156)[7]. By the standards of earlier times, then, English agriculture on the eve of massive enclosure was rich and diverse, and a device for reducing the risk of starvation might be expected to lose some of its charm.

THE LOGIC OF SAFETY FIRST

The question remains whether before enclosure the device worked. The proposition that in some degree scattering served to reduce risk is plausible on its face, as is, say, the proposition that scattering served to equalize the inheritances of siblings in some degree. The nub of the issue is, in what degree? The hypothesis of risk aversion must pass the test of quantitative bite.

The simplest way of showing that it does is to compare the total gains and losses of adopting scattered rather than consolidated holdings. And the simplest way in turn of bringing the gain in lower variability of income and the loss in lower average income into the same unit of account is to measure their contributions to avoiding disaster. On this view the peasant's purpose was to reduce the probability of his income falling below the level that exposed him to debt, hunger, disease or, in the limit, death by starvation. He sought, in short, safety first.

Figure 1. Reducing the Probability of Disaster by Reducing
Variability at the Cost of a Reduced Average.

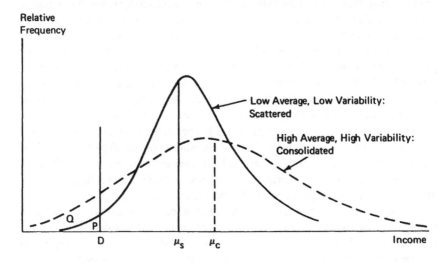

Figure 1 illustrates the choice between an income before scattering that is high on average but highly variable as well (the dotted curve), and an income, after scattering, that is lower on average but less variable (the solid curve). The level of disaster is D, and a peasant who chooses to scatter his plots, accepting the lower average income (μ_s) in exchange for the lower variability, faces a probability of disaster represented by the area under the solid curve to the left of D, area P. The peasant who chooses to consolidate his plots faces the larger probability, Q + P. In this case, then, scattering is desirable: so much lower is the variability of income that disaster is less frequent.

It need not always be so. If the loss in average income is large, or the reduction in variability small, or the level of disaster high, scattered holdings may be more rather than less dangerous than consolidated holdings. The balance of advantage for normal distributions of yields depends on whether or not scattering raises the 'distance of disaster from the average, measuring the distance in units of standard deviation. In other words, speaking of D as the disastrous income, of μ as the average income, and of σ as the standard deviation of income, scattering reduces the probability of disaster if it causes $(\mu - D)/\sigma$ to rise.

This measure in English open fields, detailed in a moment, is given in Table 1.

Table 1. The Average and Standard Deviation of Income
for Consolidated and Scattered Holdings.

				When Disaster = 50		
	Average Income	Coefficient of Variation	Standard Deviation	Distance from D	Probability of Disaster	Frequency of Disaster
Consolidated	110	.440	48.4	1.24	.108	every 9.30 years
Scattered	100	.347	34.7	1.44	.075	every 13.4 years

The results are strong. With scattered holdings peasants faced disaster—disaster not meaning, of course, starvation for everyone in the community, but misery for most that was worthy of memory, prayer and fear—about one year in thirteen. With consolidated holdings, forsaking the advantages of diversification, they would have faced it about one year in nine. To put the case another way, scattering doubled the probability of surviving twenty years and tripled the probability of surviving thirty years without disaster.

THE RISKS OF MEDIEVAL AGRICULTURE

The task now is to show that the entries in the table are correct. To begin with the entry for which the evidence is most rich, the standard deviation of income from year to year in English open fields was indeed high, certainly as high relative to an average income of 100 as 35. In plain terms, the figure asserts that in one year out of three incomes would be above 135 or below 65. The records of medieval yields on which the assertion is based, sad to say, are not ideal, for they are records from the large demesne farms worked directly by the lord's servants rather than from the small rented farms worked by the peasants. It was peasants, not lords, who were achieving insurance by scattering their plots, but the records relate to lords, and to the record-keepers among these, chiefly ecclesiastical, who would often be exceptional in other ways as well. The direction of the bias, however, is plain. The variability of yields on peasant holdings, poor land worked with poor methods, is likely to have been if anything larger than it was on the demesnes, in which case the calculated variability is a lower bound on the truth.

This lower bound, then, was high, not only because medieval farming, even of a lordly sort, was so much more vulnerable to weather and other hazards than is modern farming—protected by fertilizers, drainage pipes, rapid harvesters, and pesticides—but also because so large a share of the miserable yield had to be put back into the ground as seed. On the 102-acre demesne farm of Bladon, now near Blenheim Palace in Oxfordshire, one of a group of manors granted in 1704 to the first Duke of Marlborough by a grateful queen and country, the standard deviation relative to the gross average (that is, the coefficient of variation) of wheat produced in 1243–49 was .20.[8] In view of the uncertainties surrounding the definition of the customary "acre," yields must be expressed as yields per unit of seed, both terms of which are known from the "issue of the grange" for the year of harvest and the year of planting. The net yield of seed for next year, then, can be approximated by the gross yield per bushel of seed minus one, it being this net yield alone that is available to be eaten if one is to eat next year as well.[9] On the demesne of Bladon the gross yield of wheat was only 2.6 bushels of output per bushel of seed, on the average, implying a coefficient of variation calculated from the net yield more than half again as large as that calculated from the gross yield, namely .33 rather than .20.[10] More dramatic cases of the magnifying effect of low yields on variability are not difficult to find. On another manor of the Woodstock group, Combe, the coefficient of variation of oats produced was .32. But so low was the yield (1.69 bushels per bushel of seed) that the coefficient of variation of oats consumed was .78. For the four demesnes in the group the results are as follows:

Table 2. The Coefficient of Variation of Yields Net of Seed, Woodstock Manors 1243–49.

	Bladon	Combe	Handborough	Wooton	*Average*
		Demesne of:			
Crop:					
Wheat	.33	.41	.35	.82	.48
Barley	.16	.76	.46	.39	.44
Oats	.80	.78	.43	.53	.64
Average	.43	.65	.41	.58	.52

Source: Ballard, 1908, as compiled in Slicher van Bath, 1963.

Such figures can be supplemented elsewhere, and vary a good deal. At Oakington in Cambridgeshire, for example, the coefficient of variation in the net yield of wheat from 1362 to 1409 was .32.[11] At Hurdwick in Devon the coefficient of variation in the net yield of large oats over 13 years scattered from 1412 to 1537 was .47 (Finberg, 1951, p. 112). By far the most complete medieval English yields, however, are those of the forty or fifty demesnes of the Bishop of Winchester in the thirteenth and fourteenth centuries, compiled recently into what must be considered their definitive form by J. Z. Titow in his *Winchester Yields: A Study in Medieval Agricultural Productivity* (1972). The Bishop's estates were largely in Hampshire and neighboring counties in the south of England, a drawback when using them to infer the conditions of agriculture in the heartland of the open field further north (although the south too was in open fields), especially considering that nearly all the estates were in what Eric Kerridge describes as the Chalk Country, in which the "warm and dry" soils drained much better than did usually the "heavy, cold, wet soils on impervious and retentive bases" of the Midland Plain (Kerridge, 1973, pp. 77, 84; Kerridge, 1968, pp. 29, 42, 91). The contrast in soils, though, is likely if anything to bias the results towards a too low rather than a too high estimate of the hazards of farming.

It is tempting to calculate coefficients of variation over the entire century and a half of this magnificent collection of yields, but the temptation must be resisted. What is relevant for the behavior of peasants is the variability of income around the average income they had come to expect. Whatever the expected average may have been, it was certainly not the average calculated from 1211 to 1349, except perhaps for a 150-year old peasant with a retentive memory and little appreciation of trends in yields. What a peasant in, say, 1340 had come to expect for the yield of 1341 could be estimated as a moving average or as some more sophisticated average of past yields, but it suffices here to limit the calculations to short periods, perhaps 15 years, over which useful memory extended. In the 15 years from 1335 to 1349, for example, on demesnes that had information for all years, the results for the three major crops are:

Table 3. Average Coefficient of Variation for
Three Crops on the Winchester Demesnes, 1335–49.

	Wheat	*Barley*	*Oats*
Number of demesnes	35	28	20
Average coefficient of variation (net of seed)	.42	.35	.55
Standard deviation of the average	.09	.12	.15
Standard error of the average	.02	.02	.03

Although the variability is less in these manors in the Chalk Country, the pattern among crops is the same as it is in the Woodstock manors on the edge of the Midland Plain: barley is the least variable, oats the most; a reasonable average of all three crops for England as a whole being .46 or so.

The yields of the three, however, were not perfectly correlated from year to year, making the variability of the income from a bundle of the crops less than the variability of each. The question is, how much less? It is convenient in answering the question to develop a formula used intensively in the sequel that relates the coefficient of variation in yield of a bundle of crops (or of pieces of land) to the average coefficient of variation of the individual crops.[12] Call the variance of the entire bundle of N crops σ^2, the variance of the ith crop $s^2{}_i$, and the covariance between the ith and j^{th} crops s_{ij}. If the average output of each crop is defined to be 1.0, then s_i will be the coefficient of variation of the ith crop and σ the coefficient of variation of income. If the crops make equal contributions to income, the weight of each in the total will be 1/N. Since the definition of the correlation coefficient, R_{ij}, between the ith and j^{th} crop is $s_{ij}/s_i s_j$, one can make the substitution $s_{ij} = s_i s_j R_{ij}$. With these preparations it follows from the algebra of variances that:

$$\sigma^2 = (\frac{1}{N})^2 [\sum_{i=1}^{N} s_i^2 + \sum_{\substack{i=1 \\ i \neq j}}^{N} \sum_{j=1}^{N} s_i s_j R_{ij}] \qquad (1)$$

This equation is not as unenlightening as it looks at first. The typical term of the first sum in the brackets will be s^2, the average variance. There are N of these in the sum, suggesting that one replace the first sum by Ns^2. The typical term of the second, double sum will be $s^2 R$, the average variance multiplied by the average correlation coefficient, because $s_i s_j$ will typically be close to $s^2{}_i$ or $s^2{}_j$. There are N (N-1) of these in the double sum (not N^2, for terms like $S^2{}_3 R_{33}$ are excluded by the condition that i not equal j in the sum), suggesting that one replace the double sum by N (N-1)$s^2 R$. The result is:

$$\sigma^2 \cong (\frac{1}{N})^2 [Ns^2 + N(N-1)s^2 R] = s^2(\frac{1 + (N-1)R}{N})$$

Taking square roots:

$$\sigma = s[\frac{1 + (N-1)R}{N}]^{1/2} \qquad (2)$$

This relation between the coefficient of variation of single crops and a bundle of crops is an approximation, but its simplicity is well worth its trivial inaccuracy.[13] Observe that if R = 1 or N = 1, then σ = s; the coefficient of variation is not reduced if the yields of the various types move in lockstep or if, equivalently, only one type is held. When R = 0 the equation is simply $\sigma = s/\sqrt{N}$, the coefficient of variation falling off continuously (if at lower and lower rates) as the number of types increase. As N gets large, σ approaches $sR^{1/2}$, this being, therefore, the maximum effect of diversification in lowering the variability of income. When two types (N = 2) move exactly inversely (R = −1), then σ = 0; by holding two such types all variability of income is eliminated.[14]

All that is now required to arrive at an estimate of the variability of income is evidence on R, the average correlation among the yields of the major crops. The Winchester yields make possible the calculation of this correlation crop-by-crop, not only within a village but also—the more relevant calculation for a peasant holding plots widely scattered over the face of a large village—between two neighboring villages. For the ten villages that can be paired as neighbors, less than three miles or so from each other, the results are:

Table 4. Correlations of Crops Within and
Between Neighboring Winchester Villages, 1335–49.

	Wheat-Barley	Wheat-Oats	Barley-Oats	*Average*
Average R within the 10 villages	.38	.27	.42	.36
Average R between the 7 close pairs	.35	.21	.32	.29

Notes: The pairs are Cheriton-Beauworth, Cheriton-Sutton, Sutton-Alresford, High Clere-Woodhay, High Clere-Burghclere, Burghclere-Ecchinswell, Twyford-Stoke.

It is no surprise that the between-village correlations are less than the within-village correlations (albeit slightly so for the correlation of wheat and barley); the correlation falls with distance, a fact to be extended and applied soon. What is relevant here is that the average correlation, however it is measured, is low, with the result that the coefficient of variation of income was a good deal lower than the average coefficient of variation of individual crops (.46), in this case by the factor $\left[\frac{1+2(.29)}{3}\right]^{\frac{1}{2}}$ = .73. The coefficient of variation of total income on a scattered holding, then, was (.46)(.73) = .34. Allowing for a minor adjustment to be made later, the calculation confirms that the coefficient of variation of income was indeed .347, or near enough.

PRICES, RENTS, AND RISKS

There remain two amendments to the estimate, either of which, if potent, could make it as it stands radically misleading: first, that the risks of agriculture were price as well as yield risks; secondly, that the peasant's income was not the whole of the crop, but the residual after payment of heavy tithes and rents. As it happens, neither is potent.

Consider the risks of fluctuations in prices. If prices matter at all, it is relative not absolute prices that matter, for a doubling of all prices (general inflation) does not affect real income. In other words, the additional uncertainty of real income arising from the opportunity to exchange barley, say, for wheat depends on fluctuations in the price of barley relative to the price of wheat. The real income from barley is $(P_B/P_W)Q_B$, and the question is whether the variability of this is the same as the variability of the physical yield of barley alone, Q_B. Whether it is or not depends, clearly, on how the yield of barley is related to its price relative to wheat. On the one hand, in an isolated village trading in its own narrow market, a failure of the barley crop would drive up the relative price of barley, offsetting to some degree the drop in income (expressed in wheat) and lowering the variability of income. On the other hand, in a village trading in a wide market, a failure of its own crop would produce little offsetting. Crops elsewhere, poorly correlated with the crop in the afflicted village, could cause the price to fluctuate perversely, increasing the variability of income. To be specific, if the output of barley and its relative price are normally distributed, have a correlation coefficient, r, and have each a coefficient of variation s and c, then the coefficient of variation of their product is:[15]

$$[s^2 + 2rsc + c^2 + (1+r^2)(s^2c^2)]^{1/2} \div (1+rsc)$$

The value of s is, as was shown earlier, .46; it is the average coefficient of variation of wheat, barley and oats—"barley" standing in this discussion for any one of the crops. The value of c, the coefficient of variation of the relative price of a crop, requires prices for two crops for the same set of years. From the fragmentary evidence available for medieval England it appears to be about .25. In Oakington, Cambridgeshire for the thirteen years from 1282 to 1314 in which prices of both barley and wheat were reported, the value was .24, and for the fourteen years from 1319 to 1409 in which prices of both black peas and wheat were reported, it was .29 (Page, 1934, pp. 318–28). A longer series is available for large oats and wheat at Hurdwick, Devonshire; and for twenty-eight pairs of prices from 1398 to 1524 the coefficient of variation of the relative price of oats is .25 (Finberg, 1951, pp. 116–119). The correlation between a crop's yield and its relative price, r, requires both the prices and the yield for the same set of years, and is therefore more difficult to measure. For the seven years out of the twenty-eight at Hurdwick in which all these are available, r is −.38. The negative correlation is no surprise in view of late medieval, still less early medieval, costs of transportation. After a bad hay crop on his Sussex farm in 1777, William Marshall reflected, no doubt gratefully, that "The price of *corn* is regulated by the *crops of Europe*; but the price of *hay* is settled by those which happen within the *circuit of a few miles*" (1777, his italics). What was true of hay in the eighteenth century was true of most crops in the fourteenth century. In any event, the exact value of r, so long as it is negative, is not important. For s = .46 and for various values of c and r, the value of the expression is:

Table 5. The Coefficient of Variation of the Real Value of a Crop for Various Choices of r and c.

		Correlation between Yield and Relative Price			
		0	−.20	−.40	−.60
Coefficient of	.20	.51	.48	.45	.41
Variation of	.25	.54	.50	.47	.42
the Relative Price	.30	.57	.53	.49	.44

The most extreme values consistent with what is known about medieval agriculture produce a coefficient of variation including fluctuating prices (.57 to .41) near to the coefficient of variation excluding them (.46). Fluctuating prices did not greatly add to, or subtract from risk.

The other amendment to the simple measure of risk looks at first more potent. Peasants did not earn the gross output of their land, for in the opinion of the king, the church, and above all the lord of the manor, it was not their's to earn. The church's tithes were taken in the field, and are therefore already removed from the yields. But the lord's rents of all sorts, amounting to half of the gross yield (Postan. In Postan, [ed], 1966, p. 603) and to still more of the yield net of seed, are not. Were the rents immutable and collected in kind, their effect on the variability of peasant incomes would be similar to the effect of the fixed outlay for seed, and much stronger. The average gross yield of grains on the Bishop of Winchester's demesnes in the first half of the fourteenth century was about 3.2 per bushel of seed.[16] A coefficient of variation of income (after subtracting seed alone) of .35 or so implies a standard deviation of .78 per bushel of seed. Consequently, if the lord took in rent each year half the average gross yield (namely, (.5) (3.2) = 1.6), the coefficient of variation of the income remaining would have been (.78) ÷ (3.2−1.0−1.6) = 1.30! Were starvation half the average residual income [(.5) (.60) = .30] peasants would have starved in four years out of every ten. That they did not suggests that the reasoning is faulty.

The fault lies not in the statistics of yields or average rents, which are reasonably well founded, but in the assumption that the lord took his rents in kind. By 1300, rents all over Europe, and in particular in England, were expressed largely in money (Postan. In Postan, [ed.], 1966, p. 603; Duby, 1968, p. 238). Since the price of grain varied inversely with the size of the crop, the real, as distinct from the money burden of rents, would decline in years of crop failure. Algebraically speaking, the peasant's net income in money was $PI = PQ - M$, that is, the value of his net income (PI) was the value of his output (PQ) minus his money rents (M); his real net income, then, was $I = (PQ - M)/P = Q - (M/P)$. The output of a peasant having diverse plots in a village—note this qualification, for it will be significant when thinking of a peasant without diverse plots—would have moved up and down with the output of the village as a whole, and therefore up and down, though imperfectly correlated, with the output in the local market. The peasant's output, therefore, would have moved inversely with the price, as, say, $P = aQ^{-b}$. Consequently, the peasant's real income would have been $I = Q - (\frac{M}{a})Q^{b}$. The question is, will the coefficient of variation of real income (I) be greater than, equal to, or less than the coefficient of variation of gross output (Q)? The answer depends on b, the slope of the inverse relation between price and quantity. When its absolute value is 1.0 the peasant's real income is $I = Q - (\frac{M}{a})Q^{1.0} = Q(1 - \frac{M}{a})$, that is, real income is simply proportional to gross output and the coefficients of variation of output and of income are the same.

The absolute value of the coefficient b, in fact, appears to be near or a little below 1.0 implying that fixed money rents were equivalent to a fixed share of the crop. The most relevant evidence is for wheat, the cash crop of the peasant. Taking logarithms of both sides of the supposed relationship between price and quantity gives the equation to be fitted to the evidence, namely, $\log P = \log a + b \log Q$. The wheat output net of seed (which is what reaches the market and affects price) is, like the price, undoubtedly measured imperfectly: seed requirements changed from year to year, the output of the demesne does not reflect perfectly the output of the peasantry's land, and so forth. It is well known that errors in the independent variable in a simple regression of the sort proposed will bias the estimate of the slope, b, towards zero. The simplest solution to the problem is to regress both P on Q and Q on P, and be content with an upper and lower bound on b, thus:

Table 6. Regressions of P and Q for Wheat
at Mardon and Ecchinswell, 1297–1349.

Period	$\log P =$ $\log a + b \log Q$ $b =$	$\log Q =$ $\log a + b \log P$ $1/b =$	Average	R^2	Number of Years
1297–1318	−.61	−1.19	−.90	.51	20
(1313–1318)	−.79	− .85	−.82	.92	6
1325–1332	−.46	−4.37	−2.4	.10	3
1335–1349	−.38	−1.15	−.77	.33	15
(1337–1341)	−.28	− .53	−.40	.53	5

Source: Prices of wheat from Titow, (1969), pp. 98–99, yields net of seed the average of the two places, from Titow, (1972). The yield (calculated at the end of September in the harvest year) is matched with the price of the following year.

The lower bound is the first column, the upper bound the second, and their average (which would be the best estimate were the errors in P and Q similar in magnitude) the third. The regression is calculated for three periods instead of the entire period in order to allow, in a rough way, for trends, which would obscure the short-term relation between P and Q. The years in parentheses are sub-periods around two especially bad episodes, 1315–16 and 1339. In the regression with the best fit (1297–1318), the average of the coefficient b estimated in both ways is −.90.

The evidence for other crops, times and place is not ample because the calculation requires a set of years close enough to each other to fit the horizon of a peasant and to escape trends of inflation and deflation, both yields and prices. Oakington, Cambridgeshire meets the conditions for two crops, wheat and black peas, in the late fourteenth century.

Table 7. Regression of P and Q for
Wheat and Black Peas at Oakington.

	log P = log a + b log Q b =	log Q = log a + b log P 1/b=	Average	R^2	Number of Cases
Wheat, 1390–1408	−.28	−4.35	−2.32	.06	9
Black Peas, 1362–1375	−.23	−1.17	− .85	.27	10

Source: Page, (1934), pp. 319, 328–30.

The fits, again, are poor, but the values of b are consistent with the previous table. With results such as these it would not be impossible, of course, for the absolute value of b to be as small as, say, .50; in which case the presence of rents taking half of average output would raise the coefficient of variation from .35 to .50[17]—not the dramatic rise implied by rents fixed in real terms, but notable. The best estimate, though, is that the absolute value of b was 1.0 or a little less, perhaps .9 (which would raise the coefficient of variation from .35 to .38) or .8 (which would raise it to .41). The lord might ignore the pleas to reduce rents in a bad year, yet the rise in price would accomplish nearly the same thing. By fixing rents in money he shared with his tenants in the risks of the harvest, much as lord and tenant did in explicit agreements to sharecrop, rare though such agreements were in England. The insurance achieved by scattering was additional to the greater insurance— relative to the alternative of fixed real rents—of fixed money rents. In short, the coefficient of variation of physical output (near .35) can stand for the coefficient of variation of servile incomes.

DISASTER

Having established that the entry for the coefficient of variation of income in Table 1 of a while back is correct, the next step is to establish that the entry for the level of disaster of 50 (relative to an average income of 100) is correct. There are several ways of doing this. The first and least conclusive way is to measure yields in disastrous years. A yield in famine of one-third to two-thirds of the average is a traditional estimate, making one-half plausible.[18] The evidence for medieval England, in particular for the great famine of 1315-17, supports this judgement. One cannot merely calculate for each Winchester demesne the deficiency of the crop in a bad year, say 1316, relative to the typical yield, and then average the result over all the demesnes, because even in generally disastrous years, such as 1316, some villages were not struck by disaster. What is relevant is disaster in a village relative to normal yields when it strikes, not an average over lucky and unlucky villages. Set off from the others, midway between Portsmouth and Southampton, Fareham, for example, was lucky: while most of the villages suffered a large drop in the yield of wheat from 1314 to 1315, and many a further drop in 1316, Fareham's fell slightly in 1315 and rose sharply in 1316; its barley yield rose in both years; and only its oat yield fell, although remaining above the average of earlier years. To include Fareham or villages like it would distort the calculation. How to exclude villages, however, is uncertain. If one selects those villages in which the years 1315 and 1316 were in fact the exceptionally bad years described by contemporaries (Lucas, 1930), that is, in which the yield of at least two of the major grains was at its lowest or its next to lowest in one of these two years relative to the four years before 1315 or after 1316, there is some assurance, arbitrary though it may be, that one is looking at villages actually experiencing disaster in 1315 or 1316. Many villages did not have complete information. Since the years 1319 and 1321-23 are unavailable for any of the villages, 1320 and 1324 were taken to fill out the test of four years before and after the bad years. For the 12 villages with complete data Table 8 exhibits the ratios of incomes in 1315 and 1316 to the average incomes in the villages 1300-1324 (both terms in the ratio being simple averages of the net yields of wheat, barley and oats).

The observations with asterisks pass the test of unusual lowness of yield for that year, six passing it in each year: six out of every twelve villages does not seem unreasonable as the proportion experiencing disaster in one of the most severe famines in European history. Still, as promised, the test is inconclusive. The range in the ratio of famine income to average income in the villages that pass it is −.02 to .74, with an average of .42. The difficulty is that even if the test correctly selects only villages experiencing disaster, any average of their experiences will understate the level of disaster, some villages (in this case, patently, Ashmansworth and Ecchinswell in 1316) reaching down far below it. Were it not obvious that the level of disaster relative to the average varies from village to village the solution would

DONALD N. McCLOSKEY

Table 8. Ratio of 1315 and 1316 Yields to
Average Yields 1300–1324.

	1315 Income Relative to 1300–24	1316 Income Relative to 1300–24
Ashmansworth	.41	–.02**
Ecchinswell	.47	–.02**
West Wycombe	.37*	.32*
East Meon	.63*	.35**
Beauworth	.75	.37
Crowley	.81	.63**
Bentley	.37*	.43*
Fonthill	.64*	.81
Alresford	.74**	.84
Bitterne	.63*	1.16
Downton	.93	1.06
Fareham	1.18	1.41

Source: Titow, 1972.

* This year is worst or next worst of 1311–1324 (except other of 1315–16 pair) for at least two crops.

** This year is worst of 1311–1324 (except other of 1315–16 pair) for at least two crops.

be simple enough, namely, to select the highest level for villages certified on some other grounds as experiencing disaster (the ideal would be local testimony), in this case .74 (Alresford in 1315). As it is, one knows only that .74 is too high and .42 too low, which is a range around .50, although not a small one.

Another way to show that .50 is a reasonable estimate of disaster relative to average income is to examine disastrous consumption relative to the average. Without entering too deeply the scholarly battlefield over which partisans of one or another view of the standard of living in medieval England fight—a place of hazard for medievalists and of sure death (indeed, disaster) for non-medievalists—some rough estimates may be ventured. M. M. Postan and J. Z. Titow (partisans, admittedly, of a pessimistic view) argue that a peasant family in the thirteenth and fourteenth century, on the premise that land was its only source of income, required, to stay alive, about ten acres.[19] The average acreage with which ten acres is to be compared must be the average for peasants occupied full-time on their land and living above subsistence, because these peasants held most of the tenant land in the village and therefore determined, with the lord, the usual geography of tenant holdings. On 104 thirteenth century manors, Postan found that full virgaters holding 24 to 30 acres (27 acres, say, on average) constituted 22 percent of the tenants, half virgaters holding 12 to 15 acres (13.5 acres on average) 33 percent, and smallholders of less than 10 acres (3 acres on average) 45 percent. Numerous though the smallholders supplementing their income from land by laboring were, they held only (3) (45) ÷ [(3) (45) +

(13.5) (33) + (27) (22)] = 11 percent of the tenant land.[20] On this basis the average acreage of a tenancy above subsistence was [(13.5) (33) + (27) (22)] ÷ 55 = 18.9 acres. Since a bare subsistence yield on 18.9 acres is equivalent to the yield on a holding capable of yielding bare subsistence without outside employment—*viz*, 10 acres—subsistence was 10/18.9 = 53 percent of the relevant average.

A final way to show that disaster was 50 relative to an average income of 100 is to use the observed frequency of disaster. If the standard deviation of income is about 35 relative to 100, as has been shown, then the frequency of disaster, when disaster is 50, is about once every 13 years, and this is roughly the frequency of disaster observed before the agricultural revolution. The normality of the distribution, which is important at other stages of the argument as well, is easy to accept; indeed, what is difficult is to frame tests that have a sporting chance of rejecting it. Evidence from a demesne of 200 acres is inappropriate because, by the central limit theorem, its output may well fit a normal distribution even though 20 acre pieces from the demesne, each of which might make up a peasant's farm, fit a quite different distribution. Evidence from a long period is inappropriate as well, because it is normality over a peasant's life, not over a century, that is relevant to his decisions to insure. Yet if the period is too short there will not be enough observations to put the hypothesis of normality in jeopardy. Technically speaking, the expected frequencies in a chi-square test of goodness of fit must be at least 5 (some statisticians would say 10); the minimum number of classes that leave any degree of freedom for a test of normality when the mean and standard deviation are estimated from the data is 4; therefore the minimum number of years in a test is 20. Three cases of unusually small demesnes among the Bishop of Winchester's that have the requisite data are Bitterne in 1325–49, and Farnham in 1297–1324 and in 1335–49. Income can be calculated on these by averaging the net yields of seed of wheat, barley and oats. Peasants certainly did not grow these crops in exactly the proportions implied by a simple average, but alternative proportions give similar results. It is in any case difficult to find evidence for any assertion about what they did grow other than the useless one that they probably grew all three, wheat to sell for the rent money and the others to eat or to feed to their animals. The results (which embody the Yates correction for continuity) are contained in Table 9.

Notice that the coefficients of variation bracket the earlier figure, .35. And notice too that the larger the acreage the lower is the chi-square, confirming the remark about the central limit theorem coming into play for large acreages. It is in any case difficult on this showing to reject normality. In the peculiar manner of speaking usual when testing hypotheses statistically, were one to reject the hypothesis of normality when chi-square was greater than 1.67 or 1.48 or 1.10, one would expose oneself to a .20 or .22 or .29 probability of rejecting it when it was in fact true, a fairly skeptical position. A plausible alternative distribution—normality of the logarithms of the yield—results in somewhat higher chi-squares (2.16 for

Table 9. Chi-Square Tests for the Normality of Income.

	Number of Years with Data	Size of Demesme (acres)	Average Net Yield/Seed, Three Crops	Standard Deviation	Coefficient of Variation	Chi- Square	Probability of Falsely Reject- ing Normality if this was the Critical Level (1 degree of freedom)
Bitterne							
1325–49	22	52	2.13	.608	.29	1.67	.20
Farnham							
1297–1324	21	66	1.68	.597	.36	1.48	.22
Farnham							
1325–49	21	75	2.44	.965	.40	1.10	.29

Bitterne, 3.00 and 1.85 for Farnham) and lower risks of excessive skepticism (.14, .08, and .17) if this distribution is rejected. That the chi-squares are only "somewhat" higher testifies to the difficulty of rejecting any plausible distribution (roughly unimodal) within the constraints of the data. Still, normality is convenient, theoretically unobjectionable, and fits the facts reasonably well.

The evidence for the other half of the present demonstration that disaster was around 50 relative to an average of 100 is evidence on the frequency of disaster. It has its own ambiguities, even aside from the ambiguity in the word "disaster," because the frequency of general disaster in the absence of a perfect correlation between yields in different places would be lower than the relevant frequency, that of local disaster, and it is sometimes unclear whether a frequency is local or general. The Anglo-Saxon Chronicle, for example, speaks of fourteen harvest failures from 975 to 1124, a frequency of about one every eleven years,[21] or one every 12.5 years if failures in two successive years are counted as one, but it is unclear whether this refers to the whole kingdom (in its varying completeness) or to the part of it in which the chroniclers lived. The distinction matters, for it is shown later that the correlation between yields in distant villages within one small part of England was only .40. The effect is apparent in W. G. Hoskin's study of "Harvest Fluctuations and English Economic History, 1480–1619," (1953–54, reprinted in Minchinton, [ed.], 1968, I, pp. 113–115), which uses national average prices of wheat ranged against the literary evidence to identify years of "dearth" (as distinct from bad, deficient, average, good, and abundant harvests). In these 140 years dearth occurred in the country as a whole every 20 years (every 28 years if successive dearths are counted as one); it occurred, however, every 12.7 years (15.6 years) in a limited locale for which a continuous series is available, in Exeter. The local chronicle of Shrewsbury in the second half of the sixteenth century reports a similar interval, of 12.5 years (Hey, 1974, pp. 49–50). One year in thirteen, in short, appears to be a reasonable estimate for a single locale. Were disaster set at 40 relative to an average of 100 its frequency would be in view of such evidence unreasonably low (every 24 years); and at 60 unreasonably high (every 8 years). Disaster, then, is around 50.

THE EFFICACY OF DIVERSIFICATION

The last piece to be fitted into the evidence for Table 1 is the variability of income on a consolidated, as distinct from a scattered holding. The essential point is that a scattered holding contains many different types of land while a consolidated holding contains but one. Putting all his eggs into one basket, therefore, the coefficient of variation of the income of a peasant working a consolidated holding is higher than that of his more cautious brother working a scattered holding. To speak more quantitatively, recall first that for a single crop the coefficient of variation on medieval demesnes was about .46. Now this was itself the result of a scattered holding: even when demesnes were consolidated (some were not, perhaps the better to insure a bailiff responsible for a fixed annual return to the lord against embarassment) they were large and would contain many types of land, say 15—though it would matter little for the argument if they contained 10 or 20. Suppose that the correlation from year to year in the yields of different types of land was on the average, .60. This is the critical number. According to the formula developed earlier, the coefficient of variation on a holding of 15 types would be related to the coefficient of variation (c) on a holding of 1 type in this way: $.46 = c[[1 + 14(.60)] \div 15]^{\frac{1}{2}} = c(.79)$; from which $c = .58$. For each crop, in other words, a consolidated holding on one type of land has a coefficient of variation of .58. By contrast, a holding scattered over five types (it would make little difference if it was 4 or 6) has a coefficient of variation of $.58[[1 + 4(.60)] \div 5]^{\frac{1}{2}} = .48$. The contrast between .58 and .48 is a measure of the larger part of the insurance from scattering. The smaller part covers familiar ground. As was noted earlier, the three crops peasants grew were poorly correlated in yield. But the crops would be more poorly correlated for a scattered than for a consolidated holding, which fact adds a little to the insurance. If the correlations between pairs of the three crops (distinct from the correlation between places for a single crop, .60) was .36 for a consolidated holding and .29 for a scattered one, then the coefficients of variation of income would be:

Scattered: $.48[[1 + 2(.29)] \div 3]^{\frac{1}{2}} = .48(.73) = .35$

Consolidated: $.58[[1 + 2(.36)] \div 3]^{\frac{1}{2}} = .58(.76) = .44$

These are the figures in Table 1 given earlier. When they are proven, the table is complete.

The question is, was the correlation of yields between plots scattered over a village two miles or so square about .60? For most city folk, who reckon one bit of dirt or fall of rain much like any other, it is hard to believe such a low figure, although it is not hard for farmers and backyard gardeners. The first class of evidence is botanical and meteorological. "The common Accidents and Diseases befalling Corn in the growth of it, being Meldew, Blasting, Smut," (Enquiries of the Royal Society, 1664, in Lennard, 1932. In Minchinton, [ed.], 1968, p. 165) were fungoid diseases, local in their effects, as might be expected from the random distribution of spores by wind and rain. As Joseph Wilkinson of Yorkshire, responding in 1664 to the Royal Society, wrote: "I have observed in the same field divers parts as were cheryndred [?], some mildewed and blackish, others pure and white, the mildewed a sandy land, the pure a sharp and stony land." (Thirsk and Cooper, [eds.], 1972, p. 152; their remark on "cheryndred.") In similar fashion, birds flock and insects swarm, spotty in their depredations. Hail in England is common in the spring, rare in the ripening season, and "the usual area we should assign to an English hailstorm is a mile or two long and a few hundred yards broad" (Russell, 1893, p. 23). When hail came it could easily damage crops in one part of a village three or four thousand yards broad without damaging those in another part, although it came, on the whole, in the season when it could do the least damage. The last frost in England is frequently spotty in its incidence as well, particularly across slightly different altitudes, and variable in date. Because England's climate is wet, the change in average temperature from season to season is less sharp than it is in continental climates, and a given fall in average temperature (from a cold year or a higher altitude) will therefore produce a more radical shift in the date at which the temperature permits growth (42 degree Farenheit). As a modern student of these matters concludes, "even the several fields of a normal (i.e., non-fruit) farm have each their varying characteristics arising not merely from soil but also from the significant local variations in the incidence of frost" (Manley, 1952, p. 218).

Another, more quantitative class of evidence on the size of R is experimental. The variability of yields over small areas is notorious among agronomists. R. A. Fisher's pioneering work on *The Design of Experiments* was, in large part, devoted to precisely this problem, and one hears echoes of a cautious medieval peasant laying out elongated strips within a furlong block in one part of Fisher's advice for handling it: "each plot must . . . sample fairly the whole area of the block in which it is placed. It is often desirable, therefore . . . to let the plots lie side by side as narrow strips each running the whole length of its block" (Fisher, 1947, p. 65). He remarks, again, that even an area as small as an acre has "considerable greater soil heterogeneity" than a quarter-acre (p. 104). His elaborate techniques for minimizing the uncertainty due to such variation were fully justified by earlier spoiled experiments. In reporting the experiments in rotations on Lansome Field at Woburn beginning in 1881, for example, J.A. Voelcker complained repeatedly that despite an apparent uniformity "the soil of Lansome

Field . . . has been found to be not really uniform enough and the land not level enough to make a really satisfactory experimental field" (Voelcker, 1897, p. 640 and 1884, p. 360). Plots 1 and 4 were quarter-acres a little over 100 yards apart, treated to precisely the same unfertilized rotation. Yet the average yield from the four crops of barley taken from 1885 to 1897 was 13 percent higher on plot 4 than on plot 1; indeed, the yield on plot 4 was higher than on any of the fertilized plots. The correlation of yields on plots 1 and 4 was only .78, despite the care taken to cultivate the plots in the same thorough and expensive way, far beyond the standards of ordinary farming. Even the more successful experiments in the continuous growth of barley in the Stackyard Field at Woburn could produce a correlation of only .84 from 1877 to 1884, between the two unfertilized plots (1 and 7) 100 yards apart (Voelcker, 1897 and 1898, pp. 722, 690–97). The correlation drops sharply for plots treated with different fertilizers but cultivated otherwise in an identical careful fashion. The correlation at Rothamsted between yields of wheat grown continuously without fallow on plot 3 (unfertilized) and plot 2 (fertilized with dung) from 1844 to 1883, for example, was only .55 (Lawes and Gilbert, 1864 and 1884). Plot 2 could stand for the infield and 3 for the outfield in the variety of the open field system common in the Celtic fringe of Britain: the infield, close to the village, received intensive fertilization while the outfield received none.

The experimental evidence, however, has the defects of its virtues. Cultivation was carefully controlled and carefully recorded over a small area, but with the result that the effects of interplot variation, such as local attacks of mold and local peculiarities of drainage were minimized. Because the experimenters were attempting to isolate the effects of particular regimes of fertilization and rotation they spared no pains to eliminate others. In consequence, if the experimental correlations between plots are relevant at all they are relevant only as upper bounds on the correlations to be expected in an agriculture lacking the knowledge or resources to achieve the meticulous standards of the laboratory. The experiments, in short, imply an upper bound on R of .70 or .80.

The best evidence on R is from open field agriculture itself, scarce and ambiguous though the evidence is. Very seldom do the records for a crop of wheat, say, distinguish yields in different parts of a field or village, yet this is what is wanted. Even so methodical a record-keeper as Robert Loder, farming in Harwell, Berkshire in the early seventeenth century, kept records on separate portions of his many different crops only for hay. On three plots of hay not more than a mile or so from each other the mutual correlations 1611 to 1620 were .90, .66, and .37, for an average of .64.[22] A fall in the crop of the Padocke plot in 1612 he interpreted as "the loving and fatherly chastisements of the Lord my God" (p. 36), but the chastisements were not laid on everywhere: the yield of the Town Meade plot increased by over 50 percent in the same year.

In the absence of more evidence of this sort—which in any case could be expected to exist only in an age of literate and reflective farmers, and which therefore would be to some extent anachronistic when applied to open field farming at its height—one must turn again to the records of demesne farming in the Middle Ages. Many demesnes with records were close to others with records, making it possible to infer from the correlations between villages what the correlation might have been within them. The procedure has difficulties, to be sure. The neighboring demesnes must be quite close, no more than three miles or so apart, to be relevant to the experience of any but a long, thin village. Since few are less than two miles apart (measuring distances from church to church on the modern Ordnance Survey maps) and since, as will be shown in a moment, the correlation falls with distance, the calculated correlations may be too low to represent the correlation facing a peasant in one open field in a village. On the other hand, since the demesne usually took the best land, bottom land in a valley, for example, the correlations may be too high, because the bottom land in one village may be more similar to the bottom land in another than to the land on the village hill. Although Twyford and Stoke are the most distant pair of the Bishop of Winchester's neighboring demesnes examined in detail below (3.3 miles church-to-church) the correlation of their wheat crops is the second highest observed, .84. If these were consolidated demesnes near the center of each village the high correlation would be misleading, for the center of both is on the same bank of the River Itchen with the same (southeasterly) exposure relative to nearby hills.

The evidence, nonetheless, is suggestive. The first insight that can be wrung from it is that the correlation of yield of a crop between two villages, R, does fall as the distance between the two increases. Were this not the case it might be possible to achieve insurance without scattering, for if R were, say, .60 both at a distance of 200 yards and at 2000 yards a peasant could hold a sufficient diversity of land within a small area. One presumes that R would indeed fall with distance, and it is pleasing to have the presumption confirmed for the villages on the Winchester estates, 1335–49. Choosing the dozen less than 3.3 miles apart and setting aside the two pairs, East Meon-East Meon Church and Twyford-Stoke, which fall far off the fitted line for the good reason that they were in different parts of Hampshire from the others, the regression of R for wheat on miles of distance is:

$$R = .95 - .14d \qquad r^2 = .66$$
$$(.09) \quad (.04) \qquad n = 10$$
$$SEE = .07$$

For each mile of distance of one crop of wheat from another, therefore, the R fell 14 points.[23] It would not, of course, go on falling indefinitely. The correlations in six randomly selected pairs of villages (from 10 to 45 miles apart), compared in Table 10 with the correlations in close villages imply a lower limit on R in Hampshire for the three major crops taken together of about .40:

Table 10. Comparisons of Correlations Between Yields in Close
and Far Villages, Winchester Demesnes, 1335–49.

	Wheat	Barley	Oats	Average Equally Weighted
		Distant Villages (n=6)		
Average R	.55	.15	.38	.38
(Standard deviation)	(.18)	(.23)	(.90)	(.09)
		Near Villages (n=9)		
Average R	.68	.57	.66	.64
(Standard deviation)	(.15)	(.15)	(.22)	(.09)
Level of significance of difference	.074	.001	.01	.0001

The last line in the table gives the probability of observing such differences by mere chance if the correlations between pairs of the distant and near villages were in truth the same. That the distant villages have such definitely lower R's is additional testimony to the inverse relationship between R and distance. By this test there is more room for skepticism about the testimony on wheat than on the other crops, although by the regression test less; regressions of R against distance work poorly for barley and oats, possibly because spring crops depend more than does wheat on variations of soil and the like within distances smaller then the mile or more minimum distance church-to-church in the Winchester estates.

This last possibility finds some confirmation in still another test of the inverse relationship between R and distance, relying on correlations between different crops. If correlations fall with distance one would expect correlations between crops of, say, wheat and barley to be lower between two close villages than within each village. For instance, one would expect the correlation of the wheat crop in Alresford with the barley crop in Sutton (these two crops being about 1.5 miles apart) to be lower than the correlation of the wheat crop in Alresford with the barley crop in Alresford itself (these crops being closer, perhaps—depending on the extent of Alresford—a mile or less apart). The expectation is fulfilled:

Table 11. Correlations Between Crops Within and Between
Seven Pairs of Close Villages, Winchester Estates, 1335–49.

	Average Correlations Between:			
	Wheat-Barley	*Wheat-Oats*	*Oats-Barley*	*Average*
Within the Villages	.39	.26	.43	.36
Between the Villages	.35	.21	.32	.29

The figures in the Average column were used earlier to represent the between-crop correlations facing a peasant with a consolidated holding (.36) or a scattered holding (.29). What is relevant here is that the differences between the within-and-between village correlations for Oats-Barley (although not the correlations involving the winter crop, wheat, which display no uniform pattern) fall with greater distance. Regressing the excess of the within-village correlations of oats and barley over the between-village correlation on the church-to-church distance in miles (d) for the seven pairs gives:

$$R_{within} - R_{between} = -.16 + .12d \qquad r^2 = .61$$
$$\quad\;\; (.10) \quad (.04) \qquad SEE = .07$$

For each mile of distance, in other words, the Oats-Barley correlation falls 12 points further below the same correlation within a village.[24] Notice how similar the coefficient is to the comparable coefficient in the wheat regression given above. The correlations, then, fall with distance.

The other insight that can be wrung from the experience of neighboring demesnes is that the correlation for a single crop over the distances relevant to scattering in open fields is indeed about .60. Since the experimental correlations over small distances are often not much above this level the assertion is not surprising. On the neighboring Winchester estates, to be sure, the average (given in Table 11 above) is a little higher, about .64, implying a still higher figure at lower distances. Yet these demesnes, as was noted earlier, were located on chalk soils, inherently less variable and hazardous in their response to the weather. On the four Woodstock manors at about the same time, located on the edge of the clay soils of the Midland Plain, the average R was well below .60, as Table 12 shows.

Table 12. Correlations Between Yields of Neighboring Demesnes of the Woodstock Manors, 1243–49.

		Combe			Handborough			Wooton		
		Wheat	Barley	Oats	Wheat	Barley	Oats	Wheat	Barley	Oats
Bladon	Wheat	.12			.39			.80		
	Barley		.60			-.40			.47	
	Oats			-.29			.65			.29
Combe	Wheat				.76			.30		
	Barley					-.51			.17	
	Oats						.046			-.46
Handborough	Wheat							.50		
	Barley								.48	
	Oats									.37

Source: Ballard, 1908, as compiled in Slicher van Bath, 1963.

The average over the three crops for the six pairs (from 1.25 to 3.6 miles apart) ranges from 0 (for Combe-Wooton) to .52 (for Bladon-Wooton), the average over the six pairs for the three crops from .10 (for oats) to .48 (for wheat). The overall average correlation is .24. It is clear that the evidence justifies a choice of R as low as .60.

All the entries in the table describing the choices of a peasant facing disaster have now been confirmed. In particular, a peasant who held a scattered farm faced a standard deviation of income of 35 relative to an average of 100, whereas a peasant who held a consolidated farm faced one of 44.[25] There is, indeed, a reason for believing that the risks of a consolidated holding were even larger. Because of the imperfect correlation between yields in different parts of a village the farmer of a consolidated holding is more lonely in his struggle against hazard than is the farmer of a scattered holding. The income of an open field farmer will fluctuate in much the same way as does the income of his fellows, while an enclosed field farmer goes it alone. One consequence is that it would be difficult for a giver of charity or loans to distinguish avoidable from unavoidable accidents on a consolidated farm. The lord of the manor is more likely to forgive rents in a bad year if all his tenants ask, all with lower crops, than if only a few ask. Another consequence, at a less speculative level, is that the yield of a consolidated holding will be less well correlated with the price of corn, for a holding containing many types of land is more likely to yield well in a year of low prices generally and poorly in a year of high prices than one containing few types of land. As was argued earlier, this offsetting is critical when money rents are a large fraction of gross income. Robert Loder's hay crop in three places can illustrate the point. Table 13 gives the regression coefficients of yield on price and of price on yield for each of the three fields and for the three fields together.

Table 13. Price and Quantity Regressions, Loder's Hay Crop, 1611–20.

	Lower Bound (b in $P=a\,Q^b$)	Upper Bound (1/b in $Q=aP^b$)	Average	r^2
Town Meade	−.30	−2.56	−1.43	.12
South Marsh	−.49	− .68	− .58	.72
Padocke	−.52	− .66	− .59	.78
Whole Crop	−.67	−1.02	− .84	.68

Source: Fussell, (ed.), 1936, *passim* (e.g., pp. 5–6, 184).

Recall that the closer the coefficient b is to −1 the more completely do variations in price offset the fixity of rents, and the lower is the variability of income. The reliable regressions in the table (South Marsh and the Padocke) give upper bounds on b near the lower bound on b in the regression of the whole crop (the last line).

Had Loder held only one of these fields his income from hay after paying a 50 percent money rent typical of medieval England would have been markedly more variable than it would have been had he held all three.[26] A consolidated holding was a hazardous holding.

THE ROBUSTNESS OF THE RESULT

It is time, at last, to step back from the intricacies of the argument and assess its result. The result is that scattering reduced risk enough to offset its inefficiency: the hypothesis of risk aversion does have quantitative bite. The reader will wonder if the bite comes from some artificially sharpened tooth. Statistically speaking, the result depends on various estimates, any of which may be in error. It is difficult enough in economic history to estimate first moments, as evinced by the long list of controversies that have turned on the value of an average, from the average income of medieval peasants to the average quality of Victorian businessmen; it is still more difficult to estimate second moments, as is evinced by the equally long list of controversies, many of them hopelessly short of a conclusion, that have turned on the value of a variance or a correlation, from the price revolution of the sixteenth century to the standard of living of the early nineteenth. Yet tests of the hypothesis of risk aversion must depend on second moments, for the variability of income lies at its heart.[27] The solution is to find out how the result varies when the estimates vary. Table 14 gives high and low estimates of the variables around the best estimate.

Table 14. Alternative Values of Estimates in a Calculation of Risk.

Variable	Symbol	Low	Best	High
Correlation for one crop	R	.43	.60	.73
Correlation between crops, one village	R_c	.14	.36	.54
Correlation between crops, near pairs of villages	R_s	.07	.29	.48
Coefficient of variation of a typical crop	s	.41	.46	.60
Average income with consolidation, relative to scattered = 100	μ	107	110	113
Level of disaster relative to average income on scattered holding	d	40	50	60

The high and low estimates for R, R_c, R_s and s are meant to represent the averages of the upper and lower halves of their distributions when the best estimate is based on a sample of 15—the number of years used earlier to stand for the extent of the useful memory of peasants.[28] They would be closer to the best estimate if the procedure were permitted to reflect the larger samples on which the best estimates are in fact based. The high and low estimates of μ and d are merely plausible ranges. All possible matchings of the five high and low estimates (using R_c for consolidated holdings and R_s for scattered) yield 32 possible values for the probability of disaster on a consolidated holding and 16 possible values on a scattered holding. Table 15 arranges the values in a way that facilitates comparisons. Along a row in either the left (high d) or right (low d) panel the four variables that are involved in the calculation for both scattered and consolidated holdings (viz., s, R, D, and R_c or R_s) are the same. Along these rows, therefore, the probability of disaster for scattered and consolidated holdings can be compared.

Table 15. Probability of Disaster for High and Low Values of the Variables.

			High d			Low d		
			Scattered	Consolidated		Scattered	Consolidated	
				Low	High		Low	High
				μ	μ		μ	μ
High R	Low	Low s	.069	.078	*.064*	.013	.021	.018
	R_c or R_s	High s	.147	.171	.154	.057	.085	.079
	High	Low s	.127	.136	*.119*	.043	.057	.052
	R_c or R_s	High s	.218	.224	.209	.119	.140	.131
Low R	Low	Low s	.069	.129	.115	.013	.054	.048
	R_c or R_s	High s	.164	.221	.206	.072	.136	.127
	High	Low s	.133	.189	.174	.047	.104	.097
	R_c or R_s	High s	.224	.274	.261	.129	.195	.187

Note: The equal probabilities for four of the cases of scattering are not misprints. They are equal qu fortuitously.

The 3 probabilities in italics are the only comparisons of 32 in which a consolidated holding is superior to a scattered one. The reader may judge for himself whether the events they have in common are likely to have occured together—R as high as .73, disaster as high as 60 relative to the mean, the coefficient of variation as low as .41 (except in one of the three), and income on a consolidated holding as high as 13 percent greater than on a scattered holding. The experiment demonstrates, in any case, that risk aversion is a robust explanation of open fields, insensitive to errors in its calculation.

OPTIMAL SCATTERING AND THE NUMBER OF PLOTS

Scattering was a Good Thing: so much is by now clear. Yet it is possible to have too much or too little of a Good Thing, scattering one's land in too many or too few plots, even though the gains in insurance on the whole outweigh the losses in efficiency. To put the point another way, it would be irresponsible to offer risk aversion as a large part of the explanation of scattering, urging that it replace inheritance customs or communal plowing in the usual tales, if risk aversion could not explain some significant part of the scattering actually observed. If a peasant scatters his 20 acres in 20 plots an explanation that implies he should scatter them in only 2 plots has drawbacks as a full account of his behavior. His behavior is, as it were, underexplained, leaving the puzzle of why he overinsured. An implication that he should scatter his acres in 200 plots would be equally embarassing, suggesting as it would that something in the argument was very wrong. The argument from partible inheritance has an affliction of this second sort, since once the logic of an increase in the number of plots per holding with each generation has been accepted it is hard to see why it would stop short of agricultural chaos. Of course, arguments can be patched up and made to hobble forward. One could patch up the inheritance argument by positing—albeit contrary to its egalitarian spirit—a limit to the sacrifices of efficiency that coheirs will make on the shrine of equality. If the risk argument underexplained scattering, predicting fewer than the observed number of plots, one could patch it up, too, rather more convincingly, by positing an uncertainty in the mind of the peasant about how risky in fact was his income, uncertainty driving him to overinsure. Peasants, after all, did not have at their disposal electronic computers and statistical theory (clumsy as even these elaborate tools of inquiry are), and they could not record their yields for future analysis, had such an absurdity occured to them, because they could not write. A cautious man facing danger is perhaps especially cautious when he knows little about the danger other than that it is there.

It will prove unnecessary, however, to invoke such arguments, plausible though they may be; when the hypothesis of risk aversion is put in further jeopardy, asking it to predict not only that peasants will hold a number of plots but also what number they will hold, it predicts the correct number. The first step in showing this somewhat surprising assertion to be true is to determine the actual number of plots on a typical peasant holding; the second is to determine the predicted number.

The evidence on the actual number of plots exists in a form that makes it convenient to break down the number into three components, the acreage of a typical holding, the number of nominal plots per acre, and the effective number of plots relative to the nominal number, the product of these three being the effective number of plots per holding. The acreage of a typical holding was discussed earlier, and the conclusion there, was that the typical acreage in two samples, one centered on the year 1250 and the other on 1600, was around 20 acres, give or take

5 acres, that is, somewhere between the acreage of a full and a half virgate. An "acre," of course, is in early times not always a statute acre. A more serious difficulty with using the evidence this way is that the units of farming ownership and of farming operation may well have been different, yet it is information ownership alone (or tenancy directly from the lord of the manor) that is most often contained in field maps and in lists of holdings. In the lists of tenants of a lord "the pattern of actual economic occupation of land might differ very widely from that of official tenancies" (Brooke and Postan, [eds.], 1951, p. 133). Subleasing and absentee ownership were common early and late in the history of the open field, both of which obscure the nature of the typical operating farm: a man who owned 20 acres could lease 30 more from three absentee owners with 10 acres each to form a large and relatively consolidated farm that would appear nowhere in the records. In Eversholt, Bedfordshire in 1764, for example, there were 59 freeholders or copyholders owning lands less than 50 acres, yet of these 33 were nonresidents who could not possibly have been operating their lands as farms (Fowler, 1928–36, pp. 37–53 of 1936). And holders were often women, who could be expected to rent out their land. Jane, Countess of Shrewsbury, owning a 6-acre freehold, probably did not follow the plow in the open fields of Laxton, Nottinghamshire in 1635. The purpose in mentioning this difficulty is to draw attention to it, not to solve it. The only easily handled lists distinguishing definitely between occupiers and owners (whether lords of the manor or not; though it was the lord, if anyone, who kept records in earlier times) are those of the Tithe Commissioners in the late 1830's, but the lists are ill-timed and ill-located for a study of open fields in the Midlands before the seventeenth century. In the absence of a systematic study of this and other sources one must hope, as do other students of the subject, that official tenancies are at least approximately to the point.

The evidence on the nominal number of plots into which an acre of land was divided, of course, has the same drawback. The records of the holding and transfer of land from which the number can be inferred—surveys, glebe terriers, and grants—do not distinguish ownership from control, and the same hope, pious homage to the gods of knowledge, is all that can be offered. The records are at any rate voluminous. To illustrate what can be done with them, consider those in H. L. Gray's pioneering work on *English Field Systems* (1915, pp. 23, 140, 307n, 309, 373, 389, 423–29, 549, and Appendix II, *passim*), namely, extracts from surveys of manors, church (glebe) holdings, and grants of scraps of land in 600-odd open field villages from the twelfth to the nineteenth century. Gray collected these as evidence of multiple field systems, not of scattering, and only about a fifth of the total mention the number of parcels. At Claydon St. Botolph, Buckinghamshire in the reign of Henry VIII, for instance, a terrier of a 26-½-acre holding mentions that in the three fields the land was arranged into 15, 11, and 15 parcels (p. 455). The 130 cases of this sort can be fashioned into a representative sample of open field agriculture in England as a whole. True, many of the cases are from counties such as Dorset, Norfolk, or Herefordshire, outside the chief open field region; and the sources Gray consulted led to such peculiarities as an overrepresentation of Northamptonshire and Oxfordshire, and within Oxfordshire an overrepresentation of seventeenth-century glebe terriers. But the evidence is rich enough to allow for such biases. The cases outside the open field region, or later than the seventeenth century, can be omitted as tangentially relevant.[29] The ten cases of grants or surveys of demesne arable, usually in large blocks suitable to large-scale farming, can be omitted for the same reason.[30] The 96 that remain can be arranged as follows:

Table 16. Parcels Per Acre, 12th to 17th Century.

	1100–1400	1401–1700
Oxfordshire	1.42	1.03
n (standard error)	10(.19)	22(.11)
Northamptonshire	1.99	1.36
n (standard error)	14(.10)	6(.24)
Others	1.30	1.59
n (standard error)	23(.19)	21(.12)

Note: "Others" are in both periods Beds, Berks, Bucks, Cambs, Herts, Leics, and Yorks; in 1100–1400 also Hunts, Lincs, Notts, Warwicks; and in 1400–1700 also Wilts.

Any reasonable weighting of the sample would put more weight on "Others" than on Oxfordshire and Northamptonshire, both of which diverge fairly sharply from the rest in both periods. Weighting the three by their acreage enclosed by act of Parliament, for example—reasonable enough considering that the object is to describe the typical village in open fields—the average in the first three centuries is about 1.4 parcels per acre and in the second about 1.5, suggesting that there is no strong trend.[31] The unweighted average of all 96 cases is 1.42 and the median 1.45; it would exaggerate slightly, if anything, to say that a 20-acre holding was scattered in 30 or so parcels.

Many of these parcels, however, were clustered. When one foreign half-acre strip separates three of Christian Coxe's strips in Llancadle, Glamorgan in 1622, it is clear that no motive of risk aversion (or for that matter egalitarianism or strictly partible inheritance) could have been at work preventing consolidation, for it would have been cheap to trade lands to form a consolidated plot (or to lay them out together at the time of inheritance), were there something to be gained. It is equally clear, however, that little was to be gained; neighborhood effects are comparatively easily handled when there is only one neighbor, subleasing would be natural, joint fencing of the three Coxe plots and the one foreign plot would be cheap (and was in fact done in some villages), transportation among the three plots would be trivial. In short, for most farming purposes the three plots count, though they were not counted, as one. The difficulty is that of deciding what criterion, necessarily somewhat arbitrary, should replace the equally arbitrary but less illuminating criterion of one nominal plot counted as one effective plot. If one adopts the criterion for Llancadle that a collection of plots is to be counted as one when no piece is separated from another by more than one other owner and no part of any piece is outside a radius of 150 yards from the center of the effective plot, Coxe's 27 distinct nominal plots reduce to 12 effective plots.[32] Adopting a similar criterion for Laxton, Nottinghamshire in 1635 gives the results in Table 17.

Table 17. Nominal and Effective Numbers of Plots for Six Men at Laxton

Holder	Open Field Acres	Number of Plots		Effective/ Nominal
		Nominal	Effective	
Tho. Tailer, Sr.[a]	48	78	48	.62
Tho. Hassard[a]	34	73	44	.60
Edw. Kelsterne[a]	28	45	33	.73
Hugh Tailer[b]	25	44	31	.70
John Chapell[c]	24	23	19	.83
Robert Rosse[a]	14	23	14	.61

Average .68
(standard
error, .04)

[a] = Tenant
[b] = Tenant of the Chantry
[c] = Freeholder

Source and Notes: Orwins, 1938, pp. 137–42 and Part III (Survey and Maps). The calculation excludes closes and town land. The scale is not given in the Orwins' maps and had to be inferred from acreages. Users of this pathbreaking and much—perhaps over— used book may wish to know that the map of the town and East Field is at 257 yards per inch, the West Field at 230, the Mill Field at 284, the South Field at 232, and Laxton Moorhouse at 264.

It would not be surprising to find, therefore, that the number of effective plots was two-thirds or so of the nominal in open field England, which implies, together with the figure of 1.5 nominal plots per acre, that the number of plots was roughly equal to the number of acres in a holding. On a 20-acre holding, then, the number of plots to be predicted by risk aversion is about 20, or 6-⅔ on average in each of the three fields of a village.

THE PREDICTED NUMBER OF PLOTS

The number predicted by the theory is the number of plots, N, that makes the probability of disaster as low as possible. On the one hand a larger N reduces the probability by reducing the standard deviation of income, σ (which is dependent on N); on the other hand it raises the probability by reducing the average income achieved, μ (also dependent on N), bringing it closer to the disastrous level of income, D. Mathematically speaking, σ and μ are functions of N, and the object of the peasant is to choose the N that minimizes the distance from disaster that μ is in terms of σ, namely, $[(\mu(N)-D)/\sigma(N)]$. The way that σ varies with N is already known, namely:

$$\sigma(N) = As[\frac{1 + (1 + R)N}{N}]^{\frac{1}{2}}$$

in which A is the acreage in a holding, s is the standard deviation of the yield on an acre of one type of land, and R is the correlation of yields between types. The difference between this equation and the one used repeatedly above is that here it is expressed in standard deviations rather than in coefficients of variation. For this reason A appears in it. If the average yield on an acre of a single type is called q, the yield of a holding of A acres will be, obviously, Aq, the coefficients of variation are therefore σ/Aq and s/q, and putting these expressions into the earlier equation produces the equation here, since q cancels out.

The way that the average yield on the entire holding, $\mu(N)$, varies with N is at choice, and is the only novel ingredient in the argument. A simple and plausible choice is $\mu(N) = AcN^{-\epsilon}$, in which c is a number setting the scale that reflects the productivity of the techniques, tools and labor used on the holding, and ϵ is the percentage rate at which yield falls with each percentage increase in the number of plots. The same percentage increase in N, whether from 3 to 6 or from 15 to 30, say, reduces output further by the same percentage. Another simple choice, a straight line relationship between μ and N, is less plausible because it implies that the same absolute increase in N, whether from 5 to 6 or from 29 to 30, reduces output by the same absolute amount, even though the additions to distinct neighbors or convenient paths through growing crops or travel time to visit a scattered holding fall as N rises.

The distance from disaster to be minimized, then, is:

$$\frac{\mu(N) - D}{\sigma(N)} = \frac{AcN^{-\epsilon} - D}{As[\frac{1 + (1 - N)R}{N}]^{\frac{1}{2}}}$$

When D is replaced by $d\mu(1)$, where d is the percentage that disaster is of the maximum attainable average yield (at which $N = 1$), and terms are collected the result is:

$$(\frac{c}{s}) \frac{N^{-\epsilon} - d}{[\frac{1 + (N-1)R}{N}]^{\frac{1}{2}}}$$

Since the term c/s is constant, the whole expression will be at a minimum with respect to choices of N when the other term is. And since this other term is a quotient it will be at a minimum when the rate of change of its upper part with respect to N is equal to the rate of change of its lower part. The rates of change are:

$$\text{Upper:} \quad -\epsilon(\frac{N^{-\epsilon}}{N^{-\epsilon} - d})$$

$$\text{Lower:} \quad -1/2[\frac{1 - R}{1 - (N-1)R}]$$

When ϵ is small (it is, as will be shown in a moment), $N^{-\epsilon}$ is approximately equal to 1.0. Using this approximation, setting the two expressions equal to each other, and solving for N leads to a simple prediction:

$$N \cong (\frac{1 - R}{R}) [\frac{1 - d}{2\epsilon} - 1]$$

The clearest way of applying this equation is to a single one of the three open fields of a village, in which there were on average 6.66 of the 20 plots on a typical holding. The question is whether or not the equation implies an N of about 6.66. It was shown earlier that on a single field R was .60.[33] The appropriate value of d, the disastrous level of output relative to the best attainable average, is below the earlier appropriate value for all crops together, .50, for two reasosn. First, the value .50 is disaster relative to the average output actually achieved on a scattered holding, not, as defined here, relative to the higher average (10 percent higher, in fact) attainable on a fully consolidated holding. On this account the denominator used to calculate d must be higher. If wheat contributes on the average 33.3 units of income to the average income of 100, the denominator should be (1.10) (33.3) = 36.6, not 33.3. Secondly, because a given degree of failure in one crop of three is less serious (in view of the good chance that the other two crops will offset it) than is the same degree of failure in all three at once, the numerator is smaller. When the correlation of wheat with other crops was only .29, as it was, a peasant would for this reason look with equanimity on a crop of wheat 50 percent below normal, that is, a crop of .50 (33.3) = 16.6. A numerator of 16.6, then, is too high a level. The correct level is the answer to the following question: what, on the average, is the output of, say, wheat at which disaster, considering the various possible outputs of barley and oats, just strikes? Put another way the question is, what output of wheat corresponds on the average with the margin of disaster, i.e., an output of all crops added together just below 50? It was determined earlier that the typical coefficient of variation of wheat, barley, or oats after scattering within one field was .48 in English open fields, implying a standard deviation of 16 relative to a mean of 33.3 for a single crop; and that the typical correlation between any two crops was .29. The question posed can be answered by inserting these values into a trivariate normal distribution and calculating the frequency with which various outputs of wheat are associated with the narrow attainment of disaster overall. Weighting the outputs of wheat by these frequencies gives an expected value for wheat (or any one crop) of 12.6: this is the numerator. The appropriate value of d in one crop, then, is $12.6/36.6 = .34$.

The remaining element in the equation is ϵ, the elasticity of output with respect to the number of plots. Like d, ϵ is calculated by looking at the facts already established in another way. Output increased by ten percent when a holding scattered into twenty plots was consolidated into one. In terms of the relationship between average output and N, with N_B the number before, and N_A the number after consolidation:

$$\frac{AcN_A^{-\epsilon}}{AcN_B^{-\epsilon}} = \frac{(1)^{-\epsilon}}{(20)^{-\epsilon}} = 1.10$$

Solving for ϵ after taking logarithms implies an ϵ of .032. That is each doubling of the number of plots in each of the three open fields of the village (1, 2, 4 and so forth, producing a total number of plots of 3, 6, 12 and so forth) reduced average output by about 3 percent.

The Lord apparently favors this enterprise, for the predicted number of plots in a single field is 6.2, very close indeed to the observed number, 6.66:

$$N = (\frac{1.0 - .60}{.60}) [\frac{1.0 - .34}{2(.032)} - 1.0] = 6.2$$

What the Lord giveth, however, He can take away, by varying the parameters, and the exactness of fit between the theory and the facts is not to be taken too seriously. The predicted N varies in the following way with choices of d and ϵ around the best estimate (given $R = .60$):

Table 18. Sensitivity of Predicted N
to Alternative Values of d and ε.

		value of d		
		.40	.34	.28
value	.020	9.3	10.0	11.0
of ε	.032	5.6	6.2	6.8
	.040	4.3	4.8	5.3

These are, to be sure, large variations in the parameters, but it is nonetheless worth bearing in mind that at their extremes they imply that a 20 acre holding in three fields could be scattered in anything from 13 (= 3 × 4.3) to 33 (= 3 × 11) plots. What survives even this degree of scepticism, however, is that the equation does predict the correct order of magnitude.

It succeeds in predicting the facts in certain other ways as well. It predicts, for example, that peasants holding larger acreages and being therefore further from the margin of disaster would have lower d's and larger numbers of plots, as they did, although fewer plots per acre, as they also did.[34] True, the prediction that scattering would rise as d fell fits poorly with the drive to enclose when, in the seventeenth and eighteenth centuries, d became low. Yet the very reduction of risk that made d low on the eve of enclosure, particularly for large farmers (who were in fact the most eager to enclose) made the fear of ruin less relevant; when ruin becames a remote possibility—not one year in 13 but one in 50, say—the fear of it diminishes. And the rise during these centuries in the uniformity of yields (R) and in the gain to be had from enclosure (ε), both of which would work to reduce N whether or not the distaste for variability took the form of safety first, fit well with the history of enclosure.

ALTERNATIVE INSURANCE

Showing that scattering was efficacious insurance does not show that the insurance achieved suffices to explain scattering, although it makes the proposition appealing. In an extreme and monocausal form well beyond the ambitions of this essay the proposition would be a syllogism: medieval English peasants wished only to reduce hazard; in the Midlands in medieval times only scattering of plots would reduce hazard; therefore, medieval English peasants in the Midlands would always scatter their plots. A comparably extreme syllogism for the main alternative explanation would be: medieval English peasants wished only to achieve equity of inheritance; in the Midlands in medieval times only scattering of plots would achieve equity of inheritance; therefore medieval English peasants in the Midlands would always scatter their plots. What makes the two syllogisms extreme are the words "only" and "always." Disproving the extreme form of each step does not reduce more moderate forms of the arguments to rubble. If medieval peasants wished also to eat well in most years and to enter the Kingdom of Heaven it might still be true that their wish to reduce hazard or to achieve equity of inheritance was powerful. Yet comparing each step in the extreme forms is illuminating. If one had to choose between two simple characterizations of peasants (one does not have to, of course), that they were cautious or that they were egalitarian, which would one choose? Enough has been said here to establish that they were very cautious, with good reason. In the essay mentioned earlier (McCloskey, 1975a) it was argued that they were not very egalitarian, the chief evidence being that the distribution of land was inegalitarian, that inheritances of land were unequally distributed between sons and daughters, and that in any case inheritances in the Midlands were not in fact divided equally among sons. In the same essay it was argued that the other step in the extreme form of the syllogism—that only scattering would achieve equal inheritances—is still less plausible. Equality could have been achieved without the gratuitous burden of scattered plots, by dividing holdings instead of each plot in a holding, by making up inequities of land with more divisible assets, and, most fundamentally, by exchanging ill-situated plots in the màrket for land, which was cheap and active from the thirteenth century onwards. But the parallel step in the risk syllogism— that only scattering would reduce hazard—might face a similar difficulty, namely, a substitute for scattering as a means of achieving insurance. Did alternative and cheaper insurance exist?

In its strict definition it plainly did not. Insurance against fluctuations in the price of agricultural products has become available in modern times in the form of organized forward markets, and there is some hint in the historical record of forward selling of crops by the larger farmers. Speculative markets on any substantial scale, however, appear to be a nineteenth century innovation. Cheap insurance against fluctuations in yields (as distinct from prices) is to this day seldom available, notwithstanding the complaints of observers of the agricultural scene that farmers are driven by its absence to expensive methods of self-insurance. E. J. Russell, the director of the Rothamsted experimental farm, remarked in 1924 that "at present crop yields are uninsurable in England at any reasonable premium; if, however, there existed trustworthy tables of expectancy of crop yield, crop insurance would become as readily amenable to business management as life insurance" (Russell, 1926, delivered 1924). He was perhaps underestimating the other obstacles to the success of such a scheme, namely that farmers would take less care to avoid a bad crop when their return was guaranteed (less likely, obviously, with life insurance) and that a farmer who knew his crop was going to be bad would rush to buy insurance (as a sick man would buy life insurance). Writing in 1952, Earl Heady noted that although hail insurance had been available in the United States for many years (it was available in England from around the turn of the century), general crop insurance had been available only since 1938, and then only for a few crops. He argued that the difficulty was self-selection of poor risks in the absence of full knowledge by the insurors: a winter wheat producer on the Great Plains, for example, could predict his yield by the amount of moisture his crops had gotten in the previous autumn (Heady, 1952).

Formal insurance, however, is not the only way of insuring against disaster. Peasants could, and did, hold assets other than growing crops which, if their yields were not highly correlated with the crop, would serve to reduce the variability of total income. As was argued earlier, diversification of this sort became important in early modern times. A medieval peasant was less well placed to take advantage of a diversified portfolio of assets. To be sure, his growing crop was not the only productive asset he had: he had his lease, his labor, and his agricultural capital, above all draft animals, which in a bad year he might sell. Yet his labor would be worth little if the bad year were general, and selling his lease or his agricultural capital in a bad year would make the following years bad as well. The plow team and other moveable goods a peasant might have were in any case hazardous themselves, subject as they were to seizure and taxation. He could save money. In the thirteenth century Walter of Henley gave this advice to lords of manors anxious to improve themselves: "If you may your lands amend, either by tillage or by a stock of cattle or by any other provision above the yearly extent, put that overplus into money, for if corn fail or fire do happen or any other mischance then will that be somewhat worth to you which you have in coin" (Oschinsky, [ed.], 1971, p. 309, sixteenth-century translation, spelling modernized). The lord of the manor might follow such advice, rich and secure as he was, without his peasants being in a position to do so as well. Money was in any case a bad store of grain value. With poorly developed markets and precarious yields ten bushels given up for silver in a good year might well buy only five bushels for a peasant's table in a bad year.

The peasant could save grain itself, and did. What matters for insurance against a harvest failure, however, is the store of grain that survived a year of eating and replanting, the carryover. At the end of the seventeenth century, in an England enriched by a century or more of agricultural progress, Charles Davenant estimated the carryover at "not above four months' stock in an indifferent [i.e. average] year, which is but a slender provision against any evil accident" (Thirsk and Cooper, [eds.], 1972, p. 814), and made the perennial suggestion of constructing public granaries. In the middle of the sixteenth century the City of London, forward in all things, aimed to keep 5000 quarters of grain at the London Bridge House for this purpose (Ashley, 1914, II, p. 25). But it would have found the purpose difficult to achieve; at two-thirds of a quarter of grain per head per year (a low estimate) and with 50,000 or so Londoners (another low estimate) 5000 quarters would have been only 15 percent of minimum annual consumption, and less of the average. Storage was expensive, both in interest foregone and in spoilage: the wide flunctuations in prices over the harvest year and from harvest to harvest testify to this, as do the primitive techniques of storing grain in a wet climate and the high interest rates of the age. The stores of monks and burgers, in any case, are not necessarily stores available in a bad year to the peasant: he must have his own carryover, and probably had a trivial one. Judging from yields on the Bishop of Winchester's estates, the years leading up to the bad harvest of 1315 were reasonably good, yet by the spring after the harvest prices had doubled in England, and in Ypres (where there are statistics; the famine was European in extent) the death rate rose in the spring and remained high until the new harvest (Lucas, 1930. In Carus-Wilson, [ed.], II, pp. 55, 67).

If the peasant could not rely on borrowing, as it were, from himself, he could borrow from others. A market in loans is from one point of view a substitute for scattering. From another point of view, however, it is a complement of scattering, for the heavy indebtedness already contracted by peasants to pay entry fines, dowries and exceptional taxes (see, e.g., Duby, 1968, pp. 252–54) would make a method of avoiding still further indebtedness especially attractive. Although it is difficult to penetrate the veil thrown across the subject by the hostility to usury, the interest rates charged appear to have been very high (Pollock and Maitland, 1898, I, pp. 469, 473 and II, p. 225). And an interest rate of 40 percent on money loaned in a bad year would translate into a still higher rate in terms of grain when the loan was repaid: if the price of grain fell 50 percent between the bad year and the next, the annual rate in real terms would be 180 percent. A less formal alternative, presumably free of interest, is charity, personal or institutional. Yet the volume of sermonizing in the Middle Ages on the virtue of charity is testimony less to its abundance than to its scarcity relative to the precepts of Christian ethics. The church itself was supposed to turn back a good part of its income to the poor, but, notoriously, did not.

The substitutes for scattering as a means for achieving insurance, then, are unimpressive, less impressive than the substitutes for scattering as a means for achieving, say, equity of inheritance. As was pointed out earlier, of course, the growth of a market in cheap loans or the enrichment and diversification of agriculture does figure in the story, chiefly after the sixteenth century. In some places, earlier, it might account for the erosion of open fields, as in the Southeast of England, exposed early to the markets of London and of the northwest coast of Europe generally. It is undoubtedly false, to give again the extreme version of the proposition, that in the Midlands of England in medieval times *only* scattering of plots would reduce hazard. Yet between this extreme proposition and a more moderate one there is ample ground for believing in the efficacy of scattering for insurance.

*   *   *   *

A satisfactory explanation of the English open field must be an explanation of its persistence and decline, since the paucity of birth records of the system leaves room for unrestrained speculation on its origin. Following the principle that it is the knowable that one should seek to know, therefore, the question is: why did open fields persist from the twelfth to the nineteenth century in some places in England and disappear in the seventeenth and eighteenth centuries in most? The guiding principle in answering this question has been to ask in turn why an ordinary peasant would want to scatter his plots, for it was he—or so it is assumed in this study and in similar studies by others—who determined the usual geography of holdings. The answer offered here is that he scattered not to equalize inheritances or allotments of new village land but to insure himself against the hazards of farming before the Agricultural Revolution. It might be argued, indeed, that the alleged egalitarianism was merely a manifestation of a desire for scattered plots and the insurance they provide. In any case insurance explains the gross facts of the persistence and decline of scattering; it predicts some scattering and the amount of scattering that in fact occured; and it fits well with the view of medieval village life, long the orthodox view, that attributes self-interest as well as fellow-feeling and conservativism to medieval peasants. Peasants were conservative, to be sure, but not pointlessly so: a man is not a fool to insure himself against disaster by scattering his plots of land.

FOOTNOTES

This is a draft of a chapter in a book on *The Enclosure of English Open Fields*. I have received comments from many people, and pledge full acknowledgment in the book. I must here thank by name, however, Stephano Fenoaltea of Amherst College, whose voluminous criticisms, many of them embodied in his "Risk, Transaction Cost, and the Organization of Medieval Agriculture" (1974), have been a great stimulus to thought. The research was supported in part by a grant from the National Science Foundation.

1. The usual word for scattering in the literature, incidentally, is "fragmentation." I avoid it because it is also used for small, as distinct from scattered, farms.

2. Thompson (1963), pp. 8, 170–73. Compare Euthymios Papageorgiou in Parsons, *et al.* (1956), p. 546: "The fragmentation is not always a disadvantage, however. Where fruits, vegetables, and flowers are farmed intensively, a moderate degree of fragmentation diminishes the risk of damage from frost." In the same volume, p. 536, J. Roche makes a similar point about scattering of plots in France for those crops. And on p. 559, Setsuro Hyodo makes it for agriculture in general in Japan.

3. Personal correspondence. Thomas first heard this from farmers in the Southwest Dacca region, but later confirmed it for East Pakistan as a whole.

4. Beidelman (1971), p. 18; Netting (1972), p. 134; Johnson (1971), pp. 69–72. Further evidence on Tanzania (collected by geographers) appears in the articles by Hawkins, and by Heijnen and Kates, in White, [ed.], 1974.

5. Thomas Hitt in 1761 drew the contrast in detail with light sand or chalk soils, remarking that "two dry days render them in good order for plowing and harrowing." (Jones, 1964, p. 113.) Compare H. David, *Complete English Farmer* (1771), pp. 85–86, who warns of a common soil in England that "were it to be ploughed in a rainy season . . . would cling like mortar; and if sowed in such a situation, would produce little or no increase." (See also pp. 100, 165–72.)

6. The estimate is calculated from the median moveable wealth per acre among the eleven farmers holding 15 to 45 acres for whom the recorded acreage of fallow indicates that acreage in fallow is not being ignored. Given in F. W. Steer (1969), p. 52. The dates of the eleven range from 1666 to 1743.

7. The argument is widely applicable. M. I. Finley argues that in the fifth and fourth centuries B. C. alternative employment in the navy was "the key to Athenian freedom from agrarian troubles," in contrast with the more usual state of affairs for free peasants: "the ancient peasant was always at the margin of safety." (1973, pp. 107–108).

8. Ballard (1908), p. 459; see also Slicher van Bath, 1963, pp. 32, 37. The yields are net of tithe. Ballard records that the customary acre was 90 to 120 poles, or about two-thirds of a statute acre.

9. Subtracting by one is only an approximation because the amount of seed set aside could vary, although it would not vary if the same output on average was wanted year in and year out and if exceptionally bad crops did not require eating some seed. With the raw data from the issue of the grange one could make the calculation exactly.

10. Another consequence of low yields per bushel of seed in the Middle Ages, incidentally, is that investment in seed was a high percent of gross output. Were the yield of wheat 4.0, a quarter of the harvest would need to be invested each year in seed. Savings rates of 25 percent belie the customary assertion that peasants, medieval or other, save little or save only in the form of cathedrals and gold, not in productive investments.

11. Page (1934), pp. 329–30. The yield of the year 1394 is missing. The demesne was held in strips intermingled with those of the tenants, not in a compact block (p. 79).

12. What follows is merely a rewriting of Fama and Miller (1972), pp. 253–55.

13. How trivial may be judged as follows. Taking the standard deviations of the yields of wheat, barley and oats, at values consistent with medieval experience (the averages observed in one sample of Winchester yields 1335 to 1349, in fact), namely .38, .40 and .60, and the correlation coefficients of wheat-barley = .38, wheat-oats = .27, and barley-oats = .42 (the averages observed within each demesne in the same sample), the σ implied by the full equation, (1), is .350; that implied by the approximation, (2), when the average R and the average s (not average s^2) are arithmetic averages, is .348.

14. The equation is not defined for $[1 + (N - 1)R] < 0$, e.g. $N = 3, R = -1$, since the square root of a negative number is imaginary. It is clearly impossible to hold more than two types, each of which is perfectly inversely correlated with every other.

15. Haldane (1941–42), pp. 233–34. The assumption of normality is treated later, and verified.

16. Titow (1972), p. 4, simple average of wheat, barley and oats. Allowing for the greater weight of barley in the peasant's output than the simple average assumes (1/3) changes the average little.

17. The procedure is to simulate the variability of $I = Q - (M/a)Q^b$, when the coefficient of variation of Q is .35, a is set at 1 (to set the scale), M is chosen to take half the value of the crop at the average values of Q and P, and b is $-.5$.

18. E.g., Goubert (1970), p. 217, speaking of the "disastrous" French crop failure in 1693. See Davenant's comment on this episode in Thirsk and Cooper, (eds.), 1972, p. 813, in which the figure of one-half is used.

19. Postan (1966), p. 622; Titow (1969), p. 89. These are for a three-field system.

20. Postan (1966), p. 619. In Tawney (1912), pp. 64–65 there is a similar table of customary tenants for the late fifteenth through the early seventeenth century. In it holdings below 10 acres account for 16 percent of all land in holding up to 40 acres (a reasonable limit for farming without hiring outside laborers).

21. Darby. In Darby, (ed.) (1936), p. 196n. Cf. Genicot's estimate, apparently based on

chronicles, of 18.2 years in Languedoc in the fourteenth and fifteenth century (14.3 years in the fourteenth century alone). In Postan (ed.) (1966), p. 673.

22. Fussell, (ed.) (1936), *passim* (e.g. pp. 5–6, 184). The south part of the village was on the edge of the Berkshire Downs and could not therefore have supported hay. The north part of the village close to rivers was about a mile square.

23. Or more, in view of the errors in measurement of d (the distances between the wheat crops is not the same as the distances between churches). Reversing the regression implies an upper bound on the coefficient on d of .22.

24. That the difference is negative (rather than zero, as one would expect) when $d = 0$ should not be troubling, for the intercept is an extrapolation beyond the range of the data. To put it another way, the linear specification could easily be wrong for small distances, the true relationship flattening out at distances below the observed minimum (1.5 miles). The r^2 of $R_w - R_b = .008d^{2.72}$ is in fact a little higher, .65.

25. A minor point should be mentioned here. The calculation assumes that the coefficient of variation can be applied to the average income on a consolidated farm (110) to yield the standard deviation. This is true only if the standard deviation rises for higher averages (technically speaking, only if the distribution of yields exhibits heteroscedasticity). It does. For 22 randomly selected series of wheat yields on the Bishop of Winchester's estates 1335–49, the correlation of the yield and the standard deviation was .78 (significantly different from zero at conventional levels), while the correlation of the yield and the coefficient of variation was $-.23$ (insignificantly different from zero).

26. Cf. Jones (1964), p. 50: "Every farmer is in a state of constant uncertainty and if he is sensible will take costly measures to insure his own business against loss: the chances that his personal output will be depressed are much higher than the chances that the weather will depress the total output of agriculture."

27. Many of the alternative hypotheses, incidentally, share this difficulty, because many of them suppose that peasants were egalitarian. One cannot test the equality of inheritances or plowing dates or intakes from the waste without knowledge of the second as well as the first moment of the relevant distribution.

28. For example, s is distributed as a chi-square with 14 degrees of freedom, from which the high and low averages on either side of the median can be calculated. The procedure for the R's is similar, using Fisher's z.

29. The omitted counties are Norfolk (12 cases, all eighteenth century), Herefordshire (8 cases, all nineteenth century), Gloucestershire, Somerset, Middlesex and Essex. They have a noticeably lower number of parcels per acre on average (around 1.0) than do the remaining counties.

30. Once again, these have a low number of parcels per acre (that is, a higher number of acres per parcel), namely .39.

31. The acreages enclosed by act are given in Slater (1907), pp. 141–47. Not all open fields were enclosed by act, but the records of the many that were not are sparse.

32. The map is reproduced on pp. 504–505 of Davies. In Baker and Butlin, (eds.), 1973. Coxe was a copyholder of about 40 acres.

33. Because of the simplicity of the relationship between N and R the equation works poorly for extreme values of R: $R = 0$ implies infinite N; $R = 1$ implies zero. So long as the assumption of constant elasticity is reasonable in the range of R actually observed, however, this feature is not more troubling than are parallel features of, say, demand curves with constant elasticities.

34. As acreage increases average income rises, reducing d at the same rate. From the equation predicting N one can show that the rate of change of N (taking ϵ to be approximately zero, as it is) is $N^* = -[d/(1 - d)]d^* = [d/(1 - d)]A^*$, from which follow the assertions in the text.

REFERENCES

Agarwal, S. K. (1971), *Economics of Land Consolidation in India*, Delhi: Chand.

Ashley, W. J. (1914), *An Introduction to English Economic History and Theory*, Vol. II, London: Longmans, Green and Co.

Baker, Alan R. H. and Robin A. Butlin. (1973), *Studies of Field Systems in the British Isles*, Cambridge: Cambridge University Press.

Ballard, A. (1908), "Woodstock Manor in the Thirteenth Century," *Vierteljahrschrift für Social- und Wirtschaftsgeschichte*, 6, 424–59.

Beidelman, T. O. (1971), *The Karugu. A Matrilineal People of East Africa*, New York: Holt, Rinehart.

Bloch, Marc. (1966), *French Rural History*, Berkeley and Los Angeles: University of California Press, First published in French, 1931

Brooke, C. N. L. and M. M. Postan. (1960), *Carte Nativorum*, being *Northamptonshire Record Society Publications*, 20.

Darby, H. C. (1936), "The Economic Geography of England, A. D. 1000–1250." In Darby, (ed.), *An Historical Geography of England before A. D. 1800*, Cambridge: Cambridge University Press.

David, H. (1771), *Complete English Farmer*, London.

Deane, Phyllis and W. A. Cole. (1964), *British Economic Growth 1688–1959*, Cambridge: Cambridge University Press.

Duby, G. (1968), *Rural Economy and Country Life in the Medieval West*, Columbia: University of South Carolina Press. First published in French, 1962.

Fama, E. and M. H. Miller. (1972), *The Theory of Finance*, New York: Holt, Rinehart.

Fenoaltea, S. (December 1974), "Risk, Transaction Costs, and the Organization of Medieval Agriculture," unpublished MS, Amherst.

Finberg, H. P. R. (1951), *Tavistock Abbey*, Cambridge: Cambridge University Press.

Finley, M. I. (1973), *The Ancient Economy*, London: Chatto and Windus.

Fisher, R. A. (1947), *The Design of Experiments*, New York: Hafner. First published 1935.

Forde, C. D. (1934), *Habitat, Economy and Society*, London: Methuen.

Fowler, G. H. (1928–36), *Four Pre-enclosure Village Maps*, being *Quarto Memoirs of the Bedfordshire Historical Record Society*, 2, pts. i–iv.

Fussell, G. E. (ed.) (1936), *Robert Loder's Farm Accounts 1610–1620*, Vol. 53, Camden Society Publications, 3rd series.

Genicot, L. (1966), "Crisis: From the Middle Ages to Modern Times." In Postan, (ed.).

Goubert, P. (1970), *Louis XIV and Twenty Million Frenchmen*, New York.

Gray, H. L. (1915), *English Field Systems*, Cambridge: Harvard University Press.

Haldane, J. B. S. (1941–42), "Moments of the Distributions of Powers and Products of Normal Variates," *Biometrika*, 32, 226–42.

Heady, Earl O. (1952), *Economics of Agricultural Production and Resource Use*, New York: Prentice-Hall.

Hey, D. G. (1974), *An English Rural Community: Myddle under the Tudors and Stuarts*, Leicester: Leicester University Press.

Hoben, Alan. (c. 1972), "Social Anthropology and Development Planning: A Case Study in Ethiopian Land Reform Policy," unpublished MS, Boston University, n.d.

Homer, H. S. (1769), *An Essay on the Nature and Methods of Ascertaining Specifick Shares of Proprietors upon the Inclosure of Common Fields*, 2nd ed. Oxford.

Hoskins, W. G. (1953–54), "Harvest Fluctuations and English Economic History

1480–1619," *Agricultural History Review*, 2. Reprinted in Minchinton, (ed.), Vol. I, (1968).

Johnson, A. W. (1971), *Sharecroppers of the Sertão*, Stanford: Stanford University Press.

Jones, Eric L. (1964), *Seasons and Prices: The Role of Weather in English Agricultural History*, London: Allen and Unwin.

Kerridge, E. (1968), *The Agricultural Revolution*, New York: A. M. Kelley.

———. (1973), *The Farmers of Old England*, London: Allen and Unwin.

Laslett, T. P. R. (1965), *The World We Have Lost*, London.

Lawes, J. B. and J. H. Gilbert. (1864), "Report of Experiments on the Growth of Wheat for 20 Years in Succession on the Same Land," *Journal of the Royal Agricultural Society of England*, 25, 93–185.

———. (1884), "On the Continuous Growth of Wheat on the Experimental Plots at Rothamsted during the 20 Years, 1864 to 1883, Inclusive," *Journal of the Royal Agricultural Society of England*, 45, 391–481.

Lennard, R. V. (1932), "English Agriculture under Charles I," *Economic History Review*, 4, (1932). Reprinted in Minchinton, (ed.), 1968.

Lodge, B., (1873), (ed.) *Palladius on Husbondrie*, Vol. 52, London: Early English Text Society.

Lucas, H. S. (1930), "The Great European Famine of 1315, 1316 and 1317," *Speculum*, 5. Reprinted in E. M. Carus-Wilson, (ed.), *(1962), Essays in Economic History*, Vol. II, London: Arnold, for the Economic History Society.

Manley, Gordon. (1952), *Climate and the British Scene*, Glasgow: Collins.

Marshall, W. *Minutes of Agriculture*, entry for 15 July 1777.

Mayhew, Alan, (1973), *Rural Settlement and Farming in Germany*, London: Batsforth.

McCloskey, D. N. (1975a), "The Persistence of English Common Fields." In W. N. Parker and E. L. Jones, (eds). (1975), *European Peasants and Their Markets: Essays in Agrarian History*, Princeton: Princeton University Press.

———. (1975b), "The Economics of Enclosure: A Market Analysis," In Parker and Jones, (eds.).

Minchinton, W. E. (1968), *Essays in Agrarian History*, 2 Vols., Newton Abbot: David and Charles.

Molnar E. (ed.) (1971), *Magyarország Története*, 3rd ed., Vol. II, Budapest: Gondolat.

Netting, R. M. (1972), "Of Men and Meadows: Strategies of Alpine Land Use," *Anthropological Quarterly*, 45, 132–44.

Orwin, C. S. and C. S. Orwin. (1938), *The Open Fields*, Oxford: Clarendon Press.

Oschinsky, D. (ed.) (1971), *Walter of Henley and Other Treatises on Estate Management and Accounting*, Oxford: Clarendon Press.

Page, Frances M. (1934), *The Estates of Crowland Abbey*, Cambridge: Cambridge University Press.

Parsons, K. H.; R. J. Penn; and P. M. Raup, (eds.) (1956), *Land Tenure: Proceedings of the International Conference on Land Tenure and Related Problems in World Agriculture*, Madison: University of Wisconsin Press.

Pollock, F. and F. W. Maitland. (1968), *The History of English Law before the Time of Edward I*, 2nd ed., 2 Vols. Cambridge: Cambridge University Press. First published 1898.

Postan, M. M., (ed.) (1966), *The Cambridge Economic History of Europe*, 2nd ed., Vol. I, Cambridge: Cambridge University Press.

———. (1966), "Medieval Agrarian Society in Its Prime: England." In Postan, (ed.).

Russell, E. J. (1926), *Plant Nutrition and Crop Production*, Berkeley: University of California Press.

Russell, F. R. A. (1893), *On Hail*, London.

Slater, Gilbert. (1907), *The English Peasantry and the Enclosure of Common Fields*, London: Constable.

Slicher van Bath, B. H. (1963), *Yield Ratios, 810–1820*, being *Afdeling Agrarische Geschiedenis Bijdragen*, 10.

Steer, F. W. (1969), *Farm and Cottage Inventories of Mid-Essex 1635–1749*, 2nd ed., London and Chichester: Phillimore.

Tawney, R. H. (1912), *The Agrarian Problem in the Sixteenth Century*, London: Longmans.

Thirsk, J. (1964), "The Common Fields," *Past and Present*, 29, 3–25.

———. (1967), "Farming Techniques". In J. Thirsk, (ed.) *The Agrarian History of England and Wales*, Vol. IV, 1500–1640, Cambridge: Cambridge University Press.

———. (1973), "Field Systems of the East Midlands." In Baker and Butlin, (eds.).

Thirsk, J. and J. P. Cooper, (eds.) (1972), *17th Century Economic Documents*, Oxford: Clarendon Press.

Thompson, Kenneth. (1963), *Farm Fragmentation in Greece: The Problem and Its Setting*, Athens: Center of Economic Research, Research Monograph Series, No. 5.

Titow, J. Z. (1969), *English Rural Society 1200–1350*, London: Allen and Unwin.

———. (1972), *Winchester Yields: A Study in Medieval Agricultural Productivity*, Cambridge: Cambridge University Press.

Voelcker, J. A. (1884), "Report," *Journal of the Royal Agricultural Society of England*, 45, 337–60.

———. (1897), "The Woburn Experimental Farm," *Journal of the Royal Agricultural Society of England*, 58, 258–93, and 59 (1898): 622–55, 678–726.

White, Gilbert F., (ed.) (1974), *Natural Hazards: Local, National, Global*, New York and London: Oxford University Press.

How the gold standard worked, 1880–1913[1]

Donald N. McCloskey and J. Richard Zecher*

The monetary theory and its implications for the gold standard

Each intellectual generation since the mercantilists has revised or refined the understanding of how the balance of payments is kept in equilibrium under a system of fixed exchange rates, and all these understandings find a place in the historical literature on the gold standard of the late nineteenth century. It is difficult, therefore, to locate the orthodox view on how the gold standard worked, for it is many views. If one can find historical and economic writings describing the gold standard (and other systems of fixed exchange rates) in the manner of Hume, as a price-specie-flow mechanism, involving changes in the level of prices, one can also find writings describing it in the manner of Marshall, involving changes in the interest rate, or of Taussig, involving changes in the relative price of exportables and importables, or of Ohlin, involving changes in income. The theoretical jumble is made still more confusing by a number of factual anomalies uncovered lately.[2] Among other difficulties with the orthodox views, it has been found that the gold standard, even in its heyday, was a standard involving the major currencies as well as gold itself, and that few, if any, central banks followed the putative 'rules of the game'.

This essay reinterprets the gold standard by applying the monetary theory

*From Jacob A. Frenkel and Harry G. Johnson (eds.), *The Monetary Approach to the Balance of Payments*, London, Allen & Unwin, 1976, pp. 184–6, 192–208, abridged.

of the balance of payments to the experience of the two most important countries on it, America and Britain. Before explaining, testing and using the theory in detail, it will be useful to indicate a few of the ways in which accepting it will change the interpretation of the gold standard of the late nineteenth century. The most direct implication is that central bankers did not have control over the variables over which they and their historians have believed they had control. The theory assumes that interest rates and prices are determined on world markets, and therefore that the central bank of a small country has little influence over them and the central bank of a large country has influence over them only by way of its influence over the world as a whole.

A case in point is the Bank of England. It is often asserted, as Keynes put it, that

> During the latter half of the nineteenth century the influence of London on credit conditions throughout the world was so predominant that the Bank of England could almost have claimed to be the conductor of the international orchestra. By modifying the terms on which she was prepared to lend, aided by her own readiness to vary the volume of her gold reserves and the unreadiness of other central banks to vary the volumes of theirs, she could to a large extent determine the credit conditions prevailing elsewhere.[3]

When this musical metaphor is examined in the light of the monetary theory it loses much of its charm. If it is supposed, as in the monetary theory, that the world's economy was unified by arbitrage, and if it is supposed further that the level of prices in the world market was determined, other things equal, by the amount of money existing in the world, it follows that the Bank's potential influence on prices (and perhaps through prices on interest rates) depended simply on its power to accumulate or disburse gold and other reserves available to support the world's supply of money. By raising the interest rate (the Bank Rate) at which it would lend to brokers of commercial bills, the Bank could induce the brokers or whoever else in the British capital market was caught short of funds to seek loans abroad, bringing gold into the country and eventually into the vaults of the Bank. If it merely issued bank notes to pay for the gold the reserves available to support the supply of money would be unchanged, for Bank of England notes were used both at home and abroad as reserves. Only by decreasing the securities and increasing the gold it held – an automatic result when it discouraged brokers from selling more bills to the Bank and allowed the bills it already held to come to maturity – could the Bank exert a net effect on the world's reserves. In other words, a rise in the Bank Rate was effective only to the extent that it was accompanied by an open market operation, that is, by a shift in the assets of the Bank of England out of securities and into gold. The amounts of these two assets held by the Bank, then, provide extreme limits on the influence of the Bank on the world's money supply. Had the Bank in 1913 sold off all the securities held in its banking department it would have decreased world reserves by only 0.6 per cent; had it sold off all the gold in its issue department, it would have increased world reserves by only 0.5 per cent.[4] Apparently the Bank was no more than the second violinist, not to say the triangle player, in the world's orchestra. The result hinges on the assumption of the monetary theory that the world's economy was unified, much as each nation's economy is assumed to be in any theory of the gold standard. If the assumption is correct the historical inference is that the Bank of England had no more independent influence over the prices and interest rates it faced than, say, the First National Bank of Chicago has over the prices and interest rates it faces, and for the same reason.

A related inference from the monetary theory is that the United Kingdom, the United States, and other countries on the gold standard had little influence over their money supplies. Since money, like other commodities, could be imported and exported, the supply of money in a country could adjust to its demand and the demand would depend on the country's income and on prices and interest rates determined in the world market. The creation of money in a little country would have little influence on these determinants of demand and in consequence little influence over the amount actually supplied. How 'little' America and Britain were depends on how large they were relative to the world market, and in a world of full employment and well-functioning markets the relevant magnitude is simply the share of the nation's supply of money in the world's supply. One must depend on an assumption that the money owned by citizens of a country was in rough proportion to its income, for the historical study of the world's money supply is still in its infancy.[5] In 1913 America and Britain together earned about 40 per cent of the world's income, America alone 27 per cent.[6] A rise in the American money supply of 10 per cent, then, would raise the world's money supply on the order of 2.7 per cent; the comparable British figure is half the American. Clearly, in the jargon of international economics, America and Britain were not literally 'small countries'. Yet 2.7 per cent is far from the 10 per cent implied by the usual model, that of a closed monetary system, and the British figure is far enough from it to make it unnecessary for most purposes in dealing with the British experience to look closely into the worldwide impact of British policy.

Finally, the monetary theory implies that it matters little whether or not central banks under the gold standard played conscientiously the 'rules of the game', that is, the rule that a deficit in the balance of payments should be accompanied by domestic policies to deflate the economy. The theory argues that neither gold flows nor domestic deflation have effects on prevailing prices, interest rates and incomes. The inconsequentiality of the rules of the game may perhaps explain why they were ignored by most central bankers in the period of the gold standard, in deed if not in words, with no dire effects on the stability of the system. [...]

Did international markets work well?

If arbitrage – or, more precisely, a close correlation among national price levels brought about by the ordinary working of markets – can be shown to characterize the international economy of the late nineteenth century, many of the conclusions of the monetary theory will follow directly and the rest will gain in plausibility. In the monetary theory, the international market short-circuits the effects of domestic policy on American prices, and the expansion of the domestic supply of money spills directly into a deficit in the balance of payments.

It is essential, therefore, to examine the evidence for this short-circuiting. As a criterion of its effectiveness, we use the size of the contemporaneous correlations among changes in the prices of the same commodities in different countries. We have chosen a sample of the voluminous information on prices for examination here.[7] The statistical power of the tests is not as high as one might wish, for even if two nations shared no markets they could none the less exhibit common movements in prices if they shared similar experiences of climate, technological change, income growth or any of the other determinants of prices. In the long run, indeed, the other theories of the balance of payments imply some degree of correlation among national prices. For this reason we have resisted the temptation to improve the correlations by elaborate experimentation with lags and have concentrated on contemporaneous correlations, that is, on correlations among prices in the same year. If international markets worked as sluggishly as the other theories assume, there would be little reason to expect contemporaneous correlations to be high.

The simplest way to think about arbitrage is in terms of a single market. Given fixed exchange rates and the vigorous pursuit of profit through arbitrage, the correlation between price changes for a homogeneous commodity in two countries, say America and Britain, separated by transportation costs and tariffs, would be zero within the limits of the export and import points and unity at those points. A regression of British on American prices would test simultaneously for the lowness of the commodity's cost of transportation, including tariffs, relative to its price and the vigour with which prices were arbitraged. The good would not actually have to be traded between the two countries for the correlation to be high: the mere threat of arbitrage, or a common source of supply or demand, would be sufficient for goods with low transport costs. For goods actually flowing in trade in a uniform direction over the period 1880 to 1913, such as wheat from America to

Britain, one would expect the correlation to be perfect and the slope of the corresponding regression to be unity, no matter what the cost of transport or the level of tariffs, so long as these did not change. They both did change, of course, as exemplified by the failure of the German price of wheat to fall as far as the British or American during the 1880s, as the Germans imposed protective duties on wheat imports.[8] None the less, the average correlation among the changes in American, British and German prices of wheat is high, about 0.78. A regression of the annual change in British prices on the change in American prices (Britain had no tariffs on wheat, but the cost of ocean transport was falling sharply in the period) yields the following result (all the variables here and elsewhere in this section are measured as annual absolute changes; the figures below the coefficients in parentheses are standard errors; the levels of the variables have been converted to an index in which the average levels are equal to one).[9]

$$BWT = 0.0076 + 0.646\,AWT \qquad R^2 = 0.58$$
$$(0.0012)\ \ (0.102) \qquad\quad D.-W. = 2.02$$

One would expect errors in the independent variable to affect this and the later regressions, biasing the slope towards zero (there were changes in the source of the American wheat price, for example, and after 1890 it is a New York price alone). The value of 0.646 would be a lower bound on the true slope and the value implied by a regression of the American on the British price (1.124) an upper bound. The two bounds bracket reasonably closely the value to be expected theoretically, namely, 1.0, and the constants in both regressions (which represent the trend in the dependent price over time) are insignificantly different from zero. Not surprisingly, in short, wheat appears to have had a unified world market in the late nineteenth century; *a fortiori*, so did gold, silver, copper, diamonds, racehorses and fine art.

This conclusion can be reinforced from another direction. For wheat the reinforcement is unnecessary, for few would doubt the international character of the wheat market, but it is useful to develop here the line of argument. Because of transport costs, information costs and other impediments to a perfect correlation among changes in national prices, any use of the notion of a perfectly unified market must be an approximation, within one country as well as between two countries. For purposes of explaining the balance of payments economists have been willing to accept the approximation that within each country there is one price for each product, setting aside as a second-order matter the indisputable lack of perfect correlation between price changes in California and Massachusetts or between price changes in Cornwall and Midlothian. It is reasonable, therefore, to use the level of the contemporaneous correlation between the prices of a good in different regions within a country as a standard against which to judge the unity of the market for that good between different countries. If the correlations between the prices of wheat in America, Britain and Germany were no lower than those between the prices of wheat in, say, different parts of Germany, there would be no grounds for distinguishing between the degree of unity in the national German market and in the international market for wheat. This was in fact the case. The average correlation between changes in the prices of wheat in pairs of German cities (Berlin, Breslau, Frankfurt, Konigsberg, Leipzig, Lindau and Mannheim) from 1881 to 1912 was 0.85, quite close to the average correlation for the three countries over the same period of 0.78.

One could proceed in this fashion through all individual prices, but a shorter route to the same objective is to examine correlations across countries between pairs of aggregate price indexes. Contrary to the intuition embodied in this thought, however, there is no guarantee, at any rate none that we have been able to discover, that the correlation of the indexes is an unbiased estimator of the average degree of correlation among the individual prices or, for that matter, that it is biased in any particular direction.[10] In other words, barriers to trade could be high or low in each individual market without the aggregate correlation necessarily registering these truths. None the less, putting these doubts to one side, we will trust henceforth to the intuition.

The pioneers of the method of index numbers, Laspeyres, Jevons and others writing in the middle of the nineteenth century, produced indexes of wholesale prices – believable indexes of retail prices began to be produced only in the 1890s and implicit GNP deflators, of course, much later – and in consequence wholesale price indexes dominated empirical work on the balance of payments in the formative years of the theory. The contemporaneous correlation between annual changes in British and American wholesale prices 1880–1913 is 0.66, high enough in view of the differences in weights in the indexes and in view of the low correlation of annual changes implied by the lags operating in the orthodox theories to lend support to the postulate of a unified world market.

It is at this point, however, that supporters of the orthodox theory begin to quarrel with the argument, as did Taussig with those bold enough to suggest that world markets in more than merely traded goods were integrated in the late nineteenth century, or as did the many doubters of the theory of purchasing power parity with those who used wholesale prices to indicate the appropriate rates of exchange after World War I. The standard objection has been that wholesale price indexes are biased samples from the distribution of correlations because they consist largely of easily traded goods, ignoring nontraded services and underrepresenting nontraded goods. A large lower tail of the distribution, it is said, is left off, leading to a false impression that national price levels are closely correlated.

A point that must be made at once, however, is that traded goods, in the sense of goods actually traded and goods identical to those actually traded, were not a small proportion of national income. Historians and economists have usually thought of the openness of economies in terms of the ratio of actual exports or imports to national income, and have inferred that the United States, with a ratio of exports to national income of about 0.07 in the late nineteenth century, was relatively isolated from the influence of international prices and that the United Kingdom, with a ratio of 0.28, was relatively open to it. Yet in both countries consumption of tradable goods, defined as all goods that figured in the import and export lists, was on the order of half of national income.[11] If any substantial part of the national consumption or production of wheat, coal or cloth entered international markets in which the country in question was a small supplier or demander, the prices of these items at home would be determined exogenously by prices abroad. Wholesale indexes, if they do indeed consist chiefly of traded goods, are not so unrepresentative of all of national income as might be supposed.

But what of the other, nontradable half of national income? Surely, as James Angell wrote in 1926, 'for non-traded articles there is of course no direct equalisation [of price] at all'.[12] The operative word in this assertion is 'direct', for without it the assertion is incorrect. The price of a good in one country is constrained not only by the direct limits of transport costs to and from world markets but by the indirect constraints arising from the good's substitutability for other goods in consumption or production. This was clear to Bertil Ohlin, who asked,

> To what extent are interregional discrepancies in home market prices kept within narrow limits not only through the potential trade in these goods that would come into existence if interregional price differences exceeded the costs of transfer, but also through the actual trade in *other* goods?[13]

It is not surprising to find Ohlin asking such a question, for the analytical issue is identical to the one that gave birth to that errant child of the Heckscher–Ohlin theory, factor–price equalization. The price of the milk used as much as the wage of the labour used is affected by the international price of butter and cheese. A rise in the price of a traded good will cause substitutions in production and consumption that will raise the prices of nontraded goods. To put the point more extremely than is necessary for present purposes, in a general equilibrium of prices the fixing of any one price by trade determines all the rest. The adjustment to the real equilibrium of relative prices, which must be achieved eventually, can be slow or quick. The monetary theory assumes that it is quick.

If it were in fact slow, one would expect the contemporaneous correlation between prices for countries on the gold standard to fall sharply as more comprehensive price indexes, embodying nontraded goods, are compared. This is not the case. The correlation between the annual changes in the GNP deflators 1880–1912 for America and Britain is 0.60, to be compared with the correlation for wholesale prices alone of 0.66. The regressions of the annual changes of American on British deflators and British on American were (standard errors in parentheses; levels of the price variables converted to indexes with their averages as the base):

$$AP = 0.0002 + 0.961 \, BP$$
$$(0.0050) \quad (0.266)$$

$R^2 = 0.35$, $D. - W. = 1.98$. Standard error of the regression as a percentage of the average level of the American price $= 2.5\%$

$$BP = 0.0017 + 0.33 \, AP$$
$$(0.0028) \quad (0.089)$$

$R^2 = 0.34$, $D. - W. = 1.92$. Standard error of the regression as a percentage of the average level of the British price $= 1.4\%$

The correlations of the German GNP deflator with the American (0.40) and the British (0.45) are considerably lower, but this may be simply a reflection of the inevitable frailties of Walther Hoffman's pioneering effort to produce such a deflator, or, perhaps, a reflection of the sharp rises in German tariffs. More countries have retail price indexes (generally with weights from working-class budgets) than have reliable GNP deflators, and these statistics tell a story that is equally encouraging for the postulate of arbitrage. The correlation matrix of annual changes in retail prices for the United States, the United Kingdom, Germany, France and Sweden is shown in table 4.1. The British–American correlation (0.57) is again not markedly below the correlation of the wholesale indexes, despite the importance of such nontraded goods as housing in the retail indexes.[14]

The correlation of American with British retail prices is probably not attributable to the trade in food offsetting a lower correlation between nontraded goods, for the simple correlation between American and British food prices in the years for which it is available (1894–1913) is lower, 0.49 compared with 0.57. Against this encouraging finding, however, must be put a less encouraging one. The average correlation between the changes in food prices in five regions of the United States (North Atlantic, South Atlantic,

Table 4.1 Simple correlations between annual changes in retail prices, 1880–1912

	USA	UK	Germany	France	Sweden
USA	1.00	0.57	0.28	0.24	0.38
UK		1.00	0.53	0.42	0.57
Germany			1.00	0.45	0.62
France				1.00	0.32
Sweden					1.00

North Central, South Central and the West) for 1891–1913 is very high, 0.87, contrasted with the British–American correlation of only 0.49. If food prices were as well arbitraged between as inside countries the British–American correlation would have to be much higher than it is. Still, even with perfect unity in the market for each item of food, one would not expect countries with substantially different budget shares to exhibit close correlations in the aggregate indexes. The lower correlation between Britain and the United States than between regions of the United States, then, may well reflect international differences of tastes and income rather than lower arbitrage.

If one proceeds in this fashion further in the direction of less traded goods the results continue to be mixed, although on balance giving support to the postulate of unity in world markets. The most obvious nontraded good is labour. The correlation between changes in wages of British and American coal miners 1891–1913 is 0.42 but the correlation between those of British and American farm labourers is only 0.26. Both are lower than the correlations between changes in the wages of the two employments in each country, 0.65 in Britain and 0.53 in America. The correlation between the annual changes in Paul Douglas's index of hourly earnings of union men in American building and the changes in A.L. Bowley's index of wages in British building from 1891 to 1901 is negligible, only 0.10. On the other hand, the average correlation among bricklayers' hourly wages in four cities (Boston, Cincinnati, Cleveland and Philadelphia) selected from the mass of data for 1890–1903 in the 19th Annual Report of the US Commissioner of Labour is only 0.14. The correlations for changes in wages between countries are low, in other words, but there is reason to believe that they are nearly as low within a geographically large country like the United States as well.

The same is true for an unambiguously nontraded commodity, common brick. That it is nontraded, that is, a poor substitute for traded goods, and that it enters into the production of nontraded commodities is evident from the negligible correlation between changes in its average price in Britain and America. Yet from 1894, when the statistics first become available, to 1913, the average correlation between prices of common brick at the plant in seven scattered states of the United States (California, Georgia, Illinois, New York, Ohio, Pennsylvania and Texas) was only 0.11, and even between three states in the same region (New York, Ohio and Pennsylvania) it was only 0.13. This degree of correlation may be taken as an indicator of the correlation between regions of the United States attributable to a common experience of general inflation, technological change and growth of income rather than to the unity of markets. It is small. In any case, common brick is a good at the lower end of the distribution of goods by their correlations, and there is little evidence of greater integration of markets within than between countries.

All these tests can be much expanded and improved, and we plan to do so in later work.[15] What has been established here is that there is a reasonable case, if not at this stage an overwhelming one, for the postulate of integrated commodity markets between the British and American economies in the late nineteenth century, vindicating the monetary theory. There appears to be little reason to treat these two countries on the gold standard differently in their monetary transactions from any two regions within each country.

Money, gold and the balance of payments

If international arbitrage of prices and interest rates was thoroughgoing and if the growth of real income in a country was exogenous to its supply of money, then the country's demand for money can be estimated by relatively straightforward econometric techniques. The balance of payments – identified here with flows of gold – predicted by the monetary theory can then be estimated as the difference between the growth in the country's total predicted demand for money and the growth in its actual domestic supply. If, further, the actual flow of gold closely approximates the flow implied by the estimated change in the demand for money minus the actual change in the domestic supply of money, the monetary theory of the gold standard warrants serious consideration. In fact, to a remarkable degree the monetary theory for the United States and the United Kingdom from 1880 to 1913 passes this final test.

In table 4.2 are presented the average movements of the British and American variables to be explained (the movements, that is, in money supplies and in that part of the money supply attributable to international flows of gold) and the average movements of the variables with which the monetary theory would explain them (the movements in prices, interest rates and incomes affecting the demand for money and the movements in that part of the money supply attributable to domestic forces). The average percentage change in the money supply was decomposed in a merely arithmetical way (described in the footnote to the table) into a part reflecting how the money supply would have behaved if all gold flows into or out of the country had been allowed to affect it (by way of the multiple effects of reserves on the money supply) and a residual reflecting all other influences. Arithmetically speaking, the causes of changes in British and American money supplies differed sharply; virtually all the change in Britain was attributable to international flows of gold while virtually all the change in America was attributable to other, domestic sources of new money. Economically speaking, the differences are less sharp. Although over these three decades on average the rate of change of the money supply was far larger in America than in Britain, the difference is adequately explained in terms of the monetary theory by the faster growth of American income, given the similarity (in accord with the findings of the last

Table 4.2   Average annual rates of change 1882–1913 of American and British money supplies (domestic and international), incomes, prices and interest rates (percentages; standard errors in parentheses)

		United Kingdom	United States
1	Money supply attributable to gold flows	2.22	− 0.09
		(2.41)	(2.89)
2	Money supply attributable to other influences	0.12	5.77
		(2.51)	4.56
3	Total money supply	2.35	5.68
		(1.78)	(5.21)
4	Real income	1.84	3.69
		(2.33)	(5.35)
5	Implicit price deflator	0.24	0.23
		(1.75)	(3.09)
6	Long-term interest rates (absolute change in basis points)	2.9	− 2.3
		(2.0)	(15.0)

Sources:
Line 1. The rate of change of the money supply attributable to gold flows was calculated as:

$$100\left[\log\left(M_{t-1} + \frac{M_t}{H_t}R_t\right) - \log M_{t-1}\right]$$

where M is the total money supply, H is 'high-powered money' (M_t/H_t, therefore, is the so-called 'money multiplier') and R is the annual net flow of gold. The figures on money supply and high-powered money for the United Kingdom were taken from Sheppard (1969), p. 16; and for the United States from Friedman and Schwartz (1963), pp. 704–7. The figures on gold flows for the United Kingdom were compiled from Beach (1935), pp. 46ff. These are for England alone, excluding Scotland and Ireland, but there is little doubt that they cover the great bulk of flows into and out of the United Kingdom. Gold flows for the United States are given in US Bureau of the Census (1960), ser. U6.
Line 2 = Line 3 − Line 1.
Line 3. Source as in Line 1.
Line 4. US real gross national product is from Simon Kuznets' worksheets, reported in Lipsey (1963), p. 423; for years before 1889, the Kuznets figure Lipsey used was inferred from Lipsey's ratio of GNP to farm income and his estimate of farm income (pp. 423–4). UK real gross *domestic* product is from Feinstein (1971), appendix table 6, col. 4. Line 5. For the US the figure is from Lipsey (1963), p. 423. For the UK the figure is from Feinstein, appendix table 61, col. 7.
Line 6. The US interest rate is Macauley's unadjusted index number of yields of American railway bonds (US Bureau of the Census, 1960, ser. X332). The UK rate is the yield of consolidated government bonds (consols) in Mitchell (1962), p. 455.

section) in the behaviour of prices and given the relative fall in American interest rates.

So much is apparent from the arithmetic of the British and American experience. To go further one needs a behavioural model explaining the annual balance of payments in terms of the monetary theory. The model is simplicity itself. It begins with a demand function for money, the only behavioural function in the model, asserting that the annual rate of change in the demand for money balances depends on the rates of change of the price level and of real income and on the absolute change in interest rates (asterisks signify rates of change):

$$M_d^* = P^* + f(y^*, \Delta i)$$

And it ends with a domestic money supply function (literally, an identity using the observed money multiplier, as explained in the footnote of table 4.2) and the statement that the money not supplied domestically was supplied through the balance of payments. It is evident that the monetary theory is simply a comparative statics theory of money's supply and demand, in which the balance of payments satisfies demands for money not satisfied by domestic sources.

By virtue of the unity of world markets and the assumed exogeneity of the growth of real income to the supply of money (which is itself a consequence of market unity and the availability of an elastic supply of money abroad), there is no simultaneous equation bias in estimating the demand for money by ordinary least squares. It is convenient to estimate the demand in real terms. The result for the United States 1884–1913 of regressing the rate of change of real balances on the rate of change in real income and the absolute change in the interest rate is (*t*-statistics in parentheses):

$$(M/P)^* = 0.030 + 0.61y^* - 0.10\Delta i \qquad\qquad R^2 = 0.59$$
$$ (4.5) \quad (4.9) \qquad (2.6) \qquad\qquad D. - W. = 2.02$$

And for the United Kingdom:[16]

$$(M/P)^* = 0.014 + 0.32y^* - 0.005\Delta i \qquad\qquad R^2 = 0.27$$
$$ (2.4) \quad (2.2) \qquad (1.2) \qquad\qquad D. - W. = 1.89$$

These appear to be reasonable demand equations, although the income elasticity in the equation for the United Kingdom is low, perhaps an artifact of errors in the series for income, which, given the low variability of British income, would reduce the fitted regression coefficient. Another explanation might be the substantial ownership of British money by foreigners, which would reduce the relevance of movements in British income to the 'British' money supply. Still, both demand equations accord reasonably well with other work on the demand for money.

The acid test of the model, of course, is its performance in predicting the balance of payments as a residual from the predicted demand for money and the actual domestically determined supply. Its performance is startlingly good. The good fit of the American demand equation offsets the relative unimportance of gold flows to the American supply, while the relative importance of gold flows to the British supply offsets the poor fit of the British demand

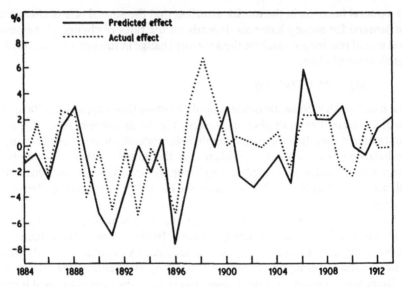

Figure 4.1 Predicted and actual effects of gold flows on the US money stock, annual rates of change, 1884–1913

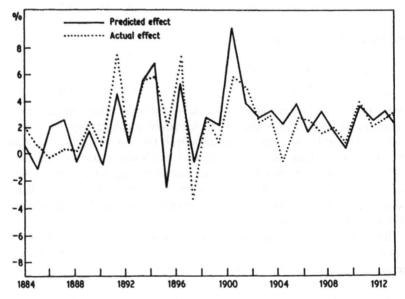

Figure 4.2 Predicted and actual effects of gold flows on the UK money stock, annual rates of change, 1884–1913

equation. Figures 4.1 and 4.2 exhibit the results, comparing the actual effect of gold flows on the American and British money supplies with the predicted effect. The actual effect is calculated annually by applying the observed ratio of money to reserves (including gold) to the actual flow of gold, the predicted effect by subtracting the domestic sources of money from the demand for money predicted by the regressions. In other words, the predicted effect is the excess demand for money predicted by the regressions in conjunction with the actual changes in the money supply due to domestic sources. One could just as well make the comparison of predicted with actual flows of gold, translating the predicted excess demand for money in each country into an equivalent demand for gold imports. The result would be the same, namely, a close correspondence between the predictions of the theory and the observed behaviour of the British and American stock of money and balance of payments.

No doubt the tests could be refined and more evidence could be examined. We believe, however, that we have established at least a prima-facie case for viewing the world of the nineteenth-century gold standard as a world of unified markets, in which flows of gold represented the routine satisfaction of demands for money. We do not claim to have rejected decisively the view of the gold standard that depends on poor arbitrage between national markets or the view that predicts an inverse rather than a positive correlation between gold inflows and income or any of the other variants of the orthodox theories. Indeed, it is perfectly possible that these variants are partly true, perhaps true in the very short run, or under special circumstances, such as mass unemployment – the monetary theory is, in the sense described earlier, an equilibrium theory, which could be consistent with any number of theories about how the British and American economies behaved out of equilibrium. But a balance-of-payments surplus or deficit is not in itself, as has often been assumed, evidence that the economy in question is in fact out of equilibrium. The monetary theory's central message is that a growing, open economy, buffeted by external variations in prices and interest rates, will have a varying demand for money, which would only fortuitously be supplied exactly from domestic sources. A country's balance of payments, in other words, could be positive or negative over the course of a year even if all asset and commodity markets in the country were continuously in equilibrium, for the flow of money into the country during the year could exactly meet the year's change in the demand for money. The source of the simplicity of the monetary theory of the gold standard is clear: the monetary theory is an equilibrium model, whereas the alternative theories are to a greater or lesser extent dynamic, dis-equilibrium models. We believe (as must be evident by now) that the simpler model yields a persuasive interpretation of how the gold standard worked, 1880–1913.

Notes

1 An earlier and longer version of this essay (available on request) was presented to the Workshop in Economic History at the University of Chicago and to the Cliometrics Conference at the University of Wisconsin. We wish to thank the participants in these meetings for their comments. The friendly scepticism of Moses Abramovitz, C.K. Harley, Hugh Rockoff, Jeffrey Williamson and our colleagues at the University of Chicago, among them Stanley Fischer, Robert J. Gordon, A.C. Harberger, Harry G. Johnson, Arthur Laffer and H. Gregg Lewis, contributed to a sharpening of the argument.

2 Many of these have been published in the Princeton Studies in International Finance. For example, Bloomfield (1963) and Lindert (1969). Bloomfield (1959) is seminal to this literature.

3 Keynes (1930), II, pp. 306–7.

4 World official reserves at the end of 1913 of $7100 million (16 per cent of which was foreign exchange, a good part of it sterling) are estimated by Lindert (1969), pp. 10–12.

5 In 1964 Robert Triffin undertook to act as midwife, but as he concedes, the infant is still in poor health (see Triffin, 1964, appendix I).

6 Needless to say, these are crude estimates: to continue the metaphor above, the historical study of world income is barely into its adolescence. The estimate of $362 billion for 1913 world income in 1955 prices begins with Alfred Maizels' compilation of figures on gross *domestic* product at factor cost for twenty-one countries, given in Maizels (1965), appendix E, p. 531. Czech and Hungarian income was estimated from Austrian income (post-1919 boundaries) on the basis of Colin Clark's ratios among the three (Clark, 1951, p. 155). Russian income was estimated by extrapolating Simon Kuznets' estimate for 1958 back to 1913 on the basis of his figure for the decennial rate of growth, 1913–58 (Kuznets, 1966, pp. 65 and 360), yielding a figure of $207 per capita in 1958 prices, which appears to be a reasonable order of magnitude. The Russian per capita figure was then applied to the population of Bulgaria, Greece, Poland, Romania and Spain, completing the coverage of Europe (boundary changes during the decade of war, 1910 to 1920, were especially important for these countries, except Spain; estimates of the relevant populations are given in Palmer (1957), p. 193). Maizels gives estimates of national income for Canada, Australia, New Zealand, South Africa, Argentina and Japan in 1913. Income per head in 1955 dollars was taken to be $50 in Africa except South Africa, $100 in Latin America except Argentina, $50 in India, and $60 in Asia except India and Japan, all on the basis of Maizels' estimates for 1929 and an assumption of little growth. Population figures for these groups of countries around 1910 were taken from Glass and Grebenik (1965), p. 58, with adjustments for the countries included in Maizels' estimates, from his population figures (1965, p. 540).

7 The sample is described in the appendix of the longer paper, available from the authors on request.

8 From 1800–2 to 1889–91 the ratio of the Berlin to the British price of wheat increased 30 per cent and remained at the higher ratio thereafter.

9 This and all subsequent regressions were subjected to the Cochrane–Orcutt iterative technique, removing in all cases understatement of the standard errors of the coefficients resulting from any autocorrelation of the residuals.

10 We have received a good deal of enlightenment on this point from H. Gregg Lewis of

78 *The Gold Standard in Theory and History*

the University of Chicago and Hugh Rockoff of Rutgers University. The issue is as follows. Suppose, to simplify at the outset, that one chooses the same set of weights $(w_1, w_2, \ldots w_N)$ to form the two indexes of prices (I_A and I_B) in the two countries (A and B). What is the relationship between the weighted average of the individual correlations,

$$w_1(\text{corr } P_1^A, P_1^B) + w_2(\text{corr } P_2^A, P_2^B) + \cdots + w_N(\text{corr } P_N^A, P_N^B),$$

and the correlation of the weighted averages, corr (I_A, I_B)(where $I_A = w_1 P_1^A + w_2 P_2^A + \cdots + w_N P_N^A)$? For the case of two prices we have written out both correlations in terms of the relevant covariances (expressing the prices in standardized form, thereby eliminating variances of the individual prices and making the corresponding covariances identical to correlation coefficients), with no very illuminating results. If no restrictions are placed on the covariances we can generate counterexamples to the proposition that the two are equal. But we suspect that we are neglecting true restrictions among the covariances (one set implying values for another set) and, further, that the case of large N would give more useful results.

11 For the calculation for the UK in 1913, see McCloskey unpublished MS), ch. 1, p. 18 (MS available on request).

12 Angell (1926), p. 381. Later Angell conceded in part the point made below, although he believed (p. 392) that 'it cannot be adequate to explain the comparatively quick adjustments [of domestic to international prices] that actually take place'.

13 Ohlin (1967), p. 104, his italics, question mark added. Contrast Viner (1924), p. 210: 'The prices of services and what may be termed "domestic commodities", commodities which are too perishable or too bulky to enter regularly and substantially into foreign trade, are wholly or largely independent of *direct* relationship with foreign prices. World price-factors influence them only through their influence on the prices of international commodities, with which the prices of domestic commodities, as part of a common price-system, must retain a somewhat flexible relationship' (his italics). Although this is an improvement on the earlier formulation by Cairnes (quoted by Viner on the next page) that 'with regard to these, there is nothing to prevent the widest divergence in their gold prices' it falls short of a full analysis of what is meant by 'direct' and 'somewhat flexible', an analysis provided by Ohlin. In long-run equilibrium the distinction between direct and indirect is beside the point and the relationship of domestic to international prices is not even somewhat flexible. Viner's work, incidentally, is one of a series of books on the balance of payments published in the Harvard Economic Studies in the 1920s and 1930s under the influence, direct or indirect, of Taussig: Williams (1920); Viner (1924); Angell (1926); Ohlin (1933); White (1933); and Beach (1935). Students of the history of economic thought will find it significant that of these Ohlin, who acknowledges explicitly his debt to the Stockholm School (among them Cassel, Heckscher and Wicksell, all of whom emphasized the intimate relationship between domestic and international prices), broke most sharply with Taussig on this issue.

14 The notion of an 'Atlantic economy', incidentally, receives support from these figures: the average correlation of French with other retail price indexes, a crude measure of the appropriateness of including a country in the Atlantic economy, is 0.36, while the same statistic for the United States is 0.37; on this reading, it would be as appropriate to exclude France from the economy of Western Europe as to exclude the United States.

15 We have passed by, for example, the issue of how unified were the markets for assets.

The correlation between the annual changes in the British and American long-term interest rates 1882 to 1913 included in the equations estimated in the next section was 0.36, and could no doubt be improved by a closer attention to gathering homogeneous data than we have thought necessary for now. Michael Edelstein (1982, p. 339) reports a correlation coefficient of 0.77 between annual changes in the levels of yields on first-class American railway bonds offered in London and New York from 1871 to 1913, a period including years before the refixing of the sterling–dollar exchange rate in 1879. The discount rates of central banks may be taken as a rough measure of the short-term interest rate. The recent revisionist literature on the gold standard has emphasized the close correlations between these rates in different countries. Triffin (1964, p. 9), for example, quotes Bloomfield (1959, p. 35) approvingly, to the effect that 'the annual averages of the discount rates of twelve [European] central banks reveal the ... interesting fact that, in their larger movements at least, the discount rates of virtually all the banks tended to rise and fall together'. Bloomfield and Triffin attribute the parallelism to a corresponding parallelism in the business cycles of the nations involved, but the finding can also be interpreted as evidence of direct or indirect arbitrage in the international capital market. Lance E. Davis's finding that the internal American capital market was poorly arbitraged in this period, suggests that for America at least arbitrage was little better within than between countries (Davis, 1971). The widely believed assertion that domestic British industry was starved of funds in favour of British investment in Argentine railways and Indian government bonds can be given a similar interpretation.

16 The evidence is described in the footnote to table 4.2. The interest rate on three-month bankers' bills (Mitchell, 1962, p. 460) performed better than the consol rate, and was used here.

References

Angell, J.W. (1926), *The Theory of International Prices*, Cambridge, Mass., Harvard University Press.

Beach, W.E. (1935), *British International Gold Movements and Banking Policy, 1881–1913*, Harvard Economic Studies, Cambridge, Mass., Harvard University Press.

Bloomfield, Arthur I. (1959) *Monetary Policy under the International Gold Standard, 1880–1914*, New York, Federal Reserve Bank of New York.

——(1963), *Short-term Capital Movements under the Pre-1914 Gold Standard*, Princeton Studies in International Finance, no. 11, Princeton, Princeton University Press.

Clark, Colin (1951), *The Conditions of Economic Progress*, 2nd edn, London, Macmillan.

Davis, Lance E. (1971), 'Capital mobility and American economic growth', in R.W. Fogel and S.L. Engerman, *The Reinterpretation of American Economic History*, New York, Harper & Row, 285–300.

Edelstein, Michael (1982), *Overseas Investment in the Age of High Imperialism*, New York, Columbia University Press.

Feinstein, C.H. (1971), *National Income, Expenditure and Output of the United Kingdom, 1855–1965*, Cambridge, Cambridge University Press.

Friedman, Milton and Anna J. Schwartz (1963), *A Monetary History of the United States, 1867–1960*, Princeton, Princeton University Press.

Glass, D.V. and E. Grebenik (1965), 'World population, 1800–1950', in H.J. Habakkuk and M. Postan, *Cambridge Economic History of Europe*, Cambridge, Cambridge University Press, vol. VI, pt 1.

Keynes, J. M. (1930), *A Treatise on Money*, London, Macmillian.

Kuznets, Simon (1966), *Modern Economic Growth*, New Haven, Yale University Press.

Lindert, Peter H. (1969), *Key Currencies and Gold, 1900–1913*, Princeton Studies in International Finance, no. 24, Princeton, Princeton University Press.

Lipsey, R.E. (1963), *Price and Quantity Trends in the Foreign Trade of the United States*, New York, National Bureau of Economic Research.

McCloskey, D.N., 'Markets abroad and British economic growth, 1820–1913', unpublished MS.

Maizels, Alfred (1965), *Industrial Growth and World Trade*, Cambridge, Cambridge University Press.

Mitchell, B.R. (1962), *Abstract of British Historical Statistics*, Cambridge, Cambridge University Press.

Ohlin, Bertil (1967), *Interregional and International Trade*, rev. edn (1st edn, 1933), Cambridge, Mass. Harvard University Press.

Palmer, R.R. (1957), *Atlas of World History*, Chicago, Rand McNally.

Sheppard, D.K. (1969), 'Asset preferences and the money supply in the United Kingdom 1880–1962', University of Birmingham Discussion Papers, ser. A, no. 111 (November),

Triffin, Robert (1964), *The Evolution of the International Monetary System: Historical Reappraisal and Future Perspectives*, Princeton Studies in International Finance, no. 12, Princeton, Princeton University Press.

US Bureau of the Census (1960), *Historical Statistics of the United States, ser. U6, Washington, D.C., US Government Printing Office*.

Viner, Jacob (1924), *Canada's Balance of International Indebtedness 1900–1913*, Cambridge, Mass., Harvard University Press.

White, Harry D. (1933), *The French International Accounts, 1880–1913*, Harvard Economic Studies, Cambridge, Mass., Harvard University Press.

Williams, J.H. (1920), *Argentine International Trade under Inconvertible Paper Money: 1880–1900*, Harvard Economic Studies, Cambridge, Mass., Harvard University Press.

[4]

Corn at Interest: The Extent and Cost of Grain Storage in Medieval England

By DONALD N. MCCLOSKEY AND JOHN NASH*

The history of storage of grain in the Middle Ages is important for understanding the past and for its contribution to other studies. It is a simple case of a complex problem in dynamic economics. At the interest rates he faced a medieval farmer seldom stored more than two years in a row; at the transport costs he faced he seldom brought grain from radically different climes. A two-period model and a closed economy are simple conditions for the study of the economics of storage, much simpler than conditions seen nowadays. Further, an assumption about the prevalence of storage underlies much of medieval economic history, and is not irrelevant to modern times. Storage was a species of insurance that could substitute for other species, such as (to pick an example quite at random) scattering of one's holdings of land (McCloskey, 1976). Scattered holdings and the desperate fear of famine they signify are common features of the modern as of the medieval countryside. The force of the economist's argument (see, for example, Theodore Schultz, 1964) that such customs are insurance rather than rural idiocy depends on a quantitative measure of at least

*Professor of Economics and of History, University of Iowa, Iowa City, IA 52242, and Assistant Professor of Economics, Texas A&M University, College Station, TX and Economist, Federal Trade Commission, Washington, D.C. We thank Richard Yntema of Chicago for excellent research assistance, and Alan Wiley and Stefano Fenoaltea for helpful comments. Earlier drafts were subjected to the friendly and productive scrutiny of seminars at the Canterbury meetings of the British Agricultural History Society, Australian National University, Berkeley, British Columbia, the California Institute of Technology, Chicago, Harvard, LaTrobe, the Law and Economics Center of Emory University, Maryland, Pittsburgh, Stanford, Texas A&M, Virginia Polytechnic Institute, and Washington. The research was supported by a grant from the Columbia University Center for the Study of Futures Markets.

one alternative. Storage is the easiest to measure.

The history of storage is important, too, for what can be discovered along the way. Most notably, a measure of the cost of storage sheds light on the prevailing rate of interest, illuminating its hitherto obscure history. The reasoning involved, examined in detail below, is that a store of grain is an investment. Wheat put into storage in October and brought out in November must pay over the month the cost of the barn and the guards, the depreciation of the grain, and the opportunity cost of the funds invested. The opportunity cost is the rate of interest. The rate was shockingly high. Stores of grain were therefore very low, and medieval men lived from hand to mouth—as one might have judged as much from their poetry as from their markets. In the sixteenth and seventeenth centuries their desperation relaxed, at the very time that interest rates fell. The last famines in England (Scotland was later) were in the 1590's (Peter Laslett, 1965, ch. 5). From the history of storage, in other words, one can infer that the interest rate had fallen quickly and deeply, an early stirring of modern economic growth.

I. The Direct Evidence that Storage was Small

The history of European storage has been neglected because the materials for its study appear so unpromising. One can learn a little from archaeological studies of grain storage, chiefly what the bins looked like, and a little from pretty tales and folklore. In 1540 at Nuremberg, for instance, Charles V tasted bread made from 118 year-old grain. It was proverbial in the fifteenth century, again, that "Winter alle etes/That summer begetes." Aside from such scraps there is little,

174

and the subject has therefore been left to bald assertion and counterassertion. A leading student of the medieval French economy, Georges Duby, asserted flatly in 1962 that medieval Europe "did not know how to store grain or accumulate reserves" (p. 135). A leading student of the medieval Swedish economy, Eli Heckscher, asserted with equal confidence in 1941 that it was on the contrary a "storage economy" (p. 10). Neither provided evidence, nor emphasized the distinction between storage for consumption during the year after the harvest and storage for consumption in later years, the "carryover." The entire crop was, of course, stored for six months on average, because it needed to be eaten, which might justify calling any economy without continuous harvests a storage economy. Yet the carryover could be zero, with no reserves accumulated on the eve of the new harvest. It is carryover that is most to the point. Carryover smooths consumption, provides insurance, and links one year economically to the next.

The direct evidence on the size of the carryover is thin, although what there is suggests that it was small. The evidence must come from those who knew how to write and who wished to write down their doings, the lords and monks and burghers. The so-called "account roll" was an annual report to the lord's auditor by his bailiff combining elements of a balance sheet and an income statement, and in particular reporting fully on the disposition of the year's harvest of grain on the lord's own farm (his "demesne"). Accounts have been published for a dozen or so English estates out of the hundreds that exist in manuscript. The simplest way to use them is to look for the amount of "old grain" on hand at the reporting date, traditionally just after the harvest, and to divide that amount by the crop. The conclusion is that the carryover was small. For example, usable accounts of wheat from 170 of the years from 1208 to 1448 at Crawley, Hampshire contain only nine mentions of old wheat in any guise (N. S. B. Gras, 1930, pp. 339–43: "old," "from the previous year," "remain," "remain in sheaf," "left over"). These nine

amount to something under 2 percent of the wheat produced in the 170 years in total.

An apparent difficulty with such evidence is that it is a lack of evidence. The rolls do not always say "old grain:nil." They often say nothing, leaving the observer to make the inference that nothing does mean nil. Yet William Beveridge was willing to make it: "Grain remaining from a previous year does not often occur, and if it does it is noted" (Beveridge, 1927, "Notes on Sources"). And more recent scholars agree: "bailiffs were appearing before auditors who had last year's account at hand. Had any corn been left on last year's account the bailiff would be required to account for what happened to it" (Eleanor Searle).

After a series of exceptionally good years, of course, the carryover might well be substantial. On the estates of the Bishop of Winchester in southern England, the years up to 1223 clearly were good ones. The manor of Wycombe carried over more quarters of grain ($246\frac{7}{8}$) than its entire crop (213), as did Ecchinswell and Burghclere (Beveridge papers, box 32, A49). The other manors carried over less, but a lot. The fifteen manors with usable accounts in 1223 had old grain of 1,561 quarters while harvesting 2,742 quarters, or carryover of fully 57 percent. But the usual case was no carryover at all. In 1220, only six out of seventeen manors had any carryover; in 1225, so soon after the remarkable prosperity of 1223, only four out of more than thirteen did; in 1236 only three out of eighteen. Not every year has usable accounts on the Winchester manors, but those that do most commonly have no single instance of carryover: 1226, 1231, 1232, 1235, 1244, and on into the century, punctuated by occasional bonanzas (such as the year 1256 at the big manor of Taunton: 624 quarters of grain "of the second year" and even 182 "of the third," as against 824 quarters fresh from the fields). The bonanzas were rare, and not to be relied upon.

These, of course, were bonanzas to the rich, not to the average man. One would like to know how if at all the other 95 percent of the population carried over grain from one harvest to the next, but the evidence is even thinner than that for the larger owners of land. Certainly there was no sharing out of what the richer folk might hold. Around 1500, a priest scolded a rich and selfish ploughman (this at Lent, incidentally, long before the next harvest):

> Thou knowest that of corn is great
>   scarceness,
> Whereby many for hunger die, doubt-
>   less,
> Because they lack their daily bread—
> Hundreds this year I have seen dead;
> And thou hast great plenty of wheat
> Which men for money now cannot get.
> [Celia Sisam and Kenneth Sisam, p. 516]

The priest proceeds to swindle the plough-man out of his plenty, for the benefit of the poor. But the poet is silent on the size of carryover.

Stefano Fenoaltea (1970) has attempted to use other sources (though still pertaining to the rich) to estimate the carryover, namely, the number and dimensions of monastic barns. He estimated the carryover to be very high, concluding that "the monastic barns alone could hold enough grain to feed England's human population for over a year and a half" (p. 139). His reasoning is in error, for it does not allow for the storage of seed, which was at medieval yields fully a quarter of the crop. The correct arithmetic is as follows. Suppose that the barn's capacity was commonly exhausted.[1] Suppose too that carryover was some fraction, c, of the year's whole consumption (taken to be 3.0 units, with 1.0 for seed, the whole output being 4.0). If the capacity of the barns was as much as 1.5 times annual consumption, the

accounting of the crop is

Barn Capacity
$$= \text{Consumption} + \text{Seed} + \text{Carryover}$$
or,
$$(1.5)(3) = \quad 3 \quad + 1 + \quad c3$$

The carryover share c implied by this capacity of one-and-one-half times consumption is $1/6$, not $1/2$.

Since carryover is calculated here as a residual it is sensitive to small errors, and the errors in estimating capacity are not small (for instance, grain was usually not threshed before being stored, but sometimes was). At a capacity of 1.33 rather than 1.50 times consumption the arithmetic implies there would be no room for carryover at all; at a capacity of 1.66 times consumption the carryover fraction would be .33. That is, the fraction varies from zero to .33 when the capacity estimate varies plus or minus by a mere one-quarter or one-fifth.

The decisive objection to a large carryover, however, is evidence on the frequency of starvation. The distribution of production is known to be normal with a standard deviation of 35 relative to an average of 100; starvation is known to have occurred at a consumption of 50 relative to 100 (Mc-Closkey, pp. 141–45). One can use tables of the normal distribution to reckon the waiting time to starvation, seeing whether large carryovers give reasonable waiting times. For example, if the carryover against crop failure was 10 compared with an average consumption of 100, then a peasant could survive any single year (i.e., consume 50) with a crop of 40 or above. A crop below 40 would cause him to starve, as would two crops in succession of, say, 44 and 44 (since the carryover, depleted by 6, could not be rebuilt before disaster hit again). But large carryovers do not give reasonable waiting times: see Table 1.

The actual waiting time calculated from the Anglo-Saxon Chronicle and other sources is on the order of 10 or 15 years (see Mc-Closkey, p. 144). The 30 to 476 years of waiting time characteristic of high carryovers

---

[1] The capacity of barns would not in fact have been exhausted, since barns were built for the *maximum maximorum*, the peak harvest year as well as the peak month within a year. Transport costs were high, implying that it would be optimal to overbuild local capacity. Almost never would there be a year using every barn in England to capacity, since each region would not have the same bumper crop. More commonly, down to early modern times in much of Europe, capacity in one region might be fully utilized while it went abegging, literally, in another.

TABLE 1—EXPECTED NUMBER OF YEARS BETWEEN
FAMINES FOR VARIOUS CHOICES OF CARRYOVER
AND THE FAMINE LINE
(Average consumption = 100)

Famine Line relative to 100	Carryover (Percent)			
	5	10	20	50
50	22	32	44	476
60	13	16	28	28+

are too long, sometimes absurdly long. Even a starvation level of 60 does not easily reconcile high carryovers with the short waits observed. That the medieval economy was haunted by starvation, in short, implies that it had little in its stores of grain.

Particular episodes of famine suggest that carryovers were at most on the order of 5 percent of consumption, not 50 percent, surely, or even 20 percent. The years leading up to the autumn of 1315, when the crop was very poor all over Europe, were not bad. Yet Henry Lucas notes that by the spring of 1316 "the old stocks became completely exhausted" and wheat sold in England for 40 shillings a quarter (compared with 5 shillings in a normal year) (1962, p. 55). He gives a table of deaths in Ypres, rising sharply in the spring. Where was the six-month buffer stock? On the demesnes of the Bishop of Winchester, net yields in the bad years 1315 and 1316 were around 45 percent of the 1314 yield. A buffer stock as large as six months of consumption would have easily permitted consumption in these 2 years at well above the starvation level (50 percent of the average consumption). Yet 1315 and 1316 was burned in men's memories, the worst famine in European history.

II. Using Prices to Show that Storage was Small

The notion of a "storage economy," then, is not favored by the usual evidence, though the usual evidence is scanty. Another class of evidence bearing on the issue, however, is available in large and elastic supply: prices of grain. For no time after the twelfth century is it difficult to get the prices at which

manorial farms, monasteries, Oxford colleges, the King's household, chartered towns, and other English institutions bought and sold wheat, barley, oats, and rye. From Poland to Portugal, indeed, medieval records yield prices in limitless array, dated, published, affixed to goods of ascertainable quality, and unused for historical purposes beyond the measurement of long-term inflation. The outmoded yet strangely resilient notion that the Middle Ages were ages of "natural economy" unused to trade, money, and prices looks odd beside such an outpouring. Here in quantities beyond the wildest dreams of intellectual avarice are the statistics of a commercial civilization.

One simple way of using prices is to ask whether the amount they fluctuated from harvest to harvest was consistent with a large and therefore price-damping carryover. They fluctuated a lot, which is inconsistent with it. Annual coefficients of variation calculated from the essentially trendless series of prices of wheat at two manors in Hampshire from 1245 to 1350 for 20-year periods ranged from .20 to .43 (J. Z. Titow, 1969, pp. 97–99). The coefficient of variation in wheat prices at Philadelphia, 1800–25, was .26, and at New York in roughly 20-year periods from 1825 to 1914 ranged from .16 to .34 (U.S. Bureau of the Census, 1975, series E123). The typical fall from medieval to modern times, then, was from about .30 to about .24: a variety of climates newly accessible by cheap transport (the Baltic, for example, in early modern times) was a substitute for a large carryover and had the same effect. The only oddity is that the effect was not even larger.

A further step along the same line of reasoning tests for the influence of carryover by regression methods. If carryovers were unusual, then in a very good year one would expect carryover stocks to be built up, depressing prices in the next crop year below what they would be had the previous crop not been good. One would expect a routine of large carryovers, on the other hand, to allow little impact on prices of a good crop. For a sample of 39 years in the thirteenth and fourteenth century in southern England, one's expectations are fulfilled, if one expected small carryovers:

$$\ln P_t = 3.59 - 1.15 \ln Q_t - 0.205 \ln Q_{t-1}$$
$$\quad\quad (0.28) \quad (0.13) \quad\quad (0.11)$$

$$- 0.301 \ln Q_{t-1}^*.$$
$$\quad (.12)$$

The fitted equation (standard errors in parentheses; $R^2 = .76$; Cochrane-Orcutt applied) says that price now (P_t) is reduced very strongly by a high yield now (Q_t), much less strongly (though definitely) by a high yield last year (Q_{t-1}) and strongly by yields last year more than one standard deviation above the mean (Q_{t-1}^*). In other words, last year's yield can be divided into two different variables, yields more and less than one standard deviation above the mean. The equation permits a kink, testing whether unusually high yields lead to unusually high carryovers and unusually great depression of next year's prices. They do. In short, carryovers existed, doubtless. But they were small and sporadic, not sustained at such high levels as 30 or 50 percent of consumption. They were probably closer to 5 percent or less, except after a spectacularly good year.

III. The Cost of Storage was High

The question is, why?—why was carryover so small? The answer is that it was expensive, which fact in its turn buttresses the shaky calculations of its smallness. As has been noted, the cost of storing a bushel of wheat is the cost of the barn per bushel plus the percentage rotting in storage plus the expected percentage loss of capital value due to falls in the price per bushel plus the opportunity cost of the interest forgone on the sum expended on the bushel. In what follows the equation will be broken down into the parts, examining what little direct evidence there is for each. At present it is necessary to accept only that the total carrying cost must be earned in equilibrium. If the storers of grain do not make systematic errors in predicting what prices will be—that is, if they are in the fashionable parlance "rational"—then the price of grain will in fact march up at the monthly carrying cost. It can behave on

average no other way. If, on the contrary, storing a bushel for four months from September to January were to earn persistently less than four times the monthly cost (suitably compounded), then storers would store less, driving the September price down and the January price up until the equality was reestablished. The harvest, or the signs of the harvest, break the logic, which begins anew at a price suitable to the size of the new crop. So it goes year upon year, in sawtooth fashion. The slope of the teeth is the cost of storage.

All that is needed is the average slope of prices within the harvest year. The account rolls again are ultimately the chief medieval source. They usually give prices without date ("of wheat sold, whereof 2 quarters the price per quarter 6s. 4d., 44 quarters $4\frac{1}{2}$ bushels the price per quarter 6s 8d" and the like). But sometimes the prices are dated, commonly by saint's days. The largest collection of raw, dated prices is J. E. Thorold Rogers' *The History of Agriculture and Prices in England*, published in 1866, and long recognized as a rich and reliable mine for data. Volume I contains about 170 pages devoted to grain prices in the late thirteenth and fourteenth centuries, or some 27,000 quotations. Some 8 percent of these, about 2,000, have more or less precise dates attached, about fourteen dated quotations on average for each year 1260–1400.

The facts for wheat are most voluminous, because wheat was the commodity of commerce. The monthly rates of change of prices can be calculated from comparisons over various pairs of months. There are 1,075 such pairs observed in the same village and the same year. For instance, one pair is the rise from May to July 1331 in the price of wheat from 6s. 8d. to 6s. 10d. per quarter of 8 bushels in Elham, Kent. There are a total of 22 cases of May to July comparisons in the Rogers data, the first in the crop year beginning in 1272 and the last in 1356, with an average ratio of 1.055 (the standard deviation around the average is high, .160; the standard error is .034). Two-thirds are from Cuxham, Oxfordshire (an Oxford college owned the village); the rest are scattered about southern England. The average

TABLE 2—ENGLISH WHEAT PRICES IN THE THIRTEENTH AND FOURTEENTH CENTURIES,
PERCENTAGE RATES OF CHANGE PER MONTH

From	October	November	December	January	To February	March	April	May	June	July	August
September	7.5	8.5	2.8	2.3	1.6	2.0	3.4	4.8	2.0	2.4	1.7
October		3.8	1.4	0.1	0.3	−0.4	1.6	1.6	0.6	3.9	0.6
November			6.4	2.2	1.5	1.2	1.6	0.8	0.7	1.5	1.4
December				6.3	6.8	2.8	2.6	2.6	2.8	0.7	0.9
January					1.9	3.2	4.0	1.4	1.5	0.1	0.8
February						3.7	4.1	4.0	2.4	2.0	2.4
March							3.6	2.2	2.1	2.6	2.8
April								1.2	0	2.8	−0.4
May									1.5	2.7	−1.5
June										4.2	4.0
July											1.5

Source: Authors' calculations, from 1,075 pairs of prices, 1260–1400.

TABLE 3—UNWEIGHTED AVERAGES BY MONTH OF ALL RATES OF CHANGE OF WHEAT PRICES,
1260–1400, ENCOMPASSING A PARTICULAR PAIR OF SUCCESSIVE MONTHS

September-October	3.55	January-February	1.91	May-June	1.52
October-November	2.25	February-March	2.04	June-July	1.78
November-December	1.85	March-April	2.12	July-August	1.29
December-January	2.03	April-May	1.78		

Source: See Table 2.

monthly rate of change of prices from May through June to July was therefore the solution, r, of $e^{2r} = 1.055$, or $r = 2.70$ percent per month, some 38 percent per year.

One way of displaying the results is in a matrix of pairs of months, as in Table 2. One way of summarizing the 66 averages is to say that their average in turn is 2.37 percent per month (32 percent per year), though with a high standard deviation (1.87 percent, a coefficient of variation of .79 around the average) and high standard error (0.23).

Another way to summarize the averages is to extract all the information in the matrix concerning a rate of change between a particular pair of consecutive months, to detect any pattern of seasons. The entries relevant to the March-April comparison, for instance, are all those northeast of the March-April entry, 3.6. Adding them together without weighting double-counts many times over and gives the same weight to an entry such as November-August, which merely passes through the March-April comparison, as to one such as March-May, which is closer to

the nub of the issue. Without theoretical light it is hard to see the merit of one average over another. For what this one is worth, the result is given in Table 3. The storage costs are high at the outset, falling to around 2 percent per month (about 30 percent a year). That the cost is lower in the spring probably reflects the arrival of definite news about the next harvest. The lowering may indicate the size of the risk premium required earlier in the year, when news is scant and long-term averages are the only guide to how prices will change.

Averages by length of the gap between months, reported in Table 4, seem also to be telling. What exactly they tell is not altogether clear. Very likely the fall as the comparisons get longer reflects the fixed cost of putting grain in storage. Possibly, too, it represents a selection bias in the evidence, since a more rapid rise in prices over a short period would cause more transactions to be undertaken by the manors and other institutions involved, and a greater likelihood that a pair of prices would fall in successive

TABLE 4—AVERAGES BY LENGTH OF GAP BETWEEN
MONTHS COMPARED

Number of Months Gap[a]	Monthly Rate of change[b]	Number of Observations	
		Actual	Expected
1	3.77	254	179
2	3.57	204	163
3	2.06	166	146
4	1.58	138	130
5	1.21	99	114
6	1.61	69	98
7	1.51	64	81
8	2.06	44	65
9	2.47	20	49
10	1.55	13	32
11	1.73	4	16

Source: Authors' calculations of wheat prices.
[a] For example, January–June = 5.
[b] Shown in percent.

months. The form of the matrix of comparisons implies the last column, the expected number of observations at each number of months gap. For example, the 11 elements on the diagonal are one-month gaps, 11 out of 66 total. That is, 11/66 of the 1,075 observations, or 179, should be one-month comparisons under the null hypothesis of equiprobability of each element. There is a marked overrepresentation of brief gaps (close to the diagonal). One could examine the runs of prices that are producing the brief gaps to see if it is plausible that they are themselves a consequence of rapid price rises. In any event, the nature of the sampling biases in the Rogers data are worth pursuing: weighted by the number of observations the average rise is a 2.55 percent per month (35 percent a year), while the average for pairs more than two months apart is only 1.75 percent (only 23 percent per year).

The tentative conclusion from even these crude methods is nonetheless plain. The whole cost of wheat storage was from about 2 to 3 percent per month, or from 27 to 43 percent per year, closer perhaps to 30 than to 40 percent.

The result is confirmed by a more elegant if less rich method, namely, a regression of prices from the same harvest year and place against the distance of days between them. It comes in two forms, depending on the placing of the constant term. Either

$$P_t = P_0 e^{rt} + c' \quad \text{or} \quad P_t = P_0 e^{c+rt}.$$

In other words, the price on the second date (P_t) is raised either by a constant cost per bushel of putting wheat in storage (c') or by a constant cost per shilling value (c). The method of estimation of the two forms is different, but their results do not differ radically in the central parameter, r, the rate of growth of prices (here, per day). The cost-per-bushel form required a nonlinear method, giving

$$P_t = P_0 \exp(.001165t).$$

The rate of change is 0.1165 percent per day, or $(1.001165)^{365} = 1.53$, or 53 percent per year. The constant-per-shilling form required logarithms and fitting by least squares, giving

$$\ln(P_t/P_0) = .0082 + .00083t.$$

The R^2 is very low (.07), unsurprisingly so. The standard error of the coefficient on t (that is, time in days) is one-half the value of the coefficient. The implied rate of change is $365(.00083) = .30$, or 30 percent a year. The econometrics echoes the ambiguity of the earlier calculations: the cost of storage is probably around or above 30 percent a year, but where exactly around or above depends on exactly how one wishes to look at the facts.

The regression results are based on 61 observations (as against 1,075 in the monthly statistics), about one-half of the exploitable pairs of dated prices in the same location and year. Little would be gained that is not captured in the monthly averages by adding observations dated simply "March" or "Spring." Were they nonetheless added, a definite downward bias from errors in variables would follow (although it is clearly no trick to estimate the error variance from saying "March" when some definite date in March is meant). Four observations of extreme drops rather than rises in prices were junked as outliers: including them turns the

TABLE 5—AVERAGE RATES OF MONTHLY GROWTH IN PRICE FOR MINOR GRAINS[a]

	Percent Rate of Change[b]	Standard Deviation	Number of Pairs of Months with Data[c]	Definition or Use
Rye	4.17 (1.31)	6.16	22	A bread grain inferior to wheat; black bread
Mixtil or Maslin	3.26 (1.36)	6.64	24	Rye and wheat sown together
Drage or Dredge	4.64 (1.51)	7.38	24	Oats and barley sown together
Malt	5.8 (2.1)	3.7	3	Sprouted barley
Drage Malt	1.		1	
Beans	2.5 (3.3)	8.8	7	Pod-bearing vines
Vetches	8.3 (3.1)	7.5	6	Mainly for animal feed
Peas	3.8 (5.)	16.	10	

Source: Authors' calculations.

[a] Thirteenth and fourteenth centuries, September through June only; excluding the famine years 1315–16.

[b] Standard errors are shown in parentheses.

[c] Except for rye, nearly equal to all the quotations.

equations into rubbish, in that the standard errors shoot up and the cost of storage becomes negative. Finally, the procedure truncated the year at 240 days after the harvest was finished (notionally, September 1), because including May, June, July, and August adds, again, more noise than music. The fact is itself significant, helping to confirm the model being used. From May onward, it would become increasingly clear how large the harvest was in fact going to be, causing prices to fan out to their ultimate destinations. No longer would the average experience of past years govern the rate of rise of prices.

Wheat was not the only grain. Barley, for example, was grown to the same or greater extent as wheat (the word "barn" derives in Anglo-Saxon from "barley"). It was used commonly for bread, occasionally for animal feed, or malted and brewed into the quantities of weak beer that made up a large part of the medieval diet. The analysis of barley gives evidence of very large price rises. The one-month comparisons beginning in September, October, November, and June, for example, average a 10 percent rise per month. The minor grains—minor at least as market-ed goods—tell a similar story. A rise in round figures of 4.0 percent per month for the minor grains appears reasonable, that is, 60 percent per year.

The results for oats (usually a bread grain) are more full, and tend to the same conclusion that the rise was very high. The average of the 42 monthly comparisons (namely, all except those ending in July and August, when the harvest began, and three months with no information) is a 5.77 percent monthly rate of rise, with a standard deviation of 4.52 and a standard error of the mean of 0.70. A 95 percent confidence interval for oats would run from 3.1 percent to 5.9 percent per month (from 45 to 99 percent per year).

That other grains have so much higher costs of storage than wheat requires explanation. It is possible that lesser grains did not store as well as wheat, or that the dealers in wheat were better placed in the capital market. The cost of storage, in other words, might actually have been higher. But there is a simpler explanation. Because the other grains had to compete with wheat for storage space, and because the space was paid for by the price rise, the absolute price rise per bushel for the other grains would have to

90   *Measurement and Meaning in Economics*

have been the same for wheat. Wheat sold for twice as much per bushel as did other grains. In percentage terms, consequently, the monthly rise would have to be higher for the lower priced grains. And wheat stored more compactly than barley. In any event, the annual cost of storage of grain was at least 30 percent per year, and could well have been higher.

IV. The Cost was High Because the Interest Rate was High

The cost of storage fell in modern times. One can duplicate the calculations for the sixteenth century and after, the data being of course plentiful. In the Oxford town market, for example, there are monthly figures from 1618 to 1644. November was the low month for wheat prices, August the high, with a rise between them of only 8.4 percent (the standard error is 3.7), or only 0.9 percent per month and 11.3 percent per year. In Namur, Belgium, 1614–92, the August to June rise for wheat is 12 percent, or only 14 percent a year. In Diest, in the Brabant province of Belgium, the rates of annual rise by crop, 1718–36, are wheat 10.9 percent, barley 14.8, rye 14.5, oats 15.4, and buckwheat 18.1. The instances could be multiplied indefinitely, with the same outcome. The cost of storage, plainly, was much lower in the seventeenth and eighteenth centuries than it had been four centuries earlier.

To explain why it fell, one must turn to the components of the cost—the percent spoilage, the barn costs, and, above all, the prevailing rate of interest. Direct scrutiny of these confirms the impression of very high costs in the Middle Ages and suggests why storage eventually became cheap.

What, then, accounts for the 30 percent cost per year or more? The rotting of grain was probably not more than 10 percent per year. This at any rate is the figure suggested by the scraps of evidence nowadays on poor countries, whose techniques of storage are little better than medieval. The latest estimate comes from a study in 1978 by the National Academy of Sciences:

Experts involved in the preparation of this report resisted extrapolating post-

harvest loss estimates to national or global levels because general estimates cannot be supported with statistically significant data. For planning purposes, however, 10 percent is cited as an average minimum overall loss figure for cereal grains and legumens.   [p. 8]

The figure is the loss from harvest to consumption, implying that it would be on average the cost for one-half year (half a year being the average time a bushel of wheat spends in storage if there is one crop a year). The annual cost, which is what is relevant here, would therefore be higher. And the 10 percent is an "average *minimum*" itself, implying again that the average average is higher. On the other hand, these are losses for tropical countries. They would be smaller in temperate countries—and indeed the same report gives 10 percent as an average (not a minimum) for Rhodesia, ranging up to 52 percent on occasion in hotter places such as India (p. 85).

No changes occurred in the character and cost of barns that would explain the fall in total costs from medieval to early modern times. Even in the sixteenth and early seventeenth centuries, Peter Bowden argues, "adequate storage facilities...were lacking," by which he means "adequate" facilities of modern type (1967, p. 816). M. W. Barley emphasizes a continuity of rural building types extending well into the late sixteenth century. It was houses, not barns, that evinced the prosperity of Elizabethan landlords. Writing of rich yeomen in East Anglia even in the early seventeenth century, he asserts that "while many such men enlarged or modernized their medieval houses, the barns they inherited were often perfectly adequate" (1967, p. 744). In the open field areas of the Midlands and the North, there were still in the seventeenth century "hovels" or "helms" or "belfries," that is, granaries on posts with adjustable roofs: but they had been "a regular feature of Germanic villages in the migration period and later; the adjustable roof is shown in manuscripts of the later Middle Ages" (Barley, p. 744). The timber (and labor) with which one might make a barn fell in price relative to grain by about 50 percent from 1450 to 1650 (Bowden's figures, p. 862), but it would be surprising if the barn costs—except perhaps on account of the high interest rate on the investment in structure—were much of a factor in storage costs to begin with.

The direct testimony on the rate of interest in the Middle Ages is not easy to interpret. The traditional usury limit in England for what amounted to pawnshop loans on good security was 2 pence per pound per week, or 43½ percent per year at simple interest and 54 percent compounded. The figure is reproduced in all discussions of medieval interest rates. So too is the history of the law of usury and its evasion. The prohibition of usury was irrelevant: that the sin of taking interest should be committed frequently is no more surprising than that the sin of adultery was. Interest rates far above 50 or 100 percent were common on personal loans, though the rates on commercial loans among the rich were at more modern levels. It is this division of the market that makes the evidence cloudy. In poor countries, seven centuries later very high interest rates by moneylenders coexisted with subsidized loans at 5 or 10 percent from government agencies (U Tun Wai, 1956, 1957). What seems clear about the European experience is that, at least in the portion of the market in which ordinary peasant cultivators found themselves, the early modern period witnessed a great fall of interest rates. By the late seventeenth century in Lincolnshire, for example, probate inventories attest that "nearly everyone with surplus cash appears to have let out at interest," at only 4½ to 6 percent per year, when rates in London were 5 percent (B. A. Holderness, 1975, pp. 108, 97). At the *haute finance* end of the scale, there is a halving of the interest rate in Northern Europe from the thirteenth to sixteenth centuries, although the clarity of the fact is muddied by the vagaries of war and the varieties of financial instruments (Sidney Homer, 1977, p. 142).

The evidence from grain prices is in important senses better than that on financial instruments. It is uniform over many centuries. It is available for all parts of Europe. And it is free of default: one cannot default on one's own investment in stored grain, or in whatever investment alternative to stored

grain was the opportunity cost of investing in grain. Such an investment is not, of course, free of risk, for stored grain faces its own hazards. One was taxes, which were assessed (usually in the fall) on any asset the taxgatherer could spot. Another was the risk of a fall in prices, since prices did not march up mechanically. More subtle calculation might extract the premium for the price risk from the data, though such subtleties are hard to take seriously. The variability of grain prices, as was noted earlier, did fall a little, though hardly enough to account for a revolution in the risk premium demanded. A measure of its size would have other uses, in suggesting how medieval people viewed the hazards of life more generally. No matter: even the pure interest rate in the Middle Ages will be found to have been very high.

V. Other Assets, such as Livestock, Reveal a High and Falling Interest Rate

The pricing of any asset embodies the interest rate. Statistics on livestock, for intance, are rich sources of indirect evidence, supporting the conclusion that the medieval interest rate was high and fell sharply by the sixteenth century. The statistics have survived because livestock were worth keeping records on—easy to steal, often put in the care of others, and frequently bought and sold. The data include herd and flock size and composition by sex and age, death rates, slaughter rates, and prices of inputs and outputs (hay, grazing land, straw; labor; milk, cheese, butter; wool, hides). All manner of ratios among these things are governed by the prevailing rate of interest, and can be forced to tell what it was.

One ratio, for example, is of net revenues to the value of the capital invested in animals. It is, of course, the interest rate. On the Crawley, Hampshire estate of the Bishop of Winchester in 26 years, with the requisite facts from 1208–09 to 1254–55, the typical yearly stock of sheep was worth about £56 (on the order of 22 man-years worth). The earnings attributable to the sheep on average each year were £4.2 from animal sales, £14 from wool, £1.5 from pelts, and £5.5 from sheep's cheese, or £25.2 in total. Since Crawley was a market-oriented place devoted largely to sheep raising, it is unlikely that much product was kept unsold for home use. The flock grew its own replacements, which sidesteps the problem of depreciation. The one significant hole in the calculation is the yearly cost of keeping the animals. Sheep are the best case if one is forced to guess, because unlike cattle they do not require intense husbandry animal-by-animal and, unlike horses, they do not (except lambs) require feed grain. The interest rate on this reckoning is 45 percent (or a little under if allowance is made for labor, grazing, and fencing costs).

A calculation that skirts the difficulty of knowing costs of upkeep asks how much interest rates fell. The claim is that the sixteenth century witnessed a great fall in interest rates. Bowden's indexes of prices of sheepish things (see p. 848ff) rise during the great inflation of the Long Sixteenth Century from 1450–99 ($=100$) to 1640–49 thus: sheep themselves, the capital good, to 681; the revenues from using the capital good, wool and sheepskins, to 396 and 372; the costs of using it, hay and straw, to 768 and 612. Note that revenue fell relative to costs. Consider that the interest earnings on an investment in one sheep are equal to annual revenue minus cost of upkeep: $iP = R - C$. By advanced algebra it follows that $i = R/P - C/P$. The change in interest, i, must equal the change of the ratios on the right. Wool and sheepskins are revenue, and fall to one-half their former value relative to the price of sheep. Hay and straw are costs, and stay the same relative to sheep (never mind labor, which falls even sharper than wool but is not a large input). If C were known, as is R and P, there would be no trick to finding i. It is not. But knowing the terminal i and the initial R is enough. Suppose (as would be easy to show) that, by 1640–49, the interest rate was, say, 15 percent on such an investment as one sheep. Take the price of that sheep to be the numeraire (thus its price is always 1.00), take the annual revenues before the fall in interest rates to be .45 relative to the price of 1.00 (recall that this was in fact the early thirteenth century ratio at Crawley), and take the fall in revenues to be a fall to one-half this level (as the price indexes imply). Thus in 1640–49, after the fall,

$$.15 = .225/1.0 - C/1.0,$$

where the .225 is half of the original .45. The value of C after the sixteenth century must be .075. The price indexes imply that it did not change relative to the price of sheep. Before the fall of relative revenues, then, the interest earnings were $2(.225) - .075 = 37.5$ percent, as against 15 percent after. The interest rate, as usual, is well above 30 percent.

This conjuring trick would warrant no great confidence standing alone. It does, however, serve to confirm the high net interest found by other methods (and, incidentally, the low costs of upkeep C per sheep relative to the medieval values of R). A more sturdy statistic, and another variation on the theme that cattle are capital more than merely etymologically, is the ratio of the hire rate to the price. A milk cow, in particular, sold for 10 shillings or so in the thirteenth and fourteenth centuries, while renting on various terms for anything from 4 to $6\frac{2}{3}$ shillings (Rogers, 1866, pp. 361, 397; 1884, p. 94, and Dorothea Oschinsky, p. 427). Roughly speaking, the figures imply interest rates from 40 to 67 percent per year. But dividing rent by price is too crude. For one thing, the owner paid for the feed (see Rogers, p. 94), so as usual the calculation runs afoul of the cost of upkeep. For another, cows were not immortal. The second point can be handled by cutting off the stream of discounted returns at the 4- or 5-year average working life of a cow. The price-rental ratio for an asset with a life of n years at an interest rate of i is $(1/i)[1 - 1/(1+i)^n]$. A price-rental ratio of 2 (price of 10s. and rental of 5s., not allowing for deductions for feed) and a life of 4 years implies an interest rate of 35 percent.

Other approaches are possible, though not pursued here. Calves grow up to be "hoggasters" and *bovetti* (heifers), and thence cows and oxen: the project of letting them grow must earn the rate of interest. The death of mature cattle and sheep is not usually an accident (though it should be remembered that cattle were raised chiefly to pull plows, not to fill plates): the optimal slaughter date also depends on the rate of interest. Plow-teams were rented: the rental-price ratio reflects the rate of interest. Land itself was both rented and sold: being a perpetuity, the rental-price ratio is the rate of interest. (By the seventeenth century, in France land often rented for 5 percent of its sale price.) It is to be expected that all these will show a remarkably high interest rate in the thirteenth century and a low rate by the sixteenth century.

VI. The Significance of High Medieval Interest Rates

The hero—or villain—of the tale, in short, is the rate of interest. A fall of interest rates from, say, something over 20 percent to something under 10 or 12 percent must have been significant for the history of Europe and for the onset of modern economic growth. An economist can easily believe this. But it is unclear exactly how it was significant. If interest rates were so high, why were Europeans so poor? A few years of moderate abstention from consumption invested at over 20 percent would make a man rich. True, men of all sorts, bond and free, did in fact scale the social ladder quickly in the Middle Ages. The economy and society are known now to have been much more fluid than was once thought. But the point is that the whole society could and would have done so. Perhaps as is commonly argued nowadays in poor countries the menu of opportunities dropped off sharply in quality after the first few items. Low savings rates might explain it, too, though the lack of savings in medieval times is easy to misapprehend. Peasants worked hard at ploughing fallow land and cleaning ditches in aid of yields quite far removed, and this was saving. Since the yield to seed ratios in the Middle Ages was only 4 or so grains returned from each planted, a quarter of the yield had to go back into the ground as investment in seed. On both counts (food being most of income), the saving entailed by medieval agriculture was enormous, albeit brief and direct. Medieval people saved a lot.

A more conclusive line of argument among several possible is that high interest rates made it difficult for peasants to depend on

the capital market at all. The reasoning is that loans would be sought before the harvest and paid back after. In the meantime the price of grain would fall, by some 30 percent in a normal year, and much more after the very years of dearth in which most loans would be made. Money that bought little grain before the harvest would have to be earned back by the borrower after the harvest by selling the grain just grown at prices that bought little money. John Waryn of Oxford borrowing 10 shilling on February 1, 1322 to buy 8 bushels of rye might pay back the debt six months later at a monthly rate of 2 percent in money, the rate earned on stored grain. But the price of rye per bushel might have fallen after the harvest from 10 shillings to 7 shillings for 8 bushels. In fact it usually did. To pay back the $10 (1.02)^6 = 11.26$ shillings on August 1, he would have to have given up $11.26 (8/7) = 12.87$ bushels of his new crop. For the 8 bushels on January 1, he would pay 12.87 bushels on July 1. The monthly interest rate is not the monetary 2 percent (27 percent per year) but 8.2 percent a month, an unpayable 260 percent per year. If the price fall after the harvest were smaller, say the 12 percent that becomes typical in early modern times, then the real interest rate is 56 percent per year, no small rate but at least potentially payable. The effect of improved storage (itself an effect of the fall in money interest rates) was to cut radically the commodity rate of interest. Before the cut, the peasant was forced back on expensive methods of self-insurance such as scattering of strips in order to avoid having to borrow. All manner of medieval institution —even serfdom itself—can be viewed as replacements for an expensive capital market. Loans among peasants were by no means unknown in medieval times, especially late medieval times (Elaine Clark, 1981). But, by the sixteenth century, they were common, the custom of scattering strips was beginning its long decline, and other medieval institutions were being cleared away.

There is one more point about the relations of medieval villagers revealed by their interest rates. If interest rates in terms of money were at the levels reported here, and higher in terms of bread, the brotherly image of the medieval countryside once taught in school and still taught in Hollywood becomes cloudy. Where is Jack's brother peasant when Jack must borrow from the moneylender at 27 percent in money and well over 100 percent in real terms to survive? The point is one more among many against the myth of the medieval community, that charming product of nineteenth-century German scholarship and speculation on the Middle Ages. The myth of the *Markgenosse*, a putative community of free Germanic citizens, and all that is alleged to follow from it has been under attack for three-quarters of a century. By now most medievalists agree with David Herlihy that "research has all but wiped from the ledgers the supposed gulf, once considered fundamental, between a medieval manorial economy and the capitalism of the modern period" (1971, pp. 154–55). So too the supposed gulf in attitudes towards one's neighbors. "You know, Ernest, the very poor in the Middle Ages were different from you and me." "Yes, Scotty, they were poorer," because of the interest on corn.

REFERENCES

Barley, M. W., "Rural Housing in England," in J. Thirsk, ed., *The Agrarian History of England and Wales*, Vol. IV, *1500–1640*, Cambridge: Cambridge University Press, 1967, 696–766.

Beveridge, W. H., "The Yield and Price of Corn in the Middle Ages," *Economic History*, May 1927, *1*, 155–67.

_____, Papers of the Project on Price History, London School of Economics, 1925–30.

Bowden, Peter, "Statistical Appendix, A: Prices of Agricultural Commodities," in J. Thirsk, *The Agrarian History of England and Wales*, Vol. IV, *1500–1640*, Cambridge: Cambridge University Press, 1967, 814–55.

Clark, Elaine, "Debt Litigation in a Late Mediaeval Village," in J. A. Raftis, ed., *Pathways to Medieval Peasants*, Toronto: Pontifical Institute of Mediaeval Studies, 1981, Papers in Mediaeval Studies 2,

247–82.

Duby, Georges, *Rural Economy and Country Life in the Medieval West*, Columbia: University of South Carolina Press, 1968 (originally published in French, 1962).

Fenoaltea, Stefano, "Risk, Transaction Cost, and the Organization of Medieval Agriculture," *Explorations in Economic History*, April 1970, *13*, 129–51.

Gras, N. S. B., *The Economic and Social History of an English Village*, Cambridge: Harvard University Press, 1930.

Heckscher, Eli F., *An Economic History of Sweden*, Cambridge: Harvard University Press, 1963 (originally published in Swedish, 1941).

Herlihy, David, "The Economy of Traditional Europe," *Journal of Economic History*, March 1971, *31*, 153–64.

Holderness, B. A., "Credit in a Rural Community, 1660–1800," *Midland History*, No. 2, 1975, *3*, 94–115.

Homer, Sidney, *A History of Interest Rates*, 2d ed., New Brunswick: Rutgers University Press, 1977.

Laslett, Peter, *The World We have Lost: England Before the Industrial Age*, New York: Charles Scribner's, 1965.

Lucas, Henry S., "The Great European Famine of 1315, 1316, and 1317," *Speculum*, 1930, reprinted in E. M. Carus-Wilson, ed., *Essays in Economic History*, Vol. II, London: Edward Arnold, 1962, 49–72.

McCloskey, Donald N., "English Open Fields as Behavior Towards Risk," in P. Uselding, ed., *Research in Economic History*, Vol. 1, Greenwich: JAI Press, 1976, 124–70.

Oschinsky, Dorothea, *Walter of Henley and Other Treatises on Estate Management and Accounting*, Oxford: Clarendon, 1971.

Rogers, J. E. Thorold, *The History of Agriculture and Prices in England*, Vol. I, London, 1866.

_____, *Six Centuries of Work and Wages*, London, 1884.

Schultz, Theodore W., *Transforming Traditional Agriculture*, New Haven: Yale University Press, 1964.

Searle, Eleanor, personal correspondence, 1982.

Sisam, Celia and Sisam, Kenneth, *The Oxford Book of Medieval English Verse*, Oxford: Clarendon, 1970.

Thirsk, Joan, *The Agrarian History of England and Wales*, Vol. IV, *1500–1640*, Cambridge: *Cambridge University Press*, 1967.

Titow, J. Z., *English Rural Society 1200–1350*, London: Allen and Unwin, 1969.

Tun Wai, U, "Interest Rates in the Organized Money Markets of Underdeveloped Countries," *International Monetary Fund Staff Papers*, August 1956, *5*, 249–78.

_____, "Interest Rates Outside the Organized Money Markets of Undeveloped Countries," *International Monetary Fund Staff Papers*, November 1957, *6*, 80–142.

National Academy of Sciences, Board on Science and Technology for International Development, *Postharvest Food Loss*, Washington, 1978.

U.S. Bureau of the Census, *Historical Statistics of the United States, Colonial Times to 1970, Bicentennial Edition*, Part 2, Washington: USGPO, 1975.

[5]

1780–1860: a survey

Donald McCloskey

Introduction

The heart of the matter is twelve. Twelve is the factor by which real income per head nowadays exceeds that around 1780, in Britain and in other countries that have experienced modern economic growth (for the international comparisons Maddison 1991; for Britain itself Feinstein 1978, 1988 and Crafts 1985a).

Such statistics are of course not perfect. What is measured by 'real income per head' does not measure all of human happiness and does not measure what it measures perfectly well. The techniques of national income were not designed for such remote comparisons: goods and services unimaginable in 1780 now crowd our lives, from air conditioning to anaesthesia; and on the other side, less weighty, the forests primaeval and the hosts of golden daffodils are rarer, if more cheaply reached. Nor is the income per head divided out perfectly fairly, then or now. But the factor of increase could be nine or fifteen or thirty, rather than twelve, and the distribution of income now less equal than it actually is, and leave the heart of the matter – the logic of the argument – undisturbed. Most conservatively measured, the average person has about twelve times more bread, books, transport and innocent amusement than the average person had two centuries ago. No previous episode of enrichment approaches modern economic growth – not China or Egypt in their primes, not the glory of Greece or the grandeur of Rome.

Observations and predictions

Britain was of course first. And Britain was also first in the study of economics, from the political arithmeticians of the seventeenth century through David Hume, Adam Smith, T. R. Malthus, David Ricardo, John Stuart Mill to the modern masters, Marshall, Keynes and Hicks. Economics was for long a British, even disproportionately a Scottish, subject. What is odd is that the British economists did not recognise the

242

factor of twelve as it was happening. The economists' theories took useful account of little changes – a 5 per cent rise of income when cotton textiles grew or a 10 per cent fall when Napoleon ruled the Continent. But they did not notice that the change to be explained, 1780 to 1860, was not 10 per cent but 100 per cent, on its way to 1,100 per cent. Only recently has the enquiry into the nature and causes of the wealth of nations begun to recognise this astonishing oversight.

Between 1780 and 1860, dates covering the classic 'industrial revolution' (a dispute breaks out from time to time about the drama in the term, but it survives in use), British national income per head doubled – this even though population also more than doubled. A much larger nation was much richer per head, the beginning of the factor of twelve.

In his *Essay on the Principle of Population* (1798) the economist T. Robert (as he preferred to be called) Malthus predicted the opposite. Malthus told a great truth about earlier history. In medieval England a rising population had become poorer and in Shakespearean England the impoverishment happened again. But in late Georgian and early Victorian England a rising population became richer, much richer. The fact was contrary to every prediction of the economists, those 'dismal scientists', in Carlyle's phrase, who saw nothing in prospect *c*. 1830 but misery for the working man and riches for the rentier.

The economists, in other words, did not notice that something entirely new was happening 1780–1860. As the demographer Wrigley put it recently to the economic historian Cameron, 'the classical economists were not merely unconscious of changes going on about them that many now term an industrial revolution: they were in effect committed to a view of the nature of economics development that ruled it out as a possibility' (personal correspondence, quoted in Cameron forthcoming). At the moment that Adam Smith and John Stuart Mill came to understand an economy in equilibrium the economy grew away from their equilibrium. It was as though an engineer had satisfied himself of the statics that kept a jumbo jet from collapsing as it sat humming on the tarmac, but did not notice when the whole thing proceeded to launch into dynamic flight.

An historian like Thomas Babington Macaulay, respectful of the economics of his day but with a longer view, could see the event better than could most of the economists. He wrote in 1830:

If we were to prophesy that in the year 1930 a population of fifty million, better fed, clad, and lodged than the English of our time, will cover these islands, that Sussex and Huntingdonshire will be wealthier than the wealthiest parts of the West Riding of Yorkshire now are, ... that machines constructed on principles yet undiscovered will be in every house, ... many people would think us insane. (1830: I, ii, 185)

244   The economic history of Britain since 1700

It has been customary to deprecate such optimism, and to characterise Macaulay in particular as hopelessly Whiggish and pro-capitalist in his sentiments. That he was, a bourgeois to the core. But Whiggish and pro-capitalist or not he was correct, down to his estimate of British population in 1930 (if one includes the recently separated Irish Republic, he was off by less than 2 per cent). The pessimists of his times – both economists and anti-economists – were wrong.

In the suggestive jargon of statistics, the startling rise of income 1780 to the present can be called the 'first moment', the *average* change. There is little historical disagreement about the first moment, at least in its order of magnitude. Macaulay was correct in prospect and so are the dozens of economic statisticians who have confirmed it in retrospect. Few doubt that by the third decade of Victoria's rule the ordinary subject was better off than eighty years before, and was about to become still better off (Lindert and Williamson 1983a).

The *second* moment is the variability of the change, its pattern of acceleration and deceleration. Second moments are more difficult to measure. You can know the average height of British women more exactly than you can know its variability. As Kuznets, the economist who pioneered the historical study of national income, once said, perhaps too gloomily, during our period 'the data are not adequate for testing hypotheses concerning the time patterns of growth rates' (1971: 41–2). An error of plus or minus 20 per cent in measuring income *c*. 1800 may not matter much for the 1,100 percentage points of change down to the present, but will matter a great deal in deciding whether working people paid for the French Wars (see ch. 13).

The second moment, in other words, is the detail of the factor of twelve, and around it the debates of British economic history gather. Has Britain done well since 1980? Did mass unemployment during the 1920s and 1930s check its growth? Did late Victorian Britain fail? And for present purposes, when exactly did the factor of twelve begin? Kuznets wrote early in the research, and we have found new sources and methods since he wrote, but the violence of controversy about such second-moment questions tends to confirm his view.

In the growth of British industry there was at least a before and after, if not a sharp discontinuity. Various emblematic dates have been proposed, down to the famous day and year: 9 March 1776, when Adam Smith's *The Nature and Causes of the Wealth of Nations* provided an ideology for the age; the five months in 1769 when Watt took out a patent on the separate condenser in his steam engine and Arkwright took out a patent on the water frame for spinning cotton; or 1 January 1760, when the furnaces at Carron Ironworks, Stirlingshire, were lit.

It sometimes seems that each economic historian has a favourite date, and a story to correspond. Carus-Wilson spoke of 'an industrial revolution of the thirteenth century': she found that the fulling mill was 'due to scientific discoveries and changes in technique' and 'was destined to alter the face of medieval England' (1941:41). Bridbury found in the late middle ages 'a country travelling slowly along the road ... that [it] travelled so very much more quickly in Adam Smith's day' (1975:xix–xx). In the eyes of Marxist writers the sixteenth was the century of discontinuity, when capitalism set off into the world to seek its fortune. Nef, no Marxist, believed he saw an industrial revolution in the same century, depending on coal (1932), though admittedly it slowed in the seventeenth century. A student of the seventeenth century itself, such as Coleman (1977), finds glimmerings of economic growth even in that disordered age.

Wider perspectives are possible, encouraging the observer to see continuity instead. Looking at the matter from 1907, the American historian Adams could see a 'movement from unity into multiplicity, between 1200 and 1900, ... unbroken in sequence, and rapid in acceleration' (1907: 498). Jones and Mokyr have taken a similar long view of European exceptionalism (Jones 1981, 1988; Mokyr 1990a). The principal modern student of the age of industrialisation, Hartwell, appealed against the jostling throng of dates (1965: 78): 'Do we need an *explanation* of the industrial revolution? Could it not be the culmination of a most unspectacular process, the consequence of a long period of economic growth?' Cameron has thrown up his hands in the face of such confusion, arguing that the very idea of an industrial revolution – so named early in the nineteenth century in explicit imitation of the upheavals of the French Revolution – is an obstacle to thought (1990 and forthcoming).

The most widely accepted period for It, whatever exactly It was that led to the factor of twelve, is the late eighteenth century, within which some emphasise the 1760s and 1770s (Mantoux 1928; Landes 1969), others later. Rostow (1960) placed the 'takeoff into self-sustained growth' in the last two decades of the eighteenth century. The dating held through the great work of Deane and Cole (1962; and the parallel project, Mitchell and Deane 1962), which first undertook comprehensive measurement. Deane and Cole, however, for all their excellences, had to build on existing evidence, especially the evidence on foreign trade and on Hoffmann's pioneering index of industrial output. The main statistical finding after their work, in the 1980s, was that the sharpness of the take-off in Britain was exaggerated by the pioneering generation of quantifiers. True, growth could be faster for the late comers. Italy and Switzerland could adopt what Britain and Belgium had invented. But the first industrial nation, rather unsurprisingly, was slow in coming. A hard coming we had of it.

The slowness is documented in the important work of Crafts (1985a) and Harley (1982). They discovered that the indexes of industrial growth put too much weight on the fastest-growing sectors. In particular, Harley noted that in Hoffmann's index the cotton textile industry, growing explosively in the 1780s and 1790s, is given more weight than its size warrants. The overweighting of cotton, Harley argues, makes an interesting sector into an important sector before its time. The bias imparted to the figures is similar to the bias from non-quantitative sources. Without some way of measuring the importance of an industry a qualitative narrative will naturally focus on its early heroes, overweighting the importance of the industry because of its later prominence. The heroism of the cotton industry came when it was devoted chiefly to producing muslin shawls for ladies of fashion. Similarly, an index like Hoffmann's overweights the early years of cotton, during which the cotton grew heroically fast, but when, after all, the industry was nothing like as important in the life of the nation as it later became.

Still, the larger change must start somewhere, and the individual industry is the place to start. As the great student of European industrialisation, Alexander Gerschenkron, once remarked,

If the seat of the great spurt lies in the area of manufacturing, it would be inept to try to locate the discontinuity by scrutinizing data on large aggregate magnitudes such as national income ... By the time industry has become bulky enough to affect the larger aggregate, the exciting period of the great spurt may well be over. (1962b: 34–5)

In a footnote he remarks that 'Walt Rostow's failure to appreciate this point has detracted greatly from his concept of the take-off.'

In other words, small beginnings (exciting as they are, perhaps over-exciting) will be hidden by the mass until well after they have become routine. Mokyr has put it as a matter of arithmetic: if the older sector of an economy is growing at a slow 1 per cent per annum, and starts with 90 per cent of output, then by mere arithmetic the modern sector, growing at 4 per cent per annum, will take three-quarters of a century to account for as much as half of output (1985c: 5). We may call it the Weighting Theorem (or the Waiting Theorem, for the wait is long when the weight is small to begin with).

Gerschenkron was hoist by his own petard. For Italian industrial output he placed his 'big spurt' in the period 1896–1908, and wished to explain it with big banks founded in the 1890s. Stefano Fenoaltea, briefly his student, applied the Weighting Theorem to the case. Surely, Fenoaltea reasoned, the components of the industrial index – the steel output and the chemical output – are the 'real' units of economic analysis. If the components started accelerating *before* the new banks appeared, becoming bulky only later, then the new banks could not have been the initiating force. The components did just this, spoiling Gerschenkron's bank-led story: the components accelerated not in the 90s but in the 80s, not after but before the banks.

Crafts (1977b) has pointed out that the detailed timing of the beginnings of modern economic growth should not anyway be the thing to be studied, because small beginnings do not come labelled with their probabilities of developing into factors of twelve. He is identifying a pitfall in storytelling. If the onset of modern economic growth fed on itself, then its start could be a trivial accident. Yet one might wonder why then it did not happen before. 'Sensitive dependence on initial conditions' is the technical term for some 'nonlinear' models – a piece of so-called 'chaos theory'. But history under such circumstances becomes untellable (McCloskey 1991).

Mokyr identifies another pitfall in storytelling (1985c: 44): rummaging among the possible acorns from which the great oak of the industrial revolution grew 'is a bit like studying the history of Jewish dissenters between 50 BC and 50 AD. What we are looking at is the inception of something which was at first insignificant and even bizarre', though 'destined to change the life of every man and woman in the West'. What is destined or not destined to change our lives will look rather different to each of us. Mokyr pointed out later (1993) that the destiny was not unified, and is therefore not well explained by a dice throw: the industrial revolution was not one event but a set of loosely related events, a trick in steam engines here, a new dock there. Something more widespread than mere chance was going on.

The slow-growth findings from Harley and Crafts do not mean that British income was low absolutely, or in any way disgraceful, merely that it grew at a stately pace. British economic development – like British population growth in the recent revisions (ch. 4) above – is therefore spread back into the early eighteenth century. The revision, again, affects the second moment, the pattern of industrial development over time, not its size in total. The factor of twelve remains; what is in dispute is whether much of it happened in a few decades in the late eighteenth century, as once believed. Again we see the difficulties with getting exact measures of the second as distinct from the first moment.

Economic and industrial structure

In any case the historians have long known that Britain was no factory in 1860. Mokyr's Weighting Theorem asserts itself: even cotton textiles, growing apace, could not absorb all the many workers in agriculture and other trades less immediately affected by the machine age. Clapham made the point in 1926, observing that still in 1850 half the population was in employment untouched by 'the first industrial revolution'. Musson's figures imply, as Cameron notes (forthcoming), that steam power in Britain increased by a factor of fully ten from 1870 to 1907, long after the dark satanic mills first enter British consciousness (Musson 1978: 8, 61, 167–8). Clapham, indeed, eschewed the very phrase 'industrial revolution', although he would not have denied that something portentous happened 1780–1860. The statistical revisionists of the 1980s, Harley and Crafts, constitute so to speak a Claphamite sect.

The Claphamite view, in summary, is that industrial change was a slow turning, no revolution if that means short and sharp. Perhaps, to get back to the puzzle, that is why it was largely invisible to economists and some others watching it – though not to many possessed of common sense and eyes to see. Macaulay wrote in 1830, 'A single breaker may recede; but the tide is evidently coming in' (1830: 185). It was not 'evident' to many classical economists, who were predicting when Macaulay wrote that landlords would take all the increase, leaving the workers in precisely the condition they began. The first edition of this book (1981) called it 'The Quiet Revolution'. By now in the thinking of economic historians the revolution is still quieter, but longer and more impressive:

> For while the tired waves, vainly breaking,
>   Seem here no painful inch to gain,
> Far back, through creeks and inlets making,
>   Comes silent, flooding in, the main.

The new estimates by Feinstein and Pollard (1988), Crafts and Harley imply a growth in what people got for their effort of a trifle over half a per cent per year, a little faster in the late eighteenth century, a little slower in the early nineteenth. (The deceleration after 1800 – the second moment again – is not surprising, considering the acceleration of population growth and an expensive war against the French.) The British people also saved and added to their equipment. All told their income per head rose at about 1 per cent per year. It takes something growing at 1 per cent a year seventy-two years to double.

It took a long time, then, at the slow rates of growth that characterised British industrialisation, to transform the economy. The fact does not make the old and new sectors into what is known in development economics as a 'dual economy'. Though Britain did come at last to have many factories, there is nothing intrinsically unprogressive about non-manufacturing sectors. For example, Karl Marx sneered at the 'idiocy of rural life,' but Britain's rural life at the time was notably unidiotic, economically speaking, at least by comparison with agriculture on the Continent. In later Victorian times it was to become technologically sophisticated, by any standard (vol. 2, ch. 6). Similarly the French physiocrats, a century before Marx, had asserted that services are somehow less genuinely productive than the making of things in factories (and that factories after all merely transform the Fundamental Goods: agricultural goods). The notion that agriculture for one reason and services for another are by nature less progressive or important has had a long life, surviving into present politics. But it is false economically, and false when applied to western European industrialisation (vol. 2, ch. 5). Danish industrialisation was led by butter, for example, Norway's by shipping services, Sweden's by timber. It just happened that Britain's was led by manufacturing.

As Berg (ch. 6 and 1985) and Hudson (1986, 1989) have noted, some technologically stagnant sectors (building, say) saw large expansion, some progressive sectors little or none (paper); some industries working in large-scale units did little to change their techniques (naval shipyards early in the period), some in tiny firms were brilliant innovators (the metal trades). Big factories in the famous sectors were not the whole of the factor of twelve.

Productivity change

The wider point notwithstanding, productivity change was fast in sectors like cotton textiles, 1780–1860. We do not have industrial censuses in Britain until well after the event (1907), and so it would appear impossible to measure productivity industry-by-industry. We can know roughly what the aggregate equipment of the nation was and how it grew (vol. 3, ch. 4; Feinstein 1978; Feinstein and Pollard, 1988). But we do not know for most industries – coal mining, for example, or pottery – how output or employment grew until well into the nineteenth century. Knowing productivity change by industry therefore would appear to be out of reach. It appears that Kuznets' gloom is justified: 'the data are not adequate for testing hypotheses concerning the time patterns of growth rates'.

But wait. We can some day, if not at present, know the details of productivity change sector-by-sector during the period, though the knowledge will require more archival research. We do not know annual quantities of china plates and steam coal, admittedly, and probably never can. On the other hand, we know practically anything we choose about the *price*. Britain was in 1800 (as in truth it had been since the danegeld) a thoroughly monetised society, with prices for everything, many of which have survived in the records of Eton, All Souls College and a hundred other archives. The technique is to measure physical productivity change

250   The economic history of Britain since 1700

Table 10.1. *The fall in the real cost of cotton cloth, 1780–1860*

	Real cost index	Annual percentage growth of productivity
c. 1780	100	
c. 1812–15	32	3·4
c. 1860	13	2·0

by the changes in prices. The two measures, physical and price-based, are connected by definition, because the value of output must be the same as the value of inputs. Productivity can therefore be measured either on the physical side (output per unit of physical input) or on the value side (real costs).

To illustrate: a piece of cotton cloth that was sold in the 1780s for 70 or 80s was by the 1850s selling for around 5s. In the process cotton cloth moved from fashionable to commonplace, in the manner a century and a half later of nylon (first called 'artificial silk') and other synthetics. A little of the decline in the price of finished cotton cloth was attributable to declines in the prices of raw cotton itself after the introduction of the cotton gin (invented in 1793) and the resulting expansion of cotton plantations in America. But in other ways the price of inputs rose: by 1860, for example, wages of cotton workers had risen markedly. Why then did the price of manufactured cloth fall? It fell because organisation and machinery were massively improved in cotton textiles, 1780 to 1860. The degree to which the price of the cloth fell relative to the price of the inputs is therefore a measure of productivity change. *Quod erat demonstrandum.*

The real costs of cotton cloth, after allowing for the changing prices of inputs, are shown in Table 10.1. In other words, cotton cloth was made with 13 per cent of the real resources in 1860 that it had been made with in 1780. Or, to put it in physical terms, productivity had increased by a factor of $100/13 = 7.7$ times. (The expression and the idea of 'real cost' are the invention of the first modern historical economist, a student of Clapham's named G. T. Jones. Jones invented what is now known as 'total factor productivity measurement' a quarter century before it was reinvented, in ignorance of Jones, by Moses Abramowitz and Robert Solow. For a demonstration that Jones' measures are precisely the 'price dual' of the measures of productivity change see McCloskey 1973: 103n.)

The case is typical in showing more about the second moment than one might at first think knowable. It shows for example that productivity growth slowed in cotton, because power weaving – which came late – was apparently less important than power carding of the raw wool and power spinning of the wool into yarn. And it shows that invention is not the same thing as innovation (ch. eleven; cf. Chapman and Butt 1988). The heroic age of invention ended by the late 1780s, by which time Hargreaves, Arkwright, Kay, Crompton and Cartwright had flourished. But the inventions saw steady improvement later – one of the main findings of quantitative economic history is that the pattern is typical, invention being only the first step (the same is true, for example, of railways, which improved in scores of small ways down to the twentieth century, with large falls in real costs). The real cost of cotton textiles had halved by the end of the eighteenth century. But it was to halve twice more down to 1860.

Few sectors were as progressive as cotton textiles. Productivity in iron grew a half to a third as fast. Productivity is not the same as production. The production of iron increased enormously in Britain 1780 to 1860 – by a factor of 56, in fact, or at 5.5 per cent per year (Davies and Pollard 1988; 'small' growth rates, as you might think 5.5 is, make for big factors if allowed to run on: 5.5 per cent is explosive industrial growth by historical standards, a doubling every $72/5.5 = 13.2$ years). The expanding British industry crowded out the iron imported from Sweden and proceeded to make Britain the world's forge. But the point is that it did so mainly by applying a somewhat improved technology (puddling) to a much wider field, not by the spectacular and continuous falls in cost that cotton witnessed. The cost of inputs to iron (mainly coal) changed little from 1780 to 1860; during the same span the price of the output (wrought-iron) fell from £20 a ton to £8 a ton. The fall in real costs, again, is a measure of productivity change. So productivity in wrought-iron making increased by a factor of about 2.5, an admirable factor of change. Yet over the same years the productivity in cotton textiles, we have seen, increased by a factor of 7.7.

Other textiles imitated the innovations in cotton (Hudson 1986), significantly cheapening their products, though less rapidly than the master industry of the age: as against cotton's 2.6 per cent productivity growth per year, worsteds (wool cloth spun into a thin yarn and woven flat, with no nap to the cloth) experienced 1.8 per cent and woollens 0.9 per cent (McCloskey 1981b: 114). Coastal and foreign shipping experienced rates of productivity growth similar to those in cotton textiles (some 2.3 per cent per year as compared with 2.6 in cotton). The figure is derived from North's estimates for transatlantic shipping during the period, rising to 3.3 per cent per year 1814–60 (1968). Again the 'low' percentage is in fact large in its cumulative effects: freights and passenger fares fell like a stone, from an index of around 200 after the Napoleonic Wars to 40 in the 1850s. Canals and railways experienced productivity growth of about 1.3 per cent

(Hawke 1970). Transportation was therefore among the more notably progressive parts of the economy.

But many other sectors, like iron as we have seen, experienced slower productivity growth. In agriculture the productivity change was slower still (ch. 5), dragging down the productivity of the economy as a whole; taking one year with another 1780–1860, agriculture was still nearly a third of national income. Productivity change varied radically from one part of the economy to the other, as it has continued to do down to the present, one sector taking the lead in driving up the national productivity while another settles into a routine of fixed technique. Agriculture itself, for example, came to have rapid productivity change in the age of the reaper and the steam tractor (vol. 2, ch. 5), and still more in the age of genetic engineering in the twentieth century. But from 1780 to 1860 textiles and transport were the leaders.

Such methods of analysis might be applied more widely, and would discipline thinking about when and where the quickening of industrial growth happened. For instance: iron machinery doubtless made possible the faster running speeds of the second and third generations of textile machines, and so iron was important in the nineteenth century as an input (ch. 11); but the industry producing the iron was not especially important. The value of iron's output relative to national income 1780–1860 was only 2 per cent.

The archival materials for seeing how productivity grew industry-by-industry are ample: prices are among the most abundant of historical statistics; an historian of ancient Mesopotamia will complain to his colleague in economic history that the cuneiform tablets are '90 per cent prices'. The collection of price statistics has been a low priority, mainly because economic historians think of the prices as useful only for calculating the standard of living. The price measure of productivity allows the prices to be used to see how the living was obtained in detail. Lindert and Williamson have done well in exploiting governmental sources (ch. 14; Lindert and Williamson 1983a; Williamson 1985), finding the wages for a range of service workers from porters to doctors (though again in aid of calculations of the standard of living). They 'urge other scholars to harvest additional wage series from the archives' (Mokyr 1985b: 183), a suggestion which can be seconded. It is a trifle scandalous that the wage estimates marching and countermarching in impossible intellectual campaigns are as old as Gilboy's (1934) for the eighteenth century and Wood's (1910) and Bowley's (1900) for the nineteenth. The price statistics are almost as old. Again Lindert and Williamson have recently improved them, by adding rents (from which one could calculate productivity change in housing per year; Jones in 1933 calculated it for housing construction) – although, as they remark, the evidential basis is slim. The collection of prices should be a high priority, in Tycho Brahean quantities. To write the history of the period without detailed prices of inputs and outputs is like studying astronomy without detailed descriptions of stars.

Some economic historians, incidentally, have formed the impression that using prices to measure productivity requires additional, and dubious, assumptions. The impression is mistaken. Physical productivity change can come from economies of scale or from monopoly. So can change in the price measure. If the price measure is misleading, so is the physical measure, and for the same reasons. In accounting the two are not merely correlated with each other; they are identical. The stars can be observed with a refracting telescope or a reflecting telescope, but are the same stars.

For the edification of the mathematical reader, a simple demonstration can be given for the case of one output and one input. (It can be generalised easily.) With one input, I, costing P_i per unit the total cost is just IP_i. The revenue from output Q at the price P_q is, similarly, QP_q. The two are equal if the accounting for inputs and outputs is complete. And so $IP_i = QP_q$. So of course $P_i/P_q = Q/I$. So the rate of change of physical productivity (which is the rate of change of Q/I) will be the same as the rate of change of the price-measured productivity (which is the rate of change of P_i/P_q). It is no chancy theorem. It is an accounting identity.

The causes of growth

Even without the requisite star maps, though, we now know enough about the second moments of growth to say some things about its causes, 1780–1860. We have learned in the past twenty years of research into the era, to put the findings in a nutshell, that reallocation was not the cause. To put the findings another way, we have learned many Nots: that industrialisation was not a matter of foreign trade, not a matter of internal reallocation, not of transport innovation, not investment in factories, not education, not science. The task of the next twenty years will be to untie the Nots.

Foreign trade

Consider foreign trade. An old tradition carried forward by Rostow and by Deane and Cole puts much emphasis on Britain's foreign and colonial trade as an engine of growth. What the recent research has discovered is that the existence of the rest of the world mattered for the British economy, but not in the way suggested by the metaphor of an 'engine of growth' (O'Brien and Engerman 1991 demur).

What has become increasingly clear from the work of Williamson and Neal (ch. 7; Williamson 1985, 1987, 1990b; Neal 1990) among others is that Britain functioned in an international market for many goods and for investment funds. More exactly, the fact has been rediscovered – it was a commonplace of economic discussion by Ricardo and the rest at the time (it became obscured in economics by the barriers to trade erected during the European Civil War, 1914–45, and aftermath just ended).

By 1780 the capital market of Europe, for example, centred in Holland and England, was sophisticated and integrated, capital flowing with ease from French to Scottish projects. True, the market dealt mainly in government debt. The old finding of Pollard (1964) and others survives: industrial growth was financed locally, out of retained earnings, out of commercial credit for inventories and out of investors marshalled by the local solicitor (Richardson 1989; ch. 7). But 'the' interest rate relevant to local projects was determined by what was happening in wider capital markets, as is plain for example in the sharp rises and falls of enclosure in the countryside with each fall and rise in the rate on Consols (ch. 5). The interest rate in the late eighteenth century also determined booms and busts in canal building. And the interest rate in turn was determined as much by Amsterdam as by London.

The same had long been true of the market in grain and other goods, as David Ricardo assumed in his models of trade *c.* 1817 as though it were obvious. The disruptions of war and blockade masked the convergence from time to time, and regulations – such as the Corn Law (ch. 12) – could sometimes stop it from working. But the European world had a unified market in wheat by the eighteenth century, as is becoming clear. Already in 1967 Braudel and Spooner had shown in their astonishing charts of prices that the percentage by which the European minimum was exceeded by the maximum price fell from 570 per cent in 1440 to a mere 88 per cent in 1760 (1967: 470). Prices continued to converge, a benefit of the rapid growth of productivity already noted in shipping and railways. The same could be said of prices of iron, cloth, wood, coal, skins and the rest of the materials useful to life around 1800. They were beginning to cost roughly the same in St Petersburg as in New York.

The reason the convergence is important is this: an economic history that imagines the British economy in isolation is wrong. If the economy of Europe is determining the price of food, for example, it makes little sense to treat the British food market as though it could set its own prices (except, of course, by protective tariffs: which until the 1840s it imposed). Purely domestic assumptions, such as those around which the controversy over agriculture's role in industrialisation have raged (Ippolito 1975), will stop making sense. The supply and demand for grain in Europe, or indeed the world, not the supply and demand in the British portion of Europe, was setting the prices faced by British farmers in 1780. Likewise for interest rates or the wages of seamen. Centuries earlier the price of gold and silver had become international.

The intrusion of the world market can become so strong that the domestic story breaks down entirely. One can tell a domestic story in the eighteenth century of how much was saved, but not a domestic story of what interest rate it was saved at. One can tell a domestic story in the early nineteenth century of the supply of labour from a slowly growing agricultural sector, but not a domestic story of the entire supply of labour to Liverpool, Glasgow and Manchester, if Ireland is not included. Nots.

Pollard, again, has argued persuasively that for many questions what is needed is a European approach, or at least a north-western European regional approach (Pollard 1973, 1981a; within Britain cf. Hudson 1989 and Crafts 1989a). He wrote in 1973 (Mokyr 1985b: 175), 'the study of industrialization in any given European country will remain incomplete unless it incorporates a European dimension: any model of a closed economy would lack some of its basic and essential characteristics'. The political analogue is that it would be bootless to write a history of political developments in Britain or Italy or Ireland 1789 to 1815 without reference to the French Revolution. Politics became international – not merely because French armies conquered most of Europe but because French political ideas became part of political thinking, whether in sympathy or in reaction. Likewise in economic matters. The world economy from the eighteenth century (and probably before) provided Britain with its framework of relative values, wheat against iron, interest rates against wages.

The point is crucial, to return again to the puzzle, for understanding why the classical economists were so wrong in their dismal predictions. Landlords, they said, would engorge the national product, because land was the limiting factor of production. But the limits on land seen by the classical economists proved unimportant, because north-west Europe gained in the nineteenth century an immense hinterland, from Chicago and Melbourne to Cape Town and Odessa. The remarkable improvement of ocean shipping tied Britain to the world like Gulliver to the ground, by a hundred tiny threads. Grain production in Ukraine and in the American Midwest could by the 1850s begin to feed the cities of an industrial Britain; but the price of wheat in Britain was constrained even earlier.

Trade, then, was important as a context for British growth. Yet it was not an engine of growth (chs. 8 and 12). For the period in question Mokyr makes the clearest case (Mokyr 1985b: 22–3 and works cited there). The underlying argument is that domestic demand could have taken the place of foreign demand (Mokyr earlier (1977) had shown likewise that the shuffling of domestic demand was no more promising). To be sure, Britons could not have worn the amount of cotton textiles produced by Lancashire at its most productive: cotton dhotis for the working people of Calcutta would not have become fashionable at the High Street Marks and Spencer. But in that case the Lancastrians would have done something else. The exporting of cotton cloth is not sheer gain. It comes at the cost of something else that its makers could have done, such as building more houses in Cheshire or making more wool cloth in Yorkshire.

In other words, the primitive conviction most people have that foreign trade is the source of wealth is wrong. Nations, or villages, do not have to trade to live. (The power of the conviction is shown nowadays by the role of fish exports in the political economy of Iceland or of exports generally in that of Japan.) Exports are not the same thing as new income. They are new markets, not new income. They are a shift of attention, not consciousness itself. Not.

The trade, of course, benefits the traders. Although not all the income earned in trade is a net gain, nonetheless there is such a gain. But – here is the nub – the gain can be shown in static terms to be small. One of the chief findings of the 'new' economic history, with its conspicuous use of economic models, is that static gains are small. Fogel's calculation of the social savings from American railways is the leading case (1984, replicated by Hawke in 1970 for Britain with broadly similar results). However essential one may be inclined to think railways were, or how crucial foreign trade to British prosperity, or how necessary the cotton mill to industrial change, the calculations lead to small figures, far below the factor of twelve.

The finding that foreign trade is a case in point, with small static gains, can stand up to a good deal of shaking of the details. Its robustness is a consequence of what is known informally among economists as Harberger's Law (after A. C. Harberger, an economist famous for such calculations). That is, if one calculates a gain amounting to some fraction from a sector that amounts to again a fraction of the national economy one is in effect multiplying a fraction by a fraction. Suppose X per cent of gain comes from a sector with Y per cent of national income. The resulting fraction, X times Y, is smaller than either of its terms. For most sectors and most events – here is the crucial point – the outcome is a small fraction when set beside the 1,100 percentage points of growth to be explained 1780 to the present, or even beside the 100 percentage points of growth to be explained 1780 to 1860.

To take foreign trade as the example, in 1841 the United Kingdom exported some 13 per cent of its national product. From 1698 to 1803 the range up and down of the three-year moving averages of the gross barter terms of trade is a ratio of 1.96, highest divided by lowest (Deane and Cole 1962; Mitchell and Deane 1962: 330); Imlah's net barter terms range over a ratio of 2.32, highest divided by lowest (1958). So the variation of the terms on which Britain traded was about 100 per cent over century-long spans like these. Only 13 per cent of any change in income, then, can be explained by foreign trade, statically speaking: $100 \times 0.13 = 13$. Another Not.

Faced with such an argument the non-economists, and some of the economists, are likely to claim that 'dynamic' effects will retrieve trade as an engine of growth. The word 'dynamic' has a magical quality. Waving it about, however, does not in itself suffice to prove one's economic and historical wisdom. One has to show that the proffered 'dynamic' effect is quantitatively strong.

For example, one might claim that the industries like cotton textiles encouraged by British trade were able to exploit economies of scale, in perhaps the making of textile machinery or the training of master designers. There: a dynamic effect that makes trade have a larger effect than the mere static gain of efficiency. Not Not.

It may be true. And in fact a smaller cotton textile industry would have been less able to take advantage of technological change nationally. After all, cotton was unusually progressive. But is the dynamic effect large?

One can answer the question by a thought experiment. If the cotton textile industry were cut in half by an absence of foreign markets 1780–1860 the importance of cotton in national productivity would have fallen from 0.07 to 0.035. Resources would have had to find other employment. Suppose that the released resources would have experienced productivity growth of 0.5 per cent per year (on the low end of the available possibilities) instead of the princely 2.6 per cent they in fact experienced in cotton. The cotton industry in the actual event contributed a large amount – namely, $(0.07)(2.6 \text{ per cent}) = 0.18$ per cent per year – to the growth of national income; this one giant contributed some 18 per cent of the total growth of income per person nationally 1780–1860. With the hypothetical cut-off of trade the resources would contribute instead $(0.035)(2.6 \text{ per cent}) + (0.035)(0.5 \text{ per cent}) = 0.11$ percentage points a year. The fall in national productivity change can be inferred from the difference between the actual 0.18 per cent attributable to cotton and the hypothetical 0.11 per cent attributable to a half-sized cotton industry and the industries its resources went to. The difference is about a 7 per cent fall in the national rate of productivity change, that is, a fall from (notionally) 1.00 per cent a year to 0.93 per cent a year. In the eighty years 1780–1860 such a lag would cumulate, however, to merely 9 per cent of national income. Remember that a 100 per cent change is to be explained. The dynamic effect sounds promising, but in quantitative terms does not amount to much. Another Not.

A 'dynamic' argument has a problem as an all-purpose intellectual strategy. If someone claims that foreign trade made possible, say, unique economies of scale in cotton textiles or shipping services, she owes it to her readers to tell why the gains on the swings were not lost on the roundabouts. Why do not the industries made *smaller* by the large extension of British foreign trade end up on the losing side? The domestic roads in Shropshire and the factories unbuilt in Greater London because of Britain's increasing specialisation in cotton textiles may themselves have had economies of scale, untapped. (The argument applies later to the worries over 'excessive' British specialisation in foreign investment, insurance and shipping; see vol. 2, chs. 7 and 8).

All this Not-saying is not to say that foreign trade was literally a nullity. Trivially, of course, some goods – the banana for the Englishman's breakfast table was the popular instance late in the nineteenth century, raw cotton the most important instance throughout – simply cannot be had in England's clime. Trade is a conduit of ideas and competitive pressures, as is best shown by the opening of Japan after 1868. And trade insures against famine, as the Raj knew in building the railways of India. A literal closing of trade is not what is contemplated: the question is, was trade a stimulus to growth in the simple, mercantilist way usually contemplated in the literature? Not.

To put the wider Not finding in a sentence: we have not discovered any single factor essential to British industrialisation. Gerschenkron a long time ago argued that the notion of essential prerequisites for economic growth is a poor one (1962a). He gave examples from industrialisation in Russia, Italy, Germany and Bulgaria that showed substitutes for the alleged prerequisites. Big banks in Germany and state enterprises in Russia, for instance, substituted for entrepreneurial ability. The British case provided the backdrop for comparison with other industrialisations. But Gerschenkron's economic metaphor that one thing can 'substitute' for another applies to Britain itself as much as to the other countries. Economists believe, with good reason, that there is more than one way to skin a cat. If foreign trade or entrepreneurship or saving had been lacking, the economist's argument goes, other impulses to growth – with some loss – could conceivably have taken their place. A vigorous domestic trade or a single-minded government or a forced saving from the taxation of agriculture could take the place of the British ideal of merchant-adventurers left alone by government to reinvest their profits in a cotton factory.

Transport

Transportation, for example, is often cast in the hero's role. The static drama is most easily criticised. Canals carrying coal and wheat at a lower price than cartage, better public roads bringing coaching times down to a mere day from London to York, and then the railway steaming into every market town were of course Good Things. But land transportation is never more than 10 per cent of national income – it was something like 6 per cent 1780–1860. Britain was well supplied with coastwise transportation and its rivers flowed gently like sweet Afton when large enough for traffic at all. Even unimproved by river dredging and stone-built harbours, Mother Nature had given Britain a low cost of transportation. The further lowering of cost by canals and railways would be, say, 50 per cent (a figure easily justified by looking at freight rates and price differentials) on the half of traffic not carried on unimproved water – say another 50 per cent. By Harberger's Law, 50 per cent of 50 per cent of 10 per cent will save a mere 2.5 per cent of national income. One would welcome 2.5 per cent of national income as one's personal income; and even spread among the population it is not to be sneezed at. But it is not by itself the stuff of 'revolution'.

Yet did not transportation above all have 'dynamic' effects? It seems not, though historians and economists have quarrelled over the matter and it would be premature to claim that the case is settled (for the pro-transport side see Szostak 1991). A number of points can be made against the dynamic effects. For one thing the attribution of dynamism sometimes turns out to be double counting of the static effect. Historians will sometimes observe with an air of showing the great effects of transport that the canals or the railways increased the value of coal lands or that they made possible larger factories – dynamic effects (the word is protean). But the coal lands and factories are more valuable simply because the cost of transporting their outputs is lower. The higher rents or the larger markets are alternative means of measuring what is the same thing, the fall in the cost of transporting coal or pottery or beer.

For another, some of the dynamic effects would themselves depend on the size of the static, 2.5 per cent effect. For example, if the 'dynamic' effect is that new income is saved, to be reinvested, pushing incomes up still further, the trouble is that the additional income in the first round is small.

For still another, as has already been stressed, the truly dynamic effects may arise from expensive as much as from cheap transportation. Forcing more industry into London in the early nineteenth century, for example, might have achieved economies of scale which were in the event dissipated by the country locations chosen under the regime of low transport costs.

The balance of swings and roundabouts has to be calculated, not merely asserted.

Enclosure

Sector by sector the older heroes have fallen before the march of Notting economists and historians. Marx put great emphasis for instance on the enclosure of open fields, which he claimed enriched the propertied classes and drove workers into the hands of industrialists. By now several generations of agricultural historians have argued, contrary to a Fabian theme first articulated eighty years ago, that eighteenth-century enclosures were equitable and did not drive people out of the villages. True, Parliament became in the eighteenth century an executive committee of the landed classes, and proceeded to make the overturning of the old forms of agriculture easier than it had been. Oliver Goldsmith lamenting The Deserted Village wrote in 1770 that 'Those fenceless fields the sons of wealth divide,/ And even the bare-worn common is denied.' But contrary to the romance of the poem, which reflects poetic traditions back to Horace more than evidence from the English countryside, the commons was usually purchased rather than stolen from the goose.

The result of enclosure was a somewhat more efficient agriculture. But was enclosure therefore the hero of the new industrial age? By no means. The productivity changes were small (McCloskey 1972; Allen 1992; ch. 5), perhaps a 10 per cent advantage of an enclosed village over an open village. Agriculture was a large fraction of national income (shrunk perhaps to a third by 1800), but the share of land to be enclosed was only half (McCloskey 1975; Wordie 1983). Harberger's Law asserts itself again: $(1/3)(1/2)(10 \text{ per cent}) = 1.6$ per cent of national income was to be gained from the enclosure of open fields. Improved road surfaces around and about the enclosing villages (straightening and resurfacing of roads went along with enclosure, but is seldom stressed) might have been more important than the enclosure itself.

Specialisation and the division of labour

Nor was Adam Smith correct that the wealth of the nation depended on the division of labour. To be sure, the economy specialised. Kussmaul's work on rural specialisation shows it happening from the sixteenth century onward (ch. 1). Berg and Hudson (ch. 6; Hudson 1989) have emphasised that modern factories need not have been large, yet the factories nonetheless were closely divided in their labour. Most enterprises were tiny, and accomplished the division of labour through the market, as Smith averred. It has long been known that metal working in Birmingham and the Black Country was broken down into hundreds of tiny firms, anticipating by two centuries the 'Japanese' techniques of just-in-time inventory and thorough sub-contracting. Division of labour certainly did happen, widely.

That is to say, the proper dividing of labour was, like transport and enclosure, efficient. Gains were to be had, which suggests why they were seized. But a new technique of specialisation can be profitable to adopt yet lead to only a small effect on productivity nationally – look again at the modest, if by no means unimportant, productivity changes from the puddling and rolling of iron. The gains were modest in the absence of dynamic effects, because the static gains from more complete specialisation are limited by Harberger's Law.

A similar thought experiment shows the force of the argument. Specialisation in the absence of technological change can be viewed as the undoing of bad locations for production. Some of the heavy clay soil of the midlands was put down to grazing, which suited it better than wheat. Or the labour of the Highlands was ripped off the land, to find better employment – higher wages, if less Gaelic spoken – in Glasgow or New York. The size of the reallocation effect can be calculated. Suppose a quarter of the labour of the country were misallocated. And suppose the misallocation were bad enough to leave, say, a 50 per cent wage gap between the old sector and the new. This would be a large misallocation. Now imagine the labour moves to its proper industry, closing the gap. As the gap in wages closes the gain shrinks, finally to zero. So the gain from closing it is so to speak a triangle (called in economics, naturally, a Harberger Triangle), whose area is half the rectangle of the wage gap multiplied by the amount of labour involved. So again: $(1/2)(1/4)(50$ per cent$) = 6.25$ per cent of labour's share of national income, which might be half, leaving a 3 per cent gain to the whole. The gain, as usual, is worth having, but is not itself the stuff of revolutions. The division of labour: Not.

Natural resources

Geography is still another Not. Some economic historians (e.g. Wrigley 1988) continue to put weight on Britain's unusual gifts from Nature. It must be admitted that coal correlates with early industrialisation: the coal-bearing swath of Europe from Midlothian to the Ruhr started early on industrial growth. But economically speaking the coal theory, or any other geographical theory, has an appointment with Harberger. Coal is important, blackening the Black Country, running the engines, heating the homes. But it does not seem, at least on static grounds, to be important enough for the factor of twelve. The calculations would be worth doing, but one suspects they would turn out like the others.

Classical models of economic growth

The claim is that the economists' static model does not explain the factor of twelve. It can tell why it did *Not* happen, a series of Nots, useful Nots, correctives to popular fable and sharpeners of serious hypotheses. But the kind of growth contemplated in the classical models, embedded now deep within modern economics as a system of thought, was not the kind of growth that overtook Britain and the world in the late eighteenth and nineteenth centuries.

One might reply that many small effects, static and dynamic, could add up to the doubling of income per head to be explained: trade, coal, education, canals, peace, investment, reallocation. No, Not. One trouble is that doubling – 100 per cent – is not enough, since in time modern economic growth was not a factor of two but a factor of twelve – not 100 per cent but 1,100 per cent. Another is that many of the effects, whether in the first or the second century of modern economic growth, were available for the taking in earlier centuries. If canals, say, are to explain part of the growth of income it must be explained why a technology available since ancient times was suddenly so useful. If teaching many more people to read was good for the economy it must be explained why Greek potters signing their amphora *c.* 600 BC did not come to use water power to run their wheels and thence to ride on railways to Delphi behind puffing locomotives. If coal is the key it must be explained why north China, rich in coal, had until the twentieth century no industrial growth. The mystery inside the enigma of modern economic growth is why it is modern.

The classical model from Smith to Mill was one of reaching existing standards of efficiency and equipment. To put it in a name: of reaching Holland. Holland was to the eighteenth century what America is to the twentieth, a standard for the wealth of nations.

The province of Holland [wrote Adam Smith in 1776] ... in proportion to the extent of its territory and the number of its people, is a richer country than England. The government there borrows at two per cent., and private people of good credit at three. The wages of labour are said to be higher in Holland than in England, and the Dutch ... trade upon lower profit than any people in Europe. (1776: I.ix.10: 108)

The emphasis on profit at the margin is characteristic of the classical school. The classical economists thought of economic growth as a set of investments, which would, of course, decline in profit as the limit was reached. Smith speaks a few pages later of 'a country which had acquired that full complement of riches which the nature of its soil and climate, and its situation with respect to other countries allowed it to acquire' (1776: I.ix.14: 111). He opines that China 'neglects or despises foreign commerce' and 'the owners of large capitals [there] enjoy a good deal of security, [but] the poor or the owners of small capitals ... are liable, under the pretense of justice, to be pillaged and plundered at any time by the inferior mandarines' (1776: I.ix.15: 112; cf. 1776: I.viii.24: 89). In consequence the rate of interest in China, he claims, is 12 rather than 2 per cent (Smith, incidentally, was off in his facts here). Not all the undertakings profitable in a better ordered country are in fact undertaken, says Smith, which explains why China is poor. Smith and his followers sought to explain why China and Russia were poorer than Britain and Holland, not why Britain and Holland were to become in the century after Smith so very much more rich. The revolution of spinning machines and locomotive machines and sewing machines and reaping machines that was about to overtake north-west Europe was not what Smith had in mind. He had in mind that every country, backward China and Russia, say, and the Highlands of Scotland might soon achieve what the thrifty and orderly Dutch had achieved. He did not have in mind the factor of twelve that was about to occur even in the places in 1776 with a 'full complement of riches'.

Smith, of course, does mention machinery, in his famous discussion of the division of labour: 'Men are much more likely to discover easier and readier methods of attaining any object, when the whole attention of their minds is directed towards the single object' (1776: I.i.8: 20). But what is striking in his and subsequent discussions is how much weight is placed on mere reallocations. The reallocations, mere efficiencies, we have found, are too small to explain what is to be explained.

In a deep sense the economist's model of allocation does not explain the factor of twelve. If allocation were all that was at stake then previous centuries and other places would have experienced what Britain experienced 1780–1860. Macaulay says, in a Smithian way, 'We know of no country which, at the end of fifty years of peace, and tolerably good government, has been less prosperous than at the beginning of that period' (1830: 183). Yes. But 100 per cent better off, on the way to 1,100 per cent better off? Not.

To put it another way, economics in the style of Adam Smith, which is the mainstream of economic thinking, is about scarcity and saving and other puritanical notions. In the sweat of thy face shalt thou eat bread. We cannot have more of everything. We must abstain puritanically from consumption today if we are to eat adequately tomorrow. Or in the modern catch-phrase: there's no such thing as a free lunch.

264   The economic history of Britain since 1700

The chief fact of the quickening of industrial growth 1780–1860 and its aftermath, however, is that scarcity was relaxed – relaxed, not banished or overcome by an 'affluent society', since whatever the size of income at any one time more of it is scarce. Modern economic growth is a massive free lunch.

In 1871, a century after Smith and at the other end of the period (but not the end of modern economic growth) John Stuart Mill's last edition of *Principles of Political Economy* marks the perfection of classical economics. Listen to Mill:

Much as the collective industry of the earth is likely to be increased in efficiency by the extension of science and of the industrial arts, a still more active source of increased cheapness of production will be found, probably, for some time to come, in the gradual unfolding consequences of Free Trade, and in the increasing scale on which Emigration and Colonization will be carried on. (1871: Bk IV, ch. ii.1: 62)

Mill was wrong. The gains from trade, though statically commendable, were trivial beside the extension of industrial arts ('science' means here 'systematic thinking', not, as it came to mean shortly afterwards, the natural sciences alone). The passage exhibits Mill's classical obsession with the principle of population, namely, that the only way to prevent impoverishment of the working people is to restrict population. His anxieties on this score find modern echo in the environmental and family-limitation movements. Whatever their wisdom today, the Malthusian ideas told next to nothing about the century to follow 1871. British population doubled again, yet income per head increased by nearly a factor of four. Nor did Mill's classical model, as we have seen, give a reasonable account of the century before 1871.

Mill again: 'It is only in the backward countries of the world that increased production is still an important object: in those most advanced, what is economically needed is a better distribution, of which one indispensable means is a stricter restraint on population' (1871: Bk IV, ch. vi.2: 114). Still more wrong, in light of what in fact happened during the century before and the century after. Mill is unaware of the larger pie to come – unaware, so strong was the grip of classical economic ideas on his mind, even in 1871, after a lifetime watching it grow larger. He says elsewhere, 'Hitherto it is questionable if all the mechanical inventions yet made have lightened the day's toil of any human being' (1871: Bk IV, ch. vi.2: 116), a strange assertion to carry into the 1871 edition, with child labour falling, education increasing, the harvest mechanising and even the work week reducing.

Mill was too good a classical economist, in short, to recognise a phenomenon inconsistent with classical economics. That the national income per head might quadruple in a century in the teeth of rising population is not a classical possibility, and so the classicals from Smith to Mill put their faith in greater efficiency by way of Harberger Triangles and a more equitable distribution of income by way of improvements in the Poor Law. It should be noted that Mill anticipated social democracy in many of his later opinions, that is, the view that the pie is after all relatively fixed and that we must therefore attend especially to distribution. That the growth of the pie would dwarf the Harberger Triangles available from efficiency, or the Tawney Slices available for redistribution, did not comport with a classical theory of political economy. Macaulay's optimism of 1830 turned out to be the correct historical point: 'We cannot absolutely prove that those are in error who tell us that society has reached a turning point, that we have seen our best days. But so said all who came before us, and with just as much apparent reason' (1830: 186). The pessimistic and puritanical classical economists, with the pessimistic and puritanical romantic opponents of industrialisation, were wrong.

Expanding the models

To account for the startling growth of income before 1860 and the still more startling growth to come it would seem that we must let our economic models expand. That economists have not explained modern economic growth is indeed something of a scientific scandal, although economists are not the only ones to blame: a hundred times more funds, perhaps a thousand times more, are spent on mapping distant galaxies or mapping the genes of E. coli than explaining the economic event that made the telescopes and the microscopes for the mappings possible. Some economists have recently turned back to questions of economic growth, questions neglected for some decades by most non-historical economists. They have tried on the blackboard to modify the economic models to fit what is by now two centuries of growth, building especially on the speculations in the 1920s by the American economist Allyn Young about economies of scale. But the new growth economists have not read more than a page or two of economic history or the history of economic thought, and so repeat the mistakes of earlier generations of economists, though exhibiting greater mathematical imagination.

Science

Turn then to less material causes, looking for some way of supplementing a materialist but unsuccessful theory in economics. Pure thought, perhaps: Science, in sense 5b in the Oxford English Dictionary, now 'the dominant sense in ordinary use', lab-coated and concerned with distant galaxies and

E. coli. Science by this modern definition, however, is another Not (Musson and Robinson 1969; Musson 1972). A powerful myth of moderns is that Science Did It, making us rich. Scientists believe it themselves, and have managed to convince the public. The finding of Not is again relatively recent. Simon Kuznets (1966) and Walt Rostow (1960) both believed that science had much to do with modern economic growth, but it is increasingly plain that they were mistaken (chs. 2 and 11). The Victorians when in an optimistic mood tended to combine technology and science together in a vision of Progress. They were mistaken as well. Workshop ingenuity, not academic science, made better machines. Chemistry made no contribution to the making of steel until the twentieth century, the reactions of a blast furnace being too complex in their details. Sciences mechanical and otherwise had little or nothing to do with inventions in textiles, which depended instead on a craft tradition of machine makers. The same could be said for the other mechanical inventions of the nineteenth century. Steam might be thought to have had a theoretical base, for it was necessary to know that an atmosphere existed before an atmospheric engine would have seemed plausible. But it is notorious among historians of physics that the steam engine affected thermodynamics, not (until very much later) the other way around (von Tunzelmann 1978). Few parts of the economy used much in the way of applied science in other than an ornamental fashion until well into the twentieth century. In short, most of the industrial change was accomplished with no help from academic science.

Literacy

Literacy, too, is a Not, though more of a Not-But than is science. Literacy was not essential for modern industry, as is apparent in its *fall* during periods of intense industrialisation (Mitch 1992; West 1978). But a mute, inglorious Watt would lie undiscovered in an illiterate nation, and doubtless did in Russia and Spain. Britain, especially north Britain, with northern Europe (and the United States), was more literate than other countries in the eighteenth century (Japan, with a more difficult form of writing, had at the time similar attainments in literacy; it appeared ready for economic growth, which was only with difficulty killed by its government).

Culture

So we have more Nots in the world of the mind. 'Cultural factors' more or less mental are promising and much studied. We have learned from Richard Roehl and Patrick O'Brien a good deal about the French/British comparison, learning for example that French agriculture was not backward, despite an old British presumption that Frenchmen simply cannot get it right. On the technological front it is notable that Frenchmen invented in the eighteenth century what Englishmen applied (ch. 2). Something was different in England that encouraged more application. Yet looked at from a distance it seems wrong to separate France from England. It was north-west Europe as a whole that developed fast, as Pollard points out. Southern France lagged, but so, after all, did southern England: Macaulay promised in 1830 that backward Sussex could some day hope to equal the West Riding. Belgian industrialisation was almost as early and vigorous as Yorkshire's and Lancashire's.

Technology and invention

Suppose then we look at the problem from a chronological distance. 'Give me a lever and a place to stand on', said boasting Archimedes, 'and I shall move the world.' What is odd about his world of the classical Mediterranean is that for all its genius it did not apply the lever, or anything much else, to practical uses. Applied technology, argue Jones (1981) and Mokyr (1990a), was a northern European accomplishment. The 'Dark Ages' contributed more to our physical well being than did the glittering ages of Pericles or Augustus. From classical times we got toy steam engines and erroneous principles of motion. From the ninth and tenth centuries alone we got the horse collar, the stirrup, and the mould-board plough.

Then from an explosion of ingenuity down to 1500 we got in addition the blast furnace, cake of soap, cam, canal lock, carrack ship, cast-iron pot, chimney, coal-fuelled fire, cog boat, compass, crank, cross-staff, eyeglass, flywheel, glass window, grindstone, hops in beer, marine chart, nailed horseshoe, overshoot water wheel, printing press, ribbed ship, shingle, ski, spinning wheel, suction pump, spring watch, treadle loom, water-driven bellows, weight-driven clock, whisky, wheelbarrow, whippletree (see 'The Wonderful One-Hoss Shay') and the windmill. Down to 1750 the pace merely slackened, without stopping: note that the pace of invention *decelerated* on the eve of the sharpest industrial change. And then came 'The Years of Miracles', as Mokyr (1990a) calls them, from 1750 to 1900.

Why? Can one give an economic account that does not run afoul of the Nots and the Harbergers?

The economist, Kirzner, has argued recently that profit is a reward for what he calls 'alertness' (1989). Sheer – or as we say 'dumb' – luck is one extreme. Hard work is the other. Alertness falls in between, being neither luck nor routine work. Pure profit, says Kirzner, earned by pure entrepreneurs, is justifed by alertness.

The story of European, and British, ingenuity can be told in Kirzner's metaphors, improving both the story and the metaphor. As many economists have emphasised – relying once again on their conviction that there is No Free Lunch – the systematic search for inventions can be expected in the end to earn only as much as its cost. The routine inventor is an honest workman, but is worthy therefore only of his hire, not worthy of supernormal profit. The cost of routine improvements in the steam engine eats up the profit. It had better, or else the improvement is not routine. Routine invention is not the free lunch experienced since the eighteenth century. Rationalisation of invention has limits, as Joseph Schumpeter and Max Weber did not appreciate. The great research laboratories can produce inventions, but in equilibrium they must spend in proportion to the value invented – or else more research laboratories will be opened until, in the way of routine investment (see Smith on Holland above), the cost rises to exhaust the value.

If hard work in invention was not the cause of the factor of twelve, is the explanation to be found at the other extreme of Kirzner's spectrum, sheer, dumb luck? No, it would seem not. After all, it happened in more than one place (in Belgium and New England as well as in Britain, for instance; in cotton as well as in pottery) but spread selectively (to northern but not southern Italy; to Japan and then Korea but not China – though time will tell). Modern economic growth seems to select countries and sectors by some characteristic.

Well, then, is it Kirzner's metaphor of 'alertness' that explains the European peculiarity? Perhaps it is. Mokyr makes a distinction between micro-inventions (such as the telephone and the light bulb), which responded to the routine forces of research and development (both the telephone and the light bulb were sought methodically by competing inventors), and macro-inventions (such as the printing press and the gravity-driven clock), which did not (Mokyr 1990a). He stresses that both play a part in the story. Yet he is more intrigued by the macro-inventions, which seem less methodical and, one might say, less economic, less subject to the grim necessicities of paying for lunch. Guttenberg just did it, says Mokyr, and created a galaxy. Macro-inventions such as these come to the alert, not to the lucky or the hard working, and macro-inventions seem to lie at the heart of the modern miracle. In short, as Mokyr says, from the technological point of view the quickening of industrial change was 'a cluster of macroinventions': the steam engine, the spinning jenny, and so to a factor of twelve.

But there is something missing in the metaphor and the story, needed to complete the theory. From an economic point of view, alertness by itself is highly academic, in both the good and the bad sense. It is both intellectual and ineffectual, the occupation of the spectator, as Addison put it, who is 'very well versed in the theory of a husband or a father, and can discern the errors of the economy, business, and diversion of others better than those engaged in them'.

Persuasion

If his alert observation of error is to be effectual the spectator has to persuade a banker. Even if he is himself the banker he has to persuade himself, in the councils of his mind. What is missing, then, from the theory of technological change is power. (Those outside the mainstream of bourgeois economic thinking will here find something to agree with.) Between the conception and the creation, between the invention and the innovation, falls the shadow. Power runs between the two. An idea without financing is just an idea. In order for an invention to become an innovation the inventor must persuade someone with the financial means or some other ability to put it into effect.

What matters, to put the point another way, are the conditions of persuasion. Europe's fragmented polity, perhaps, made for pluralistic audiences, by contrast with intelligent but stagnant China. An inventor persecuted by the Inquisition in Naples could move to Holland. The Jews of Spain, expelled in 1492, invigorated the economic life of hundreds of towns on the Mediterranean, such as far Salonika in northern Greece.

Early in his book Mokyr asserts that there is no necessary connection between capitalism and technology: 'Technological progress predated capitalism and credit by many centuries, and may well outlive capitalism by at least as long' (1990a). In the era of the factor of twelve one doubts it, and even before one might wonder, so close bound are gain, persuasion, and ingenuity. Capitalism was not, contrary to Marx's story – which still dominates the modern mind – a modern invention. As the medieval historian Herlihy put it long ago, 'research has all but wiped from the ledgers the supposed gulf, once thought fundamental, between a medieval manorial economy and the capitalism of the modern period'. And any idea requires capitalism and credit in order to become an innovation. The Yorkshireman who invested in a windmill *c.* 1185 was putting his money where his mouth was, or else putting someone else's money. In either case he had to persuade.

What makes alertness work, and gets it power, is persuasion. At the root of technological progress, one might argue, is a rhetorical environment that makes it possible for inventors to be heard. If such a hypothesis were true – and its truth is untried, and may at last end up itself on the pile of weary Nots – it would also be pleasing, for it would suggest that free speech and an openness to persuasion leads to riches. Europeans tortured, beheaded and burnt people they disagreed with in alarming numbers, to be sure, but it may be argued that their fragmented polity let new thinkers escape more often than in China or the Islamic world at about the same time. And when the Europeans, or at any rate some of them, stopped torturing, beheading and burning each other, the economy grew. No wonder that the nations where speech was free by contemporary standards were the first to grow rich: Holland, Scotland, England, Belgium and the United States.

Conclusion

The conclusion, then, is that Harberger Triangles – which is to say the gains from efficiency at the margin – cannot explain the factor of twelve. This is lamentable, because economics is much more confident about static arguments than about dynamic arguments. And yet the conclusion is not that static arguments have no role. On the contrary, they give us the means to measure what needs to be explained on other grounds. A static model of costs and revenues, for example, allows one to measure productivity change with the abundant material on prices. One can find out with static models how widespread was the ingenuity set to work in the eighteenth and nineteenth centuries. A static model of international trade allows one to see the wider context for the British economy, to see that political boundaries do not cut economies at their joints.

But going beyond the usual models, static or dynamic, appears to be necessary. In particular we need to consider the role of persuasive talk in the economy (in modern economies it is a quarter of national income). Adam Smith wrote at the beginning of the period that '[The division of labour is a] consequence of a certain propensity ... to truck, barter, and exchange ... [He could not pause to discuss] whether this propensity be one of those original principles in human nature ... or whether, as seems more probable, it be the necessary consequence of the faculties of reason *and speech*' (1776: 17). 'The faculty of reason' has been much studied by economists since then, resulting in their splendid, useful static models. But they have not taken up his phrase, 'and speech'. In his other book, *The Theory of Moral Sentiments*, he gave it prominence: 'The desire of being believed, the desire of persuading, of leading and directing other people, seems to be one of the strongest of all our natural desires. It is, perhaps, the instinct on which is founded the faculty of speech, the characteristic faculty of human nature' (1790: VII.iv.25: 336). We need an account of the age of industrialisation that admits into the tale the characteristic faculty of human nature, which is to say a combination of reason and of speech, the economic historian's calculations and the social historian's sensibilities.

Bibliography

Place of publication is London unless otherwise stated. All references to the *Economic History Review* are to the Second Series, unless otherwise stated.

Adams, H. 1907. *The Education of Henry Adams*. New York.

Allen, R. C. 1982. The efficiency and distributional consequences of eighteenth century enclosures. *Economic Journal* 92: 937–53.

1992. *Enclosure and the Yeoman: The Agricultural Development of the South Midlands, 1450–1850*. Oxford.

Berg, M. 1980. *The Machinery Question and the Making of Political Economy, 1815–1848*. Cambridge.

1985. *The Age of Manufactures: Industry, Innovation and Work in Britain 1700–1820*. Oxford.

Bowley, A. L. 1900. *Wages in the United Kingdom in the Nineteenth Century*. Cambridge.

Braudel, F., and Spooner, F. 1967. Prices in Europe from 1450 to 1750. In Rich and Wilson 1967.

Bridbury, A. R. 1975. *Economic Growth: England in the Later Middle Ages*. Brighton.

Cameron, R., ed. 1967. *Banking in the Early Stages of Industrialization: A Study of Comparative Economic History*. Oxford.

1990. La révolution industrielle manquée. *Social Science History* 14: 559–65.

Forthcoming. Misunderstanding the industrial revolution. In a Festschrift for Eric Lampard.

Carus-Wilson, E. M. 1941. An industrial revolution of the thirteenth century. *Economic History Review* 11: 39–60. Reprinted in Carus-Wilson 1954.

ed. 1954. *Essays in Economic History*.

Chapman, S. D., and Butt, J. 1988. The cotton industry, 1775–1856. In Feinstein and Pollard 1988.

Clapham, J. H. 1910. The last years of the Navigation Acts. *English Historical Review* 25; 480–501 and 687–707. Reprinted in Carus-Wilson 1954.

1926. *An Economic History of Modern Britain: The Early Railway Age, 1820–1850*. Cambridge.

Coleman, D. C. 1973. Textile growth. In Harte and Ponting 1973.

1977. *The Economy of England 1450–1750*. Oxford.

Crafts, N. F. R. 1977b. Industrial revolution in England and France: some thoughts on the question, Why was England first? *Economic History Review* 30: 429–41.

1985a *British Economic Growth during the Industrial Revolution.* Oxford.

1989a. British industrialization in an international context. *Journal of Interdisciplinary History* 19: 415–28.

Davies, R. S. W., and Pollard, S. 1988. The iron industry, 1750–1850. In Feinstein and Pollard 1988.

Deane, P., and Cole, W. A. 1962. *British Economic Growth, 1688–1959.* Cambridge. 1967. *British Economic Growth, 1688–1959.* 2nd edn. Cambridge.

Feinstein, C. H. 1978. Capital accumulation and economic growth. In Mathias and Postan 1978.

1988. National statistics, 1760–1920. In Feinstein and Pollard 1988.

Feinstein, C. H. and Pollard, S., eds. 1988. *Studies in Capital Formation in the United Kingdom, 1750–1920.* Oxford.

Floud, R. C., and McCloskey, D. N., eds. 1981. *The Economic History of Britain since* 1700, *vol. I: 1700–1860.* 1st edn, Cambridge.

Fogel, R. W. 1984. *Railroads and American Economic Growth: Essays in Economic History.* Baltimore.

Gerschenkron, A. 1962a. *Economic Backwardness in Historical Perspective.* Cambridge, Mass.

1962b. On the concept of continuity in history. *Proceedings of the American Philosophical Society* (June). Reprinted in Gerschenkron 1968.

1968. *Continuity in History and Other Essays.* Cambridge, Mass.

Gilboy, E. W. 1934. *Wages in 18th Century England.* Cambridge, Mass.

Harley, C. K. 1982. British industrialization before 1841: evidence of slower growth during the industrial revolution. *Journal of Economic History* 42: 267–89.

Harte, N. B. and Ponting, K., eds 1973. *Textile History and Economic History: Essays in Honour of Miss Julia de Lacy Mann.*

Hartwell, R. M. 1965. The causes of the industrial revolution: an essay in methodology. *Economic History Review* 18: 164–82. Reprinted in Hartwell 1967.

ed. 1967. *The Causes of the Industrial Revolution in England.*

Hawke, G. R. 1970. *Railways and Economic Growth in England and Wales 1840–1870.* Oxford.

Hudson, P. 1986. *The Genesis of Industrial Capital: A Study of the West Riding Wool Textile Industry c.1750–1850.* Cambridge.

ed. 1989. *Regions and Industries.* Cambridge.

Imlah, J. A. H. 1958. *Economic Elements in the Pax Britannica: Studies in British Foreign Trade in the Nineteenth Century.* Cambridge, Mass.

Ippolito, R. A. 1975. The effect of the agricultural depression on industrial demand in England: 1730–1750. *Economica* 2: 298–312.

James, J., and Thomas, M., eds. 1993. *Capitalism in Context: Essays in Honor of R. M. Hartwell.* Chicago.

Jones, E. L. 1981. *The European Miracle: Environments, Economics and Geopolitics in the History of Europe and Asia.* Cambridge.

1988. *Growth Recurring.* Oxford.

Jones, G. T. 1933. *Increasing Returns.* Cambridge.

Kirzner, I. 1989. *Discovery, Capitalism, and Distributive Justice.* Oxford.

Kuznets, S. S. 1966. *Modern Economic Growth: Rate, Structure and Spread.* New Haven.

Landes, D. S. 1969. *The Unbound Prometheus: Technological Change and Industrial Development in Western Europe from 1750 to the Present.* Cambridge.

Lindert, P. H., and Williamson, J. G. 1982. Revising England's social tables, 1688–1812. *Explorations in Economic History* 19: 385–408.

1983a. English workers' living standards during the industrial revolution: a new look. *Economic History Review* 36; 1–25.

Macaulay, T. B. 1830. *Southey's Colloquies on Society.* In *Macaulay's Essays* (1860 edn), vol. I.

McCloskey, D. N. 1970. Did Victorian Britain fail? *Economic History Review* 23: 446–59.

1972. The enclosure of open fields: preface to a study of its impact on the efficiency of English agriculture in the eighteenth century. *Journal of Economic History* 32; 15–35.

1973. *Economic Maturity and Entrepreneurial Decline: British Iron and Steel, 1870–1913.* Cambridge, Mass.

1975. The economics of enclosure: a market analysis. In Parker and Jones 1975.

1981b. The industrial revolution: a survey. In Floud and McCloskey 1981.

1991. History, nonlinear differential equations, and the problem of narration. *History and Theory* 30: 21–36.

Maddison, A. 1971. *Class Structure and Economic Growth.* New York.

Malthus, T. R. 1798. *An Essay on the Principle of Population.* Reprinted in Wrigley and Souden 1986.

Mantoux, P. 1905. *La Révolution industrielle au xviiie siècle.* Paris.

1928. *The Industrial Revolution in the Eighteenth Century.* 2nd edn, New York, 1961.

Mathias, P., and Pollard, S., eds. 1989. *The Cambridge Economic History of Europe, vol. III: The Industrial Economies: The Development of Economic and Social Policies.* Cambridge.

Mill, J. S. 1871. *Principles of Political Economy, with Some of their Applications to Social Philosophy* (1st edn 1848).

Mitch, D. 1992. *Education and Economic Development in England.* Princeton, N. J.

Mitchell, B., and Deane, P. 1962. *Abstract of British Historical Statistics.* Cambridge.

Mokyr, J. 1977. Demand vs supply in the industrial revolution. *Journal of Economic History* 37: 981–1008.

ed. 1985b. *The Economics of the Industrial Revolution.* Totowa, N. J.

1985c. The industrial revolution and the new economic history. In Mokyr 1985b.

1990a. *The Lever of Riches: Technological Creativity and Economic Progress.* New York and Oxford.

1993. Progress and inertia in technological change. In James and Thomas 1993.

Musson, A. E. 1972. *Science, Technology and Economic Growth in the Eighteenth Century*.

1978. *The Growth of British Industry*. New York.

Musson, A. E., and Robinson, E. 1969. *Science and Technology in the Industrial Revolution*. Manchester.

Neal, L. 1990. *The Rise of Financial Capitalism: International Capital Markets in the Age of Reason*. Cambridge.

Nef, J. U. 1932. *The Rise of the British Coal Industry*. 2 vols.

North, D. C. 1968. Sources of productivity change in ocean shipping, 1600–1850. *Journal of Political Economy* 76: 953–70.

O'Brien, P. K., and Engerman, S. L. 1991. Exports and the growth of the British economy from the Glorious Revolution to the Peace of Amiens. In Solow and Engerman 1991.

Parker, W. N., and Jones, E. L., eds. 1975. *European Peasants and their Markets: Essays in Agrarian History*. Princeton, N. J.

Pollard, S. 1963. Factory discipline in the industrial revolution. *Economic History Review* 16: 254–71.

1964. Fixed capital in the industrial revolution. *Journal of Economic History* 24: 299–314.

1973. Industrialization and the European Economy. *Economic History Review* 26: 636–48. Reprinted in Mokyr 1985b.

1981a. *Peaceful Conquest: The Industrialization of Europe, 1760–1970*. Oxford.

Rich, E. E., and Wilson, C. H., eds. 1967. *The Cambridge Economic History of Europe, vol. IV: The Economy of Expanding Europe in the Sixteenth and Seventeenth Centuries*. Cambridge.

Richardson, P. 1989. The structure of capital during the industrial revolution revisited: two case studies from the cotton textile industry. *Economic History Review* 42: 484–503.

Rostow, W. W. 1960. *The Stages of Economic Growth*. Cambridge.

Smith, A. 1776. *An Inquiry into the Nature and Causes of the Wealth of Nations*. Ed. R. H. Campbell, A. S. Skinner and W. B. Todd, 1976. Oxford.

1790. *The Theory of Moral Sentiments*. Glasgow Edition. Ed. D. D. Raphael and A. L. Macfie, Indianapolis, 1982.

Solow, B. L., and Engerman, S. L., eds. 1991. *Slavery and the Rise of the Atlantic System*. Cambridge.

Szostak, R. 1991. *The Role of Transportation in the Industrial Revolution*. Montreal.

von Tunzelmann, G. N. 1978. *Steam Power and British Industrialization to 1860*. Oxford.

West, E. G. 1978. Literacy and the industrial revolution. *Economic History Review* 31: 369–83. Reprinted in Mokyr 1985b.

Williamson, J. G. 1981. Some myths die hard – urban disamenities one more time: a reply. *Journal of Economic History* 41: 905–7.

1985. *Did British Capitalism Breed Inequality?*.

1987. Did English factor markets fail during the industrial revolution? *Oxford Economic Papers* 39: 641–78.

1990b. The impact of the Corn Laws prior to repeal. *Explorations in Economic History* 27: 123–56.

Williamson, O. 1985. *The Economic Institutions of Capitalism: Firms, Markets, Relational Contracting.*

Wood, G. H. 1910. *The History of Wages in the Cotton Trade during the Past Hundred Years.*

Wordie, J. R. 1974. Social change on the Leveson–Gower Estates, 1714–1832. *Economic History Review* 27: 593–609.

1983. The chronology of English enclosure, 1500–1914. *Economic History Review* 36: 483–505.

Wrigley, E. A. 1967. A simple model of London's importance in changing English society and economy, 1600–1750. *Past and Present* 37: 44–70.

1988. *Continuity, Chance and Change: The Character of the Industrial Revolution in England.* Cambridge.

Wrigley, E. A., and Souden, D. C., eds. 1986. *The Works of Thomas Robert Malthus.*

6

THE JOURNAL OF ECONOMIC HISTORY

VOLUME 58   JUNE 1998   NUMBER 2

Bourgeois Virtue and the History of P and S

DEIRDRE N. MCCLOSKEY

Since the triumph of a business culture a century and half ago the businessman has been scorned, and so the phrase "bourgeois virtue" sounds like an oxymoron. Economists since Bentham have believed that anyway virtue is beside the point: what matters for explanation is Prudence. But this is false in many circumstances, even strictly economic circumstances. An economic history that insists on Prudence Alone is misspecified, and will produce biased coefficients. And it will not face candidly the central task of economic history, an apology for or a criticism of a bourgeois society.

A few years ago I was standing by the front desk of Great Expectations, a bookstore in Evanston, talking to the owner. It's a good store, exhibiting bourgeois virtue: by the combined virtue of prudence and courage called Enterprise it keeps obscure university-press books in stock. Mine, for instance. I said, "You know, there are only two important European novels since 1848 that have portrayed businessmen on the job in anything like a sympathetic way. The first is Thomas Mann's tale of his north German merchant family, *Buddenbrooks* (1902). And the second . . . ." Here I paused, or rather stuttered, which people sometimes take as pausing for effect. Another customer piped up, "And the second is David Lodge's story of an affair between a university lecturer and a managing director, *Nice Work* (1988)."

Bingo. Those two, at any rate among the canon of the best that has been thought and written, are the only books with virtuous businessmen as heroes. Of course European (including American) literature talks about businessmen incidentally. The share of the talk is less than the share of life taken up in business. Love at home gets more attention in fiction than does loyalty at work. Courage on the battlefield figures more in art and literature than enterprise in the market. Henry James's characters in *The Ambassadors* (1903) are financed in their dalliances abroad by some sort of manufacturing in New England:

The Journal of Economic History, Vol. 58, No. 2 (June 1998). © The Economic History Association. All right reserved. ISSN 0022-0507.

Deirdre N. McCloskey is Tinbergen Distinguished Professor, Erasmus University of Rotterdam and John F. Murray Professor of Economics, Professor of History, and Director of the Project on Rhetoric of Inquiry, University of Iowa, Department of Economics, University of Iowa, Iowa City, Iowa 52246.

"And what *is* the article produced?"
Strether looked about him as in slight reluctance to say. . . . "I'll tell you next time."
But when the next time came he only said he'd tell her later on.[1]

And when the scene does shift to men at work the bourgeois man of the past century and a half is pilloried. The novel was a bourgeois creation of the early eighteenth century, with bourgeois writers and bourgeois readers. The middling sort was the topic, often at work, as in *Robinson Crusoe* (1719), and anyway with many sympathetically portrayed men of the bourgeoisie out in the marketplace. (The women of the bourgeoisie were another matter, in their separate sphere.) That bourgeois institution, the market, was looked on with favor. Alessandro Manzoni, the Italian Tolstoy, devoted an entire chapter of his masterpiece *The Betrothed* (1825-26, 1840; Chapter 12) to explaining the dire consequences of interfering with the grain market. You could reprint it for your class in Economics 101.

But the 1840s was the last decade of sympathy for the businessman and his market forces. *Moby Dick* (1851), especially in the first mate Starbuck, can be read as taking a liberal view of business; not *The Confidence Man* (1857). Dickens converted to a political novelist in *Hard Times* (1854), never to return to his earlier geniality about turning a profit. Since the middle of the nineteenth century, from the moment businessmen came into their own, the novelists have not let up. Mark Twain, though himself a businessman, thought of bourgeois men as thieves. Zola's *Germinal* (1885) and *Ladies' Paradise* (1883) exhibit the owners of mines and even of department stores as manipulative scoundrels. The theme reaches its height, of course, in Sinclair Lewis's *Main Street* (1920) and above all *Babbitt* (1922), which still provides some intellectuals with their only acquaintance with the American man of business. And so down to the movies of *Network* and *Wall Street*.

Something similar happened in the other arts and the other writings. Painting in seventeenth-century Holland celebrated bourgeois virtue, a celebration which cannot be found by the time of Picasso and Diego Rivera. The arts-and-crafts movement stirring in the 1860s celebrated workmen, not bosses and machinery. John Ruskin praised the Gothic in architecture as work rather than play, and wrote in 1866, "Let us, then, inquire together what sort of games the playing class in England spend their lives in playing at. The first of all English games is making money."[2] In 1910 George Bernard Shaw looked back to a Great Conversion around 1848:

The first half [of the nineteenth century] despised and pitied the Middle Ages. . . .
The second half saw no hope for mankind except in the recovery of the faith, the art,

[1] James, *Ambassadors*, p. 97.
[2] Ruskin, "Work," p. 41.

the humanity of the Middle Ages. . . . For that was how men felt, and how some of them spoke, in the early days of the Great Conversion, which produced, first, such books as the *Latter Day Pamphlets* of Carlyle, Dickens' *Hard Times*, . . . and later on the Socialist movement.[3]

As César Graña argued in 1964 in his brilliant *Bohemian versus Bourgeois*, there is hardly a French intellectual in the nineteenth century who was not simultaneously the son of a bourgeois and sternly hostile to everything bourgeois.[4] Though the son of a cotton merchant, the poet Arthur Hugh Clough felt he could sneer in 1862 at what he viewed as the businessman's decalogue:

> Thou shalt not steal; an empty feat,
> When it's so lucrative to cheat. . . .
> Thou shalt not covet, but tradition
> Approves all forms of competition.[5]

How different from Dr. Johnson a century before: "There are few ways in which a man can be more innocently employed than in getting money."

Something strange has happened since 1848, worth understanding. The cultural superstructure has contradicted the material base. Daniel Bell wrote in 1976 of the "cultural contradictions of capitalism," a theme in Schumpeter's *Capitalism, Socialism, and Democracy* as well.[6] Whether an inevitable tendency to contradiction or the autonomous force of ideas and accident explains it, this treason of the clerks, the loss of faith in the bourgeoisie at its hour of triumph, had consequences in politics beyond the economy.

In this (and some other matters) I have changed my mind. I began in economic history arguing *contra* David Landes that in my mature opinion a culture was insignificant beside technology and tastes. Age 26 in 1968, recently a Marxist and still a most enthusiastic young transportation economist, I was determined to emphasize the material rather than the spiritual, the forces of price and prudence as against what I called sociology, about which it must be said I knew very little.

I take back none of my earlier calculations, which still seem to me pretty. It is still true that Victorian Britain did not fail in steelmaking, that foreign trade is overstated as an engine of British growth, that the gold standard worked through commodity arbitrage not Lombard Street, and that medieval peasants were prudent in their open fields. I have no more patience now than 30 years ago with suppositions that people ignore gigantic opportunities for profit. As a matter of historical fact they do not. Supposing without evidence

---

[3] Shaw, "Introduction," p. 334.
[4] Graña, *Bohemian versus Bourgeois*.
[5] Clough, "Latest Decalogue," p. 1034.
[6] Bell, *Cultural Contradictions*; and Schumpeter, *Capitalism*.

McCloskey

that they do seems impious towards the glorious dead, treating them in retrospect as idiots. It is even bad sociology. But to explain how markets live, to explain where technology and tastes originate, to explain what symbolic system supported or discouraged the people living in the economies of olden days we need culture, in both the anthropologist's and the aesthete's sense.

A neglected link between the economy and culture is "bourgeois virtue." When I first planned to speak about it, at the Institute for Advanced Study at Princeton, the secretary called me up in Iowa to get the exact title. She laughed. "'Bourgeois virtue'! That's an oxymoron, isn't it?" Which puts the problem well. It will seem disorienting to talk to economic historians about ethics (not that "ethical economic historian" is an oxymoron!). But I think we are not going to get the economy right until we face the virtues and vices of its people, and we are not going to see the virtues until we face the economy.

---··•··---

We have two ancient ways of talking about the personal virtues, and seem stuck on them. One is patrician, what John Casey calls "pagan" virtues. The classical four are those of Odysseus: prudence, temperance, justice, and courage. The aristocrat is honorable, great hearted in hospitality, quick to anger. "You wine sack, with a dog's eyes, with a deer's heart," says Achilles—exhibiting more courage than prudence, temperance, or justice— "Never/ once have you taken courage in your heart to arm with your people."

The other way of virtue-talk is plebeian, the way of St. Paul. The peasant suffers yet endures. "Owe no man any thing, but to love one another." Faith, hope, and love, these three, but the greatest is love. It is a "slave morality," bending to the aristocratic virtues that Nietzsche and other Hellenizers prized.

The two vocabularies of the virtues are spoken in the Camp and Common. Achilles struts through the Camp in his Hephaestian armor, exercising a noble wrath. Jesus stands barefoot on the mount, preaching to the least of the Commoners.

And yet we live mostly now in the Town, we bourgeois, or else we are moving to townly occupations as fast as we can manage, trading the old cow for a car. The aristocracy is gone, though some intellectuals wish not. And the prediction that the proletariat at the other end would become the universal class has proven to be mistaken.

Jobs for the two older classes are disappearing. The very soldiers in bourgeois democracies are shufflers of paper. Half of employment in rich countries is white collar and rising. The proletarian production of things has become steadily cheaper, and therefore has taken few people to do it. A

Bourgeois Virtue and the History of P and S   301

barber or a professor was not much more productive in 1990 than in 1800, for that matter in 400 B.C. It still takes 15 minutes with a pair of scissors to do short back and sides and 50 minutes with a piece of chalk to convey the notion of comparative advantage. But the farmer since 1800 has become more productive in the United States by a factor of 36. We cannot eat 36 times more food (though some of us try) and so the farmer's share in employment has fallen towards nil. A piece of cotton cloth that sold for 40 shillings in the 1780s sold in the 1850s for 5 shillings and nowadays, in the same values of money, for a few pence. The cheapness led spinning out of the home, then weaving, canning, men's clothing, women's clothing, food preparation. Stanley Lebergott calculated that food preparation fell in a middle-class house from 44 hours a week in 1944 to 10 hours in 1965.[7] Calculating power itself— adding, multiplying, and carrying—that sold for $400 in 1970 sold for $4 in 1990, and pennies now. Workers on the line in American manufacturing peaked at about one-fifth of the labor force after World War II and have since been falling, at first slowly. In 50 years a maker of things on an assembly line will be as rare as a farmer. What is left is hamburger flipping on the one side and bourgeois occupations on the other.

Yet we lack a vocabulary for speaking of the virtues within this encompassing commercial, capitalist, bourgeois society. We insist on measuring temperance, prudence, justice, and courage against the soldier, and faith, hope, and love against the saint. American businessmen speak of their ethical world in sporting terms, one step from the battlefield. Their critics speak in socialist terms, one step from the nunnery. Pagan or Christian, aristocrat or peasant, the ethics we speak suits our condition poorly. We need a discourse of the bourgeois virtues: integrity, honesty, trustworthiness, enterprise, humor, respect, modesty, consideration, responsibility, prudence, thrift, affection, self-possession, prudence. We do not have it in our modern art or literature, or in our scholarship on economic history.

The modern silence is strange because in the eighteenth century the conversation started so well. I regard Hume and Smith, Locke and Montesquieu as articulating an ethical and political vocabulary for a commercial society. Adam Smith's intention was to create an ethical system for the bourgeoisie. Look for example at his very first appearance in print, in 1758, an anonymous encomium to a bourgeois friend:

To the memory of Mr. William Crauford
Merchant of Glasgow

[7] Lebergott, *Pursuing Happiness*, p. 51.

Who to that exact frugality, that downright probity and plainness of manners so
suitable to his profession, joined a love of learning . . . , an openness of hand and a
generosity of heart, . . . and a magnanimity that could support . . . the most torturing
pains of body with an unalterable cheerfulness of temper, and without once
interrupting, even to his last hour, the most manly and the most vigorous activity in
a vast variety of business . . . . Candid and penetrating, circumspect and sincere.[8]

This is not an encomium to Profit Regardless. It praises a bourgeois virtue.

An "ethic for the bourgeoisie," you see, is not the same thing as an apology for greed. Smith was hostile to the reduction of ethics to greedy interest,
which Bentham finally achieved and which was earlier recommended by
Epicurus, Hobbes, and Mandeville (whom Smith discussed explicitly and
at length). Mandeville's system, wrote Smith, "seems to take away
altogether the distinction between vice and virtue" by the simple device of
noting that people get pleasure from being thought to be good. "It is by
means of this sophistry, that he establishes his favourite conclusion, that
private vices [and in particular the vice of Vanity] are public benefits."[9]

The fallacy in the argument, which has not been spotted by modern
economists in its grip, was first noted by David Hume, followed by Smith:
"It is the great fallacy of Dr. Mandeville's book to represent every passion
as wholly vicious [that is, self-interested, a matter of vanity], which is to any
degree and in any direction."[10] Thus if I get a little utility from love, it
"follows" (say Epicurus, Mandeville, Bentham, and Gary Becker) that love
is reducible to utility, and we can abandon any account of separate virtues
and vices. But this is silly. I get utility because I love, not the other way
around. It does *not* follow that I love entirely because of utility. I may have
gotten some amusement from my children, but I did not have them and love
them with aching passion down to this bitter day entirely or even largely
because they were amusing. And it is therefore not true that virtues such as
love, justice, courage, and so forth can be reduced without remainder to
utility.

Smith of course by no means approved of every activity of the
bourgeoisie. He was suspicious of the rent-seeking of merchants, noting that
in contrast to the landlords and workers, the interests of the bourgeoisie are
"always in some respects different from, and even opposite to, that of the
publick."[11] The "clamour and sophistry of merchants and manufacturers
easily persuaded [society] that the private interest of a part, and a
subordinate part of the society, is the general interest of the whole."[12] Smith
was read this way at the time. Hugh Blair wrote on 3 April 1776

[8] Smith, *Essays*, p. 262.
[9] Smith, *Theory of Moral Sentiments*, pp. 308, 312–13.
[10] Ibid., p. 312.
[11] Smith, *Wealth of Nations*, p. 267.
[12] Ibid., p. 144.

Bourgeois Virtue and the History of P *and* S   303

commending him: "You have done great Service to the World by overturning all the interested Sophistry of Merchants, with which they have Confounded the whole Subject of Commerce."[13] As scholars on the left have noted, Smith was no Margaret Thatcher in drag.

But neither was he hostile to the values of a commercial society, something I wish my friends on the left would admit. Unlike European intellectuals since the Great Conversion, Smith wanted to make a commercial society work, not to sit outside it sneering.

The "ethical system" of Smith was not a search for a general precept of ethics, such as Kant was at the same time perfecting in his walks from home to the office in far-away East Prussia. Rules such as Kant's categorical imperative (well expressed by the bureaucrat denying you an exception: Suppose I allowed everyone to do that?) or Jesus's golden rule or the master instance in modern times, utilitarianism's rule of What's Best For All, are not what Smith sought, or found. He sought and found a system of virtues. He was influenced by classical stoicism, Epictetus the slave and Marcus Aurelius the emperor. An ethic of the virtues has been developed in recent decades by Philippa Foot, Elizabeth Anscombe, Iris Murdoch, Susan Wolf, Rosalind Hursthouse, Annette Baier, Alasdair MacIntyre, John Casey, Bernard Williams, and Martha Nussbaum. (It is the only field of modern philosophy in which women's voices predominate). But it is as old as Aristotle's *Nichomachean Ethics* and is to be set against Plato's (and Kant's and Bentham's) search for the one Good.

By the time of Smith it was conventional to think of the virtues as the four aristocratic or pagan virtues with the three peasant or theological virtues: courage, temperance, prudence, and justice, with faith, hope, and love. The analysis of all virtues into these seven was begun in classical times and completed by Aquinas, though the weight of the tradition is not a knock-down argument for thinking that the seven contain all the virtues one needs to consider. Smith may have been mistaken to adhere to these only—it may be that a bourgeois virtue is hard to discuss in terms once classical or Christian.

Smith left off Faith and Hope. I think he believed that these two of the theological virtues were inappropriate to a bourgeois society. Eighteenth-century doers and thinkers were haunted by the religious wars of the previous century, the excesses of Faith. In Britain, especially after the Gordon Riots of 1780, they were haunted, too, by the excesses of Hope. Faith you can view as backward looking: one sees it, for example, in nostalgia for the Highland clan, such an odd feature of British nation building in the late eighteenth century. Hope is forward looking, utopian in

---

[13] Smith, *Correspondence*, p. 188).

the way a saint is utopian. As Edmund Burke noted with alarm, it was embodied in the French Revolution.

If you can stand any more intellectual history in which ideas strut around like actors on a stage, one can see a revival of Faith and Hope as political ideas in the nineteenth century. An astonishing development in Britain, America, and Protestant Germany in the early nineteenth century was evangelicalism among the intelligentsia—something that would have been wholly unexpected by urbane deists such as Smith or Benjamin Franklin, or atheists such as Hume or Gibbon, or even the traditionally Anglican Dr. Johnson. The theological virtue of Hope reemerged in projects of moral reform, especially the abolition of slavery. Eventually Faith and Hope merged in a secular version of Christianity by the name of socialism and a secular version of paganism called nationalism. And all our woe.

The Smithian Five are arranged in effect along a spectrum, thus:[14]

Courage	Temperance	Prudence	Justice	Love
masculine	control of inner weather	taking care of yourself	control of outer weather	feminine
		phronesis		

It is something like a complete human. (Whatever your local pseudo-Philosopher may have told you, it is not actually a virtue in a social science that it characterize people as single-minded monsters of Prudence or Love.) Smith put Courage and Love on the edges. Not off the edge, like Hope and Faith, but away from the central virtues of a bourgeois society. It is not from the benevolence of the butcher, or the brewer, or the baker that we expect our dinner (that is, not from Love), but from their regard to their own interest (that is, Prudence). (Feminists have pointed out sardonically that someone had to *cook* the dinner, Dr. Smith [it was Mrs. Smith, his Mom], and *that* is a matter of Love.) Smith was indifferent, even hostile, to commercial courage, the virtue of enterprise. He recommended prudential investing, preferably in agriculture. As Vivienne Brown has emphasized in her amazing book on *Adam Smith's Discourse* (1994) he was not enthusiastic for the thrusting, risk-taking entrepreneurs that, say, Marx and Engels praised so. Smith was not a romantic about capitalism, as some modern defenders of it are (Ayn Rand, for example). As Albert Hirschman has said, Love and Courage were more passions than interests. It is little

---

[14] Smith, *Theory of Moral Sentiments*, pp. 216, "prudence of the great general . . . valour. . . benevolence. . . justice . . . a proper degree of self-command; p. 237, "rules of perfect prudence, of strict justice, and of proper benevolence. . . . If it is not supported by the most perfect self-command, [it] will not always enable him to do his duty" (he explains on the next page that "self-command" is Courage and Temperance combined).

Bourgeois Virtue and the History of P and S   305

wonder that a Scot witnessing the benefits of secularism and peace in a country riven so recently by the passionate virtues would take such a line. He distanced himself from the aristocratic and masculine virtues (above all Courage) and the Christian and feminine ones (above all Love).

And yet the center of the three that remain, Prudence, is not for all its coolness an ethical nullity. Prudence is simply dropped from most thinking about ethics that does not start with the concrete virtues. John Casey notes, "Philosophers here reflect common opinion: to call a judgement 'prudential' [or 'pragmatic' or 'bourgeois'] is taken by many people as meaning that it is not 'moral'." But on the contrary, Casey observes, "We can think of the man of practical wisdom as having moral imagination."[15] *Ethos* in Greek just means "character," and so it is no surprise to find the virtue of Prudence supreme in two out of Eric Erikson's eight stages of maturation, in school (Competence) and in old age (Wisdom). St. Paul in his first letter to the Corinthians says that you may talk with the voices of men and angels but if you have not Love you are as sounding brass and tinkling cymbals. The bourgeoise answers that you may express Love abiding in all your actions, but if you have not Prudence you are as a runaway truck or an exploding steam engine. Temperance, Justice, and Prudence, these bourgeois three. But the greatest is Prudence.

Something happened between Adam Smith and now. Somehow a view of Economic Man that placed him in a system of virtues and made him out to be a complete character got mislaid. The mislaying was in part an episode in the general decline of ethical philosophy, down to what Mark Johnson has called "the nadir of moral reasoning in this century," A. J. Ayers's emotivism, the notion that ethical opinions are merely opinions: "Ethical concepts are unanalysable, inasmuch as there is no criterion by which one can test the validity of the judgments in which they occur. . . . They are mere pseudo-concepts. . . . If I say to someone, 'You acted wrongly in stealing that money' . . . . it is as if I had said, 'You stole that money,' in a peculiar tone of horror."[16] Thus the undergraduate says, "That's just a matter of opinion. It's a free country. Everything's relative. *De gustibus non disputandum est*" (our undergraduate is a bit of a scholar). The earlier and specifically economistic version of such ethical nihilism is traceable I think to Bentham, viewed as a hero by recent ethical nihilists such as George Stigler, Gary Becker, or Judge Richard Posner. Bentham's *Principles of Morals and Legislation* (1789) called Prudence by his word "utility," and claimed to prove that "the only right ground of action, that can possibly subsist, is, after

---

[15] Casey, *Pagan Virtue*, pp. 145, 146.
[16] Ayer, quoted in Johnson, *Moral Imagination*, p. 137.

all, the consideration of utility."[17] It was proven, as I have noted, by taking a part of motivation for the whole, a synecdochic fallacy.

----------••◦••----------

But what of it? What do economics and economic history lose by being de-moralized? Economics since Bentham has been the science of Prudence Alone, and a wonderfully successful one. I am a Chicago School economist and still an enthusiast for this intellectual program. I once wrote an entire, long book devoted to showing how Prudence can explain, and all my work in economic history has exhibited Prudent men rushing about picking up $100 bills. But I have realized gradually that it is a scientific mistake to set the other virtues aside *even when you wish to deal mainly with Prudential consequences*. It is often possible to "economize on love," as an economist once expressed the Mandevillean/Benthamite and anti-Smithian program of modern economics. But in many important cases it is not possible, and lacking in point. And for decent history it must not be attempted.

An example is what is known in economics as the Voting Paradox. It is "paradoxical," notes the economist, that people bother to vote at all in large elections, because Prudence would keep them at home. No one vote will affect the outcome—unless the election of 1856 was literally an exact tie, a vanishingly improbable event in prospect and false in retrospect. A Prudent man would therefore never vote, if voting had (as it does) the tiniest inconvenience.

And yet people do vote, and did in 1856. Oh, oh. Hmm. Some other motive than Prudence must be explaining this very important piece of behavior. Love, perhaps. Or Justice. As George Santayana said of English liberties in America, "These institutions are ceremonial, almost sacramental. . . . They would not be useful, or work at all as they should, if people did not smack their lips over them and feel a profound pleasure in carrying them out."[18] *Sic transit* an entirely self-interested theory of voting for the Northern tariff before the Civil War, or the repeal of the British corn laws, or the free coinage of silver, or New Deal spending. It will not do to say, as the late George Stigler said to me in angry rebuttal, that if the "observable implications" of the Prudence Alone model fit, that is all we need to know. Considerations of statistical power and specification error aside, participation in elections is an observation, too, George, an observation that annihilates the anti-Smithian theory before it has had time to speak.

Another and more important example is the so-called Prisoner's Dilemma. Prudence, argued Thomas Hobbes, would lead men in a state of nature to defect from social arrangements. The Hobbes Problem has misled most

[17] Bentham, *Principles*, p. 146.
[18] Santayana, *Character*, pp. 203–04.

serious thinkers about society since he posed it. The exciting and endlessly formalizable problem is, Will a mass of unsocialized brutes form spontaneously a civil society? Hobbes's answer was, No, not without a leviathan state; otherwise one can expect society to be a war of all against all and the life of man solitary, poor, nasty, brutish, and short. Hundreds of other men have provided their own solutions.

But the Hobbes Problem, when you think of it, is very peculiar. Why would it be interesting to know about the behavior of a mass of unsocialized brutes, when every human being is in fact already socialized, already under the eye in Smith's terms of an Impartial Spectator? Such a query does not occur to most men, such as the political scientist Robert Putnam or the economic historian Douglass North. Women already know that humans, for example, are raised in families, and therefore are always already socialized. Yet men have been fixated on the Hobbes Problem, without making the slightest progress in solving it, for three centuries now. From both the left and the right it is considered clever among men to say, as they used to say in the Party, "it is no accident that" Interest reigns. As Annette Baier puts it, "preoccupation with prisoner's and prisoners' dilemmas is a big boys' game, and a pretty silly one too."[19] Or Carol Rose: "The lapse of community may occur only infrequently in our everyday lives, but this world of estrangement has had a robust life in the *talk* about politics and economics since the seventeenth century."[20] In the men's talk.

To accept Hobbes's absurd mental experiment as the frame for answering all questions of why societies hang together is a scientific mistake. Like the Voting Paradox, the Hobbes Problem is contradicted by the facts. People do not always cooperate, but neither do they always defect. The life of man is only sometimes a state of Warre. In actual experiments men and women cooperate far above the level predicted by the Solely Prudence model. (A revealing feature of the experiments is that the only people who do *not* cooperate at such levels, and who do approach the Benthamite economist's level of defection are . . . Benthamite economists.) *Sic transit* all manner of histories of the economy and polity that suppose that all we need to grasp is Prudence.

What is wrong with ignoring the system of virtues can be put econometrically. Suppose we propose to reduce all behavior, *B*—buying, borrowing, bequeathing, birthing--to a linear function of Prudence, *P*, standing for all the variables that economists since Bentham have specialized in loving: Prudence, but also profit, price, payment, property, policy,

[19] Baier, "What Do Women Want?", p. 264.
[20] Rose, *Property and Persuasion*, p. 225.

purpose, preferences, pain, punishment, the pocketbook, the Profane. We generously admit that, well, yes, there might be other springs of conduct working at the same time, in cases such as voting or the prisoners' dilemma or the raising of children, the S variables of Solidarity, but also society, sociology, sensibility, stories, speech, sanctions, shame, the soul, the spirit, the subconscious, the self, the sacrament, the Sacred. That is, econometrically speaking, we might specify:

$$B = \alpha + \beta P + \gamma S + \epsilon$$

Very nice, dear. An economist caught in the Benthamite program is going to argue as follows: "Not to worry: you see, even without inquiry into S—I leave that to those idiots over in the Department of Psychology or Sociology, or the College of Law—I can estimate the coefficient on Prudence alone, β. I can take $\gamma S + \epsilon$ as a quasi error term. Isn't *that* clever! And you know with what facility I make metaphysical assumptions about its classical properties! Give me a break: I'm not in the business of explaining all behavior. I propose merely to explain some portion, and in many cases a large portion."

But the economist is taking an econometric misstep. The estimation of the coefficients is unbiased only if the error term is uncorrelated with the included variable, P. But unless God (bless Her holy name) has arranged the world's experiment such that P and S are independent, orthogonal, unrelated in a statistical sense, the quasi error term $\gamma S + \epsilon$ will be correlated with the include variable, P. The coefficient β, the outcome of an empirical investigation that improperly ignores the S variables, will be biased. The estimate will not even be consistent, statistically speaking: large sample sizes will not make any difference, except to make the economist, by the idiocy of statistical significance, unreasonably confident that he has the explanation in P alone.

In many important cases in economic history—the Voting Paradox in 1856 and the Prisoner's dilemma in commercial trust, to take two, but others also, such as the size of coal cars on British railways around 1900, the coming of general limited liability in England, American welfare reform in the late nineteenth century, the profit from Jamaican slavery during the Industrial Revolution, the governance of Bengal after 1761, the policies of Andrew Mellon, the balance of power within the bourgeois family, the buying of public symbols such as monuments and sports arenas, the labor bargain in early Manchester, the economic history of the Wisconsin lumber industry, the Old Poor Law, child labor in the nineteenth century, family survival in the Great Depression, the treatment of slaves, American consumer credit in the 1920s, the high school movement in the North around World War I, the segregated labor markets in the South, British overseas investment around 1870, rent seeking in prerevolutionary France—the virtues buried in the error term will be correlated with Prudence positively or negatively. If the correlation is substantively large (forget about its merely statistical significance, which is irrelevant scientifically), then the attempt to get insight in the Prudence variables will be substantively ruined. Not always. Sometimes the forces of P are so large relative to those of the correlated S that the mistake is trivial. Doubtless on the foreign exchanges contemporaneous arbitrage has little to do with S. Prudence reigns. But when we think a complete character might be involved, then failing to acknowledge S explicitly will leave the experiment not properly controlled.

For example, consider the explosion of ingenuity in the first industrial nation. As Joel Mokyr, Peter Temin, and I have argued, the wave of gadgets was indeed a wave across the British economy in the eighteenth and especially the early nineteenth centuries, not a water spout here or there, as N. F. R. Crafts and Knick Harley believe. Anyway, the attempts to explain it in terms reducible to Prudence have not been great successes.[21] The history of our discipline in Britain is littered with Prudent Causes that have not worked out: capital accumulation, transport improvement, foreign trade, agricultural prosperity, patent systems. None of them is silly or to be left out of the story. They are right and proper Ps. But there is something peculiar about explaining the largest change in circumstances since the Agricultural Revolution in terms of mere, dull Prudence. Were not people prudent before? Were not canals buildable before the Canal Age? Capital accumulation possible in China? Foreign trade expansive in Mogul India?

The wave of gadgets requires S variables, not merely as afterthoughts, additional variables for a complete explanation, concessions to the fuzzy-minded among humanists, but as conditioning factors on the operation of the Ps. A simple case is trust in commercial undertakings. It is known how little groups of Old Believers or Jews or Quakers or Mennonites took advantage of co-religiosity to enforce contracts. What is remarkable about modern economic life (though not I think unprecedented: it worked in fourth-century B.C. Greece, too) is the extension of such trust to comparative strangers, not Our Crowd. If foreign trade was to expand in the eighteenth century it needed a large expansion of what might be called commercial speech—the trading of reputations and market information, the persuading of Mr. Jones in the far off Chesapeake to undertake a certain novelty in tobacco supplied that would be advantageous to his partner in Glasgow. In other words, commerce depended on virtues of conversation, the keeping of promises, speech acts. A Hobbesian analysis would miss the point that people dealing in the Atlantic economy of 1760 were socialized because it misses the point that people talk and that talk is not always empty. So the analysis of

[21] McCloskey, "Industrial Revolution."

310   *McCloskey*

Prudence would be wrong. The elasticities would be misestimated, so to speak. The variables interpenetrate. A culture is necessary for business.

Albert Hirschman, who has been making this point for some decades, puts it this way:

> What is needed is for economists to incorporate into their analysis, whenever it is pertinent, such basic traits and emotions as the desire for power or sacrifice, the fear of boredom, pleasure in both commitment and unpredictability, the search for meaning and community, and so on. . . . When one has been groomed as a "scientist" it just takes a great deal of wrestling with oneself before one will admit that moral considerations of human solidarity can effectively interfere with those hieratic, impersonal forces of supply and demand.[22]

The first thing one groomed to be a "scientist" is going to claim is that the S variables are hard to measure. Economic historians, who have more acquaintance with measurement than the average economist or the average historian, will laugh out loud at such a claim. It is less, not more, difficult to measure gender, family background, education, social class, churches attended, newspapers read, and many, many S variables than the magnitude of labor-saving technical change in the United States, the British cost of living c. 1820 including services, the rent of land in Arthur Young's England, the interest rate in eighteenth-century China, the wage gap between men and women since 1890, and many, many other P variables.

---·•●•·---

It is easy to see how P depends on S, and many dissertations in economic history could be written making the point in detail. But S also depends on P, and dissertations should be written on that subject, too. Who we are depends on what we do, our ethics depend on our business. Commerce is a teacher of ethics. The growth of the market promotes virtue, sometimes. Most intellectuals since 1848 have thought the opposite: that the market and the ethic of the bourgeoisie always erode virtue. As James Boyd White puts it in his otherwise admirable *Justice as Translation*, bourgeois growth is bad because it is "the expansion of the exchange system by the conversion of what is outside it into its terms. It is a kind of steam shovel chewing away at the natural and social world."[23] White is here stuck back with Dickens in *Hard Times*: "It was a fundamental principle of the Gradgrind philosophy," wrote, "that everything was to be paid for. . . . Gratitude was to be abolished, and the virtues springing from it were not to be. Every inch of the existence of mankind, from birth to death, was to be a bargain across a counter."[24]

---

[22] Hirschman, *Essays in Trespassing*, pp. 303–04.
[23] White, *Justice*, p. 71.
[24] Dicken, *Hard Times*, p. 212.

Bourgeois Virtue and the History of P and S   311

On the contrary, the virtues of the bourgeois are those necessary for town life, for commerce and self-government. The virtue of tolerance, for example, can be viewed as bourgeois. Its correlations in European history, such as between Spain and Holland, suggest so. The experience of uncertainty in trade creates a skepticism about certitude--the arrogant and theoretical certitude of the aristocrat or the humble and routine certitude of the peasant. As Arjo Klamer has pointed out, "the dogma of doubt" is bourgeois, an attitude suited to the vagaries of the marketplace. On the town hall of Gouda in the Netherlands is inscribed the bourgeois motto, "*Audite et alteram partem*," "Listen even to the other side."

Bourgeois charity, again, if not the "charity," meaning love, of the English bibles, runs contrary to the caricature of greed. More than the peasant or aristocrat the bourgeois gives to the poor—as in the ghettos of Eastern Europe or in the small towns of the United States. Acts of charity follow the bourgeois norm of reciprocity. Jonathan Israel points out that 1616 the city of Amsterdam helped support over 10 percent of its population from the public purse.[25] The American Gospel of Wealth, founding hospitals, colleges, and libraries wherever little fortunes were made, is a bourgeois notion, paying back what was taken in profit. Walter Annenberg gives $500 million to schools in one jolt and we are not astonished. Middle-class people in the nineteenth century habitually gave a biblical tenth of their incomes to charity. The intrusion of the state into charity deadened the impulse, remaking charity into a *taille* imposed on grumbling peasants: I gave at the office.

The market spreads American habits of cooperation with strangers. In the United States, noted Santayana, "co-operation is taken for granted, as something that no one would be so mean or short-sighted as to refuse," and it is "private interests which are the factors in any co-operation." He does not here mean that Prudence Alone makes for cooperation: "When interests are fully articulated and fixed, co-operation is a sort of mathematical problem," in the manner of Hobbes; but Santayana saw much more arising from "a balance of faculties."[26]

Above all the causal connection between P and S in the bourgeois society is a matter of rhetoric. (There: I've used the R word!) A source of bourgeois virtue and a check on bourgeois vice is the premium that a bourgeois society puts on discourse. The bourgeois must talk. The aristocrat gives a speech, the peasant tells a tale. But the bourgeois must in the bulk of his transactions talk to an equal. It is wrong to imagine, as modern economics does, that the

---

[25] Israel, *Dutch Republic*, p. 360. The population of Amsterdam was about 100,000 at the time (p. 328). Israel quotes R. B. Evenhuis as giving a figure of 2,500 families, about 10,000 souls, which is where Israel gets his 10 percent. He reckons that an equal number were "supported" by churchs and guilds, which would mean that inhabitants "receiving charitable assistance from one source or another" were 20 percent of Amsterdam's population, not 10 percent.

[26] Santayana, *Character*, pp. 196, 226, 223, 222.

market is a field of silence. "I will buy with you, sell with you, talk with you, walk with you, and so following. . . . What news on the Rialto?"

The aristocrat does not deign to bargain. Hector tries, and Achilles answers: "argue me no agreements. I cannot forgive you./ As there are no trustworthy oaths between men and lions,/ Nor wolves and lambs have spirit that can be brought into agreement." The Duke of Ferrara speaks of his last, late duchess there upon the wall, "Even had you skill/ In speech—(which I have not)--to make your will/ Quite clear to such an one . . . . / —E'en then would be some stooping; and I choose/ Never to stoop." The aristocrat never stoops; the peasant stoops silently to harvest the grain or to run the machine; the bourgeois stoops metaphorically to make his will quite clear, and to know the will and reason of the other. The aristocrat's speech is declamation, and his proofs are like commands, which is perhaps why Plato the aristocrat and some Western intellectuals after him loved them so. The proof of the irrationality of the square root of 2 convinces (*vincere*, to conquer). The bourgeois by contrast must persuade, sweetly ("*suadeo*," from the same root as English "sweet").

The bourgeois goes at persuasion with a will. About a quarter of national income nowadays in rich countries is earned from merely bourgeois and feminine persuasion: not orders or information but persuasion.[27] One thinks of advertising, but in fact advertising is a tiny part of the total, one-and-a-half percent of national income. Take instead the detailed categories of work and make a guess as to the percentage of the time in each job spent on persuasion. Out of the 115 million civilian workers it seems reasonable to assign 100 percent of the time of the 760,000 lawyers and judges to persuasion; and likewise all the public relations specialists and actors and directors. Perhaps 75 percent of the time of the 14.2 million executive, administrative, and managerial employees is spent on persuasion, and a similar share of the time of the 4.8 million teachers and the 11.2 million salespeople (excluding cashiers). Half of the effort of police, writers, and health workers, one might guess, is spent on persuasion. And so forth. The result is 28.2 million person-years, a quarter of the labor force, persuading.

The result can be checked against other measures. John Wallis and Douglass North measure 50 percent of national income as transaction costs, the costs of persuasion being part of these.[28] Not all the half of American workers who are white-collar talk for a living, but in an extended sense many do, as for that matter do many blue-collar workers persuading each other to handle the cargo just so and pink collar workers dealing all day with talking customers and cooks. Of the talkers a good percentage are per-

---

[27] The calculation is given in more detail in McCloskey and Klamer, "One-Quarter of GDP is Persuasion."

[28] Wallis and North, "Measuring the Transaction Sector."

suaders. The secretary shepherding a document through the company bureaucracy is called on to exercise sweet talk and veiled threats. The bureaucrats and professionals who constitute most of the white-collar workforce are not themselves merchants, but they do a merchant's business inside and outside their companies. Note the persuasion exercised the next time you buy a suit. Specialty clothing stores charge more than discount stores not staffed with rhetoricians. The differential pays for the persuasion: "It's you, my dear" or "The fish tie makes a statement." As Adam Smith said in his lectures on jurisprudence, "every one is practising oratory . . . [and therefore] they acquire a certain dexterity and address in managing their affairs, or in other words in managing of men; and this is altogether the practise of every man in most ordinary affairs. . . , the constant employment or trade of every man."[29] Not constant, perhaps, but in Smith's time a substantial percentage and in modern times fully 25 percent.

Is the persuasive talk of the bourgeoisie "empty," mere comforting chatter with no further economic significance? No. It can not be. If that was all it was then the economy would be engaging in an expensive activity to no purpose. By shutting up we could pick up a $100 bill (or more exactly a $1,750,000,000,000 bill). A quarter of national income is a lot to pay for economically functionless warm and fuzzies. The fact would not square with the most modest claims of economics. *S* matters, but if gigantic amounts of *P* are supposed to be sacrificed for what looks like a small gain in *S* the economist is right to complain. The businesspeople circling La Guardia on a rainy Monday night could have stayed home. The crisis meeting in the plant cafeteria between the managers and the workers would lack point.

Adam Smith as usual put the matter well. The division of labor is the "consequence of a certain propensity . . . to truck, barter, and exchange. . . [I cannot pause here to consider] whether this propensity be one of those original principles in human nature, of which no further account can be given; or whether, as seems more probable, it be the necessary consequence of the faculties of reason *and speech*."[30] *The Wealth of Nations* did not again mention the faculty of speech in a foundational role, though Smith, who began his career as a freshman English teacher, did remark frequently on how business people and politicians talked together. In *The Theory of Moral Sentiments* he called speech "the characteristic faculty of human nature."[31]

Half of the Smith formula, the faculty of reason, became in time the characteristic obsession of economists. Smith himself did not much pursue it. Economic Man, restlessly seeking, is not a Smithian character. It was later economists, especially Paul Samuelson during the 1940s, who reduced

[29] Smith, *Lectures on Jurisprudence*, p. 352.
[30] Smith, *Wealth of Nations*, p. 25; cf. *Lectures on Jurisprudence*, pp. 352, 493.
[31] Smith, *Theory of Moral Sentiments*, p. 336.

economics to the reasoning of a constrained maximizer, Seeking Man, *Homo petens*. Samuelson's seeking has a peasant cast to it: the maximization of known utility under known constraints sounds more like Piers Ploughman than Robinson Crusoe. The utilitarian reduction of all the virtues to one maximand makes all virtues into Prudence. The wind-up mice of modern economic theory know nothing of humor, affection, integrity, and self-possession. Smith's notion of *Homo loquans*, Speaking Man, squares better with the varied virtues of the bourgeoisie.

The world of the bourgeoisie is jammed with institutions for making relationships and declaring character, from credit bureaus to business schools. The aristocracy and the peasantry got their characters ready-made by status, and in any case did not need to persuade. Tom Buddenbrook bitterly scolds his unbusinesslike brother, a harbinger of bohemianism in the family: "In a company consisting of business as well as professional men, you make the remark, for everyone to hear, that, when one really considers it, every businessman is a swindler--you, a business man yourself, belonging to a firm that strains every nerve and muscle to preserve its perfect integrity and spotless reputation."[32]

The bourgeoisie works with its mouth, and depends on word of mouth. Tom most enjoys "trade he came by through his own personal efforts. Sometimes, entirely by accident, perhaps on a walk with the family, he would go into a mill for a chat with the miller, who would feel himself much honoured by the visit; and quite *en passant*, in the best of moods, he could conclude a good bargain."[33] The firm's motto, challenged in the nineteenth century by Greed and Art, is, "My son, attend with zeal to thy business by day, but do none that hinders thee from they sleep at night."[34] Doing well by talking well, and doing therefore good.

-------------••••••-------------

A change is overdue. To admire bourgeois virtue is not to admire greed. Capitalism needs encouragement, being the hope for the poor of the world and being in any case the practice of what we were and who we are. But capitalism need not be hedonistic or monadic, and certainly not unethical. An aristocratic, country-club capitalism, well satisfied with itself, or a peasant, grasping capitalism, hating itself, are both lacking virtue. And neither works in town. They lead to monopoly and economic failure, alienation and revolution. We need a capitalism that nurtures communities of good townsfolk, in South Central Los Angeles as much as in Iowa City. We encourage it by taking seriously the bourgeois virtues.

[32] Mann, *Buddenbrooks*, p. 262.
[33] Ibid., p. 222.
[34] Ibid, p. 146 and throughout.

Bourgeois Virtue and the History of P and S   315

One can think of people and countries to stand as models. Benjamin Franklin and the United States lead the pack. Graña recounts the venom against Franklin in the writings of D. H. Lawrence, Stendhal, and Baudelaire: "a knave in Franklin's style," writes Baudelaire, was part of "the rising bourgeoisie come to replace the faltering aristocracy," which otherwise a new aristocracy of intellectuals would resupply. It is natural to think of millionaires in imagining an ideal bourgeois, the "vital few," as Jonathan Hughes put it: Henry Ford, for example, or Sam Walton of Walmart or Bill Gates of Microsoft. But it is not necessary: Franklin, Macaulay, Whitman, Lincoln, Twain, Frost, Orwell were bourgeois, and in their best moods unashamed of it. Being ashamed of being bourgeois has for a long time amounted to being ashamed of America. Scratch a pro-American and you find a pro-bourgeois. The sneerers at Franklin like Baudelaire and Lawrence were antidemocrats and anti-Americans. Dickens came to detest the United States as much as he came to detest businessmen.

A myth of recency has made the virtues arising from towns seem those of a shameful parvenu, such as Franklin and the United States. In economic history dependent on Marx, such as Weber's *General Economic History* or Karl Polanyi's *The Great Transformation*, the market is seen as a novelty. "Market economy," claimed Polanyi on little evidence, "is an institutional structure which, as we all too easily forget, has been present at no time except our own."[35] From this historical mistake arose the fairytales of lost paradises for aristocrats or peasants, and a reason for ignoring the bourgeois virtues.

It has taken a century of professional history to correct the mistake. The late David Herlihy put it this way in 1971: "research has all but wiped from the ledgers the supposed gulf once considered fundamental, between a medieval manorial economy and the capitalism of the modern period."[36] Medieval men bought and sold everything from grain to bishoprics. The Vikings were traders, too. Greece and Rome were business empires. The city of Jericho dates to 8000 B.C. The emerging truth is that we have lived in a world market for centuries, a market run by the bourgeoisie. Time to recognize the fact—to study a bourgeois virtue, and recognize its tangled history of *P* and *S*.

[35] Polanyi, *Great Transformation*, p. 37.
[36] Herlihy, "the Economy of Traditional Europe," p. 155.

REFERENCES

Baier, Annette. "What Do Women Want with a Moral Theory?" In *Virtue Ethics*, edited by R. Crisp and M. Slote, 263–77. Oxford Readings in Philosophy. Oxford: Oxford University Press, 1997.
Bell, Daniel. *The Cultural Contradictions of Capitalism*. New York: Basic Books, 1976.

Bentham, Jeremy. *A Fragment on Government, with an Introduction to the Principles of Morals and Legislation*. Edited by W. Harrison. Oxford: Basil Blackwell, 1948.

Brown, Vivienne. *Adam Smith's Discourse*. London: Routledge, 1994.

Casey, John. *Pagan Virtue: An Essay in Ethics*. Oxford: Clarendon Press, 1990.

Clough, Arthur Hugh. "The Latest Decalogue." In *The Norton Anthology of English Literature*, Vol. 2, edited by H. H. Abrams et al., 1034. New York: Norton, 1962.

Dickens, Charles. *Hard Times*. London: Bradbury and Evans, 1854.

Graña, César. *Bohemian versus Bourgeois: French Society and the French Man of Letters in the Nineteenth Century*. New York: Basic Books, 1964.

Herlihy, David. "The Economy of Traditional Europe." this JOURNAL 31, no. 1 (1971): 153–64.

Hirschman, Albert O. *Essays in Trespassing: Economics to Politics and Beyond*. Cambridge: Cambridge University Press, 1981.

_____. *The Passions and the Interests: Political Arguments for Capitalism before Its Triumph*. Princeton: Princeton University Press, 1977.

Israel, Jonathan. *The Dutch Republic: Its Greatness, Rise, and Fall, 1477–1806*. Oxford: Clarendon Press, 1995.

James, William. *The Ambassadors*. 1903. London: Penguin, 1986.

Johnson, Mark. *Moral Imagination: Implication of Cognitive Science for Ethics*. Chicago: University of Chicago Press, 1993.

Lebergott, Stanley. *Pursuing Happiness: American Consumers in the Twentieth Century*. Princeton: Princeton University Press, 1993.

Lodge, David. *Nice Work*. London: Penguin, 1988..

Mann, Thomas. *Buddenbrooks*. Trans. H. T. Lowe-Porter. New York: Vintage, 1992.

Manzoni, Alessandro. *The Betrothed [I promessi sposi]*. 1825–26; 1840. Reprint, Harvard Classics. New York: Collier, 1909.

McCloskey, Deirdre. *The Applied Theory of Price*. 2d ed. New York: Macmillan, 1985.

_____. "The Industrial Revolution." In *The Economic History of Britain since 1700*, Vol. 1, *1700–1860*, edited by R. C. Floud and D. N. McCloskey, 242–70. Cambridge: Cambridge University Press, 1994.

McCloskey, Deirdre, and Arjo Klamer. "One Quarter of GDP is Persuasion." *American Economic Review* 85, no. 2 (May 1995): 191–95.

Polanyi, Karl. *The Great Transformation*. Boston: Beacon Press, 1944.

Rose, Carol M. *Property and Persuasion: Essays on the History, Theory, and Rhetoric of Ownership*. Boulder: Westview, 1994.

Ruskin, John. "Work," in *Crown of Wild Olives*. 1866. Reprint, New York: Hurst, no date.

Santayana, George. *Character and Opinion in the United States*. 1920. Reprint, New York: Norton, no date.

Schumpeter, J. A. *Capitalism, Socialism and Democracy*. 1942. 3rd. ed. New York: Harper and Row, 1950.

Shaw, George Bernard. "Introduction to *Hard Times*." 1912. Reprinted in Charles Dickens, *Hard Times*, edited by G. Ford and S. Monod, 333–40. Norton Critical Edition. New York: Norton, 1990.

Smith, Adam. *The Theory of Moral Sentiments*. Edited by D. D. Raphael and A. L. Macfie. Glasgow Edition. Oxford: Oxford University Press, 1976.

Smith, Adam. *Correspondence of Adam Smith*. Edited by E. C. Mossner and I. S. Ross. Glasgow Edition. Oxford: Oxford University Press, 1977.

_____. *Lectures on Jurisprudence*. Edited by R. L. Meek, D. D. Raphael, and P. G. Stein. Glasgow Edition. Oxford: Oxford University Press, 1978.

_____. *An Inquiry in the Nature and Causes of the Wealth of Nations*. Edited by R. H.

Campbell, A. S. Skinner, and W. B. Todd. Glasgow Edition. 2 vols. Oxford: Oxford University Press, 1979.

_____. *Essays on Philosophical Subjects*. Edited by W. P. D. Wightman and J. J. Bryce. Glasgow Edition. Oxford: Oxford University Press, 1980.

Wallis, John Joseph, and Douglass North. "Measuring the Transaction Sector in the American Economy, 1870–1970." In *Long-Term Factors in American Economic Growth*, edited by S. L. Engerman and R. E. Gallman, 95–161. Chicago: University of Chicago Press for the National Bureau of Economic Research.

White, James Boyd. *Justice as Translation*. Chicago: University of Chicago Press, 1989.

PART II

WRITING ECONOMICS AND HISTORY AS IF MEANING MATTERED

7

REVIEW OF SOCIAL ECONOMY

VOLUME XLVII   FALL, 1989   NUMBER 3

WHY I AM NO LONGER A POSITIVIST*

By Donald N. McCloskey**
University of Iowa

In 1964 all the good people were positivists, or so a first-year graduate student in economics was likely to think,

True, among philosophers the doctrines of strict positivism were mostly dead. Philosophical positivism had long since had its day, a glorious one, in the 1920s. One of the headings of Karl Popper's splendid intellectual autobiography, *Unended Quest* [1976 (1974), p. 87f] asks "Who Killed Logical Positivism?" He answers, "I fear that I must admit responsibility." His book of 1934, written when he was about 30 and translated into English 25 years later as *The Logic of Scientific Discovery*, was the death knell. He quotes the Australian philosopher John Passmore as writing in 1967 that "Logical positivism, then, is dead, or as dead as a philosophical movement ever becomes." [Passmore, p. 56] Even the broader doctrines of empiricism under which logical positivism sheltered had been under attack for a long time. W. V. Quine's "Two Dogma's of Empiricism" had in 1951 dynamited the distinction inherited from Kant between analytic and synthetic statements. Over in the philosophy department, then, no one earned prestige by declaring himself to be a positivist. Not in 1964.

Over in the economics department, however, there was still prestige to be earned by sneering at the soft little qualitative people. No one in economics at Harvard had heard that positivism was dead, or if they had heard they weren't telling. The division of "soft" and "hard" was irresistible to a 22-year old. A beginning graduate student wanted to be hard as nails, of course: that was why one studied economics rather than history or, perish

*0034-6764/89/0901-225/$1.50/0.

**Originally delivered to the conference on Economics, Truth and Logic: The Impact of Logical Positivism on Economics, University of Wisconsin, March 4, 1989. I thank the participants for their comments.

the thought, English. The economists, like many other academics around 1964, espoused a positivism cruder than the philosophical kind.

Now, a quarter of a century later, the crude version persists. An economist who uses "philosophical" as a cuss word ("That's rather philosophical, don't you think?") and does not regard philosophical argument as relevant to his business will of course not reexamine the philosophy he lives by, regardless of what is going on in the philosophy department. Even grown-up economists, therefore, do not have an occasion to rethink their youthful positivism. Economists young and old still use the positivist way of arguing. They talk a lot about verifiability, observable implications, meaningful statements, science *vs.* pseudo-science, the love of physics, the unity of sciences, the fact/value split, prediction and control, hypothetico-deductive systems, and the formalization of languages. Logical positivism of the crude sort had charmed the young men of the 1920s and 1930s. It charmed the young men of the 1960s. It still charms the young men of the 1980s (the young women find it less attractive). Milton Friedman's famous article of 1953, usually interpreted as straightforward positivism [contrast de Marchi and Hersh, forthcoming] and confusingly named "positive economics" by Milton himself, is all that most economists think about what they do. Sentences from Milton's pen still provide the philosophical stage directions for the field. Until something changes, as it has shown recently a few signs of doing, the history and appeal of positivism will continue to be news in economics.

So the data about the graduate student of 1964 may help think about the story of positivism in economics. I do not want to laugh too harshly at the young man I once was. Professors forget that from Olympus they are all pretty funny looking. And I want to emphasize at the outset that I do not regard positivism as a useless or silly movement. In its time it did a great deal of good. In 1938 Terence Hutchison argued effectively against the a priorism of the 1920s and 1930s; in 1953 Friedman argued effectively against the refusal to examine facts of the 1940s and 1950s. But its time has passed; its values require scrutiny; it has become an oppressive rather than a liberating force in field after field, in economics, in sociology, in political science. We must grow beyond a fanatical adolescence, which is not to say that the adolescence was worthless or unnecessary.

Why then was our young man a positivist?

A young non-philosopher who declares himself to be a positivist in 1964 must be seen as declaring an allegiance vaguely understood. The young are good at vague allegiances (something we should bear in mind when teaching them) but not so good at doctrine. The same young man was beginning to stop thinking of himself as a socialist, yet even during his socialist phase had not read much of *Capital* or much else of the doctrine. On the positivist front he seems to have owned a copy of A. J. Ayer, ed. *Logical Positivism* [1959], but internal evidence suggests that he did not read it until later, and never more than a couple of essays. (At the head of the essay by Otto Neurath he wrote in pencil "This paper reeks of metaphysics," which is either a complaint from a positivist against backsliding or a sophisticated anti-positivist observation that logical positivism requires metaphysics to live; probably the former.) A year or so into graduate school, following the economist John R. Meyer, his mentor, he read the first half of R. B. Braithwaite's book [1953] and fancied himself to be daringly advanced about hypothetico-deductive systems in science. At about the same time, having decided to study economic history, he read Carl Hempel's "The Function of General Laws in History" [1942] and decided that storytelling could be reduced to model testing. He therefore believed that hypothetico-deductive testing of models covered what was of value in human thought, and he tried to force his work on British economic history into the plan. He had been taken by Friedman's article, especially the part about leaves on trees not having to know that they "want" to face towards the sun, and remembered Hendrick Houthakker's diffident lecture on the matter to the first-year students of price theory.

His grasp of the doctrines of the new religion, then, was weak in book learning. Yet one did not need book learning in 1964 to be a thoroughgoing positivist. The intellectual world then was positivist. A sense in which it was positivist was soon to be demonstrated in the Vietnam War: here were social engineers, committed to the observable and the verifiable, armed with falsifiable hypotheses deduced from higher order propositions, unencumbered by the value half of the fact/value split, seeking passionately for dispassionate data and body counts from the river patrols. Positivistic thinking, if not philosophical positivism, pervaded intellectual life [for painting and economics see Klamer 1988].

Amateur positivism fitted with the trend of Western philosophy, or at any rate the trend as discerned by the logical positivists themselves, the best of the philosophical crop 1920-1950 and the writers of the books that young men bought and admired. Our young man of 1964 had browsed on the non-technical works of Bertrand Russell in the local Carnegie library when in high school. He had at least picked up Russell's scornful attitude towards the past. Logical positivism could be seen as a culmination. Glorious if muddled Greek beginnings; Christian fall back; then the ascent to Descartes, Hume, Kant, and Russell.

Positivism, therefore, appealed to a young man's desire to be up-to-date. And it was clearly scientific. A touching faith in what science could do seemed justified — scientism. Science seemed then, as it still seems to people who have not examined the history, to have been the main engine of economic progress since 1700. And the history of science had not yet established that the rational reconstructions of which philosophers talked had nothing to do with how science worked. The sociology of science that looked closely at laboratory life was still a decade away. Even in 1964 the doubts may have occurred to scholars working in the history of science, but they had not occurred to outsiders. Someone trying to become an economic scientist was going to latch on to a theory of how to be scientific. How do I know what Scientific Economics is? Positivism tells me what, right here in this book.

Being Scientific means in English being different from the common herd. Demarcating Science from other thought was the main project of the positivist movement. Perhaps the mixing of the English definition ("science" in other languages means merely "inquiry") with the positivistic program of demarcation explains why positivism of a sort has stuck so firmly to the English-speaking world. English-speaking people even now worry a good deal about whether they are scientific or not. Witness the sneers that journalists in America and Britain adopt against social "science." In Italian by contrast *un scienziato* is merely "a learned one," and mothers use it to brag about their studious little boys. A graduate student in 1964 had less desire to be "learned" than to be "scientific," in the English, honorific, lab-coated, hard-nosed, and masculine sense of the world [the desire of students has not changed: see Colander and Klamer 1987].

Importantly in 1964, as I have said, the exemplary scientists were positivists. I mentioned John Meyer, whose work with Alfred Conrad on the economics of slavery and on quantitative economic history had come out as papers a few years before. The graduate student in question had been a research assistant for Meyer, helping him put the papers into *The Economics of Slavery and Other Studies in Econometric History* [1964]. Bliss was it in that dawn to be alive/But to be young [and positive] was very heaven!

The student was soon to meet his next model, the economic historian Alexander Gerschenkron, and to get another dose of an admired scholar talking positivism (while doing something else, but the point here is the official doctrine, not the behavior). Near the beginning of Gerschenkron's famous essay "Economic Backwardness in Historical Perspective," he declared that "historical research consists essentially in application to

empirical material of various *sets of empirically derived hypothetical gener-
alizations* and in *testing the closeness of the resulting fit*, in the hope that in
this way certain *uniformities*, certain typical situations, and certain *typical
relationships among individual factors* in these situations can be ascertained." [1952, *aet.* 48 (reprinted 1962, p. 6), italics added] The sentence has
a whiff of Bacon in it but could pass for the usual positivism of the chair. And
elsewhere he said repeatedly that the concept of relative backwardness is
"an operationally usable concept." ["An Approach," p. 354]

Avant-garde-ism, hero worship, being scientific, joining in the ceremo-
nies of scientism, then, partly explained our student's youthful positivism.
The certainty of its doctrines was half the rest. Eric Hoffer wrote in *The
True Believer* that "The effectiveness of a doctrine does not come from its
meaning but from its certitude. No doctrine however profound and sublime
will be effective unless it is presented as the embodiment of the one and
only truth." [1963 (1951), p. 83f]

The remaining charm was efficiency. Even to a graduate student it was
clear that positivism saved effort. It was economical in ways attractive to the
young and impatient. Here was a method of being an economic historian, for
example, that required no tiresome involvement with "all the sources" (as
the people in the Department of History kept saying so irritatingly). No.
One needed merely to form an "observable implication" of one's "higher
order hypothesis," then proceed to "test" it. Most of the facts of the matter
could be ignored, since most could be construed as not bearing on the
hypothesis under test. No tacit knowledge was necessary, no sense of the
landscape, no feel for the story. A young historian of the British iron and
steel industry did not have to learn broadly about the iron and steel
industry. (He did in fact learn more than was required on properly positivistic grounds, but only because he was thrown into a company of historians at
the London School of Economics while doing his research, and anyway he
had a non-positivistic father, also an academic, who from time to time would
remark mildly to his technocratic son that one needs to know something to
write about it.) Nothing could be simpler than the positivistic formula. In
fact, nothing was: the proliferation of normal science in economics has
shown how simple it is.

The simplicity of positivism has great appeal to the young. To put it
harshly, it is a 3″ × 5″ card philosophy of science. Its doctrines can be stated
briefly and understood shortly thereafter. Once understood they can be
applied to everything, and most particularly they can be applied by the
young and ignorant. The young can be forgiven, having few enough weapons against the old. Game theory has such charm these days; econometrics

once had it; tomorrow it will be computer simulations.

Positivism avowedly and from its beginnings tried to narrow the grounds on which scholars could converse to the observable, to the numerical, to the non-tacit. The physicist Ernst Mach famously attacked the very idea of the electron, as a non-observable figment. His slogan was "the observable." The economic slogans are equally unargued: "macro-economics must be expressed as microeconomics"; "ethical discussions are meaningless." Positivism is one of the great sloganeering movements. So it is with movements attractive to young intellectuals. The German classicist, Ulrich von Wilamowitz-Moellendorff, wrote of his own youthful fascination with the Method of his age:

> *Philology had [in 1870] the highest opinion of itself, because it taught method, and was the only perfect way of teaching it. Method,* via ac ratio, *was the watchword. It seemed the magic art, which opened all closed doors; it was all important, knowledge was a secondary consideration.*

He remarked ruefully fifty years on, "Gradually the unity of science ["inquiry" in German] has dawned on me. . . . Let each do what he can, . . . and not despise what he himself cannot do." [1928 (1930), p. 115; cf. 1927 (1982), p. 136]

The Harvard graduate student's attitude towards the *via ac ratio* in 1964 is best illustrated by the motto he affixed a couple of years later over the doorway of the Economic History Workshop, in the attic of a building just off Harvard Square: "Give us the data and we will finish the job." It seemed clever at the time. Economists would not need to be concerned with the mundanities of *collecting* the data. And there was nothing beyond quantifiable, observable implications to be known from a phenomenon.

By way of contrast, consider the great biologist Barbara McClintock, who approached Nature with the idea, as Evelyn Fox Keller puts it in her account of McClintock's career, that

> *Organisms have a life and an order of their own that scientists can only begin to fathom. . . . [McClintock said] "there's no such thing as a central dogma into which everything will fit." . . . The need to "listen to the material" follows from her sense of the order of things . . . [T]he complexity of nature exceeds our own imaginative possibilities. . . . Her major criticism of contemporary research is based on what she sees as inadequate humility. . . . [The usual] dichotomies of subject-object, mind-matter, feeling-reason, disorder-law . . . are directed towards a cosmic unity typically excluding or devouring one of the pair [1985, pp. 162-63]*

Perhaps positivism is a male method. The style of empirical inquiry that spends six years on the aberrant pigmentation of a few kernels of corn is rare in economics. Yet no one is surprised to find it disproportionately among female economists: Margaret Reid of Chicago, for example, or Dorothy Brady of Pennsylvania and of the Women's Bureau at the Department of Labor, or Anna Jacobson Schwartz of New York University and the National Bureau of Economic Research. "The thing is dear to you for a period of time; you really [have] an affection for it," said McClintock. [Keller, 1985, p. 164] What is dear to male economists, by contrast, is quick fits to models. "Testing hypothesis," after all, is easier than thinking and much easier than making the thing "dear to you for a period of time."

One could reverse the old calumny on socialism: Anyone who is not a positivist before 25 has no brain; anyone who is still a positivist after age 40 has no heart. But that is not quite right. The brain/heart distinction is itself a piece of positivism, dividing up the world into what we know and what we feel, science and passion. Positivism is a young man's passion about what he feels positively he knows.

Einstein wrote to his friend Michele Angelo Besso about Ernst Mach's positivism: "I do not inveigh against Mach's little horse; but you know what I think about it. It cannot give birth to anything living; it can only exterminate harmful vermin." [13 May 1917, cited in Jeremy Bernstein's book on Einstein; self-cited in his essay on Besso in the *New Yorker* Feb. 27, 1989, p. 86f] That seems about right. Positivism was a reaction to German idealism. Harmful or not, idealism was exterminated in the English-speaking world for fifty or sixty years. It is coming back as something more grownup, as pragmatism or rhetoric or other projects after virtue, finding its reality in social discourse rather than in the transcendental spirit or in data seen clearly and distinctly by a lone observer. In the meantime positivism did not give birth to anything living. Our theories of the economy are more precise than they were before positivism and claim to be more observable, at least by a narrow standard of observability. But our living understanding of the economy has not much advanced. In some brains it has retrogressed.

The graduate student of 1964 went on to get his Ph.D. from Harvard, becoming there a Chicago economist in method and in politics, and in 1968 began twelve years teaching at the University of Chicago. Gradually, very gradually, his student positivism faded. Such intellectual growth will come as a surprise to people who cannot think of the Chicago School of Economics as anything but the incarnation of all evil (such people are surprisingly common, though it turns out that they do not know the Good Old Chicago School of Frank Knight, T. W. Schultz, Margaret Reid, and Ronald Coase).

The positivism faded when the method talk of other Chicago economists stopped sounding fresh and new. It took ten years. At Chicago the positivism was laid on thick, and conversations with George Stigler were likely to be terminated abruptly by a positivist ukase and a sneer.

One conversation with Stigler was especially eye opening to an associate professor beginning at last in 1978 to doubt the epistemological claims of positivism. George was holding forth on the merits of behaviorist theories of voting in which people are said to vote their pocketbooks. His younger colleague, who had just read Brian Barry's devastating attack on such models [1978] and for ten years had been teaching first-year graduate students about the small man in a large market, following George's exposition in *The Theory of Price*, noted that people would be irrational to go to the polls in any case. Since the people were nuts to begin with, it would be strange if they voted their pocketbooks when they got inside the booth. The argument struck a nerve, and Stigler became as was his custom abusively positivistic, declaring loudly that all that mattered were the observable implications. To the doubting positivist, though, the argument seemed to throw away some of the evidence we have. That did not seem right to him: throw away some of the evidence and then proceed to examine the evidence. He noticed, too, that Stigler refused to talk any more about the matter. By 1978 Milton Friedman had left Chicago for the Hoover Institution, Harry Johnson was dead, Robert Fogel was at Harvard, and T. W. Schultz was long retired. The ethics of conversation at Chicago was being governed by Stigler. One began to wonder whether a method that resulted in such irrational ends to conversations was all that it was cracked up to be.

A conversation with Gary Becker a year or so later opened the eyes of the apostate positivist still further. The Lord works in mysterious ways, and it may be significant that the conversation took place at the regular Economics luncheon in the cafeteria of the Episcopal Theological Seminary. The Chicago economists were talking about the economics of capital punishment (conversations at Chicago were always about economics, which is why it was the best place to be an assistant or associate professor, though maybe not such a good place to be a full professor, if you wanted to grow intellectually). Gary was explaining the result from his colleague and student Isaac Erlich that from a cross-section of states one execution appeared to deter seven murders. The now definitely apostate colleague (he was reading philosophy of science again) remarked that an execution was not the same as a murder. He did not express it very clearly at the time, and Gary may not have followed the point (Becker was more open-minded than Stigler on such matters). The point was that an execution is an elevation of the state to life-and-death power, whereas a murder is an individual's act. The two are not morally comparable. It would be like deterring truancy by shooting the parents: shooting would work, no doubt, probably in a ratio about seven to one, but would not, therefore, be morally desirable. Becker was greatly annoyed (again that conversation rupturing feature of positivism). In a positivistic and utilitarian spirit he broke off the discussion, muttering repeatedly, "Seven to one! Seven to one!"

And so it went, quickly. At about this time (the end of the 1970s) the former positivist picked up a copy of Feyerabend's *Against Method* at the Chicago bookstore, found Stephen Toulmin's book *The Uses of Argument* [1958] in a New Orleans second-hand shop, and finally in 1980 was asked by the English professor Wayne Booth to give a talk on "The Rhetoric of Economics," whatever that was. The invitation probably came on the strength of a reputation for knowing more people outside economics than most economists at Chicago did and being marginally less inclined to sneer at non-economists than the rest of the Department. The economist read hurriedly Booth's *Modern Dogma and the Rhetoric of Assent* and Michael Polanyi's *Personal Knowledge* in his mother-in-law's house in Vermont over Christmas 1980. He gave the lecture and wondered what he was talking about.

In the spring came the final break with Chicago's version of positivism. An otherwise excellent graduate student gave a thesis seminar consisting of "observable implications" which massively ignored evidence and reasoning that did not fit into a positivistic mold. The associate professor, having by this time declared that he was going to leave Chicago, made himself a pain in the neck at the seminar, grilling the candidate and the faculty supervisor on why they did not want to look at all the evidence.

*   *   *   *   *

Later the other arguments against positivism became important. Positivism has long claimed to be a sword and buckler against totalitarianism. The Demarcation Criterion was taken to demarcate civilization from the darkness. As Terence Hutchison expressed the notion in 1938:

> *The most sinister phenomenon of recent decades for the true scientist, and indeed to Western civilization as a whole, may be said to be the growth of Pseudo-Sciences no longer confined to hole-in-corner cranks.... [Testability is] the only principle or distinction practically adoptable which will keep science separate from pseudoscience.* [pp. 10-11]

This rhetorical turn has been popular since the 1930s. It was the convention of the 1950s to associate fascism, somehow, with Hegel and Neitzsche and even with the anti-fascist Croce. The turn is still in use — witness the use of the late Yale critic Paul de Man's fascist past (the fact of it is in dispute) as a way of attacking recent trends in literary criticism. Think of it as intellectual McCarthyism. I hold in my hand a list of intellectuals with plain connections to the enemies of civilization.

The turn has parallels in many fields. Peter Novick in *That Noble Dream: The "Objectivity Question" and the American Historical Profession* discusses its use in academic history and observes that "as early as 1923 Bertrand Russell [consider the source] had made a connection between the pragmatic theory of truth and rigged trials in the Soviet Union. In a 1935 discussion of the ancestry of fascism he made it clear that doubts about the existence of objective truth [or Objective Truth, McC.] figured prominently in that genealogy." [1988, p. 289]

The viciousness of the assaults on "relativism," and the willingness to tar people of good will with fascism or Stalinism, conceals a weakness in the case. The weakness is that totalitarianism can be more plausibly connected with positivism than with relativism. One can reply, in other words, *tu quoque*. Hutchison was attacking, of course, the pseudoscience of racism. What he failed to notice was that this particular pseudoscience was itself a product of early positivism. The political analysis here, echoed even now in rearguard actions by neo-positivists, was always weak. Especially so it was weak, I am saying, because the positivists themselves (for example, Karl Pearson) devised the pseudosciences of which Hutchison speaks — eugenics, for example, and racial anthropology, the sciences of the extermination camps. A day at Auschwitz does not put one in mind of Hegel or Nietzsche. It puts one in mind of factories and laboratories and record-keeping, the measuring of skulls and the testing of human tolerance for freezing water.

I am not claiming that positivists are fascists. I am suggesting merely that they cannot in all fairness claim that their opponents are. The trick of saying that anyone who does not agree with a particularly narrow version of French rationalism or British empiricism is an "irrationalist" [Stove 1982] and is, therefore, in cahoots with Hitler needs to be dropped. One of many awful truths about Nazism and the Holocaust is that they came from Western civilization, from its best as from its worst, from positivism itself as much as from Valley-girl irrationalism. The positivists have long been accustomed to shouting angrily that open discourse leads to totalitarianism. Perhaps their anger defends them from a wordless guilt.

Positivism, then, claims to contribute to human freedom. I must say I have not noticed such results. The narrowing of argument down to a nub of first-order predicate logic and the results of controlled experiments makes people more not less intolerant and more not less willing to use violence in support of their ideas. One is reminded of the sometime chief rabbi of the British Empire of whom it was said he never used reasoning until he had exhausted violence. The violence with which economists outside the main stream excluded from the conversation is one example (though our National Science Foundation has in fact been admirably tolerant, to its cost). A physicist who works on the paranormal (that is, works on it, not "believes in it") is instantly ostracized from science. [Collins and Pinch, 1982]

A case can be made, in fact, that positivism is a denial of human freedom, a step beyond freedom and dignity. It is a subordination of individuals to the rare systematic genius. John Ruskin, the 19th-century critic of architecture, noted that the search for a crystalline ideal has been an incubus on classical and Renaissance (and now modernist) architecture. He attacked the tyranny of the lonely genius, seeking by contemplation in his warm room a universal system to impose upon us all. Of the Renaissance he wrote:

> *[I]ts main mistake . . . was the unwholesome demand for* perfection *at any cost. . . . Men like Verrocchio and Ghiberti [try Marx or Samuelson] were not be had every day. . . . Their strength was great enough to enable them to join science with invention, method with emotion, finish with fire. . . . Europe saw in them only the method and the finish. This was new to the minds of men, and they pursued it to the neglect of everything else. "This," they cried, "we must have in our work henceforward;" and they were obeyed. The lower workman secured method and finish, and lost, in exchange for them, his soul. [1853 (1960), pp. 228-229]*

Consider whether Ruskin's argument does not apply to positivism in economics, seeking an all-embracing, testable Theory quite apart from the practical skills of the statesman, the craftsman, or, indeed, the economic scientist. An "interpretative economics," as Arjo Klamer and Don Lavoie are calling it, would turn the other way, as economists really do in most of their work. It is in Ruskin's terms "Gothic economics," an end to searching for a Grail of a unified field theory, an awakening from Descartes' Dream. As Ruskin said again,

> *[I]t requires a strong effort of common sense to shake ourselves quit of all that we have been taught for the last two centuries, and wake to the perception of a truth. . .: that great art . . . does not say the same thing over and over again. . . . [T]he Gothic spirit . . . not only dared, but delighted in, the infringement of every servile principle. [1853 (1960), pp. 166-167]*

Positivism has the young man's willingness to enslave himself to a $3'' \times 5''$ card principle and the corresponding intolerance. A few years ago A. J. Ayer, the importer of a simplified form of Vienna positivism into the English-speaking world, gave a speech at the University of York. His subject, astonishingly, was tolerance (it was a series, not his own choice of topic). He used religion as the example of intolerance, as befits the condition of the West that positivism helped cure. At the reception after the talk he was asked if he had been tolerant of non-positivists in the 1930s. He did not seem startled by the question: "No," he said, "I was not tolerant."

Toleration is not the strong point of positivism. The philosopher Clark Glymour amused many of his colleagues by beginning his *Theory and Evidence* with the following: "If it is true that there are but two kinds of people in the world — the logical positivists and the god-damned English professors — then I suppose I am a logical positivist." [1980, p. ix] That most philosophers find this funny is a measure of how far they have wandered from the love of truth. Another philosopher, Stanley Rosen, noted that "the typical practitioner of analytic philosophy" succumbs "to the temptation of confusing irony for a refutation of opposing views." [1980, p. xiii] To Glymour I say in reply that if there are but two such kinds of scholars, and one loftily scornful of what can be learned from the other, then I suppose I am a goddamn English professor.

Many economists I admire talk in positivist terms — Friedman, Armen Alchian, Harold Demsetz, Robert Fogel. But I think this only suggests that it is possible to be a good economist and a poor philosopher. My habit is to avoid picking fights with such people on their philosophy, sticking to the economics. The philosophy may be pretty weak, but it seems to give them the strength to go on. We need inspiriting in academic life because the rewards come so late. If an illogical philosophy makes an economist courageous in collecting facts and ideas about the economy, then no one should object. The other English professors and I are willing to be more tolerant of the positivists than they were of others.

If some good economists espouse positivism, the question arises how economics would be different without it. Not much [see Klamer *et al.*, 1988]. An economist without the $3'' \times 5''$ card would take questionnaires more seriously. Right now a confused argument that people sometimes (shockingly) do not tell the whole truth suffices to kill questionnaires in economics. He would be more serious about analyzing his introspection. Right now the introspection comes in by the back door. He would recognize his metaphors and his stories [McCloskey, 1988b]. Right now he calls them models and time series, thinking himself superior to the humanists. He would reassess his devotion to value-freedom, without abandoning the distinction entirely. Right now the values run the wizard's show from behind the curtain. He would be less enamoured of utilitarianism. Right now utilitarianism seems to most economists to be the same as thinking. He would look at all the evidence. Right now his positivism allows him to narrow the evidence to certain mismeasured numbers and certain misspecified techniques. [McCloseky, 1989] Economics would become less rigidly childish in its method. I do not know what changes in conclusions would follow. If I did I would be rich. [McCloskey, 1988a]

Positivism, in short, is not a philosophy for an adult in science. Young men — especially young *men* — can believe it because they can believe any crazy thing. Recall the title. Why am I no longer a positivist? Because finally the graduate student of 1964, in this one matter at any rate, was able to put away his childish toys.

REFERENCES

Ayer, A. J., ed.   *Logical Positivism.* New York: Free Press, 1959.
Barry, Brian.   *Sociologists, Economists and Democracy.* Chicago: University of Chicago Press (London: Collier-Macmillan, 1970), 1978.
Braithwaite, Richard B.   *Scientific Explanation.* Cambridge: Cambridge University Press, 1953.
Colander, David and Arjo Klamer.   "The Making of an Economist." *Journal of Economic Perspectives* (Fall 1987).
Collins, Harry and Trevor Pinch.   *Frames of Meaning: The Social Construction of Extraordinary Science.* London: Routledge and Kegan Paul, 1982.
Conrad, Alfred H. and John R. Meyer.   *The Economics of Slavery and Other Studies in Econometric History.* Chicago: Aldine, 1964.
Friedman, Milton.   "The Methodology of Positive Economics." In his *Essays in Positive Economics.* Chicago: University of Chicago Press, 1953.
Gerschenkron, Alexander.   "Economic Backwardness in Historical Perspective." Reprinted pp. 5-30 in *Economic Backwardness in Historical Perspective: A Book of Essays.* Cambridge: Harvard University Press, 1952 (1962).
——— "The Approach to European Industrialization: A Postscript." In *Economic Backwardness*, (1962), pp. 353-366.
Glymour, Clark.   *Theory and Evidence.* Princeton: Princeton University Press, 1980.
Hempel, Carl G.   "The Function of General Laws in History." In P. Gardiner, ed., *Theories of History* (New York: Free Press, 1959), 1942.
Hoffer, Eric.   *The True Believer: Thoughts on the Nature of Mass Movements.* New York: Time, Inc., 1963 (1951).
Hutchison, Terence.   *The Significance and Basic Postulates of Economic Theory,* 2nd ed. New York: Kelley, 1960 (1938).
Keller, Evelyn Fox.   *Reflections on Gender and Science.* New Haven: Yale University Press, 1985.
Klamer, Arjo, Donald N. McCloskey, Robert M. Solow (eds.).   *The Consequences of Economic Rhetoric.* New York: Cambridge University Press, 1988.
Klamer, Arjo.   *Conversations with Economists: New Classical Economists and Opponents Speak Out on the Current Controversy in Macroeconomics.* Totawa, N.J.: Rowman and Allanheld, 1983.

_____. "The Advent of Modernism in Economics." MS, University of Iowa, 1987.

Klamer, Arjo, D. N. McCloskey, and Robert Solow, eds. *The Consequences of Rhetoric.* Cambridge: Cambridge University Press, 1988.

McCloskey, D. N. "The Limits of Expertise: If You're So Smart, Why Ain't You Rich?" *The American Scholar*, 57 (Summer 1988a), pp. 393-406.

_____. "The Storied Character of Economics." *Tijdschrift voor Geschiedenis*, 101 (4, 1988b), pp. 643-654.

_____. "Formalism in Economics, Rhetorically Speaking." *Ricerche Economiche*, forthcoming, March, 1989.

Marchi, Neil de and Abraham Hersh. "Milton Friedman's Pragmatism." Unpublished paper.

Novick, Peter. *That Noble Dream: The 'Objectivity Question' and the American Historical Profession.* Cambridge: Cambridge University Press, 1988.

Passmore, John. "Logical Positivism." art. P. Edwards, ed. *The Encyclopedia of Philosophy.* New York and London: Macmillan and Collier Macmillan, 1967.

Popper, Karl. *Unended Quest: An Intellectual Autobiography.* London: Fontana. (First published in *The Philosophy of Karl Popper*, 1974), 1976.

Rosen, Stanley. *The Limits of Analysis.* New York: Basic, 1980.

Ruskin, John. *The Stones of Venice.* Abridged by J. G. Links. New York: Farrar, Strauss & Giroux, paperback edition of 1983 (New York: Da Capo Press), 1863 (1960).

Stove, David. *Popper and After: Four Modern Irrationalists.* Oxford: Pergamon, 1982.

Wilamowitz-Moellendorff, Ulrich von. *My Recollections*, trans. G. C. Richards. London: Chatto & Windus, 1930 (1928).

Journal of Economic Literature
Vol. XXI (June 1983), pp. 481–517

The Rhetoric of Economics

By DONALD N. MCCLOSKEY

The University of Iowa

The length of the acknowledgments here testifies to an unexplored feature of the rhetoric of economics, the role of the audience: like oratory, scholarship depends for its virtues on the virtues of its audience. I have been fortunate in mine. I must apologize for my amateurish understanding of what is happening in philosophy, mathematics, literary criticism, rhetorical studies, and other places beyond my competence, and ask that practitioners in these fields assist in my further education. For their early attempts I thank Evan Fales, Paul Hernadi, John Lyne, Michael McGee, Allan Megill, John Nelson, and Jay Semel of the Colloquium on Applied Rhetoric at The University of Iowa; Wayne Booth, Ira Katznelson, and others at the University of Chicago in the program in Politics, Rhetoric and Law, before which the earliest version was delivered; Robert Boynton, Bernard Cohn, John Comaroff, Otis Dudley Duncan, James O. Freedman, Clifford Geertz, William Kruskal, Donald Levine, Laura McCloskey, Richard Rorty, Renato Rosaldo; and the Humanities Society at the University of Iowa. That the economists on whom I have inflicted the argument have reacted with such intelligent skepticism and generous encouragement suggests, as the paper does, that we are better scholars than our methodology would allow. I thank my colleagues in economics at Iowa, especially the Sanctuary Seminar in Economic Argument; Seminars at the World Bank and the National Science Foundation; my colleagues at the Institute of Advanced Studies and the Faculty of Economics at the Australian National University; seminars at the universities of Adelaide, Auckland, Melbourne, New South Wales, Tasmania and Western Australia; at Monash, and Iowa State universities; Victoria University of Wellington; and an assemblage of economists elsewhere: William Breit, Ronald Coase, Arthur Diamond, Stanley Engerman, J. M. Finger, Milton Friedman, Allan Gibbard, Robert Goodin, Gary Hawke, Robert Higgs, Albert Hirschman, Eric Jones, Arjo Klamer, Harvey Leibenstein, David Levy, Peter Lindert, Neil de Marchi, Michael McPherson, Amartya Sen, Robert Solow, Larry Westphal, Gordon Winston, and Gavin Wright. Thomas Mayer's encouragement at an early stage and his detailed comments as referee for this Journal *at a later stage were exceptionally heartening and useful.*

481

ECONOMISTS DO NOT FOLLOW the laws of enquiry their methodologies lay down. A good thing, too. If they did they would stand silent on human capital, the law of demand, random walks down Wall Street, the elasticity of demand for gasoline, and most other matters about which they commonly speak. In view of the volubility of economists the many official methodologies are apparently not the grounds for their scientific conviction.

Economists in fact argue on wider grounds, and should. Their genuine, workaday rhetoric, the way they argue inside their heads or their seminar rooms, diverges from the official rhetoric. Economists should become more self-conscious about their rhetoric, because they will then better know why they agree or disagree, and will find it less easy to dismiss contrary arguments on merely methodological grounds. Philosophy as a set of narrowing rules of evidence should be set aside in scientific argument, as even many philosophers have been saying now for fifty years.

Economics will not change much in substance, of course, when economists recognize that the economic emperor has positively no clothes. He is the same fellow whether philosophically naked or clothed, in reasonably good health aside from his sartorial delusion. But the temper of argument among economists would improve if they recognized on what grounds they were arguing. They claim to be arguing on grounds of certain limited matters of statistical inference, on grounds of positive economics, operationalism, behaviorism, and other positivistic enthusiasms of the 1930s and 1940s. They believe that these are the only grounds for science. But in their actual scientific work they argue about the aptness of economic metaphors, the relevance of historical precedents, the persuasiveness of introspections, the power of authority, the charm of symmetry, the claims of morality. Crude positiv-

ism labels such issues "meaningless" or "nonscientific" or "just matters of opinion." Yet even positivists actually behave as though the matters are discussable. In fact, most discussion in most sciences, and especially in economics, arises from them. Nothing is gained from clinging to the Scientific Method, or to any methodology except honesty, clarity, and tolerance. Nothing is gained because the methodology does not describe the sciences it was once thought to describe, such as physics or mathematics; and because physics and mathematics are not good models for economics anyway; and because the methodology is now seen by many philosophers themselves to be uncompelling; and because economic science would stop progressing if the methodology were in fact used; and, most important, because economics, like any field, should get its standards of argument from itself, not from the legislation of philosopher kings. The real arguments would then be joined.

I. Rhetoric Is Disciplined Conversation

These points, elaborated below, amount to an appeal to examine the rhetoric of economics. By "rhetoric" is not meant a verbal shell game, as in "empty rhetoric" or "mere rhetoric" (although form is not trivial, either: disdain for the form of words is evidence of a mind closed to the varieties of argument). In *Modern Dogma and the Rhetoric of Assent* Wayne Booth gives many useful definitions. Rhetoric is "the art of probing what men believe they ought to believe, rather than proving what is true according to abstract methods"; it is "the art of discovering good reasons, finding what really warrants assent, because any reasonable person ought to be persuaded"; it is "careful weighing of more-or-less good reasons to arrive at more-or-less probable or plausible conclusions—none too secure but better than would be arrived at by chance or unthinking impulse"; it is the "art of discovering warrantable beliefs and improving those beliefs in shared discourse"; its purpose must not be "to talk someone else into a preconceived view; rather, it must be to engage in mutual inquiry" (Booth, 1974, pp. xiii, xiv, 59, 137). It is what economists, like other dealers in ideas, do anyway: as Booth says elsewhere, "We believe in mutual persuasion as a way of life; we live from conference to conference" (Booth, 1967, p. 13). Rhetoric is exploring thought by conversation.

The word "rhetoric" is doubtless an obstacle to understanding the point, so debased has it become in common parlance. If "pragmatism" and "anarchism" had not already suffered as much, unable to keep clear of irrelevant associations with the bottom line or the bomb, the title might better have been "Pragmatism's Conception of Truth in Economics" or "Outline of an Anarchistic Theory of Knowledge in Economics" (William James, 1907; Paul Feyerabend, 1975). But the enemies of sophisticated pragmatism and gentle anarchism, as of honest rhetoric, have used the weapons at hand. The results discourage onlookers from satisfying the curiosity they might have had about alternatives to coercion in philosophy, politics, or method. A title such as "How Economists Explain" (Mark Blaug, 1980; but see below) or "Why Methodology Is a Bad" would perhaps have been meeker and more persuasive.[1] Still, "rhetoric" like the others is a fine and ancient word, whose proper use ought to be more widely known among economists and calculators.

The rhetoric here is that of Aristotle, Cicero, and Quintilian among the ancients, reincarnated in the Renaissance, crucified by the Cartesian dogma that only the indubitable is true; which in the third

century after Descartes rose from the dead. The faith built on these miracles is known in literary studies as the New Rhetoric, new in the 1930s and 1940s from the hands of I. A. Richards in Britain and Kenneth Burke in America (Richards, 1936; Burke, 1950). In philosophy John Dewey and Ludwig Wittgenstein had already begun to criticize Descartes' program of erecting belief on a foundation of skepticism. More recently Karl Popper, Thomas Kuhn, and Imre Lakatos among others have undermined the positivist supposition that scientific progress does in fact follow Descartes' doubting rules of method. The literary, epistemological, and methodological strands have not yet wound into one cord, but they belong together. On the eve of the Cartesian revolution the French philosopher and educational reformer, Peter Ramus (*fl.* 1550), brought to completion a medieval tendency to relegate rhetoric to mere eloquence, leaving logic in charge of reason. In the textbooks that Descartes himself read as a boy probable argument was made thus for the first time wholly subservient to indubitable argument. Hostile to classical rhetoric, such a reorganization of the liberal arts was well suited for the Cartesian program extending over the next three centuries to put knowledge on foundations built by philosophy and mathematics. The program failed, and in the meantime probable argument languished. In Richard Rorty's words, following Dewey, the search for the foundations of knowledge by Descartes, Locke, Hume, Kant, Russell, and Carnap was "the triumph of the quest for certainty over the quest for wisdom" (Rorty, 1979, p. 61; *cf.* John Dewey, 1929, pp. 33, 227). To reinstate rhetoric properly understood is to reinstate wider and wiser reasoning.

The reaction to the narrowing of argument by the Cartesian program is by now broad. Its leading figures range from professional philosophers (Stephen Toulmin,

---

[1] After recognizing the intent, Colin Forster of Australian National University suggested the title "The Last Paper on Methodology." But ambition must have limits.

Paul Feyerabend, Richard Rorty) to a miscellany of practitioners-turned-philosophers in chemistry (Michael Polanyi), law (Chaim Perelman), and literary criticism (Wayne Booth). The reach of the idea nowadays that argument is more than syllogism is illustrated well by the lucid treatment of it in what would seem an unlikely place, by Glenn Webster, Ada Jacox, and Beverly Baldwin in "Nursing Theory and the Ghost of the Received View" (1981, pp. 25–35). The reach, however, has not extended to economics. Austrian, institutionalist, and Marxist economists, to be sure, have for a century been attacking certain parts of positivism as the basis for economic knowledge. But they have seized on other parts with redoubled fervor, and have so expressed their remaining doubts as to make them unintelligible to anyone but themselves. In their own way they have been as narrowing as thoroughgoing positivists—the rejection of econometrics, for instance, would be reasonable only if its more naive claims were taken seriously. For the rest, economists have let philosophical scribblers of a few years back supply their official thinking about what a good argument is.

II. *The Official Methodology of Economics Is Modernist*

Economists have two attitudes towards discourse, the official and unofficial, the explicit and the implicit. The official rhetoric, to which they subscribe in the abstract and in methodological ruminations, declares them to be scientists in the modern mode. The credo of Scientific Method, known mockingly among its many critics as the Received View, is an amalgam of logical positivism, behaviorism, operationalism, and the hypothetico-deductive model of science. Its leading idea is that all sure knowledge is modeled on the early 20th century's understanding of certain pieces of 19th century physics. To empha-

size its pervasiveness in modern thinking well beyond scholarship it is best labeled simply "modernism," that is, the notion (as Booth puts it) that we know only what we cannot doubt and cannot really know what we can merely assent to.

Among the precepts of modernism are:

(1) Prediction (and control) is the goal of science.
(2) Only the observable implications (or predictions) of a theory matter to its truth.
(3) Observability entails objective, reproducible experiments.
(4) If (and only if) an experimental implication of a theory proves false is the theory proved false.
(5) Objectivity is to be treasured; subjective "observation" (introspection) is not scientific knowledge.
(6) Kelvin's Dictum: "When you cannot express it in numbers, your knowledge is of a meagre and unsatisfactory kind."[2]
(7) Introspection, metaphysical belief, aesthetics, and the like may well figure in the discovery of an hypothesis but cannot figure in its justification.
(8) It is the business of methodology to demarcate scientific reasoning from non-scientific, positive from normative.
(9) A scientific explanation of an event brings the event under a covering law.
(10) Scientists, for instance economic scientists, have nothing to say as scientists about values, whether of morality or art.

---

[2] From Sir William Thomson (Lord Kelvin), *Popular Addresses*, edition of 1888–1889, quoted in Kuhn, 1977, p. 178n. An approximation to this version is inscribed on the front of the Social Science Research Building at the University of Chicago. Frank Knight, the famous University of Iowa economist, is said to have remarked on it one day: "Yes, and when you *can* express it in numbers your knowledge is of a meagre and unsatisfactory kind."

(11) Hume's Fork: "When we run over libraries, persuaded of these principles, what havoc must we make? If we take in our hand any volume—of divinity or school metaphysics, for instance—let us ask, *Does it contain any abstract reasoning concerning quantity or number?* No. *Does it contain any experimental reasoning concerning matter of fact and existence?* No. Commit it then to the flames, for it can contain nothing but sophistry and illusion" (italics his [1748], 1955, p. 173).

Few in philosophy now believe as many as half of these propositions. A substantial, respectable, and growing minority believes none of them. But a large majority in economics believes them all.

For instance, the leading methodologists in economics do. It is odd but true that modernism in economic methodology is associated with the Chicago School.[3] The main texts of economic modernism, such as Milton Friedman's "The Methodology of Positive Economics" (1953) or Gary Becker and George Stigler's *"De Gustibus Non Est Disputandum"* (1977), bear a Chicago postmark; and the more extreme interpretations of the texts flourish among economists bearing a Chicago degree. What is odd about it is that a group so annoying to other economists in most of its activities should have their assent in the matter of official method: Oddly, a watered down version of Friedman's es-

say is part of the intellectual equipment of most economists, and its arguments come readily to their lips.

Premeditated writings on method, not excluding Chicago's own, are more careful than the remark in the course of other business that reveals modernism in its rawer form. In precept one can be vague enough to earn the assent of everyone; in practice one must make enemies. Kalman Cohen and Richard Cyert, to take one among many examples of first-chapter methodology in economics texts, present in their book an outline of modernism, which they assert is the method "used in all scientific analyses" (1975, p. 17). The "method" they then outline, with a bibliography heavily weighted towards logical positivism and its allies, reduces to an appeal to be honest and thoughtful. Only when such a phrase as "at least in principle testable by experiment and observation" (p. 23) is given content by practice do we know what is at stake. To be sure, vague precepts are not without their uses. When Friedman wrote, for instance, the practice of economics was split into theory without fact and fact without theory. His modernist incantations, supported by choruses of philosophers, were at the time probably good for the souls of all concerned.

Friedman's essay was even then more post-modernist than one might suppose from slight acquaintance with its ideas. He did, for example, mention with approval the aesthetic criteria of simplicity and fruitfulness that an economist might use to select among a multiplicity of theories with the same predictions, though in the next sentence he attempted to reduce them to objective matters of prediction (p. 10). He accepted that questionnaires, forbidden to the modernist in economics, are useful for suggesting hypotheses, though in the next sentence he asserted that they are "almost entirely useless as a means of *testing* the validity of eco-

---

[3] Nothing in this essay is meant to give comfort to the enemies of Chicago. Having long been a victim of their anti-Chicago dogmatism, I am not impressed by the assertion that Chicago economics is peculiarly dogmatic. Chicago is merely a particularly clear and candid version of a dogmatic impulse common to all economics, expressing itself in methodological imperatives. Economists appear to believe that economics is too important to be left to the open-minded, and especially must never be left to anyone lacking faith in some approved formula for achieving knowledge. Chicago is no worse than the rest. *Immo, civis Chicagonus sum, subspecies TP (cf.* Melvin Reder, 1982).

nomic hypotheses" (p. 31n). He emphasized the role of the rhetorical community
to which the scientist speaks in producing
conviction—whether made up of sociologists, say, or of economists—though in the
next sentence he returned to an "objective" theory of testing. Like Karl Popper,
Friedman appeared to be struggling to escape the grip of positivism and its intellectual traditions, though with only sporadic
success. Perhaps that the *locus classicus*
of economic modernism contains so much
that is anti-modernist indicates that modernism cannot survive intelligent discussion even by its best advocates.

The unpremeditated remark in the heat
of economic argument, however, usually
has a crudely modernist content, often in
Friedman's very words. An article by
Richard Roll and Stephen Ross on finance,
for instance, asserts that "the theory
should be tested by its conclusions, not
by its assumptions" and that "similarly,
one should not reject the conclusions derived from firm profit maximization on the
basis of sample surveys in which managers
claim that they trade off profit for social
good" (1980, p. 1093 and footnote). The
same can be found elsewhere, in nearly
identical terms, all dating back to Friedman's essay: William Sharpe (1970, p. 77),
for instance, writing on the same matter
as Roll and Ross, takes it as a rule of polite
scientific behavior that "the realism of the
assumptions matters little. If the implications are reasonably consistent with observed phenomena, the theory can be said
to 'explain' reality" (1970, p. 77). Repeated
often, and exhibiting modernism as well
in their devotion to objective evidence,
quantifiable tests, positive analysis, and
other articles of the faith, such phrases
have the ring of incantation. Modernism
is influential in economics, but not because its premises have been examined
carefully and found good. It is a revealed,
not a reasoned, religion.

III. *Modernism Is a Poor Method*

Modernism Is Obsolete in Philosophy

There are a great many things wrong
with modernism as a methodology for science or for economic science.[4] Even when
philosophically inclined, economists appear to read about as much in professional
philosophy as philosophers do in professional economics. It is unsurprising, then,
that the news of the decline of modernism
has not reached all ears. From a philosopher's point of view the worst flaw in the
hostility to the "metaphysics" that modernism sees everywhere is that the hostility is itself metaphysical. If metaphysics
is to be cast into the flames, then the methodological declarations of the modernist
family from Descartes through Hume and
Comte to Russell and Hempel and Popper
will be the first to go. For this and other
good reasons philosophers agree that strict
logical positivism is dead, raising the question whether economists are wise to carry
on with their necrophilia.[5]

In the economic case the metaphysical
position akin to logical positivism is not
well argued, probably because its roots lie
more in the philosophizing of physicists
from Mach to Bridgeman than in the parallel thinking of professional philosophers.
It is at least obscure what might be the
appeal of "operationally meaningful statements" (Paul Samuelson, 1947, p. 3 and

[4] The overdiscussed question of whether there can
be a value-free social science will not be much discussed here, but it must be accounted one of the
chief failings of modernism that it places moral argument outside the pale of rational discussion. In this
connection it should be more widely known that
Morris Schlick, the founder of the Vienna Circle of
logical positivism and a vigorous lecturer on the
theme that moral knowledge is no knowledge at all,
was murdered in 1936 by one of his students.

[5] See John Passmore, 1967. Karl Popper quotes
Passmore with approval for the motto of a chapter
of his own entitled "Who Killed Logical Positivism?"
(Popper, 1976, pp. 87–90), in which he confesses to
the murder.

throughout) or "valid and meaningful predictions about phenomena not yet observed" (Friedman, p. 7) as standards against which all but mathematical assertions are to be judged. Samuelson, Friedman, or their followers do not present reasons for adopting such metaphysical positions, except for confident assertions, at the time correct, that they were the received views of philosophers on the method of science. The trust in philosophy was a tactical error, for the philosophy itself has since changed. Some philosophers now doubt the entire enterprise of epistemology and its claim to provide foundations for knowledge (Richard Rorty, 1982b). A great many doubt the prescriptions of modernist methodology.

Falsification Is Not Cogent

A prescription that economic methodologists have in common, for instance, is an emphasis on the crucial falsifying test, supposedly the hallmark of scientific reasoning. But philosophers have recognized for many decades that falsification runs afoul of a criticism made by the physicist and philosopher Pierre Duhem in 1906, evident at once without philosophical reading to an economist who has tried to use falsification for science. Suppose that the hypothesis H ("British businessmen performed very poorly relative to Americans and Germans in the late 19th century") implies a testing observation O ("Measures of total factor productivity in iron and steel show a large difference between British and foreign steelmaking"); it implies it, that is, not by itself, but only with the addition of ancillary hypotheses H_1, H_2, and so forth that make the measurement possible ("Marginal productivity theory applies to Britain 1870-1913"; "British steel had no hidden inputs offsetting poor business leaderships"; and so forth). Then of course not-O implies not-H—or not-H_1 or not-H_2 or any number

of failures of premises irrelevant to the main hypothesis in question. The hypothesis in question is insulated from crucial test by the ancillary hypotheses necessary to bring it to a test. This is no mere possibility but the substance of most scientific disagreement: "Your experiment was not properly controlled"; "You have not solved the identification problem"; "You have used an equilibrium (competitive, single-equation) model when a disequilibrium (monopolistic, 500-equation) model is relevant." And even if the one hypothesis in question could be isolated, the probabilistic nature of hypotheses, most especially in economics, makes crucial experiments non-crucial: chance is the ever present alternative, the H_n that spoils falsificationism.

Prediction Is Impossible in Economics

The common claim that prediction is the defining feature of a real science, and that economics possesses the feature, is equally open to doubt. It is a cliché among philosophers and historians of science, for instance, that one of the most successful of all scientific theories, the theory of evolution, has no predictions in the normal sense, and is therefore unfalsifiable by prediction. It is at least suggestive of something odd in prediction as a criterion for useful economics that Darwin's theory was inspired by classical economics, a system as it happens erroneous in most of the predictions it made. With no apparent awareness of the incongruity, Friedman quoted Alchian's revival of the connection (Armen Alchian, 1950) in the midst of his most famous piece of predictionist metaphysics ("the leaves are positioned as if each leaf deliberately sought to maximize the amount of sunlight it receives").

In any event, predicting the economic future is, as Ludwig von Mises put it, "beyond the power of any mortal man" (1949, p. 867). What puts it beyond his power is the very economics he uses to make the prediction. When the economist for a big bank predicts lower interest rates after Christmas, and has not before the prediction placed his net worth in margin loans on bonds, properly hedged and insured against variance, he is behaving either irrationally or self-deceivingly. If he knows the expected value of the future, he for some reason chooses not to take the unlimited wealth that such Faustian knowledge can surely bring, and is willing for some reason instead to dissipate the opportunity by the act of telling others about it. If he does not really know, then he faces no such unexploited opportunity. But then he has perhaps no business talking as though he does. Predictionism cannot be rescued by remarking that the big bank economist makes only conditional predictions. Conditional predictions sell for their value in a soft market: if the sea were to disappear, a rock would accelerate in falling from sea level to the sea floor at about 32.17 feet per second per second. But a serious prediction has serious boundary conditions. If it does it must answer again the American Question: If you're so smart why aren't you rich? At the margin (because that is where economics works) and on average (because some people are lucky) the industry of making economic predictions, which includes universities, earns only normal returns.

Modernism Itself Is Impossible, and Is Not Followed

The most damaging, however, of these lesser criticisms of the modernist methodology is that if taken at its word it is narrow to absurdity. Consider again the steps to modernist knowledge, from predictionism through Kelvin's Dictum to Hume's Fork. If economists (or physicists) confined themselves to economic (or physical) propositions that literally conformed to such steps they would have nothing to say. Cartesian or Humean skepticism is too

corrosive a standard of belief for a real human. As the chemist and philosopher Michael Polanyi put it, the methodology of modernism sets up "quixotic standards of valid meaning which, if rigorously practiced, would reduce us all to voluntary imbecility" (1962, p. 88). Modernism promises knowledge free from doubt, metaphysics, morals, and personal conviction; what it delivers merely renames as Scientific Method the scientist's and especially the economic scientist's metaphysics, morals, and personal convictions. It cannot, and should not, deliver what it promises. Scientific knowledge is no different from other personal knowledge (Polanyi, 1962). Trying to make it different, instead of simply better, is the death of science.

In other words, the literal application of modernist methodology cannot give a useful economics. The best proofs are historical. In his *Against Method* (1975) Paul Feyerabend uses an interpretation of Galileo's career to attack the claims of prescriptive methodology in physics; the same point can be made about economics. Had the modernist criterion of persuasion been adopted by Galileo's contemporaries, he argues, the Galilean case would have failed. A grant proposal to use the strange premise that terrestrial optics applied also to the celestial sphere, to assert that the tides were the sloshing of water on a mobile earth, and to suppose that the fuzzy views of Jupiter's alleged moons would prove, by a wild analogy, that the planets, too, went around the sun as did the moons around Jupiter would not have survived the first round of peer review in a National Science Foundation of 1632, at any rate if that one (unlike ours) were wedded to modernist ideology. The argument applies widely to the history of physics: observational anomalies in the experiments testing Einstein's theories were ignored for many years, to be revealed as errors of measurement long after the theories had been embraced, embraced on grounds of "the reason of the matter," as Einstein was fond of saying (Feyerabend, 1975, pp. 56–57).

Historians of biology have uncovered one after another case of cooking the statistical results to fit modernist precepts of what counts as evidence, from Pasteur and Mendel down to the present. The measurement of IQ has been a scandal of self-deception and bold fraud in the name of scientific method from its beginning (Stephen Jay Gould, 1981). Perhaps modernism fits poorly the complexities of biology and psychology: straining after evidence of a sort typically available only in the simplest experiments in physics may not suit their frontiers. It suits the frontiers of economics poorly enough. For better or worse the Keynesian revolution in economics would not have happened under the modernist legislation recommended for the method of science. The Keynesian insights were not formulated as statistical propositions until the early 1950s, well after the bulk of younger economists had become persuaded they were true. By the early 1960s liquidity traps and accelerator models of investment, despite failures in their statistical implementations, were taught to first-year students of economics as matters of scientific routine. Modernist methodology would have stopped all this in 1936: where was the evidence of an objective, statistical, controlled kind?

Nor was the monetarist counterrevolution a success for modernist methodology, though so powerful had the methodology become by the 1960s in the minds of economists and especially of monetarist economists that most of the explicit debate took place in its terms. Yet in truth crude experiments and big books won the day, by their very crudeness and bigness. The Kennedy tax cut boosted the Keynesians to their peak of prestige; the inflation of the 1970s brought them down again, leaving the monetarists as temporary kings of

the castle. An important blow for monetarism was Friedman and Schwartz' big book, *A Monetary History of the United States, 1867–1960*. It established a correlation, which Keynesians would not deny, between money and money income. The significance of the correlation, however, depended on the assumption that money caused prices and that money was determinable by the monetary authority (in 1929–1933, for example) despite the openness of the American economy to trade in both goods and money itself. Nonetheless, what was telling in the debate was the sheer bulk of the book—the richness and intelligence of its arguments, however irrelevant most of the arguments were to the main point.

A modernist method thoroughly applied, in other words, would probably stop advances in economics. What empirical anomaly in the traditional tale inspired the new labor economics or the new economic history? None: they were merely realizations that the logic of economics had not exhausted its applicability at conventional borders. What observable implications justify the investment of intellect since 1950 in general equilibrium theory? For all the modernist talk common among its theorists, none; but so what? Could applications of economics to legal questions rely entirely on objective evidence? No; but why would one wish to limit the play of understanding? And so forth. There is nothing to be gained and a great deal to be lost by adopting modernism in economic methodology.

The very point is economic. In order for an economic theory to be tested, Ronald Coase points out, some economists must care enough about it to bother. They care only when it is believed by some investigators—they and their allies or some significant group of opponents. Only when many believe is there a demand for tests. Fortunately, "economists, or at any rate enough of them, do not wait to discover whether a theory's predictions are accurate before making up their minds"; to wait in proper modernist style "would result in the paralysis of scientific activity" (Coase, 1982, p. 14) because no one would have an incentive to choose one out of the infinite number of hypotheses for test. Even quantitative studies, he argues, rely heavily on pre-quantitative arguments founding belief, and he quotes with approval T. S. Kuhn's remark that "the road from scientific law to scientific measurement can rarely be traveled in the reverse direction" (Coase, p. 18, quoting Kuhn, 1977, p. 219). The laws come from a rhetoric of tradition or introspection, and in physics as in economics "quantitative studies . . . are explorations with the aid of a theory" (Coase, p. 17), searches for numbers with which to make specific a theory already believed on other grounds (see Edward Leamer, 1978, and the discussion below). Modernism is impractical.

Any Method Is Arrogant and Pretentious

The objections to modernist method so far, however, are lesser ones. The greater objection is simply that modernism *is* a method. It sets up laws of argument drawn from an ideal science or the underlying history of science or the essence of knowledge. The claim is that the philosopher of science can tell what makes for good, useful, fruitful, progressive science. He knows this so confidently that he can limit arguments that worthy scientists make spontaneously, casting out some as unscientific, or at best placing them firmly in the "context of discovery." The philosopher undertakes to second-guess the scientific community. In economics the claim of methodological legislation is that the legislator is not merely expert in all branches of economic knowledge within sound of his proclamations but expert in all possible future economics, limiting the growth of economics now in order to

make it fit a philosopher's idea of the ultimate good.

It is hard to take such claims seriously. Einstein remarked that "Whoever undertakes to set himself up as a judge in the field of Truth and Knowledge is shipwrecked by the laughter of the gods" (Einstein, 1953, p. 38). Modernism sets up a court of the Red Queen ("Normative argument," she says, "off with his head"), and the gods laugh merrily. Any methodology that is law-making and limiting will do so. It will do so with the noblest intentions, but economists are fond of pointing out in like cases that noble intentions can have bad consequences. The methodologist fancies himself the judge of the practitioner. His proper business, though, is an anarchistic one, resisting the rigidity and pretension of rules. I. A. Richards applied the point to the theory of metaphor: "Its business is not to replace practice, or to tell us how to do what we cannot do already; but to protect our natural skill from the interference of unnecessarily crude views about it" (1936, p. 116).

The crudeness of modernist methodology, or of any methodology reducible to rigid precept, is bad; but that it is allowed to interfere with practice is worse. The custom of methodological papers in economics is to scold economists for not allowing it to interfere more. Mark Blaug's useful book summarizing the state of play of economic methodology in 1980, *The Methodology of Economics: Or How Economists Explain*, is a recent case in point. It would be better subtitled "How the Young Karl Popper Explained," since it repeatedly attacks extant arguments in economics for failing to comply with the rules Popper laid down in *Logik der Forschung* in 1934. Blaug's exordium is typical of the best of the methodologists in economics: "Economists have long been aware of the need to defend 'correct' principles of reasoning in their subject; although actual practice may bear little relationship to what is preached, the preaching is worth considering on its own ground" (Blaug, p. xii). Words like these flow easily from a modernist's pen. But why would preaching unrelated to actual practice be worth considering at all? Why do economists have to defend in the abstract their principles of reasoning, and before what tribunal? A case for having a methodology—whether logical positivist or Popperian or Austrian or Marxist—would be expected to give answers to the questions of why, but commonly does not. Recent philosophy of science and ordinary good sense suggest that it cannot. Blaug's peroration is frankly prescriptive, taking economic rhetoric directly from philosophy:

> What methodology can do is to provide criteria for the acceptance and rejection of research programs, setting standards that will help us to discriminate between wheat and chaff. The ultimate question we can and indeed must pose about any research program is the one made familiar by Popper: what events, if they materialize, would lead us to reject that program? A program that cannot meet that question has fallen short of the highest standards that scientific knowledge can attain [1980, p. 264].

It sounds grand, but Einstein's gods are rolling in the aisles. Why should a dubious epistemological principle be any test of practice, much less the ultimate test? And doesn't science take place most of the time well short of the ultimate?

Anyone would commend the vision of science that Popper and his followers have—of science as a self-correcting exploration verging on the dialectic otherwise so foreign to the analytic tradition in philosophy. For an economic scientist to adopt an obdurate refusal to consider objections and to resist offering hostages to evidence, though as common in modernist as in nonmodernist circles, is not merely unscientific; it is cowardly. So much one can take from the idea of falsification by evidence. The problem comes, and the modernist preaching begins, with

the word "evidence." Should it all be "objective," "experimental," "positive," "observable"? Can it be? In *The Open Society and Its Enemies* (1945) Popper closes the borders of his society to psychoanalysts and Marxists on the grounds that they do not conform to the modernist notion of evidence prevalent there. He would also have to close it to physicists from Galileo Galilei to particle charmers. An economist bracero, surely, would be deported on the next truck from such an open intellectual society.

Other Sciences Do Not Follow Modernist Methods

For all its claims to the scientific priesthood, then, economics is different from the man-in-the-street's image of Science. Economists should be glad that their subject fits poorly with this image and well with the New Rhetoric, as do studies long foreign to economics such as the study of literature or law or politics. Economics, in other words, is not a Science in the way we came to understand that word in high school.

But neither, really, are other sciences. Other sciences, even the other mathematical sciences, even the Queen herself, are rhetorical. Mathematics appears to an *incognoscento* to be the limiting example of objectivity, explicitness, and demonstrability. Surely here is bedrock for belief. Yet standards of mathematical demonstration change. The last fifty years have been a disappointment to followers of David Hilbert and his program to put mathematics on indubitable foundations. The historian of mathematics, Morris Kline, wrote recently that "it is now apparent that the concept of a universally accepted, infallible body of reasoning—the majestic mathematics of 1800 and the pride of man—is a grand illusion." Or again:

> There is no rigorous definition of rigor. A proof is accepted if it obtains the endorsement of the leading specialists of the time and employs

492   *Journal of Economic Literature, Vol. XXI (June 1983)*

the principles that are fashionable at the moment. But no standard is universally acceptable today [1980, pp. 6, 315].

The recent flap over a computerized proof of the four-color proposition is one example. The more fundamental example is said to be Kurt Gödel's proof fifty years ago that some true and statable propositions in mathematics are unprovable. The point is controversial. John van Heijenoort writes that "the bearing of Gödel's results on epistemological problems remains uncertain. . . . [T]hey should not be rashly called upon to establish the primacy of some act of intuition that would dispense with formalization" (1967, p. 357). To be sure. But one need not dispense with formalization and flee to an unexamined act of intuition to think that formalization has limits.

Kline's opinions are somewhat loosely expressed, and unpopular among mathematicians. Apparently less so are those of Philip J. Davis and Reuben Hersh, whose recent book *The Mathematical Experience* (1981) was described in the *American Mathematical Monthly* as "one of the masterpieces of our age." Davis and Hersh speak of the crisis of confidence in modern mathematical philosophy, however, in terms nearly identical with Kline's. In the work of The Ideal Mathematician "the line between complete and incomplete proof is always somewhat fuzzy, and often controversial" (p. 34; cf. p. 40). They quote a living Ideal Mathematician, Solomon Feferman, who writes "it is also clear that the search for ultimate foundations via formal systems has failed to arrive at any convincing conclusion" (p. 357). Without using the word, Davis and Hersh argue that what is required is a rhetoric of mathematics:

The dominant style of Anglo-American philosophy . . . tends to perpetuate identification of the philosophy of mathematics with logic and the study of formal systems. From this standpoint, a problem of principal concern to the

mathematician becomes totally invisible. This is the problem of giving a philosophical account . . . of preformal mathematics. . . , including an examination of how [it] relates to and is affected by formalization [1981, p. 344].

They assert that "informal mathematics *is* mathematics. Formalization is only an abstract possibility which no one would want or be able actually to carry out" (p. 349). Real proofs "are established by 'consensus of the qualified' " and are "not checkable . . . by any mathematician not privy to the gestalt, the mode of thought in the particular field. . . . It may take generations to detect an error" (p. 354). They conclude:

The actual experience of all schools—and the actual daily experience of mathematicians— shows that mathematical truth, like other kinds of truth, is fallible and corrigible. . . . It is reasonable to propose a different task for mathematical philosophy, not to seek indubitable truth, but to give an account of mathematical knowledge as it really is—fallible, corrigible, tentative, and evolving, as is every other kind of human knowledge [p. 406].

Not much in this line has been done, though one astounding piece has shown what can be: Imre Lakatos' *Proofs and Refutations: The Logic of Mathematical Discovery* gives an account for a theorem in topology of the rhetoric of mathematics.

It appears, then, that some deep problems facing mathematics are problems of rhetoric, problems in "the art of probing what men believe they ought to believe." Similar points can be made about other sciences, such as paleontology. The sudden proliferation of species at the beginning of the Cambrian period, one of the great puzzles in evolution, was explained by Steven Stanley in 1973 by supposing the sudden arrival of forms of life that fed on other forms of life, single-celled herbivores, as it were, in a grassy sea. Their grazing on the dominant forms allowed new forms to survive the competition from the previously dominant ones, which in turn resulted in new grazers. Stephen Jay Gould remarks of the arguments offered in support of this brilliant and persuasive theory that:

> . . . they do not correspond to the simplistic notions about scientific progress that are taught in most high schools and advanced by most media. Stanley does not invoke proof by new information obtained from rigorous experiment. His second criterion is a methodological presumption, the third a philosophical preference, the fourth an application of prior theory. . . . Science, at its best, interposes human judgment and ingenuity upon all its proceedings. It is, after all (although we sometimes forget it), practiced by human beings [Gould, 1977, p. 125].

One can even say the same of physics, that favorite of outsiders seeking a prescription for real, objective, positive, predictive science. The sequence Carnap-Popper-Lakatos-Kuhn-Feyerabend represents in the history and philosophy of physics a descent, accelerating recently, from the frigid peaks of scientific absolutism to the sweet valleys of anarchic rhetoric (see Popper, 1934, 1976; Lakatos, 1970; Kuhn, 1970; Feyerabend, 1975, 1978). If economics should imitate other sciences, imitate even the majesty of physics and mathematics (there is, to be sure, considerable doubt that it should), then it should officially open itself to a wider range of discourse.

IV. The Unofficial Rhetoric Is Honorable But Unexamined

Econometric Rhetoric Is Too Narrow

But unofficially it does. The second attitude towards discourse is that adopted in actual scientific work in economics. It is different from the official, modernist rhetoric. What is alarming about the workaday rhetoric is not its content but that it is unexamined, and that in consequence the official rhetoric pops up in mischievous ways. Economists agree or disagree—their disagreements are exaggerated—but they

do not know why. Any economist believes more than his evidence of a suitably modernist and objective sort implies. A recent poll of economists, for example, found that only three percent of those surveyed flatly disagreed with the assertion that "tariffs and import quotas reduce general economic welfare." Only two percent disagreed with the assertion that "a ceiling on rents reduces the quantity and quality of housing available." Only eight percent disagreed with the assertion that "the taxing and spending of government has a significant impact on the income of a partly idle economy" (J. R. Kearl, Clayne Pope, Gordon Whiting, and Larry Wimmer, 1979). You probably fall into the 97, 98, and 92 percent majorities. The evidence for the assertions, however, is obscure. How do economists know these statements are true? Where did they acquire such confidence? The usual answer is that "theory tells us." But great social questions are not answered by looking at a diagram on a blackboard, because it is trivially easy to draw a diagram that yields the opposite answer. The factual experience of the economy, certainly, has little to do with their confidence. No study has shown in ways that would satisfy a consistent modernist, for example, that high tariffs in America during the 19th century, on balance, hurt Americans. Yet it is believed that tariffs hurt then and now.[6] No study has shown that an inadvertent policy of fiscal ease brought unemployment down during the War. Yet it is believed on all sides. Economists have not considered their rhetoric.

Everywhere in the literature of economics one is met with premises that are unargued, tricks of style masquerading as reason ("it is evident that"), forms of evidence that ignore the concerns of the au-

[6] Charles Peirce, the founder of pragmatism, related in 1877 how he had been "entreated not to read a certain newspaper lest it might change my opinion upon free-trade" (p. 101).

494   *Journal of Economic Literature, Vol. XXI (June 1983)*

dience, and other symptoms of a lack of self-consciousness in rhetoric. The lack is most evident in quarrels across research paradigms. Some economists (I am one) believe that peasants are rational. The mass of modernist proofs, originating largely from Chicago, that resistance to the "Green Revolution" or persistence in scattering plots of land are rational leave many other economists cold. Some economists (I am one) believe that competition is a robust characterization of the modern American economy. The mass of modernist proofs, originating largely from Chicago, that, for instance, advertising has small effects on profits leaves the others cold. Why? Why do Chicago proofs leave Texas institutionalists or NYU Austrians or Massachusetts Marxists or even Berkeley neoclassicists cold? The non-Chicago economists, of course, believe they have modernist evidence of their own. But part of the problem is that they also believe, without thinking about it much, that they have evidence of a non-modernist sort: stories of peasants and their lumpish character in the flesh; self-awareness of the force of advertising. A good part of the disagreement is over evidence that is not brought openly into the discussion, though it is used.

Even in the most narrowly technical matters of scientific discussion economists have a shared set of convictions about what makes an argument strong, but a set which they have not examined, which they can communicate to graduate students only tacitly, and which contains many elements embarrassing to the official rhetoric. A good example is the typical procedure in econometrics. From economic theory, politics, and the workings of the economist's psyche, all of which are in the rhetorical sense unexamined, come hypotheses about some bit of the economy. The hypotheses are then specified as straight lines, linear models being those most easily manipulated. The straight lines are fitted to someone else's collection of facts. So far the official and workaday rhetoric correspond, and the one might with justice be called a guide to the other. Presently, however, they diverge. If the results of the fitting to the data are reasonable, on grounds that are not themselves subject to examination, the article is sent off to a journal. If the results are unreasonable, the hypothesis is consigned to a do loop: the economic scientist returns to the hypotheses or the specifications, altering them until a publishable article emerges. The product may or may not have value, but it does not acquire its value from its adherence to the official rhetoric. It violates the official rhetoric blatantly.

But why shouldn't it? Even at the level of tests of statistical significance the workaday rhetoric violates the philosopher's law. But so what? It is a cliché of cynicism in economics and related statistical fields to point out that a result significantly different from one that may have been gotten by chance does not have the significance it claims if the hypothesis has been manipulated to fit the data. That only significant results get published has long been a scandal among statistical purists: they fear with some reason that at the five percent level of significance something like five percent of the computer runs will be successful. The scandal is not, however, the failure to achieve modernist standards of scientific purity. The scandal is the failure to articulate reasons why one might want to ignore them.

It would be arrogant to suppose that one knew better than thousands of intelligent and honest economic scholars what the proper form of argument was. The Received View is arrogant in this way, laying down legislation for science on the basis of epistemological convictions held with vehemence inversely proportional to the amount of evidence that they work. Better to look hard at what is in fact done. In an important book that is an exception to the general neglect of rhetorical considerations in economics Edward Leamer asks what purpose the workaday procedures in econometrics may be serving (Leamer, 1978, esp. p. 17). Instead of comparing them with a doctrine in the philosophy of science he compares them with reasons that ought to persuade a reasonable person, with what really warrants assent, with, in short, economic rhetoric. As Christopher Sims points out in a review, "there is a myth that there are only two categories of knowledge about the world—'the' model, given to us by 'economic theory,' without uncertainty, and the parameters, about which we know nothing except what the data, via objectively specified econometric methods, tells us. . . . The sooner Leamer's cogent writings can lead us to abandon this myth, to recognize that nearly all applied work is shot through with applications of uncertain, subjective knowledge, and to make the role of such knowledge more explicit and more effective, the better" (Sims, 1979, p. 567). Yes. The very title of Leamer's book is an outline of rhetoric in econometrics: *Specification Searches: Ad Hoc Inference with Nonexperimental Data.*

Examples of the search abound. It is common in a seminar in economics for the speaker to present a statistical result, apparently irrefutable by the rules of positive economics, and to be met by a chorus of "I can't believe it" or "It doesn't make sense." Milton Friedman's own Money Workshop at Chicago in the late 1960s and the early 1970s was a case in point. Put in statistical language, the rhetorical context that creates such skepticism can be called a priori beliefs and can be analyzed in Bayesian terms. It seldom is, but such a step would not be enough even if it were taken. That the rhetorical community in economics might reject "solid" results, for instance that oil prices appear in a regression explaining inflation, and accept "flimsy" ones, for instance that money causes inflation, shows the strength of prior beliefs. (The beliefs can be reversed without changing the example.) To leave the discussion at prior beliefs, however, perhaps formalizing them as prior probability distributions, is to perpetuate the fact-value split of modernism, leaving most of what matters in science to squeals of pleasure or pain. What is required is an examination of the workaday rhetoric that leads to the prior beliefs. It is not enough, as Thomas F. Cooley and Stephen F. LeRoy do in their recent, penetrating paper on "Identification and Estimation of Money Demand" (1981) to merely stand appalled at the infection of econometric conclusions by prior beliefs. If econometric argument does not persuade it is because the field of argument is too narrow, not because the impulse towards thoughtfulness and explicitness which it embodies is wrong. The arguments need to be broadened, not merely dismissed.

The Controversy Over Purchasing Power Parity Is an Example of Unexamined Rhetoric

A good example of how the official rhetoric—in the absence of an examinaton of the workaday rhetoric—can lead a literature in economics astray, especially in econometric matters, is the debate about purchasing power parity. It is worth examining in detail as a case study in unexamined rhetoric and the need to broaden it (Donald McCloskey and J. Richard Zecher, 1982). The question is: is the international economy more like the economy of the Midwest, in which Iowa City and Madison and Champaign all face given prices for goods; or is it more like the solar system, in which each planet's economy is properly thought of in isolation? If the Iowa City view is correct, then the prices of all goods will move together everywhere, allowing for exchange rates. If the Martian view is correct they will move differently. If the Iowa City view is correct, then all closed models of economies, whether Keynesian or monetarist or rationally expecting, are wrong; if the Martian view is correct, then economists can (as they do) go on testing macroeconomic faiths against American experience since the War.

The question of whether prices are closely connected internationally, then, is important. The official rhetoric does not leave much doubt as to what is required to answer it: collect facts on prices in, say, the United States and Canada and . . . well . . . test the hypothesis (derived in orthodox fashion from a higher order hypothesis, using objective data, looking only at observable facts, controlling the experiment as much as possible, and so forth, according to the received view). A large number of economists have done this. Half of them conclude that purchasing power parity works; the other half conclude that it fails. A misleading but nonetheless superb paper by Irving Kravis and Robert Lipsey on the subject concludes that it fails, in terms that are worth repeating:

> We think it *unlikely* that the *high* degree of national and international commodity arbitrage that many versions of the monetarist [sic] theory of the balance of payments contemplate is *typical* of the real world. This is not to deny that the price structures of the advanced industrial countries *are linked* together, but it is to suggest that the links are *loose* rather than *rigid* [1978, p. 243, italics added].

Every italicized word involves a comparison against some standard of what constitutes unlikelihood or highness or typicality or being linked or looseness or rigidity. Yet here and elsewhere in the tortured literature of purchasing power parity no standard is proposed.

The narrowest test of purchasing power parity, and the one that springs most readily to a mind trained in the official rhetoric, is to regress the price in the United

States (of steel or of goods-in-general, in levels or in differences) against the corresponding price abroad, allowing for the exchange rate. If the slope coefficient is 1.00 the hypothesis of purchasing power parity is said to be confirmed; if not, not. Kravis and Lipsey perform such a test. Being good economists they are evidently made a little uncomfortable by the rhetoric involved. They admit that "Each analyst will have to decide in the light of his purposes whether the purchasing power parity relationships fall close enough to 1.00 to satisfy the theories" (p. 214). Precisely. In the next sentence, however, they lose sight of the need for an explicit standard if their argument is to be cogent: "As a matter of general judgment we express our opinion that the results do not support the notion of a tightly integrated international price structure." They do not say what a "general judgment" is or how one might recognize it. The purpose of an explicit economic rhetoric would be to provide guidance. The guidance Kravis and Lipsey provide for evaluating their general judgment is a footnote (p. 214) reporting the general judgments of Houthakker, Haberler, and Johnson that deviations from parity of anything under 10 to 20 percent are acceptable to the hypothesis. It happens, incidentally, that the bulk of the evidence offered by Kravis and Lipsey passes rather than fails such a test, belying their conclusions. But accepting or rejecting one unargued standard by comparing it with another unargued standard does not much advance the art of argument in economics.

Kravis and Lipsey, to be fair, are unusually sensitive to the case for having some standard, more sensitive than are most economists working the field. They return repeatedly to the question of a standard, though without resolving it. On page 204 they reject in one irrelevant sentence the only standard proposed in the literature so far, the Genberg-Zecher criterion, described below. On pages 204–05 and on 235 and again on 242 they draw a distinction between the statistical and the economic significance of their results. So frequently do they make the point that it must be counted one of the major ones in the paper. On page 205 they remark, for example, that even small differences between domestic and export prices can make a big difference to the incentive to export: "this is a case in which statistical significance [that is, a correlation of the two prices near 1.0, which one might mistakenly suppose to imply that they were insignificantly different] does not necessarily connote economic significance." Yet they do not turn the sword on themselves. No wonder: without a rhetoric of *economic* significance, and in the face of a modernist rhetoric of statistical significance with the prestige of alleged science behind it, they are unaware they are wielding it.

The abuse of the word "significant" in connection with statistical arguments in economics is universal. Statistical significance seems to give a standard by which to judge whether a hypothesis is true or false that is independent of any tiresome consideration of how true a hypothesis must be to be true enough. The point in the present case is that the "failure" of purchasing power parity in a regression of the usual type is not measured against a standard. How close does the slope have to be to the ideal of 1.00 to say that purchasing power parity succeeds? The literature is silent. The standard used is the irrelevant one of statistical significance. A sample size of a million yielding a tight estimate that the slope was .9999, "significantly" different from 1.00000, could be produced as evidence that purchasing power parity had "failed," at least if the logic of the usual method were to be followed consistently. Common sense, presumably, would rescue the scholar from asserting that an estimate of .9999 with

a standard error of .0000001 was significantly different from unity in a significant meaning of significance. Such common sense should be applied to findings of slopes of .90 or 1.20. It is not.[7]

The irrelevance of the merely statistical standard of fit does not undermine only that half of the empirical literature that finds purchasing power parity to be wrong. Towards the end of a fine article favorable to purchasing power parity, Paul Krugman writes:

> There are several ways in which we might try to evaluate purchasing power parity as a theory. We can ask how much it explains [that is, R-square]; we can ask how large the deviations from purchasing power parity are in some absolute sense; and we can ask whether the deviations from purchasing power parity are in some sense systematic [1978, p. 405].

The defensive usage "in some absolute sense" and "in some sense" betrays his unease, which is in the event justified. There is no "absolute sense" in which a description is good or bad. The sense must be comparative to a standard, and the standard must be argued.

Similarly, Jacob Frenkel, an enthusiast for purchasing power parity as such things go among economists but momentarily bewitched by the ceremony of regression, says that "if the market is efficient and if the forward exchange rate is an unbiased forecast of the future spot exchange rate, the constant [in a regression of the spot rate today on the future rate for today quoted yesterday] . . . should not differ *significantly* from unity." In a footnote on the next page, speaking of the standard

---

[7] An example is J. D. Richardson's paper, "Some Empirical Evidence on Commodity Arbitrage and the Law of One Price" (1978). He regresses Canadian on American prices multiplied by the exchange rate for a number of industries and concludes: "It is notable that the 'law of one price' fails uniformly. The hypothesis of *perfect* commodity arbitrage is rejected with 95 percent confidence for every commodity group" (p. 347, italics added). The question is, why in an imperfect world would it matter that *perfect* arbitrage is rejected?

errors of the estimates for such an equation in the 1920s, he argues that "while
these results indicate that markets were
efficient and that on average forward rates
were unbiased forecasts of future spot
rates, the 2–8 percent errors were *significant*"(1978, pp. 175–76, italics added). He
evidently has forgotten his usage of "significant" in another signification. What he
appears to mean is that he judges a 2–8
percent error to be large in some unspeci-
fied economic sense, perhaps as offering
significant profits for lucky guessers of the
correct spot rate. In any event, it is unclear what his results imply about their
subject, purchasing power parity, because
significance in statistics, however useful
it is as an input into economic significance,
is not the same thing as economic significance.

The point is not that levels of significance are arbitrary. Of course they are.
The point is that it is not known whether
the range picked out by the level of significance affirms or denies the hypothesis.
Nor is the point that econometric tests are
to be disdained. Quite the contrary. The
point is that the econometric tests have
not followed their own rhetoric of hypothesis testing. Nowhere in the literature of
tests of purchasing power parity does
there appear a loss function. We do not
know how much it will cost in policy
wrecked or analysis misapplied or reputation ruined if purchasing power parity is
said to be true when by the measure of
the slope coefficient it is only, say, 85 percent true. That is, the argument due to
Neyman and Pearson that undergirds
modern econometrics has been set aside
here as elsewhere in favor of a merely
statistical standard, and an irrelevant one
related to sampling error at that. We are
told how improbable it is that a slope coefficient of .90 came from a distribution centered on 1.00 in view of the one kind of
error we claim we know about (unbiased
sampling error with finite variance), but

we are not told whether it matters to the
truth of purchasing power parity where
such limits of confidence are placed.

Silence on the matter is not confined
to the literature of purchasing power parity. Most texts on econometrics do not
mention that the goodness or badness of
a hypothesis is not ascertainable on merely
statistical grounds. Statisticians themselves are more self-conscious, although
the transition from principle to practice
is sometimes awkward. A practical difficulty in the way of using the Neyman and
Pearson theory in pure form, A. F. Mood
and F. A. Graybill say, is that

> the loss function is not known at all or else it
> is not known accurately enough to warrant its
> use. If the loss function is not known, it seems
> that a decision function that in some sense min-
> imizes the error probabilities will be a reason-
> able procedure [1963, p. 278].

The phrase "in some sense" appears to
be a marker of unexplored rhetoric in the
works of intellectually honest scholars. In
any event, the procedure they suggest
might be reasonable for a general statistician, who makes no claim to know what
is a good or bad approximation to truth
in fields outside statistics. It is not reasonable for a specialist in international trade
or macroeconomics. If the loss function
is not known it should be discovered. And
that will entail a study of the question's
rhetoric.

One standard of economic significance
in questions of parity, for example, might
be the degree to which the customary regressions between countries resembled
similar regressions within a single country.
We agree, for purposes of argument, that
the United States is to be treated as a single point in space, as one economy across
which distances are said not to matter for
the purposes of thinking about inflation
or the balance of payments. Having done
so we have a standard: is Canada economically speaking just as closely integrated
with the United States as is California with

Massachusetts? Is the Atlantic Economy as closely integrated as the American Economy? The standard is called the Genberg-Zecher criterion, after its inventors (Hans Genberg, 1976; McCloskey and Zecher, 1976). It is not the only conceivable one. The degree of market integration in some golden age (1880–1913 perhaps; or 1950–1970) might be a standard; the profits from arbitrage above normal profits might be another standard; the degree to which an X percentage deviation from purchasing power parity does or does not disturb some assertion about the causes of inflation might be still another. The point is to have standards of argument, to go beyond the inconclusive rhetoric provided by the pseudo-scientific ceremony of hypothesis-regression-test-publish in most of modern economics.

V. *The Rhetoric of Economics Is a Literary Matter*

Even a Modernist Uses, and Must Use, Literary Devices

The mere recognition that the official rhetoric might be dubious, then, frees the reason to examine how economists really argue. Obscured by the official rhetoric the workaday rhetoric has not received the attention it deserves, and the knowledge of it is therefore contained only in seminar traditions, advice to assistant professors, referee reports (a promising primary source for its study), and jokes. It is significant that George Stigler, a leader of modernism in economics, chose to express his observations about the rhetoric of economics in a brilliantly funny "The Conference Handbook" ("Introductory Remark number E: 'I can be very sympathetic with the author; until 2 years ago I was thinking along similar lines' ") rather than as a serious study in one of the several fields he has mastered, the history of economic thought (1977). The attitude of the Handbook is that rhetoric is mere rhetoric, mere game playing in aid of ego gratification; the serious business of Science will come on that happy day when the information theory of oligopoly or the vulgar Marxist theory of the state is brought to a critical test under the auspices of naive falsificationism.

Economists can do better if they will look soberly at the varieties of their arguments. The varieties examined here can only be crude preliminaries to a fuller study, a study that might dissect samples of economic argument, noting in the manner of a literary or philosophical exegesis exactly how the arguments sought to convince the reader. It is not obvious a priori what the categories might be; in view of the methodological range of modern economics they doubtless would vary much from author to author. A good place to start might be the categories of classical rhetoric, Aristotle's divisions into invention, arrangement, delivery, and style, for instance, with his paired sub-headings of artificial (i.e., argumentative) and inartificial (i.e., factual) proofs, syllogism and example, and the like. A good place to continue would be the procedures of modern literary critics, bright people who make their living thinking about the rhetoric of texts.

The purpose would not be to make the author look foolish or to uncover fallacies for punishment by ridicule—fallacymongering is evidence of a legislative attitude towards method, and it is no surprise that Jeremy Bentham, confident of his ability to legislate for others in matters of method as in education, prisons, and government, had compiled from his notes *The Book of Fallacies* (1824). David Hackett Fischer's book, *Historians' Fallacies* (1970), has this flaw: that it takes as fallacious what may be merely probable and supporting argument.

The purpose of literary scrutiny of economic argument would be to see beyond the received view on its content. Two pages (pp. 122–23) chosen literally at random from that premier text of the received view, and a local maximum in economic scholarship, Samuelson's *Foundations*, will suffice for illustration:

(1) To begin with he gives a general mathematical form from which detailed results in comparative statics can be obtained by reading across a line. The implication of the lack of elaboration of the mathematics is that the details are trivial (leading one to wonder why they are mentioned at all). An "interesting" special case is left "as an exercise to the interested reader," drawing on the rhetorical traditions of applied mathematics to direct the reader's mind in the right directions. The mathematics is presented in an offhand way, with an assumption that we all can read off partitioned matrices at a glance, inconsistent with the level of mathematics in other passages. The air of easy mathematical mastery was important to the influence of the book, by contrast with the embarrassed modesty with which British writers at the time (Hicks most notably) pushed mathematics off into appendices.

Samuelson's skill at mathematics in the eyes of his readers, an impression nurtured at every turn, is itself an important and persuasive argument. He presents himself as an authority, with good reason. That the mathematics is so often pointless, as here, is beside the point. Being able to do such a difficult thing (so it would have seemed to the typical economist reading in 1947) is warrant of expertise. The argument is similar in force to that of a classical education conspicuously displayed. To read Latin like one's mother tongue and Greek like one's aunt's tongue is extremely difficult, requiring application well beyond the ordinary; therefore—or so it seemed to Englishmen around 1900—men who have acquired such a skill should have charge of a great empire. Likewise—or so it seemed to economists

around 1983—those who have acquired a skill at partitioned matrices and eigenvalues should have charge of a great economy. The argument is not absurd or a "fallacy" or "mere rhetoric." Virtuosity *is* some evidence of virtue.[8]

(2) There are six instances of appeal to authority (C. E. V. Leser, Keynes, Hicks, Aristotle, Knight, and Samuelson; appeal to authorities is something of a Samuelsonian specialty). Appeal to authority is often reckoned as the worst kind of "mere" rhetoric. Yet it is a common and often legitimate argument, as here. No science would advance without it, because no scientist can redo every previous argument. We stand on the shoulders of giants, and it is a perfectly legitimate and persuasive argument to point this out from time to time.

(3) There are several appeals to relaxation of assumptions. The demand for money is "really interesting . . . when uncertainty . . . is admitted." Again, the implicit assumption in Hicks that money bears no interest is relaxed, unhitching the interest rate from the zero return on money. Relaxation of assumptions is the literature generating function of modern economics. In the absence of quantitative evidence on the importance of the assumption relaxed it is no modernist evidence at all. Samuelson is careful to stick to the subjunctive mood of theory (money *"would* pass out of use"), but no doubt wants his strictures on a theory of the interest rate based merely on liquidity preference (that is, on risk) to be taken seriously as comments on the actual world. They are, surely, but not on the operationalist grounds he articulates when preaching methodology.

(4) There are several appeals to hypo-

---

[8] The limiting case is spelling. Most college teachers will agree that those who do not know how to spell "consensus" lose some of their authority to speak on it.

thetical toy economies, constrained to one or two sectors, from which practical results are derived. This has since Ricardo been among the commonest forms of economic argument, the Ricardian vice. It is no vice if done reasonably. "It would be quite possible to have an economy in which money did not exist, and in which there was still a substantial rate of interest." Yes, of course.

(5) There is, finally, one explicit appeal to analogy, which is said to be "not . . . superficial." Analogy, as will be shown in detail in a moment, pervades economic thinking, even when it is not openly analogical: transaction "friction," yield "spread," securities "circulating," money "withering away" are inexplicit examples here from one paragraph of live or only half-dead metaphors. Yet analogy and metaphor, like most of the other pieces of Samuelson's rhetoric, have no standing in the official canon.

Most of the Devices Are Only Dimly Recognized

The range of persuasive discourse in economics is wide, ignored in precept while potent in practice. At the broadest level it is worth noting that the practice of economic debate often takes the form of legal reasoning, for, as Booth put it, "the processes developed in the law are codifications of reasonable processes that we follow in every part of our lives, even the scientific" (1974, p. 157). Economists would do well to study jurisprudence, then, with some other aim than subordinating it to economic theory. For instance, economists, like jurists, argue by example, by what Edward Levi calls "the controlling similarity between the present and prior case" (1967, p. 7).

The details of the pleading of cases at economic law have little to do with the official scientific method. Without self-consciousness about workaday rhetoric

they are easily misclassified. A common argument in economics, for example, is one from verbal suggestiveness. The proposition that "the economy is basically competitive" may well be simply an invitation to look at it this way, on the assurance that to do so will be illuminating. In the same way a psychologist might say "we are all neurotic"—it does not mean that 95 percent of a randomly selected sample of us will exhibit compulsive handwashing; rather, it is merely a recommendation that we focus attention on the neurotic ingredient "in us all" (Passmore, 1966, p. 438). To misunderstand the expression as a properly modernist hypothesis would be to invite much useless testing. The case is similar to $MV=PT$ understood as an identity. The equation is the same term-for-term as the equation of state of an ideal gas, and has the same status as an irrefutable but useful notion in chemistry as it has in economics. The identity *can* be argued against, but not on grounds of "failing a test." The arguments against it will deny its capacity to illuminate, not its modernist truth.

Another common argument in economics with no status in the official rhetoric is philosophical consistency: "If you assume the firm knows its own cost curve you might as well assume it knows its production function, too: it is no more dubious that it knows one than the other." The argument, usually inexplicit though signalled by such a phrase as "it is natural to assume," is in fact characteristic of philosophical discourse (Passmore, 1970). It is analogous to symmetry as a criterion of plausibility, which appears in many forms and forums. A labor economist tells a seminar about compensating differentials for the risk of unemployment, referring only to the utility functions of the workers. An auditor remarks that the value of unemployment on the demand side (that is, to the firm) is not included.

The remark is felt to be powerful, and a long discussion ensues of how the demand side might alter the conclusions. The argument from the-other-side-is-empty is persuasive in economics, but economists are unaware of how persuasive it is.

Likewise (and here we reach the border of self-consciousness in rhetoric), "ad hoccery" is universally condemned by seminar audiences. An economist will cheerfully accept a poor R^2 and terrible and understated standard errors if only she "has a theory" for the inclusion of such-and-such a variable in the regressions. "Having a theory" is not so open and shut as it might seem, depending for instance on what reasoning is prestigious at the moment. Anyone who threw accumulated past output into an equation explaining productivity change before 1962 would have been accused of ad hoccery. But after Arrow's essay on "The Economics of Learning By Doing" (which as it happened had little connection with maximizing behavior or other higher order hypotheses in economics), there was suddenly a warrant for doing it.

An example of the rhetoric of economics which falls well within the border of self-consciousness is simulation. Economists will commonly make an argument for the importance of this or that variable by showing its potency in a model with back-of-the-envelope estimates of the parameters. Common though it is, few books or articles are devoted to its explication (but, see Richard Zeckhauser and Edith Stokey, 1978). It would be as though students learned econometrics entirely by studying examples of it—no bad way to learn, but not self-conscious in grounding the arguments. What is legitimate simulation? Between A. C. Harberger's modest little triangles of distortion and Jeffrey Williamson's immense multiequation models of the American or Japanese economies since 1870 is a broad range. Economists have no vocabulary for criticizing

any part of the range. They can deliver summary grunts of belief or disbelief but find it difficult to articulate their reasons in a disciplined way.

VI. *Economics Is Heavily Metaphorical*

Models Are Metaphors

The most important example of economic rhetoric, however, falls well outside the border of self-consciousness. It is the language economists use, and in particular its metaphors. To say that markets can be represented by supply and demand "curves" is no less a metaphor than to say that the west wind is "the breath of autumn's being." A more obvious example is "game theory," the very name being a metaphor. It is obviously useful to have in one's head the notion that the arms race is a two-person, negative-sum cooperative "game." Its persuasiveness is instantly obvious, as are some of its limitations. Each step in economic reasoning, even the reasoning of the official rhetoric, is metaphor. The world is said to be "like" a complex model, and its measurements are said to be like the easily measured proxy variable to hand. The complex model is said to be like a simpler model for actual thinking, which is in turn like an even simpler model for calculation. For purposes of persuading doubters the model is said to be like a toy model that can be manipulated quickly inside the doubter's head while listening to the seminar. John Gardner wrote:

> There is a game—in the 1950s it used to be played by the members of the Iowa Writers' Workshop—called 'Smoke.' The player who is 'it' [thinks of] some famous person . . . and then each of the other players in turn asks one question . . . such as 'What kind of weather are you?'. . . Marlon Brando, if weather, would be sultry and uncertain. . . . To understand that Marlon Brando is a certain kind of weather is to discover something (though something neither useful nor demonstrable) and in

the same instant to communicate something [Gardner, 1978, pp. 118–19].

On the contrary, in economics the comparable discovery is useful and by recourse to rhetorical standards demonstrable.

Metaphors in Economics Are Not Ornamental

Metaphor, though, is commonly viewed as mere ornament. From Aristotle until the 1930s even literary critics viewed it this way, as an amusing comparison able to affect the emotions but inessential for thought. "Men are beasts": if we cared to be flat-footed about it, the notion was, we could say in what literal way we thought them beastly, removing the ornament to reveal the core of plain meaning underneath. The notion was in 1958 common in philosophy, too:

> With the decline of metaphysics, philosophers have grown less and less concerned about Godliness and more and more obsessed with cleanliness, aspiring to ever higher levels of linguistic hygiene. In consequence, there has been a tendency for metaphors to fall into disfavour, the common opinion being that they are a frequent source of infection [H. J. N. Horsburgh, 1958, p. 231].

Such suspicion toward metaphor is widely recognized by now to be unnecessary, even harmful. That the very idea of "removing" an "ornament" to "reveal" a "plain" meaning is itself a metaphor suggests why. Perhaps thinking is metaphorical. Perhaps to remove metaphor is to remove thought. The operation on the metaphoric growth would in this case be worse than the disease.

The question is whether economic thought is metaphorical in some nonornamental sense. The more obvious metaphors in economics are those used to convey novel thoughts, one sort of novelty being to compare economic with noneconomic matters. "Elasticity" was once a mind-stretching fancy; "depression" was depressing; "equilibrium" compared an economy to an apple in a bowl, a settling idea; "competition" once induced thoughts of horseraces; money's "velocity" thoughts of swirling bits of paper. Much of the vocabulary of economics consists of dead metaphors taken from noneconomic spheres.

Comparing noneconomic with economic matters is another sort of novelty, apparent in the imperialism of the new economics of law, history, politics, crime, and the rest, and most apparent in the work of that Kipling of the economic empire, Gary Becker. Among the least bizarre of his many metaphors, for instance, is that children are durable goods. The philosopher Max Black pointed out that "a memorable metaphor has the power to bring two separate domains into cognitive and emotional relation by using language directly appropriate to the one as a lens for seeing the other" (1962, p. 236). So here: the subject (a child) is viewed through the lens of the modifier (a durable good). A beginning at literal translation would say, "A child is costly to acquire initially, lasts for a long time, gives flows of pleasure during that time, is expensive to maintain and repair, has an imperfect second-hand market. . . . Likewise, a durable good, such as a refrigerator. . . ." That the list of similarities could be extended further and further, gradually revealing the differences as well—"children, like durable goods, are not objects of affection and concern"; "children, like durable goods, do not have their own opinions"— is one reason that, as Black says, "metaphorical thought is a distinctive mode of achieving insight, not to be construed as an ornamental substitute for plain thought" (p. 237). The literal translation of an important metaphor is never finished. In this respect and in others an important metaphor in economics has the quality admired in a successful scientific theory, a capacity to astonish us with implications yet unseen.[9]

But it is not merely the pregnant quality of economic metaphors that makes them important for economic thinking. The literary critic I. A. Richards was among the first to make the point, in 1936, that metaphor is "two thoughts of different things *active together, . . . whose meaning is a resultant of their interaction*" (Richards, 1936, p. 93, my italics; Black, 1962, p. 46; Owen Barfield, 1947, p. 54). A metaphor is not merely a verbal trick, Richards continues, but "a borrowing between and intercourse of *thoughts*, a transaction between contexts" (p. 94, his italics). Economists will have no trouble seeing the point of his economic metaphor, one of mutually advantageous exchange. The opposite notion, that ideas and their words are invariant lumps unaltered by combination, like bricks (Richards, p. 97), is analogous to believing that an economy is a mere aggregation of Robinson Crusoes. But the point of economics since Smith has been that an island-full of Crusoes trading is different from and often better off than the mere aggregation.

Another of Becker's favorite metaphors, "human capital," illustrates how two sets of ideas, in this case both drawn from inside economics, can thus mutually illuminate each other by exchanging connotations. In the phrase "human capital" the field in economics treating human skills was at a stroke unified with the field treating investment in machines. Thought in

---

[9] A good metaphor depends on the ability of its audience to suppress incongruities, or to wish to. Booth gives the example of:

'All the world's a stage' . . . [The reader must make a choice only if the incongruities—failures of fit—come too soon]. Usually they arrive late and without much strength. . . . [W]e have no difficulty ruling from our attention, in the life-stage metaphor, the selling of tickets, fire insurance laws, the necessity for footlights [1961, p. 22f].

The appreciation of "human capital" requires the same suspension of disbelief.

both fields was improved, labor economics by recognizing that skills, for all their intangibility, arise from abstention from consumption; capital theory by recognizing that skills, for all their lack of capitalization, compete with other investments for a claim to abstention. Notice by contrast that because economists are experts only in durable goods and have few (or at any rate conventional) thoughts about children, the metaphor that children are durable goods has so to speak only one direction of flow. The gains from the trade were earned mostly by the theory of children (fertility, nuptiality, inheritance), gaining from the theory of durable goods, not the other way around.

Economic Metaphors Constitute a Poetics of Economics

What is successful in economic metaphor is what is successful in poetry, and is analyzable in similar terms. Concerning the best metaphors in the best poetry, comparing thee to a summer's day or comparing *A* to *B*, argued Owen Barfield,

> We feel that *B*, which is actually said, ought to be necessary, even inevitable in some way. It ought to be in some sense the best, if not the only way, of expressing *A* satisfactorily. The mind should dwell on it as well as on *A* and thus the two should be somehow inevitably fused together into one simple meaning [Barfield, 1947, p. 54].

If the modifier *B* (a summer's day, a refrigerator, a piece of capital) were trite—in these cases it is not, although in the poem Shakespeare was more self-critical of his simile than economists usually are of theirs—it would become as it were detached from *A*, a mechanical and unilluminating correspondence. If essential, it fuses with *A*, to become a master metaphor of the science, the idea of "human capital," the idea of "equilibrium," the idea of "entry and exit," the idea of "competition." The metaphor, quoth the poet, is the "consummation of identity."

Explicit-ness	Extent	
	Short	Long
Explicit	simile (The firm behaves as if it were one mind maximizing its discounted value.)	tiresome caution (repeat the simile)
Middling	metaphor (human capital)	allegory (economics of education using human capital)
Implicit	symbol (income) (demand curve)	a symbol system: a mathematics; a theory (Keynesian theory of income determination) (supply and demand analysis)

Figure 1. Analogical Thinking Has Two Dimensions (And Economic Cases in Point)

Few would deny, then, that economists frequently use figurative language. Much of the pitiful humor available in a science devoted to calculations of profit and loss comes from talking about "islands" in the labor market or "putty-clay" in the capital market or "lemons" in the commodity market. The more austere the subject the more fanciful the language. We have "turnpikes" and "golden rules" in growth theory, for instance, and long disquisitions on what to do with the "auctioneer" in general equilibrium theory. A literary man with advanced training in mathematics and statistics stumbling into *Econometrica* would be astonished at the metaphors surrounding him, lost in a land of allegory.

Allegory is merely long-winded metaphor, and all such figures are analogies. Analogies can be arrayed in terms of explicitness, with simile ("as if") the most explicit and symbol ("the demand curve") the least explicit; and they can be arrayed by extent.

Economists, especially theorists, are for-

ever spinning "parables" or telling "stories." The word "story" has in fact come to have a technical meaning in mathematical economics, though usually spoken in seminars rather than written in papers. It means an extended example of the economic reasoning underlying the mathematics, often a simplified version of the situation in the real world that the mathematics is meant to characterize. It is an allegory, shading into extended symbolism. The literary theories of narrative could make economists self-conscious about what use the story serves. Here the story is the modifier, the mathematics the subject. A tale of market days, traders with bins of shmoos, and customers with costs of travel between bins illuminates a fixed point theorem.

Even Mathematical Reasoning Is Metaphorical

The critical question is whether the opposite trick, modifying human behavior with mathematics, is also metaphorical. If it were not, one might acknowledge the metaphorical element in verbal economics about the "entrepreneur," for instance, or more plainly of the "invisible hand," yet argue that the linguistic hygiene of mathematics leaves behind such fancies. This indeed was the belief of the advanced thinkers of the 1920s and 1930s who inspired the now-received view in economic method. Most economists subscribe to the belief without doubt or comment or thought. When engaging in verbal economics we are more or less loose, it is said, taking literary license with our "story"; but when we do mathematics we put away childish things.

But mathematical theorizing in economics is metaphorical, and literary. Consider, for example, a relatively simple case, the theory of production functions. Its vocabulary is intrinsically metaphorical. "Aggregate capital" involves an analogy of "capital" (itself analogical) with something—sand, bricks, shmoos—that can be "added" in a meaningful way; so does "aggregate labor," with the additional peculiarity that the thing added is no thing, but hours of conscientious attentiveness; the very idea of a "production function" involves the astonishing analogy of the subject, the fabrication of things, about which it is appropriate to think in terms of ingenuity, discipline, and planning, with the modifier, a mathematical function, about which it is appropriate to think in terms of height, shape, and single valuedness.

The metaphorical content of these ideas was alive to its inventors in the 19th century. It is largely dead to 20th-century economists, but deadness does not eliminate the metaphorical element. The metaphor got out of its coffin in an alarming fashion in the Debate of the Two Cambridges in the 1960s. The debate is testament, which could be multiplied, to the importance of metaphorical questions to economics. The very violence of the combat suggests that it was about something beyond mathematics or fact. The combatants hurled mathematical reasoning and institutional facts at each other, but the important questions were those one would ask of a metaphor—is it illuminating, is it satisfying, is it apt? How do you know? How does it compare with other economic poetry? After some tactical retreats by Cambridge, Massachusetts on points of ultimate metaphysics irrelevant to these important questions, mutual exhaustion set in, without decision. The reason there was no decision was that the important questions were literary, not mathematical or statistical. The continued vitality of the idea of an aggregate production function in the face of mathematical proofs of its impossibility and the equal vitality of the idea of aggregate economics as practiced in parts of Cambridge, England in the face of statistical proofs of its impracticality would otherwise be a great mystery.

Even when the metaphors of one's economics appear to stay well and truly dead there is no escape from literary questions. The literary man C. S. Lewis pointed out in 1939 that any talk beyond the level of the-cow-standing-here-is-in-fact-purple, any talk of "causes, relations, of mental states or acts . . . [is] incurably metaphorical" (1962, p. 47). For such talk he enunciated what may be called Screwtape's Theorem on Metaphor, the first corollary of which is that the escape from verbal into mathematical metaphor is not an escape:

> when a man claims to think independently of the buried metaphor in one of his words, his claim may . . . [be] allowed only in so far as he could really supply the place of that buried metaphor. . . . [T]his new apprehension will usually turn out to be itself metaphorical [p. 46].

If economists forget and then stoutly deny that the production function is a metaphor, yet continue talking about it, the result is mere verbiage. The word "production function" will be used in ways satisfying grammatical rules, but will not signify anything. The charge of meaninglessness applied so freely by modernists to forms of argument they do not understand or like sticks in this way to themselves. Lewis' second corollary is that "the meaning in any given composition is in inverse ratio to the author's belief in his own literalness" (p. 27). An economist speaking "literally" about the demand curve, the national income, or the stability of the economy is engaging in mere syntax. Lewis cuts close to the bone here, though sparing himself from the carnage:

> The percentage of mere syntax masquerading as meaning may vary from something like 100 percent in political writers, journalists, psychologists, and economists, to something like forty percent in the writers of children's stories. . . . The mathematician, who seldom forgets that his symbols are symbolic, may often rise for short stretches to ninety percent of meaning and ten of verbiage [p. 49].

If economists are not comparing a social fact to a one-to-one mapping, thus bringing two separate domains into cognitive and emotional relation, they are not thinking:

I've never slapped a curved demand;
I never hope to slap one.
But this thing I can tell you now:
I'd rather slap than map one.

Literary Thinking Reunifies the Two Cultures

Metaphor, then, is essential to economic thinking, even to economic thinking of the most formal kind. One may still doubt, though, whether the fact matters. For it is possible for rhetoricians as well as unreconstructed modernists to commit the Philosophizing Sin, to bring high-brow considerations of the ultimate into discussions about how to fix a flat tire. Pushkin's poetry may be ultimately untranslatable, in view of the difference in language, to be sure, but also the difference in situation between a Pushkin in Russia in the early 19th century and a bilingual translator in New York in the late 20th century. Because he was a different man speaking to a different audience even Nabokov's brilliant translation, in the words of the economist and litterateur, Alexander Gerschenkron, "can and indeed should be studied but . . . cannot be read" (in Steiner, 1975, p. 315). Our intrinsic loneliness will make some nuance dark. Yet crude translation, even by machine, is useful for the workaday purposes of informing the Central Intelligence Agency (for instance, "out of sight, out of mind" = "blind madman"). Likewise, the intrinsic metaphors of language may make it ultimately impossible to communicate plain meaning without flourishes—the flourishes *are* the meaning. But the economist may be able to get along without full awareness of his meaning for the workaday purposes of advising the Central Intelligence Agency.

So it might be argued. But it should be argued cautiously. Self-consciousness about metaphor in economics would be an improvement on many counts. Most obviously, unexamined metaphor is a substitute for thinking—which is a recommendation to examine the metaphors, not to attempt the impossible by banishing them.[10] Richard Whately, D.D., Archbishop of Dublin, publicist for free trade as for other pieces of classical political economy, and author of the standard work in the 19th century on *The Elements of Rhetoric*, drew attention to the metaphor of a state being like an individual, and therefore benefiting like an individual from free trade. But he devoted some attention, not all of it ironic, to the question of the aptness of the figure:

To this is it replied, that there is a great difference between a Nation and an Individual. And so there is, in many circumstances . . . [he enumerates them, mentioning for instance the unlimited duration of a Nation] and, moreover, the transactions of each man, as far as he is left free, are regulated by the very person who is to be a gainer or loser by each,—the individual himself; who, though his vigilance is sharpened by interest, and his judgment by exercise in his own department, may chance to be a man of confined education, possessed of no general principles, and not pretending to be versed in philosophical theories; whereas the affairs of a State are regulated by a Congress, Chamber of Deputies, etc., consisting perhaps of men of extensive reading and speculative minds [1894, p. 63].

The case for intervention cannot be put better. And the metaphor is here an occasion for and instrument of thought, not a substitute.

Metaphors, further, evoke attitudes that are better kept in the open and under the control of reasoning. This is plain in the ideological metaphors popular with parties: the invisible hand is so very discrete, so soothing, that we might be inclined to accept its touch without protest;

---

[10] An example of a naïve attack on economic metaphors, and of a failure to realize that economic theory is itself armed with metaphor, is the first page of McCloskey (1981).

the contradictions of capitalism are so very portentous, so scientifically precise, that we might be inclined to accept their existence without inquiry. But it is true even of metaphors of the middling sort. The metaphors of economics convey the authority of Science, and often convey, too, its claims to ethical neutrality. It is no use complaining that we didn't *mean* to introduce moral premises. We do. "Marginal productivity" is a fine, round phrase, a precise mathematical metaphor that encapsulates a most powerful piece of social description. Yet it brings with it an air of having solved the moral problem of distribution facing a society in which people cooperate to produce things together instead of producing things alone. It is irritating that it carries this message, because it may be far from the purpose of the economist who uses it to show approval for the distribution arising from competition. It is better, though, to admit that metaphors in economics can contain such a political message than to use the jargon innocent of its potential.

A metaphor, finally, selects certain respects in which the subject is to be compared with the modifier; in particular, it leaves out the other respects. Max Black, speaking of the metaphor "men are wolves," notes that "any human traits that can without undue strain be talked about in 'wolf-language' will be rendered prominent, and any that cannot will be pushed into the background" (1962, p. 41). Economists will recognize this as the source of the annoying complaints from non-mathematical economists that mathematics "leaves out" some feature of the truth or from non-economists that economics "leaves out" some feature of the truth. Such complaints are often trite and ill-formed. The usual responses to them, however, are hardly less so. The response that the metaphor leaves out things in order to simplify the story temporarily is disingenuous, occurring as it often does

in contexts where the economist is simultaneously fitting 50 other equations. The response that the metaphor will be tested eventually by the facts is a stirring promise, but seldom fulfilled (see again Leamer, throughout). A better response would be that we like the metaphor of, say, the selfishly economic person as calculating machine on grounds of its prominence in earlier economic poetry plainly successful or on grounds of its greater congruence with introspection than alternative metaphors (of people as religious dervishes, say, or as sober citizens). In *The New Rhetoric: A Treatise on Argumentation* (1967), Chaim Perelman and L. Olbrechts-Tyteca note that "acceptance of an analogy . . . is often equivalent to a judgment as to the importance of the characteristics that the analogy brings to the fore" (p. 390). What is remarkable about this unremarkable assertion is that it occurs in a discussion of purely literary matters, yet fits so easily the matters of economic science.

This is in the end the significance of metaphors and of the other rhetorical machinery of argument in economics: economists and other scientists are less separate from the concerns of civilization than many think. Their modes of argument and the sources of their conviction—for instance, their uses of metaphor—are not very different from Cicero's speeches or Hardy's novels. This is a good thing. As Black wrote, discussing "archetypes" as extended metaphors in science: "When the understanding of scientific models and archetypes comes to be regarded as a reputable part of scientific culture, the gap between the sciences and the humanities will have been partly filled" (p. 243).

VII. *Be Not Afraid*

The Alternative to Modernism Is Not Irrationalism

It will be apparent by now that the objectivity of economics is overstated and, what is more important, overrated. Pregnant economic knowledge depends little on, as Michael Polanyi put it, "a scientific rationalism that would permit us to believe only explicit statements based on tangible data and derived from these by a formal inference, open to repeated testing" (1966, p. 62). A rhetoric of economics makes plain what most economists know anyway about the richness and complexity of economic argument but will not state openly and will not examine explicitly.

The invitation to rhetoric, however, is not an invitation to irrationality in argument. Quite the contrary. It is an invitation to leave the irrationality of an artificially narrowed range of arguments and to move to the rationality of arguing like human beings. It brings out into the open the arguing that economists do anyway—in the dark, for they must do it somewhere and the various official rhetorics leave them benighted.

The charge of irrationalism comes easily to the lips of methodological authoritarians. The notion is that reasoning outside the constricted epistemology of modernism is no reasoning at all. Mark Blaug, for instance, charges that Paul Feyerabend's book *Against Method* "amounts to replacing the philosophy of science by the philosophy of flower power" (1980, p. 44). Feyerabend commonly attracts such dismissive remarks by his flamboyance. But Stephen Toulmin and Michael Polanyi are nothing if not sweetly reasonable; Blaug lumps them with Feyerabend and attacks the Feyerabend-flavored whole. On a higher level of philosophical sophistication Imre Lakatos' *Methodology of Scientific Research Programmes* (1978, from articles published from 1963 to 1976) repeatedly tars Polanyi, Kuhn, and Feyerabend with "irrationalism" (e.g., Vol. 1, pp. 9n1, 76n6, 91n1, 130 and 130n3), emphasizing their sometimes aggressively expressed case against rigid rationalism and ignoring their moderately expressed case

for wider rationality. The tactic is an old one. Richard Rorty notes that "the charges of 'relativism' and 'irrationalism' once leveled against Dewey [were] merely the mindless defensive reflexes of the philosophical tradition which he attacked" (1979, p. 13; Rorty, 1982a, Ch. 9). The position taken by the opponents of Dewey, Polanyi, Kuhn, and the rest is "if the choice is between Science and irrationality, I'm for Science." But that's not the choice.

The Barbarians Are Not at the Gates

Yet still the doubt remains. If we abandon the notion that econometrics is by itself a method of science in economics, if we admit that our arguments require comparative standards, if we agree that personal knowledge of various sorts plays a part in economic knowledge, if we look at economic argument with a literary eye, will we not be abandoning science to its enemies? Will not scientific questions come to be decided by politics or whim? Is the routine of Scientific Method not a wall against irrational and authoritarian threats to inquiry? Are not the barbarians at the gates?

The fear is a surprisingly old and persistent one. In classical times it was part of the debate between philosophy and rhetoric, evident in the unsympathetic way in which the sophists are portrayed in Plato's dialogues. Cicero viewed himself as bringing the two together, disciplining rhetoric's tendency to become empty advocacy and trope on the one hand and disciplining philosophy's tendency to become useless and inhuman speculation on the other. The classical problem was that rhetoric was a powerful device easily misused for evil ends, the atomic power of the classical world, and like it the subject of worrying about its proliferation. The solution was to insist that the orator be good as well as clever: Cato defined him as *"vir bonus dicendi peritus,"* the good man skilled at speaking, a Ciceronian ideal as well. Quintilian, a century and a half after Cicero, said that "he who would be an orator must not only *appear* to be a good man, but cannot *be* an orator unless he *is* a good man" (*Institutio* XII, 1, 3). The classical problem looks quaint to moderns, who know well that regressions, radios, computers, experiments, or any of the now canonized methods of persuasion can be and have been used as methods of deceit. There is nothing about anaphora, chiasmus, metonymy, or other pieces of classical rhetoric that make them more subject to evil misuse than the modern methods. One can only note with regret that the Greeks and Romans were more sensitive to the possibility, and less hypnotized by the claims of method to moral neutrality.

The 20th century's attachment to limiting rules of inquiry solves a German problem. In the German Empire and Reich it was of course necessary to propound a split of fact from values in the social sciences if anything was to be accomplished free of political interference. And German speculative philosophy, one hears it said, warranted a logical positivist cure. The German habits, however, have spilled over into a quite different world. It is said that if we are to avoid dread anarchy we cannot trust each scientist to be his own methodologist. We must legislate a uniform though narrowing method to keep scholars from resorting to figurative and literal murder in aid of their ideas. We ourselves could be trusted with methodological freedom, of course, but the others cannot. The argument is a strange and authoritarian one, uncomfortably similar to the argument of, say, the Polish authorities against Solidarity or of the Chilean authorities against free politics. It is odd to hear intellectuals making it. Perhaps their low opinion of the free play of ideas comes from experiences in the faculty senate: the results of academic democracy,

it must be admitted, are not so bad an argument for authoritarianism, at least until one looks more closely at the results of authoritarianism. Surely, though, the alternative to blindered rules of modernism is not an irrational mob but a body of enlightened scholars, perhaps more enlightened when freed to make arguments that actually bear on the questions at issue.

There Is No Good Reason to Wish to Make "Scientific" As Against Plausible Statements

The other main objection to an openly rhetorical economics is not so pessimistic. It is the sunny view that scientific knowledge of a modernist sort may be hard to achieve, even impossible, but all will be well on earth and in heaven if we strive in our poor way to reach it. We should have a standard of Truth beyond persuasive rhetoric to which to aspire. In Figure 2 all possible propositions about the world are divided into objective and subjective, positive and normative, scientific and humanistic, hard and soft. The modernist supposes that the world comes divided nicely along such lines.

scientific	humanistic
fact	opinion
objective	subjective
positive	normative
vigorous	sloppy
precise	vague
things	words
cognition	intuition
hard	soft

Figure 2. The Task of Science Is to Move the Line

According to the modernist methodologist the scientist's job is not to decide whether propositions are useful for understanding and changing the world but to classify them into one or the other half, scientific or nonscientific, and to bring as many as possible into the scientific portion. But why? Whole teams of philosophical surveyors have sweated long over the placing of the demarcation line between scientific and other propositions, worrying for instance about whether astrology can be demarcated from astronomy; it was the chief activity of the positivist movement for a century. It is not clear why anyone troubled to do so. People are persuaded of things in many ways, as has been shown for economic persuasion. It is not clear why they should labor at drawing lines on mental maps between one way and another.

The modernists have long dealt with the embarrassment that metaphor, case study, upbringing, authority, introspection, simplicity, symmetry, fashion, theology, and politics serve to convince scientists as they do other folk by labeling these the "context of discovery." The way scientists discover hypotheses has been held to be distinct from the "context of justification," namely, proofs of a modernist sort. Thomas Kuhn's autobiographical reflections on the matter can stand for puzzlement in recent years about this ploy:

> Having been weaned intellectually on these distinctions and others like them, I could scarcely be more aware of their import and force. For many years I took them to be about the nature of knowledge, and . . . yet my attempts to apply them, even *grosso modo*, to the actual situations in which knowledge is gained, accepted, and assimilated have made them seem extraordinarily problematic [Kuhn, 1970, p. 9].

The methodologist's claim is that "ultimately" all knowledge in science can be brought into the hard and objective side of Figure 2. Consequently, in certifying propositions as really scientific there is great emphasis placed on *"conceivable falsification"* and *"some future test."* The apparent standard is the Cartesian one that we can find plausible only the things we cannot possibly doubt. But even this curious standard is not in fact applied: a conceivable but practically impossible test takes over the prestige of the real test, but free of its labor. Such a step needs to be challenged. It is identical to the one involved in equating as morally similar the actual compensation of those hurt during a Pareto optimal move with a hypothetical compensation not actually paid, as in the Hicks-Kaldor test; and it is identically dubious. A properly identified econometric measurement of the out-of-sample properties of macroeconomic policy is "operational," that is, conceivable, but for all the scientific prestige the conceivability lends to talk about it, there are grave doubts whether it is practically possible. While economists are waiting for the ultimate they might better seek wisdom in the humanism of historical evidence on régime changes or of introspection about how investors might react to announcements of new monetary policies. And of course they do.

The point is that one cannot tell whether an assertion is persuasive by knowing at which portion of the scientific/ humanistic circle it came from. One can tell whether it is persuasive only by thinking about it. Not all regression analyses are more persuasive than all moral arguments; not all controlled experiments are more persuasive than all introspections. Economic intellectuals should not discriminate against propositions on the basis of race, creed, or epistemological origin. There are some subjective, soft, vague propositions that are more persuasive than some objective, hard, precise propositions.

Take, for instance, the law of demand. The economist is persuaded that he will buy less oil when its price doubles better than he or anyone else is persuaded of the age of the universe. He may reasonably be persuaded of it better than he is that the earth goes around the sun, because not being an astronomer with direct knowledge of the experiments involved he has the astronomical facts only from the testimony of people he trusts, a reliable though not of course infallible source of knowledge.[11] The economic fact he has mostly from looking into himself and seeing it sitting there. The ceremony of the official rhetoric to the contrary, it is not because the law of demand has predicted well or has passed some statistical test that it is believed—although such further tests are not to be scorned. The "scientific" character of the tests is irrelevant. It may be claimed in reply that people can agree on precisely what a regression coefficient means but cannot agree precisely on the character of their introspection. Even if true (it is not) this is a poor argument for ignoring introspection if the introspection is persuasive and the regression coefficient, infected with identification problems and errors in variables, is not. Precision means low variance of estimation; but if the estimate is greatly biased it will tell precisely nothing.

An extreme case unnecessary for the argument here will make the point clear. You are persuaded that it is wrong to murder better than you are persuaded that inflation is always and everywhere a monetary phenomenon. This is not to say that similar techniques of persuasion will be applicable to both propositions. It says merely that each within its field, and each therefore subject to the methods of honest persuasion appropriate to the field, the one achieves a greater certainty than the other. To deny the comparison is to deny that reason and the partial certitude it can bring applies to nonscientific subjects, a common but unreasonable position. There is no reason why specifically scientific persuasiveness ("at the .05 level the coeffi-

cient on M in a regression of prices in 30 countries over 30 years is insignificantly different from 1.0") should take over the whole of persuasiveness, leaving moral persuasiveness incomparably inferior to it. Arguments such as that "murder violates the reasonable moral premise that we should not force other people to be means to our ends" or that "from behind a prenatal veil of ignorance of which side of the murderer's revolver we would be after birth we would enact laws against murder" are persuasive in comparable units. Not always, but sometimes, they are, indeed, more persuasive, better, more probable (Toulmin, 1958, p. 34). We believe and act on what persuades us—not what persuades a majority of a badly chosen jury, but what persuades well educated participants in our civilization and justly influential people in our field. To attempt to go beyond persuasive reasoning is to let epistemology limit reasonable persuasion.

VIII. *The Good of Rhetoric*

Better Writing

Well, what of it? What is to be gained by taking the rhetoric of economics seriously? The question can be answered by noting the burdens imposed by an unexamined rhetoric.

First of all, economics is badly written, written by a formula for scientific prose. The situation is not so bad as it is in, say, psychology, where papers that do not conform to the formula (introduction, survey of literature, experiment, discussion, and so forth) are in some journals not accepted. But economists are stumbling towards conventions of prose that are bad for clarity and honesty. The study of rhetoric, it must be said, does not guarantee the student a good English style. But at least it makes him blush at the disdain for the reader that some economics exhibits (Walter Salant, 1969).

[11] The astronomical "fact" that the earth goes around the sun, of course, is not even a properly modernist fact, though it is commonly treated as one in such discussions. Which goes around which is a matter of the point of view one chooses. It is the aesthetics of the simpler theory, not the "facts," that leads to heliocentrism.

The economist's English contains a message, usually that "I am a Scientist: give way." Occasionally the message is more genial: Zvi Griliches' irony says "Do not make a fetish out of these methods I am expounding: they are mere human artifices." Milton Friedman's style, so careful and clear, has to an exceptional degree the character of the Inquirer. We will not raise up a race of Dennis Robertsons, Robert Solows, George Stiglers, or Robert Lucases by becoming more sensitive to the real messages in scientific procedure and prose, but maybe we will stunt the growth of the other kind.

Better Teaching

A second burden is that economics is badly taught, not because its teachers are boring or stupid, but because they often do not recognize the tacitness of economic knowledge, and therefore teach by axiom and proof instead of by problem-solving and practice. To quote Polanyi yet again:

> . . . the transmission of knowledge from one generation to the other must be predominately tacit. . . . The pupil must assume that a teaching which appears meaningless to start with has in fact a meaning that can be discovered by hitting on the same kind of indwelling [a favorite Polanyi expression] as the teacher is practicing [1966, p. 61].

It is frustrating for students to be told that economics is not primarily a matter of memorizing formulas, but a matter of feeling the applicability of arguments, of seeing analogies between one application and a superficially different one, of knowing when to reason verbally and when mathematically, and of what implicit characterization of the world is most useful for correct economics. Life is hard. As a blind man uses his stick as an extension of his body, so whenever we use a theory "we incorporate it in our body—or extend our body to include it—so that we come to dwell in it." Problem-solving in economics

is the tacit knowledge of the sort Polanyi describes.[12] We know the economics, but cannot say it, in the same way a musician knows the note he plays without consciously recalling the technique for executing it. A singer is a prime example, for there is no set of mechanical instructions one can give to a singer on how to hit a high C. Al Harberger often speaks of so-and-so being able to make an economic argument "sing." Like the directions to Carnegie Hall, the answer to the question "how do you get to the Council of Economic Advisors?" is "practice, practice."

Better Foreign Relations

A third burden placed on economics by its modernist methodology is that economics is misunderstood and, when regarded at all, disliked by both humanists and scientists. The humanists dislike it for its baggage of antihumanist methodology. The scientists dislike it because it does not in reality attain the rigor that its methodology claims to achieve. The bad foreign relations have many costs. For instance, as was noted above, economics has recently become imperialistic. There is now an economics of history, of sociology, of law, of anthropology, of politics, of political philosophy, of ethics. The flabby methodology of modernist economics simply makes this colonization more difficult, raising irrelevant methodological doubts in the minds of the colonized folk.

Better Science

A fourth burden is that economists pointlessly limit themselves to "objective" facts, admitting the capabilities of one's own or others' minds as merely sources of hypotheses to be tested, not as themselves arguments for assenting to hypotheses. The modernist notion is that common sense is nonsense, that knowledge must somehow be objective, not *verstehen* or

---

[12] On this score, and some others, I can heartily recommend McCloskey, 1982.

introspection. But, to repeat, we have much information immediately at our disposal about our own behavior as economic molecules, if we would only examine the grounds of our beliefs. The idea that observational proofs of the law of demand, such as the Rotterdam School's multi-equation approach, are more compelling than introspection is especially odd. Even the econometrics itself would be better, as Christopher Sims has recently argued:

> If we think carefully about what we are doing, we will emerge, I think, both more confident that much of applied econometrics is useful, despite its differences from physical science, and more ready to adapt our language and methods to reflect what we are actually doing. The result will be econometrics which is more scientific [by which he means "good"] if less superficially similar to statistical methods used in experimental sciences [Sims, 1982, p. 25].

The curious status of survey research in modern economics is a case in point. Unlike other social scientists, economists are extremely hostile towards questionnaires and other self-descriptions. Secondhand knowledge of a famous debate among economists in the late 1930s is part of an economist's formal education. The debate concerned the case of asking businessmen if they equalized marginal cost to marginal revenue. It is revealing that the failure of such a study—never mind whether that was indeed the study—is supposed to convince economists to abandon all self-testimony. One can literally get an audience of economists to laugh out loud by proposing ironically to send out a questionnaire on some disputed economic point. Economists are so impressed by the confusions that might possibly result from questionnaires that they abandon them entirely, in favor of the confusions resulting from external observation. They are unthinkingly committed to the notion that only the externally observable behavior of economic actors is admissable evidence in arguments concerning eco-

nomics. But self-testimony is not useless, even for the purpose of resolving the marginal cost-average cost debate of the 1930s. One could have asked "Has your profit margin always been the same?" "What do you think when you find sales lagging?" (Lower profit margin? Wait it out?) Foolish inquiries into motives and foolish use of human informants will produce nonsense. But this is also true of foolish use of the evidence more commonly admitted into the economist's study.

Better Dispositions

A fifth and final burden is that scientific debates in economics are long-lasting and ill-tempered. Journals in geology are not filled with articles impugning the character of other geologists. They are not filled with bitter controversies that drone on from one century to the next. No wonder. Economists do not have an official rhetoric that persuasively describes what economists find persuasive. The mathematical and statistical tools that gave promise in the bright dawn of the 1930s and 1940s of ending economic dispute have not succeeded, because too much has been asked of them. Believing mistakenly that operationalism is enough to end all dispute, the economist assumes his opponent is dishonest when he does not concede the point, that he is motivated by some ideological passion or by self-interest, or that he is simply stupid. It fits the naive fact-value split of modernism to attribute all disagreements to political differences, since facts are alleged to be, unlike values, impossible to dispute. The extent of disagreement among economists, as was mentioned, is in fact exaggerated. The amount of their agreement, however, makes all the more puzzling the venom they bring to relatively minor disputes. The assaults on Milton Friedman or on John Kenneth Galbraith, for example, have a bitterness that is quite unreasonable. If one cannot reason about values, and if most of what matters is placed in the value half of the fact-value split, then it follows that one will embrace unreason when talking about things that matter. The claims of an overblown methodology of Science merely end conversation.[13]

A rhetorical cure for such disabilities would reject philosophy as a guide to science, or would reject at least a philosophy that pretended to legislate the knowable. The cure would not throw away the illuminating regression, the crucial experiment, the unexpected implication unexpectedly falsified. These too persuade reasonable scholars. Non-argument is the necessary alternative to narrow argument only if one accepts the dichotomies of modernism. The cure would merely recognize the good health of economics, disguised now under the neurotic inhibitions of an artificial methodology of Science.

REFERENCES

ALCHIAN, ARMEN. "Uncertainty, Evolution, and Economic Theory," *J. Polit. Econ.*, June 1950, *58*(3), pp. 211–21.

BARFIELD, OWEN. "Poetic Diction and Legal Fiction," in *Essays presented to Charles Williams*. London: Oxford U. Press, 1947; reprinted in *The importance of language*. Ed.: MAX BLACK, Englewood Cliffs, NJ: Prentice-Hall, 1962, pp. 51–71.

BECKER, GARY S. AND STIGLER, GEORGE J. "De Gustibus Non Est Disputandum," *Amer. Econ. Rev.*, Mar. 1977, *67*(2), pp. 76–90.

BENTHAM, JEREMY. *The book of fallacies from unfinished papers*. London: Hunt, 1824.

BLACK, MAX. *Models and metaphors: Studies in language and philosophy*. Ithaca, NY: Cornell U. Press, 1962.

BLAUG, MARK. *The methodology of economics: Or how economists explain*. Cambridge, U.K.: Cambridge U. Press, 1980.

BOOTH, WAYNE C. *The rhetoric of fiction*. Chicago, IL: U. of Chicago Press, 1961.

———. "The Revival of Rhetoric," in *New rhetorics*.

[13] Listen to Harry Johnson: "The methodology of positive economics was an ideal methodology for justifying work that produced apparently surprising results without feeling obliged to explain why they occurred" (Johnson, 1971, p. 13). I do not need to think about your evidence for widespread monopolistic competition because my methodology tells me the evidence is irrelevant.

Ed.: MARTIN STEINMANN, JR. NY: Scribner's, 1967.

———. *Modern dogma and the rhetoric of assent*. Chicago, IL: U. of Chicago Press, 1974.

BURKE, KENNETH. *A rhetoric of motives*. Berkeley: U. of California Press, 1950.

COASE, RONALD. "How Should Economists Choose?" The G. Warren Nutter Lectures in Political Economy. Washington, DC: American Enterprise Institute, 1982.

COHEN, KALMAN AND CYERT, RICHARD. *Theory of the firm*. 2nd ed. Englewood Cliffs, NJ: Prentice-Hall, 1975.

COOLEY, T. F. AND LEROY, S. F. "Identification and Estimation of Money Demand," *Amer. Econ. Rev.*, Dec. 1981, *71*(5), pp. 825–44.

DAVIS, PHILIP J. AND HERSH, REUBEN. *The mathematical experience*. Boston, MA: Houghton Mifflin, 1981.

DEWEY, JOHN. *The quest for certainty*. NY: Putnam, [1929] 1960.

EINSTEIN, ALBERT. "Aphorisms for Leo Baeck," reprinted in *Ideas and opinions*. NY: Dell, [1953] 1973.

FEYERABEND, PAUL. *Against method: Outline of an anarchistic theory of knowledge*. London: Verso, [1975] 1978.

———. *Science in a free society*. London: New Left Books, 1978.

FISCHER, DAVID HACKETT. *Historians' fallacies*. NY: Harper & Row, 1970.

FRENKEL, JACOB. "Purchasing Power Parity: Doctrinal Perspectives and Evidence from the 1920s," *J. Int. Econ.*, May 1978, *8*(2), pp. 169–91.

FRIEDMAN, MILTON. "The Methodology of Positive Economics," in *Essays in positive economics*. Chicago, IL: U. of Chicago Press, 1953.

FRIEDMAN, MILTON AND SCHWARTZ, ANNA J. *A monetary history of the United States*. Princeton, NJ: Princeton U. Press, 1963.

GARDNER, JOHN. *On moral fiction*. NY: Basic Books, 1978.

GENBERG, A. HANS. "Aspects of the Monetary Approach to Balance-of-Payments Theory: An Empirical Study of Sweden," in *The monetary approach to the balance of payments*. Eds.: JACOB A. FRENKEL AND HARRY G. JOHNSON. London: Allen & Unwin, 1976.

GOULD, STEPHEN JAY. *Ever since Darwin*. NY: Norton, 1977.

———. *The mismeasure of man*. NY: Norton, 1981.

VAN HEIJENOORT, JOHN. "Gödel's Proof," in *The encyclopedia of philosophy*. NY: Macmillan & Free Press, 1967.

HORSBURGH, H. J. N. "Philosophers Against Metaphor," *Philosophical Quart.*, July 1958, *8*(32), pp. 231–45.

HUME, DAVID. *An inquiry concerning human understanding*. Ed.: CHARLES W. HENDEL. Indianapolis: Bobbs & Merrill, [1748] 1955.

JAMES, WILLIAM. "Pragmatism's Conception of Truth" reprinted in *Essays in pragmatism by William James*. Ed.: CASTELL ALBUREY. NY: Hafner, [1907] 1948.

JOHNSON, HARRY G. "The Keynesian Revolution and

the Monetarist Counterrevolution," *Amer. Econ. Rev.*, May 1971, *61*(2), pp. 1–14.

KEARL, J. R.; POPE, CLAYNE; WHITING, GORDON AND WIMMER, LARRY. "A Confusion of Economists?" *Amer. Econ. Rev.*, May 1979, *69*(2), pp. 28–37.

KLINE, MORRIS. *Mathematics: The loss of certainty.* NY: Oxford, 1980.

KRAVIS, IRVING B. AND LIPSEY, ROBERT E. "Price Behavior in the Light of Balance of Payments Theories," *J. Int. Econ.*, May 1978, *8*(2), pp. 193–246.

KRUGMAN, PAUL R., "Purchasing Power Parity and Exchange Rates: Another Look at the Evidence," *J. Int. Econ.*, Aug. 1978, *8*(3), pp. 397–407.

KUHN, THOMAS. *The structure of scientific revolutions.* 2nd ed. Chicago: U. of Chicago Press, 1970.

————. *The essential tradition: Selected studies in scientific tradition and change.* Chicago: U. of Chicago Press, 1977.

LAKATOS, IMRE. *Proofs and refutations: The logic of mathematical discovery.* Cambridge: Cambridge U. Press, 1976.

————. *The methodology of scientific research programmes.* From articles 1963–1976. Cambridge, NY and London: Cambridge U. Press, 1978.

———— AND MUSGRAVE, ALAN. *Criticism and the growth of knowledge.* Cambridge: Cambridge U. Press, 1970.

LEAMER, EDWARD. *Specification searches: Ad hoc inferences with nonexperimental data.* NY: Wiley, 1978.

LEVI, EDWARD. *An introduction to legal reasoning.* Chicago, IL: U. of Chicago Press, [1948] 1967.

LEWIS, C. S. "Buspels and Flansferes," in *Rehabilitations and other essays.* London: Oxford U. Press, 1939; reprinted in *The importance of language.* Ed.: MAX BLACK. Englewood Cliffs, NJ: Prentice-Hall, 1962.

McCLOSKEY, DONALD N. "The Loss to Britain from Foreign Industrialization," reprinted in his *Enterprise and trade in Victorian Britain.* London: Allen & Unwin, [1970] 1981.

————. *The applied theory of price.* NY: Macmillan, 1982.

———— AND ZECHER, J. RICHARD. "How the Gold Standard Worked, 1880–1913," in *The monetary approach to the balance of payments.* Eds.: J. FRENKEL AND H. G. JOHNSON. London: Allen & Unwin, 1976.

———— AND ZECHER, J. R. "The Success of Purchasing Power Parity," in *A retrospective on the classical gold standard.* Eds.: MICHAEL BORDO AND ANNA J. SCHWARTZ. NBER conference, 1982. Forthcoming.

MISES, LUDWIG VON. *Human action.* New Haven, CT: Yale U. Press, 1949.

MOOD, A. F. AND GRAYBILL, F. A. *Introduction to the theory of statistics.* 2nd ed. NY: McGraw Hill, 1963.

PASSMORE, JOHN. *A hundred years of philosophy.* 2nd ed. London: Penguin, 1966.

————. "Logical Positivism," in *The encyclopedia of philosophy.* NY: Macmillan, 1967.

————. *Philosophical reasoning.* 2nd ed. London: Duckworth, 1970.

PEIRCE, CHARLES. "The Fixation of Belief," reprinted in *Values in a universe of chance: Selected writings of Charles S. Peirce.* Ed.: P. P. WIENER. Garden City, NJ: Doubleday, [1877] 1958.

PERELMAN, CHAIM AND OLBRECHTS-TYTECA, L. *The new rhetoric: A treatise on argumentation.* Eng. trans. Notre Dame: Notre Dame U. Press, [1958] 1967.

POLANYI, MICHAEL. *Personal knowledge: Towards a post-critical philosophy* Chicago, IL: U. of Chicago Press, 1962.

————. *The tacit dimension.* Garden City, NY: Doubleday, 1966.

POPPER, KARL. *The logic of scientific discovery.* Eng. trans. NY: Harper, [1934] 1959.

————. *The open society and its enemies.* London: Routledge, 1945.

————. *Unended quest: An intellectual autobiography.* London: Collins, 1976.

QUINTILIAN, MARCUS F. *Institutio oratoria.* Cambridge, MA: Harvard U. Press, [c. 100 AD] 1920.

REDER, MELVIN. "Chicago Economics: Permanence and Change," *J. Econ. Lit.*, Mar. 1982, *20*(1), pp. 1–38.

RICHARDS, I. A. *The philosophy of rhetoric.* NY: Oxford U. Press, 1936.

RICHARDSON, J. D. "Some Empirical Evidence on Commodity Arbitrage and the Law of One Price," *J. Inter. Econ.*, May 1978, *8*(2), pp. 341–51.

ROLL, RICHARD AND ROSS, STEPHEN. "An Empirical Investigation of the Arbitrage Pricing Theory," *J. Finance*, Dec. 1980, *35*, pp. 1073–1103.

RORTY, RICHARD. *Philosophy and the mirror of nature.* Princeton NJ: Princeton U. Press, 1979.

————. *Consequences of pragmatism (Essays: 1972–1980).* Minneapolis: U. of Minnesota Press, 1982a.

————. "The Fate of Philosophy," *The New Republic*, Oct. 18, 1982b, *187*(16), pp. 28–34.

SALANT, WALTER. "Writing and Reading in Economics," *J. Polit. Econ.*, July-Aug. 1969, *77*(4, Pt. I), pp. 545–58.

SAMUELSON, P. A. *The foundations of economic analysis.* Cambridge, MA: Harvard U. Press, 1947.

SEN, AMARTYA. "Behaviour and the Concept of Preference," Inaugural Lecture. London School of Economics and Political Science, 1973.

SHARPE, WILLIAM. *Portfolio theory and capital markets.* NY: McGraw Hill, 1970.

SIMS, CHRISTOPHER. "Review of *Specification searches: Ad hoc interference with nonexperimental data.* By Edward E. Leamer." *J. Econ. Lit.*, June 1979, *17*(2), pp. 566–68.

————. "Scientific Standards in Econometric Modeling," Unpub. paper for the 25th anniversary of the Rotterdam Econometrics Institute, Apr. 1982.

STEINER, GEORGE. *After Babel: Aspects of language.* London: Oxford U. Press, 1975.

STIGLER, GEORGE J. "The Conference Handbook," *J. Polit. Econ.*, Apr. 1977, *85*(2), pp. 441–43.

TOULMIN, STEPHEN. *The uses of argument.* Cambridge: Cambridge U. Press, 1958.

————. "The Construal of Reality: Criticism in Modern and Postmodern Science," *Critical Inquiry,* Autumn 1982, *9*(1), pp. 93–110.

WEBSTER, GLENN; JACOX, ADA AND BALDWIN, BEVERLY. "Nursing Theory and the Ghost of the Received View," in *Current issues in nursing.* Eds.: JOANNE MCCLOSKEY AND HELEN GRACE.

Boston, MA: Blackwell Scientific, 1981, pp. 16–35.

WHATELY, RICHARD. *Elements of rhetoric.* 7th ed. London: [1846] 1894.

ZECKHAUSER, RICHARD AND STOKEY, EDITH. *A primer for policy analysis.* NY: Norton, 1978.

[9]
Storytelling in Economics

DONALD N. McCLOSKEY

It is good to tell the story of science and art, economics and the nineteenth-century novel, the marginal productivity theory of distribution and the tradition of the Horatian ode as similarly as possible. I intend to do so. Economists are tellers of stories and makers of poems, and from recognizing this we can know better what economists do.

There seem to be two ways of understanding things; either by way of a metaphor or by way of a story, through something like a poem or through something like a novel. When a biologist is asked to explain why the moulting glands of a crab are located just as they are he has two possibilities. Either he can call on a model – a metaphor – of rationality inside the crab, explaining that locating them just *there* will maximize the efficiency of the glands in operation; or he can tell a story, of how crabs with badly located glands will fail to survive. If he is lucky with the modelling he will discover some soluble differential equations. If he is lucky with the storytelling he will discover a true history of some maladapted variety of crabs, showing it dying out. Metaphors and stories, models and histories, are the two ways of answering 'why'.

It has probably been noticed before that the metaphorical and the narrative explanations answer to each other. Suppose the biologist happens first to offer his metaphor, his hypothetical individual crab moving bits of its body from here to there in search of the optimal location for moulting glands. The listener asks, 'But why?' The biologist will answer with a story: he says, 'The reason why the glands must be located optimally is that if

5

DONALD N. McCLOSKEY

crabs did a poor job of locating their glands they would die off as time passed.' A story answers a model.

But likewise a model answers a story. If the biologist gives the evolutionary story first, and the listener then asks, 'But why?', the biologist will answer with a metaphor: 'The reason why the crabs will die off is that poorly located glands would serve poorly in the emergencies of crabby life . . . .' The glands would not be located according to the metaphor of maximizing: that's why.

Among what speakers of English call the sciences, metaphors dominate physics and stories dominate biology. Of course, the modes can mix. That we humans regard metaphors and stories as antiphonal guarantees they will. Mendel's thinking about genetics is a rare case in biology of pure modelling, answered after a long while by the more usual storytelling. In 1902 W.S. Sutton observed homologous pairs of grasshopper chromosomes. He answered the question put to a metaphor – '*Why* does the Mendelian model of genes work?' – with a story: 'Because, to begin with, the genes are arranged along pairs of chromosomes, which I have seen, one half from each parent.'

The modes of explanation are more closely balanced in economics. An economist explains the success of cotton farming in the antebellum American South indifferently with static, modelling arguments (the South in 1860 had a comparative advantage in cotton) or with dynamic, storytelling arguments (the situation in 1860 was an evolution from earlier successes). The best economics, indeed, combines the two. Ludwig von Mises' famous paper of 1920 on the impossibility of economic calculation under socialism was both a story of the failures of central planning during the recently concluded war and a model of why any replacement for the market would fail (Lavoie 1985: 49).

The metaphors are best adapted to making predictions of tides in the sea or of shortages in markets, simulating out into a counterfactual world. (One could use here either an evolutionary story from the history of science or a maximizing model from the sociology or philosophy of science.) Seventeenth-century physics abandoned stories in favour of models, giving up the claim to tell in a narrative sense how gravity reached up and pulled things down; it just did, according to such-and-such an equation – let me show you the model. Similarly a price control on apartments will yield shortages; don't ask how it will in sequence; it just will,

Storytelling in Economics

according to such-and-such an equation – let me show you the model.

On the other hand the storytelling is best adapted to explaining something that has already happened, like the evolution of crabs or the development of the modern corporation. The Darwinian story was notably lacking in models, and in predictions. Mendel's model, which offered to explain the descent of man by a metaphor rather than by a story, was neglected for thirty-four years, all the while that evolutionary stories were being told.

The contrast carries over to the failures of the two modes. When a metaphor is used too boldly in narrating a history it becomes ensnared in logical contradictions, such as those surrounding counterfactuals (McCloskey 1987). If a model of an economy is to be used to imagine what would have happened to Britain in the absence of the industrial revolution then the contradiction is that an economy of the British sort did in fact experience an industrial revolution. A world in which the Britain of 1780 did not yield up an industrial revolution would have been a very different one, before and after 1780. The model wants to eat the cake and have all the ingredients, too. It contradicts the story. Likewise, when a story attempts to predict something, by extrapolating the story into the future, it contradicts some persuasive model. The story of business cycles can organize the past, showing capitalist economies bobbing up and down. But it contradicts itself when it is offered as a prediction of the future. If the models of business cycles could predict the future there would be no surprises, and consequently no business cycles.

The point is that economists are like other human beings in that they both use metaphors and tell stories. They are concerned both to explain and to understand, *erklären* and *verstehen*. I am going to concentrate here on storytelling, having written elsewhere about the metaphorical side of the tale (McCloskey 1985). What might be called the poetics or stylistics of economics is worth talking about. But here the subject is the rhetoric of fiction in economics.

I propose to take seriously an assertion by Peter Brooks, in his *Reading for the Plot*: 'Our lives are ceaselessly intertwined with narrative, with the stories that we tell, all of which are reworked in that story of our own lives that we narrate to ourselves . . . . We are immersed in narrative' (Brooks 1985: 3). As the historian J.H. Hexter put it, storytelling is 'a sort of knowledge we cannot live

DONALD N. McCLOSKEY

without' (Hexter 1986: 8). Economists have not lived without it, not ever. It is no accident that the novel and economic science were born at the same time. We live in an age insatiate of plot.

Tell me a story, Dr Smith. Why, of course:

A pension scheme is proposed for the nation, in which 'the employer will pay half'. It will say in the law and on the worker's salary cheque that the worker contributes 5% of his wages to the pension fund but that the employer contributes the other 5%. The example is a leading case in the old quarrel between lawyers and economists. A law is passed 'designed' (as they say) to have such-and-such an effect. The lawyerly mind goes this far, urging us therefore to limit the hours of women workers or to subsidize shipping. The women, he thinks, will be made better off; as will the ships. According to the lawyer, the workers under the pension scheme will be on balance 5% better off, getting half of their pension free from the employer.

An economist, however, will not want to leave the story of the pension plan in the first act, the lawyer's and legislator's act of laws 'designed' to split the costs. She will want to go further in the drama. She will say: 'At the higher cost of labour the employers will hire fewer workers. In the second act the situation created by the law will begin to dissolve. At the old terms more workers will want to work than the employer wishes to hire. Jostling queues will form outside the factory gates. The competition of the workers will drive down wages. By the third and final act a part of the "employer's" share – maybe even all of it – will sit on the workers themselves, in the form of lower wages. The intent of the law', the economist concludes, 'will have been frustrated.'

Thus in Chicago when a tax on employment was proposed the reporters asked who would pay the tax. Alderman Thomas Keane (who as it happens ended in jail, though not for misappropriation of economics) declared that the City had been careful to draft the law so that only the employers paid it. 'The City of Chicago', said Keane, 'will never tax the working man.'

Thus in 1987, when Senator Kennedy proposed a plan for American workers and employers to share the cost of health insurance, newspapers reported Kennedy as estimating 'the overall cost at $25 billion – $20 billion paid by employers and $5 billion by workers'. Senator Kennedy will never tax the working man. The manager of employee relations at the US Chamber of Commerce

8

Storytelling in Economics

(who apparently agreed with Senator Kennedy's economic analysis of where the tax would fall) said, 'It is ridiculous to believe that every company . . . can afford to provide such a generous array of health care benefits.' The US Chamber of Commerce will never tax the company.

The case illustrates a number of points about economic stories. It illustrates the delight that economists take in unforeseen consequences, a delight shared with other social scientists. It illustrates the selection of certain consequences for special attention: an accountant or political scientist would want to hear how the pension was funded, because it would affect business or politics in the future; economists usually set such consequences to the side. It illustrates also the way economists draw on typical scenes – the queues in front of the factory – and typical metaphors – workers as commodities to be bought and sold. Especially it illustrates the way stories support economic argument. Since Adam Smith and David Ricardo, economists have been addicted to little analytic stories, the Ricardian vice. The economist says, 'Yes, I see how the story starts; but I see dramatic possibilities here; I see how events will develop from the situation given in the first act.'

It is not controversial that an economist is a storyteller when telling the story of the Federal Reserve Board or of the industrial revolution. Plainly and routinely, ninety per cent of what economists do is such storytelling. Yet even in the other ten per cent, in the part more obviously dominated by models and metaphors, the economist tells stories. The applied economist can be viewed as a realistic novelist or a realistic playwright, a Thomas Hardy or a George Bernard Shaw. The theorist, too, may be viewed as a teller of stories, though a non-realist, whose plots and characters have the same relation to truth as those in *Gulliver's Travels* or *A Midsummer Night's Dream*. Economics is saturated with narration.

The analogy on its face seems apt. Economics is a sort of social history. For all their brave talk about being the physicists of the social sciences, economists do their best work when looking backwards, the way a biologist or geologist or historian does. Journalists and politicians demand that economists prophesy, forecasting the social weather. Sometimes, unhappily, the economists will take money for trying. But it is not their chief skill, any more than earthquake forecasting is the chief skill of seismologists, or election

9

DONALD N. McCLOSKEY

forecasting the chief skill of political historians. Economists cannot predict much, and certainly cannot predict profitably. If they were so smart they would be rich (McCloskey 1988). Mainly economists are tellers of stories.

Well, so what? What is to be gained by thinking this way about economics? One answer can be given at once, and illustrates the uses of the literary analogy, namely: storytelling makes it clearer why economists disagree.

Disagreement among scientists is suggestive for the rhetoric of science in the same way that simultaneous discovery is suggestive for its sociology. The lay person does not appreciate how much economists agree, but he is not entirely wrong in thinking that they also disagree a lot. Economists have long-lasting and long-disagreeing schools, more typical of the humanities than of the sciences. Why then do they disagree?

When economists themselves try to answer they become socio-logical or philosophical, though in ways that a sociologist or philosopher would find uncongenial. When in a sociological mood they will smile knowingly and explain that what drives monetarists or Keynesians to 'differentiate their product', as they delight in putting it, is self-interest. Economists are nature's Marxists, and enjoy uncovering and then sniggering at self-interest. When they are in a more elevated and philosophic mood they will speak sagely of 'successive approximations' or 'treating a theory merely *as if* it were true'. Some have read a bit of Popper or Kuhn, and reckon they know a thing or two about the Methodology of Science. The stories that result from these ventures into ersatz sociology and sophomore philosophy are unconvincing. To tell the truth, the economists do not know why they disagree.

Storytelling offers a richer model of how economists talk and a more plausible story of their disagreements. The disagreement can be understood from a literary perspective in more helpful ways than saying that one economist has divergent material interest from another, or a different 'crucial experiment', or another 'paradigm'.

It is first of all the theory of reading held by scientists that permits them to disagree, and with such ill temper. The over-simple theory of reading adopted officially by economists and other scientists is that scientific texts are transparent, a matter of 'mere communication', 'just style', simply 'writing up' the 'theoretical

Storytelling in Economics

results' and 'empirical findings'. If reading is so free from difficulties, then naturally the only way our readers can fail to agree with us is through their ill will or their dimness. (Leave aside the unlikely chance that it is we who are dim.) It's right there in black and white. Don't be a dunce.

A better theory of reading, one that admitted that scientific prose like literary prose is complicated and allusive, drawing on a richer rhetoric than mere demonstration, might soothe this ill temper. The better theory, after all, is the one a good teacher uses with students. She knows well enough that the text is not transparent to the students, and she does not get angry when they misunderstand. God likewise does not get angry when His students misunderstand His text. In fact, like scientists and scholars, God writes obscurely in order to snare us. As Gerald Bruns has noted, St Augustine viewed the obscurity of the Bible as having 'a pragmatic function in the art of winning over an alienated and even contemptuous audience' (Bruns 1984: 157). He quotes a remark of Augustine about the difficulty of the Bible that might as well be about the latest proof in mathematical economics: 'I do not doubt that this situation was provided by God to conquer pride by work and to combat disdain in our minds, by which those things which are easily discovered seem frequently to be worthless.'

One source of disagreement, then, is a naïve theory of reading, the theory that would ask naïvely for the 'message' in a poem, as though poems were riddles in rhyme. Another source of disagreement is likewise a source of disagreement about literature: compression, a lack of explicitness. Partly this is economic. Had she but world enough and time the writer could make everything explicit. In a world of scarcity, however, she cannot. Yet explicitness is no guarantee of agreement, because if the writer has all the time in the world the reader does not. I cannot listen long enough to understand some of my Marxist friends (though I ask them to keep trying). Similarly, the mathematician in economics has an expository style based on explicitness and a zero value of time. Everything will be clear, he promises earnestly, if the readers will but listen carefully to the axioms. The readers grow weary. They cannot remember all the axioms and anyway cannot see why one would wish to doubt them. They do not have the toleration for such speech that the mathematician has.

The point involves more than the economic scarcity of journal

DONALD N. McCLOSKEY

space and of the leisure time to read. It involves the anthropology of science, the customs of its inhabitants and their ability to read a language. A scientist convinced of what she writes will come from a certain background, supplied with a language. Unless her reader knows roughly the same language – that is, unless he has been raised in approximately the same conversation – he will misunderstand and will be unpersuaded. This is an unforgivable failure only if it is an unforgivable failure to be, say, non-Javanese or non-French. The reader comes from another culture, with a different tongue. The training in reading English that a D.Phil. in English provides or the training in reading economics that a Ph.D. in economics provides are trainings in rapid reading, filling in the blanks.

A third and final source of disagreement in literature and in economics, beyond the naïve theory of reading and the limits on understanding foreign speech, is an inability of the reader to assume the point of view demanded by the author. A foolishly sentimental poem has the same irritating effect on a reader as does a foolishly libertarian piece of economics. The reader refuses to enter the author's imaginative world, or is unable to. A literary critic said, 'A bad book, then, is a book in whose mock reader we discover a person we refuse to become, a mask we refuse to put on, a role we will not play' (Gibson 1950: 5). The reader therefore will of course misread the text, at least in the sense of violating the author's intentions. We do not submit to the authorial intentions of a badly done greeting card. In a well-done novel or a well-done scientific paper we agree to submit to the authorial intentions, so far as we can make them out. The entire game in a science such as biology or chemistry or economics is to evoke this submission to authorial intentions. Linus Pauling commands attention, and his readers submit to his intentions, at least outside of vitamin C; Paul Samuelson likewise, at least outside of monetary policy.

The argument can be pushed further. An economist expounding a result creates both an 'authorial audience' (an imagined group of readers who know that this is fiction) and a 'narrative audience' (an imagined group who do not). As Peter Rabinowitz explains (Rabinowitz 1980: 245) 'the narrative audience of "Goldilocks" believes in talking bears'; the authorial audience knows it is fiction. The split between the two audiences created by the author seems weaker in economic science than in explicit fiction, probably

Storytelling in Economics

because we all know that bears do not talk but we do not all know that marginal productivity is a metaphor. In science the 'narrative audience' is fooled, as in 'Goldilocks'. But the authorial audience is fooled, too (and commonly so also is the literal audience, the actual readers as against the ideal readers the author wishes into existence). Michael Mulkay (1985) has shown how important is the choice of authorial audience in the scholarly correspondence of biochemists. The biochemists, like other scientists and scholars, are largely unaware of their literary devices, and become puzzled and angry when their audience refuses to believe in talking bears. Small wonder that scientists and scholars disagree, even when their rhetoric of 'What the facts say' would appear to make disagreement impossible.

Taking economics as a kind of writing, then, explains some of the disagreements of economists. Economists go on disagreeing after the 'theoretical results and empirical findings', as they put it, have been laid out for inspection not merely because they are differentiating their product or suffering from inflammation of the paradigm but because they read a story or a scientific paper written in an unfamiliar language inexpertly, yet do not realize it. They are like the British tourist in Florence who believes firmly that Italians really do understand English, and can be made to admit it if one speaks very slowly and very loudly: 'WHERE . . . IS . . . YOUR . . . STORY??!'

Telling the stories in economics as matters of beginnings, middles, and ends has many attractions. One can start with pure plot, breaking 100 economic stories down into their components as Vladimir Propp did in 1928 for 100 Russian folk tales (Propp 1968: 19–24): the capitalization of Iowa corn prices tale, the exit from and entry to computer selling in the 1980s tale, the correct incidence of the Kennedy health insurance tale, and so forth. The tales can then be analysed into 'functions' (Propp's word for actions). And, to Proppize it entirely, one can ask whether the sequences of functions prove to be constant, as they are in Russia.

The task sounds bizarre. But in a way economics is too easy a case. Economics is already structural, as Ferdinand de Saussure suggested long ago (Saussure 1916: 79, 113). The actions of an economistic folklore are few: entry, exit, price setting, orders within a firm, purchase, sale, valuation, and a few more. It is indeed this self-consciously structural element that makes

DONALD N. McCLOSKEY

economics so irritating to outsiders. Economists say over and over again: 'action X is *just like* action Y' – labour is just like a commodity, slavery is just like capitalization, children are just like refrigerators, and so forth. The economist's favourite phrase would please Claude Lévi-Strauss: 'Underneath it all.' Underneath it all, international trade among nations is trade among individuals, and can be modelled in the same way. Underneath it all, an inflated price is earned by someone as an inflation wage, leaving average welfare unchanged. Underneath it all, we owe the national debt to ourselves, though the people who pay the taxes might wonder about this. In such a highly structured field, whose principles of storytelling are so well known by the main storytellers, it would be surprising to find as many as thirty-one distinct actions, as Propp found in his 100 Russian folk tales (Propp 1968: 64). He found seven characters (ibid: 80). That seems more likely: David Ricardo in his economic tales got along with three.

Tale-telling in economics follows the looser constraints of fiction, too. The most important is the sense of an ending, as in the story of the pension scheme. Go all the way to the third act. The 5% pension gained by the workers is 'not an equilibrium', as economists say when they do not like the ending proposed by some unsophisticated person. Any descendant of Adam Smith, whether by way of Marx or Marshall or Menger, will be happy to tell you the rest of the story.

Many of the disagreements inside economics turn on this sense of an ending. To an eclectic Keynesian the story idea 'Oil prices went up, which caused inflation' is full of meaning, having the merits that stories are supposed to have. But to a monetarist it seems incomplete, no story at all, a flop. As A.C. Harberger says, it doesn't make the economics 'sing'. It ends too soon, half-way through the second act: a rise in oil prices without some corresponding fall elsewhere is 'not an equilibrium'. From the other side, the criticism of monetarism by Keynesians is likewise a criticism of the plot line, complaining of an ill-motivated beginning rather than a premature ending: where on earth does the money *come* from, and why?

There is more than prettiness in such matters of plot. There is moral weight. The historian Hayden White has written that 'The demand for closure in the historical story is a demand . . . for moral reasoning' (White 1981: 20). A monetarist is not morally

Storytelling in Economics

satisfied until she has pinned the blame on the Bank of England. The economist's ending to the pension story says, 'Look: you're getting fooled by the politicians and lawyers if you think that specifying the 50–50 share in the law will get the workers a 50% cheaper pension. Wake up; act your age; look beneath the surface; recognize the dismal ironies of life.' Stories impart meaning, which is to say worth. A *New Yorker* cartoon shows a woman looking up anxiously from the telly, asking her husband, 'Henry, is there a moral to *our* story?'

The sense of adequacy in storytelling works in the most abstract theory, too. In seminars on mathematical economics a question nearly as common as 'Haven't you left off the second subscript?' is 'What's your story?' The story of the pension scheme can be put entirely mathematically and metaphorically, as an assertion about the incidence of a tax on a system of supply-and-demand curves in equilibrium:

$$w^\star = - [E_d/ (E_d + E_s)] T^\star$$

The mathematics here is so familiar to an economist that he will not require explanation beyond the metaphor. But in less familiar cases he will. Like the audience for the biologist explaining moulting glands in crabs, at the end of all the modelling he will ask insistently *why*; 'What's your story?' His question is an appeal for a lower level of abstraction, closer to the episodes of human life. It asks for more realism, in a fictional sense, more illusion of direct experience. It asks to step closer to the nineteenth-century short story, with its powerful and unironic sense of *being there*.

And of course even the most static and abstract argument in economics, refusing to become storylike and insisting on remaining poetic and metaphorical, is part of 'that story of our own lives which we narrate to ourselves'. A scholar has a story in which the work in question is an episode: this is why seminars so often begin with 'how I came to this subject', because such a fragment of autobiography gives meaning to it all. You will hear mathematicians complain if a seminar has not been 'motivated'. The motivation is a story, frequently a mythic history about this part of mathematics or about this speaker. The audience wishes to know why the argument might matter to the speaker, or to the audience itself. The story will then have a moral, as all good stories do.

Economics-as-story provides some places from which to see the plot of economics. To repeat, the author is either a narrator or a poet, a user of either a story or a metaphor. But the reader, too, figures in economic thought. A distinction has been drawn by Louise Rosenblatt between *aesthetic* and *efferent* reading. In efferent reading (*effero*, carry off) the reader focuses on what she will carry off from the reading. Efferent reading is supposed to characterize model-building and science. In aesthetic reading the reader focuses on her experience at the time of the reading, which is supposed to characterize storytelling and art. Yet an aesthetic reading of a scientific text commonly carries the argument. The feeling 'Yes: this is right' in the last stanza of 'Among school children' resembles the feeling that comes upon one when concluding the ancient proof that the square root of 2 cannot be expressed as the ratio of two whole numbers. Rosenblatt supposes that 'To adopt an aesthetic stance . . . toward the directions for constructing a radio is possible, but would usually be very unrewarding' (Rosenblatt 1978: 34). Well, yes, usually. Yet the computer repairman takes an aesthetic attitude toward the schematics for a Murrow computer: 'A nice little machine', he says, and smiles, and is brought to this or that solution. The physicist Steven Weinberg argues that aesthetic readings govern the spending of millions of dollars in research money (Weinberg 1983). The pleasure of the text is sometimes its meaning, even in science.

Rosenblatt anticipates such an argument, noting that theories of literature that do not stress the reader's role are left puzzled by pleasurable nonfiction, such as *The Decline and Fall of the Roman Empire* or, one might add, the best applied economics. The reader's response gives a way of keeping track of the aesthetic readings when they matter. The usual theory of scientific reading claims that they never do.

The telling of artful stories has its customs, and these may be brought to economics, too. Take for instance the bare notion of genre, that is, of types of literary production, with their histories and their interrelations. The scientific report is itself a genre, whose conventions have changed from time to time. Kepler wrote in an autobiographical style, spilling his laboratory notes with all their false trails onto the page; Galileo wrote in urbane little dramas. It was Newton, in some other ways also an unattractive man, who insisted on the cramping literary conventions of the

Storytelling in Economics

Scientific Paper (Medawar 1964). An economist should be aware that he adopts more than a 'mere' style when he adopts the conventions.

Pure theory in economics is similar to the literary genre of fantasy. Like fantasy it violates the rules of 'reality' for the convenience of the tale, and amazing results become commonplace in a world of hypothesis. That animals exhibit the foibles of human beings is unsurprising in a world in which animals talk. No blame attaches. The task of pure theory is to make up fantasies that have a point, in the way that *Animal Farm* has a point. Pure theory confronts reality by disputing whether this or that assumption drives the result, and whether the assumption is realistic. The literary analogy, by the way, puts the debate about the realism of economic assumptions into a strange light. Is it the talking animals or the flying carpets, both of which are unrealistic, that makes *The Arabian Nights* on the whole 'unrealistic'? The question is strange to the point of paradox, but economists talk routinely as though they can answer it.

To speak of pure theory as fantasy, I repeat, is not to put it at a low value. *Gulliver's Travels* is fantasy, too, but pointed, instructive, useful fantasy for all that. Theorists usually know what genre they are writing. Their awareness reveals itself in their little jokes, of 'turnpikes' along the way to economic growth and 'islands' of labour in the economy. Yet the Ricardian vice is most characteristic of high theory: the vice of allowing fancy too free a rein. Auden remarks, 'What makes it difficult for a poet not to tell lies is that, in poetry, all facts and all beliefs cease to be true or false and become interesting possibilities' (quoted in Ruthven 1979: 175). The hundredth possible world of international trade gives the impression of a poetry gone to Bedlam. Economists would do well to know what genre they are reading or writing, to avoid misclassifying the fantasy and to assure that they are doing it well.

Good empirical work in economics, on the other hand, is like realistic fiction. Unlike fantasy, it claims to follow all the rules of the world. (Well . . . all the *important* ones.) But of course it too is fictional.

The modernist schoolmasters so long in charge of our intellectual lives would reply crossly that it is my analysis that is the fantasy and the fiction. They will complain that the proper scientist *finds* the story; no fiction about it.

DONALD N. McCLOSKEY

The answer to such an assertion has long been understood. The storyteller cloaks himself in Truth – which is what annoyed Plato about alleged imitations of life in sculpture or poetry. Just 'telling the story as it happened' evades the responsibility to declare a point of view. Realist fiction does this habitually – which shows another use for the literary analogy, to note that realist 'fiction' in science can also evade declaring a point of view. Michael Mulkay notes in the epistolary arguments of biologists a Rule 11: 'Use the personal format of a letter . . . but withdraw from the text yourself as often as possible so that the other party continually finds himself engaged in an unequal dialogue with the experiments, data, observations and facts' (Mulkay 1985). The evasion is similar in history: 'the plot of a historical narrative is always an embarrassment and has to be presented as "found" in the events rather than put there by narrative techniques' (White 1981: 20).

Admitting that the Battle of Waterloo has more promising material than today's breakfast, still it is true that nothing is given to us by the world in story form already. *We* tell the stories. John Keegan has nicely illustrated the point in reference to Waterloo in his book *The Face of Battle* (1977). He speaks of the 'rhetoric of battle history' (ibid: 36) as demanding that one cavalry regiment be portrayed as 'crashing' into another, a case of 'shock' tactics. Yet an observant witness of such an encounter at Waterloo reported that 'we fully expected to have seen a horrid crash – no such thing! Each, as if by mutual consent, opened their files on coming near, and passed rapidly through each other' (ibid: 149). A story is something told to each other by human beings, not something existing ready-told in the very rocks or cavalry regiments or mute facts themselves. Niels Bohr once remarked that physics is not about the world but about what we as human beings can say about the world.

Stories, in other words, are selective. In this they are similar to metaphors and models, which must select, too. We cannot portray anything literally completely, as another Niels Bohr story illustrates. He asked his graduate class to *fully* describe a piece of chalk, to give *every* fact about it. As the students found, the task is impossible unless radically selective. We cannot know about the history of every atom in the chalk, or the location of every atom that bears any relation to the atoms in the chalk, since every atom bears some relation, if only by not being that atom in the chalk

Storytelling in Economics

We decide what matters, for *our* purposes, not for God's or Nature's.

The fictional writer selects like the scientist, and invites the reader to fill in the blanks. Stories or articles can give only a sample of experience, because experience is overwhelmed by irrelevance: taking out the rubbish, bumping the table, scratching the back of one's head, seeing the title of the book one was not looking for. What distinguishes the good storyteller and the good scientific thinker from the bad is a sense of pointedness.

The vaunted parsimony of scientific stories is not the result of some philosophy commending parsimony. It is a result of the way we read science, our ability to fill the blanks, telling stories in our culture. The economist can read the most unreadable and compressed production of his fellows, but only if they participate in the same community of speech. Wholly fictional stories are parsimonious in the same way.

Skilful fiction, whether in the form of *Northanger Abbey* or *The Origin of Species*, 'stimulates us to supply what is not there', as Virginia Woolf remarked of Austen: 'What she offers is, apparently, a trifle, yet is composed of something that expands in the reader's mind and endows with the most enduring form of life scenes which are outwardly trivial' (Woolf 1953: 142). Remarking on Woolf in turn, Wolfgang Iser put it this way:

> What is missing from the apparently trivial scenes, the gaps arising out of the dialogue – this is what stimulates the reader into filling the blanks with projections [the image is of the reader running a motion picture inside his head, which is of course why novels can still compete with television] . . . . The 'enduring form of life' which Virginia Woolf speaks of is not manifested on the printed page; it is a product arising out of the interaction between text and reader.
>
> (Iser 1980: 110–11)

As Arjo Klamer (1987) has shown for the postulate of economic rationality, scientific persuasion, too, is like that. Persuasion of the most rigorous kind has blanks to be filled at every other step, if it is about a difficult murder case, for example, or a difficult mathematical theorem. The same is true of a difficult piece of economic storytelling. What is unsaid – but not unread – is more important to the text as perceived by the reader than what is there on the page. As Klamer puts it (ibid: 175), 'The student of the rhetoric of economics faces the challenge of speaking about the unspoken,

DONALD N. McCLOSKEY

filling in the "missing text" in economic discourse.'

The running of different motion pictures in our heads is going to produce different texts as perceived. The story here circles back to disagreement. Tzvetan Todorov makes the point: 'How do we explain this diversity [of literary readings]? By the fact that these accounts describe, not the universe of the book itself, but this universe as it is transformed by the psyche of each individual reader' (Todorov 1980: 72). And elsewhere: 'Only by subjecting the text to a particular type of reading do we construct, from our reading, an imaginary universe. Novels do not imitate reality; they create it' (ibid: 67f.). Economic texts also are made in part by the reader. Obscure texts are often therefore influential. Keynes left many opportunities for readers to run their own internal motion pictures, filling in the blanks.

What, then, is to be done? Should economists go on pretending that scientific texts are transparent and complete in themselves? If economists read texts differently, and know that they do, is economics left in chaos? Will admitting that economics like other sciences depends on storytelling lead to the war of all against all, and low wages?

No. In grim little wars of misreading the chaos already exists. A literary turn might bring a peace of toleration and trade. A community of readers is built the same way a community of listeners to music or a community of businesspeople is built, by making them sophisticated readers and listeners and businesspeople, willing to try other ways of reading or listening or dealing.

Perhaps there is something to treating economics as stories. The advantage would be self-consciousness, though self-consciousness itself is disparaged by certain economists anxious to manipulate the rules of conversation. Economists would do better to know what they are talking about. Looking on economics as poetry or fiction – or for that matter, as history – gives the economist a place to look in from outside. It is a better place than is provided by the usual philosophies of science; it is a great deal better than the homespun sociologies and philosophies that economists commonly use.

There is another advantage, to the larger culture. Economics should come back into the conversation of mankind. It is an extraordinarily clever way of speaking, which can do much good. The way to bring it back is to persuade economists that they are not so very different from poets and novelists. They do not have to abandon their lovely mathematics. For a long time now they have been standing aside, believing they have only the mathematical sciences as models. They practise a physics-worship that misunderstands both physics and themselves. Economists could get their gods from poetry or history or philology and still do much the same job of work, with a better temper and with better results.

Reunifying the conversation of mankind is best accomplished with hard cases. Economics is a hard case, wrapped in its prideful self-image as Science. If even economics can be shown to be fictional and poetical and historical its story will be a better one. Technically speaking it will be a comedy, comprising words of wit, an amused tolerance for human folly, stock characters colliding at last in the third act, and, most characteristic of the genre, a universe in equilibrium and a happy ending.

Bibliography

Brooks, Peter (1985) *Reading for the Plot: Design and Intention in Narrative*, New York: Vintage.

Bruns, Gerald L. (1984) 'The problem of figuration in antiquity', pp. 147–64 in G. Shapiro and A. Sica (eds) *Hermeneutics: Questions and Prospects*, Amherst: University of Massachusetts Press.

Gibson, Walker (1950) 'Authors, speakers and mock readers', *College English* 11 (Feb. 1950), reprinted pp. 100–6 in Jane P. Tompkins (ed.) (1980) *Reader-Response Criticism*, Baltimore: Johns Hopkins University Press.

Hexter, J.H. (1986) 'The problem of historical knowledge', unpublished MS, Washington University, St Louis.

Iser, Wolfgang (1980) 'The interaction between text and reader', pp. 106–19 in Susan R. Suleiman and Inge Crosman (eds) *The Reader in the Text: Essays on Audience and Interpretation*, Princeton: Princeton University Press.

Keegan, John (1977) *The Face of Battle*, New York: Vintage Books.

Klamer, Arjo (1987) 'As if economists and their subjects were rational', pp. 163–83 in John Nelson, Allan Megill, and D.N. McCloskey (eds) *The Rhetoric of the Human Sciences*, Madison: University of Wisconsin Press.

Lavoie, Don (1985) *Rivalry and Central Planning: The Socialist Calculation Debate Reconsidered*, Cambridge: Cambridge University Press.

DONALD N. McCLOSKEY

McCloskey, D.N. (1985) *The Rhetoric of Economics*, Madison: University of Wisconsin Press, in the Series on the Rhetoric of the Human Sciences.

———— (1987) 'Counterfactuals', article in *The New Palgrave: A Dictionary of Economic Theory and Doctrine*, London: Macmillan.

———— (1988) 'The limits of expertise: if you're so smart, why ain't you rich?', *The American Scholar*, spring.

Medawar, Peter (1964) 'Is the scientific paper fraudulent?', *Saturday Review* Aug. 1, pp. 42–3.

Mulkay, Michael (1985) *The Word and the World: Explorations in the Form of Sociological Analysis*, Winchester, Massachusetts: Allen & Unwin.

Propp, V. (1968 (1928)) *Morphology of the Folktale*, 2nd edn. trans. L. Scott and L.A. Wagner, American Folklore Society, Austin: University of Texas Press.

Rabinowitz, Peter J. (1980) '"What's Hecuba to us?" The audience's experience of literary borrowing', pp. 241–63 in Susan R. Suleiman and Inge Crosman (eds) *The Reader in the Text: Essays on Audience and Interpretation*, Princeton: Princeton University Press.

Rosenblatt, Louise M. (1978) *The Reader, the Text, the Poem: The Transactional Theory of the Literary Work*, Carbondale: Southern Illinois University Press.

Ruthven, K.K. (1979) *Critical Assumptions*, Cambridge: Cambridge University Press.

Saussure, F. de (1916) *Course in General Linguistics*, trans. R. Harris (1983) London: Duckworth.

Todorov, Tzvetan (1980 (1975)) 'Reading as construction', pp. 67–82 in Susan R. Suleiman and Inge Crosman (eds) *The Reader in the Text: Essays on Audience and Interpretation*, Princeton: Princeton University Press.

Weinberg, Steven (1983) 'Beautiful theories', revision of the Second Annual Gordon Mills Lecture, unpublished MS, University of Texas, Austin.

White, Hayden (1981) 'The value of narrativity in the representation of reality', pp. 1–24 in W.J.T. Mitchell (ed.) *On Narrative*, Chicago: University of Chicago Press.

Woolf, Virginia (1953 (1925)) *The Common Reader. First Series*, New York and London: Harcourt Brace Jovanovich.

[10]

HOW TO DO A RHETORICAL

ANALYSIS OF ECONOMICS,

AND WHY

It's Not Philosophical Reading, It's Rhetorical

Start with an example taken from a book with which I mostly agree, the first edition of Richard Posner's *Economic Analysis of Law*:

> Our survey of the major common law fields suggests that the common law exhibits a deep unity that is economic in character. . . . The common law method is to allocate responsibilities between people engaged in interacting activities in such a way as to maximize the joint value . . . of the activities. . . . [T]he judge can hardly fail to consider whether the loss was the product of wasteful, uneconomical resource use. In culture of scarcity, this is an urgent, an inescapable question. (Posner 1972, pp. 98f.)

Posner is urging us to see the common law as economically efficient. That's the philosophical way of reading the passage, seeing through. But look at the surface, the rhetoric.

The argument is carried in part by the equivocal use of economic vocabulary. "Allocate," "maximize," "value," and "scarcity" are technical words in economics, with precise definitions. Here they are used also in wider senses, to evoke Scientific power, to claim precision without necessarily using it. The sweetest turn is the use of "uneconomical," which is not a technical word in economics, but encapsulates Posner's argument that in their courtrooms the judges follow economic models because to do otherwise would be "wasteful." The "economical/uneconomical" figure of speech supports the claim that economic arguments (arguments about efficiency) are pervasive in the law. The claim is hammered home by treble repetition (technically in classical rhetoric, *com-*

3

4
_____

How to Do a Rhetorical Analysis of Economics, and Why

moratio): first in this word "uneconomical"; then in the reference to a culture of scarcity (a nice echo of "a culture of poverty," that, from the other side of the tracks); and finally in the repetition of "urgent, inescapable."

People involved mutually in automobile accidents or breaches of contract are said to be "engaged in interacting activities." That's on the surface of the words, yet the surface has philosophical importance. The "interaction" Posner talks about does not extend to the political or moral systems of the society. A rancher and a railroad "interact," but a judge does not "interact" with people who think that big enterprises like railroads are blameworthy or that people have inalienable rights. A vocabulary of "engaging in interacting activities" makes an appeal to the character of Scientist or Observer (technically, an "ethical" argument).

Again, on the surface the passage uses the metaphor of "deepness" in unity, as do other arguments trying to change the way we categorize the world. The left-wing radicals in American law, the critical legal theorists, will tell you that the "deep" structure of law is an apology for capitalism. The right-wing radicals, here Richard Posner, will tell you that the "deep" structure is on the contrary a celebration of capitalism.

As I say, I come down on Posner's side, though I have realized at last that a jurisprudence without a notion of rights is lunacy, a specifically Benthamite lunacy. But that I agree with many of Dick Posner's applications of economics to law does not make him, or me, or Milton Friedman immune from rhetorical scrutiny. The rhetorical reading is at least richer than the reading invited by the passage itself, which claims to represent the world. Posner wants us to read philosophically, which is good. But he does not want us to read rhetorically, which is bad. As the literary critic Richard Lanham has put it (1994), we need to do both, to be educated to "toggle" between philosophical and rhetorical readings, to know what the passage says but also how it achieves its end, persuasion.

The Old World "Rhetoric" Is a Good One

Science is an instance of writing with intent, the intent to persuade other scientists, such as economic scientists. The study of such writing with intent was called by the Greeks "rhetoric." Until the seventeenth century it was the core of education in the West and down to the present it remains, often unrecognized, the core of humanistic learning. A science like economics should be read skillfully, with a rhetoric, the more explicit the better. The choice here is between an implicit and naïve rhetoric or an explicit and learned one, the naïve rhetoric of significance tests, say, versus a learned rhetoric that knows what it is arguing and why.

Rhetoric could of course be given another name—"wordcraft," perhaps, or "the study of argument." The book that in 1987 began the "rhetoric of inquiry" was subtitled "Language and Argument in Scholarship and Public Affairs." Yet it revived the old "R" word in the main title, *The Rhetoric of the Human Sciences*. Why? The word "rhetoric" after all is used by newspapers as a synonym for the many words in English that sneer at speech: ornament, frill, hot air, advertising, slickness, deception, fraud. Thus the *Des Moines Register* headline: "Senate Campaign Mired in Rhetoric."

But the newspapers vulgarized, too, the word "pragmatism" shortly after its birth, by understanding it as unprincipled horse-trading. They defined "anarchism" as bomb-throwing nihilism. They defined "sentiment" as cheap emotionalism, "morality" as prudery, and "family values" as social reaction. They defined "science" as something no scientist practices. Not all usage should be decided by the newspapers, or else their views will be all we have. We need a scholarly word for wordcraft. The ancient and honored one will do.

The point of a rhetorical analysis is merely to read with understanding. Attending graduate school will somewhat educate an economist to read, supplying her with an implicit rhetoric for understanding. But the rhetoric in graduate school is incomplete and the understanding partial, a beginning but not the whole of economic science. What distinguishes good from bad economists, or even old from young economists, is additional sophistication about the rhetoric. It is the ability to read the depth and the surface of the text at the same time, to toggle. Robert Solow or Milton Friedman or Herbert Stein do not know anything of classical rhetoric—they grew up at the nadir of rhetorical education—but they can spot when a formal assumption is being used well or badly, and can sense when this or that verbal device is appropriate. And the wordcraft that the best economists exercise by instinct can be taught, at least a little.

Classical rhetoric was merely a list of terms with some thinking attached. A classical architecture without terms for architrave, echinus, guttae, mutule, quoin, and triglyph cannot see the Old Capitol in Iowa City (a Doric temple with Corinthian capital) as anything other than vaguely pretty (Summerson 1963, pp. 16, 47–52). Likewise we need terms to describe scientific argument, or else we are reduced to the vague and unexamined aesthetics of "deep," "rigorous," "elegant," "convincing." Gerard Debreu, for example, uses such terms to defend abstract general equilibrium analysis: it "fulfills an intellectual need of

6

How to Do a Rhetorical Analysis of Economics, and Why

many contemporary economic theorists, who therefore seek it for its own sake"; "simplicity and generality" are "major attributes of an effective theory"; "their aesthetic appeal suffices to make them desirable ends in themselves for the designer of a theory" (Debreu 1984). The aesthetics here is vague, unlearned, inexplicit. Debreu's is a dress-designer's vocabulary for scientific argument. No, that's unfair: Debreu's rhetoric is less precise and less self-critical than that of the better dress designers.

A rhetorical vocabulary is more rigorous than airy talk about rigor, though really only a list with some thinking attached. Literary thinking is like that. The best introduction to the schools of criticism is called *Critical Terms for Literary Study* (Lentricchia and McLaughlin, eds. 1990), listing among others Structure, Narrative, Figurative Language, Author, Value/Evaluation, Determinacy/Indeterminacy, Canon, Ideology, and Rhetoric. The best way to understand the rhetorical school 427 B.C. to the present is to supply oneself with a copy of Richard Lanham, *A Handlist of Rhetorical Terms* (2nd ed. 1991), and another work that makes use of it on a familiar text, such as George A. Kennedy, *New Testament Interpretation Through Rhetorical Criticism* (1984). The best comprehensive modern treatments are Edward P. J. Corbett, *Classical Rhetoric for the Modern Student* (1971 and later editions), which is a thoughtful list of terms with readings attached, and Sharon Crowley's excellent *Ancient Rhetorics for Contemporary Students* (1994). An early and good use of rhetorical criticism to make an argument is Wayne C. Booth, *Modern Dogma and the Rhetoric of Assent* (1974a). Booth, too, works with the original handlists dating back to Aristotle and Quintilian.

That's encouraging for beginners like you and me. By contrast, to do a useful piece of *economic* analysis you need to have finished the course. The noneconomists imagine it's enough to have some first-week idea of what "oligopoly" means. Economics is in fact a good example of the "hermeneutic circle": you need to know the argument overall to understand the details, and the details to understand the argument. But many literary techniques, and in particular the techniques of rhetorical analysis, come piecemeal, item by item, and can be put to use at once even by tyros. In this they are like some of the empirical methods of economics, such as national income analysis. Obviously a master in literary study like Booth or Lanham (compare in economics Kuznets or Denison) is going to do a better job than you or me. But even you and I can start.

I am not suggesting that educated people come equipped to do a rhetorical analysis without study. The results of attempting to do so are as embarrassing as criticizing economics without knowing any. I can name some embarrassing examples of both. Come on, Professor, do the homework. The point is simply that in rhetorical analysis even students can do useful work almost immediately. A rhetorical analysis can start with any part of "writing with intent" and proceed. It's like unraveling a sweater: start with a loose bit of yarn and keep pulling. A student is unlikely to find a poem or novel that a professor of English cannot unravel blindingly quicker. But the writings in sciences like economics are frayed sweaters waiting to be unraveled, the better to be understood, and in some respects a professor of economics is likely to know better where to pull.

Here then is a partial and preliminary handlist of rhetorical terms for students of economic literature.

The Scientist Must Establish Her "Ethos"

Ethos, the Greek word simply for "character," is the fictional character an author assumes. It is the same as the Latin *persona* or the modern "implied author." No one can refrain from assuming a character, good or bad. An author without good character will not be credited. The exordium, or beginning, of any speech must establish an ethos worth believing. An established ethos is the most persuasive of scientific arguments, and scientists are therefore very busy establishing it.

Consider, for example, the implied authors created by these opening lines in the *American Economic Review*'s issue of March 1989: "Two decades of research have failed to produce professional consensus on the contribution of federal government civil rights activity to the economic progress of black Americans" (Heckman and Payner 1989, p. 138). The implied authors here are policy-oriented, precise but awkward (look at the nominal phrase "federal government civil rights activity"), aware of the longer trends in scholarship, scholarly (with a Latinate vocabulary), dignified yet decisive, men who will succeed where others have "failed." The reader has to be an economist for the sentence to have these effects, just as the listener had to be a fourth-century Athenian for Demosthenes's appeals to his good ethos to have their effects.

Or, "After a period of intensive study of optimal indirect taxation, there has been a renewed interest in recent years in the problem of optimal income taxation, with particular emphasis on capital income taxation and economic growth" (Howitt and Sinn 1989, p. 106). Here the implied authors are modest (contrast the ringing "Two decades of research have failed" above or the unconscious arrogance of "Consider . . . the setting" below), concerned to fill gaps rather than take on once more the great questions of the age, academic rather than political ("re-

8
_____

How to Do a Rhetorical Analysis of Economics, and Why

newed interest," as there might be renewed interest in the satellites of Jupiter), but again Latinate in vocabulary, anonymous, American academic writers.

Or, "Consider the following stylized setting" (Lewis and Sappington 1989, p. 69). These two are mathematical, uninterested in facts, followers of a certain fashion, pretending to be direct but staying firmly in the lecture room, unaware of how funny the first sentence sounds to most economists, how pathetically stuck in blackboard economics. The writers of course need not be aware of every effect their writing has on the audience, no more than poets need be.

Finally, "There is good reason to think that the market for single-family homes ought to be less efficient than are capital markets" (Case and Shiller 1989, p. 125). These are candid, direct, practical, better writers than "After a period of intensive study," interested in explaining an empirical phenomenon, up-to-date in financial theory.

Everyone makes an appeal to ethos, if only an ethos of choosing never to stoop to such matters as ethos. No speech with intent is "nonrhetorical." Rhetoric is not everything, but it is everywhere in the speech of human persuaders.

It is a commonplace that formal complexity, for example, is a claim to the ethos of the Deep Thinker, a powerful appeal in modern economics. But any figure of speech can be pointedly reversed for ironic effect. Thus, complexity has been used in the literature on British economic "failure" as the opposite of an authoritative ethos, as evidence of disauthority. A paper by the historical economist Stephen Nicholas in 1982 tries to cast doubt on calculations of total factor productivity change in Victorian Britain. After a lucid prose survey of the debate on failure from Landes down to 1982, Nicholas "explains" the calculation of total factor productivity. He says, "It is assumed [note at once the style borrowed from mathematics] that the economic unit is a profit maximizer, subject to a linear homogeneous production function and operating in perfectly competitive product and factor markets. Given these limiting assumptions, the marginal productivity theory of distribution equates marginal products to factor rewards. It follows by Euler's theorem . . . ," etc., etc. (Nicholas 1982, p. 86).

To most of his readers he might as well have written "it is assumed that the blub-blub is a blub maximizer, blub-blub blub-blub-blub and blub in perfectly blub and blub blub. Given these limiting assumptions, the blub blub blub blub blub blub blub. It follows by blub blub . . ." The audience that can understand the argument is the audience of people who already understand it, leaving you to wonder why the argument was necessary in the first place. The people who do not understand it gain only the impression that "limiting assumptions" are somehow involved (they are not, by the way). The rhetorical form of the passage is explanation; its effect in the pages of the *Economic History Review* is to terrify the onlookers, convincing them that the "neoclassical" analysis makes a lot of strange and unconvincing assumptions. By the mere statement of the "assumptions" said to underlie the "neoclassical" calculation one can cast doubt on the calculation in the eyes of all historians and many economists.

In replying to a sharp rebuttal by Mark Thomas in a later issue of the *Review,* Nicholas repeats the turn. The last sentence of his exordium makes the argument explicit: *"The long list of restrictive assumptions* cautions the economic historians that, at best, the Solow index is a crude measure from which to draw conclusions about historical change" (Nicholas 1985, p. 577, italics supplied). The ethos here is of the Profound Thinker defending the innocents from other Profound (but Irresponsible) Thinkers.

Point of View Is a Scientific Choice

The implied author, in other words, chooses a vantage point, such as Huck in *Huckleberry Finn,* a first-person narrator who in this case is portrayed as not knowing what is happening beyond his sight; or the author in *Anna Karenina,* who can hear aloud what people are thinking and can travel from Moscow to St. Petersburg without a ticket. In the modern novel the suppression of the "authorial I" has resulted in a technique peculiar to literature, "represented speech and thought." Grammarians call it "unheralded indirect speech," the French *style indirect libre.* Any page or two of Jane Austen serves to illustrate, as in *Persuasion:* "Sir Walter had taken a very good house in Camdenplace, a lofty dignified situation, such as becomes a man of consequence" (1818, p. 107; Sir Walter's words ["dignified . . . a man of consequence"] in Austen's mouth). "Could Anne wonder that her father and sister were happy? She might not wonder, but she must sigh that her father should feel no degradation in his change" (p. 108; Anne's words ["sigh . . . no degradation"] in Austen's mouth.)

The parallel technique in science might be called "represented reality" or "unheralded assertion" or *"style indirect inévitable."* The scientist says, It is not I the scientist who make these assertions but reality itself (Nature's words in the scientist's mouth). When the audience applauded Fustel de Coulanges's inaugural lecture at the University of Paris long ago he put up his hand for silence: "Do not applaud me. It is not I who

10

How to Do a Rhetorical Analysis of Economics, and Why

speak. It is the Voice of History speaking through me." Redoubled applause. Scientists, including economic scientists, pretend that Nature speaks directly, thereby effacing the evidence that they, the scientists, are responsible for the assertions. It's just there. The result is similar in fiction: "We (as readers) cannot question the reliability of third-person narrators. . . . Any first-person narrative, on the other hand, may prove unreliable" (Martin 1986, p. 142). Thus Huck Finn, a narrator in the first person, misapprehends the Duke and we the readers know he does. The scientist avoids being questioned for his reliability by disappearing into a third-person narrative of what really happened.

The sociologist Michael Mulkay notes in the epistolary arguments of biologists a Rule 11: "Use the personal format of a letter . . . but withdraw from the text yourself as often as possible so that the other party continually finds himself engaged in an unequal dialogue with the experiments, data, observations and facts" (1985, p. 66). The technique is similar in history: "The plot of a historical narrative is always an embarrassment and has to be presented as 'found' in the events rather than put there by narrative techniques" (White 1973, p. 20). It is widespread in economics, of course.

"Mere" Style Is Not Mere

The Greeks and Romans divided rhetoric into Invention (the finding of arguments), Arrangement, and Style (they included fourth and fifth categories, Memory and Delivery, less important in a literate and electronic culture). "Style versus content" is a rhetorical commonplace of our post-rhetorical culture, most common since the seventeenth century. But the modern premise that content can be split from expression is mistaken. The two are yoke and white in a scrambled egg. Economically speaking, the production function for thinking cannot be written as the sum of two subfunctions, one producing "results" and the other "writing them up." The function is not separable.

Tony Dudley-Evans and Willie Henderson, for example, have studied intensively the style of four articles from the *Economic Journal* over a century of publication. "Taxation Through Monopoly" by C. F. Bastable (1891), for example, "strikes one immediately as having been written for a highly educated reader [the implied reader] who happens also to be interested in economic matters" (1987, p. 7). And Bastable, they note, "frequently uses 'and,' 'but' and 'again' in initial position" (an ornament in modern English). Again he uses in initial position "elegant adverbial phrases," such as "So much is this the case" or "Alike in classical and medieval times" (p. 8). Alike in his scientific and his journalistic work, "Bastable based his writing not upon shared technical knowledge but on a shared understanding of an educated culture more widely defined" (p. 15).

Modern economics is quite different, obscure in style. The obscurity of the style is necessary to defend scientific ethos. St. Augustine, as the literary critic Gerald Bruns noted, viewed the obscurity of the Bible as having "a pragmatic function in the art of winning over an alienated and even contemptuous audience" (Bruns 1984, p. 157). Obscurity is not rare in religion and science. Bruns quotes Augustine (who might as well be justifying the obscurities of a mathematical economist proving the obvious): "I do not doubt that this situation was provided by God to conquer pride by work and to combat disdain in our minds, to which those things which are easily discovered seem frequently to be worthless" (p. 157).

Style Is Often an Appeal to Authority

Economic style appeals in various ways to an ethos worthy of belief. For example, a test claiming authority uses the "gnomic present," as in the sentence you are reading now, or in the Bible, or repeatedly in the historian David Landes's well-known book on modern economic growth, *The Unbound Prometheus* (1969). Thus in one paragraph on p. 562, "large-scale, mechanized manufacture *requires* not only machines and buildings . . . but . . . social capital. . . . These *are* costly, because the investment required *is* lumpy. . . . The return on such investment *is* often long deferred." Only the last sentences of the paragraph connect the rest to the narrative past: "the burden *has tended* to grow."

The advantage of the gnomic present is its claim to the authority of General Truth, which is another of its names in grammar. The gnomic present is Landes's substitute for explicit economic theory (of which he is innocent), a function the gnomic present serves in sociology and in much of the literature of economic development, too.

Note the tense in Landes's essay at p. 563, for example, after some *aporia* (rhetorical doubt) concerning whether it is true or not: "Where, then, the gap between leader and follower *is* not too large to begin with . . . the advantage *lies* with the latecomer. And the more so because the effort of catching up *calls* forth entrepreneurial . . . responses." That in general and as an economic law the advantage *lies* with the latecomer is offered as a deductive conclusion. And in truth it does follow deductively from

12

How to Do a Rhetorical Analysis of Economics, and Why

the earlier assertions, themselves expressed in the gnomic present (for instance on p. 562, "There *are* thus two kinds of related costs").

The disadvantage is that it sidesteps whether it is asserting an historical fact (that in fact the return on "such investment" in 1900 was by some relevant standard long deferred) or a general truth (that in economies of the sort we are talking about most such returns will be long deferred), or perhaps merely a tautology (that the very meaning of "social capital" is investment of a generally useful sort with long-deferred returns). The one meaning borrows prestige and persuasiveness from the other. The usage says, "I speak as an historian, the Voice of History, who is telling you of the facts, this being one of them; but I am also an Economist in command of the best and timeless theorizing on the matter; and if you don't like that, consider that what I assert is anyway true by definition."

Economists Are Poets

The ancients spoke of "figures" as the surface of prose, dividing them into "figures of ornament" (such as the parallelism in the present sentence) and "figures of argument" (such as the metaphor of a "surface" of prose). The most well known of the figures of argument is metaphor, which, since the philosophers Max Black (1962a, 1962b) and Mary Hesse (1963) wrote on the subject, has been recognized as synonymous with the scientist's "model."

An example is a book, *The Zero-Sum Solution* (1985) by Lester Thurow, an economist and dean of the business school at M.I.T. The book is sporting. "To play a competitive game is not to be a winner—every competitive game has its losers—it is only to be given a chance to win. . . . Free market battles can be lost as well as won, and the United States is losing them on world markets" (p.59). One chapter is entitled "Constructing an Efficient Team." Throughout there is talk about America "competing" and "beating" the rest of the world with a "world-class economy." Thurow complains that more people don't appreciate his favorite metaphor, and calls it a "reality": "For a society which loves team sports . . . it is surprising that Americans won't recognize the same reality in the far more important international economic game" (p. 107). In more aggressive moods he slips into a military uniform: "American firms will occasionally be defeated at home and will not have compensating foreign victories" (p. 105). Foreign trade is viewed as the economic equivalent of war.

Three metaphors govern Thurow's story: the metaphor of the international zero-sum "game," a metaphor of the domestic "problem," and a metaphor of "we." *We* have a domestic *problem* of productivity that leads to a *loss* in the international *game*. Thurow has spent a long time interpreting the world with these linked metaphors. The we-problem-game metaphors are not the usual one in economics. The metaphor of exchange as a zero-sum game has been favored by anti-economists since the eighteenth century. Economists have replied that the metaphor is inapt. The subject after all is the exchange of goods and services. If exchange is a "game" it might better be seen as one in which everyone wins, like aerobic dancing. No problem. Trade in this view is *not* zero sum.

The example is not meant to suggest that metaphors are somehow optional or ornamental or unscientific. Although I disagree with Thurow's argument here, what is wrong about it is not that he uses a metaphor—no scientist can do without metaphors—but that his metaphor is inapt, as could be shown in various ways both statistical and introspective. The novice's mistake is to suppose that a rhetorical criticism is merely a way of unveiling Error. If we snatch away the veil of ornament, the novice thinks, we can confront the Facts and the Reality direct. The numerous books called "Rhetoric and Reality," such as Peter Bauer's collection of prescient essays (1984), commit this mistake.

True, devices of rhetoric such as metaphors can be veils over bad arguments. But they are also the form and substance of good arguments. I agree, for example, with most of Gary Becker's metaphors, from criminals as small businessman to the family as a little firm. Becker is an economic poet, which is what we expect of our theorists.

And Novelists

The word "story" is not vague in literary criticism. Gerald Prince used some ingenious mental experiments with stories and nonstories to formulate a definition of the "minimal story," which has

> three conjoined events. The first and third events are stative [such as "Korea was poor"], the second is active [such as "then Koreans educated themselves"]. Furthermore, the third event is the inverse of the first [such as "Then as a result Korea was rich"]. . . . The three events are conjoined by conjunctive features in such a way that (a) the first event precedes the second in time and the second precedes the third, and (b) the second event causes the third. (Prince 1973, p. 31)

14
_____

How to Do a Rhetorical Analysis of Economics, and Why

Prince's technique isolates what is storied about the tales that we recognize as stories.

Is this a story? *A man laughed and a woman sang.* No, it does not feel like one—in the uninstructed sense we learned at our mother's knee. (Of course in a more instructed way, after Joyce and Kafka, not to speak of writers of French detective fiction, anything can be a "story.") The following sounds more like an old-fashioned story: *John was rich, then he lost a lot of money.* At least it has the claim of sequence of consequence, "then." And it has the inversion of status ("rich . . . poor"). But it doesn't quite make it. Consider, *A woman was happy, then she met a man, then, as a result, she was unhappy.* Right. If feels like a complete story, as "generally and intuitively recognized" (Prince 1973, p. 5). Contrast: *Mary was rich and she traveled a lot, then, as a result, she was rich.* Something is screwy. What is screwy is that her status is not inverted from what it was.

One can use Prince's examples to construct stories and non-stories in economics. Test the pattern:

> *Poland was poor, then it adopted capitalism, then as a result it became rich.*
> *The money supply increased this year, then, as a result, productivity last year rose and the business cycle three decades ago peaked.*
> *A few firms existed in chemicals, then they merged, and then only one firm existed.*
> *Britain in the later nineteenth century was capitalistic and rich and powerful.*

The pattern is story/nonstory/story/nonstory.

Stories end in a new state. If a 5 percent tax on gasoline is said by some congressman or journalist to be "designed" to fall entirely on producers the economist will complain, saying "It's not an equilibrium." "Not an equilibrium" is the economist's way of saying that she disputes the ending proposed by some untutored person. Any descendant of Adam Smith, left or right, whether by way of Marx or Marshall, Veblen or Menger, will be happy to tell you a better story.

Many of the scientific disagreements inside economics turn on this sense of an ending. To an eclectic Keynesian, raised on picaresque tales of economic surprise, the story idea *Oil prices went up, which caused inflation* is full of meaning, having the merits that stories are supposed to have. But to a monetarist, raised on the classical unities of money, it seems incomplete, no story at all, a flop. As the economist A. C. Harberger likes to say, it doesn't make the economics "sing." It ends too soon, half-way through the second act: a rise in oil prices without some corresponding fall elsewhere is "not an equilibrium."

From the other side, the criticism of monetarism by Keynesians is likewise a criticism of the plot line, complaining of an ill-motivated beginning rather than a premature ending: where on earth does the money you think is so important come from, and why? Our jargon word for this in economics is "exogenous": if you start the story in the middle the money will be treated as though it is unrelated to, exogenous to, the rest of the action, even though it's not.

There is more than prettiness in such matters of plot. There is moral weight. Hayden White has written that "the demand for closure in the historical story is a demand . . . for moral reasoning" (White 1981, p. 20). A monetarist is not morally satisfied until she has pinned the blame on the Federal Reserve. The economist's ending to the story of the gasoline tax falling entirely on producers says, "Look: you're getting fooled by the politicians and lawyers if you think that specifying that the refiners pay the tax will let the consumers off. Wake up; act your age; look beneath the surface; recognize the dismal ironies of life." Stories impart meaning, which is to say worth. A *New Yorker* cartoon shows a woman looking up worried from the TV, asking her husband, "Henry, is there a moral to *our* story?"

The sense of adequacy in storytelling works in the most abstract theory, too. In seminars on mathematical economics a question nearly as common as "Haven't you left off the second subscript?" is "What's your story?" The story of the gasoline tax can be put entirely mathematically and metaphorically, as an assertion about where the gasoline tax falls, talking of supply and demand curves in equilibrium thus:

$$w^* = -(E_d/(E_d+E_s))T^*$$

The mathematics here is so familiar to an economist that she will not need explanation. In less familiar cases, at the frontier of economic argument, where we are arguing about what is important and what is not, the economist will need more conversation. That is, she will need a story. At the end of all the mathematics she will ask insistently *why*. In seminars on economics the question "What's your story?" is an appeal for a lower level of abstraction, closer to the episodes of human life. It asks for more realism, in a fictional sense, more illusion of direct experience. It asks to step closer to the nineteenth-century novel, with its powerful and nonironic sense of Being There.

Be Not Afraid of Deconstruction and Other Terrors

When Richard Posner wanted in a recent book to terrify his lawyer-readers about Reds in the English department, you can

16

How to Do a Rhetorical Analysis of Economics, and Why

imagine the school of literary criticism he began with: "Deconstruction and Other Schools of Criticism" (1988, p. 211). Deconstruction, by merest chance the most frightening version of literary criticism that could be brought before conservative readers, is "least well understood by lawyers, and . . . is therefore an appropriate starting point" (p. 211). Ho, ho.

Deconstruction, for all the calls to arms against it from the ignorant (and proud of it), constitutes only a tiny part of criticism. It is not even the most recent of fashions in literary theory (feminism and the new historicism are, with the new economic criticism on the horizon). It is merely one of a score of partially overlapping ways to do literary criticism. A partial list in historical order would include rhetorical, philological, Aristotelian, belletristic, hermeneutic, historical, new critical, psychoanalytic, neo-Aristotelian, archetypical, neorhetorical, Marxist, reader-response, deconstructive, linguistic, feminist, and new historicist criticism. In the same way you could divide economics into Good Old Chicago School, eclectic econometric macro, nouvelle Chicago, highbrow general equilibrium, and policy oriented micro.

But the journalistic interest in the word is so great that it cannot be ignored even in a brief list (a good treatment for economists is Rossetti 1990, 1992). One insight that the deconstructionists are properly credited with is the notion of verbal "hierarchy." The point is simply that words carry with them a ranking with respect to their opposites, as the word "infidel" calls to mind "Muslim," and "black" calls to mind "white." A sentence will achieve some of its effect through playing on these rankings. The hierarchies expose the politics (so to speak) in writing.

In economics long ago, for example, Wesley Clair Mitchell wrote, "it must never be forgotten that the development of the social sciences (including economics) is still a social process. Recognition of that view . . . leads one to study these sciences . . . [as] the product not merely of sober thinking but also subconscious wishing" (quoted in Rossetti 1992, p. 220). The passage contains at least these half-spoken hierarchies ready for liberating deconstruction (reading back to front, the terms in square brackets being those implied but not mentioned): sober/subconscious; thought/wishing; product/[mere ephemera]; sciences/[mere humanities]; study/[beach reading]; one/[you personally]; leads/[compels]; view/[grounded conviction]; sciences/[mere] processes; development/[mere chaotic change]; and must/[can]. The first term of each is the privileged one—except that in the pairs leads/[compels] and view/[grounded conviction] they are in fact polite self-deprecation, with ironic force: Mitchell is on the contrary claiming the commanding heights of compelling and grounded conviction, not the soft valleys of mere gently leading "views." Literary people speak of "deprivileging" the superior term in such pairs, which in economics would be, for example, "microfoundations/macroeconomics" or "general/partial" or "rigorous/informal."

In the vernacular, the economist Mitchell is playing mind games on us readers, and we'd better watch out. Mitchell, of course, is not special. It's easier to see the mind games played by writers long ago than in our own time, but you can depend on it that writing with intent has them.

The deeper point deconstruction makes is that among the mind games in which all writing participates is the claim that the writing *is* the world. The realistic novel is the plainest example, but scientific writing is another (for which see again Mulkay 1985). For example, the phrase "it is obvious that" conveys certitude in mathematics and in economics. One eight-page article in the *Journal of Political Economy* (Davies 1989) uses expressions such as "it is obvious that," "obviously," "it is evident," "doubtless," "easily seen," "needs no discussion," and "we may expect" some forty-two times. But nothing is "obvious" on a printed page except that certain marks have been made on a white field. The "easily seen" is evoked in the mind's eye.

Writing Is Performance

The point is not peculiar to deconstruction. In a way it is one of the chief findings of humanism. Books do not "reproduce" the world. They evoke it. Skillful fiction, whether in the form of *Northanger Abbey* or *The Origin of Species*, "stimulates us to supply what is not there," as Virginia Woolf remarked of Austen. "What she offers is, apparently, a trifle, yet is composed of something that expands in the reader's mind and endows with the most enduring form of life scenes which are outwardly trivial" (1925, p. 142). Commenting on her remark in turn, the critic Wolfgang Iser put it this way: "What is missing from the apparently trivial scenes, the gaps arising out of the dialogue—this is what stimulates the reader into filling the blanks with projections. [Iser's image is of the reader running a motion picture inside his head, which is, of course, why novels can still compete with television.] . . . The 'enduring form of life' which Virginia Woolf speaks of is not manifested on the printed page; it is a product arising out of the interaction between text and reader" (1980, pp. 110–11).

As Arjo Klamer (1987) has shown for the postulate of economic rationality, scientific persuasion, too, is like that. Persuasion of the most rigorous kind has blanks to be filled at every other step, whether it is

18
―――――――

How to Do a Rhetorical Analysis of Economics, and Why

about a difficult murder case, for example, or a difficult mathematical theorem. The same is true of a debate about economic policy. What is unsaid—but not unread—is more important to the text as perceived by the reader than what is there on the page. As Klamer puts it, "The student of the rhetoric of economics faces the challenge of speaking about the unspoken, filling in the 'missing text' in economic discourse" (1987, p. 175).

The running of different motion pictures in our heads is going to produce different texts as perceived. Tzvetan Todorov asks, "How do we explain this diversity [of readings]? By the fact that these accounts describe, not the universe of the book itself, but this universe as it is transformed by the psyche of each individual reader" (1975, p. 72). And, "Only by subjecting the text to a particular type of reading do we construct, from our reading, an imaginary universe. Novels do not imitate reality; they create it" (pp. 67f.). Economic texts also are made in part by the reader. Obscure texts are often therefore influential. The crafty John Maynard Keynes, for example, most influentially in *The General Theory of Employment, Interest and Money*, left many opportunities for readers to run their own internal motion pictures, filling in the blanks.

The argument can be pushed. An economist expositing a result creates an "authorial audience" (an imagined group of readers who know this is fiction) and at the same time a "narrative audience" (an imagined group of readers who do not know it is fiction). As the critic Peter Rabinowitz explains, "the narrative audience of 'Goldilocks' believes in talking bears" (1968, p. 245). The "authorial" audience realizes it is fiction.

The difference between the two audiences created by the author seems less decisive in economic science than in explicit fiction, probably because we all know that bears do not talk but we do not all know that the notion of "marginal productivity" in economics is a metaphor. The narrative audience in science, as in "Goldilocks," is fooled by the fiction, which is as it should be. But in science the authorial audience is fooled, too (and, incidentally, so is part of the literal audience, the actual readers as against the ideal readers the author seems to want to have). Michael Mulkay, again, has shown how important the inadvertent choice of authorial audience is in the scholarly correspondence of biochemists. Biochemists like other scientists and scholars are largely unaware of their literary devices, and become puzzled and angry when their literal audience refuses to believe in talking bears (Mulkay 1985, ch. 2). They think they are merely stating facts, not making audiences. Small wonder that scientists and scholars disagree, even when their rhetoric of "what the facts say" would seem to make disagreement im-

19

How to Do a Rhetorical Analysis of Economics, and Why

possible. Science requires more resources of the language than raw sense data and first-order predicate logic.

It requires what may be called the Rhetorical Tetrad (McCloskey 1994, pp. 61–63). Fact and logic also come into the economics in large doses. Economics is a science, and a jolly good one, too. But a serious argument in economics will use metaphors and stories as well—not for ornament or teaching alone but for the very science. Fact, logic, metaphor, and story.

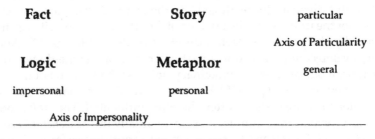

Figure 1. The Rhetorical Tetrad: The Four Human Arguments

The reasons to do a rhetorical analysis of an economic text are various: to understand it, to admire it, to debunk it, to set it beside other works of persuasion in science, to see that science is not a new dogma but is thoroughly and respectably part of the old culture. Rhetorical sophistication is an alternative to reading scientific texts the way the implied reader does, a reader who believes for example in talking bears. If we are to get beyond nursery school as scientific readers we need such a rhetoric applied to economic science.

BIBLIOGRAPHY

Austen, Jane. 1818. *Persuasion*. New York: Houghton Mifflin, 1965.

Bauer, Peter. 1984. *Reality and Rhetoric: Studies in the Economics of Development*. Cambridge, Mass.: Harvard University Press.

Black, Max, ed. 1962a. *The Importance of Language*. Englewood Cliffs, N.J.: Prentice-Hall.

Black, Max. 1962b. *Models and Metaphors: Studies in Language and Philosophy*. Ithaca, N.Y.: Cornell University Press.

Booth, Wayne C. 1974a. *Modern Dogma and the Rhetoric of Assent*. Chicago: University of Chicago Press.

Bruns, Gerald L. 1984. "The Problem of Figuration in Antiquity." In G. Shapiro and A. Sica, eds., *Hermeneutics: Questions and Prospects*, pp. 147–164. Amherst: University of Massachusetts Press.

Case, K. E., and R. J. Shiller. 1989. "The Efficiency of the Market for Single-Family Homes." *American Economic Review* 79 (March).

Corbett, Edward P. J. 1971. *Classical Rhetoric for the Modern Student*, 3d ed. New York: Oxford University Press.

Crowley, Sharon. 1994. *Ancient Rhetorics for Contemporary Students*. Boston: Allyn and Bacon.

Davies, G. R. 1989. "The Quantity Theory and Recent Statistical Studies." *Journal of Political Economy.*

Debreu, Gerard. 1984. "Economic Theory in the Mathematical Mode." *American Economic Review* 74 (June): 267–78.

Dudley-Evans, T., and W. Henderson. 1987. "Changes in the Economics Article." Department of Extramural Studies, University of Birmingham, England.

Heckman, J. J., and B. S. Payner. 1989. "Determining the Impact of Antidiscrimination Policy on the Economic Status of Blacks: A Study of South Carolina." *American Economic Review* 79 (March): 138–77.

Hesse, Mary. 1963. *Models and Analogies in Science*. South Bend, Ind.: University of Notre Dame Press.

Howitt, Peter, and Hans-Werner Sinn. 1989. "Gradual Reform of Capital Income Taxation." *American Economic Review* 79 (March): 106–24.

Iser, Wolfgang. 1980. "The Interaction Between Text and Reader." In Susan R. Suleiman and Inge Crosman, eds., *The Reader in the Text*, pp. 106–19. Princeton, N.J.: Princeton University Press.

Kennedy, George A. 1984. *New Testament Interpretation Through Rhetorical Criticism*. Chapel Hill: University of North Carolina Press.

Klamer, Arjo. 1987. "As if Economists and Their Subjects Were Rational . . ." In John Nelson et al., eds. *Rehetoric of the Human Sciences*, pp. 163–83. Madison: University of Wisconsin Press.

Landes, David. 1969. *The Unbound Prometheus; Technological Change and Industrial Development in Western Europe from 1750 to the Present.*

Cambridge: Cambridge University Press. (Reprinting, with additions, his book-length essay, "Technological Change and Development in Western Europe, 1750–1914." In *Cambridge Economic History of Europe*. Vol. VI. Cambridge: Cambridge University Press, 1965.)

Lanham, Richard. 1991. *A Handlist of Rhetorical Terms*. 2d ed. Berkeley: University of California Press.

Lanham, Richard A. 1994. *The Electronic Word: Democracy, Technology, and the Arts*. Chicago: University of Chicago Press.

Lentricchia, Frank, and Thomas McLaughlin, eds. 1990. *Critical Terms for Literary Study*. Chicago: University of Chicago Press.

Lewis, T., and D. E. M. Sappington. 1989. "Inflexible Rules in Incentive Problems." *American Economic Review* 79 (March): 69–84.

Martin, Wallace. 1986. *Recent Theories of Narrative*. Ithaca, N.Y.: Cornell University Press.

McCloskey, D. N. 1994. *Knowledge and Persuasions in Economics*. Cambridge: Cambridge University Press.

Mulkay, Michael. 1985. *The Word and the World: Explorations in the Form of Sociological Analysis*. Winchester, Mass.: Allen and Unwin.

Nicholas, Stephen. 1982. "Total Factor Productivity Growth and the Revision of Post-1870 British Economic History." *Economic History Review* 2d ser. 25 (February): 83–98.

Nicholas, Stephen. 1985. "British Economic Performance and Total Factor Productivity Growth, 1870–1940." *Economic History Review* 2d ser. 38 (November); 576–82.

Posner, Richard A. 1972. *Economic Analysis of Law*. Boston: Little, Brown.

Posner, Richard A. 1988. *Law and Literature: A Misunderstood Relation*. Cambridge, Mass.: Harvard University Press.

Prince, Gerald. 1973. *A Grammar of Stories*. Paris: Mouton.

Rabinowitz, Peter J. 1968. "'What's Hecuba to Us?' The Audience's Experience of Literary Borrowing." In Susan R. Suleiman and Inge Crosman, eds., *The Reader in the Text*, pp. 241–63. Princeton, N.J.: Princeton University Press, 1980.

Rossetti, Jane. 1990. "Deconstructing Robert Lucas." In Warren J. Samuels, ed., *Economics as Discourse*, pp. 225–43. London: Kluwer Academic.

Rossetti, Jane. 1992. "Deconstruction, Rhetoric, and Economics." In Neil de Marchi, ed., *The Post-Popperian Methodology of Economics: Recovering Practice*, pp. 211–34. Boston: Kluwer and Neijoff.

Samuels, Warren, J. ed. 1990. *Economics as Discourse: An Analysis of the Language of Economists*. London: Kluwer Academic.

Summerson, John. 1963. *The Classical Language of Architecture*. Cambridge, Mass.; M.I.T. Press.

Thurow, Lester. 1985. *The Zero-Sum Solution: Building a World-Class American Economy*. New York: Simon and Schuster.

Todorov, Tzvetan. 1975. "Reading as Construction." In Susan R. Suleiman and Inge Crosman, eds., *The Reader in the Text*, pp. 67–82. Princeton, N.J.: Princeton University Press, 1980.

White, Hayden. 1973. *Metahistory: The Historical Imagination in Ninetenth Century Europe*. Baltimore: Johns Hopkins University Press.

White, Hayden. 1981. "The Value of Narrative in the Representation of Reality." In W. J. T. Mitchell, ed. *On Narrative*, pp. 1–24. Chicago: University of Chicago Press.

Woolf, Virginia. 1925. *The Common Reader. First Series*. New York: Harcourt Brace Jovanovich. 1953.

[11]

HISTORY, DIFFERENTIAL EQUATIONS, AND THE PROBLEM OF NARRATION

DONALD N. MCCLOSKEY

The talk of engineers and the talk of historians connects in the way that metaphors connect with stories. Though both make use of both (because we cannot live otherwise in the world), engineers specialize in metaphors and historians in stories.

In the abstract it is a matter of definitions. Take the essence of the metaphor to be comparison and the essence of the story to be time. (And let the definitions ride; they break down soon enough if they are wrong.) A comparison can be put as a timeless law, such as that apples and the moon fall to earth or that imperial hubris usually gets punished. The moon is like an apple; Athens in the Peloponnesian War was like a proud man. A history, on the other hand, can be stated as a sequence of connected events. The moon was here on January 1, and therefore will be just so on April 2, eclipsing the sun; Athens overreached to Sicily in the sixteenth summer, and therefore only a few returned out of many.

The engineer and historian do not deal in mere comparison or mere time, no more than poets or novelists do. Aimless comparison is bad poetry and bad engineering; one damned thing after another is bad fiction and bad history. The point is pointedness, which will vary with the purpose in mind. (The point, incidentally, need not be simple or realistic or of any other kind especially approved by the nineteenth century.) Comparing a pendulum to the wavering of the beloved's affection may have a point in a certain poem, but to have a point as engineering the pendulum needs to be compared with, say, an ideal falling body constrained by an ideal shaft. A bare chronology likewise makes no history, unless pointed by the context and the questions. The dated sequence of winning numbers on the Iowa lottery from 1987 to 1990 is a chronology, but can be read as history only in the imaginings of an numerologist.

Metaphor and story, then, are two ways of arguing. Place pure metaphor at one end, containing no element of story, "timeless" as I have said. I shall compare thee to any old summer's day, not to the remarkable events of May 21-28, 1595. At the other end place a mere listing of the events in order: "May 23, midday, rough winds; at sunset, gold complexion dimmed."

The two ends are linked by a theme. That is the first point here. A list of events in World War I or in the market for hogs is not much of a story; maybe it is not a story at all, a sheer chronicle. But when thematized — by "God favors big battalions," for instance — the story can be told persuasively. Letting in a trace of metaphor gives shape to the chronicle and pushes it towards a good story. It works from the other end, too. That God favors big battalions is a pure metaphor, and rather lacking in point. When clothed in time it begins to look more story-like. Themes can be good or bad. God may favor the big battalions only in the very long run, over a century of battle, say. Such a slow-working model will be a poor theme in a story of World War I. To tell the story we will have to seek some other thematizing commonplace, such as that God favors the smarter generals or that God favors the British Empire or, as many of the combatants came to believe, that God did not give a damn after all.

A thematized story, or a dynamized model, stands between the pure (and mere) metaphor and the pure (and mere) story. The good middle ground seems to be an allegory, which persuades on both grounds: the Christian life is like a journey, and Christian's actual journey in time to the Heavenly City brings the metaphors to a life. Thus, a metaphor that people are calculating machines, when applied to the market for wheat, might lead an economist to a little equation that speaks of time: the rate of change of price, she says, is equal to some number multiplied by the gap between the actual and the long-run price. The number tells how quickly the market responds. It is a thematized story, most useful in life. How sluggish is the market for hogs? A large number in the economist's equation will have the market leaping smartly to it; a small one and the market lingers abed.

Again, the physicist's metaphor of the point mass falling under gravity leads to that splendid theme, Force equals mass times acceleration, etched on the shields of physicists. When applied to a pendulum, $F = ma$, itself a metaphor (though speaking quietly about time in mentioning acceleration), leads to a theme still more explicitly historical: how the next step in the history of a swinging pendulum will depend on gravity and the resistance of the fluid in which it swings. The new equation is closer to history. The equation is story-like because it speaks of time and therefore organizes experience in time, at least implicitly. The time-speaking themes will shape the raw experience, as a story does when it is more than a mere unthematized chronicle.

Such themes in engineering that quietly mention time carry the imposing title of Differential Equations. Not all differential equations need speak of time, but many in engineering and physics and economics do. They say, "The rate of change of X depends on various matters, among them the time that the situation has been developing." A differential equation involving time is in a sense neither fish nor fowl, neither a timeless metaphor nor a pure story. Notions such as that people are calculating machines or that the pendulum is rigidly fixed are the timeless metaphors, true at all times and therefore not making reference to time ($F = ma$, to repeat the example, is a metaphor already on the way to a story, since it speaks of speeding up per unit of time, the acceleration). The differential equation that is derived from the metaphors is the middle type, a link between pure metaphors and pure stories. It is an allegory with inexplicit meaning; the analyst makes it explicit.

The idea of a differential equation can be grasped simply, although whole libraries filled with mathematics have been devoted to the complications. An example of a differential equation is: "The world's population is increasing by 80 million people a year." It gives a thematized story about how something will change. Population is said to be just like a series of numbers that rise by 80 million in each year. Time is mentioned, quietly—the equation has no dates in it, but the dates are implicit. In 1991 the change will be 80 million people, in 1992 another 80 million, and so forth. (Needless to say the differential equations in the libraries are not so simple. And in fact this particular one, though popular in the newspapers, is not very sensible as demography. It says that population will go on growing, like a frictionless pendulum in a vacuum will go on swinging, despite forces to the contrary.)

Algebraically speaking, the differential equation is that the population next year, or time $t+1$, is the population now, time t, plus 80 million: $P_{t+1} = P_t +$ 80 million. To put it another way, the way that differential equations are in fact often put, the *change* in P (called "dP") per year (that is, divided by "dt," the change in time) is 80 million. As the mathematicians have said since Leibniz, $dP/dt = 80$ million.

The time path of population is going to be whatever it is in 1990 (called in the trade "the initial conditions") plus 80 million, then plus 80 million, and so forth. The time path is the pure story, the mere chronicle unthematized: the world in 1990 has 4,500 million, the world in 1991 will have 4,580 million, the world in 1992 will have 4,660 million, and so forth into an ecological disaster or a flowering of world civilization, depending on one's other beliefs. Without a theme the set of numbers is just one damned thing after another, the purest story.

The shape of the chronology is more apparent in what is known officially as the "solution" to the differential equation. The solution characterizes the chronology. In this case, obviously (as the mathematician in the joke said about the step that had taken him six months of contemplation to believe), the solution is: the population in a year that is t years after the initial year is the initial population plus t times 80 million. That is, $P_t = P_0 + t$ (80 million).

None of this is higher math, but it illustrates the essence of some very high math indeed. You can always simply mount the differential equation on a computer, start somewhere, and then grind out a future. Start at 4,500 million people, note that the differential equation says that the annual change is 80 million, and then calculate successively 4,580 million then 4,660 million and so forth. The set of numbers about the future is the brute chronology, which you can look at and perhaps impose interesting themes upon.

When differential equations have solutions (and the first surprising fact about the higher math is that it is very easy to write down ones that do not) the themes are fully explicit. Just to show that the "solutions" are by no means always as trivial as the example of population change, think of a pendulum swinging in a fluid. An engineer might come to think about the angle ø that a moderately swinging pendulum (as in a clock) deviates from the straight up and down at any time t. Suppose he signifies the rate of change of ø as ø' (note the prime: it signals the " first derivative" of ø with respect to time). Consequently the acceleration rate of change of the rate of change, or the second derivative, will be called ø". If he thinks extremely perspicaciously about the situation it turns out that he will come to believe that the angle ø must satisfy always the differential equation:

*
$$\text{ø}'' + k_1\text{ø}' + k_2\text{ø} = 0.$$

(The k's are constants related to the force of gravity and the viscosity of the fluid, such as air, in which the pendulum swings.) If he has gotten this far by unaided intellect he is probably the great Swiss mathematician Leonhard Euler (1707–1783) and can write down directly the astounding solution, that is to say, an equation that gives you the time path of the pendulum for every future (or past) time, t. It is the theme in the motion for ø as time goes by. It involves sines and cosines, those high school horrors, and a number e, about 2.71828, which Euler showed keeps coming up in mathematics:

Solution to *: $\text{ø} = (c_1 e^{bt} \sin at) + (c_2 e^{bt} \cos at)$.

Like the terms of most human histories, most solutions of differential equations in this explicit form (called "analytic solutions") cannot be achieved mechanically. They have to be guessed at, then confirmed by showing they correspond with the original equations, which is to say with the partially thematized chronologies that we call history. Even the ones that do not have analytic solutions often have approximate solutions in terms of what are called, alarmingly, "infinite series." The successive terms of such series are approximate themes. For instance, the large first term in an infinite series of themes for World War I might be "God favors the bigger battalions," to which might be added the somewhat less important second term (". . . and the better generals"), to which might be added the third (". . . and the British Empire"), and so on, out to the limit of the historian's or the engineer's need for thematization. (The engineer uses the thematization to characterize and predict, the historian to characterize and explain, but otherwise they are doing much the same job: one is predicting, the other postdicting.)

So the solution to the differential equation * is a more direct and flat-footed story, shaping experience more explicitly, than the differential equation itself. And finally a particular, numerical history derived from either the differential equation or its solution — such as "when time is at 1.0 the pendulum is at ø = +15°, when time is at 1.1 it is at 12°," and so forth — is the most flatfooted and chronological of all, the Cliff Notes, so to speak, laying out the plot of *The Mayor of Casterbridge*.

The differential equation itself might be looked on as the model/metaphor. Alternatively, and I think better, the honor of the word "metaphor" might be reserved for the timeless physical or economic or historical idea behind the equation, such as that the moon falls towards the earth or that people pursue profits in buying wheat or that the men of Athens were very fools in their imperial might. The actual numerical time paths from the solution of a differential equation is the narration in time, and the solution (which can also generate the numerical path) is the thematized narrative — transparent or muddy depending on how neat the solution is, when it exists. The analytic solutions correspond to simply predictable histories, that is, histories that can be reexpressed as equations. The differential equations embody what we think we know about societies as theory, such as a Marxist theory. The solution then characterizes a particular historical path. If the path can be expressed in terms of what the mathematicians call elementary functions, then what is being asserted is that history is in every sense elementary. The law of surplus value leads, the Marxist historian/engineer asserts, to a falling rate of profit and a crisis of capitalism, as the night will follow day.

Such talk undermines the claim that natural science and historical science have two separate modes of apprehension. The separation seems less consequential if it is viewed merely as the metaphor as against the story, and if in good metaphors and good stories the two are linked by a differential equation. The old question—Clio, Science or Muse?—loses its gripping interest if sciences use stories and art uses number.

But why bother with all this? All right, history and engineering can be made both to lie down on a Procrustean bed of the differential equation. But why on earth would one wish to speak in such a way?

The answer is this: speaking so makes it possible for each of the two modes of thinking to criticize the other. "Criticize," I say, not "lambast" or "sneer at" or even "blindly worship," which are some of the present ways the two cultures deal with each other. I am arguing that there is a similarity between the most technical scientific reasoning and the most humanistic literary reasoning.

I have given some economic examples in *The Rhetoric of Economics* (1985) and *If You're So Smart* (1990). Here I want to give another example, of how life gets difficult for the engineer and the historian when the differential equation does.

The big difficulty shows up when the differential equations are "nonlinear." The word means simply that the variables described by the equation and their "derivatives," the rates of change of the variables, are squared or sined or in some other way blown up beyond their simple, linear selves, plain ϕ or ϕ' or ϕ''. The change turns out to be important. As a good textbook on differential equations put it in 1972, "The theory of *linear* differential equations has been studied deeply and extensively for the past 200 years, and is a fairly complete and well-rounded body of knowledge. However, very little of a general nature is known about *non*linear equations."[1] A lot has been learned since 1972, some of it under the name of "chaos."[2] One gathers that a lot remains to be learned.

The commonest theme of battle history, the horseshoe nail, is a case of a nonlinear differential equation: For want of a nail the shoe was lost. / For want of the shoe the horse was lost. / For want of the horse the rider was lost. / For want of the rider the battle was lost. / For want of the battle the kingdom was lost. / And all for the want of a horseshoe nail. The rate of loss feeds on itself.

1. George F. Simmons, *Differential Equations, with Applications and Historical Notes* (New York, 1972), 290, italics added.

2. See James Glieck, *Chaos: Making a New Science* (New York, 1987), an enthralling popular history of the recent work.

Battle history is not held in high regard by historians precisely because it so obviously depends on tiny chances of this sort. The popular history magazine *American Heritage* will turn to them when explaining the battle of Chancellorsville: "Only the failure of one inept Confederate officer saved the Federal army from unmitigated disaster."[3]

But the disdain for assigning large events small causes is not rational in a world partly nonlinear. A recent book by the economist and historian Robert Fogel argues that there was nothing inevitable about Lincoln's election and the resulting secession. Like many historians before him he emphasizes the precarious balance of American politics in the 1850s, which could have been turned one way or the other by minor events. In the late 1850s:

The Republican party was not wrecked by the panic of 1857 and by 1860 it had lured most of the former Know-Nothings into its ranks. However, neither outcome was inevitable. . . . It is doubtful that party leaders could have continued to suppress the nativist impulses of so many of its members if immigration had returned to the 1854 rate. . . . If the party would have conceded these demands, some of the Germans and the more conservative Whigs would have been alienated. Only relatively small defections were needed to deny power to the anti-slavery coalition in 1860.[4]

And during the fateful month of May, 1856 in bloody Kansas:

a sheriff who had proprietory interests in a rival town not far from Lawrence, and who was an impulsive extremist, took unauthorized command of the posse. The mob that he led burned the hotel that served as the headquarters for the New England Emigrant Aid Society. . . . Two days later, in retaliation for the "sack of Lawrence," John Brown and his sons killed "five helpless and unprepared pro-slavery settlers." . . . As the posse moved toward Lawrence, Senator Charles Sumner (R, MA) delivered a searing indictment. . . . of leading Democratic members of the Senate, including Stephen A. Douglas (D, IL) and Andrew P. Butler (D, SC). Butler was absent from the chamber during Sumner's speech but Preston S. Brooks, a relative and a member of the House from South Carolina, brooded over the insults to his aged kinsmen and to his state. . . . Brooks entered the Senate chamber after it adjourned on May 22 and delivered a series of blows to Sumner's head and shoulders with his cane.[5]

Fogel identifies other turning points, too. He is trying to show that the end of slavery was by no means determined by massive and unstoppable forces, such as its alleged unprofitability or its alleged inconsistency with industrialization. "The overarching role of contingent circumstances in [the] ultimate victory [of the antislavery movement] needs to be emphasized. There never was a moment between 1854 and 1860 in which the triumph of the antislavery coalition was assured."[6]

James McPherson's recent history of the same era provides military examples. "The third critical point came in the summer and fall of 1863 when Gettysburg,

3. Robert K. Krick, "Lee's Greatest Victory," *American Heritage* 41 (March, 1990), 74.
4. Robert Fogel, *Without Consent or Contract: The Rise and Fall of American Slavery* (Boston, 1989), 385–386.
5. *Ibid.*, 379.
6. *Ibid.*, 322.

Vicksburg, and Chattanooga turned the tide toward ultimate northern victory."[7] Vicksburg was settled by many things — one is put in mind of the much-abused term "over-determination" — but among them was a disagreement before the siege between the Confederate generals Joe Johnston and John C. Pemberton.

Johnston urged Pemberton to unite his troops with Johnston's 6,000 survivors north of Jackson [Mississippi], where with expected reinforcements they would be strong enough to attack Grant. . . . Pemberton disagreed. He had orders to hold Vicksburg and he intended to do so. . . . Before the two southern generals could agree on a plan, the Yankees made the matter moot by slicing up Pemberton's mobile force on May 16 at Champion's Hill.[8]

At Gettysburg one of numerous turning points was the desperate defense of Little Round Top on July 2 by Colonel Joshua L. Chamberlain of the twentieth Maine. Chamberlain (who not incidentally was in civilian life a professor of rhetoric) ordered his men, ammunition exhausted, to attack with bayonets the massing Confederates down the hill. "(T)he two Round Tops dominated the south end of Cemetery Ridge. If the rebels had gotten artillery up there, they could have enfiladed the Union left. . . . (S)hocked by the audacity of this bayonet assault, the Alabamians surrendered by scores to the jubilant boys from Maine."[9]

In Michael Shaara's fine historical novel about Gettysburg, *The Killer Angels*, one can list the contingencies on which the battle depended: John Buford's eye for good ground on which the Federals could stand; the bullet that had already killed Stonewall Jackson; Richard Ewell's hesitation, which kept the Confederates from taking Cemetery Ridge before it was fortified; Lee's heart disease slowing his decisions; Jeb Stuart's failure to stay in touch with Lee's headquarters; Longstreet's inability to persuade Lee to move left; Longstreet's decision not to disobey Lee; and so forth.[10] Only a novelist's touches? They had better be an historian's too, if he wants to tell the story.

In the conclusion to his book McPherson writes, "Northern victory and southern defeat in the war cannot be understood apart from the contingency that hung over every campaign, every battle, every election, every decision during the war. This phenomenon of contingency can best be presented in a narrative format."[11] Precisely. Fogel and McPherson and Shaara are telling the usual horseshoe-nail story.

Little events can have big consequences in some parts of history. The parts are described by models that are nonlinear in the events and whose consequences feed on themselves. In other words, a little event affecting one of the equations yields a large consequence, which is then fed back as input. "Nothing succeeds like success" is such a model, and certainly applies to the decade 1856–1865 in the United States. It was the strategy of both the Union and Confederacy for much of the war to win one more battle in order to bring Britain or France in on the correct side.

7. James M. McPherson, *The Battle Cry of Freedom: The Civil War Era* (New York, 1988), 858.
8. *Ibid.*, 630.
9. *Ibid.*, 659.
10. Michael Shaara, *The Killer Angels* (New York, 1974).
11. McPherson, 858.

The point is not that great oaks from little acorns grow. They do, as did Christianity and the Industrial Revolution. The right acorn is impossible to see before the event. The historical economist Joel Mokyr identifies a common pitfall in storytelling: rummaging among the possible acorns from which the great oak of the Industrial Revolution grew "is a bit like studying the history of Jewish dissenters between 50 B.C. and 50 A.D. What we are looking at is the inception of something which was at first insignificant and even bizarre," albeit "destined to change the life of every man and woman in the West."[12] Any one of numberless acorns may be chosen by chance. Chance of this unconventional sort is similarly difficult to narrate. But at least after the acorn is chosen it grows slowly from acorn to sprout to sapling to tree, shaped by the great forces of its environment and at each stage more prominent. Mokyr misspeaks in saying that the party of Jesus was "destined" to win. Much had to happen before it did.

The point here is rather that in some modeled worlds an acorn produces by itself a great tree in an instant. Such a world is unstable, as in the world of the United States in 1856–1865. The models need not be complicated. As students of chaos theory since Poincaré have pointed out, simple models can generate astonishingly complicated patterns. The slightest perturbation can yield an entirely different history. (And in catastrophe theories, quickly.) Confederate success depended on recognition by Great Britain, which depended on . . . Confederate success. It depended on, among other things, human wills at Lawrence, Kansas or Little Round Top.

The basic model is $x_{t+1} = f(x_t)$, a one-period difference equation, where the function f is nonlinear (for example, squared). The simplest equation is the hump: $x_{t+1} = \beta x_t[1 - x_t]$, where β is the so-called "tuning parameter" to give some variation in how the hump looks. It might tell you how the population of rabbits in year $t+1$ depends on the population in year t (considering that wolves, who eat rabbits, depend, too, on how many rabbits there are). Look at Figure 1.[13] The 45° line serves merely to translate x_{t+1} back into a new x_t to get stuck into the equation again for another iteration. A few iterations are shown, starting at point A in the year-t rabbit population. The rule is: all horizontal moves are to the 45° line, all vertical ones back to the humped curve. Just follow out the sequence vertical-horizontal-vertical-horizontal and so forth, forever. The succession of value below the emphasized dots are how the rabbit population changes, the chronological history deriving from the differential equation.

Written out the equation is $x_{t+1} = \beta x_t - \beta x_t^2$, the squared term signaling the nonlinearity. The equation says that the next value of the variable x (which can be the population of rabbits or the offer at the arms control negotiations) is proportional to the value now, but gets driven down (by the squared term) if it gets too high. Too many rabbits will give scope for too many wolves, with a consequent crash in rabbit populations. The humped curve is the equation; the sharper

---

12. Joel Mokyr, *The Economics of the Industrial Revolution* (Totowa, N.J., 1985), 44.
13. From William Baumol and Jess Benhabib, "Chaos: Significance, Mechanism, and Economic Applications," *Journal of Economic Perspectives* 3 (Winter, 1989), 82.

HISTORY, DIFFERENTIAL EQUATIONS, NARRATION   29

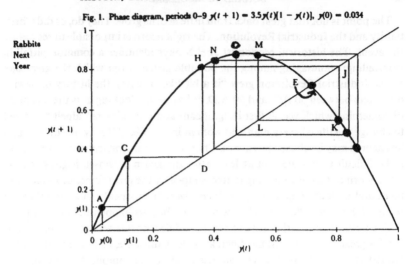

Fig. 1. Phase diagram, periods 0–9 $x(t + 1) = 3.5x(t)(1 - x(t))$, $x(0) = 0.034$

Figure 1:
How a Population Changes According to
a Nonlinear Differential Equation

is the hump the higher is β. The more humped the more violently nonlinear is the differential equation. Notice that by first-year calculus the rate of change of x, dx_{t+1}/dx_t, is just $\beta(1 - 2x_t)$, β being the violence number. Notice too that the mathematics is not exactly "feeding on itself": it is more like gnawing on itself, reducing its rate of change as it (whatever it is) gets larger.

Look at Figure 2.[14] It consists of the plots of the first fifty iterations on the same equation, with β at 3.94 in the top one and only slightly different, 3.935, in the bottom. At first the two look alike. But they soon diverge: look for example at the strange stability from point B to point C in the bottom plot.

The jargon is "sensitive dependence on initial conditions." In a nonlinear world the history depends sensitively on where you start. A point A' a little bit away from A would yield eventually an entirely different time path of rabbits. Another nice bit of jargon is the "average rate of local trajectory spreading," which is to say how fast two points originally close to each other split apart. A world in 1863 without a Colonel Joshua Lawrence Chamberlain is easy to imagine, since it is close to the actual world in which he commanded on Little Round Top. A case can be made that his action prevented Confederate victory at the Battle of Gettysburg, in which case the local trajectory spreading is very great. In 1931 the Right Honorable Winston S. Churchill, viewing a hypothetical world in which Lee *had* won, described a socialist Britain, an Americanized Mexico, and a Continental Europe on the brink of unification under Wilhelm II.[15]

14. *Ibid.*, 94–95, from an experiment by the economist Richard Quandt.
15. Winston S. Churchill, "If Lee Had Won the Battle of Gettysburg," in J. C. Squire *et al.*, *If: Or, History Rewritten* (New York, 1931), 259–284.

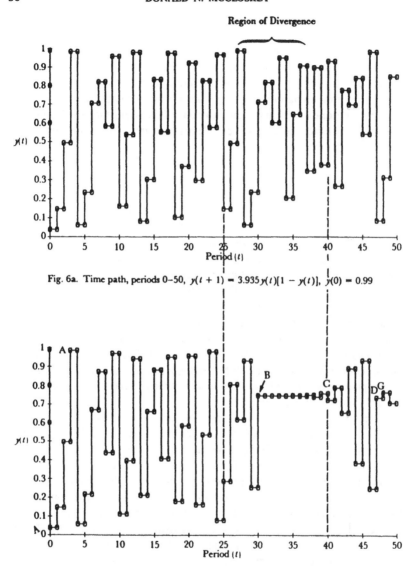

Fig. 6a. Time path, periods 0–50, $y(t + 1) = 3.935y(t)[1 - y(t)]$, $y(0) = 0.99$

Fig. 6b. Time path, periods 0–50, $y(t + 1) = 3.94y(t)[1 - y(t)]$, $y(0) = 0.99$

Figure 2

Nine caroms of a billiard ball are enough to make the gravitational field of a spectator in the room significant to the shot.[16] The meteorologist Edward Lorenz, who is responsible for the notion, called it the butterfly effect. The flapping of a butterfly's wings in China can eventually produce a hurricane in Jamaica. In

16. Ivar Ekeland, *Mathematics and the Unexpected* (Chicago and London, 1988), 68.

nonlinear systems it is possible for extremely small horseshoe nails to have extremely large effects.

People are willing to believe such models because they see butterflies in their own lives. A fluttering impulse suggested to three young men on a summer's day in 1962 that the porch of Alpha Theta would be a better place to finish the next beer, just in time to hail three young women who just happened to be passing by at the time, one of whom became later one of the young men's wife of twenty-five years. The history of a nation, people reason, cannot be so different. In truth it is hard to deny.

But the attraction of the chaotic is also the attraction of magic. The accident has the power of magic, a childish omnipotence of thought in which I can change the world with a word. Each stage of mathematical education begins with magical surprises: it was surprising to most of us at 10 years old that 7 times 8 equals 56; at 14 that a quadratic equation in algebra has a formulaic solution; at 16 that an angle can be bisected with compass and straight edge; at 17 that sines and tangents are connected numerically; at 19 (an emotional high point of any mathematical education) that Kepler's Laws of Motion can be derived from Newton's laws of motion; at 21 that $e \exp i(\text{pi}) + 1 = 0$.

At first such propositions have the arbitrary character of magic. Anyone who does not see in these an image of mysterious wisdom won by toil is intellectually dead. Tiny errors in a magical ceremony can make it go wrong. "If the Hindu magicians are to be believed, some of their rites could be practiced successfully only once every forty-five years."[17] Naturally: if magic could be done on any day, in any place, it would not have the scarcity that protects its claim of efficacy. It would merely be engineering.

Education, though, consists of demystifying the wonders and making them into non-scarce knowledge suitable for engineering. Years of training in the human and physical sciences will finally drive out the belief in magic. An historian will stop telling history in the style of popular military history and strive for social significance (our freshmen are properly groping for such generality when they write "In France, during the Revolution, you were under tremendous pressure to be revolutionary"; or "The industrial revolution wasn't totally good because the machines that were invented sometimes cut off fingers and hands"; or "France is considered an isolated country. They considered themselves as Iowans do."). An engineer at some point during a long education will stop looking on a physical system as incomprehensibly organic, and will start believing that every system can be broken down into known pieces, as in the immortal paper, "Stress Analysis of a Strapless Evening Gown." He has started to think like an engineer.

The common opinion of those educated in a rhetoric of linear differential equations is that large results must have large causes. Certainly in economics the opinion is powerful. I have made a living for twenty years retailing it, attacking again and again the notion that little causes in economic history can have large effects. Most of my book reviews draw on the opinion at least once.

17. Marcel Mauss, *A General Theory of Magic* [1902–1903] (New York, 1972), 46.

But the common opinion is merely a rhetorical dogma, a way of arguing not often reflected upon, identical to the dogma of social causation in history. It can be called The Dogma of Large-Large. Large results, it says, must have large causes. A.-A. Cournot, a French savant of the nineteenth century (not irrelevantly, one of the inventors of mathematical economics, well-trained in the mathematics of engineering) wrote in 1875:

> But philosophic history, the great history, concerns itself little with these microscopic causes. It seeks a sufficient reason for great events, that is to say, *a reason the importance of which is proportionate to the importance of the events.* . . . [T]he philosophic historian . . . will leave as pasture-ground for a frivolous curiosity those boudoir facts which are in themselves insignificant but which figure in the chain of causes and which we must assign to the realm of chance.[18]

The fall of American slavery must depend on large motives of profit, not individual morality. Capitalism must arise from irresistible social forces. A large swing of a pendulum must arise from a large push. In linear models the doctrine is true. But it can be radically false in the parts of the world that are nonlinear.

The Dogma of Large-Large, by the way, is not particular to quantification. What one admires in Marx or Tocqueville is precisely their insight into the large causes of large events, quite without mention of differential equations. By 1851, wrote Marx,

> [t]he roots that small-holding property struck in French soil [had] deprived feudalism of all nutriment. . . . [I]n the course of the nineteenth century . . . aristocratic landed property was replaced by bourgeois capital. . . . The condition of the French peasantry provides us with the answer to the riddle of the general elections of December 20 and 21. . . . Manifestly the bourgeoisie had now no choice but to elect Bonaparte.[19]

Tocqueville's chapter titles leave little to chance: "Part 2. Chapter 2. How administrative centralization was an institution of the old régime and not, as is often thought, a creation of the Revolution or the Napoleonic period"; "Pt. 2. Chp. 9. How, though in many respects so similar, the French were split up more than ever before into small, isolated, self-regarding groups"; "Pt. 3. Chp. 8. How, given the facts set forth in the preceding chapters, the Revolution was a foregone conclusion." Such Large-Large metaphors and stories satisfy an intellect trained in history or engineering more than does the hero-worship of Carlyle or the national epic of Michelet.

Chaos pleases us, then, by reintroducing a sense of magic, a sense of many possibilities. Chaotic motion is to be distinguished from randomness. Big randomness in models of the economy leads to fatalism. Chaos—which is to say, very strong effects generated wholly within the model, but giving random-looking results—can lead to activism. The president hoping that his jawboning will end a depression is a nonlinear dynamist: he thinks that little actions of his own can

---

18. S. W. Floss, *An Outline of the Philosophy of Antoine-Augustin Cournot*. Ph.D. dissertation (Philadelphia, 1941), 99–100, italics added.
19. Karl Marx, "The Eighteenth Brumaire of Louis Napoleon" [1852], in Lewis S. Feuer, *Marx and Engels: Basic Writings on Politics and Philosophy* (New York, 1959), 341–342, 345.

overwhelm the natural randomness.[20] Or alternatively a grasp of chaos can lead to proper caution: small lags in pushing brakes or the accelerator can be disastrous on Route 80, and on the troubled route of economic policy, too.[21]

The economists William Baumol and Jess Benhabib note that in regions of chaos "a time path is sometimes extremely sensitive to microscopic changes in the values of the parameters—a change in, say, the fifth decimal place of one parameter can completely transform the fifth qualitative character or the path."[22] We do not know the fifth digit (much less the fifth decimal point) of most statistics. To achieve such accuracy the 1990 Census in the United States would have to be accurate to plus or minus 10,000 people (which it is not difficult to imagine as the number of homeless or illegals uncounted in New York City alone). As Oskar Morgenstern wrote in 1963, in an unsuccessful attempt to persuade economists to adopt the error-conscious precision of engineers and physicists, "[s]tatements concerning month-to-month changes in the growth rate of the nation are nothing but absurd."[23]

The butterfly can take flight either in the parameters (that is, in the confidence about the model imposed) or in the initial conditions (that is, in the confidence about the observations of the world's condition). Both yield large differences out of small differences. Only unreasonable dogmatism about the model or unreasonable dogmatism about acuity can restore one's confidence in the Dogma of Large-Large.

The problem (and this is the main point) is that in nonlinear parts of the world the idea of storytelling is cast into doubt. "This is why long-range weather forecasting is so difficult: everything, absolutely everything, must be taken into account."[24] American history 1856–1865, in the opinion of two careful students, was in such a precarious state that small events could have a big effect. The rogue sheriff and the bold professor of rhetoric "changed history," as we say.

But in that case *any* of an unbounded set of little people and little events could be brought into the story. Unknown to history, a certain John Jones in Kansas, who alone had the moral authority to stop the sheriff, failed to arrive in the posse (he had a bad cold and was in bed). Likewise unknown to history, a political general named Robert Smith in 1861 had assigned Chamberlain to the twentieth Maine quite by accident—Chamberlain should have been put in the second, not the twentieth, but it was late at night when Smith did the job, and the orders had to go out by the next morning, leaving no time to check them. George Burns said on his TV show once, "George S. Kaufman is responsible for the skit tonight: I asked him to write it, he refused, and so I had to do it."

20. William A. Brock, "Introduction to Chaos and Other Aspects of Nonlinearity" [1987]. Working paper, Department of Economics, University of Wisconsin. Published as Chapter 10 in *Differential Equations, Stability, and Chaos in Dynamic Economics*, ed. W. A. Brock and A. G. Malliaris (New York, 1988), 9.

21. Baumol and Benhabib, 80.

22. *Ibid.*, 79.

23. Oskar Morgenstern, *On the Accuracy of Economic Observations*, 2nd ed. (Princeton, 1963), 304.

24. Ekeland, 66, speaking of Lorenz.

In some counterfactual world the Civil War and its outcome might have been governed by big, simple, linear metaphors — slavery might have been steadily less profitable despite southern sentiments, the North might have been destined to win despite southern generalship. The success of Christianity, likewise, depended on the Roman Empire, and the Industrial Revolution on the freedoms of north-western Europe. But if, as Fogel and McPherson and many historians before them have persuasively argued, the correct models for 1856–1865 are models of non-linear feedback then the story becomes unmanageable, untellable. It is a paradox, beyond the common opinion of Large-Large.

What we can do is look for times that seem chaotic and be forewarned. That is what engineers do. In regions or times that seem chaotic they note the pattern of onset but do not otherwise try to predict the motion of the swirling water.

Are we in a nonlinear and even chaotic world and if so what can be done to go on telling stories in it? I have already discussed one way of knowing whether we face chaotic systems, namely, by building up a model from horseshoe nail to kingdom. Engineers and ecologists use the technique, starting with a nonlinear equation in which they have acquired confidence and noting that for observed values of its parameters it does indeed imply chaotic behavior.

If one already knows the laws of motion then the strategy of simulation (which is what it is called) is fine. But it has difficulties for historical narration, where what we know of a metaphorical and model-building sort does not come usually with laboratory-fitted magnitudes.

The alternative to simulation as a method of reasoning in science is look-see. You can either build a model of a star on the blackboard from first principles and see how the model behaves or you can go up the mountain to the telescope. Whether or not you have a believable and numerical model of evolution you can merely look at the results and see. But the look-see evidence for chaos is sometimes hard to assess. The economists who doubt that chaos has much to do with the macroeconomic features of the economy (growth rates, unemploy-ment, inflation, and the like) point to the stability of certain magnitudes, such as the saving rate (when correctly measured) and the real interest rate; and they point to the tendency of the economy to return to its trend after being disturbed.[25] Fair enough: if the economy does not exhibit erratic and nonrandom motion like that in Quandt's second experiment above then all may be well. But the economy sometimes *does* exhibit such motion, as most famously in the Great Depression of 1929–1939. Is it chaos?

The most direct way to untangle the chaos and to make look-see work is to guess, by God's grace, what the order of the differential equation is. The "order" is how many derivatives it has, that is, how many rates of change of rates of change. The first-order *linear* differential equation of the simplest sort marches up by 80 million a year. Plotting its tth value again against its $t+1^{th}$ will show a straight line. If the *non*linear equation is of first order, similarly, you can plot the succes-sive points on a graph of x_t and x_{t+1}. The nonlinear hump will appear out of

25. Brock, "Introduction to Chaos," 7–8.

the gloom (look at the heavy dots in Figure 1 above, tracing out the hump), and the same is true of higher orders in the underlying differential equation. The feature is called "dimension," or as the mathematical economist William Brock puts it, "the minimal number of lags of x that one would need to describe the dynamic behavior of x(t) in the long run."[26] For a system that God has told you has only one lag (the first-order system, in which x_{t+1} can be fully determined by knowing x_t) the dimension is officially 1, and a two-dimensional diagram plotting x_t and x_{t+1} achieved is enough to fully reveal the structure.

The trouble is that you have to have God's grace. You have to guess what the lags are in the world's equation. As Baumol and Benhabib point out, "this problem is no different from that in choosing the structure of a model for econometric estimation," that is, the usual statistical problem.[27] Attempts to solve the problem without recourse to rhetoric (that is, by absolute and nonhuman standards) have driven econometricians insane, because the problem of choosing the model is that of choosing a human point of view. It is something done by us, not by God, and is therefore not absolute and not nonhuman. One is going to be driven insane if one tries to find a nonhuman point of view from within a hopelessly human problem. (The rhetoric of the scientific conversation, I have argued elsewhere, provides the practical solution, and keeps one's sanity.)

The problem is that a simple model with horse-kick randomness looks much like a wholly deterministic but chaotic model. You often cannot tell the difference between old-fashioned randomness — which, God knows, is prevalent in this life — and new-fashioned chaos. Chaotic randomness is often jerky: it looks random and deterministic by turns, exhibiting what economists call "régime changes" from time to (unpredictable) time. Some types of randomness, though, could look jerky, too.

Low dimension chaos is the only kind worth worrying about, because of the difficulties of measuring anything without error. "Low dimensional chaos" means essentially a return to the neighborhood of a given point after a certain number of periods — high dimensional chaos would be indistinguishable from randomness (randomness is infinite dimensional chaos, so to speak[28]). Well short of high dimensional chaos the cycles in a nonlinear system become so mind-boggling that in practical terms they cannot be known. Only in a system without appreciable error of measurement or appreciable pure randomness could a mathematical technique extract them infallibly; the alternatives are statistical techniques, but short of experimental perfection they always face some probability of false positives. Chaos, technically speaking, is a limiting case, in which the pattern of repeating values has, so to speak, an infinite number of cycles, with the effect that no point is exactly repeated, ever. Parts of the chaotic regions will show patterns, with the points clustering. In other regions the Small-Large will hold.

26. William A. Brock, "Chaos and Complexity in Economic and Financial Science," in *Acting under Uncertainty: Multidisciplinary Conceptions*, ed. George M Furstenberg (Boston, 1989), 424.
27. Baumol and Benhabib, 101.
28. See Brock, "Introduction to Chaos," 8.

The ambition to spot low-dimension nonlinearity faces, however, an impossibility theorem. It stops the narrative again. Brock points out that in stock markets a low dimension chaos would be searched out and used to make money.[29] The chartists and other technical elves in the stock market, he notes, are essentially claiming to detect recurring patterns by suitable choice of lags. But the claim is unbelievable. If they were so smart they would be rich.

The criticism is devastating to any pretensions to see simple patterns in history. I would add only that more than stock markets have this problem of claiming (unbelievably) to know how a differential equation works. If the patterns of chaos were so simple then the actors in the history would see them, and would eliminate them by making use of their knowledge. Historians need to discipline their stories by making sure that they do imply such stupidity as even Haig or Louis XVI would see through.

The problem of chaos, then, is the problem of unpredictable and inexplicable behavior. Such behavior does not arise simply because God plays dice but because we mortals cannot monitor His/Her dice playing closely enough, in nonlinear cases, to predict even the larger events. The problem is intrinsic to narrating human life. The literary critic Peter Brooks observes that "our lives are ceaselessly intertwined with narrative, with the stories that we tell, all of which are reworked in that story of our own lives that we tell to ourselves. . . . We are immersed in narrative."[30] We has met the "we," however, and they is us. The fossils do not tell a story about the Cambrian explosion: we tell it. For the human sciences the case is worse. The water molecules in even a turbulent flow are not listening to the story, and for all the principles of least action they are not telling stories about their own lives.

Perhaps chaos is merely the historian's way of thinking getting into science. It is a new way of arguing in economics and other mathematical fields, but in the end it comes down to Cleopatra's nose: if she had had a different nose, unattractive to Roman generals, the battle of Actium might not have happened,[31] and that could have made all the difference. Narration in a nonlinear world is difficult regardless of whether the problem is numerical or not. One does not avoid nonlinearities by not knowing what they are called. When success breeds success, when variables feed back into themselves, we have an exciting story to tell, but unless we know its metaphors already we have no way to tell it.

University of Iowa

29. Brock, "Chaos and Complexity," 427.

30. Peter Brooks, *Reading for the Plot: Design and Intention in Narrative* (New York, 1985), 8.

31. J. B. Bury, "Cleopatra's Nose," in *Selected Essays of J. B. Bury*, ed. Harold Temperley (Cambridge, Eng., 1930).

[12]

THE RHETORIC OF SCIENTISM

HOW JOHN MUTH PERSUADES

Muth's Article Was Ill-Written but Important

Consider another example in detail, less charming than Solow's but as important. In 1961 John Muth published a paper in *Econometrica* (the leading journal of statistical and mathematical economics, and the very embodiment of modernism in economics) entitled "Rational Expectations and the Theory of Price Movements." For years economists ignored it. Robert Lucas and Thomas Sargent, who were chiefly responsible for its later fame, wrote in 1981 (p. xi) that the paper had "a remarkably quiet first decade," which is no rash assessment. Although early accorded, like Solow's paper, the honor of inclusion in Arnold Zellner's *Readings in Economic Statistics and Econometrics* (1968), it was for a long time little read. The pattern of citations to the paper is unusual in a field that models itself so self-consciously on the urgent bustle of physics (Table 2). Seventy-four citations in 1982: even such an important paper as Solow's reached, at most, thirty in a year. There was a tiny flash, and long afterwards a boom.

Table 2. Annual Citations, 1966–1982, of Muth's 1961 Article

Year	Citations	Year	Citations
1966	5	1975	20
1967	3	1976	33
1968	2	1977	41
1969	2	1978	47
1970	4	1979	44
1971	2	1980	71
1972	9	1981	56
1973	10	1982	74
1974	10		

Source: *Social Science Citation Index.* The index begins in 1966.

The paper took a long time to be recognized as important because it was badly written. It is a good bet that most of the citers of the article have never laid eyes on it, and would not understand it if they did. The

52

53
_____
The Rhetoric of Scientism

case illustrates, by an argument from contraries, the importance of good writing in successful science. Galileo was a master of Italian prose; Poincaré, Einstein, and Keynes influenced science and society almost as much with their pens as with their mathematics.

Even by the undemanding standards of American academic life Muth's prose was not masterful or influential. It was badly organized, with ill-motivated digressions and leaps from large claims to lame examples. Little distinction was made between minor points of form and major revisions of economic thinking. Though no reader of *Econometrica* would have stumbled over the inelegant mathematics involved, she probably did wonder what exactly it was supposed to prove.

The paper bore some of the marks of professional excellence, such as an easy familiarity with mathematical statistics at a time when not many economists could claim it, and a wide-ranging bibliography. But even a serious reader of the journal could easily have dismissed it as mere muttering. Apparently most did. While richer in invention even than it seemed, it was too obviously clumsy in arrangement to warrant much investment by its readers.

Yet Muth was making an important argument. The trouble with the prevailing explanation of hog cycles or inventory accumulation and other dynamics was that it implied that economic actors are less perceptive than economics professors. The actors were supposed to be slow to change, but the professors were said to know the actors' slowness, and to be able to trace their slow adjustment. The audience claimed to know the lines better than the players. Before Muth's theory the prevailing explanation was that people get a more or less correct idea of what the future will bring and then gradually adjust to it. Muth's notion was that the professors, even if correct in their model of man, could do no better in predicting than could the hog farmer or steelmaker or insurance company. The notion is one of intellectual modesty. The professors declare themselves willing to attribute to economic actors at least as much common sense as is embodied in professional theories. The common sense is "rationality": therefore Muth called the argument "rational expectations."

What made Muth's version of the argument especially important was its application, at first by Stephen Turnovsky and Robert Lucas and later by many others, to the matter of macroeconomics. Muth's paper became the holy writ for one of the sects that sweep macroeconomics every five years. In the Keynesian or monetarist models of the 1960s and before the economic actor was perpetually astonished, the perfect rube: [Seizes newspaper.] "My word! The government has just reduced taxes in depression!" [Eyes bug out.] "Holy cow! The government has

54

The Rhetoric of Scientism

trimmed the growth of money after a long period of inflation! Gosh!"
[Faints.] It would be easy to manipulate such a dunce, from which grew
the conviction in the 1940s and 1950s that it was easy to manipulate the
economy—to "fine-tune" it, as the journalists said. The models of rational expectations in the 1970s went to the opposite extreme. They
viewed the economic actor as a man of the world: "Oh, yes, a tax cut."
[Yawns, lights cigarette in a golden holder.] "Hmm: I see that inflation
has been going on for some months." [Settles into club chair.] "About
time for the Fed to do its tight money act." [Calls broker, sips scotch,
dozes off under his copy of *Barron's*.]

Muth's Main Points Can
Be Expressed in English

By what means does Muth persuade? The question is a
critical not an historical one. The critical issue doesn't depend on the
usual questions in the history of economic thought—who influenced
Muth's paper, how it circulated in draft, what circumstances in macroeconomics made it an idea whose time had come, and whether it was
anticipated in Austrian economics, Chicago-school finance, or growth
theory. Its history is relevant only to the extent that the history illuminates the way it achieves its effect now. In Saussure's jargon, the issues
here are synchronic not diachronic.

Below are reproduced the crucial sentences in the paper. It would be
easy to persuade economists that the selection here is the core.

Muth:

[A] The objective of this paper is to
outline a theory of expectations and
to show that implications are—as a
first approximation—consistent with
the relevant data. (Muth 1961, as
cited in Zellner, 1968, p. 536)

[B] I should like to suggest that expectations, since they are informed
predictions of future events, are essentially the same as the predictions
of the relevant economic theory. At
the risk of confusing this purely de-

Translation:

The paper asks how people guess
about what the future will bring. The
answer is tested against some of the
facts in agricultural markets.

The guesses people make are probably no better or worse than the
guesses economists would make. I'll
call such guesses "rational," to distinguish them from the irrational—
that is, unreasonable, foolish—

scriptive hypothesis with a pronouncement as to what firms ought to do, we call such expectations "rational." It is sometimes argued that the assumption of rationality in economics leads to theories inconsistent with, or inadequate to explain, observed phenomena, especially changes over time (e.g., Simon 1959). Our hypothesis is based on exactly the opposite point of view: that dynamic economic models do not assume enough rationality. (p. 537)

guesses that present theories posit. Hostility to "rationality" is common among the critics of economics. I wish to go in the other direction: to see how far one can get by supposing that people are as rational in guessing about the future as in buying bread in the present.

[C] The hypothesis asserts three things: (1) Information is scarce, and the economic system generally does not waste it. (2) The way expectations are formed depends specifically on the structure of the relevant system describing the economy. (3) A "public prediction," in the sense of Grunberg and Modigliani (1954), will have no substantial effect on the operation of the economic system (unless it is based on inside information). This is not quite the same thing as stating that the marginal revenue product of economics is zero, because expectations of a single firm may still be subject to greater error than the theory. (p. 537)

In other words, I'm saying that people take appropriate care with their guesses, and economists should credit them with such caretaking. If people take care in guessing, talk about the future will be pointless: people will have allowed for the effects being talked about. For instance, declarations that prosperity is just around the corner will have no impact, unless the declarer really does know something we all don't know. Economists do know something, though not as much as their present notions about guessing imply: they know that a bunch of guesses by individuals average out over a large group to less quirky guesses.

[D] It does *not* assert that the scratch work of entrepreneurs resembles the system of equations in any way; nor does it state that predictions of entrepreneurs are perfect or that their expectations are all the same. (p. 537)

Business people do not have to be trained in mathematical economics to do about as well as economists can do in guessing the future. Nor do they have to guess perfectly or all in the same way.

[E] If the prediction of the theory were substantially better than the ex-

The notion of rational guessing makes a lot of sense. If economists

56
―――――

The Rhetoric of Scientism

pectations of the firms, then there would be opportunities for the "insider" to profit from the knowledge—by inventory speculation if possible, by operating a firm, or by selling a price forecasting service to the firms. The profit opportunities would no longer exist if the aggregate expectation of the firms is the same as the prediction of the theory: ... The expected price equals the equilibrium price. (p. 539)

[F] It is rather surprising that expectations have not previously been regarded as rational dynamic models, since rationality is assumed in all other aspects of entrepreneurial behavior. From a purely theoretical standpoint, there are good reasons for assuming rationality. First, it is a principle applicable to all dynamic problems (if true). Expectations in different markets and systems would not have to be treated in completely different ways. Second, if expectations were not moderately rational there would be opportunities for economists to make profits in commodity speculation, running a firm, or selling the information to present owners. Third, rationality is an assumption that can be modified. Systematic biases, incomplete or incorrect information, poor memory, etc., can be examined with analytical methods based on rationality. (p. 550)

[G] The only real test, however, is whether theories involving rationality explain observed phenomena any better than alternative theories. In this section we shall therefore compare some of the empirical im-

could do better than business people, the economists would be rich. They are not. A farmer guessing about the price of hogs will arrive on average at the price the market does: he'd better.

It is asymmetric for economists to treat people as rational economic men in buying bread or building ships but not in guessing the future. On aesthetic grounds it would be better to use one principle of rationality. As I said, if economists were smart enough to know how business people were failing to be rational, the economists would be rich. Furthermore, rationality is usually a good place to start thinking about human affairs, especially economic affairs. You can add later whatever allowance for ignorance or foolishness seems justified in each case.

But these arguments I've made so far are just frosting, and are not good scientific method. The cake is the ability of my notion to make better sense of the world than some competing notion. In agricultural mar-

plications of the rational expectations hypothesis with those of the cobweb "theorem." The effects of rational expectations are particularly important because the cobweb theorem has often been regarded as one of the most successful attempts at dynamic economic theories (e.g., Goodwin 1947). Few students of agricultural problems or business cycles seem to take the cobweb theorem very seriously, however, but its implications do occasionally appear. For example, a major cause of price fluctuations in cattle and hog markets is sometimes believed to be the expectations of farmers themselves. As a result, the prediction of the cobweb theory would ordinarily have the sign opposite to that of the firms. (p. 551)

kets especially (though also in the study of general booms and busts) the competing notion is called the "cobweb theorem." No one actually takes the "theorem" very seriously, perhaps because they recognize without thinking about it much that it's not rational. In any event, it says that each single farmer thinks prices will stay high when they are high, and that he will therefore raise lots of hogs to take advantage of the high price. By the time the little hogs become big hogs, however, every other farmer has also raised lots of hogs; the price is in fact low, contrary to what he expected. The farmer, poor fool, never learns.

[H] There is some direct evidence concerning the quality of expectations of firms. Heady and Kaldor (1954) have shown that for the period studied, average expectations were considerably more accurate than simple extrapolation. (p. 552)

Heady and Kaldor showed that the firms do learn, or at least that they learn better than this.

[I] It often seems that reported expectations underestimate the extent of changes that actually take place. . . . Such findings are clearly inconsistent with the cobweb theory, · which ordinarily requires a negative coefficient. (p. 553)

Other writers have found that farmers do not expect prices to move as much as the prices actually do move, but that they at least predict the right direction: the cobweb theorem says they would predict the wrong direction.

[J] The evidence for the cobweb model lies in the quasi-periodic fluctuations in prices of a number of commodities. The hog cycle is perhaps the best known, but cattle and potatoes have sometimes been cited as others which obey the

The whole notion of the cobweb is based on the ups and downs of, say, hog prices. But hog prices take much longer to go up and down than it takes to raise hogs. Something is wrong. What is wrong, I'll venture, is that the irrational theory of how

58
_____

The Rhetoric of Scientism

"theorem.". . . That the observed hog cycles were too long for the cobweb theorem was first observed in 1935 by Coase and Fowler (1935, 1937). The graph of cattle prices given by Ezekiel (1938) as evidence for the cobweb theorem implies an extraordinarily long period of production (5–7 years). The interval between successive peaks for other commodities tends to be longer than three production periods. (pp. 553–54)

farmers make guesses about the future is mistaken.

Muth's Article Engages in the Usual Appeals to Scientific Method

The question is how such a wretchedly expressed argument achieves credence. Its obscurity of course became a rhetorical advantage once it had been made into holy writ. It is composed in a foreign language, but the language is a sacred one, like Old Church Slavonic.

Its style is the key to its rhetorical appeal, because it is the style of scientism. Lucas and Sargent, the most prominent users of the argument, are persuaded that it is "one of the most carefully and compactly written papers of recent vintage: every sentence in the introduction [not reproduced here] counts, and many have since been expanded into entire articles. Muth introduces the hypothesis at a general, verbal level, motivating it as a corollary of the general principles of economic equilibrium, and then turns to specific, certainty-equivalent examples" (1981, p. xvii). The praise is itself scientistic and draws on the stylistic rhetoric of modernism. The language of "introduc[ing] the hypothesis at a general, verbal level, motivating it as a corollary of . . . general principles" is undiluted modernism. You deduce lower-level hypotheses from general principles, and the test of the lower hypothesis is therefore an indirect test of the principles. The talk of corollaries is part of the same tradition (and so too, incidentally, is the special virtue attributed to care and compactness, the virtues of mathematics in the Math Department, not in Engineering). The hypotheses come from the context of discovery, before the rigor of justification. You "motivate" a proof in mathematics—the language used here—by stepping for a little while outside the rigorous mode of proof-making to show the groundlings what's afoot.

The Rhetoric of Scientism

Muth himself makes similar remarks, also couched in modernist language, about what should warrant belief. In the first sentence of the selection he implicitly declares that most of his arguments to follow in the paper are, by his own standards, epistemologically lame. Showing that "the implications are . . . consistent with the relevant data" (paragraph A) is indeed the positivist criterion of truth in science, but little of the paper does it. He does show that if he is careful his notion does not lead to manifest absurdity, such as a condition that speculators in hogs entered the business to lose rather than to gain money. These are the quality of the "data" he shows "consistent" with his argument. Toward the end, after much argument that would find no place in the epistemology of positivism, he turns impatiently on himself with a positivist *ukase*: "The only real test, however, is whether theories involving rationality explain observed phenomena any better than alternative theories" (paragraph G). The words are redolent of the received view. The richness of scientific persuasion is to be reduced to a crucial experiment, a "real test" (*pace* Duhem and the dilemma that no test is crucial). Since the alternative views are "theories," the job of science is to upend or uphold them (*pace* Kuhn and the history of normal science fitting fact to invariant theory). The relevant test depends on "observed phenomena," the hard, objective data so much to be desired (*pace* Polanyi and the truth that scientific knowledge is not epistemologically special).

The appeals to the method of science in Muth's paper are mainly matters of style, arising out of a modernist conversation. The paper does not achieve credence by axiomatic proof or statistical curve-fitting, though written in the genre recommended by modernism. What is modernist in it is not the turns of argument but the style.

The conflict between the "nonrhetorical" ideology of modernism and the actual practice of modernists has been apparent from the beginning, showing up repeatedly in matters of style. Amelie Oksenberg Rorty observes of Descartes that "despite his austere recommendations about the methods of discovery and demonstration, he hardly ever followed those methods, hardly ever wrote in the same genre twice" (1983, p. 548). She notes that his attacks on the common topics of argument, such as authority or the appeal to common knowledge, have an ironic air, for he "found himself using the very modes he intended to attack" (p. 548). Since Bacon and Descartes and the creators later in the seventeenth century of the scientific paper, any scientist who wished to persuade had to adopt the modernist style, as Muth did. Darwin is the leading case. The student of rhetoric John Campbell has argued that Darwin took "care to redescribe his path to discovery so that it appeared to conform with conventional standards of Baconian induction-

60
———————

The Rhetoric of Scientism

ism" (1984, p. 15); and Edward Manier writes that "the early drafts of
the theory do not conform to the 'hypothetico-deductive model' of scientific explanation, although they indicate Darwin's intent to represent
his views as if they did conform to that model" (Campbell 1984, p. 77,
and p. 76, where Manier is quoted).

The style of Muth's article makes an ethical and emotional appeal, an
appeal to his character as a Scientist and to the self-image of his audience as fellow scientists. The word "I" occurs twice only (once in the selection), in keeping with the convention that kings, editors, people with
tapeworms, and honest-to-goodness scientists are permitted to use the
more dignified "we" instead. The style is often indirect in other ways,
as suits a Scientist (one can make insecure scientists still more insecure
by violating such stylistic conventions). Ten of the thirty sentences in
the selection have their main clauses in the passive voice. Amidst much
that is self-confident and even cocky there are soothing words of proper
scientific modesty: "as a first approximation" (A) the theory works; "I
would like to suggest" (B), not assert; "it is rather surprising" (F) that
the theory has been overlooked; "it often appears" (I) that behavior is
inconsistent with the alternative theories. And throughout the essay
the reader is treated to dollops of scientific vocabulary from the classical languages: "purely descriptive hypotheses," "observed phenomena," "objective probability distributions of outcomes," "analytical
methods," and the like. Northrop Frye observes that "much of the difficulty in a philosophical [and scientific] style is rhetorical in origin, resulting from a feeling that it is necessary to detach and isolate the intellect from the emotions" (1957, p. 330). He examines a characteristically
opaque sentence from James Mill, translates it in the style of the translation of Muth above, and wonders, as you do about Muth, "why, if
James Mill meant that, he could not have said it." The answer is that
"the style is motivated by a perverse, bristling intellectual honesty. *He*
will not condescend to employ any of the pretty arts of persuasion,
sugar-coated illustrations or emotionally-loaded terms; he will appeal
only to the cold logic of reason itself—reinforced, to be sure, by a peculiarly Victorian sense that the more difficult the style, the tougher the
moral and intellectual fibre one develops in wrestling with it" (p. 330).
On the page before he remarks, "All of these are clearly at least in part
endeavours to purify verbal communication of the emotional content of
rhetoric; all of them, however, impress the literary critic as being themselves rhetorical devices" (p. 329).

Well, of course. The form of Muth's article seeks to persuade. Not to
fool: to persuade. Put clearly or modestly or, above all, unscientifically,
it would not have been in the end a success as a scientific paper. If he

had written in the plain style I have translated it into, no one would have made it into a holy text. In a word, the article, like any other piece of scientific work, is rhetorical, even in its stylistic appeal to a rhetoric of not having a rhetoric.

Muth's Appeal Is in Fact to the Community of Scholars

The theory of knowledge put forward by the objective, data-respecting, sober style of modernism in Muth's paper is that the privileged form of knowing is knowing by the lone person himself, *solus ipse*. That is, real knowing is said to be individual and solipsistic, not social. No one needs to *say* anything to you, the Cartesian says, to persuade you of the ancient proof of the irrationality of the square root of two. There is nothing social about your assent to it.

But on the contrary, persuasive knowledge is social. It is a social event that Muth's arguments came to be credible. The arguments were not written in the heavens or, as Descartes imagined, in the soul of the self-regarding man. The astronomer relies for his convictions on "a sequence of instrument makers and astronomers and nuclear physicists, specialist in this and that, each of whom he must trust and believe. All this knowledge, all our knowledge, has been built up communally. The fallacy which imprisons the positivist and the analyst [in philosophy] is the assumption that he can test what is true and false without consulting anyone but himself" (Bronowski 1965, p. 57).

The evidence for the social character of knowledge is that not everyone of Muth's society has been persuaded. A particular society of economists, not the ages, was to be persuaded. Not all were persuaded, and those who were have identifiable characteristics. His arguments, to use the modernist word, were not altogether "compelling." They did not compel assent the way some (but not all) of the simplest and oldest proofs in mathematics do, or the way some (but not all) of the simplest and most dramatic controlled experiments in physics do. This may be seen in the refusal of such intelligent economists as Robert Gordon, James Tobin, and Benjamin Friedman, among many others, to give their assent to Muth's arguments.

The official rhetoric of the paper allows no room for anything but unanimous assent, since the paper claims to be a certified piece of positivism "consistent with the facts." But noncompulsion in scientific argument is, of course, commonplace. When honest and well-informed biologists disagree about the strength of a tendency to inherited altru-

62
_____

The Rhetoric of Scientism

ism among human blood relatives or when honest and well-informed physicists disagree about the significance of Bell's Theorem, they must be using arguments that do not compel assent in the conclusive way required by modernist method.

Muth's paper has in fact few modernist certitudes. The main argument, as I have said, is that rational expectations applies more widely a principle of entry used daily by economists elsewhere. The usual models "do not assume enough rationality" (B); "rationality is assumed in all other aspects of entrepreneurial behavior" (F), so why not here? It is an appeal to a figure of speech discussed earlier, philosophical consistency. Muth is simply pointing to an oversight in the application of economic theory. It is as though for some reason astronomers who grasped Newton's theory had not noticed that the motions of the earth's moon could be brought under it. A paper pointing out that this too could be fitted into a theory that explained the motions of the earth, Jupiter, and Mars, and even of Ganymede and Phobus, would be instantly plausible to many. Likewise in Muth's case.

The analogy was not persuasive to all economists, I have noted. Yet it had magical power over others. Some of Muth's audience were persuaded as much as they were ever going to be as soon as they understood the argument, that is to say (if they were among the tiny group who saw through its "compactness"), by about the second page. Compare the rapidity with which Solow persuaded his audience, or at least the part of it that believed anyway the metaphor of the production function. There is nothing unscientific about such ready if partial assent.

Nor did Muth break with the traditions of science when he turned to little mathematical simulations that seemed to behave well—not simulations that "predict well" in properly modernist style, but that compute and fit and lie still beside the existing theory without exploding. Thomas Kuhn, in contrasting his views on the "logic of discovery or psychology of research" with Popper's, argued that for the most part a scientist is concerned rather with evaluating his "best guesses about the proper way to connect his own research problem with the corpus of accepted scientific knowledge. The scientist must *premise* current theory as the rules of the game" (Kuhn 1977, p. 270, his italics). Science, to repeat, is not "testing" its theories against predictions. The attempts at simulation are mostly puzzles the scientist poses which are "like crossword puzzles, challenges only to his ingenuity. *He* is in difficulty, not current theory" (p. 271n, his italics).

The role of simulation in science is evident in the conversation about the extinction of the dinosaurs. The new explanation argues that a comet hit the earth scores of millions of years ago, creating a natural version of the nuclear winter. As a reviewer of a book on the subject wrote, "The chief difficulty is in rendering it quantitative. We must hope that someone will now produce a numerical simulation that extinguishes/perpetuates all the right species in all the right numbers" (McCrea 1983). A related conversation has been taking place in astronomy since the early 1980s, using identical rhetorical devices. One astronomical argument, beginning with the observation that there are regular mass extinctions, is that the sun has a mate, a star called Nemesis, whose orbit periodically disturbs the comet fields surrounding the sun, causing comets to rain into the solar system. Or perhaps the disturbing body is a Planet X:

> Although the Planet X model also appears to explain the periodic mass extinctions adequately, Mr. Whitmire says he does not consider it to be better than the Nemesis model. Nemesis, he noted, has so far withstood many detailed calculations. But if the Planet X model can withstand similar calculations, "I think it will be a better model than Nemesis" for two reasons, he added. The most important reason, he said, is that the existence of Planet X has long been postulated, so scientists "would not be inventing anything new." The second reason is that the orbit of the planet is closer to the sun than that proposed for Nemesis, which means it would be much more likely to be stable. (*Chronicle of Higher Education*, February 20, 1985)

When the puzzle is solved, the scientific community applauds, but it is not applauding an event in the hypothetico-deductive model of science. The situation is similar in economics and in Muth.

The Explicit Arguments
Are Rhetorically Complex

Having shown that his instance can be simulated without gross violation of the facts, Muth is ready to make more direct arguments for it. Early on he remarks that "information is scarce, and the economic system generally does not waste it" (paragraph C; compare the remark on the "marginal revenue product of economics" in the same paragraph, which makes the same point). Such remarks are common in economics: economists delight in posing deep but tough little examination questions for their colleagues, just as classicists delight in posing for theirs apt but difficult quotations from *The Greek Anthology*. The correct reaction is a show of effortless understanding.

64
_____

The Rhetoric of Scientism

In Muth's case the understanding is that he is comparing information about the future of hog prices with any other good that can be bought and sold. If the analogy persuades, then you will believe that business people buy information to the optimal extent—or at any rate to the extent of optimality that they exhibit in their other and more ordinary purchases. Their purchases of trucking services or space in feedlots do not leave any gaps between the cost of the last units of such things and the marginal value in use. There is no waste, no misallocation. Nor, Muth is saying, is there misallocation in purchasing information about the future, which implies that there is no gap for mere economists to exploit. When business people have done their jobs, the future will in fact bring what *on average* they had expected it would bring. The argument does not "state that the predictions of entrepreneurs are perfect" (C). They do not hit the bull's-eye every time. But at least their hits are distributed around the bull's-eye in such a way that no economist could profitably advise them to aim higher in shooting (E, F near the middle).

His three further arguments "from a purely theoretical standpoint" (F) are revealing. They are purely aesthetic, which is what economists mean when they call an argument "theoretical." As I have noted, when economists are asked why almost all of them believe in free trade, they will say that it is a "theoretical" argument that persuades them. Further inquiry will reveal that it is in fact a pretty diagram that persuades them. Evidence that would persuade a consistent positivist is absent. So here, which probably explains why Muth immediately turns on himself with the stern injunction to seek positive virtue and "explain observed phenomena."

The arguments are arguments from symmetry and suitability and personal character, distant from the rules of modernism. His notion of rational expectations would be a unified theory of expectations, Muth argues, symmetrical in all its applications. The appeal is to a uniformity in social nature—or, more accurately, to a desire to understand social nature uniformly. He argues again that economists would be rich if they were as smart as alternative theories posit (E again). The argument is practically *ad hominem* and has the reflexive character that the Frankfurt School of philosophers associates with critical, as against scientific, theories.

He argues finally that rational expectations can be conveniently modified to fit the imperfections of the social world. Flexibility is frequently praised in scientific theories and of course should be. But flexibility is simply a promise that the theory will be able to evade crucial tests, surviving unscathed from positivist tortures. Nothing could be further from naïve falsification. All the arguments he uses are, as Muth

says, "good reasons"; but they do not fit with the narrowing epistemology that many scientists still believe.

Even when he has jerked himself back to "real tests," Muth cannot
follow the modernist line. His "observations" (H, I, J) are all reports of
other people's work, once removed from the virtue of primary experiment. They are, in fact, mainly attacks on the plausibility of one among
the infinite number of possible alternatives to rationality, not the full,
fair horse race among alternatives imagined in positivist folklore. The
Heady and Kaldor paper cited by Muth used self-reporting of expectations by the farmers themselves, which is forbidden in the economist's
version of positivist method. The regression coefficients discussed in
paragraph I are open to numerous objections, as Muth well understood.
And the observation in J that cycles in Hog prices are in fact much
longer than the gestation period of hogs (the gestation period is important to the other theories of expectation) is hardly decisive, as Muth
himself remarks: "Positive serial correlation of the exogenous distur-
bances" means that farmers may have a series of several bad years in a
row, lengthening the apparent cycle beyond the period it takes to raise
a hog. The rejection of the nonrational hog cycle may be merely apparent. The test Muth proposes, to put it technically, is underidentified.

To say that Muth's "observations" would not persuade consistent
modernists is not, however, to say that they do not persuade reasonable
economists. Economists cannot be consistent modernists and remain
reasonable. The persuasiveness of Muth's paper comes from the richness
and catholicity of its unofficial arguments, well beyond the official narrowness. Among economists an argument from axiomatic demonstration, statistical test (regression in particular), or appeal to the competitive model all have prestige. None is logically compelling, nor even
very persuasive by itself. You can object to each that garbage in implies
garbage out. Yet the most hostile economist, if properly socialized, will
want to yield to the form. She will be pleased by their success at a formal level—"Gosh, what a clever argument that is: What a neat proof/
statistical test/appeal to the intellectual traditions of economics"—
even if she wants to disbelieve their substance.

To claim that Muth persuades by rhetorical means is not of course a
criticism. Quite the contrary: it is inevitable, and even good. Outside of
a rather small group of specialists in speech communication, theatre
arts, and related fields the study of the rhetoric of a text is usually a
preface to debunking it. There is a rhetoric of the analysis of rhetoric.
An outsider reading "Sweet Talk: The Moral Rhetoric Against Sugar"
by Elizabeth Walker Mechling and Jay Mechling, published in 1983 in the
Central States Speech Journal, aches for the demonstration that the dia-

66

The Rhetoric of Scientism

tribes against sugar, analyzed rhetorically in the paper, are in fact misled. But the demonstration does not come. The expectation that it must come is naïve. Critical thinking is not necessarily "critical" in the common sense.

Muth's article is typical of the literature of economics, with its rich and unexplored rhetoric. That is the point: economists are not aware of the rhetorical riches buried in their style of talk. The richness is not astonishing, of course. That economists persuade the way other professional arguers do is no more astonishing than that arguers now use much the same common topics as were current in Cicero's time (Burke 1950, p. 56). True, you might be equally astonished by both facts, and study them with wondering respect. An anthropologist, for instance, would do well, as some have, to study rhetoric among the Sherpas or the Ilongot, to see if the same figures of argument carry conviction there as with us. In any case a study of rhetoric among the Econ need not encourage bad rhetoric any more (or less) than the study of econometrics encourages bad econometrics.

Muth's Rhetoric Is Indistinguishable from That in Other Fields

Muth's rhetoric ought to be familiar, because it uses figures of speech common to our civilization. Different fields of study pick from the same list of figures of speech. The list is issued with an education.

Imagine the figures of speech stuffed into a storeroom: twelve dozen appeals to authority here, a gross of syllogisms there, 157 metaphors (few of them fresh) on the top shelf, a dozen urn models stuck in behind the metaphors, and one argument from design, apparently secondhand, over by the window. These and others are available for use. A field such as economics will at one time make large use of the argument from design, say, and little use of appeals to the character of Scientist; at another time it will use a different bundle, having put the used ones back in the storeroom. None of the items are epistemologically privileged. To be proud that you achieve human persuasion by using existence theorems as against analogies does not make much sense, especially considering that the bundle of figures used is not permanent. Today's user of an argument from experiment will be tomorrow's user of an appeal to authority.

In short, any field, such as economics, differs from another, such as history or physics, in two respects. It uses for a while a somewhat different selection from the common store of figures of speech. Much overlap can be expected. And it studies different objects. A science is a class of objects and a way of conversing about them, not a way of knowing truth.

The overlap of argument especially requires factual demonstration. You do not after all see engineers using the metaphor of the invisible hand every day or theologians using Brouwer's fixed-point theorem (though each could). You can see the overlap by getting down into the details of argument in fields different from economics, showing the similarity point by point to Muth's argument.

Three fields that among them must surround economics, whatever coordinates you might use, are paleontology, pure mathematics, and the study of Latin literature. If we accept the modernism that correlates what is out there with how we know, these surely will be the realms of plain fact, indubitable proof, and mere opinion. It will develop that they are not.

For paleontology I have already remarked on how the conversation about mass extinctions uses simulation, a figure of speech whose use in economics has grown as the price of computer time has fallen. Even when away from their computers the economists use it, to think about the effect of withholding the grain crop on prices, for example. It is mathematical analogizing. In this, unsurprisingly, economists are not different from other scientific poets. Another case is described by Stephen Jay Gould. The sudden proliferation of species at the beginning of the Cambrian period, one of the great puzzles in evolution, was explained by Steven Stanley in 1973 by positing the sudden arrival of forms of life that fed on other forms of life, single-celled herbivores, as it were, in a grassy sea. Their grazing on the dominant forms allowed the new forms to survive the competition from the previously dominant ones, which in turn resulted in new grazers. For the similarity of Stanley's explanation to the analysis of Muth, Gould's description is worth quoting at length:

> Stanley did not develop his theory from empirical studies of Precambrian communities. It is a deductive argument based on an established principle of ecology that does not contradict any fact of the Precambrian world and seems particularly consistent with a few observations. In a frank concluding paragraph, Stanley presents four reasons for accepting his theory: (1) "It seems to account for what facts we have about Precambrian life"; (2) "It is simple, rather than complex or contrived"; (3) "It is purely biological, avoiding *ad hoc* invocation of external controls";

68
_____

The Rhetoric of Scientism

and (4) "It is largely the product of direct deduction from an
established ecological principle."

Such justifications do not correspond to the simplistic notions
about scientific progress that are taught in most high schools and
advanced by most media. Stanley does not invoke proof by new
information obtained from rigorous experiment. His second criterion is a methodological presumption, the third a philosophical
preference, the fourth an application of prior theory. Only Stanley's first reason makes any reference to Precambrian facts, and it
merely makes the weak point that his theory "accounts" for what
is known (many other theories do the same). But creative thought
in science is exactly this—not a mechanical collection of facts and
induction of theories, but a complex process involving intuition,
bias, and insight from other fields. Science, at its best, interposes
human judgment and ingenuity upon all its proceedings. (Gould
1977, p. 125)

That the theory "accounts for what [few] facts we have" (as Stanley
put it, in the usual phrase) is exactly Muth's claim too, buttressed immediately—lest we pause too long over the paucity of these facts and become depressed—by appeals to the traditions of reasoning in the field
and the aesthetic pleasure of the simpler argument. It is not strange to
find evolution and economics using identical rhetorical devices, for
they are identical twins raised separately. In any case, Muth's and Stanley's theories are similar in the rhetorical appeals they make.

In pure mathematics the case is one described by Mark Steiner in 1975,
suggested in turn by George Polya's book on the rhetoric of number and
quantity, *Induction and Analogy in Mathematics* (1954). The great Swiss
mathematician Leonhard Euler wished to find a simple expression,
supposing one existed, for the infinite sum $1 + 1/4 + 1/9 + 1/16 + \ldots$ and
so forth forever, the sum of the reciprocals of successive squares of the
positive integers. To those unfamiliar with infinite sums, the logic of
which was not developed in full rigor until long after Euler wrote, there
is no obvious reason why the sum should exist (although a little calculation makes it very plausible that it does and is somewhere around
1.64). What Euler showed is typical of the rabbits that eighteenth-century mathematicians were always pulling out of hats: that the sum is
exactly $(\pi)^2/6$. To nonmathematicians it is astonishing that π turns up
so often in expressions apparently unrelated to circles.

The argument that Euler developed depended on many things,
among them, as Steiner puts it, precisely that "he knew that a constant
like π on the basis of past experience, was likely to show up in such a

context" (1975, p. 105). Likewise, Muth knew on the basis of past experience that rational models were easy to manipulate and likely to give especially simple results. Euler felt his result to be "simple and esthetic" (Steiner's words, p. 105), as Muth did. Euler could see no alternative, as Muth could see no merit and many demerits in the cobweb theorem. Euler, a famous calculator, showed the formula to be empirically correct to twenty decimal places. Muth had less precise material, but made an identical argument, dressed up for purposes of modernist epistemology as "the only real test."

The most important strand in Euler's web of persuasion was an algebraic derivation of the equality. But the derivation depends on a crucial "inductive 'leap'. . . unjustified by anything so far presented" (Steiner 1975, p. 103). The leap was an analogy between finite equations like $0 = 3 + 4x - 10x^2$, of the second degree, and equations like
$$0 = x/1 - x^3/(3)(2) + x^5/(5)(4)(3)(2) - x^7/(7)(6)(5)(4)(3)(2) + \ldots.$$
Euler explained that these should be viewed as equations of the "infinite" degree, yet as Steiner notes, "no axiomatization, or even formalization, of 'infinite addition' existed at the time" (1975, p. 106). It was "Euler's genius and his painstaking verifications" by numerical simulation that made fruitful this notion of "exploiting the analogy between finite and infinite" (p. 106). Even by the standards of eighteenth-century mathematics "Euler had not proved his results." But—and this is the crucial point—"we must admit that Euler had a right to be confident in his discovery, beyond any doubt" (p. 106).

So too Muth. His discovery, though clearly more doubtful than Euler's, also rested on an unproven analogy, between ordinary goods and information about the future. He claimed, with approximately as much prior warrant as Euler, that both were objects of production, allocation, and lucid plan. The analogy, like Euler's, carried much of the weight of persuasion. Like Euler, Muth had a warrant for using the analogy that in other applications a similar analogy "yields other results that are also verified to many decimal places," and that it is "an analogy that brings forth previously proved theorems" (Steiner 1975, p. 107). This is the burden of Muth's use of the word "rational." He is pointing out that other applications of the analogy between human action and methodical calculation have proven fruitful in understanding. And of course they have. The mathematician, like the paleontologist, does not argue in a way much different from the economist.

Another theorem of Euler was the subject of Imre Lakatos's experiment in the rhetorical study of mathematics (Lakatos 1976; it would have irritated Lakatos and the Lakatosians to describe it as a "rhetorical study"). The conversation about the Descartes-Euler theorem on

The Rhetoric of Scientism

polyhedra witnessed many correct but contradictory proofs, though a purely modernist line would demand only one. As the Teacher in Lakatos's dialogue says, "Proofs, even though they may not prove, certainly do help to improve our conjecture" (Lakatos 1976, p. 37). Muth's demonstrations do not "prove" the theorem of rational expectations in any final, ultimate, modernist sense, any more than Euler's proved his theorem: they illuminate it and improve it, with an audience in mind.

In Latin literature the example is a striking new understanding of the arrangement of poetry books in the late republic and early empire. Helena R. Dettmer (1983 and later works) has discovered that the poets arranged their books with methodical care (one might say rationally), going so far as to impose numerical patterns on the sums of lines in corresponding sections. Her treatise on the structure of Horace's *Odes*, for instance, discovers in them an immense structure of nested rings, linking poems hundreds of lines distant from each other. *Odes* 1.1 corresponds (as has long been known) to *Odes* 3.30 in theme and meter, *Odes* 1.2 to *Odes* 3.29 in theme (as had not been suspected, significant though it is for understanding Horace's attitude to the peace-giver and liberty-taker Octavius Augustus Caesar). Likewise, 1.3 corresponds to 3.27 (a slight irregularity), 1.4 to 3.28, 1.5 to 3.26, and so on and on in dazzling and unsuspected symmetry.

Certain poems stand out by their tightness of symmetry in the arrangement as "structural," and for these Dettmer discovered dozens of astonishing arithmetical truths: the fourteen structural poems in the first half of the book have in sum (not individually) exactly the same number of lines as the fourteen corresponding ones in the second half (348 lines); the five structural poems on one side of the midpoint have in sum 124 lines, as do the five corresponding ones on the other side. As Dettmer says, difficult though it may be to believe, "The mathematical symmetry is highly significant because it furnishes clear and compelling evidence that all the structural poems have been identified" (1983, pp. 525, 531; note that Dettmer, with no training in statistics, here uses the word "significant" in exactly its statistical sense, as a low probability of rejecting the hypothesis of no symmetry if it were true).

Other Latin poets of late republican and early imperial times used similar artifice. In Catullus's little book, for example, Dettmer has discovered a series of numerical theorems no less astonishing than Euler's and more precise than Muth's (Dettmer 1984a). Divide the middle (long) poems on the basis of theme and evident verbal echoes into sets labeled A (which is poem 64), B (poems 61 and 62), B' (68a and 68b), A' (65 and 66), C (63), and C' (67). Note a lemma (which, like Euler's algebra, Stanley's cropping theory, and Muth's rationality, "yields other results that are also verified") that Roman poets arranged their poetry in balanced rings, as Dettmer has shown to be true of Horace, Vergil, Propertius, Ovid, and others. Signify the number of lines in a section by its letter. THEOREM: A - B + A' - B' = C + C'

It takes the breath away. You can believe almost anything about π, precambrian organisms, or hog farmers, but had imagined that poets were of different stuff. This and many scores of other instances detailed by Dettmer change the conception of Latin poets, increasing admiration for their artfulness, if not their art. The embedding of the poetry in verified structures can resolve numerous textual and interpretative doubts, from the validity of the conjecture *"o patrona virgo"* in line 9 of *"Cui domo lepidum novum libellum"* to the understanding of how the Romans thought.

What is chiefly important here is the character of the argument. Dettmer's book on Horace is 550 pages long and assesses methodically hundreds upon hundreds of verbal echoes and thematic clues, embedding them in the two-thousand-year-old conversation of scholarship about Horace. It is wholly "scientific" if the word means "precise, numerical, thorough, crushingly persuasive." Dettmer realizes that she will have trouble making the numerical symmetries believable to many classicists, who identify as dogmatically with the literary side of the cultural chasm between literature and science as most economists identify with its mathematical side:

> Whether one likes numbers or not (and many do not), the fact remains that they exist. It is true that numbers and their implications, the [poet indulging in] addition or deletion of verses to make patterns, do indeed destroy our romantic illusions of a poet posed with stilus and wax tablet sitting beneath a spreading plane tree, invoking the Muse for inspiration. [But numerical patterns] furnish an invaluable tool for the literary critic. (Dettmer 1983, pp. 7–8)

Their use can be denied only by an epistemological theory that forbids numerical figures of speech in the study of poetry. The official epistemology gets in the way of the science. Few classicists have understood or believed Dettmer's work, though she has by now demonstrated overwhelmingly that similar structures appear in the books of Catullus and other Latin poets. Her discovery is in her own field comparable to genetics or plate tectonics, yet most classicists have never heard of it. That Dettmer is right does her no good in a rhetorical community in which people can get away with dismissing numbers because they are not words. Similarly, on epistemological grounds economists like Muth

72

The Rhetoric of Scientism

deny official status to arguments from introspection and authority, and dismiss words because they are not numbers.

Dettmer's scientific precision, though expressed more in "numbers" than most, is characteristic of the best classical scholarship. Steele Commager in "Notes on Some Poems of Catullus" (1965) or Ronald Syme on "Piso and Veranius in Catullus" (1956) argue in a similarly exact way. They argue, to be sure, about literary and historical matters, such as the impression that a certain line of poetry makes in view of the linguistic evidence on usage in republican Rome or the identity of a certain governor of Macedonia in 60–59 B.C. in view of the political evidence on families and parties. But in their use of figures of speech they might as well be arguing about the usages of hog farmers in A.D. 1950 or the identity of a herbivore in 600,000,000 B.C. Subjects do not entail epistemologies. If "science" means "indubitable," then there is no science in science. If it means "very persuasive," then much clear and honest thinking is scientific.

The contrary notion, shared by literary and scientific modernists, is that only certain subjects can be scientific, and that their study will always depend on certain invariant figures of speech. Modernist methodism, exhibited in Muth's paper, asserts that only experiment, statistical procedures, or axiomatization are "scientific."

Methodism infects classical textual criticism, too, and is as unhelpful there as it is in economics. One methodological rule in textual criticism, for example, embodied in various Latin maxims, is to honor the text. Every surviving manuscript of Macrobius's *Saturnalia* 1.6, line 14, speaking of an article of clothing, reads *totam*. A thoughtless scientism, of the sort that measures regardless or axiomatizes regardless, would therefore resist the emendation *togam*, the well-known article of male clothing, even though this other, alleged *totam* would be the sole occurrence of such a word in Latin literature (James Willis 1972, p. 7, who is eloquent on the point).

Such voluntary imbecility in the application of rules of methodology infuriated the poet and textual critic A. E. Housman. On the rule that "The More Sincere Text Is the Better" (even if erroneous and senseless), he wrote,

> The best way to treat such pretentious inanities is to transfer
> them from the sphere of textual criticism . . . into some sphere
> where men are compelled to use concrete and sensuous terms,
> which force them, however reluctantly, to think. I ask him to tell
> me which weighs most, a tall man or a fat man. *Tall* and *fat* are
> adjectives that transport even a textual critic from the world of

73
___

The Rhetoric of Scientism

humbug into the world of reality, a world inhabited by
comparatively thoughtful people, such as butchers, grocers, who
depend on their brains for their bread. (Housman 1922, p. 1063)

The best way to treat such pretentious inanities as that economics is distinct from other fields by virtue of a unique methodology is to translate them into comparatively concrete and sensuous terms. Which is the more persuasive evidence, a correlation coefficient of .90 or an uncontroversial piece of introspection? A rule of methodology claims to say, in general. But there is no point in knowing such a thing in general. An economist does not do economics in general. She does it in particular. Surely if she does it well she uses particular figures of speech from the common store.

BIBLIOGRAPHY

Bronowski, Jakob. 1965. *Science and Human Values*. Rev. ed. New York: Harper and Row.

Burke, Kenneth. 1950. *A Rhetoric of Motives*. Berkeley: University of California Press, 1969.

Campbell, John Angus. 1987. "Charles Darwin: Rhetorician of Science." In John Nelson, et al., eds., *Rhetoric of the Human Sciences*, pp. 69–86. Madison: University of Wisconsin Press.

Commager, Steele. 1965. "Notes on Some Poems of Catullus." *Harvard Studies in Classical Philology* 70: 83–110.

Dettmer, Helena. 1983. *Horace: A Study in Structure*. Altertumswissenschaftliche Texte und Studien, Bd. 12. Hildensheim, West Germany: Olms.

Dettmer, Helena. 1984a. "The Design of the Catullan Corpus." Manuscript, Department of Classics, University of Iowa.

Frye, Northrop. 1957. *An Anatomy of Criticism*. New York: Atheneum, 1967.

Gould, Stephen Jay. 1977. *Ever Since Darwin*. New York: Norton.

Housman, A. E. 1922. "The Application of Thought to Textual Criticism." In J. Diggle and F. R. D. Goodyear, eds., *The Classical Papers of A. E. Housman*, vol. 3, pp. 1058–69. Cambridge: Cambridge University Press.

Kuhn, Thomas. 1977. *The Essential Tension: Selected Studies in Scientific Tradition and Change*. Chicago: University of Chicago Press.

Lakatos, Imre. 1976. *Proofs and Refutations: The Logic of Mathematical Discovery*. Vol. 1. Cambridge: Cambridge University Press.

Lucas, Robert E., Jr., and Thomas J. Sargent, eds. 1981. *Rational Expectations and Econometric Practice*. Vol. 1. Minneapolis: University of Minnesota Press.

McCrea, W. H. 1983. "Review of Allaby and Lovelock, *The Great Extinction*." *Times Literary Supplement* (July 19).

Mechling, Elizabeth Walker, and Jay Mechling. 1983. "Sweet Talk: The Moral Rhetoric Against Sugar." *Central States Speech Journal* 34 (Spring): 19–32.

Muth, John F. 1961. "Rational Expectations and the Theory of Price Movements." *Econometrica* 29 (July): 315–35. Reprinted in Arnold Zellner, ed., *Readings in Economic Statistics and Econometrics*, pp. 536–56. Boston: Little, Brown, 1968.

Polya, George. 1954. *Induction and Analogy in Mathematics*. Vol. 1 of *Mathematics and Plausible Reasoning*. Princeton, N.J.: Princeton University Press.

Rorty, Amelie Oksenberg. 1983. "Experiments in Philosophic Genre: Descartes' *Meditations*." *Critical Inquiry* 9 (March): 545–65.

Steiner, Mark. 1975. *Mathematical Knowledge*. Ithaca, N.Y.: Cornell University Press.

Syme, Ronald. 1956. "Piso and Veranius in Catullus." *Classica and Mediaevalia* 17: 129–34.

Willis, James. 1972. *Latin Textual Criticism*. Urbana: University of Illinois Press.

Zellner, Arnold, ed. 1968. *Readings in Economic Statistics and Econometrics*. Boston: Little, Brown.

[13]

THE LAWYERLY RHETORIC

OF COASE'S "THE NATURE

OF THE FIRM"

Coase Solved His Problem of Ethos
by Appeal to Axiom and Proof

An author, twenty-seven years old in 1937, of an essay called imposingly "The Nature of the Firm," an author who had not published a line when he drafted the article (early summer 1934; see Coase 1988c, p. 19; it was based closely on a lecture he gave in October 1932, at age twenty-one), "a young man who knew virtually no economics" (Coase 1988d, p. 35), had a problem. The problem was to establish in the reader's mind a character worth listening to. In 1960, by contrast, forty-nine years old and well-known if not yet famous in economics, he had no such problem, and could start in a more offhand, self-deprecating way, using even the deadly beginning "This paper": "This paper is concerned with those actions of business firms which have harmful effects on others" (Coase 1960, p. 95).

For his exordium Ronald Coase declared that "Economic theory has suffered in the past from a failure to state clearly its assumptions" (Coase 1937, p. 32). He was drawing on the rhetoric of axiomatization, the French claim since Descartes that we know what we mean only if we know what axioms we have started with. Such claims were helpful for a young economist even in 1937, and have since become compulsory. Coase acknowledged with a citation to Nicholas Kaldor (among appeals in the paragraph to the authority of five other well-known economists) "a trend in economic theory towards starting analysis with the individual firm and not with the industry" (Coase 1937, p. 32), a tendency pronounced in Hicks's *Value and Capital* (1939) and brought to perfection as the main method of economics by Paul Samuelson. Assume a maximizing individual self-aware of his constraints and tastes, and proceed. You will then know what you mean. Many econ-

87

88

The Lawyerly Rhetoric of Coase's "The Nature of the Firm"

omists cannot now understand an argument unless it is expressed axiomatically.

But Coase did not in the article or in his later work actually carry out the Cartesian program of his exordium. In the event, his was a British, empirical, and nonmathematical approach, altogether scrappier and less formal. He got into economics, he has said, through courses in "works and factory management" in 1930–1931, "for which I was singularly ill-suited, but what else was there for someone to do who did not know Latin and did not like mathematics?" (Coase 1988b, p. 5; at Coase 1998d, p. 45, he remarks, "fortunately for me, 1932 saw the height of the Depression, there were no jobs in industry, and I went to Dundee [School of Economics and Commerce] and became an economist"). Coase has never been an economist in the Samuelsonian mode, in love with rigor of a mathematical kind. He was as enthusiastic as any young economist in the 1930s about the new apparatus, which "has the advantage that one could cover the blackboard with diagrams [later with equations] and fill the hour in one's lectures without the need to find out anything about what happened in the real world" (Coase 1988c, p. 22). But he outgrew it. When George Stigler started in the 1960s calling his misunderstanding of one of Coase's propositions in the celebrated article of 1960 "Coase's Theorem," Paul Samuelson snorted, "Where's the theorem"? Where is the axiom system from which an if-then statement can be rigorously derived, the only way of knowing what we mean? Not in "The Problem of Social Cost," nor in "The Nature of the Firm."[1]

Coase also speaks the language of highbrow economic science, establishing an ethos worth believing, when late in the paper he ponderously generalizes: "Other things being equal, therefore, a firm will tend

1. I should mention my longstanding conviction that the misnamed "Coase's Theorem" (it is Smith's or Edgeworth's or Arrow-Debreu's Theorem, misnamed by that fine student of economic thought, George Stigler) is not the point of Coase's article in 1960 (see McCloskey 1985, pp. 335–40; and the full argument in McCloskey 1997b). The article was *not* meant to show that we live already in the best of all possible worlds (as Stigler was inclined to assume in this and other cases) but, on the contrary, that if we did live in such a world there would of course be no need for policy, as economists have been pointing out since Smith. In fact, as Coase argued also in the 1937 article, transaction costs put our world far away from the blackboard optimum. But I have given up hope of persuading any other economist of this interpretation, since the only economist who shares it is R. H. Coase (Coase 1988a, pp. 15, 174), and we know how unpersuasive he has been. Coase's chief contribution to economics has been to remind economists, as he does when complaining about Kaldor assuming "all relevant prices" are known, "but this is clearly not true of the real world" (Coase 1937, p. 38n. 18). The misunderstanding of the Coase Theorem arises from economists thinking that Coase is trying, like them, to flee the world.

The Lawyerly Rhetoric of Coase's "The Nature of the Firm"

to be larger: (a.) the less the costs of organzing" and so forth. The "other things being equal," "therefore," and "tend" are careful and conventional boilerplate in the contract between reader and economic Scientist. When claiming the ethos of Scientist the young Coase was especially fond of "tend to," the phrase becoming virtual anaphora on p. 46 (Coase 1937), repeated in all six of the complete sentences on the page and once in the footnotes.

Such a treatise-rhetoric was popular in economics at the time. Likewise Coase indulged in outlining, anticipation, and summary, the curse of modern prose, borrowed from the Germanic textbooks of an earlier age: phrases like "The point has been made in the previous paragraph" (Coase 1937, p. 44); "The problem which has been investigated in the previous section" (p. 47); "This point is further discussed below" (p. 51n. 41); and "The factors mentioned above" (p. 53) litter the essay. Economics had developed a rhetoric of close outlining, treatise-like, the better to win the victory on the blackboard, which may be seen in works like Marshall's *Principles* (1920) or in its most tedious form in Irving Fisher's *The Theory of Interest* (1930): "First Summary," "Introduction," "The Theory in Words," "The Theory in Mathematics," "Further Discussion," "Second Summary," "The Theory in Words," "The Theory in Mathematics," . . . "First Approximation in Geometric Terms," "Second Approximation in Geometric Terms," "Third Approximation," and so forth (Fisher 1930, pp. xiii–xiv). Economists regard Fisher's great but unreadable book as a masterpiece of exposition, which is a measure of the discipline's understanding of exposition.

But Coase Was an Advocate, Not a Prover

Coase's core rhetoric, however, as becomes apparent after a page or two, is not really Cartesian or Scientific or Treatise-like. It is lawyerly. That's the main point about Coasean rhetoric: it takes as much from the Law School as from the Department of Economics, and promises therefore a new style of economic science.

The paper reads like a brief. Unusually for an economist trained in the English-speaking world (it was commonplace on the Continent), Coase was immersed from the beginning in the study of the law. He testified that during his two years in residence as an undergraduate at the London School of Economics, 1929–1930, "I took no course in economics, and although some of the courses had an economic content, most did not. The courses to which I devoted the most time were those on law, particularly industrial law. I was fascinated by the cases and by legal

The Lawyerly Rhetoric of Coase's "The Nature of the Firm"

reasoning" (1988b, p. 6). The lawyerly rhetoric was no youthful fancy. It has defined the Coasean approach.

One lawyerly feature of his rhetoric, for example, is its disputatiousness. Coase repeatedly and firmly rejects this or that line of argument, after thorough enumeration of the possibilities (called *diallage* in Greek rhetoric), as when he turns back the claims of Frank Knight (an economist similar to Coase in many ways), "But those [like Knight] . . . would appear to be introducing a point which is irrelevant to the problem" (Coase 1937, pp. 40–41). Or, "The reason given by [the Marxist] Maurice Dobb is therefore inadmissable" (p. 47). The essay is filled with such sharp disputation, usually with a name attached: "This is surely incorrect" (p. 50); "Austin Robinson's conclusion . . . would appear to be definitely wrong" (p. 51n. 44); and so forth. The definiteness cannot have endeared the young man to the establishment in British economics, skewered thus in lawyerly cross-examination.

The adversarial rhetoric shows in the details, such as Coase's fondness for starting sentences with "But." "But . . . why is such organization necessary?" (p. 35); "But this is clearly not true in the real world" (p. 38n. 18); "But he does not develop the idea" (p. 39n. 19); "But it is difficult to believe that it is measures such as those . . . which have brought firms into existence" (p. 41). Three more times on p. 44, twice on p. 50 contradicting Knight, twice in the paragraph beginning at the bottom of p. 51 contradicting Kaldor, Austin Robinson, and Joan Robinson. It shows too in the overuse of "not only . . . but" (an ornament of Latin origin, though Coase disclaims Latin: "*non solum . . . sed etiam*"), as twice in the first paragraph.

Another lawyerly habit is Coase's frequent appeals to political relevance, against the academic rhetoric by then typical of economics. In this he was not unusual. The waste of the 1930s had made many economists, and even many poets, politically alert. The alternative of socialism was always on their minds: the puzzle of planning can "be summed up in one word, Russia" (1988b, p. 8). Thus, "Those who object to economic planning on the grounds that the problem is solved by price movements can be answered by pointing out that there is planning within our economic system which is quite different from the individual planning mentioned above [by which he means 'individuals . . . exercise foresight and choose between alternatives' (p. 34)], and which is akin to what is normally called economic planning" (Coase 1937, p. 35).

Coase is an attorney of economics in the arrangement, too. He follows the model of forensic speech, the six parts of a classical oration (for which see Lanham 1991, p. 171). The *exordium* catches the reader's at-

The Lawyerly Rhetoric of Coase's "The Nature of the Firm"

tention and is accomplished in his paper in the unnumbered paragraph preceding Section I. The *narratio* sets forth the facts and is followed by a *partitio* dividing controversial from uncontroverial propositions in explanation of the facts. Coase does both in Section I. The fact is the existence of the firm, which can be "explained" uncontroversially by positing an "entrepreneur" who organizes it (Coase 1937, p. 35). We must, however, narrow down the point of controversy to the "islands of conscious power in this ocean of unconscious co-operation like lumps of butter," in a memorable phrase of Dennis Robertson's, memorable mainly because Coase quoted it so aptly (p. 35). "The distinguishing mark of the firm is the supersession of the price mechanism" (p. 36). All right: Why supercede it? The answer is the *probatio*, the proof, given in the long Section II, ten pages out of twenty-two. The proposition is that "the main reason why it is profitable to establish a firm would seem to be that there is a cost of using the price mechanism" (p. 38). The proof imitates the rhetoric of law rather than that of mathematics except at the end, a peroration in the middle of an oration, which is expressed in the language of Scientific Law. In classical form, Sections III and IV constitute a *refutatio*, telling "why the reasons given above . . . are to be preferred to the other explanations," such as Knight's notion of "uncertainty" or the rising cost curve (p. 47, at the beginning of Section III). Section V is a *peroratio*, appealing briefly to the rhetoric of scientific test, and then claiming that the new way of looking at the firm is scientifically "manageable."

The peroration is in fact curiously muted, a British touch (thus the last paragraph of the two-page announcement of the discovery of DNA was devoted to thanking the sources of funding). The final sentence in the essay deprecates what has gone before: "But an elaboration of this point would take us far from our comparatively simple task of definition and clarification," the comparatively simple task of reorienting economics. A barrister might end her case so before the court of Queen's Bench; a French *avocat* or an American lawyer would not be able to resist the temptation to bluster.

The Lawyerly Rhetoric Appeals to the Facts

Another lawyerly (and British) feature of Coase's rhetoric is that facts or alleged facts of the world are repeatedly brought in to settle matters. You might imagine that economics would appeal to facts anyway, as a science. But economists are social philosophers as

92
_____

The Lawyerly Rhetoric of Coase's "The Nature of the Firm"

much as social historians, and have developed various rhetorical ex-
cuses to stay on the blackboard as long as possible. The mathematical
economist Tjalling Koopmans argued in his influential tract *Three Essays
on the State of Economic Science* (1957) for a program of research in economics of accumulating blackboard results strictly separated from facts,
"for the protection of both. It recommends the postulational method
[Descartes again] as the principal instrument by which this separation
is secured" (p. viii). Economists will routinely claim that they have
fewer facts to conjure with than do, say, physicists (the claim is false),
and must therefore rely on postulation methods. Another mathematical economist, Gerhard Debreu, argued so in his presidential address to
the American Economic Association. The physicists who economists
imagine they are emulating do not care about postulational consistency,
Debreu admitted, but economics is "denied a sufficiently secure experimental base," and therefore, "economic theory has had to adhere to the
rules of logical discourse and must renounce the facility of internal inconsistency" and stay on the blackboard (Debreu 1991, p. 2).

Not Coase, who has inveighed often against "blackboard economics"
(Coase 1988a, pp. 19, 28). Coase has been from the beginning of his career a keen visitor of economic sites, an astronomer of the business
world, engaging for example in economic sociology in his trip to America in 1932 while he was wrestling with the theory of the firm: "I still
remember one most instructive day spent in the office of a purchasing
agent, I think Union Carbide, listening to his telephone conversation"
(1988b, pp. 8–9). He quotes a letter he wrote to a friend at the time boasting that "I am quite a lawyer in my craftiness of putting questions. I can
get admissions regarding costs out of [businesspeople] without them
realizing that they have done so. . . . I can always get almost whatever I
want" (1988b, p. 14). Coase, contrary to the method economists espouse, actually talked to businesspeople. Shocking, really. In 1932, "I
confirmed that the risk [of exploitation of suppliers who had invested
to supply one demander] was real by discussion with businessmen. . . .
[But] I found that the problem worried me more than the businessmen
who had to deal with it" (Coase 1988d, p. 44).

And again the mere diction in "The Nature of the Firm" shows the
empirical lean. Coase for example favors the ugly phrase "the fact
that," though in fact employing it usually to introduce a logical consideration, not a fact (Coase 1937, pp. 35, 37, 52). A Cartesian rhetoric would
focus on consistencies and inconsistencies of logic in a strict sense, as
economics has under Samuelson-Koopmans-Debreu. The frequency of
Coase's appeal to facts is more lawyerly than it is late-twentieth-
century economistic. The sentence, "In fact, nothing could be more di-

verse than the actual transactions which take place in our modern world" (Coase 1937, p. 45), is one that Paul Samuelson could not have written.

And a Scientific rhetoric would confine the facts, if any, to the end of the paper, as a Test of the Hypothesis. Coase's paper seems to have been influenced in this regard by a Scientific model, propounded by Lionel Robbins at the London School of Economics. As I have noted, Section V, the *peroratio*, announces itself as asking how the theory "fits in with . . . the real world" (Coase 1937, p. 53). The received arrangement of modern articles in economics is, first, many pages of Theory and then, after a long time, the Test, in imitation of what the economists conceive to be Scientific Method. Coase's turn here seems parallel. But the effect of the "fit" in Section V is odd, since the paper is filled from beginning to end in a lawyerly way with appeals to the world's facts. Again and again the appeal is to the "relevance" of arguments (p. 53: "The factors mentioned above would seem to be the relevant ones"). Coase does not here, or ever in his career, launch out into model space far from the gravity of the world's facts. (Half of the articles in the more prestigious journals in economics nowadays achieve escape velocity [Leontief 1982]; it is notable that in 1932 Coase visited Leontief, who had just emigrated from Russia, and discussed the problem of the firm with him [Coase 1988b, p. 12]). And his end-game "fitting" with the world takes the form of a long quotation from a law book, which would hardly seem a clincher in the quantitative rhetoric of economics now. The recognition that laws are evidence is one of the fruits of the law and economics movement. Such evidence has never fit well with the 3-by-5 card version of Scientific Method that economists carry about, according to which a mere word is a nullity and numbers alone constitute Tests.

Thus Coase rejects the notion that people might set up firms for the sheer pleasure of bossing by noting that bosses normally make more than their subordinates (that is, the bosses do not seem to be paying for their pleasures, as the hypothesis of sheer pleasure would lead one to expect) and that firms exist in places where the pleasures of bossing must be small (Coase 1937, p. 38 and p. 38n. 16; cf. p. 43n. 26). The argument is not logically or empirically decisive. It is no theorem, certainly, in a Samuelsonian sense. And it is not a knock-down Scientific Test. Businesspeople speak often of their pleasure in being the boss, saying that they collect the salary merely to keep score. Yet as one argument in a legal case for a transaction-cost theory of the firm, Coase's little argument is fine. As Aristotle put it, such arguments are "enthymemes," that is, incomplete syllogisms of the sort that all science and law depend on.

The Lawyerly Rhetoric of Coase's "The Nature of the Firm"

And Yet Coase Is Indubitably an Economist

The third part of classical rhetoric, after Style and Arrangement, is Invention, the finding of arguments. By contrast with his style and arrangement, Coase's art of invention is not lawyerly. It is thoroughly and unblinkingly economistic. If his style and arrangement puzzle economists, his invention puzzles lawyers. Puzzling people is not a good way to get readers. Coase was creating—with a lag, he notes, of "thirty or forty years" (Coase 1988d, p. 33)—a new audience that could appreciate a lawyerly style of respect for facts and disputation combined with an economistic choice of postulates. Like Fogel, he was, in the French word popular with literary critics, an *auteur*, a maker of new forms. Coase's implied audience of lawyerly economists or economistic lawyers did not exist in 1937.

What is so deeply economistic and unlawyerly about Coase's reasoning is its apparent turning away from the matter at hand in order to settle it by looking at the alternatives. It would be as though a lawyer defending a thief were to argue that after all the man could have been a murderer, too, and should therefore be given credit for his restraint. An economist looks always at the other possibilities in a world of imagination, the opportunity cost, the alternatives forgone by the action in question. If the young man writing a lecture on the firm in 1932 "knew virtually no economics" he knew this lesson better than many professors of the subject do. In his paper discussing the meaning of the article Coase admires some notes of his around 1934 where he examined the prevention of fraud as a reason for making a firm. He argues from alternatives forgone: "a wholesaler may specialize on [*sic*] discovering who are reliable . . . and thus by using him, a consuming firm may eliminate the effects of fraud. But it is a cost and may be eliminated . . . by integration," that is, by making the consuming firm and the supplying firm into one big firm (Coase 1988c, p. 30). This sort of reasoning is at the heart of "The Nature of the Firm."

The reasoning is counterfactual, in a way that lawyers and historians find unsettling but economists like Coase (and Fogel and Muth and the rest) think is the only way of thinking. A lawyer thinking about someone violating a contract looks for what Aristotle called "efficient" causes, the immediate gain to be had, for example. An economist will look for "final" causes, the ultimate purpose served by taking one road rather than another diverging in a yellow wood.

Coase's rhetoric, in short, is mixed and therefore disorienting, which explains the long lag between the publication of the article and its influence. Although in some ways a typical piece of 1930s economics, its

The Lawyerly Rhetoric of Coase's "The Nature of the Firm"

rhetoric is quite lawyerly. Yet it was equally fervent in its devotion to economic reasoning (Coase attributes it to his teacher Arnold Plant: "I was the beneficiary of an extraordinary piece of luck" [Coase 1988b, p. 6], Plant's appointment to the London School of Economics in 1930). So Coase did not in 1937 have an audience of lawyers, either.

His Article Was about the Rhetoric in the Economy

There is another sense of the "rhetoric" of "The Nature of the Firm." Coase's work extends economics out into the world in which people speak to each other, that is, in which they practice rhetoric. Adam Smith, as usual, put the issue well two centuries ago. The division of labor, he wrote, is the "consequence of a certain propensity . . . to truck, barter, and exchange. . . . [I will not further consider] whether this propensity be one of those original principles in human nature . . . or whether, as seems more probable, it be the necessary consequence of the *faculties of reason and speech*" (1776, p. 17). *The Wealth of Nations* does not again mention the faculty of speech in a foundational role, though Smith, who began as a professor of rhetoric, did remark frequently on how business people and politicians talked. Half of his foundational formula, the faculty of reason, became in time the characteristic obsession of economists, though again Smith did not much pursue it. Economic Man is not a Smithian character. It was later economists, especially Paul Samuelson, who reduced economics to the reasoning of a constrained maximizer, Seeking Man. *Speaking* Man never figured much, by contrast, even among institutionalist economists. A man acted silently, by and for himself. That is what utility functions or institutions or social classes or property rights are about, said the economists before Coase. As Coase summarized it, "The consumer [in conventional economic theory] is not a human being but a consistent set of preferences. . . . We have consumers without humanity, firms without organization, and even exchange without markets" (1988a, p. 3). No need to speak.

Smith would not have agreed. In his other book he dug behind the faculty of speech (which led to the propensity to exchange, which led to the division of labor, which led to the wealth of nations). He connected it to persuasion, which is to say, speech meant to influence others: "The desire of being believed, the desire of persuading, of leading and directing other people, seems to be one of the strongest of all our natural desires. It is, perhaps, the instinct on which is founded the faculty of speech, the

The Lawyerly Rhetoric of Coase's "The Nature of the Firm"

characteristic faculty of human nature" (1790, VII.iv.25, p. 336); Smith was the sort of writer who would have been well aware that he was using the same phrase here in *The Theory of Moral Sentiments* as he used in *The Wealth of Nations.*

The faculty of speech, so much the stock-in-trade of lawyers, is a mystery to economists. But it is a startlingly large part of economic activity and cannot continue to be ignored. Take the categories of employment and make an educated guess as to the percentage of time spent on persuasion in each category. The preliminary result (see Klamer and Mc-Closkey 1995) is that 28.2 million out of 115 million civilian employees, or about a quarter of the labor force, is devoted to persuasion.

The result can be confirmed in other measures. Wallis and North measure 50 percent of national income as Coasean transaction costs, negotiation costs being part of these. Similarly, over half of American workers are white-collar. Some do not talk for a living, but in an extended sense many do, as for that matter do many blue-collar and especially pink-collar workers. And of the talkers a good percentage are persuaders. The secretary shepherding a document through the company bureaucracy is often called on to exercise sweet talk and veiled threats. Or notice the persuasion exercised the next time you buy a suit. Specialty clothing stores charge more than discount stores not staffed with rhetoricians. The differential pays for the persuasion: "It's you, my dear" or "The fish tie makes a statement." As Smith says (1762–1763, p. 352, spelling modernized), "everyone is practising oratory . . . [and therefore] they acquire a certain dexterity and address in managing their affairs, or in other words in managing of men; and this is altogether the practise of every man in most ordinary affairs . . . , the constant employment or trade of every man" and woman. Not constant, perhaps, but in Smith's time a substantial percentage and in modern times fully 25 percent.

Coase in other words is returning to the Smithian rhetorical program. He is extending the wholly silent economics of Marshall (which Axel Leijonhufvud has characterized, not without sympathy, as an economics of wind-up toys) to the faculty of speech. Coase's transactions costs are in fact the costs of talking. What makes for low transaction costs is exactly what makes for smooth conversation, the common tongue, the "precise definition" of the mathematician. What lies behind the phrase "transaction costs" are precisely the talk of businesspeople. "I will buy with you, sell with you, talk with you, and so following. . . . What news on the Rialto?" Talk establishes the relationships for doing business. You might say that it establishes a repeated game—or at least the atmosphere of a repeated game, reassuring peo-

The Lawyerly Rhetoric of Coase's "The Nature of the Firm"

ple that they have implicitly promised to act as though they were friends with the other. Imagine a blackjack table without banter. The economic purpose of the table is to separate the sucker from his money in a pleasant way. If the dealer were merely coldly efficient then the machines that simulate blackjack would be just as popular as the live tables. They are not.

Coase's bridge between institutions and neoclassical economics is of course what has come to be called "transaction costs" (he called them "marketing costs"; Coase 1937, pp. 40, 42, 43, 43 n.24). These are the costs of "discovering what the relevant prices are" (p. 38), "negotiating and concluding a separate contract for each transaction" (pp. 38–39), "forecasting" (p. 39), "uncertainty" (p. 40), and sales taxes and price controls (p. 41). By his own account, "The solution [to the problem of why firms were necessary, considering that markets made decisions automatically] was to realize that there were costs of making transactions in a market economy and that it was necessary to incorporate them into the analysis" (1988b, p. 17).

But Coase's extension of economics into the world of lawyerly talk is cautious, keeping the faculty of reason constantly in view. Coase asks what a reasoning manager would do when faced by an offer from the market to produce crank shafts at a lower price than his own plant. The analysis looks into the firm, but the viewpoint is still that of the bourse. For example, the desires for independence or mastery do not function alone. Coase puts them in a market, noting as an economist reflexively would that workers enjoying subordination "would accept less work under someone" and that bosses enjoying bossing "might be willing to give up something in order to direct others" (1937, p. 38).

The older institutionalists in Germany and the United States had noted before the First World War that neoclassical economics ignores institutions. But they made a mistake that the slow development of a Coasean institutionalism has avoided. The leap to the direct study of institutions, though obvious and understandable, proved to be a mistake because it unnecessarily abandoned the Faculty of Reason in order to better pursue the Faculty of Speech. It was lawyerly without being also economistic. Most of the law professors critical of the law and economics movement have this problem, that they have not mastered as Coase had at age twenty-one the reasoning of opportunity cost. A modern embodiment of the mistake, for example, is the work of the business historian Alfred Chandler, who knows as much about economic reasoning as a Samuelsonian economist knows about business speech. Both are glad of their ignorance. A Coasean economics, by contrast, learns both.

___

The Lawyerly Rhetoric of Coase's "The Nature of the Firm"

Coasean Economics Is Anti-Modernist, "Gothic," Postmodern in Its Rhetoric

I have said that Coasean economics as exhibited even in the article of 1937 is British, lawyerly, empirical; not French, Samuelsonian, and mathematical. John Ruskin, the nineteenth-century critic of architecture (I do not recommend his views on economics), noted that the search for a crystalline Ideal has been an incubus on classical and Renaissance, and now we may say modernist, architecture. He attacked the tyranny of the lonely genius, seeking by contemplation in his warm room a system to impose upon us all. Of the Renaissance he wrote,

> Its main mistake . . . was the unwholesome demand for perfection at any cost. . . . Men like Verrocchio and Ghiberti [consider Marx or Samuelson] were not to be had every day. . . . Their strength was great enough to enable them to join science with invention, method with emotion, finish with fire. . . . Europe saw in them only the method and the finish. This was new to the minds of men, and they pursued it to the neglect of everything else. "This," they cried, "we must have in our work henceforward"; and they were obeyed. The lower workman secured method and finish, and lost, in exchange for them, his soul. (Ruskin 1851–1853, pp. 228–29)

Ruskin's argument fits positivism in economics and elsewhere, which seeks an all-embracing, testable Theory apart from the practical skills of the statesman, the craftsman, or the economic scientist. An "interpretive economics," as Arjo Klamer, Metin Cosgel, and Don Lavoie began to call it at the end of the 1980s, would turn the other way, as economists do in practical work (see Lavoie 1990, Cosgel and Klamer 1990). It is in Ruskin's terms "Gothic economics," an end to searching for a grail of a unified field theory, an awakening from Descartes' Dream. As Ruskin said again, "It requires a strong effort of common sense to shake ourselves quit of all that we have been taught for the last two centuries, and wake to the perception of a truth . . . : that great art . . . does *not* say the same thing over and over again. . . . [T]he Gothic spirit . . . not only dared, but delighted in, the infringement of every servile principle" (Ruskin 1851–1853, pp. 166–67).

And that is the point of Coase's rhetoric, evident even in his maiden effort. He inverts the hierarchy of theory and practice. Most people have a simple theory of theory, in which mere dolts apply to practice the "method and finish" of theorists. But it is a servile theory. The Gothic spirit is seen in the best works of applied economics, from the economic

The Lawyerly Rhetoric of Coase's "The Nature of the Firm"

historian Robert Fogel, say, or the agricultural economist Theodore Schultz; from the financial economist Robert Shiller or the statistical economist Edward Leamer; and above all in the legal economics of Ronald Coase. It is not seen in the routine science of the field, servile to the undoubted genius of Paul Samuelson, Kenneth Arrow, and Lawrence Klein.

George Stigler and other methodologists who huddled around the corpse of logical positivism in the 1950s and 1960s succeeded in overcoming such common sense. Positive economics was useful for a time, up to about 1965, in forcing economists into a narrow program worth attempting. But it was and is a sort of voluntary imbecility, as the crystallographer and philosopher Michael Polanyi described the 3-by-5 card theory of Scientific Method. It was the bad rhetoric that only a narrow range of reasoning is needed because only the narrow reasoning is properly Scientific. Under such a methodology it does not matter whether an argument is rich or relevant or persuasive. We are to be nourished on certain scraps of utilitarian ethics, certain demonstrably irrelevant statistical tests, and certain rules of evidence enshrined in the oldest handbooks of positivism and behaviorism. The rhetoric has had a disastrous effect on scholarly standards in Chicago School economics, and if it had been even more strenuously enforced would have made Ronald Coase's career impossible.

Coase's "Gothic" economics, on the contrary—to revive another word much maligned that embodies common sense and common morality—is "casuistic" rather than universalist, common law rather than jurisprudential. It is a case-by-case approach: if you think on the blackboard the lighthouses are perfect examples of pure public goods, pull down the books, take depositions, and examine the actual case (thus Coase 1974). If you think that beekeepers and orchardmen are perfect examples of the impossibility of solving externalities by contract, do the same (Cheung 1973). Albert Jonsen and Stephen Toulmin have rescued the word "casuistic" from the contempt into which it has fallen (compare "rhetoric," "pragmatism," "anarchism"). They take it as a throughly modern approach to ethics, in the context of the revival of the Aristotelian studies of the particular virtues (Jonsen and Toulmin 1988). Coase's approach to economics is in this sense precisely casuistic, looking for the stories and metaphors and facts and logics that fit the case at hand, and avoiding the unreasonable obsession with one of them alone. A style of ethical storytelling that insists that cases matter as much as principles is foreign to most of modern economics. As Coase has argued since 1937, largely unheeded, economics and law need a rhetoric that is lawyerly and economistic at the same time.

BIBLIOGRAPHY

Cheung, Steven N. S. 1973. "The Fable of the Bees." *Journal of Law and Economics* 16 (April): 11–13.

Coase, Ronald H. 1937. "The Nature of the Firm." *Economica* 4 (November): 386–405. Reprinted in Coase 1988a, to which reference is made.

Coase, Ronald H. 1960. "The Problem of Social Cost." *Journal of Law and Economics* 3 (1960): 1–44. Reprinted in Coase 1988a, to which reference is made.

Coase, Ronald H. 1974. "The Lighthouse in Economics." *Journal of Law and Economics* 17 (October): 357–376. Reprinted in Coase 1988a.

Coase, Ronald H. 1988a. *The Firm, the Market, and the Law*. Chicago: University of Chicago Press.

Coase, Ronald H. 1988b. "The Nature of the Firm: Origin." *Journal of Law, Economics, and Organization* 4 (Spring): 3–17.

Coase, Ronald H. 1988c. "The Nature of the Firm: Meaning." *Journal of Law, Economics, and Organization* 4 (Spring): 19–32.

Coase, Ronald H. 1988c. "The Nature of the Firm: Influence." *Journal of Law, Economics, and Organization* 4 (Spring): 33–47.

Cosgel, Metin, and Arjo Klamer. 1990. "Entrepreneurship as Discourse." Manuscript,Departments of Economics, University of Connecticut/George Washington University.

Debreu, Gerard. 1991. "The Mathematization of Economic Theory." *American Economic Review* 81 (March): 1–7.

Hicks, J. R. 1939. *Value and Capital*. Oxford: Oxford University Press.

Jonsen, Albert R., and Stephen Toulmin. 1988. *The Abuse of Casuistry: A History of Moral Reasoning*. Berkeley: University of California Press.

Klamer, Arjo, and D. N. McCloskey. 1995. "One-Quarter of GDP is Persuasion." *American Economic Review* 92 (May): 191–95.

Koopmans, Tjalling. 1957. *Three Essays on the State of Economic Science*. New York: McGraw-Hill.

Lanham, Richard. 1991. *A Handlist of Rhetorical Terms*. 2d ed. Berkeley: University of California Press.

Lavoie, Don C., ed. 1990. *Economics and Hermeneutics*. London: Routledge.

Leontief, W. 1982. "Letter: Academic Economics." *Science* 217: 104, 107.

Ruskin, John. 1851–1853. *The Stones of Venice*. 3 Vols. New York: Peter Fenelon Collier, 1890.

Smith, Adam. 1776. *An Inquiry into the Nature and Causes of the Wealth of Nations*. R. H. Campbell, A. S. Skinner, and W. B. Todd, eds. 2 Vols. Indianapolis: Liberty Classics, 1981.

[14]

Donald N. McCloskey

Some Consequences of a Conjective Economics

Let a man get up and say, "Behold, this is the truth," and instantly I
perceive a sandy cat filching a piece of fish in the background. Look, you
have forgotten the cat, I say.

Virginia Woolf, *The Waves* (1931)

Arjo Klamer (1990) has a way of describing what is peculiar about modern economics. He draws a square to stand for the rigid, axiomatic method that dominates most journals in the field. The square, he points out, is the ideal shape of modernist architecture and painting, of Mondrian and Mies van der Rohe. Squares are about facts and logic. Show me the theorem. Then he draws a circle some distance from the square. Circles are about metaphor and story. Circle reasoning is the other half. Tell me your story. Since the seventeenth century, and especially during the mid-twentieth century, the square and the circle have stood in nonoverlapping spheres, sneering at each other.

Klamer's diagrammatic parable, of course, has a feminist interpretation. Whether or not there is any truth to it, the myth of our culture says that men do the squares and women the circles. Regardless of what men and women actually do statistically speaking, the claims about what they do exist as cultural objects. It may or may not be correct that women in our culture have deeper friendships than men. But in any case the stereotype exists and can be used to criticize a foursquare economics that has no room for friendships, deep or otherwise. It may or may not be correct that women communicate

I thank the participants in the conference at the University of Iowa on Women's Bodies/Women's Voices: The Power of Difference, a seminar at Iowa's Project on Rhetoric of Inquiry, and the CSWEP session at the Southern Economic Association meetings in San Antonio for their comments. I have benefited from written comments by Barbara Bergmann, Kathleen Biddick, Eleanor Birch, Paula England, Susan Feiner, Tara Gray, Sarah Hanley, Katherine Hayles, Jane Humphries, Evelyn Fox Keller, Linda Kerber, Joanne McCloskey, Laura McCloskey, Marjorie McElroy, Julie Nelson, Elyce Rotella, Sibyl Schwarzbach, Diana Strassmann, and an anonymous referee for the University of Chicago Press. They do not agree with everything I say. Some of the themes in the paper are explored further in *If You're So Smart: The Narrative of Economic Expertise* (Chicago: University of Chicago Press, 1990) and in *Knowledge and Persuasion in Economics* (Cambridge: Cambridge University Press, 1993).

with stories of somebody's life, men with unnarrated facts such as astounding baseball trivia.[1] But in any case the stereotype can be used to criticize an economics that does not realize it depends on stories. The round, "feminine" arguments can be construed as "modes of argument suppressed by modern economics," which is square.

Klamer points out how crazy it is to insist that the only arguments that are really scientific are the square ones. Crazy, but common. His point can be put economically: argumentative styles, like countries, have different endowments and tastes; some trade between them would therefore be mutually advantageous.

That is, because men and women live somewhat differently they differ on average in their ways of approaching economics. The way certain women actually or might or should approach economics is good. Some of the limitations of economics can be traced to its square masculinity, understanding "masculinity" to be a cultural not a biological product. A feminine economics would in some ways be better. Above all, both modes of argument, round or square, should be available to economists, male or female, and both should be accorded scientific prestige.

That "feminine" qualities are not unique to women does not prevent an inquiry into a difference, as long as there is a notable difference on average. There is no need to take a stand on nature *versus* nurture to admit that for some reason men and women at present think rather differently, especially about society. The assertion is no more controversial than an assertion that Japanese and Americans at present think rather differently, especially about society. Yet women often think and act in ways that we stereotypically associate with men, and vice versa. Characteristics of women and men, Americans and Japanese, overlap, as in body weights and lengths of hair. We are mainly human beings, not women or Japanese. For most purposes a difference in gender or nationality is less important than what we have in common— human language, mathematics, history, social origin, passion, intelligence. For most scholarly purposes male and female economists have more in common with each other than with male and female classicists.

And yet the gender differences might be worth noting for describing the science. A "tetrad" in Greek is a set of four things. "Rhetoric" is the art of argument, good or bad, from Pythagoras to advertising. Sciences use four things to argue, the four of the "rhetorical tetrad": fact, logic, metaphor, and story. Half of the tetrad is the methodical dyad of fact and logic, that is, Klamer's square. The other half is the creative dyad of metaphor and story, Klamer's circle. But thinking requires both dyads, the whole tetrad: $2 + 2 = 4$ in a complete science. In truth, all four parts of the tetrad participate in me-

1. What major league pitcher retired every batter he faced for twelve innings yet lost the game? Answer: Harvey Haddix of the Pirates, May 26, 1959. He lost on an error, a walk, and a hit in the thirteenth inning. Wow!

thodicalness and in creativity. As it was put by the philosopher of science Mary Hesse, one of the early contributors to the new understanding of science, "rationality consists just in the continuous adaption of our language to our continually expanding world, and metaphor is one of the chief means by which this is accomplished" (1966, 176–77). Story, too. "We are storytelling animals," says Stephen Jay Gould, and shows the fact with the history of paleontology (1989, 70; 1980, ch. 3). All his works shows the storied character of evolution: "In the steretyped image, scientists rely upon experiment and logic [—] a middle aged man in a white coat (most stereotypes are sexist). . . . But many sciences do not and cannot work this way. As a paleontologist and evolutionary biologist, my trade is the reconstruction of history" (1980, 27).

Pieces of the tetrad are not enough. The allegedly scientific and masculine half of the tetrad, the fact and logic, falls short of an adequate economic science, or even a science of stars or arthropods. The allegedly humanistic and feminine half falls short of an adequate art of economics, or even a criticism of form and color. Scientists, scholars, and artists had better be factual and logical. But they had also better be literary. The scientists had better devise good metaphors and tell good stories about the first three minutes of the universe or the last three months of the economy. A scientist with only half of the rhetorical tetrad is going to mess up her science.

It is easy to catch economists, as good scientists, in the act of using metaphors and stories for their science. Outsiders will find this easier to see than the economists will because the economists are trained to think of themselves as fact and lógic users. They do not realize that they are also the poets and novelists of the ordinary business of life. To an outsider it is obvious that economists are using metaphors (analogies, similes, comparisons of one realm with another) when they speak of the demand "curve" for housing in New York City or the "human capital invested in a child, which is of course a durable good." It is obvious to the outsider that economists are using stories about a hog market once upon a time out of equilibrium or about the causes in the olden days of modern economic growth.

It is not an attack on ecoríomics to say that like other sciences it uses the whole of the tetrad. Let "God" be a metaphor of certitude beyond day-to-day persuasion (the God metaphor was lively and potent before the sea of faith receded, and nostalgia for its certitude remains). The truth is that not this "God" but we humans make the metaphors and tell the stories; not God but humans identify the facts and choose the logics (note the plurals). No part of the tetrad is wholly God-given and nonhuman, whether in physics or in economics. The models and histories in economics are not facts made by nature or logic immanent in the universe but words made by human art.

The art does not make them arbitrary; it merely makes them various. To admit that what we say in science is socially constructed is not to fall into

Valley-girl, touchy-feely relativism or to advocate anything goes. Niels Bohr, who was not a touchy-feely, said, "It is wrong to think that the task of physics is to find out how nature is. Physics concerns what we can say about nature. . . . We are suspended in language. . . . The word 'reality' is also a word, a word which we must learn to use correctly" (quoted in Moore 1966, 406).

In any event it is a crazy dualism to insist that *either* we merely read what God's Reality presents to us *or* we construct the world wholly without reference to the facts of the matter. The better model is fishing. The fish are there by God's command, and if they were not then no human ingenuity in making nets would bring them up. But likewise a sea full of fish does not feed humans without nets made by human hands. We need both to eat on Fridays.

A paleontologist, for example, is constrained by what in fact happened to life, and by what he thinks are relevant logics.[2] Nonetheless, with the same choice of fact and logic he can tell the story in varied ways—to use the words in paleontology, he can tell it as "gradualist" or "catastrophist." The movie can be run in dignified slow motion or in frantic lurches. The same sort of thing happens in economics. The workplace can be seen with a metaphor of conflict, as in Marxian economics, or with a metaphor of exit and entry to markets, as in neoclassical economics. How we judge the two depends on their fit with the facts, with the logic, with the story, and with the other metaphors we have found useful. The variety of metaphors and stories does not make all of them equally good or equally important for every purpose, any more than the variety of facts or logics makes all of them equally good or important for every purpose. No one is proposing, to repeat, that anything goes, merely that a life in science is more complicated than checking first-order predicate logic against uncontroversial facts. To criticize the varieties of facts, logics, metaphors, and stories you have to recognize that they are being constructed and postulated and imagined and told.

For about fifty years economists have believed themselves to be users only of fact and logic, the square rather than the circle, half of the rhetorical tetrad, the masculinist half. During the 1940s they shared belatedly in the temporary narrowing of Western culture called "positivism" or "modernism" (Booth 1974; Klamer 1990, 1987). Modernism has roots as deep as Descartes and Plato, but it became the whole of what we call thinking only in the early twentieth century. As Virginia Woolf said in 1924, "On or about December 1910, human character changed" (Woolf 1967 [1924], 320). Certain male philosophers in the West came suddenly to believe that their whole subject could be narrowed down to an artificial language; certain male architects narrowed

---

2. In the late twentieth century "logics," to repeat, are plural, like geometries. They are Aristotelian, first-order predicate, fuzzy, deontic, modal, relevant, multivalued, informal, epistemic, paraconsistent, and so on and so forth through the various ways that people can formalize what they are saying.

their whole subject to a cube; certain male painters narrowed their whole subject to a surface. Out of this narrowness was supposed to come insight and certitude.

Insight did come (not certitude, alas). After modernism in philosophy we know more about languages lacking human speakers. In architecture we know more about buildings lacking tops. In painting we know more about pictures lacking depth of field. When news of modernism got out to economics around 1940 it yielded some worthwhile insight, too. In economics after modernism, after the masculinist programs of Paul Samuelson and Tjalling Koopmans, we know more about economic models lacking contact with the world.

On the whole the narrowing did not work out very well. The failure of modernism in economics and elsewhere in the culture does not say it was a bad or stupid idea to try. And it certainly does not say that we should now abandon fact and logic, surface and cube, and surrender to the irrational. We are all very glad to keep whatever we have learned from the Bauhaus or the Vienna Circle or the running of rats. We in economics are all very thankful to Smith, Marx, and Marshall for inspiring those wonderfully theorems by Arrow, Robinson, and Samuelson. It says merely that we should turn back to the work at hand equipped now with the full tetrad of fact, logic, metaphor, and story.

The modernist experiment in getting along with fewer than all the resources of human reasoning puts one in mind of the Midwestern rural expression, "a few bricks short of a load." It means cracked, irrational. A masculinist economics, such as we have had in most refined form since the 1940s, is irrational. To admit now that metaphor and story also matter in human reasoning does not entail becoming less rational and less reasonable, dressing in saffron robes, or tuning into "New Directions." On the contrary it entails becoming more rational and more reasonable, because it puts more of what persuades serious people under the scrutiny of reason. Modernism was rigorous about a tiny part of reasoning and angrily (one might say hysterically) unreasonable about the rest. The typical article on international economics is arranged in the modernist form: scandalously vague motivation, rigorous middle, and vague, even reckless, "implications for policy."[3]

Modernism seized the word "science" for its purposes. In English the word for a long time has been a club with which to beat on arguments the modernists did not wish to hear. "Science" has been a verbal weapon within the intelligentsia. English speakers over the past century and a half have used it in a peculiar way, as in British academic usage, arts and sciences, the "arts" of literature and philosophy as against the "sciences" of chemistry and geology. A historical geologist in English is a scientist; a political historian is not. The

---

3. I have in mind some recent work by William Milberg (1991) and Hans Lind (1992), who have analyzed the rhetorical structure of typical articles in international economics.

usage in English would puzzle an Italian father boasting of his studious daughter, *mia scienziata*, my learned one. He does not mean that she is a nuclear physicist. Italian and other languages use the science word to mean simply "systematic inquiry," as do French, Spanish, German, Dutch, Icelandic, Norwegian, Swedish, Greek, Gaelic, Polish, Hindi, Bengali, Tamil, Hungarian, Turkish, Korean, and Hebrew. Only English, and only the English of the past century, has made physical and biological science (definition 5b in the old *Oxford English Dictionary* [Oxford, 1933]) into, as the *Supplement* (1982; compare *OED*, 2d ed., 1989) describes it, "the dominant sense in ordinary use." It would be a good idea to reclaim the word for reasonable and rigorous argument.

The English and modernist error, to put it another way, is thinking of science and literature as two cultures. The author of the phrase, the scientist-novelist C. P. Snow, can hardly be blamed, since he lived and wrote at the peak of an anxious masculinism in British and American science—evinced, for example, in the mistreatment of Rosalind Franklin in the uncovering of DNA. Literature since romanticism and most particularly since aestheticism was written off as airy-fairy. The very work of middle-class men was paper shuffling and feminine. Only tough science and Hemingwayesque literature could assuage their dread. As Barbara Laslett has argued persuasively in writing of William Fielding Ogburn (1886–1959), one of the founders of the Chicago school of sociology and in his uncertain youth an advocate of quantitative methods, "Science so defined simultaneously offered a cultural space to which men could aspire without threat to their masculinity and provided a gatekeeping mechanism that limited women's entry" (1990, 429).

The two-cultures talk is not written in the stars, though it is common enough and encouraged by the faculty and the deans. The dualism drips with sexist mythology, and the women co-opted by such dualism are not immune. A dean of research at a large state university gave a talk a couple of years ago in which she spoke of the humanities as what is left over after the (physical and biological) sciences, and then after them the social sciences, have expended their eloquence. The humanities in her mind are a residuum for the mystical and the ineffable, the stuff of circles, not squares. The dean, who was a social scientist, thought she was being good natured. The bad-natured remarks muttered from each side are worse: that if we mention metaphors we are committed to an arty irrationalism; that if we mention logic we are committed to a scientific autism.

One is tempted to shake them both and say, "Get serious." The sciences, such as economics, require supposedly humanistic and "feminine" methods in the middle of their sciences; likewise, the arts and humanities require fact and logic, right in the middle of their own systematic inquiries. It is not so much that metaphor is an alternative to fact (true though this sometimes is) as that the construction of facts requires metaphors—for example, the metaphor of light as quanta, as against waves, is essential for certain measurements in physics. Without the metaphor no one would have thought to do the measurements. So, too, in economics: without the metaphor of the nation as a business enterprise the measurement of the "national accounts" would not happen; without the story line of "development" the historical measurement of income would not happen. The items in the rhetorical tetrad work together, each necessary for the job of the other. Leonardo da Vinci used stories and logic; Newton used logic and metaphors; Darwin used facts and stories. Science is literary, requiring metaphors and stories in its daily work.

Speaking of a science such as economics in literary terms, of course, inverts a recent and anxiety-producing hierarchy. Science is masculine and high status; art is feminine and low status; therefore, for God's sake, let's demarcate science from art. But contrary to the century-long program to demarcate science from the rest of the culture—a strange program when you think of it—science is after all a matter of arguing. The ancient categories of argument still apply. Satisfying stories are recognized in a complete psychology (Gergen and Gergen 1986; Bruner 1986); beautiful metaphors in a complete physics (Weinberg 1983); so, too, in economics after modernism (Klamer, McCloskey, and Solow, eds. 1988).

The dualisms square/circle, fact/story, logic/metaphor, science/art, numbers/words, cognition/feeling, rigor/intuition, truth/opinion, fact/value, hard/soft, positive/normative, objective/subjective may be useful as tentative descriptions. Certainly they come up a lot in methodological disputes, usually as conversation stoppers. But they are crazy when they are imagined, as the modern byword has it, to cut the universe at its joints. Such dualisms, it need hardly be emphasized, reenact the Mother of All Dualisms, male/female, as Julie Nelson, Ann Jennings, and others point out in their essays in this volume. Men insist on square, fact, logic, science, numbers, cognition, rigor, truth, hardness, positiveness, and the objective with a comical, anxious rigidity of the sort the comedian John Cleese makes fun of. The anxiety resembles nothing more than a man worrying that he might be taken for a woman.

The distinction objective/subjective, for example, does not withstand much scrutiny. The modern usage (a reversal, incidentally, of the medieval usage) was popularized by Kant in the late eighteenth century and came into English with Coleridge in the early nineteenth century. For scientific purposes it is useless. We cannot know what is objective, if it means the Reality that is in the mind of God. In the twentieth century we humans are alone with the universe and have to make of it what we can with our human ways of seeing and talking. Two-and-a-half millennia of attempts since the Greeks to vault to a higher realm in which we will *know* the objective, will have *solved* the problem of epistemology, will *hear* what God is whispering to us, have failed.

Similarly, we cannot know what is subjective, if it means the wholly personal place from which each of us looks out. We cannot, after Freud, know it even in our own minds, and certainly never completely in someone else's.

What we can and do know, to coin a term, is the *conjective*. It is neither the square nor the circle, neither the objective nor the subjective. It is what we know together, by virtue of a common life and language. It is what economists know about the definition of the money supply or the prevalence of marginal cost pricing. It is what men and women know in their conversations, together or apart. As the mathematician Armand Borel noted, for practical purposes "something becomes objective . . . as soon as we are convinced that it exists in the minds of others in the same form that it does in ours, and that we can think about it and discuss it together" (1983, 13). Helen Longino, quoted in the introduction to this volume, gives the same social spin to "objectivity": it is "dependent upon the depth and scope of the transformative interrogation that occurs in any given scientific community." For practical purposes, in other words, we have only the "conjective."

The conjective is the milieu in which Klamer's square and circle sit. Imagine an amoebalike shape encompassing both the masculine square and the feminine circle, a fluid of words and symbols in which the two must float. That is where science actually goes on, never in the square or the circle alone but in the conversations that surround them. The conversations are subject to rigorous appraisal, more rigorous than the phony rigor of wholly square proofs or wholly round faiths. We do it daily in a science like economics, assessing a new paper on the basis of its fit in detail with our earlier conversations.

All right, so what? What is to be gained by such talk? This: a conjective economics, which admitted the "feminine" alongside the "masculine," would be better science because it would be more complete and persuasive. It would constitute a higher standard for a science, one of coherence in story as much as in axioms; of relevance in Bureau of Labor Statistics questionnaires administered as much as in its regressions.

The prefeminist economics I can speak of most convincingly is the neoclassical, a hard case in all senses. Compared with other schools of economics the neoclassicals are notably butch. They are a motorcycle gang among economists, strutting about the camp with clattering matrices and rigorously fixed points, sheathed in leather, repelling affection. They are not going to like being told that they should become more feminine.

Looking at the economy from a conjective point of view, putting the allegedly feminine and the allegedly masculine into conversation with each other, will, I say, enrich neoclassical economics. The project is enrichment, not impoverishment. I would *not* argue that economics is worthless in its square and masculine moods. But even the "conservative" and Chicago-school economics that I espouse, which seems to me admirably masculine, is open to feminine revision.

The purpose, in other words, is to encompass and extend what has been learned from men, not to dynamite it unthinkingly. As was noted recently by J. A. Boone, a feminist critic of literature, "the solution isn't simply to discard all 'offending' texts. . . . If we are to hang on to our Norman Mailers as well as our Margaret Atwoods, we need a more sophisticated means of evaluation than simply judging a book's contents in terms of its 'political correctness'" (1988, 2). He's right. We want to hang onto our Gary Beckers as well as our Joan Robinsons.

At a modest level one can beat masculine economics at its own game (pardon me) by a more conjective choice of postulates. Consider the economics of the family, explored by Becker and his associates (Becker 1981). In common with other Chicago economists working on law, history, politics, and economic development, Becker saw that economic reasoning could be applied to events beyond the usual, to families as much as to firms. Lucidity has come from this, and a welcome turn of economics to wide subjects.

For all its brilliance as a pioneering effort, though, Becker's program is constrained by its masculinity. For instance the family in Becker's world has one purpose, one utility function—guess whose?—unproblematically unified in the way that the neoclassical firm is supposed to be (see Folbre and Hartmann 1988, 188ff; and elsewhere in the present volume). Ironic commentary on the postulate of mastership within the family comes from a surprising direction. The late George Stigler, Becker's greatest fan and the very model of a modern Chicago economist, wrote: "It would of course be bizarre to look upon the typical family—that complex mixture of love, convenience, and frustration—as a business enterprise." Quite right. But then, with Stiglerian irony, he says truly that "therefore economists have devoted much skill and ingenuity to elaborating this approach" (1966, 21).

One neoclassical way to get beyond a masculine mastership has been illustrated by Marjorie B. McElroy and Mary Jean Horney in "Nash-Bargained Household Decisions: Towards a Generalization of the Theory of Demand" (1981). They view the household as a bargaining game among two players over the allocation of public and private goods. Consider it as double solitaire. To anyone in a family the setup has a familiar sound. The results of the McElroy-Horney model are detailed and plausible, yielding clean implications for labor force participation by women and by teenage children. It brings market solutions into the family (see, however, Brian Cooper's thorough and feminist commentary on such arguments [1990]).

A Darwinian route to the same result has been suggested by Howard Margolis in *Selfishness, Altruism, and Rationality: A Theory of Social Choice* (1982). He argues that for good evolutionary reasons a person is public spirited as well as narrowly selfish, having virtually two selves trading with each other. Margolis would probably agree that the argument applies literally to families: for some purposes (child-minding) the wife tends to be public spirited and the husband selfish; for others (protection) the man tends to be the public spirited one and the woman selfish.

Susan Feiner (1984), to give another example, takes a nonmarket view of the matter, making use of an analogy of families with serfdom. The analogy is again useful, though it would be more so if the Marxist economists would read more history. In the way that the serfdom of women threatens to break down under advanced capitalism, so, too, the serfdom of men in Western Europe broke down when it was pushed into contact with markets. (The push happened not in the sixteenth century, as a much-beloved piece of Marxist folklore says, but in the thirteenth.)

Another element in a conjective economics is taking difference seriously. From an Austrian perspective, for example, Karen Vaughn has questioned the neoclassical disdain for the committee, that ubiquitous and irritating institution, which so obviously does not achieve the efficient solution:

> The Austrian emphasis on the particularized and personalized qualities of knowledge are especially helpful to anyone who has ever worked closely with a group of people to get a job done, whether it be volunteer work in the neighborhood or church, organizing a project at work or running a family. People are all different, and women, I believe, are more tuned-in to that fact than most men. . . . Economists are predisposed to hate this kind of compromise since it probably isn't "the efficient solution." But the Austrian insight reminds us that for most problems where the welfare of many are concerned, there is no efficient solution. The committee is one way both to gather decentralized information and to get the affected parties to buy into the decision finally arrived at. (1988, 14–15)

I admit to harboring dark thoughts about committees myself, and have said frequently that the optimal size of an academic committee is one: all power to the deans. Dictatorship has been the man's model of society since Plato, or for that matter since the caves. Put a good man in charge. After all, says he, a football team has a quarterback who calls the plays and takes the blame. But the point made by Vaughn, presumably not the left guard of her high school football team, has merit as description and as democracy, in contrast to the military and sporting contexts in which men grow up.

Still further along the way to a conjective economics, and economics of what we know together, is taking solidarity seriously. After all, Adam Smith did: the book we economists all know is his book about greed; but his other great book, *The Theory of Moral Sentiments* (1759, 1790), is about love. I repeat that nothing biological is assumed in solidarity. In their essay on the sexist rhetoric of neoclassical and Marxist economics Nancy Folbre and Heidi

Hartmann quote with approval J. S. Mill's advanced views of 1869: "If women are better than men in anything it surely is in individual self-sacrifice for those of their own family. But I lay little stress on this, so long as they are universally taught that they are born and created for self-sacrifice" (1988, 194). Precisely. And I repeat that nothing especially virtuous about the stereotypical woman is being assumed either. Solidarity sounds like a swell idea until one reflects that Tojo, Hitler, and Mussolini raised empires by calling on it.

Anyway, neoclassical economics does not take solidarity seriously, except implicitly within the family and within the firm, and neither do any of the other schools. No wonder. *Vir economicus* sporting around the marketplace is stereotypically male: rule driven, simplemindedly selfish, uninterested in building relations for their own sake.[4] A cross between Rambo and an investment banker, our *vir economicus* has certain boyish charms, but a feminine solidarity is not one of them. When it suits his convenience he routinely defects from social arrangements, dumping externalities on the neighbors. *Femina economica,* by contrast, would more often walk down the beach to dispose of her McDonald's carton in a trash bin—not because she reasons in the manner of Kant (and again of men) that one must test one's behavior by hypothetical universalization ("Suppose *everyone* dumped their trash on their neighbors?") but because she feels solidarity with others. It is simply not done to dump trash on the beach; we do not treat our neighbors that way.

James Buchanan (another unexpected direction, this) has noted a consequence of taking *femina economica* and her solidarity seriously. If people

> do, in fact, behave in accordance with some version of the Kantian imperative [note that there is a conjective route to this], potential externalities, in the normal usage of this term, will tend to be internalized within the calculus of the actors. Individuals will tend to take into account the effects of their own actions on the situation of others than themselves. Hence [here is the remarkable turn], in such a world there can be no need for corrective collective or governmental intervention in the private decision process. It becomes impossible to observe "market failure" in the standard sense. (1979, 70ff)

A feminine economy would have less need of a paternalistic government. If everyone behaved like people do in Iowa, then socialism would have less to recommend it.

A related technical example in economics concerns the value of a human

4. By the way, Latin like many languages, but unlike modern English, had two words for man: *vir,* which means a "male adult" or "husband," like *Mann* in German or *anēr* in Greek, as distinct from *femina* or *mulier;* and *homo,* which means (and is cognate with the word) "human," like *Mensch* in German or *anthropos* in Greek. In patriarchal societies, of course, the distinction was a fine one. But *homo economicus* literally means "economic human," not "economic man."

life. The usual strategy is to infer the value from how individuals act when they buy insurance or choose risky but well-paying jobs. If a coal miner gets five dollars an hour more than a waiter/waitress of similar skill, and if enough people can move between the mine and the restaurant (a big if), then evidently the person just barely willing to switch to mining puts a value of five dollars on the dangers of the mine relative to work in the restaurant. The statistics of injury and death measure the danger she is actually facing. Therefore the implicit value she puts on her life, assuming she values it methodically and that there are no other amenities or disamenities of the two jobs, can be calculated. The same reasoning applies to more straightforward gambles with one's life, especially the gamble of life insurance. Alan Dillingham (1985) has summarized the estimates, arriving at a figure in the United States nowadays of one million dollars plus or minus half a million.

It has sometimes been noted, however, that individual self-valuation is only part of the value of a life (Usher 1985, 183). In a society with solidarity a life is technically speaking a public good, to be valued by summed values that the citizenry places on it. The whole value is the sum of all valuations of the life, by its owner and by others. Yet most economists have not noticed how it matters that the life is valued by him or her or thee. No human is an island; any human's death diminishes me because I am involved in humankind.

Remarkably, the only value of other lives recognized in the present literature is not the great misery of seeing others die but the cash *advantage* that accrues to the survivor through inheritance and the like. As an empirical matter these merely pecuniary advantages are probably dwarfed by the misery. Janet Guthrie may value her own life at $1,000,000, and enter formula-one auto racing with that figure in mind. But Jack Guthrie values her life, too, at $1,500,000, say, and Janet's mother values it at $2,000,000, her father at another $2,000,000, her best friend at another $1,000,000, and so on, down to the single dollar from that anonymous other part of humankind who never sends to know for whom the bell tolls.

The upshot is that the value of life calculated on the assumption of *vir economicus* is probably a small fraction of the correct, conjective measure, the result of our knowing value together, not as isolates. Janet is worth millions, not the one million at which she values herself. The consequences are grave. A value of human life, like it or not, must be used in designing roads and, when the courts allow more than earning power, in deciding personal injury cases. That's just economics. But a conjective economics would use a much higher figure than a masculine economics would, interfering more with the devil-may-care attitude of males, especially young ones, zooming about helmetless on their Kawasakis. Consequently, though a feminine economy would need spontaneously less interference, the interference that did take place would be more thorough—one might say, more motherly.

A conjective economics has other consequences, large and small. Hannah

Arendt once remarked that only a man would ignore a hurt to our grandchildren, which is to say that men might at present discount the future too much in pursuing present glory. Again, the omission of housework from the national income does not survive conjective scrutiny (see Folbre 1991; although even among male economists the omission has long seemed strange).[5] A conjective theory of labor relations, which would draw attention to the social meaning of employment and wages, might push farther down a road that men have tentatively explored, with their tortured and masculine notion of the "implicit contract" between worker and employer. A conjective view of immigration might find it harder to take the nationalist, I'm-all-right-Jack position that motivates present policy (Roback 1981). Economists better equipped than I am to see the economy with feminine eyes will think of twenty other ways in which an economics amended by women would differ from the male-centered version we now have.

Looking at the economy with feminine eyes, however, is made more difficult than it has to be by certain masculine rules of engagement. A conjective economics, valuing stereotypically feminine perspectives as much as stereotypically masculine perspectives, will be hobbled, corseted, awkwardly hoopskirted at the start if it accedes without protest to the man-made rules of the game. The masculine rules need to be resisted.

For example, questionnaires are disdained on methodological grounds in a masculine economics. Robin Bartlett (1985) suggests quite plausibly that a conjective economics, using what we know together, would make more use of questionnaires than economics nowadays does; in her presidential address to the Eastern Economic Association Barbara Bergmann (1975) had made the same point. The small percentage of papers in the *American Economic Review* that depend on questionnaires would startle other social scientists.

The reason economists give is, "If you just *ask* someone what they are doing they will tell you lies." Male economists use the argument reflexively whenever someone proposes to ask businesspeople why they are hiring or to ask consumers why they are buying. But hostility to questionnaires among men, and their eagerness to reduce questionnaires to numbers before considering the very words, appears to reflect a masculine idea of the ends and means of conversation. To the masculine argument against questionnaires a woman might reply that the response of course needs to be probed, considered, interpreted; but that doesn't make it unscientific, or even, come to think

5. I once asked the great economist Margaret Reid, the actual implementer of household economics (invented by her Ph.D. supervisor Hazek Kirk), a friend and colleague of mine at Chicago, whether she thought the housewife's work should be included in national income. I was disappointed by her answer, which was the conventional one that it is difficult to estimate (which of course is also true of the value of owner-occupied houses, governmental services, and most capital goods, each included in national income).

of it, different from other evidence. The "nonquestionnaire" evidence, after all, comes from responses about one's state of employment spoken to the interviewer from the Department of Labor.

The responses are more than mute facts. As Karen Vaughn has pointed out, in the masculine and neoclassical view of the world the only information comes from bumping up against constraints. Nobody *tells* anyone anything. You can see the neoclassical assumption in the way the new experimental economists talk about their work: they could if they wished examine the rhetoric of markets but usually they prefer to keep their "market" participants in isolation booths. About a fellow economist who claimed that he never "preached" at his children, but merely presented them with the "correct incentive structure" (if you foul up, you get punished, and presumably learn), Vaughn remarks, "My reaction was, first of all, I didn't believe him. . . . Children do not only learn by doing, they also learn by exhortation, conversation, story-telling and example. The advantage of verbal learning over learning by doing is that it saves the child's time" (1988, 16–17). Vaughn is speaking as a mother; I agree as a father, though as a father I can see what her colleague had in mind. I do not know if learning by fouling up is an especially male way of behaving, but there can be little doubt that it is an especially male way of seeing behavior. Show me the budget constraint and then shut up. Where in economics have you heard that before?[6]

The reduction of empirical work in economics to statistical fitting of formal models is another saver of masculine labor. The male economist confronted with facts will immediately subordinate them to a model, then to a statistical mechanism, which, he will claim stoutly in the face of most scientific experience, "tests" the model (my own work in economic history has this character). Evelyn Fox Keller recalls the metaphor used by the men of the early seventeenth century, so skilled in torture: Nature is to be put on the rack and tortured until she confesses her formulas. (In the end Dame Nature almost always confesses to formulas surprisingly consistent with the male investigator's model, and so in the end did the witch confess to the male suggestion that she rode through the air on a broom.)

Consider by way of contrast the great biologist, Barbara McClintock, who approached Nature with the idea that, as Keller puts it in writing of McClintock,

> organisms have a life and an order of their own that scientists can only begin to fathom. . . . [McClintock said] "there's no such thing as a central dogma into which everything will fit." . . . The

---

6. Arjo Klamer and I have estimated that persuasion—managers persuading employees, entrepreneurs persuading bankers, retailers persuading customers, professors persuading students—amounts to about a quarter of national income (Klamer and McCloskey 1991). So the "feminine" matter of persuasion is not optional.

> need to "listen to the material" follows from her sense of the or-
> der of things. . . . The complexity of nature exceeds our own
> imaginative possibilities. . . . Her major criticism of contempo-
> rary research is based on what she sees as inadequate humil-
> ity. . . . [The dualisms of] subject-object, mind-matter, feeling-
> reason, disorder-law . . . are directed towards a cosmic unity
> typically excluding or devouring one of the pair. (1985, 162–63)

The style of empirical inquiry that spends six years on the aberrant pigmentation of a few kernels of corn is rare in economics, but no one is surprised to
find it disproportionately among female economists: Margaret Reid of Iowa
State and Chicago, for example, in her studies of the consumer spending and
death rates, or Mary Jean Bowman of Chicago in her studies of education, or
Dorothy Brady of Pennsylvania and of the Women's Bureau at the Department
of Labor in her studies of consumer spending in the distant past, or Anna
Jacobson Schwartz of the National Bureau of Economic Research and New
York University in her studies of money. "The thing was dear to you for a
period of time, you really had an affection for it," said McClintock (Keller
1985, 164). What is dear to male economists is not the thing itself but their
model of the thing. Disproportionately they scorn the rich and multiple stories
of the thing itself, the sandy cat in Woolf's perception filching a piece of fish.
The men want to impose their favorite metaphors on the world, not to remain
"content with multiplicity as an end in itself" (Keller 1985, 163). "I start with
the seedling," said McClintock, "and I don't want to leave it. I don't feel I
really know the story [note the word] if I don't watch the plant all the way
along" (Keller 1983, 198).

The point is that economics is at present dominated by a masculinist methodology, defended since Plato by a philosophical doctrine overstating its practical importance. To repeat, even male economists depend on analogy, storytelling, *verstehen*, appeals to authority, mucking about with the raw data, the
other half of the rhetorical tetrad; and they depend on them even in their most
logical and factual moods. The alternative is not to throw away proof and
curve fitting, which deserve a place of honor. The alternative is to make them
fruitful by recognizing that we economists already use massively another, parallel, more conjective and more feminine rhetoric.

The use of storytelling is a case in point. The literary critic Peter Brooks
says rightly that "our lives are ceaselessly intertwined with narrative, with the
stories that we dream or imagine or would like to tell, all of which are reworked in that story of our own lives that we narrate to ourselves. . . . We are
immersed in narrative" (1985, 1). Yet male economists sneer at the anecdote,
though it gives them most of their factual beliefs, and do not recognize that
they use storytelling conventions in their science daily (McCloskey 1990). An
eclectic Keynesian will tell the story that "oil prices caused inflation." To this
a monetarist will reply that "it is not an equilibrium," namely, that the curtain

has been lowered prematurely near the beginning of the second act: if aggregate demand is not changed by the oil prices, why would not other nominal prices fall? The Keynesian will reply in turn with his own drama criticism: "Well, you damned monetarists start the drama in the middle; where does all that money come from, before your play begins?"

In her recent book on biography, *Writing a Woman's Life*, Carolyn Heilbrun notes that "lives do not serve as models; only stories do that" (1988, 37). Her point is that "there will be narratives of female lives only when women no longer live their lives isolated in the houses and the stories of men" (47). An economics with its stories made explicit would be unable to carry on with merely masculine tales.

School librarians attest that girls disproportionately read stories, boys nonfiction. When the big boys reach economics they prefer metaphors of maximization to stories of entry and exit. Notice that there is no epistemological ranking between the two, a metaphor being just as humanistic, if that's how you want to put it, as a story. If a seventeenth-century Darwin had published *The Origin of Species* in 1687 and some Newton had waited until 1859 to publish *Philosophae naturalis principia mathematica* we would now perhaps think of stories as hard science and metaphors as soft. A conjective rhetoric of economics would exploit the Darwinian niche provided by the neglect of explicit storytelling in economics. Joan Robinson, who admittedly is a hard case, converted around 1940 from modeling maximization, at which she excelled, to the telling of evolutionary and Marxist stories, at which she also excelled. The exemplar of a "feminine" economics would be biology, not physics, and McClintock's biology at that, not a biochemistry revolutionized by guilty but still model-building physicists after the Second World War (as Keller has argued elsewhere).

Discussions of economic methodology involve few women participants. Men more than women tend to be fascinated by the rules of the game (Klant 1985). Women economists often appear to find the discussion vacuous, though most seem to have been persuaded to obey its conclusions. The literary critics Annis V. Pratt and Mary Daly attack "methodolatry" (Pratt's word): "the insistence on a single method is not only dysfunctional but an attribute of the patriarchy" (quoted in Ruthven 1984, 25). "Methodocide" (Daly's word) is a good option. But if we insist on continuing the conventional conversation of methodology, at least the conversation should be opened.

In an illuminating study, "Sex Differences in Games Children Play," Janet Lever noted that "boys were seen quarreling all the time, but not once was a game terminated because of a quarrel. . . . The P.E. teacher in one school noted that the boys seemed to enjoy the legal debates every bit as much as the game itself. Even players who were marginal because of lesser skills or size took equal part in these recurring squabbles" (1976, 482). The boys' game went on, and on, and on, through recess, through every quarrel. By contrast, "most girls interviewed claimed that when a quarrel begins [among them], the game breaks up. . . . And some complained that their [girl] friends could not resolve the basic issues of choosing up sides, deciding who is to be captain, which team will start, and sometimes not even what game to play" (483).

Methodological disputes in economics and elsewhere run parallel to disputes about kickball and Monopoly. The Swiss psychologist Jean Piaget noted in 1932 a contrast between the "polymorphism and tolerance" of girls' games and "the splendid codification and complicated jurisprudence of the [boys'] game of marbles" (76, 70). Men and boys decide rules of the game and decide to discuss the rules endlessly because they think rules are important, the only important thing. As Carol Gilligan (1982) noted in her discussion of this literature of games, girls and women could not care less. My daughter's girl friends gather in social clusters on the soccer field while the boys quarrel passionately about the rules or bury themselves in lonely fantasies of sporting greatness. Girls and women in our culture, it seems, stress community, conversation, solidarity, and other nonrule values, of the sort that Richard Rorty has embraced as the values of the "new fuzzies" (1987, 41; see Laura McCloskey 1987 on the conversation of girls and boys). When the game no longer serves these values they abandon it. They therefore are defined as incompetent in a game not of their choosing.

The point is to imagine a conversation among economists ruled in this cooperative, antiauthoritarian, anarchopacifist, conjective way, what we know together. Susan Feiner, Barbara Morgan, and Bruce Roberts, in a paper taking a Marxist look at race and gender in introductory economics texts (1988), quote Richard Rorty on the matter a good deal. Certainly Richard Rorty has it right. But I recommend, too, Amelie Oksenberg Rorty. In writing on Descartes' strange and masculine rhetoric of science she argued that what is crucial in distinguishing genuine intellectual life from system-building lunacy is "our ability to engage in continuous conversation, testing one another, discovering our hidden presuppositions, changing our minds because we have listened to the voices of our fellows. Lunatics also change their minds, but their minds change with the tides of the moon and not because they have listened, really listened, to their friends' questions and objections" (1983, 562). A conversation in which economists listened, really listened, to their friends' questions and objections would not sound much like a conversation of men.

Masculine rhetoric in economics has long possessed certain conversation stoppers, notably mathematical proof. The alleged superiority of mathematical proof favors men, who more commonly believe it and believe it deeply. It is notable, by the way, that physicists do not believe it. Contrary to what mathematical economists tell their students, physicists are irritated and embarrassed by the mathematical attitudes of the mathematics department. Math-department mathematics is qualitative, not quantitative. It does not depend on actual measurements, merely existence (see McCloskey 1993, ch. 9).

By contrast, in economics one encounters repeatedly the rhetorical turn of a "disproof" of marginal productivity theory (e.g., Feiner, Morgan, and Roberts 1988, 15–19) or a "proof" of the existence and stability of competitive equilibrium (e.g., Hahn 1986). One finds, that is, a man with chalk dust on his jacket trying to persuade you that *set theory shows* that people do not earn their worth under capitalism or that *game theory shows* that capitalism is after all a workable social arrangement.

The notion that one can prove or disprove a great social truth by standing at a blackboard is a peculiarly masculine delusion. The women can do the math, of course. But they are less inclined to accept it as all there is. It is something of which women students of economics are disproportionately skeptical, I think, though usually silent in their skepticism. Men, especially young men, are typically able to believe any crazy abstraction about society, and stand ready to impose it by force of arms because they do not know what a "society" is. Many more women know, even when young, and are appalled by the shallow summaries of society displayed in the words and graphs and mathematics of economics. Perhaps this contributes to their lack of enthusiasm for economics as presently taught.

I am not suggesting that there is some error in the proofs that competitive equilibrium can be derived from axioms of choice or, to name another male obsession since Hobbes, that there is some error in the proofs that civil society can be derived from axioms of selfishness. They are "right" when they are right. But they are right in such a narrow sense, so removed from the concerns of a community that already has approximate equilibrium and already has a semblance of civility, that someone not half in love with easeful narrowness would wonder what the fuss is all about.

The mathematical economist Frank Hahn, for instance, a man's man in this line of work, wrote that Arrow and Debreu "*demonstrated . . .* the logical possibility of the truth of [Adam] Smith's claims." Many male economists, like Hahn, take this Arrow-Debreu theorem to be the essence of modern economics: "these were remarkable achievements not only for what had been *demonstrated* but for the *conclusive manner* in which it was done. . . . The theory . . . is *all we have of honest and powerful thinking* on the subject [of how economies might behave]" (Hahn 1986, 833; my emphasis). What in fact was done was to show in a couple of pages that certain mathematical objects called "economies" can be looked at mathematically in two ways at least. Using a style of proof fashionable circa 1910, a certain mathematical expression was shown to be equivalent to another.

Worthwhile as the equivalence is—the point here is not to abandon mathematics, considering as I have noted that identical points can be made about wholly nonmathematical work in the tradition of Hobbes—it is limited as science. No historical evidence was adduced; no common experience was reinterpreted; no new way of viewing society was revealed; no deep insight into human behavior was put forward. Without the substance of economics the proof is just not very useful. Only a man, and a man in love with blackboards, would be likely to be caught saying that such writing was "all we [economists] have of honest and powerful thinking."

Looking at the formalisms of economics in a conjective way can help. For instance, the vocabulary of the neoclassical "production function," as a self-consciously conjective style of reasoning would recognize, is intrinsically analogical: we imagine that production is a function of capital and labor. I am arguing that self-consciousness about analogizing and storytelling are feminine in our culture; literalism, a belief in the Reality of this or that analogy or story, is masculine. As Roslyn Willett notes:

> For reasons that are not entirely clear, men seem to fantasize more than women. . . . Men tend to impose abstract structures on reality, and then to perceive reality in terms of their abstractions. . . . Economic theory [for example] is elaborated but quite often fails to be predictive, although that is its ostensible purpose. . . . The whole male-dominated world shows symptoms of a progressive removal from the real world with its stubborn ad-hoc-ness and variability. (1972, 526, 528; compare McClintock's words above)

"Aggregate capital" involves an analogy of "capital" (itself analogical) with something—sand, bricks, shmoos—that can be "added" in a meaningful way; so does "aggregate labor," with the additional peculiarity that the thing added is not a thing but hours of conscientious attentiveness. The very idea of a "production function" involves the astonishing analogy of the subject, the fabrication of things, about which it is appropriate to think in terms of ingenuity, discipline, and planning, with the modifier, a mathematical function, about which it is appropriate to think in terms of height, shape, and single valuedness. The metaphorical content of these ideas was alive to their inventors in the nineteenth century. It is largely dead to twentieth-century male economists. The men do not notice that they are perceiving reality in terms of their metaphorical fantasies.

During the 1960s the dead metaphor of the production function got out of its coffin Bela Lugosi style for the debate of the two Cambridges. The Marxist economists of Cambridge, England, who did not believe in production functions, battled with the neoclassical economists of Cambridge, Massachusetts, who did. (The British group was led of course by that same Joan Robinson.) All sides agree that after a few quarters of play Cambridge, England was ahead on points, although penalized frequently for eye-gouging and groin-kicking. But suddenly, on account of injuries and the lack of a crowd, to the dismay of the Cambridge, England group, the game was abandoned.

The game itself was testimony to the importance of metaphorical questions in economics. Its very violence suggests that boys' rules were in force, and that something beyond simple fact or elementary logic was at stake. The combatants hurled logic at each other. The important and unanswered questions, however, were those one would ask of a metaphor, which could be asked only with a conjective self-consciousness about such matters—is the metaphor of a production function illuminating, is it satisfying, is it apt? How do you know? How does it compare with other economic poetry? After some tactical retreats by Cambridge, Massachusetts on matters of ultimate metaphysics irrelevant to these important questions, mutual boredom and exhaustion set in, without decision.

The reason there was no decision was that the important questions were literary, not logical. No one noticed this, and the game therefore breaks out in back alleys from time to time under the old rules. The Cambridge Marxists are properly irritated about the lack of outcome, because after all they won the game fair and square on a logical field laid out by their opponents. Yet they lost the larger argument. The continued vitality of the idea of an aggregate production function in the face of logical proofs of its impossibility can only be explained this way: that logical proof, the masculine weapon, is not a perfect winner of arguments.

Nor should it be, on the frequent occasions when the main issue is not a matter of properly translating one expression deductively into another. The "proofs" of the possibility or impossibility of an aggregate production function are equivalent to telling Shakespeare that he must abandon a metaphor because, you know, it is logically "impossible." "You are being illogical, my dear William, to compare your beloved to a summer's day: a human being is surely flesh and blood—a fact indeed that I have proven experimentally. It is not rough winds and darling buds. Break off this madness, dearest Will, and return to the sure path of literal experiment and conclusive proof." Francis Bacon and Descartes, eloquent against rhetoric, could almost have argued so.

The question between neoclassicals and Marxists in the Cambridge Controversy, in short, was a question of metaphor. Can you write down a blueprint for a factory (one of Samuelson's self-conscious metaphors for a production function) and expect to get it built? No, not if the carpenters and electricians and secretaries on the job do not possess "kinds of skills [that] could not even in principle be written down" (Vaughn 1988, 10). The visualization of the metaphor in action is a more persuasive criticism of it than the logic. Nothing was settled forever and ever by hauling in the logic and declaring the matter resolved.

In discussing another "one of the most perfect examples in the history of economic thought of a total failure of a conversation to take place," the Hayek/Lange debate about the feasibility of socialism, Vaughn notes that Oskar Lange "thought the whole debate concerned and could be settled by mathematical reasoning" (1988, 8). He was that kind of guy. The figure of speech "you-are-inconsistent-and-that's-all-I-need-to-show" dominates the rhetoric of masculine argument, as many wives have had occasion to note. Consistency is not the hobgoblin only of little minds; it is more particularly the hobgoblin of little masculine minds. The demonstration that this or that neoclassical idea is incoherent mathematically by a narrow definition of "coherence" settles something worth settling. But it is after all not much. It is sometimes interesting and occasionally important. Hardly ever is it decisive.

Likewise the usual demonstrations that Marxist economics leaves something to be desired "empirically," by which the man using the word will mean "according to some 3 × 5-card definition of consulting The Facts," is not decisive. Nor should it be. There are many reasons for adopting one or the other view, and all are subject to conversation. The actual conversation of science and scholarship leads to conclusions more definite than those achieved by the narrow and official and nonconjective methods—this contrary to the main virtue alleged for the official methods, that they are supposed to yield conclusions. Name the conclusion produced by highbrow mathematical or econometric means since the Second World War. Go ahead: no fair merely citing the literature; tell me the substantive gain to economic thinking that has come by the highbrow route. The test is embarrassing to the overblown promise of formalism in economics. The plan to reduce all science to authoritarian pronouncements of true theorems and nonfalsified predictions reflects a masculine notion of life's simplicity. It overvalues "that mass of small intellectual tricks, that complex of petty knowledge, that collection of cerebral rubber stamps, which constitute the chief mental equipment of the average male" (Mencken 1963 [1922], 8). It is a 3 × 5-card philosophy of inquiry.

The usual criticisms in economics of other people's research programs are notably simpleminded, and notably masculine. Men tend to think it satisfactory to find one loose end and pull hard. The young Karl Popper advocated just such a procedure, a thought-saver beloved ever since by young men. It makes scholarship into a game of marbles, scoring points under the rules of falsification and quitting promptly when time is called. It rejects the notion of an agreement arrived at through long and serious discussion. If you can falsify Marxist economics by "proving" that "Marx's predictions were wrong" or falsify Chicago economics by "proving" that "a full set of contingent markets are necessary for efficiency," then you can quit early and go have a beer. There is no need—a conjective need, creative of scholarly community—to synthesize, to compromise, to hear the other person's opinion, to spend time listening, really listening, to one's colleagues' questions and objections.

A conjective economics might humanize economics and enlarge it, and it might make economists better scholars. Economics through feminine eyes would not lack seriousness or rigor, unless the women economists allow the feminine to be defined as marginal, pushing Virginia Woolf, Joan Robinson, Emily Dickinson, and Margaret Reid off to one side in favor of Serious Work.

Men and women already must use a wide and conjective rhetoric in doing economics, but are not aware of it. If they became aware of it they would do their economics better and would keep their tempers better. They could speak then in their own voice but with a tolerant confidence, without shouting or sneering. And perhaps they could speak better in the voice of the other, too.

References

Bartlett, Robin L. 1985. "Integrating the New Scholarship on Women into an Introductory Economics Course." Paper presented at session on Gender and Race in the Economics Curriculum, meetings of the American Economic Association, December, New York.

Becker, Gary. 1981. *A Treatise on the Family.* Cambridge, Mass.: Harvard University Press.

Bergmann, Barbara. 1975. "Have Economists Failed?" *Eastern Economic Journal* 2 (July): 16–24.

Boone, Joseph A. 1988. "Feminist Criticism and the Study of Literature: What Difference Does Difference Make?" *Harvard Graduate Society Newsletter* (Spring): 1–3.

Booth, Wayne C. 1974. *Modern Dogma and the Rhetoric of Assent.* Chicago: University of Chicago Press.

Borel, Armand. 1983. "Mathematics: Art and Science." *Mathematical Intelligencer* 5 (4): 9–17.

Brooks, Peter. 1985. *Reading for the Plot: Design and Intention in Narrative.* New York: Vintage.

Bruner, Jerome. 1986. *Actual Minds, Possible Worlds.* Cambridge, Mass.: Harvard University Press.

Buchanan, James M. 1979. "Professor Alchian on Economic Method." In *What Should Economists Do?*, 65–79. Indianapolis: Liberty Press.

Cooper, Brian. 1990. "Marital Problems: A Reconsideration of Neoclassical Models of Household Decision-Making." Manuscript, Department of Economics, Harvard University.

Dillingham, Alan E. 1985. "The Influence of Risk Variable Definition in Value-of-Life Estimates." *Economic Inquiry* 24 (April): 277–94.

Feiner, Susan F. 1984. "The Household Class Process and Imperialism: An Alternative View of the Family Wage." Manuscript, Department of Economics, Virginia Commonwealth University.

———, Barbara A. Morgan, and Bruce B. Roberts. 1988. "Hidden by the Invisible Hand: Race and Gender in Introductory Economics Texts." Paper for session on Gender and Race in the Economics Curriculum, American Economic Association meetings, and for the CSWEP session, Southern Economic Association; November, San Antonio.

Folbre, Nancy. 1991. "The Unproductive Housewife: Her Evolution in Nineteenth-Century Economic Thought." *Signs* 16 (3): 463–84.

————, and Heidi Hartmann. 1988. "The Rhetoric of Self-Interest: Ideology and Gender in Economic Theory." In *The Consequences of Economic Rhetoric*, ed. Arjo Klamer, Donald N. McCloskey, and Robert M. Solow, 184–203. New York: Cambridge University Press.

Gergen, Kenneth J., and Mary M. Gergen. 1986. "Narrative Form and the Construction of Psychological Science." In *Narrative Psychology: The Storied Nature of Human Conduct*, ed. T. R. Sarbin, 22–44. New York: Praeger.

Gilligan, Carol. 1982. *In a Different Voice: Psychological Theory and Women's Development.* Cambridge, Mass.: Harvard University Press.

Gould, Stephen Jay. 1980. *The Panda's Thumb.* New York: W. W. Norton.

————. 1989. *Wonderful Life: The Burgess Shale and the Nature of History.* New York: W. W. Norton.

Hahn, Frank. 1986. "Living with Uncertainty in Economics: A Review of Kenneth Arrow's Collected Papers." *Times Literary Supplement.* 1 August, 833–34.

Heilbrun, Carolyn G. 1988. *Writing a Woman's Life.* New York: Ballantine Books.

Hesse, Mary. 1966. *Models and Analogies in Science.* South Bend, Ind.: University of Notre Dame Press.

Keller, Evelyn Fox. 1983. *A Feeling for the Organism: The Life and Work of Barbara McClintock.* New York: Freeman.

Keller, Evelyn Fox. 1985. *Reflections on Gender and Science.* New Haven, Conn.: Yale University Press.

Klamer, Arjo. 1987. "The Advent of Modernism in Economics." Manuscript, Department of Economics, George Washington University.

————. 1990. "Towards the Native's Point of View: The Difficulty of Changing the Conversation." In *Economics and Hermeneutics,* ed. Don Lavoie, 19–33. London and New York: Routledge.

————, Donald N. McCloskey, Robert M. Solow, eds. 1988. *The Consequences of Economic Rhetoric.* New York: Cambridge University Press.

———— and D. N. McCloskey. 1991. "The Economy as a Conversation." Manuscript, Department of Economics, University of Iowa.

Klant, J. J. 1985. *The Rules of the Game.* Cambridge: Cambridge University Press.

Laslett, Barbara. 1990. "Unfeeling Knowledge: Emotion and Objectivity in the History of Sociology." *Sociological Forum* 5 (3): 413–33.

Lever, Janet. 1976. "Sex Differences in Games Children Play." *Social Problems* 23:478–87.

Margolis, Howard. 1982. *Selfishness, Altruism, and Rationality: A Theory of Social Choice.* Chicago: University of Chicago Press.

McCloskey, Donald N. 1990. *If You're So Smart: The Narrative of Economic Expertise.* Chicago: University of Chicago Press.

———. 1993. *Knowledge and Persuasion in Economics.* Cambridge: Cambridge University Press.

McCloskey, Laura A. 1987. "Gender and Conversation: Mixing and Matching Styles." In *Current Conceptions of Sex Roles and Sex Typing: Theory and Research,* ed. D. B. Carter, 139–53. New York: Praeger.

McElroy, Marjorie B., and Mary Jean Horney. 1981. "Nash-Bargained Household Decisions: Towards a Generalization of the Theory of Demand." *International Economic Review* 22 (2): 333–49.

Mencken, H. L. 1963 [1922]. *In Defense of Women.* New York: Time Inc.

Moore, Ruth. 1985 [1966]. *Niels Bohr: The Man, His Science, and the World They Changed.* Cambridge, Mass.: MIT Press.

Oxford. 1933. *The Oxford English Dictionary,* vol. 9, S–Soldo. Oxford: Clarendon Press.

Oxford. 1982. *A Supplement to the Oxford English Dictionary,* vol. 3, O–Scz. Oxford: Clarendon Press.

Oxford. 1989. *The Oxford English Dictionary.* 2d ed. Vol. 14, Rob–Sequyle. Oxford: Clarendon Press.

Piaget, Jean. 1932. *The Moral Judgment of the Child.* Trans. Marjorie Gabain. London: Routledge and Kegan Paul.

Roback, Jennifer. 1981. "Immigration Policy: A New Approach." Policy analysis paper, Cato Institute.

Rorty, Amelie Oksenberg. 1983. "Experiments in Philosophical Genre: Descartes' *Meditations.*" *Critical Inquiry* 9 (March): 545–65.

Rorty, Richard. 1987. "Science as Solidarity." In *The Rhetoric of the Human Sciences: Language and Argument in Scholarship and Public Affairs,* ed. J. S. Nelson, A. Megill, and D. N. McCloskey, 38–52. Madison: University of Wisconsin Press.

Ruthven, K. K. 1984. *Feminist Literary Studies: An Introduction.* Cambridge: Cambridge University Press.

Stigler, George. 1966. *The Theory of Price.* 3d ed. New York: Macmillan.

Usher, Dan. 1985. "The Value of Life for Decision Making in the Public Sector." In *Ethics and Economics,* ed. Ellen Frankel Paul, F. D. Miller, Jr., and J. Paul, 168–91. London: Basil Blackwell, for the Social Philosophy and Policy Center, Bowling Green State University.

Vaughn, Karen I. 1988. "Austrian Economics/Feminine Economics." Paper presented to the CSWEP session, Southern Economic Association, November, San Antonio.

Weinberg, Steven. 1983. "Beautiful Theories." Revision of the Second Annual Gordon Mills Lecture on Science and the Humanities, University of
Texas, 5 April. Typescript.

Willett, Roslyn S. 1972. "Working in 'A Man's World': The Woman Executive." In *Woman in Sexist Society,* ed. Vivian Gornick and Barbara K.
Moran, 511–32. New York: Mentor.

Woolf, Virginia. 1931. *The Waves.* New York: Harcourt, Brace.

———. 1967 [1924]. *Collected Essays.* Vol. 1. New York: Harcourt, Brace,
and World.

[15]

Economic Science: A Search Through the Hyperspace of Assumptions?

Donald N. McCloskey
University of Iowa

It would of course be silly to object to the mere existence of mathematics in economics. No one wants to return to the time, not so distant, in which economists could not keep straight the difference between the movement of a curve and a movement along it.[1] Economics made progress without mathematics, but has made faster progress with it. Mathematics has brought transparency to many hundreds of economic arguments. The metaphor of the production function, the story of economic growth, the logic of competition, the facts of labor force participation would rapidly become muddled without mathematical expression. In fact muddled they once were. Most economists and I agree with Léon Walras, who wrote in 1900, "As for those economists who do not know any mathematics, who do not even know what is meant by mathematics and yet have taken the stand that mathematics cannot possibly serve to elucidate economic principles, let them go their way repeating that 'human liberty will *never* allow itself to be cast into equations' or that 'mathematics ignores frictions which are *everything* in social science" [p. 47].

But economists know that a qualitative argument for something does not automatically fix its optimal quantity. When America has market power in some exportable, and takes a selfish view, the economist can assert qualitatively that some tariff would improve on free trade. But an argument for the existence of an optimal tariff does not automatically tell how large the tariff should be, quantitatively speaking. Likewise, if some industries are monopolized, then forcing other industries to price exactly at marginal cost may be a bad idea, as a matter of qualitative, logical, on-off, what-might-possibly-happen truth. But the scientific question is quantitative. How far from competitive is the economy? What closeness to marginal cost would trigger the second best? How much marginal cost pricing can the economy stand?

In other words, economists do not need more existence theorems about the role of mathematics in economics – "there does not exist a mathematical economics that can take account of human liberty" or "there does not exist a rigorous economic argument unless in Bourbaki-style mathematics." To answer the quantitative question about the role of mathematical formalism in economics we need quantitative standards.

Comparison provides a quantitative standard. On several grounds, physics is a good standard for comparison. For one thing, economists share some human qualities with physicists. Economists like to think of themselves as the physicists of the social sciences, and they are. Like physicists they are political animals, in love with conferences and competition. They are hedgehogs, not foxes; they know one big thing ($F = ma$; $e = mc^2$; $P = MC$; $MV = PT$) not a large number of little things. They like to colonize other fields, the way biology was colonized after the War by physicists ashamed of making bombs. And economists are approximately as arrogant about the neighboring fields as physicists are.[2] The jokes that economists tell about sociologists and political scientists, without knowing anything about sociology or political science, are matched in physics by jokes about chemists and engineers. The chemist in the Manhattan Project who made the trigger for the bomb (a brilliant trick, without which no bomb) was praised by one of the physicists: "George, you're an absolutely first-rate chemist – which is to say, a good third-rate physicist!" Very funny.

For another, economists admire physicists and judge themselves, as do most people in our culture, to be intellectually inferior to the physicists. Like philology in the centuries of Scaliger, Erasums, and Bentley, physics nowadays is at the top. Physicists have the most prestige among intellectual workers. The peculiarly English word "Science" (all other languages use the word to mean "systematic inquiry") has come to mean "a field of study close to what non-physicists imagine physics is like." The first-rate economists imagine themselves to be good third-rate physicists. Comparisons with sociology, then, would not be to the point, since economists, without knowing any sociologists, imagine sociologists to be inferior to economists. The standard of comparison should be the field we look up to rather than the one we look down upon.

Robert Solow has a good story on the matter. He was complaining at lunch one day to the Nobel laureate Victor Weisskopf about the dearth of really bright people in economics, "unlike physics," said Solow, in a bit of ill-advised humility. Weisskopf replied that such a situation did not sound like an equilibrium: if there were too few bright people in economics, then some of the marginally bright in physics could move over into economics and make their intellectual fortunes. So in equilibrium the marginal person would be equally bright. Solow was stunned and embarrassed. Here was a physicist inventing on the spot the economist's favorite argument and using it better than Solow himself to show that self-deprecation was not in order. The story says either that physicists *are* brighter than economists or, at another level,

that they are not, and likewise for sociology. It's that way in the human sciences.

Most economists would accept physics as a standard for the use of mathematics. The empirical result of applying it is this: physics is less mathematical than modern economics.

The proposition sounds crazy. The average economist knows a lot less mathematics than the average physicist, as is apparent from the courses both take in college. Walk the aisles of the college bookstore and open some of the upper-division undergraduate books in physics (or in the much-despised civil engineering, for that matter). It makes the hair stand on end. Even the mathematically more sophisticated economists know less math than comparable physicists, if by "knowing math" one means "knowing about Bessel functions" or "knowing six ways to solve an ordinary differential equation" or even "knowing a lot about the theory of groups."

The proposition, however, does not say that economics *uses* more math; it says that economics is "more mathemaitcal." In the Economics Department the Spirit of the Math Department reigns. The spirit is different over in the Physics Department. The great theoretical physicist Richard Feynman, for example, introduced a few simple theorems in matrix algebra into his first-year class at Cal Tech with considerable embarrassment [1963, Vol. I, 22-1]: "What is mathematics doing in a physics lecture? ..... Mathematicians are mainly interested in how various mathematical facts are demonstrated ..... They are not so interested in the result of what they prove." Feynman's rhetorical question startles an economist. In most first-year graduate programs in economics it would be rather "What else but mathematics should be in an economics lecture?" In physics the familiar spirit is Archimedes the experimenter. But in economics, as in mathematics, it is theorem-proving Euclid who paces the halls.

Economists know little about how physics operates as a field, and the physicists are amazed at the math-department character of economics. The new Santa Fe Institute, which brings the two groups together for the betterment of economics, has made the cultural differences plain. In 1989 *Science* described the physical scientists there as "flabbergasted to discover how mathematically rigorous theoretical economists are. Physics is generally considered to be the most mathematical of all the sciences, but modern economics has it beat" [Pool, p. 701]. The physicists do not regard the mathematical rigor as something to be admired. To the seminar question asked by an economist, "where are your proofs?", the physicist replies, "You can whip up theorems, but I leave that to the mathematicians" [701]. A physicist at the Institute solved a problem with a computer simulation, approximately, while the economist found an analytic solution. Who is the more mathematical?

Economists think that science involves axiomatic proofs of theorems and then econometric tests of the QED, which therefore will test the axioms. In truth the physicists could care less about mathematical proofs. Even the theoreticians in physics spend much of their time reading the physical equivalent of agricultural economists or economic historians. Pencil-and-paper guys are uncommon in physics departments. Physics is finding driven. Economics is theorem driven. Ask your local physicist what he thinks about proofs. He'll say, "Well, I prefer to depend on an existence theorem about existence theorems: if the mathematicians tell me they exist, fine; I reckon they know. but it ain't physics."

The economists, to put it another way, have adopted the intellectual values of the Math Department – not the values of the Departments of Physics or Electrical Engineering or Biochemistry they admire from afar. The situation is odd on its face. Philip Anderson, the distinguished physicist who brought the Sante Fe Institute together, explained the differences with "the differences in the amount of data available to the two fields" [701]. But economists are drenched in data, as hard as they want them to be. Odd.

No one would make the absurd claim, of course, that axiom and proof have no place of honor in economic reasoning. They do, and should, though economists might be more sensitive to Alfred Marshall's remark long ago that "the function then of analysis and deduction in economics is not to forge a few long chains of reasoning, but to forge rightly many short chains and single connecting links" [1920, p. 773]. We had better know that assumption A leads to conclusion C, although it would be a poor economics that only knew this.

But at the heart of axiom and proof as practiced in economics is a rhetorical problem, a failure to ask how large is large. As our own William Brock put it in 1988:

We remark, parenthetically, that when studying the natural science literature in this area it is important for the economics reader, especially the economic theorist brought up on the tradition of abstract general equilibrium theory, to realize that many natural scientists are not impressed by mathematical arguments showing the "anything can happen" in a system loosely disciplined by general axioms. Just showing existence of logical possibilities is not enough for such skeptics. The parameters of the system needed to get the erratic behavior must conform to parameter values established by empirical studies or the behavior must actually be documented in nature. (p. 2 of typescript).

The problem, to put it formally, is that economists have fallen in love with existence theorems, the beloved also of the Math Department. There *exists* a canopener, somewhere. the most famous of these theorems is of course Arrow-Debreu, though I intend the word "existence theorem" to apply to all the qualitative theorems with which economists wile away their hours between 8:00 and quitting time. Significantly, what are commonly regarded as the first formal proofs of the existence of a competitive equilibrium, advanced during the 1920s and 1930s, were devised by professional mathematicians, John von Neumann and Abraham Wald. (Equally significantly, one could plausibly claim that Edgeworth had already proven the theorem; for merely N = 2, of course, but so what?)

From everywhere outside of economics except the Department of Mathematics the proofs of existence of competitive equilibrium, just to take them as concrete examples, will seem strange. They do not claim to show that an actual existing economy is in equilibrium, or that the equilibrium of an existing economy is desirable. The blackboard problem thus solved derives more or less vaguely from Adam Smith's assertion that capitalism is self-regulating and good. But the proofs of existence do not prove or disprove Smith's assertion. They show that certain equations describing a certain blackboard economy have a solution, but they do not give the solution to the blackboard problem, much less to an extant economy. Indeed, the problem is framed in such general terms that no specific solution even to the toy

Methodus   June 1991

economy on the blackboard could reasonably be expected. The general statement that people buy less of something when its price goes up cannot yield specific answers, such as $4598 billion.³ The proofs state that somewhere in the mathematical universe there exists a solution. Lord knows what it is; we humans only know that it exists.

The usual way the quest for existence is justified is to say that, after all, we had better know that solutions exist before we go looking for them. Ask an economist why she's so interested in existence theorems and this is the answer you will get. Of course, the economist giving it does not then go out and look for parameterized and empirical solutions. But nobody's perfect. The answer anyway sounds reasonable: if you can't actually find it, nonetheless know that what you're looking for exists. Judging again from physics, however, it is not reasonable. Physicists have happily used the Schrödinger equation since 1926 without knowing whether it has solutions in general. The three-body problem in Newtonian physics does not possess known solutions in general. Yet astronomers can tell you with sufficient accuracy for most of the questions they ask where the moon will be next year. For that matter, poets can write particular *terza rima* poems without knowing whether the form has in general a solution possessing optimal properties. Whether a solution under assumption A exists in general is irrelevant if the physical or economic or poetic question has to do with a particular finite case under assumption A' merely close to A.

The way the mathematical rhetoric has been transformed into economic rhetoric has been to *define* the economic problem as dealing with a certain kind of (easily manipulable) mathematics. One searches under the lamppost because the light there is good. The notions of "equilibrium" and "maximization" in economics have been treated in such a way [Weintraub 1991; Mirowski 1990]. Many economists have claimed that Adam Smith's question *is* the mathematical one of existence. The move is doubtful as intellectual history. Smith used the phrase "the invisible hand" only once (albeit in each of his books) and it is not until the coming of mathematical values in economics that the matter of existence was considered to be important.

But what is more unhappy is that a proof of existence leaves every concrete question unresolved, while enticing some of the best minds in the business into perfecting the proofs. With certain assumptions about preferences and technology one can write down equations which can be shown to have somewhere out there a solution (and sometimes, more to the point, even a stable solution, insensitive to trembling hands). Naturally the result, which is about the equations, not about the economy, depends on the assumptions. The task has been to vary the assumptions and see what happens. Unsurprisingly, under some assumptions the equilibrium does exist and under others it does not; under some assumptions the equilibrium is efficient and under others it is not.

Well, so what? Sometimes it rains and sometimes it does not. In some universes the moon is made of green cheese and in others it is not. None of the theorems and countertheorems of general equilibrium theory has been surprising in a qualitative sense. *But this is the only sense they have.* They are not quantitative theorems. They are mathematics without numbers, of great and proper interest inside the Department of Mathematics, but of little interest to quantitative intellectuals.

The problem is that the general theorem does not relate to anything an economist would actually want to know. We already know for example that if the world is not perfect the outcomes of the world cannot be expected to be perfect. This much we know by being adults. But economists arguing over the federal budget next year or the stability of capitalism forever want to know *how big* a particular badness or offsetting goodness will be. Will the distribution of income be radically changed by the abandonment of interest? Will free trade raise American national income? It is useless to be told that if there is not a complete market in every commodity down to and including chewing gum then there is no presumption that capitalism will work efficiently. Yet that is a typical piece of information from the mathematical front lines. It does not provide the economic scientist with a scale against which to judge the significance of the necessary deviations from completeness. Chewing gum or all investment goods: it does not matter for the proof.

Practical people, including most economists, understand Adam Smith's optimism about the economy as asserting something like this: economies that are approximately competitive are approximately efficient, if approximate externalities and approximate monopolies and approximate ignorance do not significantly intervene; and anyway they are aprpoximately progressive in a way that the static assertion does not pretend to deal with, even approximately. The claim has analogies to the theorems of general equilibrium theory (say: similar fuzzy but highly relevant claims are made in other parts of economics). But except on the knife edge of exact results, where a set of measure zero lives, the theorems are not rigorously relevant. If we are going to be rigorous we should be rigorous, not rigorous about the proof and extremely sloppy about its range of application.[4] The theorems are exact results, containing no definition of the neighborhood in which they are approximately correct.

The exact existence theorems may be worth having, though why exactly it is worth having needs to be argued more rigorously than it has been so far – a matter of rhetorical, not mathematical, rigor, but rigor all the same. Mathematical economics has not been sufficiently rigorous about its arguments.

To put it rigorously, the procedure of modern economics is too much a search through the hyperspace of conceivable assumptions. In the second of his *Three Essays on the State of Economic Science* (1957) Tjalling Koopmans argued for precisely such a program of research, referring to a "card file" of logical results connecting a sequence of assumptions A, A', A", A''', ..., Aᴺ to the corresponding conclusions C, C', C", and so forth. He specifically wished to separate blackboard economics from empirical economics, "for the health of both." Economists should have a theoretical branch and an empirical branch (which he thought was going to result in an imitation of physics). The theoretical branch should devote itself to "a sequence of models".

Koopmans' program has been widely accepted. In 1984, for example, Frank Hahn thought he was answering the objection that anything can happen in general theorising by saying: "It is true that often many things can be the case in a general theory but not that anything can be. Everyone who knows the textbooks can confirm that" (p. 6). What he means is that the textbooks line up the sequence of assumptions A, A', A", ... with the conclusions C, C', C", ... True enough. But of course it is not an answer to the objection that in economic theorizing, contrary to its declared love of rigor, in fact anything goes. I conjecture the following important

Metatheorem on Hyperspaces of Assumptions

For each and every assumption A implying a conclusion C and for each alternative conclusion C' arbitrarily far from C (for example, disjoint with C), there exists an alternative assumption A' arbitrarily close to the original assumption A, such that A' implies C'.

I have not been able to devise a proof, but you can whip one up; anyway, as an empirical scientist, I leave that to the mathematicians. The empirical evidence is overwhelming. Name a conclusion, C, in recent but not last year's formal economics – say, that rational expectations obviates government policy or that interaction in many different markets makes for closer collusion of oligopolists. Observe that by now there have appeared numerous proofs that alternative assumptions A' or A", which for most purposes look awfully close to the original A, result in C' or C" – that government policy outwits rational expectations or that the oligopolists are nonetheless unable to achieve collusion.[5]

The problem, to repeat, is a rhetorical one. The prestige of mathematical argument led economists to believe, contrary to their discipline, that the economist could get something intellectually for nothing, proving or disproving great social truths by writing on a blackboard. Programs of research since the 1940s that focused on existence theorems have for a time been rhetorically successful, until the economist have realized once again that after all nothing has been concluded. Besides the general equilibrium program itself, one can mention the $2 \times 2 \times 2$ program of international trade, the theory of international finance, and the rational expectations revolution in macroeconomics. The economists responsible for these excellent ideas have wandered off into a discussion of whether or not an equilibrium exists for this or that "setting" and what its character might be, qualitatively speaking.

They have seldom asked in ways that would persuade other economists how large the effects were. They have not asked how large is large. Eventually they have gotten bored with the formal tool of the day and have walked off to develop a new one. For example, game theory is beginning (for the third time in its brief history) to bore economists; evolutionary theory stands enticingly ready to fuel careers and then to be abandoned in its turn. The economists, though

Methodus   June 1991

they talk about it quite a lot, and sneer at lesser breeds without the law such as lawyers and sociologists, have not taken the rhetoric of science seriously, and have retreated from the library and laboratory to the blackboard. The research in many fields of economics does not cumulate. It circles.

The problem was brought into focus by the philosopher Allan Gibbard and the mathematical economist Hal Varian some time ago. "Much of economic theorizing," they noted (without intent to damn it), "consists not ..... of forming explicit hypotheses about situations and testing them, but of investigating economic models" [1978, p. 676]. That's right. Economic literature is largely speculative, an apparently inconclusive exploration of possible worlds. In defending the excess of speculation over testing in economics journals Gibbard and Varian use a phrase heard a lot in the hallways: "When we vary the assumptions of a model in this way to see how the conclusions change, we might say we are *examining the robustness of the model*" [same page]. Economists commonly defend their chief activity by saying that running through every conceivable model will show them the crucial assumptions. They have embarked so to speak on a fishing expedition in the hyperspace of possible worlds.

The trouble is that they have not caught any fish with the theoretical line. The activity works as science only when it gets actual numbers to fish in. But economic speculation does not use actual numbers. It makes qualitative arguments, such as existence theorems. (Paul Samuelson, who founded the present paradigm in economics, spent a good deal of time in his book of marvels published in 1947 trying to derive *qualitative* theorems; he did not show the way to empirical work. Maybe for all his astounding excellences Samuelson in this respect set economics off in the wrong direction.)

What economics needs, say Gibbard and Varian, is a quantitative rhetoric, telling how large is large:

> When a model is applied to a situation as an approximation, an aspiration level epsilon is set for the degree of approximation of the conclusions. What is hypothesized is this: there is a delta such that (i) the assumptions of the applied mdoel are true to a degree of approximation delta, and (ii) in any possible situation to which the model could be applied, if the assumption of

> that applied model were true to degree of approximation delta, its conclusions would be true to degree epsilon. [pp. 671-72]

That sounds good. Yet they realize that the degree of approximation of this desirable, physical, engineering rhetoric to economics is poor. In the next sentence they concede that "Of course ..... few if any of the degrees of approximation involved are characterized numerically" [p. 672]. Oh, oh. Wasn't that the point? If the literature of economics consists largely of *qualitative* explorations of possible models, what indeed *is* its point? Don't we already know that there exist an unbounded number of solutions to an unbounded number of equations? Where, one might ask, will it end?

Gibbard and Varian are uneasily aware of how crushing their remark is. They conclude lamely "but the pattern of explanation is, we think, the one we have given" [same page]. Well, be quantitative. Within what neighborhood of radius epsilon does economic theory, high-brow or low, approximate the quantitative procedures that are routine in physics, applied math, labor economics, or quantitative economic history?

Varying the assumptions of economic models with no rhetorical plan in mind – because "it's interesting to see what happens" when assumption A is replaced by assumption A' – is not science but mathematics. It is th search through the hyperspace of assumptions. A long time ago I helped interview a young man who had written a thesis weakening one of the assumptions in Arrow's Impossibility Theorem. We asked him mildly what the scientific uses of such a result might be. The youth waxed worth: "What! Don't you understand? I have *weakened* an assumption in *Arrow's Impossibility Theorem!*" Here was someone from the Math Department, at least in spirit.

Scientists think differently. When the economic historian Robert Fogel varies an assumption he plans to strengthen his economic case by biasing the findings against himself. When Richard Feynman cut the safety seals of the space shuttle engine with a kitchen knife he also had an *a fortiori* plan in mind. The most prestigious research method in modern economics, imitated at all levels of mathematical competence in the field, has no such rhetorical plan.

The rhetorical problem, to repeat, is that economists have taken over the intellectual values of the wrong subjects. It is not that the values or the subjects are intrinsically bad. No reasonable person could object to such values flourishing within the Department of Mathematics. Splendid. Some of all our best friends are mathematicians. Capital. The problem comes when the economists abandon an economic question in favor of a mathematical one, and then forget to come back to the Department of Economics. Questions of existence or questions that ring the changes on the mathematical object itself might be of interest to mathematics, regardless of how remote. Unless they can be shown to bear directly on a dispute in economic science, however, they are not of interest to economics.

The problem lies in the sort of mathematics used, which is to say the details of the formal methods. Physicists and engineers routinely state the bounds within which their assertions hold approximately true and then they tell how true. Listen to page 3 of one of the leading textbook, in engineering mechanics:

In mechanics models or idealizations are used in order to simplify application of the theory ..... A *particle* has a mass but a size that can be neglected. For example, the size of the earth is insignificant compared to the size of its orbit ..... *Rigid Body*. ..... In most cases, the actual deformations occurring in structures ..... are relatively small ..... *Concentrated Force* ..... We can represent the effect of the loading by a concentrated force, providing the area ..... is *small* compared to the overall size of the body. (Hibbeler, 1989, p. 3)

Such talk about magnitudes is foreign in economics. It is surprising to both their students and to their colleagues in physics and engineering that in what economists regard as their chief scientific work they do not talk about magnitudes at all. Of course, when they come to advise on policy or reconstruct past economies the bounds of error must be stated, and often are, with wonderful skill. On the blackboard, where they spend most of their time, however, economists routinely forget to say how large is large. They have taken over unawares the intellectual ideals of that admirable, excellent department where existence is all important and magnitude is irrelevant. The economists are in love with the wrong mathematics, the pure rather than the applied.

It is not fair, in other words, to blame the Department of Mathematics for the economist's love of existence theorems. In fact, it is not fair to blame the mathematical economists themselves. Even non-mathematical economists have always loved existence theorems. It is said that economists would have had to reinvent the calculus for their own lovely marginal analysis if it had not already been invented; likewise they would have had to reinvent fixed point lemmas.

It's not a matter of the use of mathematical notation. A mathematical spirit pervades the works of David Ricardo (Schumpeter called the spirit The Ricardian Vice), who used no mathematics. The physiocrats, too, were attempting to solve great social questions by manipulating definitions. The Ricadian Vice has little or nothing to do with the use of *mathematical* formalism. It is formalism, whether of words or statistics or mathematics, that creates the false hope that the blackboard is all we need. The wholly verbal Austrian economists are as much in love with their own sort of formalism, and hostile to the notion that science might have to come off the blackboard, as is the most math-besotted graduate of Berkeley or Minnesota. The older sort of Marxian economists are, too. System is what people want, as Francis Bacon promised in sounding the bell that gathered the wits, "the business done as if by machine."

Among the oldest questions in economics, after all, is a theorem about whether, as Bernard Mandeville put it in the early 18th century, private vice can be a public benefit: "Thus every Part was full of Vice. Yet the whole Mass a Paradise." Are social systems automatically virtuous as well as automatically stable? No numbers are expected in the answer, which is a tip-off that social philosophy, not social physics, is in question. It is to be done at the blackboard or the lecture podium, not in the world of measurement. A modern student of the matter, known as the Hobbes Problem, is the non-mathematical but Nobel economist James Buchanan; and another the philosopher Robert Nozick; and another the lawyer and judge Richard Posner; and scores of lesser lights, none of whom can be accused of making a fetish out of mathematics. The non-mathematical existence theorems are as peculiar as the mathematical ones. Why would it matter for a worldly philosophy whether or not a knife-edge existence theorem could be proven? Unless it concerns the relevant quantitative questions – *how* full of vice, *how* paradisical – the theorem will not enlighten economics. The problem,

Methodus   June 1991

again, is not the presence of logic or mathematics – plainly, systematic imagination will often need them. The problem, as one can see clearly in these non-mathematical cases, is the strange rhetoric of existence theorems.

The classic but largely definition of economics is Marshall's: "a study of mankind in the ordinary business of life" (p. 1). The literary critic Northrup Frye would extend the definition: "The fundamental job of the imagination in ordinary life ..... is to produce, out the society we have to live in, a vision of the society we want to live in" (1964, p. 140). Mathematical economics, and indeed theory generally, should be viewed as poetry in this act of imagination. Poets are not more luxuries. We need their constructs – although it should be noted that we do not need large numbers of third-rate constructs any more than we need lots of third-rate poetry. The third rate in empirical work is still useful, something on which one can build. The third rate in theoretical work is perfectly useless, even bad for one's soul, the way that Edgar Guest or even Robert Bridges is.

The advantage of looking at theorists this way is that they are cut off from their false claim of physics-mimicking scientificity. They are bards, imaginaries, mathematicians. One of them, Brock again, speaks of his work explicitly in such terms, as for example (1989, p. 443), "chaos theory unfetters our imagination ..... [L]ike much of abstract economic theory, it may give us a hint of how to formulate better empirical models even though the guidance is still rather limited".

The intellectual values of poets are not to be taken as a guide to science. The rhetoric of existence theorems elevates consistency to the only intellectual virtue – not merely the most important or the one necessary, but the only one. "A foolish consistency," the American philosopher said, "is the hobgoblin of little minds, adored by little statesmen and philosophers and divines." The singleminded pursuit of consistency is the Math Department's value. In economics is it too often a foolish consistency.

Alan Turing, the great mathematician, had a good-natured debate in 1939 with Ludwig Wittgenstein, the still greater philosopher (who was trained, not incidentally, as an aeronautical engineer):

Wittgenstein: the question is: Why are people afraid of contradictions? It is easy to understand why they should be afraid of contradictions in orders, descriptions, etc., *outside* mathematics. The question is: Why should they be afraid of contradictions inside mathematics? Turing says, "Because something may go wrong with the application." But nothing need go wrong. [D.N. Mc.: the word "need" in the sentence should probably be emphasized; cf. Friedman's methodology.] And if something does go wrong – if the bridge breaks down – then your mistake was of the kind of using a wrong natural law .....

Turing: You cannot be confident about applying your calculus until you know that there is no hidden contradiction in it.

Wittgenstein: There seems to be an enormous mistake there ..... Suppose I convince Rhees of the paradox of Liar, and he says, "I lie, therefore I do not lie, therefore I lie and I do not lie, therefore we have a contradiction, therefore 2 × 2 = 369." [D.N.Mc.: Wittgenstein here refers to the logical proposition that an accepted contradiction allows one formally to prove any false proposition whatever.] Well, we should not call this "multiplication," that is all .....

Turing: Although you do not know that the bridge will fall if there are no contradictions, yet it is almost certain that if there are contradictions it will go wrong somewhere.

Wittgenstein: But nothing has ever gone wrong that way yet .....

Andrew Hodges, a mathematical physicist and the biographer of Turing, writes of this exchange:

But Alan would not be convinced. For any pure mathematician, it would remain the beauty of the subject, that argue as one might about its meaning, the system stood serene, self-consistent, self-contained. Dear love of mathematics! Safe, secure world in which nothing could go wrong, no trouble arise, no bridges collapse! So different from the world of 1939. *[p. 154]*

The mathematician's mad pursuit of consistency (for which in the 1920s and 1930s the gods rewarded him, in part through this very Alan Turing, with rigorous proofs of its ultimate impossibility) is aesthetic, not practical. The poet's values surface again. Whatever may be its merits in mathematics (and there are doubters even there; Kline 1980, p. 352), the aestheticization of science is bad. The main argument that economists appear to have in favor of an argument is that it is "deep" or "elegant," as against "ad hoc." I would suggest that the reason they have such a non-rigorous vocabulary of persuasion is that they are not aware they are persuading. In any event, taking over the persuasive rhetoric of the Math Department is not a good idea. Economics is a science, not a branch of mathematics.

In the end the engineer's criterion is what matters: does it work? Quantitatively speaking, has the formalism of economics resulted in good science? the question is complicated, but by now, after forty years of rigorous trial it is fair to ask what has been learned. It is not fair to claim in answer simply the number of theorems or papers. The mathematician Stanislaw Ulam calculates that some 200,000 theorems are proven annually in mathematics (1976, p. 288). The NSF reckons that some 2,000,000 articles are published each year in science, from 20,000 journals. Such figures suggest the question whether much of it matters. What ideas that matter have come out of the formalization of economics?

In 1965 one could stand back from the program of formalization in economics and remark wisely that economics needed to invest a little in searching the hyperspace of assumptions, because perhaps in 50 years one of the theorems will become empirically relevant. We should tolerate the mathematical economists for a while. After all, said the tolerant sages, non-Euclidean geometry was useless at its birth but proved to be just what Einstein needed.

There are three practical problems with such tolerance. First, it is no longer 1965. It is 25 years on, and we have still yet to see the payoff. In the meantime the empirical parts of economics have taught us all manner of things, that we now will always know, about how economies actually work. The second problem is that economists think that being a social physicist means not having to read anything that is older than the last round of xerox preprints. So economists reinvent the wheel, and the claim that old theorems will come back into use is undermined. Monopolistic competition, for example, keeps getting reinvented. Likewise, economists reinvent every few years the point that pure bargaining, being language (which always can be trumped by itself), has no solution. There is no point piling up theorems whose half-life is six month. Or more exactly, to recur to the quantitative theme, the number of them we presently produce seems grossly non-optimal. Wassily Leontief recently categorized the articles in the leading journals in physics, chemistry, economics, and sociology. In physics and chemistry the theoretical paper were about 10 or 15 percent of the total. In economics (and sociology, perish the thought) the figure was about 50 percent.

I hesitate to articulate the third practical problem with continuing to tolerate the large scale of formalization in economics, because it will seem mean spirited. It probably is. I feel mean about it. But someone has to say it, because everyone knows it is true: A dominant coalition of the formalizers are not themselves tolerant of science. It is an open secret that they *want* economics to become a branch of the Math Department. What is most objectionable about their want is that they are willing to act as *homines economici* in a rigorous sense to achieve it. One economics department after another has been seized by the formalists and marched off to a Gulag of hyperspace searching. Few graduate programs in economics teach economics, especially to first-year students. They teach "tools," tools which become obsolete every five years or so.

Partly this is because of the vocabulary we use. The leading middle-aged economists laugh when Gary Becker is described as a "theorist" and the leading young economists do not even think it is funny. The way first-year graduate programs are structured is a direct result of such terminological confusion. If you do not know anything about any actual economy, the argument goes, perhaps you had better be assigned to the "theory" sequence. "Theory" will at least be your comparative advantage.

Whatever the merits of the argument for static allocation, it has had dismal effects dynamically speaking. It has resulted in a graduate students who believe (until experience drives the madness out) that economics is about certain mathematical objects called "economies". The students have no incentive to learn about the economy. When Arjo Klamer and David Colander asked graduate students whether having a thorough knowledge of the

$\mathcal{M}\!e\!x\!\mathcal{H}\!o\!d\!u\!s$ June 1991

economy was a very important thing to have for academic success in economics only 3.4 percent said it was [1990, p. 18]. Nor do the students have an incentive to learn about economic theory beyond that embodied · in certain mathematical books (only 10 percent said it was very important to have a knowledge of the literature of economics). Such students become teachers and practitioners who do not understand economics: micro teachers, say, who do not grasp opportunity cost and cannot think about entry; macroeconomists who have not read Keynes; policymakers who do not know the history of their section of the economy.

Their ignorance is commonly defended by saying that, well, they certainly did acquire in their education a lot of "tools". But the tool kit turns out to be filled mainly with bits of mathematics that in five years will become unfashionable again (in favor of other "tools": witness the history of linear programming in economics). Broken power routers and defective power jigsaws have crowded out the hammers and nails.

The problem of a training in technique that does not deal with life appears to be a widespread modern problem. Look at modern art, School of Manhattan, if you can, or modern architecture, from Bauhaus to our house. In a recent essay the critic John Aldridge attacks what is known in English departments as "the workshop writer," that is, the product of one of the numerous programs that teach writing in imitation of the University of Iowa's original Workshop. His description of "that odd species of bloodless fiction so cherished by the editors of *the New Yorker*" would fit most graduate programs in economics. Try substituting "academic economists" for "writers," "economic research" for "writing," and "economics" for "literature":

> [W]hat finally counts ..... is not the quality of the work produced but the continued existence and promotion of writers. Any question raised about quality would surely be considered a form of treason or self-sabotage ..... [I]t is entirely possible for a young writer to be graduated from one of these programs in almost total ignorance of the traditions of his craft and, for that matter, with only superficial knowledge of literature ..... [O]ften the promise they show is the variety most young people show up to the age of about

twenty-five, while other qualities more essential to the continued productivity of writers are not so immediately detectable ..... [T]hese writers are not only estranged from their culture but seem to have no impressions of, or relations to it at all. In fact, they show no symptoms of having vital social and intellectual interests of any kind or any sense of belonging to a literary tradition ..... [A]ny of their novels and stories might conceivably have been written by almost any one of them. (pp. 31, 32, 33, 37)

The benefits, I claim, have been meagre. The physics standard shows that something is wrong. Another standard is the scale of promised and then boldly claimed accomplishments. To hear mathematical economists say it, you would think that mathematical economics would bring us to a Newtonian stage in the science. In a review of Kenneth Arrow's collected works Frank Hahn made the following assertion: "The theory which Arrow and his coevals and successors have built is all we have of honest and powerful thinking on the subject." "The subject" appears to be economics. Suppose, to be generous, that Hahn means rather "the subject" to be the narrower matter of thinking about the desirability of capitalism since Adam Smith. Even so, his claim that general equilibrium has afforded "that precise formulation which would allow [Adam Smith's arguments] to be evaluated and their range of applicability discussed" will seem unreasonable to many economists. It is similarly unreasonable to say that "the case for modern economics" rests on the achievements of one who "has only concerned himself with establishing what it is that can be claimed as true if certain assumptions are made," when the "assumptions" are formal only, the product of the blackboard rather than of the library or of the world.

To ask the question of what we have learned from formalization since the War is to suggest that the yield has been rather modest.[6] We have learned more in economics from our continuing traditions of political arithmetic and economic philosophy. Human capital, the economics of law and society, historical economics, and the statistics of economic growth have come from economists who trade with someone besides the Math Department.

This is not, I repeat, to set *The Journal of*

Economic Theory below its proper value. Surely we should have people doing some sort of philosophical job, finding out how much can be wrung from this or that convenient assumption, though we should not assign quite so many people to the job as at present. We are all very thankful to Smith and Marx and Keynes for having inspired those fine theorems by Hahn and Arrow and Samuelson. But we should not be thankful for the reduction of "theory" to a certain brand of mathematics.

In other ways, however, I stand four square with Frank Hahn: "[A]ll these 'certainties' and all the 'schools' which they spawn are a sure sign of our ignorance ..... [I]t is obvious to me that we do not possess much certain knowledge about the economic world and that our best chance of gaining more is to try in all sorts of directions and by all sorts of means. This will not be furthered by strident commitments of faith" [pp. 7-8].

And I stand, too, with our sainted Léon, he of general economic equilibrium a century ago. He attacked then (p. 48) "the idea, so bourgeois in its narrowness, of dividing education into two separate compartments: one turning out calculators with no knowledge whatsoever of sociology, philosophy, history, or [even, McC.] economics; and the other cultivating men of letters devoid of any notion of mathematics. The twentieth century, which is not far off, will feel the need, even in France, of entrusting the social sciences to men of general culture who are accustomed to thinking both inductively and deductively and who are familiar with reason as well as experience." The 21st century hurries near. We may hope by then, after a century of experiments in educational compartments, that Walras' vision of an undivided economics may be fulfilled.

Notes

1. Look for instance at the presidential address of Harry A. Millis to the American Economic Association (delivered December, 1934), especially pp. 4-5 on marginal productivity and the labor problem. Because he did not understand the notion of a function Millis misunderstood Hicks' *Theory of Wages*.

2. Richard Palmer, a physicist from Duke University recalling a conference of physicists and economists, told Robert Pool, "I used to think physicists were the most arrogant people in the world. The economists were, if anything, more arrogant" [1989, 700].

3. I am speaking of neoclassical economics; but anti-neoclassicals should not therefore rejoice. They do the same thing. In Marxian economics, for example, the general statement that commodities are made with

commodities cannot be expected to yield specific answers to any question worth asking, either. The various impossibility theorems that make institutional economists happy ("But after all the economy is obviously not competitive and so all that neoclassical talk is rubbish") are equally vacuous.

4. The recent works of William Milberg at the University of Michigan-Dearborn and of Hans Lind at the University of Stockholm have noted the lack of rigor in the opening and closing paragraphs of theoretical papers. Great rigor in the middle; touchie-feelie on the ends.

5. For that last see Fisher 1989, p. 122.

6. A full catalogue is examined in Henry Woo's book, *What's Wrong with Formalizaiton in Economics*.

References

Aldridge, John W. 1990. "The New American Assembly-Line Fiction: An Empty Blue Center." *American Scholar* Winter: 17-38.

Brock, W. A. 1988. "Introduction to Chaos and Other Aspects of Nonlinearity." In W. A. Brock and A. G. Malliaris, eds. *Differential Equations, Stability, and Chaos in Dynamic Economics*. NY: North Holland, (October 30, 1987 draft, Department of Economics, University of Wisconsin).

Brock, William A. 1989. "Chaos and Complexity in Economic and Financial Science". Pp. 421-447 in George M. Furstenberg, ed. *Acting Under Uncertainty: Multidisciplinary Conceptions*. Boston: Kluwer Academic.

Feynman, Richard. 1963. *The Feynman Lectures on Physics*. Reading, Massachusetts: Addison-Wesley, Vol. I.

Fisher, Franklin M. 1989. "Games Economists Play: A Noncooperative View." *RAND Journal of Economics* 20 (Spring): 113-124.

Hahn, Frank. 1984. *Equilibrium and Macroeconomics*. Oxford: Basil Blackwell.

Hahn, Frank. 1986. "Review of Collected Works of Kenneth Arrow." *Times Literary Supplement* (August).

Hibbeler, R. C. 1989. *Engineering Mechanics: Statics and Dynamics*. 5th ed. New York: Macmillan.

Hodges, Andrew. 1983. *Alan Turing: The Enigma*. New York: Simon and Schuster.

Klamer, Arjo, and David Collander. 1990. *The Making of an Economist*. Boulder: Westview Press.

Kline, Morris. 1980. *Mathematics: The Loss of Certainty*. New York: Oxford University Press.

Marshall, Alfred. 1920. *Principles of Economics*. London: Macmillan.

Millis, Harry A. 1935. "The Union in Industry: Some Observations on the Theory of Collective Bargaining." *American Economic Review* 25 (March): 1-13.

Mirowski. 1989. *More Heat Than Light*. NY: Cambridge University Press.

Pool, Robert. "Strange Bedfellows." *Science* 245 (18 August 1989): 700-703.

Walras, Léon. *Elements of Pure Economics*. Fourth Ed. (1926).trans. William Jaffé. Homewood, Ill.: Irwin, 1954 (Orion reprint, 1984).

Weintraub, Roy. 1991. *Stabilizing Dynamics: Constructing Economic Knowledge*. Cambridge: Cambridge University Press.

Frye, Northrup. 1964. *The Educated Imagination*. Bloomington: Indiana University Press.

Woo, Henry K. H. 1986. *What's Wrong with Formalization in Economics? An Epistemological Critique*. Newark, California: Victoria Press.

Journal of Economic Literature
Vol. XXXIV (March 1996), pp. 97–114

The Standard Error of Regressions

By DEIRDRE N. MCCLOSKEY

and

STEPHEN T. ZILIAK

University of Iowa

Suggestions by two anonymous and patient referees greatly improved the paper. Our thanks also to seminars at Clark, Iowa State, Harvard, Houston, Indiana, and Kansas State universities, at Williams College, and at the universities of Virginia and Iowa. A colleague at Iowa, Calvin Siebert, was materially helpful.

THE IDEA OF statistical significance is old, as old as Cicero writing on forecasts (Cicero, *De Divinatione*, I. xiii. 23). In 1773 Laplace used it to test whether comets came from outside the solar system (Elizabeth Scott 1953, p. 20). The first use of the very word "significance" in a statistical context seems to be John Venn's, in 1888, speaking of differences expressed in units of probable error:

> They inform us which of the differences in the above tables are permanent and significant, in the sense that we may be tolerably confident that if we took another similar batch we should find a similar difference; and which are merely transient and insignificant, in the sense that another similar batch is about as likely as not to reverse the conclusion we have obtained. (Venn, quoted in Lancelot Hogben 1968, p. 325).

Statistical significance has been much used since Venn, and especially since Ronald Fisher.

The problem, and our main point, is that a difference can be permanent (as Venn put it) without being "significant" in other senses, such as for science or policy. And a difference can be signifi-

cant for science or policy and yet be insignificant statistically, ignored by the less thoughtful researchers.

In the 1930s Jerzy Neyman and Egon S. Pearson, and then more explicitly Abraham Wald, argued that actual investigations should depend on substantive not merely statistical significance. In 1933 Neyman and Pearson wrote of type I and type II errors:

> Is it more serious to convict an innocent man or to acquit a guilty? That will depend on the consequences of the error; is the punishment death or fine; what is the danger to the community of released criminals; what are the current ethical views on punishment? From the point of view of mathematical theory all that we can do is to show how the risk of errors may be controlled and minimised. The use of these statistical tools in any given case, in determining just how the balance should be struck, *must be left to the investigator.* (Neyman and Pearson 1933, p. 296; italics supplied)

Wald went further:

> The question as to how the form of the weight [that is, loss] function . . . should be determined, *is not a mathematical or statistical one.* The statistician who wants to test

97

certain hypotheses must first determine the relative importance of all possible errors, *which will depend on the special purposes of his investigation.* (1939, p. 302, italics supplied)

To date no empirical studies have been undertaken measuring the use of statistical significance in economics. We here examine the alarming hypothesis that ordinary usage in economics takes statistical significance to be the same as economic significance. We compare statistical best practice against leading textbooks of recent decades and against the papers using regression analysis in the 1980s in the *American Economic Review.*

I. An Example

The usual test of purchasing power parity regresses prices at home (P) on prices abroad $(P*)$, allowing for the exchange rate (e). Thus: $P = a + \beta \, (eP*) +$ error term (cf., McCloskey and J. Richard Zecher 1984). The equation can be in levels or rates of change or in some more complex functional form. An estimated coefficient β is of course a random variate, and the accuracy of its estimated mean depends on the properties of the error term, the specification of the model, and so forth. But to fix ideas suppose that all the usual econometric problems have been solved. In tests of purchasing power parity the null hypothesis is usually thought of as "β equal to 1.0." Suppose an unbiased estimator of β yields not exactly 1.000 but very close, say 0.999. That is, prices at home rise by very nearly the same rate as prices abroad for most purposes of science or policy. (Not for all purposes: the point of thinking as Wald did in terms of loss functions is that for *some* purposes a difference that in some metric looks "small" might in another metric be important.) If the sample size were large enough, however, even a coefficient of 0.999

might prove to be a *statistically* significant divergence from exactly 1.000. Under purely statistical procedures the investigator would conclude, as many have, that the hypothesis of purchasing power parity had failed.

The hypothesis does not in truth predict that the coefficient will be 1.000 to many decimal places. It predicts that β will be "about 1." The economically relevant null hypothesis is a range around 1.000, not the point itself in isolation from its neighborhood. The investigator would not want to assert that if $\beta = 0.999$ with a standard error of 0.00000001 we should abandon purchasing power parity, or run our models of the American economy without the world price level. Yet the literature on purchasing power parity has ordinarily used the null of 1.000 exactly. The procedure is not defensible in statistical theory. The table of t will not tell what is "close." Closeness depends, in Wald's words, on the special purposes of the investigation—good enough for inflation control, say, if $\beta = 0.85$, though not good enough to make money on the foreign exchange market unless $\beta = 0.99998$.

Just how the balance should be struck, as Neyman and Pearson put it, must be left to the investigator. A coefficient of 0.15, say, would for most purposes reject "β = about 1." Accepting the null hypothesis may be reasonable or unreasonable, but it depends on economic context. The point is that it does not mainly depend on the value of the test statistic. The uncertainty of the estimate that arises from sampling error—the only kind of uncertainty the test of significance deals with—is still of scientific interest. But low or high uncertainty (more or less "permanence" in Venn's terms) does not by itself answer the question how important the variable is, how large is large. In tests of purchasing power parity, for example, one should ask if $\beta =$

0.999 is close enough for scientific purposes to the null. How should the answer be adjusted if there are 20,000 observations (cf. Richard Rudner 1953, p. 3; Scott Gordon 1991, pp. 664–65)? If the estimate is not taken to be close to the null, what makes it "interestingly different" or what is the "scientific intuition" of one's "public" (Edwin Boring 1919, p. 337)? These are not easy questions. But they are the questions relevant to scientific discovery.

II. *The Evidence: Textbooks*

The late Morris DeGroot ([1975] 1989), a statistician with sophistication in economics, was emphatic on the point:

> It is extremely important . . . to distinguish between an observed value of *U* that is statistically significant and an actual value of the parameter . . . In a given problem, the tail area corresponding to the observed value of *U* might be very small; and yet the actual value . . . might be so close to [the null] that, for practical purposes, the experimenter would not regard [it] as being [substantively] different from [the null]. (p. 496)
> [I]t is very likely that the *t*-test based on the sample of 20,000 will lead to a statistically significant value of *U* . . . [The experimenter] knows in advance that there is a high probability of rejecting [the null] even when the true value . . . differs [arithmetically] only slightly from [the null]. (p. 497)

But few other econometrics textbooks distinguish economic significance from statistical significance. And fewer emphasize economic significance. In the econometrics texts widely used in the 1970s and 1980s, when the practice was becoming standard, such as Jan Kmenta's *Elements of Econometrics* (1971) and John Johnston's *Econometric Methods* ([1963] 1972, 1984), there is no mention of economic as against statistical significance. Peter Kennedy, in his *A Guide to Econometrics* (1985), briefly mentions that a large enough sample always gives statistically significant differences. This

is part of the argument but not all of it, and Kennedy in any case relegates the partial argument to an endnote (p. 62).

Among recent econometrics books Arthur Goldberger's is the most explicit. His *A Course in Econometrics* (1991) gives the topic "Statistical versus Economic Significance" a page of text (pp. 240–41), quoting McCloskey's little article of 1985. Goldberger's page has been noticed as unusual. Clive Granger, reviewing in the March 1994 issue of this *Journal* four leading books (Goldberger; Russell Davidson and James G. MacKinnon 1993; William H. Greene 1993; William E. Griffiths, R. Carter Hill, and George G. Judge 1993), notes that

> when the link is made [in Goldberger between the economics and the technical statistics] some important insights arise, as for example the section discussing "statistical and economic significance," a topic not mentioned in the other books. (1994, p. 118)

That is, most beginning econometrics books even now, unlike DeGroot and Goldberger and before them the modern masters of statistics, do not contrast economic and statistical significance.

Nor do the present-day advanced handbooks and textbooks. The three volumes of the *Handbook of Econometrics* contain one mention of the point, unsurprisingly by Edward Leamer (p. 325 of Volume I, Zvi Griliches and Michael D. Intriligator, ed. 1983). In the 762 pages of the recent companion work, Volume 11 of the *Handbook of Statistics* (1993), there is one sentence about the level of the test in its relation to sample size (Jean-Pierre Florens and Michel Mouchart 1993, p. 321).

One might defend contemporary usage by arguing that the advanced texts assume their readers already grasp the difference between economic and statistical significance. Economy of style would dictate the unqualified word "significance," its exact meaning, economic or statistical, to be supplied by thè sophisticated reader. Under such a hypothesis the contemporary usage would be no more than a shorthand way to refer to an estimated coefficient. The implied reader would be educated enough to supply the appropriate caveats about *economic* significance.

The hypothesis is not borne out by the evidence. To take one example among many, Takeshi Amemiya's advanced textbook in econometrics does not itself draw a distinction between economic and statistical significance (Amemiya 1985). The book makes little claim to teaching empirical methods, but presumably the theory of econometrics is supposed to connect to empirical work. Amemiya recommends that the student prepare "at the level of Johnston, 1972" (preface). Does the recommendation cover the matter of statistical versus substantive significance?

No. Johnston as we have seen makes no mention of the point. He uses the term "economic significance" once only, without contrasting it to the statistical significance on which he lavishes attention: "It is even more difficult to attach economic significance to the linear combinations arising in canonical correlation analysis than it is to principal components" (p. 333), In an extended example of hypothesis testing, spanning pages 17 to 43, Johnston tests in the conventional way the hypothesis that "sterner penalties" for dangerous driving caused fewer road deaths, concluding "[t]he computed value [of the *t*-statistic] *is suggestive of a reduction*, being *significant* at the 5 per cent, *but not at the one per cent*, level" (p. 43, italics supplied). He is saying that at a high level of rigor the policy of sterner penalties might be doubted to have desirable effects. Statistically the usage is unobjectionable (except that he uses the universe of road casualties in the United Kingdom 1947–1957 as

though it were a sample of size 11 from some universe). But the 100,000 lives that were saved in the reduction as measured are not acknowledged as "significant." Johnston has merged statistical and policy significance. At what level the significance level should be set, considering the human cost of ignoring the effect of sterner penalties, is none of Johnston's concern. He leaves the question of how large is large to statistics. As Wald said in 1939, however, the question "is not a mathematical or statistical one."

Johnston does recommend "The Cairncross Test" (1984, pp. 509–10). That is, after computing assorted test statistics the researcher should ask if the model would satisfy the discerning judgment of Sir Alec Cairncross. "Would Sir Alec be willing to take this model to the Riyadh?" But that is our point. If judgments about economic significance are not made at the keyboard they need to be brought into the open, before reaching Sir Alec. The researcher wastes the time of Cairncross if the statistically significant does not correspond to what Sir Alec, and the Riyadh, want: economic significance.

A tenacious defender of contemporary usage might argue further that Johnston, in turn, presumes the reader already understands the difference between economic and statistical significance, having acquired it in elementary courses on statistics. The argument is testable. In his preface Johnston directs the reader who has difficulty with his first chapter to examine a "good introductory" book on statistics, mentioning Paul G. Hoel's *Introduction to Mathematical Statistics* (1954), Alexander M. Mood's *Introduction to the Theory of Statistics* (1950), and Donald A. S. Fraser's *Statistics: An Introduction* (1958) (p. ix). These are fine books: Mood, for example, gives a good treatment of power functions, pointing to their relevance in applied work. But none of them make a distinction between substantive and statistical significance. Hoel writes that

[t]here are several words and phrases used in connection with testing hypotheses that should be brought to the attention of students. When a test of a hypothesis produces a sample value falling in the critical region of the test, the result is said to be *significant*; otherwise one says that the result is *not significant*. (p. 176, his italics)

The student from the outset of her statistical education, therefore, is led to believe that economic (or substantive) significance and statistical significance are the same thing. Hoel explains: "This word ['not significant'] arises from the fact that such a sample value is not compatible with the hypothesis and therefore signifies that some other hypothesis is necessary" (p. 176). The elementary point that "[t]here is no sharp border between 'significant' and 'insignificant,' only increasingly strong evidence as the P-value decreases" (David S. Moore and George P. McCabe 1993, p. 473) is not found in most of the earlier books from which most economists learned statistics and econometrics. The old classic by W. Allen Wallis and Harry V. Roberts, *Statistics: A New Approach*, first published in 1956, is an exception:

It is essential not to confuse the statistical usage of "significant" with the everyday usage. In everyday usage, "significant" means "of practical importance," or simply "important." In statistical usage, "significant" means "signifying a characteristic of the population from which the sample is drawn," regardless of whether the characteristic is important. (Wallis and Roberts [1956] 1965, p. 385)

The point has been revived in elementary statistics books, though most still do not emphasize it. In their leading elementary book the statisticians David Freedman, Robert Pisani, and Roger Purves (1978) could not be plainer. In

one of numerous places where they make the point they write:

This chapter . . . explains the limitations of significance tests. The first one is that "significance" is a technical word. A test can only deal with the question of whether a difference is real [permanent in Venn's sense], or just a chance variation. *It is not designed to see whether the difference is important.* (p. 487, italics supplied)

The distinction is also emphatic in Ronald J. Wonnacott and Thomas H. Wonnacott (1982, p. 160) and in Moore and McCabe (1993, p. 474).

III. The Instrument: A Survey of Practice in Significance

The evidence, then, is that econometricians are not in their textbooks emphasizing the difference between economic significance and statistical significance. What is practice?

We take the full-length papers published in the *American Economic Review* as an unbiased selection of best practice (we will not say "sample" and will not therefore use tests of statistical significance). We read all the 182 papers in the 1980s that used regression analysis (and record our impression that in most matters these are superb examples of economic science). Each paper was asked 19 questions about its use of statistical significance, to be answered "yes" (sound statistical practice) or "no" (unsound practice) or "not applicable."

The survey questions are:

1. *Does the paper use a small number of observations, such that statistically significant differences are not found at the conventional levels merely by choosing a large number of observations?* The power of a test is high if the significance level at $N = 30,000$ is carried over from situations in which the sample is 30 or 300. For example, in Glen C. Blomquist, Mark C. Berger, and John P. Hoehn, $N =$

34,414 housing units and 46,004 individuals (Mar. 1988, p. 93). At such large sample sizes the authors need to pay attention to the tradeoff between power and the size of the test, and to the economic significance of the power against alternatives.

2. *Are the units and descriptive statistics for all regression variables included?* Empirical work in economics is measurement. It is elementary to include units of the variables, and then also to give means.

3. *Are coefficients reported in elasticity form, or in some interpretable form* relevant for the problem at hand and consistent with economic theory, so that readers can discern the economic impact of regressors? Wallis and Roberts long ago complained that "sometimes authors are so intrigued by tests of significance that they fail even to state the actual *amount* of the effect, much less to appraise its practical importance" (1956, p. 409). In some fields (not much in economics, though we did find one example) the investigator will publish tables that consist only of asterisks indicating levels of significance.

4. *Are the proper null hypotheses specified?* The commonest problem would be to test against a null of zero when some other null is to the point. Such an error would be the result of allowing a canned program to make scientific decisions. If a null hypothesis is $\beta_1 + \beta_2 = 1$, there is not much to be gained from testing the hypothesis that each coefficient is statistically significantly different from zero. The most fruitful application of the Neyman-Pearson test specifies the null hypothesis as something the researcher believes to be true. The only result that leads to a definitive conclusion is a rejection of the null hypothesis. Failing to reject does not of course imply that the null is therefore true. And rejecting the null does not imply that the alternative hypothesis is true: there may be other alternatives (a range that investigators agree is relevant, for example) which would cause rejection of the null. The current rhetoric of rejection promotes a lexicographic procedure of "regress height income country age"; inspect *t*-values; discard as unimportant if $t < 2$; circulate as important if $t > 2$.

5. *Are coefficients carefully interpreted?* Goldberger has an illustration similar to many issues in economic policy (Goldberger 1991, p. 241). Suppose the dependent variable is "weight in pounds," the large coefficient is on "height," the smaller coefficient is on "exercise," and the estimated coefficients have the same standard errors. Neither the physician nor the patient would profit from an analysis that says height is "more important" (its coefficient being more standard errors away from zero in this sample), offering the overweight patient in effect the advice that he's not too fat, merely too short for his weight. "The moral of this example is that statistical measures of 'importance' are a diversion from the proper target of research—estimation of relevant parameters—to the task of 'explaining variation' in the dependent variable" (Goldberger, p. 241).

6. *Does the paper eschew reporting all t- or F-statistics or standard errors, regardless of whether a significance test is appropriate?* Statistical computing software routinely provide *t*-statistics for every estimated coefficient. But that programs provide it does not mean that the information is relevant for science. We suspect that referees enforce the proliferation of meaningless *t*- and *F*-statistics, out of the belief that statistical and substantive significance are the same.

7. *Is statistical significance at the first use, commonly the scientific crescendo of the paper, the only criterion of "impor-*

tance"? By "crescendo" we mean that place in the paper where the author comes to what she evidently considers the crucial test.

8. *Does the paper mention the power of the tests?* For example, Frederic S. Mishkin does, unusually, in two footnotes (June 1981, pp. 298 n11, 305 n27; lack of power is a persistent difficulty in capital-market studies, but is seldom faced). As DeGroot pointed out, the power of a test may be low against a nearby and substantively significant alternative. On the other hand, power may be high against a nearby and trivial alternative.

9. *If the paper mentions power, does it do anything about it?* It is true that power can only be discussed relative to an explicit alternative hypothesis, making power analysis difficult for some of the alternatives. An example is the Durbin-Wu-Hausman test for whether two estimators are consistent. (The survey accounts for the difficulty by coding the relevant papers "not applicable.")

10. *Does the paper eschew "asterisk econometrics,"* that is, ranking the coefficients according to the absolute size of *t*-statistics?

11. *Does the paper eschew "sign econometrics,"* that is, remarking on the sign but not the size of the coefficients? There is a little statistical theory in the econometrics books lying behind this customary practice (Goldberger, ch. 22; Greene, ch. 8), though for the most part the custom outstrips the theory. But sign is not *economically* significant unless the magnitude is large enough to matter. Statistical significance does not tell whether the size is large enough to matter. It is not true, as custom seems to be arguing, that sign is a statistic independent of magnitude.

12. *Does the paper discuss the size of the coefficients?* That is, once regression results are presented, does the paper make the point that some of the coefficients and their variables are *economically* influential, while others are not? Blomquist, Berger, and Hoehn do in part, by giving their coefficients on housing and neighborhood amenities in dollar form. But they do not discuss whether the magnitudes are scientifically reasonable, or in some other way important. Contrast Christina Romer, in a 19-page, exclusively empirical paper: "Indeed, correcting for inventory movements reduces the discrepancy . . . by approximately half. This suggests that inventory movements are [economically] important" (June 1986, p. 327). M. Boissiere, J. B. Knight, and R. H. Sabot reflect the more typical practice: "In both countries, cognitive achievement bears a highly significant relationship to educational level . . . In Kenya, secondary education raises H by 11.75 points, or by 35 percent of the mean" (Dec. 1985, p. 1026). They make ambiguous use of the word "significance," then draw back to the relevant question of economic significance. Later in the paragraph they recur to depending on statistical significance alone: "significantly positive" and "almost significantly positive" become again their only criteria of importance.

Daniel Hamermesh, by contrast, estimates his crucial parameter K, and at the first mention says, "The estimates of K are quite large, implying that the firm varies employment only in response to very large shocks. . . . Consider what an estimate this large means" (Sept. 1989, p. 683). The form is here close to ideal: it gets to the scientific question of what the size of a magnitude means. Two paragraphs down he speaks of "fairly large," "very important," "small," and "important" without merging these with statistical significance. In Goldberger's terms, he focuses on "the proper target of research—estimation of relevant parameters." (Later, though, Hamermesh falls back to average practice: "The $\hat{K}$ for the aggregated data in Table 2 are insignificant," though he adds wisely, "and very small; and the average values of the $\hat{p}$ are much higher than in the pooled data"; p. 685.)

13. *Does the paper discuss the scientific conversation within which a coefficient would be judged "large" or "small"?* Romer, for example, remarks that "The existence of the stylized fact [that is, the scientific consensus] that the economy has stabilized implies a general consensus" (p. 322).

14. *Does the paper avoid choosing variables for inclusion solely on the basis of statistical significance?* The standard argument is that if certain variables enter the model significantly, the information should not be spurned. But such an argument merges statistical and substantive significance.

15. *After the crescendo, does the paper avoid using statistical significance as the criterion of importance?* The referees will have insisted unthinkingly on a significance test, the prudent author will have acceded to their insistence, but will after reporting them turn to other and scientifically relevant criteria of importance.

16. *Is statistical significance decisive, the conversation stopper, conveying the sense of an ending?* Romer and Jeffrey Sachs (Mar. 1980) both use statistical significance, and misuse it—in both cases looking to statistical significance as a criterion for how large is large. But in neither paper does statistical significance run the empirical work. The misuse in Michael Darby (June 1984) is balder: his only argument for a coefficient when he runs a regression is its statistical significance (pp. 311, 315), but on the other hand his findings do not turn on the regression results.

17. *Does the paper ever use a simulation (as against a use of the regression as an input into further argument) to determine whether the coefficients are reasonable?* To some degree Blomquist, Berger, and Hoehn do. They simulate the rankings of cities by amenity, and if the coefficients were quite wrong the rankings would be themselves unreasonable. Santa Barbara does rank high, though the differential value of amenities worst to best, at $5,146, seems low (Mar. 1988, p. 96). Simulations using regression coefficients can be informative, but of course should not use statistical significance as a screening device for input.

18. *In the "conclusions" and "implications" sections, is statistical significance kept separate from economic, policy, and scientific significance?* In Boissiere, Knight, and Sabot (Dec 1985) the effect of ability is isolated well, but the economic significance is not argued.

19. *Does the paper avoid using the word "significance" in ambiguous ways, meaning "statistically significant" in one sentence and "large enough to matter for policy or science" in another?* Thus Darby (June 1984): "First we wish to test whether oil prices, price controls, or both has a significant influence on productivity growth" (p. 310). The meanings are merged.

IV. Results of the Survey of the American Economic Review

Some of the *AER* authors, such as Romer and Hamermesh, show that they are aware of the substantive importance of the questions they ask, and of the futility of relying on a test of statistical significance for getting answers. Thus Kim B. Clark: "While the union coefficient in the sales specification is twice the size of its standard error, it is substantively small; moreover, with over 4,600 observations, the power of the evidence that the effect is different from zero is not

TABLE 1

THE *AMERICAN ECONOMIC REVIEW* IN THE 1980s HAD NUMEROUS ERRORS IN THE USE OF STATISTICAL
SIGNIFICANCE

Survey Question	Total for which the question applies	Percent Yes
Does the Paper . . .		
8. Consider the power of the test?	182	4.4
6. Eschew reporting all standard errors, *t*-, and *F*-statistics, when such information is irrelevant?	181	8.3
17. Do a simulation to determine whether the coefficients are reasonable?	179	13.2
9. Examine the power function?	12	16.7
13. Discuss the scientific conversation within which a coefficient would be judged large or small?	181	28.0
16. Consider more than statistical significance decisive in an empirical argument?	182	29.7
18. In the conclusions, distinguish between statistical and substantive significance?	181	30.1
2. Report descriptive statistics for regression variables?	178	32.4
15. Use other criteria of importance besides statistical significance after the crescendo?	182	40.7
19. Avoid using the word "significance" in ambiguous ways?	180	41.2
5. Carefully interpret coefficients? For example, does it pay attention to the details of the units of measurement, and to the limitations of the data?	181	44.5
11. Eschew "sign econometrics," remarking on the sign but not the size of the coefficients?	181	46.7
7. At its first use, consider statistical significance to be one among other criteria of importance?	182	47.3
3. Report coefficients in elasticities, or in some other useful form that addresses the question of "how large is large"?	173	66.5
14. Avoid choosing variables for inclusion solely on the basis of statistical significance?	180	68.1
10. Eschew "asterisk econometrics," the ranking of coefficients according to the absolute size of the test statistic?	182	74.7
12. Discuss the size of the coefficients?	182	80.2
1. Use a small number of observations, such that statistically significant differences are not found merely by choosing a very large sample?	182	85.7
4. Test the null hypotheses that the authors said were the ones of interest?	180	97.3

Source for Tables 1–5: All full-length papers using regression analysis in the *American Economic Review,* 1980–1989, excluding the Proceedings.

Notes: "Percent Yes" is the total number of Yes responses divided by the relevant number of papers (never exceeding 182). Some questions are not generally applicable to particular papers and some questions are not applicable because they are conditional on the paper having a particular characteristic. Question 3, for example, was coded "not applicable" for papers which exclusively use nonparametric statistics. Question 19 was coded "not applicable" for papers that do not use the word "significance."

overwhelming" (Dec 1984, p. 912). And Griliches:

> Here and subsequently, all statements about statistical "significance" should not be taken literally. Besides the usual issue of data mining clouding their interpretation, the "sample" analyzed comes close to covering completely the relevant population. Tests of significance are used here as a metric for discussing the relative fit of different versions of the model. In each case, the actual magnitude of the estimated coefficients is of more interest than their precise "statistical significance." (Dec 1986, p. 146)

Griliches understands that populations should not be treated as samples, and that statistical significance is not a substitute for economic significance. (He does not say why statistical significance is a scientifically relevant "metric for discussing the relative fit of the different versions of the model.")

But most authors in the *AER* do not understand these points. The results of applying the survey to the papers of the 1980s are displayed in Table 1.

The principal findings of the survey are:

- 70 percent of the empirical papers in the *American Economic Review* papers did not distinguish statistical significance from economic, policy, or scientific significance.

- At the first use of statistical significance, typically in the "Estimation" or "Results" section, 53 percent did not consider anything but the size of *t*- and *F*-statistics. About one third used only the size of *t*- and *F*-test statistics as a criterion for the inclusion of variables in future work.

- 72 percent did not ask "How large is large?" That is, after settling on an estimate of a coefficient, 72 percent did not consider what other authors had found; they did not ask what standards other authors have used to determine "importance"; they did

not provide an argument one way or another whether the estimate $\beta = 0.999$ is economically close to 1.0 and economically important even though "statistically different from one." Awareness that scientific inquiry takes place in a conversation about how large is large seemed to improve the econometric practice. Of 131 papers that did *not* mention the work of other authors as a quantitative context for their own, 78 percent let statistical significance decide questions of substantive significance. Of 50 papers that did mention the work of other authors as a context, only 20 percent let statistical significance decide.

- 59 percent used the word "significance" in ambiguous ways, at one point meaning "statistically significantly different from the null," at another "practically important" or "greatly changing our scientific opinions," with no distinction.

- Despite the advice proffered in theoretical statistics, only 4-percent considered the power of their tests. One percent examined the power function.

- 69 percent did not report descriptive statistics—the means of the regression variables, for example—that would allow the reader to make a judgment about the economic significance of the results.

- 32 percent admitted openly to using statistical significance to drop variables (question 14). One would have to have more evidence than explicit admissions to know how prevalent the practice is in fact. One-third is a lower bound.

- Multiple-author papers, as one might expect from the theory of common property resources, more

TABLE 2
MULTIPLE AUTHORS APPEAR TO HAVE COORDINATION PROBLEMS, MAKING THE ABUSES WORSE
MEASURED BY PERCENT YES

Survey Question	Multiple Author Papers	Single Author Papers
Does the paper . . .		
7. At its first use, consider statistical significance to be one among other criteria of importance?	42.2	53.4
10. Eschew "asterisk econometrics," the ranking of coefficients according to the absolute size of the test statistic?	68.8	79.2
12. Discuss the size of the coefficients?	76.7	84.1
1. Use a small number of observations, such that statistically significant differences are not found merely by choosing a very large sample?	77.8	84.8

Notes: "Percent Yes" is the total number of Yes responses divided by the relevant number of papers.

often spoke of "significance" in ambiguous ways, used sign econometrics, did not discuss the size of estimated coefficients, and found nothing more than the size of test statistics to be of importance at the first use of statistical significance (Table 2).

• Authors from "Tier 1" schools did in some respects a little better, but whether the difference justifies the invidious terminology of "tiers" is a scientific, not a statistical, question and must be left to the investigator (Table 3; the terminology is that of the most recent National Research Council assessment and includes Chicago, Harvard, MIT, Princeton, Stanford, and Yale.)

Though we do not here report the results, we found on the other hand that papers written by faculty at Tier 1 schools were proportionally more likely to use sampling theory on entire populations, and to treat as probability samples what are in fact samples of convenience. The substantive significance of such practices can be made more vivid by ex-

amining a few of the papers in some depth.

The first is a case of not thinking about the economic meaning of a coefficient. The authors estimate benefit-cost ratios for the state of Illinois following the implementation of an unemployment insurance experiment. In one experiment a control group was given a cash bonus for getting a job quickly and keeping it for several months. In another experiment, the "Employer Experiment," *employers* were given a cash-bonus if claimants found a job quickly and retained it for some specified amount of time (Sept. 1987, p. 517). The intent of the "Employer Experiment" was to "provide a marginal wage-bill subsidy, or training subsidy, that might reduce the duration of insured unemployment" (p. 517). Here is how the conclusion is presented:

The fifth panel also shows that the overall benefit-cost ratio for the Employer Experiment is 4.29, but it is not statistically different from zero. The benefit-cost ratio for white women in the Employer Experiment, however, is 7.07, and is statistically different from zero. Hence, a program modeled on the Employer Experiment also might be attrac-

TABLE 3
AUTHORS AT TIER 1 DEPARTMENTS DO BETTER THAN OTHERS IN MANY CATEGORIES
MEASURED BY PERCENT YES

Survey Question	Tier 1 Departments	Other Departments
Does the paper . . .		
1. Use a small number of observations, such that statistically significant differences are not found merely by choosing a very large sample?	91.3	83.9
12. Discuss the size of the coefficients?	87.0	78.9
10. Eschew "asterisk econometrics," the ranking of coefficients according to the absolute size of the test statistic?	84.8	71.4
7. At its first use, consider statistical significance to be one among other criteria of importance?	65.5	41.2
5. Carefully interpret coefficients? For example, does it pay attention to the details of the units of measurement, and to the limitations of the data?	60.0	37.5
19. Avoid using the word "significance" in ambiguous ways?	52.4	37.5
18 In the conclusions, distinguish between statistical and substantitive significance?	50.0	23.1

Notes: According to the most recent National Research Council assessment, the tier 1 departments are Chicago, Harvard, MIT, Princeton, Stanford, and Yale.
"Percent Yes" is the total number of Yes responses divided by the relevant number of papers.

tive from the state's point of view if the program did not increase unemployment among nonparticipants. Since, however, the Employer Experiment affected only white women, it would be essential to understand the reasons for the uneven effects of the treatment on different groups of workers before drawing conclusions about the efficacy of such a program. (p. 527)

Here "affected" means that the estimated coefficient is statistically significantly different from a value the authors believe to be the relevant one. The 4.29 benefit-cost ratio for the whole Employer Experiment is, according to the authors, *not useful or important for public policy*. The 7.07 ratio for white women is said to "affect"—to be important—because it passed an arbitrary significance test. That is, 7.07 *affects*, 4.29 does not. It is true that 4.29 is a realization from a noisy random variable, whereas 7.07 is from a more quiet one.

Though the authors do not say so, the 4.29 benefit-cost ratio is marginally discernible from zero at about the 12 percent level (p. 527). Yet for policy purposes even a noisy benefit-cost ratio is worth talking about. The argument that the 4.29 figure does not "affect" is unsound, and could be costly in employment foregone.

Another paper offers "an alternative test of the CAPM and report[s] . . . test results that are free from the ambiguity imbedded in the past tests" (Jan. 1980, p. 660). The authors are taking exception, they say, to Richard Roll's comment that "there is practically no possibility that such a test can be accomplished in the future" (p. 660). So they test five hypotheses: the intercept equals zero; the slope coefficients differ from zero; the adjusted coefficient of determination should be near one; there is no trend in the intercept; and there is no'trend in the adjusted coefficient of determination (pp. 664–65). On several time-series they run least squares regressions to estimate coefficients. Nowhere in the text is the size of the estimated coefficients discussed (a common mistake in the capital-market literature). Instead, the authors *rank* their results according to the number of times the absolute value of the *t*-statistic is greater than two (p. 667). Three out of four of their tables of estimation results have a column called "No. of Times *t* > 2," another column with "Average *t*-statistics," and one with "Adjusted R^2." They do not report coefficient estimates in the three tables, merely the *t*-statistics (Tables 1, 2, and 3, pp. 667–68). The only "Yes" that the paper earned in our survey was for specifying the null according to what their theory suggests.

Using ambiguously the very word "significance" implies there is no difference between economic significance and statistical significance, that nothing or little else matters. Of the 96 papers that use only the test of statistical significance as a criterion of importance at its first use, 90 percent imply—or state—that it is decisive in an empirical argument, and 70 percent use the word "significance" ambiguously. Of the other 86 papers in the survey less than half use the word ambiguously. The 96 unsound papers continue making inappropriate decisions at a higher rate than the 86 papers that acknowledge some criterion other than statistical significance. Only seven of the 96 distinguish statistical significance from economic or policy or scientific significance in the conclusions and implications sections, while 47 of the 86 make the distinction (Table 4).

Here is an extreme case of ambiguity:

The statistically significant [read: (1) sampling theory] inequality aversion is in addition to any unequal distribution of inputs re-

sulting from different social welfare weights for different neighborhoods. The KP results allowing for unequal concern yield an estimate of *q* of -3.4. This estimate is significantly [read: (2) some numbers are smaller than others] less than zero, indicating aggregate outcome is not maximized. At the same time, however, there is also significant [read: (3) a moral or scientific or policy matter] concern about productivity, as the inequality parameter is significantly [read: (4) a joint observation about morality and numbers] greater than the extreme of concern solely with equity. (AER Mar. 1987, p. 46)

In a piece on Ricardian Equivalence, statistical significance decides nearly everything:

Notice the least significant of the variables in the constrained estimation is the second lagged value of the deficit in the government purchases equation. A natural course would be to reestimate the model for the case of two lagged values of government spending and one lagged value of the government deficit. . . . Although the elimination of [the variable] raises the confidence level at which the null hypothesis can be rejected, it remains impossible to argue that the data provides evidence against the joint proposition of Ricardian equivalence and rational expectations at conventional levels of significance. (AER Mar. 1985, p. 125)

Another paper reports "significant" results on the relation between unemployment and money:

The coefficient is significant at the 99 percent confidence level. Neither the current money shock nor all 12 coefficients as a group are significantly different from zero. The coefficient on *c* is negative and significant and the distributed lag on *c* is significant as well. In column (2) we report a regression which omits the insignificant lags on money shocks. The *c* distributed lag is now significant at the 1 percent confidence level. . . .

We interpret these results as indicating that the primary factor determining cyclical variations in the probability of leaving unemployment is probably heterogeneity. Inventory innovations appear to play some role and surprisingly, money shocks have no significant impact. (AER Sept. 1985, p. 630)

TABLE 4
IF ONLY STATISTICAL SIGNIFICANCE IS SAID TO BE OF IMPORTANCE AT ITS FIRST USE (QUESTION 7),
THEN MANY OTHER INAPPROPRIATE DECISIONS ARE MADE
MEASURED BY PERCENT YES

Survey Question	If only statistical significance is important	If more than statistical significance is important
Does the paper . . .		
12. Examine the power function?	0	28.6
6. Eschew reporting all standard errors, t-, and F-statistics, when such information is irrelevant	3.2	14.0
8. Consider the power of the test?	4.2	4.7
17. Do a simulation to determine whether the coefficients are reasonable	6.3	17.9
18. In the conclusions, distinguish between statistical and substantive significance	7.3	55.3
16. Consider more than statistical significance decisive in an empirical argument?	10.4	51.2
5. Carefully interpret coefficients? For example, does it pay attention to the units of measurement, and to the limitations of the data?	13.7	77.9
13. Discuss the scientific conversation within which a coefficient would be judged large or small?	17.7	38.8
11. Eschew "sign econometrics," remarking on the sign but not the size of the coefficients?	21.9	74.1
2. Report descriptive statistics for regression variables?	26.3	36.1
15. Use other criteria of importance besides statistical significance after the crescendo?	30.2	52.3
19. Avoid using the word "significance" in ambiguous ways?	29.5	52.9
3. Report coefficients in elasticities, or in some other useful form that addresses the question "how large is large?"	51.6	80.0
14. Avoid choosing variables for inclusion solely on the basis of statistical significance?	59.0	77.7
10. Eschew "asterisk econometrics," the ranking of coefficients according to the size of the test statistic?	66.7	83.7
12. Discuss the size of the coefficients, making points of substantive significance?	66.7	96.5
1. Use a small number of observations, such that statistically significant differences are not found merely by choosing a very large sample?	86.5	84.8
4. Test the null hypotheses that the authors say are the ones of interest?	94.7	100

Notes: "Percent Yes" is the total number of Yes responses divided by the relevant number of papers. Some questions are not generally applicable because they are conditional on a paper having a particular characteristic. Question 3, for example, was coded "not applicable" for papers which exclusively use nonparametric statistics. Question 19 was coded "not applicable" for papers that do not use the word "significance."

TABLE 5
THE EASE OF COMPUTING STATISTICAL SIGNIFICANCE IN THE LATE 1970s MAY HAVE HAD ILL EFFECTS ON THE
USE OF REGRESSION ANALYSIS
MEASURED BY PERCENT YES

	Does the Paper . . .		
Date of Ph.D. Conferral	Distinguish Among Kinds of Significance in the Conclusions (Question 18)	Eschew Ambiguous Usage of the Very Word (Question 19)	Consider More Than Statistical Significance Decisive in Empirical Argument (Question 16)
1940–1969	29	61	26
1970–1974	33	37	31
1975–1979	17	29	13
1980–1984	33	45	33

Notes: The number of papers published by each cohort is 31, 48, 24, and 24. Multiple author papers were dated by the first name listed on the published article.

Such misuses of statistical significance appear to depend in part on a vintage effect, measured by date of Ph.D. conferral. The papers authored by Ph.D.'s conferred between 1975 and 1979, when inexpensively generated *t*-tests first reached the masses, were considerably worse than the papers of others at making a distinction between economic and statistical significance. They used the word "significance" in ambiguous ways more often than did early or later Ph.D.'s and they were less likely to separate statistical significance from other kinds of significance in the sections on scientific and policy implications (Table 5).

V. *Taking the Con Out of Confidence Intervals*

In a squib published in the *American Economic Review* in 1985 one of us claimed that "[r]oughly three-quarters of the contributors to the *American Economic Review* misuse the test of statistical significance" (McCloskey 1985, p. 201). The full survey confirms the claim, and in some matters strengthens it.

We would not assert that every economist misunderstands statistical significance, only that most do, and these some of the best economic scientists. By way of contrast to what most understand statistical significance to be capable of saying, Edward Lazear and Robert Michael wrote 17 pages of empirical economics in the *AER*, using ordinary least squares on two occasions, without a single mention of statistical significance (*AER* Mar. 1980, pp. 96–97, pp. 105–06). This is notable considering they had a legitimate sample, justifying a discussion of statistical significance were it relevant to the scientific questions they were asking. Estimated coefficients in the paper are interpreted carefully, and within a conversation in which they ask how large is large (pp. 97, 101, and throughout).

The low and falling cost of calculation, together with a widespread though unarticulated realization that after all the significance test is not crucial to scientific questions, has meant that statistical significance has been valued at its cost. Essentially no one believes a finding of statistical significance or insignificance.

This is bad for the temper of the field. My statistical significance is a "finding"; yours is an ornamented prejudice. Contrary to the decisive rhetoric of rejection in the mechanical test, statistical significance has not in fact changed the minds of economic scientists. In a way the insignificance of significance tests in scientific debate is comforting. Economists have not been fooled, even by their own mistaken beliefs about statistical significance. To put it another way, no economist has achieved scientific success as a result of a statistically significant coefficient. Massed observations, clever common sense, elegant theorems, new policies, sagacious economic reasoning, historical perspective, relevant accounting: these all have led to scientific success. Statistical significance has not.

What should replace a lessened attention to statistical significance is serious attention to the scientific question. The scientific question is ordinarily "How large is large in the present case?" This is the question that geologists thinking about continental drift and astrophysicists thinking about stellar evolution spend their days answering.

The question "How large is large?" requires thinking about what coefficients would be judged large or small in terms of the present conversation of the science. It requires thinking more rigorously about data—for example, asking what universe they are a "sample" from. (Carelessness in such matters is more common than one might have expected. Of the 107 papers using cross-sectional data, for example, 20 percent used tests of statistical significance on the entire population or on a sample of convenience. Only two of these offered some justification for the usage.)

Most scientists (and historians) use simulation, which in explicit, quantitative form is becoming cheaper in economics, too. It will probably become the main empirical technique, following other observational sciences. Econometrics will survive, but it will come at last to empha-

size economic rather than statistical significance. We should of course worry some about the precision of the estimates, but as Leamer has pointed out the imprecision usually comes from sources other than too small a sample.

Simulation, new data sets, and quantitative thinking about the conversation of the science offer a way forward. The first step anyway is plain: stop searching for economic findings under the lamppost of statistical significance.

REFERENCES

AMEMIYA, TAKESHI. *Advanced econometrics.* Cambridge: Harvard U. Press, 1985.

AMES, EDWARD AND REITER, STANLEY. "Distributions of Correlation Coefficients in Economic Time Series," *J. Amer. Statist. Assoc.*, Sept. 1961, 56(295), pp. 637–56.

BAKAN, DAVID. "The Test of Significance in Psychological Research," *Psychological Bulletin*, Dec. 1966, 66(6), pp. 423–37.

BARRETT, WILLIAM. *The illusion of technique.* Garden City, NY: Anchor Press, 1978.

BEHRMAN, JERE R. AND CRAIG, STEVEN G. "The Distribution of Public Services: An Exploration of Local Government Preferences," *Amer. Econ. Rev.*, Mar. 1987, 77(1), pp. 37–49.

BLOMQUIST, GLENN C.; BERGER, MARK C. AND HOEHN, JOHN P. "New Estimates of Quality of Life in Urban Areas," *Amer. Econ. Rev.*, Mar. 1988, 78(1), pp. 89–107.

BOISSIERE, M.; KNIGHT, J.B. AND SABOT, R.H. "Earnings, Schooling, Ability, and Cognitive Skills," *Amer. Econ. Rev.*, Dec. 1985, 75(5), pp. 1016–30.

BORING, EDWIN G. "Mathematical versus Scientific Significance," *Psychological Bulletin*, Oct. 1919, 16(10), pp. 335–38.

CICERO, MARCUS TULLIUS. *De divinatione* [45 BC]; in *De senectute; De amicitia; De divinatione.* Ed. and trans. WILLIAM A. FALCONER. Cambridge: Harvard U. Press, 1938.

CLARK, KIM B. "Unionization and Firm Performance: The Impact on Profits, Growth, and Productivity," *Amer. Econ. Rev.*, Dec. 1984, 74(5), pp. 893–919.

COHEN, JACOB. "The Statistical Power of Abnormal-Social Psychological Research: A Review," *J. Abnormal and Social Psychology*, Sept. 1962, 65(3), pp. 145–53.

COOLEY, THOMAS F. AND LEROY, STEPHEN F. "Identification and Estimation of Money Demand," *Amer. Econ. Rev.*, Dec. 1981, 71(5), pp. 825–44.

DARBY, MICHAEL R. "The U.S. Productivity Slowdown: A Case of Statistical Myopia," *Amer. Econ. Rev.*, June 1984, 74(3), pp. 301–22.

DAVIDSON, RUSSELL AND MACKINNON, JAMES G. *Estimation and inference in econometrics.* Oxford: Oxford U. Press, 1993.

DAVIS, PHILIP J. AND HERSH, REUBEN. "Rhetoric and Mathematics," in *The rhetoric of the human sciences.* Eds.: JOHN S. NELSON, ALLAN MEGILL, AND DONALD N. MCCLOSKEY. Madison: U. of Wisconsin Press, 1987, pp. 53–68.

DEGROOT, MORRIS H. *Probability and statistics.* Reading, MA: Addison-Wesley, [1975] 1989.

DENTON, FRANK T. "Data Mining as an Industry," *Rev. Econ. Statist.*, Feb. 1985, 67(1), pp. 124–27.

——— "The Significance of Significance: Rhetorical Aspects of Statistical Hypothesis Testing in Economics," in *The consequences of economic rhetoric.* Eds.: ARJO KLAMER, DONALD N. MCCLOSKEY, AND ROBERT SOLOW. New York: Cambridge U. Press, 1988, pp. 163–83.

FEIGE, EDGAR. "The Consequences of Journal Editorial Policies and a Suggestion for Revision," *J. Polit. Econ.*, Dec. 1975, 83(6), pp. 1291–95.

FISHER, RONALD A. *Statistical methods for research workers.* Edinburgh: Oliver and Boyd, 1925.

FLORENS, JEAN-PIERRE AND MOUCHART, MICHEL. "Bayesian Testing and Testing Bayesians," in *Handbook of statistics.* Vol. 11. *Econometrics.* of Eds.: G. S. MADDALA, C. R. RAO, AND H. D. VINOD. Amsterdam: North-Holland, 1993, pp. 303–91.

FRASER, DONALD A. S. *Statistics: An introduction.* New York: Wiley, 1958.

FREEDMAN, DAVID; PISANI, ROBERT AND PURVES, ROGER. *Statistics.* New York: Norton, 1978.

GIGERENZER, GERD. "Probabilistic Thinking and the Fight Against Subjectivity." Unpublished paper, Department of Psychology, Universität Konstanz, no date.

GOLDBERGER, ARTHUR S. *A course in econometrics.* Cambridge: Harvard U. Press, 1991.

GORDON, SCOTT. *The history and philosophy of social science.* London: Rontledge, 1991.

GOULD, STEPHEN JAY. *The mismeasure of man.* New York: Norton, 1981.

GRANGER, CLIVE W. J. "A Review of Some Recent Textbooks of Econometrics," *J. Econ. Lit.*, Mar. 1994, 32(1), pp. 115–22.

GREENE, WILLIAM H. *Econometric analysis.* New York: Macmillan, [1990] 1993.

GRIFFITHS, WILLIAM E.; HILL, R. CARTER AND JUDGE, GEORGE G. *Learning and practicing econometrics.* New York: Wiley, 1993.

GRILICHES, ZVI. "Productivity, R&D, and Basic Research at the Firm Level in the 1970's," *Amer. Econ. Rev.*, Mar. 1986, 76(1), pp. 141–54.

GRILICHES, ZVI AND INTRILIGATOR, MICHAEL D. *Handbook of econometrics.* Vols. I, II, and III. Amsterdam: North-Holland, 1983, 1984, 1986.

GUTTMAN, LOUIS. "What Is Not What in Statis-

tics?" in *Multidimensional data representations: When and why.* Ed.: INGWER BORG. Ann Arbor: Methesis Press, 1981, pp. 20–46.

——— "The Illogic of Statistical Inference for Cumulative Science," *Applied Stochastic Models and Data Analysis*, July 1985, 1(1), pp. 3–10.

HAMERMESH, DANIEL S. "Labor Demand and the Structure of Adjustment Costs," *Amer. Econ. Rev.*, Sept. 1989, 79(4), pp. 674–89.

HOEL, PAUL G. *Elementary statistics.* New York: Wiley, 1966.

HOGBEN, LANCELOT T. *Statistical theory: The relationship of probability, credibility, and error.* New York: Norton, 1968.

HOGG, ROBERT V. AND CRAIG, ALLEN T. *Introduction to mathematical statistics.* 4th ed. New York: Macmillan, 1978.

JOHNSTON, JOHN. *Econometric methods.* 2nd ed.. New York: McGraw-Hill, [1963] 1972.

——— *Econometric methods.* 3rd ed. New York: McGraw-Hill, 1984.

KENDALL, MAURICE G. AND STUART, ALAN.*The advanced theory of statistics.* Vol. 2., 3rd ed. London: Griffin, 1951.

KENDALL, MAURICE G.; STUART, ALAN AND ORD, J. KEITH. *The advanced theory of statistics.* Vol. 3, 4th ed. *Design and analysis, and time-series.* New York: Macmillan, 1983.

KENNEDY, PETER. *A guide to econometrics.* Cambridge: MIT Press, [1979] 1985.

KMENTA, JAN. *Elements of econometrics.* New York: Macmillan, 1971.

KRUSKAL, WILLIAM. "Significance, Tests of," *International encyclopedia of statistics.* Eds.: WILLIAM H. KRUSKAL AND JUDITH M. TANUR. New York: Macmillan, [1968] 1978a, pp. 944–58.

——— "Formulas, Numbers, Words: Statistics in Prose," *The American Scholar*, Spring 1978b, 47(2), pp. 223–29.

KURTZ, ALBERT K. AND EDGERTON, HAROLD A., eds. *Statistical dictionary of terms and symbols.* New York: Wiley, 1939.

LAZEAR, EDWARD P. AND MICHAEL, ROBERT T. "Family Size and the Distribution of Real Per Capita Income," *Amer. Econ. Rev.*, Mar. 1980, 70(1), pp. 91–107.

LEAMER, EDWARD E. *Specification searches: Ad hoc inferences with nonexperimental data.* New York: Wiley, 1978.

——— "Let's Take the Con Out of Econometrics," *Amer. Econ. Rev.*, Mar. 1983, 73(1), pp. 31–43.

LOVELL, MICHAEL C. "Data Mining," *Rev. Econ. Statist.*, Feb. 1983, 65(1), pp. 1–12.

MADDALA, G. S. *Introduction to econometrics.* New York: Macmillan, [1988] 1992.

MAYER, THOMAS. "Selecting Economic Hypotheses by Goodness of Fit," *Econ. J.*, Dec. 1975, 85(340), pp. 877–83.

MCCLOSKEY, DONALD N. "The Loss Function Has Been Mislaid: The Rhetoric of Significance Tests," *Amer. Econ. Rev.*, May 1985, 75 (2), pp. 201–05.

McCLOSKEY, DONALD N. AND ZECHER, J. RICH-ARD. "The Success of Purchasing Power Parity," in *A retrospective on the classical gold standard, 1821–1931.* Eds.: MICHAEL D. BORDO AND ANNA J. SCHWARZ. Chicago and London: U. of Chicago Press, 1984, pp. 121–50.

MEEHL, PAUL E. "Theory Testing in Psychology and Physics: A Methodological Paradox," *Philosophy of Science*, June 1967, 34(2), pp. 103–15.

MISHKIN, FREDERIC S. "Are Market Forecasts Rational?" *Amer. Econ. Rev.*, June 1971, 71(3), pp. 295–305.

MOOD, ALEXANDER M. *Introduction to the theory of statistics.* 1st ed. New York: McGraw-Hill, 1950.

MOOD, ALEXANDER M. AND GRAYBILL, FRANK-LIN A. *Introduction to the theory of statistics.* 2nd ed. New York: McGraw-Hill, 1963.

MOORE, DAVID S. AND McCABE, GEORGE P. *Introduction to the practice of statistics.* 2nd ed. New York: Freeman, 1993.

MORRISON, DENTON E. AND HENKEL, RAMON E. "Significance Tests Reconsidered," *Amer. Sociologist*, May 1969, 4(2), pp. 131–39.

———. *The significance test controversy: A reader.* Chicago: Aldine, 1970.

MOSTELLER, FREDERICK AND TUKEY, JOHN W. *Data analysis and regression.* Reading, MA: Addison-Wesley, 1977.

NEYMAN, JERZY AND PEARSON, EGON S. "On the Problem of the Most Efficient Tests of Statistical Hypotheses," *Philosophical Transactions of the Royal Society* A, 1933, 231, pp. 289–337.

OHTA, MAKOTA AND GRILICHES, ZVI. "Automobile Prices Revisited: Extensions of the Hedonic Hypothesis," in *Household production and consumption.* Studies in Income and Wealth, vol. 40. Ed.: NESTOR E. TERLECKYJ. New York: National Bureau of Economics Research, 1976, pp. 325–90.

ROMER, CHRISTINA D. "Is the Stabilization of the Postwar Economy a Figment of the Data?" *Amer. Econ. Rev.*, June 1986, 76(3), pp. 314–34.

RUDNER, RICHARD. "The Scientist Qua Scientist Makes Value Judgments," *Phil. Science*, Jan. 1953, 20(1), pp 1–6.

SACHS, JEFFREY D. "The Changing Cyclical Behavior of Wages and Prices: 1880–1976," *Amer. Econ. Rev.*, Mar. 1980, 70 (1), pp. 78–90.

SCOTT, ELIZABETH. "Testing Hypotheses," in *Statistical astronomy.* Ed.: ROBERT J. TRUMPLER AND HAROLD F. WEAVER. New York: Dover, 1953, pp. 220–30.

TUKEY, JOHN W. "Sunset Salvo," *The American Statistician*, Feb. 1986, 40(1), pp. 72–76.

TULLOCK, GORDON. "Publication Decisions and Tests of Significance—A Comment," *J. Amer. Statist. Assoc.*, Sept. 1959, 54(287), p. 593.

———. *The organization of inquiry.* Durham, NC: Duke U. Press, 1966.

WALD, ABRAHAM. "Contributions to the Theory of Statistical Estimation and Testing Hypotheses," *Annals of Mathematical Statistics*, Dec. 1939, 10(4), pp. 299–326.

WALLIS, W. ALLEN AND ROBERTS, HARRY V. *Statistics: A new approach.* New York: Macmillan, 1956.

WONNACOTT, RONALD J. AND WONNACOTT, THOMAS H. *Statistics: Discovering its power.* New York: Wiley, 1982.

WOOFTER, T. J., JR. "Common Errors in Sampling," *Social Forces*, May 1933, 11(4), pp. 521–25.

Appendix: The Publications of Deirdre Nansen McCloskey, 1968–2000

BOOKS

Economic History

Economic Maturity and Entrepreneurial Decline: British Iron and Steel, 1870–1913. Harvard Economic Studies. Harvard University Press, 1973. (David A. Wells Prize)

Enterprise and Trade in Victorian Britain: Essays in Historical Economics. Allen and Unwin, 1981; reprinted 1993 by Gregg Revivals (Godstone, Surrey, England).

Econometric History. British Economic History Society. Macmillan UK, 1987. Trans. into Japanese 1992.

Criticism in Economics and History

The Applied Theory of Price. Macmillan, 1982; second revised edition, 1985. International student edition 1985; Spanish trans. Teoria de Precios Aplicada (Mexico: CECSA: Compania Editorial Continental, SA), 1990. Czech trans. Aplikovaná Teorie Ceny (Praha: Státni pedagogické, 1993).

The Writing of Economics. NY: Macmillan, 1986, a 90-page libellus from the article 'Economical Writing' below. Second Revised Edition as *Economical Writing*, Prospect Heights, IL: Waveland Press, 1999.

The Rhetoric of Economics. University of Wisconsin Press, 1985. British edition: Wheatsheaf, 1986. Italian trans., *La Retorica dell' Economia: Scienza e letturatura nel discorso economico*, with an introduction by Augusto Graziani (Torino: Giulio Einaudi, 1988; trans. Bianca Maria Testa; series Nuovo Politecnico no. 165); Spanish (Alianza, 1990); Japanese (Harvest Sha, 1992). Second revised edition, 1998. Hungarian trans., Europa Publishing, forthcoming 2000.

If You're So Smart: The Narrative of Economic Expertise. University of Chicago Press, 1990; paperback Spring 1992. Spanish trans., *Si eres tan listo: La narrativa de los expertos en economía* (Madrid: Alianza, 1993), trans. Graciela Sylvestre and Victoriano Martin. Chinese trans. said to be forthcoming, Chien Hua Publishing. (Chapter 11 reprinted in Daniel Klein (ed.), *What Do Economists Contribute?*, Macmillan Press, 1998.)

Knowledge and Persuasion in Economics. Cambridge University Press, 1994.

The Vices of Economists; The Virtues of the Bourgeoisie. University of Amsterdam Press and University of Michigan Press, 1997.

How to Be Human* *Though an Economist. University of Michigan Press, 2000.

Other

Crossing: A Memoir. University of Chicago Press, 1999. Named December 1999 among *New York Times* 'Notable Books of 1999.' Excerpts published in *Reason* magazine (December 1999); *Chicago Tribune* Sunday Magazine, January 30, 2000. Japanese trans., Bungie Shunju Ltd, forthcoming 2001.

BOOKS EDITED

Economic History

Essays on a Mature Economy: Britain after 1840. Methuen, 1971; and Princeton University Press, 1971.

[with Roderick Floud] *The Economic History of Britain, 1700–Present*. 2 vols, Cambridge University Press, 1981; second revised edition (3 vols) 1994.

[with George Hersh, Jr] *A Bibliography of Historical Economics to 1980*. Cambridge University Press, 1990.

Second Thoughts: Myths and Morals of US Economic History. Oxford University Press, 1992; paperback 1994.

Rhetoric of Inquiry

[with John Nelson and Allan Megill] *The Rhetoric of the Human Sciences: Language and Argument in Scholarship and Public Affairs*. University of Wisconsin Press, 1987.

[15] [with Arjo Klamer and Robert Solow] *The Consequences of Economic Rhetoric*. Cambridge University Press, 1988.

ARTICLES

British Enterprise in the 19th Century

'Productivity Change in British Pig Iron, 1870–1939', *Quarterly Journal of Economics*, **82** (May 1968): 281–96.

'Review of Birch's *British Iron and Steel*', *Business History Review*, **43** (Fall 1969): 412–14.

'The British Iron and Steel Industry', *Journal of Economic History*, **29** (March 1969): 173–5.

'Did Victorian Britain Fail?', *Economic History Review*, **23** (December 1970): 446–59.

'Victorian Growth: A Rejoinder [to Derek Aldcroft]', *Economic History Review*, **27** (May 1974): 275–7.

'No It Did Not: A Reply to Craft [to his Comment on "Did Victorian Britain Fail?"]', *Economic History Review*, **32** (November 1979): 538–41.

'A Counterfactual Dialogue with William Kennedy on Late Victorian Failure or the Lack of It', pp. 119–26 in McCloskey, *Enterprise and Trade in Victorian Britain* (1981) [1993].

'Discussion' (of William Kennedy and William Phillips), *Journal of Economic History*, **42** (March 1982): 117–18.

'International Differences in Productivity? Coal and Steel in America and Britain Before World War I', in *Essays on a Mature Economy* (1971), cited above, Chapter 8, pp. 285–304.

'An Exchange with David Landes', pp. 305–9, in *Essays on a Mature Economy* (1971).

[with L.G. Sandberg] 'From Damnation to Redemption: Judgments on the Late Victorian Entrepreneur', *Explorations in Economic History*, **9** (Fall 1971): 89–108.

'Review of Sandberg's *Lancashire in Decline*', *Journal of Political Economy*, **84** (February 1976): 198–200.

'Review of Hannah's *The Rise of the Corporate Economy: The British Experience*', *American Historical Review*, **82** (December 1977): 1258–9.

'Review of Matthews, Feinstein, and Odling-Smee, *British Economic Growth 1855–1973*', *Times Literary Supplement*, **462** (6 May 1983).

'Review of Kennedy's *Industrial Structure, Capital Markets, and the Origins of British Economic Decline*', *Economic History Review*, **42** (February 1989): 141–3.

'Is America in Decline?', *Des Moines Register*, September 1990. A revised version in *The Key Reporter*, **60** (2, Winter 1994–5): 1–3. Trans. and distributed by United States Information Service in Bangladesh.

'Review of Thurow's *The Zero-Sum Solution*', *Des Moines Register*, 9 January 1986.

'Competitiveness and the Anti-Economics of Decline', pp. 167–73 in McCloskey (ed.), *Myths and Morals of U.S. Economic History* (Oxford 1992).

British Foreign Trade in the 18th and 19th Centuries

'Britain's Loss from Foreign Industrialization: A Provisional Estimate', *Explorations in Economic History*, **8** (Winter 1970–71): 141–52.

'Magnanimous Albion: Free Trade and British National Income, 1841–1881', *Explorations in Economic History*, **17** (July 1980): 303–20; reprinted Forrest Capie (ed.), *Protectionism in the World Economy* (Elgar, 1992).

'Reply to Peter Cain', *Explorations in Economic History*, **19** (April 1982): 208–10.

'From Dependence to Autonomy: Judgments on Trade as an Engine of British Growth', in McCloskey, *Enterprise and Trade in Victorian Britain* (1981), pp. 139–54.

[with R.P. Thomas] 'Overseas Trade and Empire, 1700–1820', Chapter 4 in Floud and McCloskey, *The Economic History of Britain, 1700–Present* (1981), vol. 1, pp. 87–102.

[with C.K. Harley] 'Foreign Trade: Competition and the Expanding International Economy, 1820–1914', Chapter 17 in Floud and McCloskey, *The Economic History of Britain, 1700–Present* (1981), vol. 2, pp. 50–69.

The History of International Finance

'Review of Ramsey's *The Price Revolution in 16th Century England*', *Journal of Political Economy*, **80** (November/December 1972): 1332–5.

[with J. Richard Zecher] 'How the Gold Standard Worked, 1880–1913', in J.A. Frenkel and H.G. Johnson (eds), *The Monetary Approach to the Balance of Payments* (Allen and Unwin, 1976), pp. 357–85; reprinted as pp. 63–80 in B. Eichengreen (ed.), *The Gold Standard in Theory and History* (Methuen, 1985).

[with J. Richard Zecher] 'The Success of Purchasing Power Parity: Historical Evidence and Its Implications for Macroeconomics', in Michael Bordo and Anna J. Schwartz (eds), *A Retrospective on the Classical Gold Standard 1821–1931* (NBER, University of Chicago Press, 1984), pp. 121–50.

'Mars Collides with Earth? Review of Volcker and Gyohten's *Changing Fortunes: The World's Money and the Threat to American Leadership*', *Reason*, **24** (10 March 1993): 60–62.

'The Gulliver Effect', *Scientific American* (September 1995): 44.

'Review of Gray's *False Dawn* and Friedman's *The Lexus and the Olive Tree*' for the *Minnesota Journal of Global Trade* (a new journal from the Law School at the University of Minnesota), 2000, 20 pp.

Open Fields and Enclosure in England

'The Enclosure of Open Fields: Preface to a Study of Its Impact on the Efficiency of English Agriculture in the Eighteenth Century', *Journal of Economic History*, **32** (1 March 1972): 15–35.

'Review of Williams' *Draining of the Somerset Levels*', *Journal of Economic History*, **32** (4 December 1972): 1021–3.

'The Persistence of English Common Fields', in E.L. Jones and William Parker (eds), *European Peasants and Their Markets: Essays in Agrarian Economic History* (Princeton University Press, 1975), pp. 73–119.

'The Economics of Enclosure: A Market Analysis,' in Jones and Parker, as cited, pp. 123–60.

'English Open Fields as Behavior Towards Risk', *Research in Economic History*, **1** (Fall 1976): 124–70.

'Fenoaltea on Open Fields: A Comment', *Explorations in Economic History*, **14** (October 1977): 402–4.

'A Reply to Professor Charles Wilson', *Journal of European Economic History*, **8** (Spring 1979): 203–7.

'Another Way of Observing Open Fields: A Reply to A.R.H. Baker', *Journal of Historical Geography*, **5** (October 1979): 427–9.

'Scattering in Open Fields: A Comment on Michael Mazur's Article', *Journal of European Economic History*, **9** (Spring 1980): 209–14.

'Review of Popkin's *The Rational Peasant* and Macfarlane's *The Origins of English Individualism*', *Journal of Political Economy*, **89** (August 1981): 837–40 [reprinted in UCLA Writing Program, Ellen Strenski (ed.), *Cross-Disciplinary Conversations about Writing* (NY: St Martin's Press, 1989)].

'Comment on Petras and Havens' *Peasant Behavior and Social Change – Cooperatives and Individual Holdings*', in Clifford S. Russell and N.K. Nicholson (eds), *Public Choice and Rural Development* (Washington, DC, 1981), pp. 226–31.

'Theses on Enclosure', pp. 56–72 in Papers Presented to the Economic History Society Conference at Canterbury, 1983. Agricultural History Society.

[with John Nash] 'Corn at Interest: The Extent and Cost of Grain Storage in Medieval England', *American Economic Review*, **74** (March 1984): 174–87.

'Conditional Economic History: A Reply to Komlos and Landes', *Economic History Review*, **44** (1 February 1991): 128–32.

'Review of Turner's, *English Enclosures*', *Journal of Economic History*, 1982.

'Open Field System', brief entry in Eatwell, Milgate, and Newman (eds), *The New Palgrave: A Dictionary of Economic Thought and Doctrine* (Macmillan UK, 1987).

'The Open Fields of England: Rent, Risk, and the Rate of Interest, 1300–1815', in David W. Galenson (ed.), *Markets in History: Economic Studies of the Past* (Cambridge: Cambridge University Press, 1989), pp. 5–51.

'The Prudent Peasant: New Findings on Open Fields', *Journal of Economic History*, **51** (2 June 1991): 343–55.

The Industrial Revolution

'Review of Hohenberg's *Economic History of Europe*', *Kyklos* (November 1971): 147.

'Review of Hawke's *Railways and Economic Growth in England and Wales, 1840–1870*', *Economic History Review*, **24** (August 1971): 493–5.

'Review of Hughes' *Industrialization and Economic History: Theses and Conjectures*', *Journal of Modern History*, **44** (March 1972): 97–8.

'Review of Davis, Easterlin, Parker et al., *American Economic Growth: An Economist's History of the United States*', *Journal of Economic History*, **32** (December 1972): 963–6.

'Review of Williamson's *Late Nineteenth-Century American Development*', *Times Literary Supplement* (December 12, 1975).

'Review of David's *Technology and Nineteenth-Century Growth*', *Economic History Review*, **29** (May 1976): 340–42.

'Review of Reed's *Investment in Railways in Britain*', *American Historical Review*, **82** (February 1977): 102.

'Review of Coleman's *The Economy of England, 1450–1750*', *Journal of Economic Literature*, **16** (March 1978): 108–10.

'The Industrial Revolution, 1780–1860: A Survey', Chapter 6 in Floud and McCloskey (eds), *The Economic History of Britain, 1700–Present* (1981), vol. 1, pp. 103–27, reprinted in J. Mokyr (ed.), *Economic History and the Industrial Revolution* (Rowman and Littlefield, 1985).

'Review of Rosenberg and Birdzell's *How the West Grew Rich*', *New York Times Sunday Book Review*, February 1986.

'Beyond the Margin: Review of Joel Mokyr's *The Lever of Riches: Technological Creativity and Economic Progress*', *Reason*, **22** (10 March 1991): 56–7.

'Review of Robert Reich's *The Work of Nations*', *Chicago Tribune Book World*, 10 March, 1991, p. 3.

'1780–1860: A Survey', a new essay, in Floud and McCloskey (eds), *The Economic History of Britain, 1700–Present*, 2nd edition, 1994.

'Once Upon a Time There was a Theory', *Scientific American* (February 1995): 25.
'Squashing the Politically Correct in History (Review of David Landes, *Wealth and Poverty of Nations*)', *Reason*, June 1998.

Other Historical Subjects

'New Perspectives on the Old Poor Law', *Explorations in Economic History*, **10** (Summer 1973): 419–36.
'Review of Wrigley's (ed.), *Nineteenth Century Society* and Singer's and Small's *The Wages of War, 1816–1965*', *Journal of the American Statistical Association* (March 1974).
'A Mismeasurement of the Incidence of Taxation in Britain and France, 1715–1810', *Journal of European Economic History*, **7** (1, Spring 1978): 209–10.
'Comment on Hartwell's "Taxation During the Industrial Revolution"', *Cato Journal*, **1** (1, Spring 1981): 155–9.
'Little Things Matter: Review of Robert W. Fogel, *Without Consent or Contract*', *Reason*, **22** (2 June 1990): 51–3.

Criticism in History and Economic History

'The New Economic History: An Introduction', *Revista Storica Italiana* (March 1971: 5–22; in Italian); and *Revista Espanola de Economia* (May–August 1971) in Spanish).
'Introduction' to special issue of *Explorations in Economic History*, **11** (Summer 1974): 317–24.
'The New Economic History in Britain' (in Italian), *Quaderni Storici,* **31** (December 1976): 401–8.
'Does the Past Have Useful Economics?', *Journal of Economic Literature*, **14** (June 1976): 434–61. Translated into Russian for *Thesis*, **1** (1, Spring 1993): 107–36. Reprinted in Diana Betts and Robert Whaples (eds), *Readings in American Economic History*, 1994.
'The Achievements of the Cliometric School', *Journal of Economic History*, **38** (1 March 1978): 13–28.
'The Problem of Audience in Historical Economics: Rhetorical Thoughts on a Text by Robert Fogel', *History and Theory*, **24** (1, 1985): 1–22.
'Review of Boland's *The Foundations of Economic Method*', *Journal of Economic Literature*, **23** (June 1985): 618–19.
[with Allan Megill] 'The Rhetoric of History', in Nelson, Megill, and McCloskey (eds), *The Rhetoric of the Human Sciences* (University of Wisconsin Press, 1987), pp. 221–38.
'Counterfactuals', article in Eatwell, Milgate, and Newman (eds), *The New Palgrave: A Dictionary of Economic Thought and Doctrine* (Macmillan, 1987).
'Continuity in Economic History', article in *The New Palgrave: A Dictionary of Economic Thought and Doctrine* (Macmillan, 1987), pp. 623–6.
'The Storied Character of Economics', *Tijdschrift voor Geschiedenis*, **101** (4, 1988): 543–654.

'History, Differential Equations, and the Problem of Narration', *History and Theory*, **30** (1, 1991): 21–36.

'Ancients and Moderns' [presidential address, Social Science History Association, Washington, DC, 1989]. *Social Science History*, **14** (3 January 1991): 289–303.

'Introduction' to McCloskey and Hersh (eds), *A Bibliography of Historical Economics to 1980*, Cambridge University Press, 1991, pp. ix–xii.

'Kinks, Tools, Spurts, and Substitutes: Gerschenkron's Rhetoric of Relative Backwardness', Chapter 6 in Richard Sylla and Gianni Toniolo (eds), *Patterns of European Industrialization: The Nineteenth Century* (London: Routledge, 1991).

'Looking Forward into History.' Introduction (pp. 3–10) to McCloskey (ed.), *Second Thoughts: Myths and Morals of U.S. Economic History* (Oxford, 1992).

'The Economics of Choice: Neoclassical Supply and Demand', in Thomas Rawski (ed.), *Economics and the Historian* (Berkeley and Los Angeles: University of California Press, 1995): 122–58.

'1066 and a Wave of Gadgets: The Achievements of British Growth', in Penelope Gouk (ed.), *Wellsprings of Achievement: Cultural and Economic Dynamics in Early Modern England and Japan* (Variorum, 1995).

[with Santhi Hejeebu] 'The Reproving of Polanyi', forthcoming 2000, *Critical Review*.

Criticism in Economics

'The Rhetoric of Economics', *Journal of Economic Literature*, **31** (June 1983): 482–517; reprinted in B.J. Caldwell (ed.), *Appraisal and Criticism in Economics* (Allen and Unwin, 1985); translated into Japanese, *Contemporary Economics*, **61** (Spring 1985), pp. 156–84.

'Reply to Caldwell and Coats', *Journal of Economic Literature*, **22** (June 1984): 579–80.

'Sartorial Epistemology in Tatters: A Reply to Martin Hollis', *Economics and Philosophy*, **1** (April 1985): 134–7.

'The Character of Argument in Modern Economics: How Muth Persuades', in *Proceedings of the Third Summer Conference on Argumentation*, sponsored by the Speech Communication Association and the American Forensic Association, Annandale, VA, Fall 1983; revised for *The Rhetoric of Economics*.

'The Literary Character of Economics', *Daedalus*, **13** (3, Summer 1984): 97–119.

'A Conversation with McCloskey About Rhetoric', *Eastern Economic Journal* (October–December 1985): 293–6.

'The Rhetoric of Economics', *Social Science*, **71** (2/3, Fall 1986): 97–102 (prepared by Frank Moore from a talk at the Institute in Social Science, University of North Carolina, January 1986).

'Economics as a Historical Science', pp. 63–9 in William Parker (ed.), *Economic History and the Modern Economist* (NY: Basil Blackwell, 1986; Italian trans., 1988, Liters Editore).

'Rhetoric', in *The New Palgrave: A Dictionary of Economic Thought and Doctrine* (Macmillan, 1987).

'The Rhetoric of Economic Development: Rethinking Development Economics', *Cato Journal*, **7** (Spring/Summer 1987): 249–54; reprinted with minor revisions in James Dorn and A.A. Walters (eds), *The Revolution in Development Economics*, 1993.

'Towards a Rhetoric of Economics', pp. 13–29 in G.C. Winston and R.F. Teichgraeber III (eds), *The Boundaries of Economics*, Murphy Institute Studies in Political Economy. Cambridge University Press, 1988.

'Thick and Thin Methodologies in the History of Economic Thought', pp. 245–57 in Neil de Marchi (ed.), *The Popperian Legacy in Economics* (Cambridge University Press, 1988).

[with Arjo Klamer] 'Economics in the Human Conversation', pp. 3–20 in Klamer, McCloskey, and Solow (eds), *The Consequences of Rhetoric* (Cambridge University Press, 1988).

'The Consequences of Rhetoric', pp. 280–94 in Klamer, et al. (eds), *The Consequences of Rhetoric*, Cambridge University Press, 1988 [reprinted in *Fundamenta Scientiae*, **9** (2/3, 1988): 269–84 (a Brazilian journal)].

'Their Blackboard, Right or Wrong: A Comment on Contested Exchange', *Politics and Society*, **18** (2 June 1990): 223–32.

'Storytelling in Economics', pp. 5–22 in Christopher Nash and Martin Warner (eds), *Narrative in Culture* (Routledge 1990); and pp. 61–75 in Don C. Lavoie (ed.), *Economics and Hermeneutics* (Routledge 1990). An earlier version, with discussion, appeared in Orace Johnson (ed.), *Methodology and Accounting Research: Does the Past Have a Future?* (Proceedings of the 8th Annual Big Ten Accounting Doctoral Consortium, May, 1987: 69–76).

'Telling Stories Economically', *The Ludwig von Mises Lecture Series: Economic Education*, **22**: 83–107.

'Formalism in Economics, Rhetorically Speaking', *Ricerche Economiche*, **43** (1989), 1–2 (January–June): 57–75. Reprinted with minor revisions in *American Sociologist*, **21** (1, Spring 1990): 3–19.

'Reply to Peter Mueser', *American Sociologist*, **21** (1, Spring 1990): 26–8.

[with Arjo Klamer] 'The Rhetoric of Disagreement', *Rethinking Marxism*, **2** (Fall 1989): 140–61. Reprinted in D.H. Prychitko (ed.), *Why Economists Disagree*, Albany: SUNY Press, 1998.

[with Arjo Klamer] 'Accounting as the Master Metaphor of Economics', *European Accounting Review*, **1** (1 May 1992): 145–60.

'Agon and Ag Ec: Styles of Persuasion in Agricultural Economics', *American Journal of Agricultural Economics*, **72** (December 1990): 1124–30.

'The Rhetoric of Economic Expertise', pp. 137–47 in Richard H. Roberts and J.M.M. Good (eds), *The Recovery of Rhetoric: Persuasive Discourse and Disciplinarity in the Human Sciences*, (Charlottesville: University of Virginia Press, 1993). In French as 'La rhétorique de l'expertise économique', in Vincent de Coorebyter (ed.), *Rhétorique de la Science Paris*: Presse Universitaires de France, in the series 'L'interrogation philosophique', M. Meyer (ed.), pp. 171–88.

'Mere Style in Economics, 1920 to the Present', *Economic Notes*, **20** (1, 1991): 135–48.

'Economic Science: A Search Through the Hyperspace of Assumptions?', *Methodus*, **3** (1 June 1991): 6–16.

'The Arrogance of Economic Theorists' [Die Arroganz der Wirtschaftstheorie: Okonomische Rechenkunste im Zwielicht], *Neue Zurcher Zeitung*, 31 August/1 September 1991, p. 85, in the series Themen und Thesen der Wirtschaft, reprinted (in English) in *Swiss Review of World Affairs*, **41** (no. 7, October 1991): 11–12.

'Les Métaphores de la Science Economique', *Le Monde*, 28 April 1992, p. 39.
'The Rhetoric of Finance', for the *New Palgrave Dictionary of Money and Finance*, 1992: 350–52.
'Review of de Marchi and Blaug, eds., *Appraising Economic Theories*', *Journal of Economic Literature*, **31** (1 March 1993): 229–31.
'Review of Samuels, ed. *Economics as Discourse*', *Journal of Economic History*, **53** (1 March 1993): 204–6.
'Review of Rosenberg's *Economics: Mathematical Politics?*', *Isis*, **84** (4 December 1993): 838–9.
'How to Do a Rhetorical Analysis of Economics, and Why', in Roger Backhouse (ed.), *Economic Methodology* (London: Routledge, 1994): 319–42.
'Economics and the Limits of Scientific Knowledge', in Robert Goodman and Walter Fisher (eds), *Rethinking Knowledge: Reflections Across the Disciplines* (Albany: State University of New York Press, 1995).
'Fun in Econ 101: Review of John Kenneth Galbraith's *A Journey Through Economic Time: A Firsthand View*', *Chicago Tribune Book World*, 25 September 1994, Sec. 14, p. 4.
[with Arjo Klamer] 'One Quarter of GDP is Persuasion', *The American Economic Review*, **85** (2 May 1995): 191–5.
'How Economists Persuade', *Journal of Economic Methodology*, **1** (1 June 1994): 15–32.
'The Discreet Charm of the Bourgeoisie, comment on Sandra Harding's "Can Feminist Thought Make Economics More Objective?"', *Feminist Economics*, **1** (3, Fall 1995): 119–24.
'Metaphors Economists Live By', *Social Research*, **62** (2, Summer 1995): 215–37.
'Simulating Barbara', *Feminist Economics*, **4** (3, Fall, 1998): 181–6.
'Ask What the Boys in the Sandpit Will Have', (London) *Times Higher Education Supplement*, 1996.
'The Genealogy of Postmodernism: An Economist's Guide'. Forthcoming, Steven Cullenberg (ed.), *Postmodernism and Economics*, NY and London: Routledge, 2000.

Invited Replies to Reviews of *The Rhetoric of Economics* and Other Rhetorical Works

'The Two Cultures and Methodology [A Reply to Mark Blaug]', *Critical Review*, **1** (3, Summer 1987): 124–7.
'Responses to My Critics: A Mild Response to William Butos; An Agreeable Reply to A.W. Coats; A Disagreeable Reply to Steven Pressman', *Eastern Economic Journal*, **13** (July–September 1987): 308–11.
'Two Replies and a Dialogue on the Rhetoric of Economics' [Rosenberg, Rappaport, and Mäki], *Economics and Philosophy*, **4** (1988): 150–66.
'Rhetoric as Morally Radical: Reply to Klamer, Stewart, and Gleicher', *Review of Radical Political Economy*, **19** (3): 87–91. Translated into Spanish, Estudios Economicos [El Colegio de Mexico].
'Splenetic Rationalism: Hoppe's Review of Chapter 1 of The Rhetoric of Economics', *Market Process*, **7** (1), (Spring 1989): 34–41, reprinted in Peter J. Boettke and

David L. Prychitdo (eds), *The Market Process: Essays on Contemporary Austrian Economics* (Elgar, 1994), pp. 187–200.

'Commentary [on Rossetti and Mirowski]', pp. 261–71 in Neil de Marchi (ed.), *Post-Popperian Methodology of Economics: Recovering Practice*. Boston: Kluwer, 1992.

'Reply to Munz', *Journal of the History of Ideas*, **51** (1, January/March 1990): 143–7.

'Modern Epistemology Against Analytic Philosophy: A Reply to Maki', *Journal of Economic Literature*, **33** (September 1995): 1319–23.

'Review of Mirowski's *Natural Images in Economic Thought: "Markets Read in Tooth and Claw"*', *Isis*, 1996.

The Rhetoric of Inquiry

[with Allan Megill and John Nelson] 'Rhetoric of Inquiry', pp. 3–18 in Nelson, Megill, and McCloskey (eds), *The Rhetoric of the Human Sciences* (University of Wisconsin Press, 1987).

'The Limits of Expertise: If You're So Smart, Why Ain't You Rich?', *The American Scholar*, **57** (3), (Summer 1988): 393–406; reprinted as pp. 92–111 in J. Lee Auspitz, W.W. Gasparski, M.K. Mlicki, and K. Szaniawski (eds), *Praxiologies and the Philosophy of Economics*. Spanish translation as 'Si de verdad eras tan listo . . . (I)' in *Revista de Occidente*, **83** (April 1988): 71–86. Reprinted in B.J. Caldwell (ed.), *The Philosophy and Methodology of Economics*, Vol. II (Edward Elgar, 1993).

'An Economic Uncertainty Principle', *Scientific American* (November 1994): 107.

'Computation Outstrips Analysis', *Scientific American* (July 1995): 26.

'The Very Idea of Epistemology: A Comment on Hausman and McPherson's "Standards"', *Economics and Philosophy*, **5** (Spring 1989): 1–6.

'The Dismal Science and Mr. Burke: Economics as a Critical Theory', pp. 99–114 in H.W. Simons and T. Melia (eds), *The Legacy of Kennneth Burke* (Wisconsin: University of Wisconsin Press, 1989).

'Why I Am No Longer a Positivist', *Review of Social Economy*, **47** (3, Fall, 1989): 225–38.

'Review of Wayne Booth's *The Company We Keep: An Ethics of Fiction*', *Chicago Tribune Book World*, 25 December 1988, Sec. 14, p. 5.

'Review of Allan Bloom's *Giants and Dwarfs: Essays, 1960–1990*', *Chicago Tribune Book World*, October 1990.

'Keeping the Company of Sophisters, Economists, and Calculators', in Fred Antczak (ed.), *Keeping Company: Rhetoric, Pluralism and Wayne Booth* (Columbus: Ohio State University Press, 1994).

'Forward' to Robert H. Nelson, *Reaching for Heaven on Earth: The Theological Meaning of Economics*. Savage, Maryland: Rowman and Littlefield, 1991, pp. xi–xvii.

'Voodoo Economics', *Poetics Today*, **12** (2, Summer 1991): 287–300.

'Platonic Insults: "Rhetorical"', *Common Knowledge*, **2** (2, Fall 1993): 23–32.

'The Unquashed Masses: Review of John Carey's *The Intellectuals and the Masses: Pride and Prejudice among the Literary Intelligentsia 1880–1939*', *Reason*, **26** (3 July 1994): 60–61.

'Big Rhetoric, Little Rhetoric: Gaonkar on the Rhetoric of Science', in Alan G. Gross and William M. Keith (eds), *Rhetorical Hermeneutics, Invention and Interpretation in the Age of Science* (Albany: State University of New York Press, 1997): pp 101–12.

'Exchange of Letters on The Consequences of Pragmatism', *Times Literary Supplement*, 26 August 1983.

Significance Testing and Econometrics

'The Loss Function Has Been Mislaid: The Rhetoric of Significance Tests', *American Economic Review*, Supplement 75 (2 May 1985): 201–5.

'Why Economic Historians Should Stop Relying on Statistical Tests of Significance, and Lead Economists and Historians into the Promised Land', *Newsletter of the Cliometric Society*, 2 (2 November 1986): 5–7.

'Rhetoric Within the Citadel: Statistics', pp. 485–90 in J.W. Wenzel et al. (eds), *Argument and Critical Practice: Proceedings of the Fifth SCA/AFA Conference on Argumentation* (Annandale, VA: Speech Communication Association, 1987); reprinted in C.A. Willard and G.T. Goodnight (eds), *Public Argument and Scientific Understanding* (1993).

'The Bankruptcy of Statistical Significance', *Eastern Economic Journal*, **18** (Summer 1992): 359–61.

'The Art of Forecasting, Ancient to Modern Times', *Cato Journal*, **12** (1, Spring/ Summer 1992): 23–43.

'The Insignificance of Statistical Significance', *Scientific American* (April 1995): 32–3.

[with Stephen Ziliak] 'The Standard Error of Regressions', *Journal of Economic Literature*, March 1996: pp. 97–114; version reprinted as Chapter 8 in *The Rhetoric of Economics*, 2nd edition.

'Aunt Deirdre's Letter to a Graduate Student', *Eastern Economic Journal*, **23** (2, Spring 1997): 241–4.

'Cassandra's Open Letter to Her Economist Colleagues', *Eastern Economic Journal*, **25** (3, Summer 1999).

'Beyond Merely Statistical Significance', Statement of editorial policy, *Feminist Economics*, forthcoming, 2000.

Teaching Composition in Economics

'Economical Writing', *Economic Inquiry*, **24** (2) (April 1985): 187–222.

'Reply to Jack High', *Economic Inquiry*, **25** (3) (July 1987): 547–48.

'Writing as a Responsibility of Science: A Reply to Laband and Taylor', *Economic Inquiry*, **30** (October 1992): 689–95.

'Duty and Creativity in Economic Scholarship', in Michael Szenberg (ed.), *Passion and Craft: Economists at Work*, Ann Arbor: University of Michigan Press, 1995.

The Rhetoric of Law

'The Rhetoric, Economics, and Economic History of Michelman's "Republican Tradition: A Commentary"', *Iowa Law Review*, **72** (5 July 1987): 1351–3.

'The Rhetoric of Law and Economics', *Michigan Law Review*, **86** (4 February 1988): 752–67.

[with John Nelson] 'The Rhetoric of Political Economy', pp. 155–74 (Chapter 8) in James H. Nichols, Jr and Colin Wright (eds), *Political Economy to Economics – And Back?* (San Francisco: Institute for Contemporary Studies Press, 1990).

'The Essential Rhetoric of Law, Literature, and Liberty' [review of Posner's *Law as Literature*, Fish's *Doing What Comes Naturally* and White's *Justice as Translation*], *Critical Review*, **5** (1, Spring 1991): 203–23.

'Minimal Statism and Metamodernism: A Reply to Jeffrey Friedman', *Critical Review*, **6** (1 December 1992): 107–12.

'The Lawyerly Rhetoric of Coase's "The Nature of the Firm"', *Journal of Corporation Law*, **18** (2, Winter 1993): 424–39.

'The Good Old Coase Theorem and the Good Old Chicago School: Comment on the Medema-Zerbe Paper', *Coasean Economics: The New Institutional Economics and Law and Economics* (Steven G. Medema, ed.) Boston: Kluwer Publishing, 1997, pp. 239–48.

'The Rhetoric of Liberty', *Rhetoric Society Quarterly*, **1** (11, 1995): pp. 9–27.

'Review of Gaskins on Law and Rhetoric', *Social Services Review*, **70** (3 September 1996): 482–9.

'Happy Endings: Law, Gender, and the University', *Journal of Gender, Race and Justice*, **2** (1, Fall 1998): 77–85.

Teaching Economics

'9th Edition of Samuelson's Economics', *Challenge*, **16** (September/October 1973): 65–6.

[with John Siegfried, Robin Bartlett, W. Lee Hansen, Allen Kelley, and Thomas Tietenberg] 'The Status and Prospects of the Economics Major', *Journal of Economic Education*, **22** (3, Summer 1991): 197–224.

[with John Siegfried, W. Lee Hansen, Robin Bartlett, Allen Kelley, and Thomas Tietenberg] 'The Economics Major: Can and Should We Do Better than a B–?', *American Economic Review*, **81** (2 May 1991): 20–25.

'Why Economics is Tough for Ten-Year-Olds', *Social Studies Review* (American Textbook Council), **10** (Fall 1991): 8–11.

'Contribution to Special Book Section on books to recommend to undergraduate economics Students', *Reason*, **26** (7 December 1994): 42.

Academic Policy

'The Theatre of Scholarship and the Rhetoric of Economics', *Southern Humanities Review*, **22** (Summer, 1988): 241–9.

'The Poverty of Letters: The Crushing Case Against Outside Letters for Promotion', *Change*, **20** (5 September 1988): 7–9.

'The Invisible Colleges and Economics: An Unacknowledged Crisis in Academic Life', *Change*, **23** (6, November/December 1991): 10–11, 54.

'A Small College Aura for Large Institutions', *Chronicle of Higher Education*, **38**

(5, 25 September 1991): p. B3.

'Review of Bowen and Rudenstine's *In Pursuit of the PhD*: A Review Article', *Change*,
26 (1, January/February 1994) and *Economics of Education Review*, **4** (1993):
pp. 359–65.

Intellectual Biography

'Review of Robert Skidelsky's *John Maynard Keynes: Hopes Betrayed, 1883–1920*',
Washington Post Book World, May 25 1986.

'Earl Hamilton', in *The New Palgrave: A Dictionary of Economic Thought and
Doctrine* (Macmillan, 1987).

'Charles P. Kindleberger', in *The New Palgrave*, 1987.

'Robert William Fogel: An Appreciation by an Adopted Student', pp. 14–25, in Claudia
Goldin and Hugh Rockoff (eds), *Strategic Factors in Nineteenth-Century American
Economic History: A Volume to Honor Robert W Fogel* (Chicago and London:
University of Chicago Press, 1992).

'Alexander Gerschenkron: By a Student', *The American Scholar*, **61** (2, Spring 1992):
241–6.

'Review of James Buchanan's *Better Than Plowing*', *Constitutional Political Economy*,
1993.

'Fogel and North: Statics and Dynamics in Historical Economics', *Scandinavian
Journal of Economics* (2, 1994).

'The Persuasive Life: Review of *Hayek on Hayek* (Eds. Stephen Kresge and Leif
Wener)', *Reason*, **26** (4, August/September 1994): 67–70.

'Chicago School of Economics', *Encyclopedia of Chicago History*, Spring 1999.

Sociology of Science

'[A Post-Modern Rhetoric of Sociology:] Review of D.W. Fiske and R.A. Shweder's
Metatheory in Social Science', *Contemporary Sociology*, **15** (6 November 1986).

'Review of Michael Mulkay's *The Word and the World: Explorations in the Form of
Sociological Analysis*', *American Journal of Sociology*, **93** (September 1987): 467–
9.

'A Strong Programme in the Rhetoric of Science' [Review of H.M. Collins, *Changing
Order: Replication and Induction in Scientific Research*], *Journal of Economic
Psychology* (1986): 128–33.

'Review of M.C. LaFollete's *Stealing into Print*', *Journal of Economic Literature*, **32**
(September 1994): 1226–9.

The Rhetoric of the Virtues

'Bourgeois Virtue', *American Scholar*, **63** (2, Spring 1994): 177–91; reprinted in
Occasional Papers of the Centre for Independent Studies, New South Wales (short
version reprinted in the *Phi Beta Kappa Key Reporter*, Fall 1994).

'Bourgeois Blues', *Reason*, **25** (1 May 1993): 47–51.

'Bourgeois Virtue', pp. 44–6 in Patricia Werhane and E.R. Freeman (eds), *Blackwell*

Encyclopedic Dictionary of Business Ethics (Blackwell: Maldon, MA and London, 1997).

'Procedural Justice', pp. 509–10, for *Blackwell Encyclopedic Dictionary of Business Ethics*.

'Breakthrough Books: The Market', *Lingua Franca*, July/August 1995.

'Missing Ethics in Economics', pp. 187–201 in Arjo Klamer (ed.), *The Value of Culture on the Relationships Between Economics and Arts* (Amsterdam: Amsterdam University Press, 1996).

'Bourgeois Virtue and the History of *P* and *S*', Presidential Address, presented at the Economic History Association, New Brunswick, NJ, Sept 1997 and *The Journal of Economic History*, **58** (2 June 1998): 297–317.

Gender

'Some Consequences of a Conjective Economics', pp. 69–93 in Julie Nelson and Marianne Ferber (eds), *Beyond Economic Man: Feminism and Economics* (Chicago: University of Chicago Press, 1993).

'Some News That At Least Will Not Bore You', *Eastern Economic Journal*, **21** (4, Fall 1995): 551–3; reprinted in *Lingua Franca*, early spring 1996; shortened version in *Harper's*, July 1996.

'The Discreet Charm of the Bourgeoisie: Comment on Sandra Harding's "Can Feminist Thought Make Economics More Objective?"', *Feminist Economics*, **1** (3, Fall 1995): 119–24.

'Love and Money: A Comment on the Markets Debate', *Feminist Economics*, **2** (2, Summer 1996): 137–40.

'Femmes Fiscales', *Times Higher Education Supplement*, 31 May 1996.

'It's Good to be a Don if You're Going to be a Deirdre', *Times Higher Education Supplement*, 23 August 1996, 1 page.

'Transformation', *Iowa Alumni Quarterly*, Summer 1997, p. 49.

'Simulating Barbara', *Feminist Economics*, **4** (3, Fall 1998): 181–6.

'Becoming Stories', pp. 112–17 in Linda Roodenburg (ed.), *Photowork(s) in Progress/Constructing Identity* (Rotterdam, The Netherlands, 1997), Dutch section, pp. 118–23.

'Happy Endings: Law, Gender, and the University', *Journal of Gender, Race and Justice*, **2** (1, Fall 1998): 77–85.

'Slate Diary, Nov 29, 1999–Dec 3, 1999' [invited week of five diary entries, focusing on gender], slate.com.

'Post-Modern Free-Market Feminism: A Conversation with Gayatri Chakravorty Spivak', forthcoming, *Rethinking Marxism*, 2000.

'Crossing Economics', *The International Journal of Transgenderism*, forthcoming 2000.

Other Brief Academic Items

'Review of Stratton and Brown's *Agricultural Records in Britain*', *Journal of Economic History*, c. 1978: 189.

'Fungibility', in *The New Palgrave*, 1987; reprinted *New Palgrave Dictionary of Money and Finance* (Macmillan UK; Stockton), 1992.

'Gresham's Law', for the *New Palgrave Dictionary of Money and Finance*, 1992.

'Reading the Economy', *Humane Studies Review*, **70** (2, Spring 1992): pp. 1, 10–13.

'Other Things Equal' (Columns in the *Eastern Economic Journal*; those on economics as an academic field are reprinted in *How to Be Human* * [*Though an Economist*]):

1. 'The Natural', **18** (2, Spring 1992): 237–9.
2. 'The Bankruptcy of Statistical Significance', **18** (3, Summer 1992): 359–61.
3. 'Schelling's Five Truths of Economics', **19** (1, Winter 1993): 109–12.
4. 'The A-Prime, C-Prime Theorem', **19** (2, Fall 1993): 235–8.
5. 'Reading I've Liked', **19** (3, Summer 1994): 395–9.
6. 'Economics: Art or Science or Who Cares?', **20** (1, Winter 1994): 117–20.
7. 'How to Organize a Conference', **20** (2, Spring 1994): 221–4.
8. 'Why Don't Economists Believe Empirical Findings?', **20** (3, Summer 1994).
9. 'To Burn Always with a Hard, Gemlike Flame, Eh Professor?', **20** (4, Fall 1994): 479–81.
10. 'He's Smart, and He's a Nice Guy Too', **21** (1, Winter 1995): 109–12.
11. 'How to Host a Seminar Visitor', **21** (2, Spring 1995): 271–4.
12. 'Kelly Green Golf Shoes and the Intellectual Range from M to N', **21** (3, Summer 1995): 411–14.
13. 'Some News That At Least Will Not Bore You', **21** (4, Fall 1995): 551–3.
14. 'Love or Money', **22** (1, Winter 1996): 97–100.
15. 'Keynes Was a Sophist, and a Good Thing, Too', **22** (2, Spring 1996).
16. 'Economic Tourism', **22** (3, Summer 1996).
17. 'One Small Step for Gary', **23** (1, Winter 1997): 113–16.
18. 'Aunt Deirdre's Letter to a Graduate Student', **23** (2, Spring 1997): 241–4.
19. 'The Rhetoric of Economics Revisited', **23** (3, Summer 1997): 359–62.
20. 'Polanyi Was Right, and Wrong', **23** (4, Fall 1997): 483–7.
21. 'Quarreling with Ken', **24** (1, Winter 1998): 111–15.
22. 'Small Worlds, or, the Preposterousness of Closed Economy Macro', **24** (2, Spring 1998): 229–32.
23. 'The So-Called Coase Theorem', **24** (3, Summer 1998): 367–71.
24. 'Career Courage', **24** (4, Fall 1998): 525–8.
25. 'Learning to Love Globalization', **25** (1, Winter 1999): 117–21.
26. 'Economical Writing: An Executive Summary', **25** (2, Spring 1999).
27. 'Cassandra's Open Letter to Her Economist Colleagues', **25** (3, Summer 1999).
28. 'Christian Economics?', **25** (4, Fall 1999).
29. 'Alan Greenspan Has No Influence on Interest Rates', **26** (1, Winter 2000).

Name index

Abramowitz, M. 104
Adams, H. 99
Agarwal, S.K. 20
Alchian, A. 164, 173
Aldridge, J. 330
Allen, R.C. 114
Amemiya, T. 335
Anderson, P. 323
Angell, J. 70, 79
Annenberg, W. 144
Anscombe, E. 136
Arendt, H. 307–8
Aristotle 136, 169, 185, 186, 189, 225, 287, 288
Arrow, K. 188, 293, 300, 313, 323, 326, 330, 331
Ashley, W.J. 56
Auden, W.H. 216
Ayer, A.J. 138, 155, 163

Bacon, F. 265–6, 315, 327
Baier, A. 136, 140
Baldwin, B. 170
Ballard, A. 26, 43, 59
Barfield, O. 190
Barley, M.W. 90
Barry, B. 160
Bartlett, R. 308
Bastable, C.F. 229–30
Baudelaire, C.P. 148
Bauer, P. 232
Baumol, W. 249, 254, 256
Beach, W.E. 74, 79
Becker, G. 135, 138, 160–61, 171, 189, 190, 232, 304, 329
Beidelman, T.O. 58
Bell, D. 132
Benhabib, J. 249, 254, 256
Bentham, J. 135, 136, 138–9, 140, 185
Berg, M. 103, 114
Berger, M.C. 336–7, 338, 339
Bergmann, B. 308
Besso, M.A. 159
Beveridge, W. 83
Black, M. 189, 190, 194, 231
Blair, H. 135–6
Blaug, M. 169, 176–7, 195
Bloch, M. 19

Blomquist, G.C. 336–7, 338, 339
Bloomfield, A.I. 78
Bohr, N. 217–18, 299
Boissiere, M. 338
Boone, J.A. 304
Booth, W.C. 161, 168–9, 170, 187, 190, 225, 299
Borel, A. 303
Boring, E. 334
Bowden, P. 90, 92
Bowley, A.L. 14, 106
Bowman, M.J. 310
Brady, D. 159, 310
Braithwaite, R.B. 155
Braudel, F. 108
Bridbury, A.R. 99
Bridgeman 172
Brock, W.A. 254, 255, 256, 257, 323, 327
Bronowski, J. 267
Brooke, C.N.L. 48
Brooks, P. 206, 257, 310
Brouwer 273
Brown, V. 137
Bruner, J. 302
Bruns, G. 210, 230
Buchanan, J. 306, 327
Burke, E. 137
Burke, K. 169
Butt, J. 105

Cairnes 79
Cairncross, A.K. 9, 10, 335
Cameron, R. 97, 102
Campbell, J. 265–6
Campion, H. 10
Carnap 169, 179
Carus-Wilson, E.M. 99
Case, K.E. 227
Casey, J. 133, 136, 138
Cassell 79
Cato 195–6
Chandler, A. 291
Chapman, S.D. 105
Cheung, S.N.S. 293
Churchill, W.S. 250
Cicero 169, 194, 195, 332
Clapham, J.H. 102
Clark, C. 78

Economists of the Twentieth Century

Monetarism and Macroeconomic
Policy
Thomas Mayer

Studies in Fiscal Federalism
Wallace E. Oates

The World Economy in Perspective
Essays in International Trade and European
Integration
Herbert Giersch

Towards a New Economics
Critical Essays on Ecology, Distribution and
Other Themes
Kenneth E. Boulding

Studies in Positive and Normative
Economics
Martin J. Bailey

The Collected Essays of Richard E.
Quandt (2 volumes)
Richard E. Quandt

International Trade Theory and Policy
Selected Essays of W. Max Corden
W. Max Corden

Organization and Technology in Capitalist
Development
William Lazonick

Studies in Human Capital
Collected Essays of Jacob Mincer, Volume 1
Jacob Mincer

Studies in Labor Supply
Collected Essays of Jacob Mincer, Volume 2
Jacob Mincer

Macroeconomics and Economic Policy
The Selected Essays of Assar Lindbeck
Volume I
Assar Lindbeck

The Welfare State
The Selected Essays of Assar Lindbeck
Volume II
Assar Lindbeck

Classical Economics, Public Expenditure
and Growth
Walter Eltis

Money, Interest Rates and Inflation
Frederic S. Mishkin

The Public Choice Approach to Politics
Dennis C. Mueller

The Liberal Economic Order
Volume I Essays on International Economics
Volume II Money, Cycles and Related Themes
Gottfried Haberler
Edited by Anthony Y.C. Koo

Economic Growth and Business Cycles
Prices and the Process of Cyclical Development
Paolo Sylos Labini

International Adjustment, Money and
Trade
Theory and Measurement for Economic Policy
Volume I
Herbert G. Grubel

International Capital and Service Flows
Theory and Measurement for Economic Policy
Volume II
Herbert G. Grubel

Unintended Effects of Government
Policies
Theory and Measurement for Economic Policy
Volume III
Herbert G. Grubel

The Economics of Competitive Enterprise
Selected Essays of P.W.S. Andrews
Edited by Frederic S. Lee
and Peter E. Earl

The Repressed Economy
Causes, Consequences, Reform
Deepak Lal

Economic Theory and Market Socialism
Selected Essays of Oskar Lange
Edited by Tadeusz Kowalik

Trade, Development and Political
Economy
Selected Essays of Ronald Findlay
Ronald Findlay

General Equilibrium Theory
The Collected Essays of Takashi Negishi
Volume I
Takashi Negishi

The History of Economics
The Collected Essays of Takashi Negishi
Volume II
Takashi Negishi

Studies in Econometric Theory
The Collected Essays of Takeshi Amemiya
Takeshi Amemiya